.95

ADMIRAL OF THE OCEAN SEA

Ideal Portrait of Columbus

*From the Henri Lefort etching of the modern portrait
in the Naval Museum of Madrid*

ADMIRAL
OF THE OCEAN SEA

A Life of Christopher Columbus

BY

SAMUEL ELIOT MORISON

Maps by Erwin Raisz

Drawings by Bertram Greene

An Atlantic Monthly Press Book

LITTLE, BROWN AND COMPANY · BOSTON

1942

/

ATLANTIC-LITTLE, BROWN BOOKS
ARE PUBLISHED BY
LITTLE, BROWN AND COMPANY
IN ASSOCIATION WITH
THE ATLANTIC MONTHLY PRESS

PRINTED AND BOUND IN THE UNITED STATES OF AMERICA
BY THE HADDON CRAFTSMEN, INC., CAMDEN, N. J.

To My Shipmates

OF THE

Harvard Columbus Expedition
Barkentine *Capitana*
Ketch *Mary Otis*
1939–1940

Spanish Coins of the Columbian Era and Their Equivalents

	In maravedis	Number to the mark *	Weight of gold content in grams	Value in U.S. pre-1934 dollars
Copper blanca	0.5			$0.0035
Copper maravedi	1.	96		.007
Silver real (1475)	30.	67		.133
Gold ducat	375.	65⅛	3.48	$2.32
Gold castellano or peso d'oro	435.	50	4.55	$3.025
Gold excelente (1475)	870.	25	9.1	$6.05

The above figures are based on the monetary legislation of 1475 and 1497.

* The mark (Sp. *marco*) was a weight equivalent to 230.04½ grams.

GOLD PIECE OF 20 EXCELENTES OF
FERDINAND AND ISABELLA

Preface

THIS book arose out of a desire to know exactly where Columbus sailed on his Four Voyages, and what sort of seaman he was. No previous work on the Discoverer of America answers these questions in a manner to satisfy even an amateur seafarer. Most biographies of the Admiral might well be entitled "Columbus to the Water's Edge." The authors either cared little about the Discoverer's career on his chosen element, or expended so much space on unprofitable speculation about his birth, character and early life that no room was left to tell where and how he sailed. The earliest writers, such as Peter Martyr, Oviedo, Ferdinand Columbus and Las Casas, have more sense of proportion, but take too much knowledge for granted, and of course do not identify places by their modern names. Von Humboldt, Murdock and Irving cleared up a few points, and Charcot sized up Columbus's seamanship correctly, but neither Irving nor Charcot visited the West Indies, and the great Von Humboldt, with the universe for his field, had little time for this subject.

Popular interest in Columbus, which was slight in the colonial era, became progressively greater as the Americas won their independence and forced Europe to recognize their importance. The entire Western World joined in celebrating the four hundredth anniversary of 1492. European libraries and archives were searched for any and every scrap of contemporary information about the early voyages, and the Italian government's monumental source collection, the *Raccolta di Documenti e Studi*, was the imposing result. Navarrete's *Colección de los Viages* had, early in the century, presented the most important documents from Spanish archives, and from time to time investigators like Harrisse, Gould, Assereto, and the Duchess of Berwick and Alba made significant finds. Thus, material for the Four Voyages is both abundant and

available; yet little of it has been used to any advantage. For no
biographer of Columbus appears to have gone to sea in quest of
light and truth. And you cannot write a story out of these fifteenth-
and sixteenth-century narratives that means anything to a modern
reader, merely by studying them in a library with the aid of maps.
Such armchair navigation is both dull and futile. It may be compared with those ancient books on natural science that were compiled without field work or experimentation.

Francis Parkman, the greatest North American historian, was
not content to study the documentary history of Canada in his
Boston library. He followed the routes of the French explorers,
camped in the primeval forest, and lived among primitive Indians.
This field work, combined with historical imagination and a lively
narrative style, gives Parkman's *History of France in the New
World* a peculiar depth and vividness. It is no mere flat land map
of words out of other words on paper, but a fresh creation in three
dimensions, a story in which the reader is conscious of space and
light, of the earth underfoot, the sky overhead, and God in His
Heaven.

That, in a modest way, is what I have tried to do for Columbus.
One winter's sail in a chartered yawl along the line of the Windward and Leeward Islands provided me with a living commentary
on the contemporary narratives of Columbus's Second Voyage,
and proved that Parkman's outdoor methods could profitably be
applied at sea. So I sought ways and means for following the routes
of Columbus's other voyages under sail. Paul Hammond and a
number of his friends and mine organized for that purpose the
Harvard Columbus Expedition. We purchased and fitted out the
barkentine *Capitana*, near enough to Columbus's larger ships in
rig and burthen to enable us to cross the ocean under conditions
very similar to those of his day, and to view islands and coasts as
through his eyes. William D. Stevens contributed his 45-foot ketch
Mary Otis as the *Niña* of our expedition. Departing separately in
August and September, 1939, we dropped down near enough to
the latitude of Columbus's first homeward passage to check his

observations of weather, birds and gulfweed. At the Azores we met, and examined very thoroughly the island of Santa Maria where Columbus had unhappy experiences; then sailed by the track of his First Voyage to Lisbon, Cape St. Vincent and Palos. Thence by way of Sanlúcar and Cadiz we caught the winter northerlies to Porto Santo, Madeira and the Canary Islands, all associated with Columbus. Our ocean crossing from Gomera to Trinidad was approximately on the route of his Third Voyage, and we made exactly the same Trinidad landfall on December 12, 1939, as he did on July 31, 1498. With somewhat more trepidation than his Journal exhibits, we sailed through the Boca de la Sierpe into the Gulf of Paria. On the northern (Venezuelan) shore of that gulf we ascertained the place where Columbus first made contact with the American continent, and where he took possession *por Castilla y por León.* Passing out through the Bocas del Dragón, we followed the route of the Third Voyage to Margarita, visited Cartagena, and joined the route of Columbus's Fourth Voyage at the entrance to the Gulf of Darien, where he took his last departure from the mainland. The somewhat confused accounts of the Fourth Voyage became clear as we reconnoitered the Caribbean shores of Panama and Costa Rica; and with the aid of a native sloop we effected the difficult landing at the mouth of the Rio Belén, where Columbus attempted a mainland settlement. After identifying the passage between Almirante Bay and Chiriqui Lagoon which Columbus expected would lead to the Indian Ocean, we called at his "Cariai" in Costa Rica, and proceeded to Jamaica, where our *Capitana* paid homage to the ghost of his, at her last resting place in St. Ann's or Santa Gloria Bay.

During the summer of 1940 Captain Stevens and I sailed *Mary Otis* along Columbus's course of the First Voyage from the San Salvador landfall through the Bahamas to Cuba, and along the beautiful Oriente Province to Cape Maisi. There we picked up the route of his Cuban exploring voyage of 1494. *Mary Otis* took us into Guantanamo Bay and Santiago de Cuba, around Cape Cruz, through El Jardín de la Reina and past the Sierra de Trinidad to

Cienfuegos. We drew too much water to follow the remainder of that Columbian Voyage, and my reconnaissance of the "Province of Mangi" was successfully completed aboard a shoal-draught and hospitable Cuban gunboat.

On other occasions in 1938 and 1939 I sailed in government patrol boats, native sloops, or anything I could pick up, along the shores of Hispaniola, the Virgin Islands and Puerto Rico. Nicaragua and Honduras I had reserved for another voyage; but war conditions have indefinitely postponed that pleasure, and it seemed best to conclude this biography without completing the work of re-exploration.

Although I have not neglected the problems connected with the nationality, birth, early life and objectives of Columbus, the emphasis in this book is on what he did, where he went, and what sort of seaman he was. I am greatly indebted to the works of marine archeologists such as Ernesto D'Albertis, Cesare Fernández Duro, my patient correspondent D. Julio Guillén y Tato, and my late lamented friend Capitão A. Fontoura da Costa, for a knowledge of the technical side of seafaring in 1492 — the design and rig of vessels, how they sailed, methods of navigation, and the routine and ritual of the sea. I trust that my chapters on these subjects are clear and simple enough so that anybody, seaman or landsman, can understand the conditions of navigation in those days and appreciate the excellent work that Columbus and his shipmates performed.

The reader may be disappointed at finding no "authentic portrait" of Columbus; but none there is. He may also wonder why I have no general chart showing the Four Voyages of Columbus out and home, since other and less ambitious biographies of the Admiral generally provide one. The reason again is that no authentic materials exist for tracing the ocean crossings, except those of the First Voyage, and, with some approximation, the outward passage of the Third. Of these, especially the First, a careful study has been made by the expert navigators of the Expedition, and new charts provided. For the five other ocean crossings we know only the point of departure and the landfall; any attempt to trace the actual course, considering that the vessels were propelled by sail, would be pure guesswork. But our sailing experience in the Caribbean has made it possible to follow Columbus's routes along American coasts and among the islands with reasonable accuracy, to mark his anchorages and identify the points that he named. A complete series of charts of Columbus's Caribbean voyages has been drafted under my direction by Dr. Erwin Raisz of the Harvard Institute of Geographical Exploration and by my nephew Bertram Greene. These charts and diagrams, representing an immense amount of labor and research, are copyrighted and may not be reproduced without my permission.

Outside the monumental *Raccolta*, accurate printed texts of the sources of Columbus's voyages are not easy to find, and trustworthy translations (bad ones are plenty) do not exist. Accordingly I have made my own translations, and these, with selected texts, will be published separately in a volume entitled *Journals of Columbus and Other Documents on His Life and Voyages*.

The persons and organizations who have helped this work of historical reconstruction are so numerous that I cannot name them all. President Franklin D. Roosevelt and the Foreign Service of the United States; President Augusto S. Boyd and the government of the Republic of Panama; President Laredo Bru and the government of the Republic of Cuba; the foreign offices and naval officials of Portugal, Spain, Colombia, Costa Rica, Haiti and the Dominican Republic; the Governors and Administrators of the Azorean Islands, Madeira, the Grand Canary, Gomera, Trinidad, Jamaica, the Virgin Islands, St. Croix, and of several islands in the Bahamas; the Historical, Scientific, Geographical and Columbian Societies of Lisbon, the Niebla, Las Palmas, Trinidad, Panama, Santiago de Cuba, Havana, and San José; and the United Fruit Company, all gave assistance of various kinds. Many port officials, scholars, antiquarians, and other gentlemen in these countries and islands co-operated in the most generous manner to aid us in acquiring the information that we sought, and entertained us splendidly ashore. The Carnegie Corporation, the Mellon Educational Foundation of Pittsburgh, the Milton Research Fund of Harvard University, and several firms and individuals contributed money, labor and materials to the Harvard Columbus Expedition. Among the individuals to whom I am particularly indebted are Mr. and Mrs. Paul Hammond for organizing the Expedition, William D. Stevens for the indispensable and ubiquitous *Mary Otis*, and my "staff" of secretaries — Captain John W. McElroy and Albert Harkness, Jr. (both seagoing), Dr. Milton V. Anastos (research), and Miss Florence Berlin (permanent). I wish also to thank collectively and severally the gentlemen of the Press in the United States, Portugal, Spain, Latin America and the British possessions in the West Indies, for their sympathetic and abundant publicity, which enabled us to meet local experts, and to acquire many important facts.

The present volume is a condensation of my two-volume *Admiral of the Ocean Sea*, published at the same time. All the notes have been omitted, and a good many pages of navigational data; a chapter on Ships and Sailing and one on the origin of syphilis have been summarized. Otherwise the two editions are identical. Readers who wish to learn my authority for this or that statement, or the exact source of a quotation, are respectfully referred to the two-volume edition, which is liberally annotated.

S. E. MORISON

HARVARD UNIVERSITY
1942

THE FIRST FORTY YEARS

*— Así es — replicó Sansón —; pero uno es escribir como
poeta, y otro como historiador: el poeta puede contar o
cantar las cosas, no como fueron, sino como debían ser; y el
historiador las ha de escribir, no como debían ser, sino como
fueron, sin añadir ni quitar a la verdad cosa alguna.*

I am of your opinion, said Samson; but it is one thing to
write like a poet, and another thing to write like an historian.
The poet can tell or sing of things, not as they were but as
they ought to have been, whereas the historian must describe
them, not as they ought to have been but as they were, without exaggerating or suppressing the truth in any particular.
— Don Quixote part ii ch. 3

CHAPTER I

Prologue

AT THE END of the year 1492 most men in Western Europe felt exceedingly gloomy about the future. Christian civilization appeared to be shrinking in area and dividing into hostile units as its sphere contracted. For over a century there had been no important advance in natural science, and registration in the universities dwindled as the instruction they offered became increasingly jejune and lifeless. Institutions were decaying, well-meaning people were growing cynical or desperate, and many intelligent men, for want of something better to do, were endeavoring to escape the present through studying the pagan past.

Islam was now expanding at the expense of Christendom. Every effort to recover the Holy Sepulchre at Jerusalem, touchstone of Christian prestige, had been a failure. The Ottoman Turks, after snuffing out all that remained of the Byzantine Empire, had overrun most of Greece, Albania and Serbia; presently they would be hammering at the gates of Vienna. For half a century each successive pope had proclaimed a new crusade, but Europe regarded these appeals to duty as a mere device to raise money; and no wonder, since papal diplomacy was as cynical as any. Innocent VIII even used a Turkish prince as hostage to extort money and support from the sultan in order to checkmate France, whose king was showing unmistakable signs of embarking on the easy adventure of invading Italy instead of the hard one of fighting Turks. One great scandal of Christendom, the great schism, had indeed been overcome, but only at the cost of suppressing reforms within the Church, thus rendering the greater and more permanent Protestant schism inevitable; and in 1492 the papacy touched bottom when Rodrigo Borgia, a corrupt ecclesiastical politician, was elected to the throne of Saint Peter as Alexander VI.

If one turned to the Holy Roman Empire, secular counterpart to the Catholic Church, the picture was no brighter. The amiable but listless Emperor Frederick III, driven from his Austrian lands by the king of Hungary, had finally retired to dabble in astrology and alchemy; his son Maximilian was full of promise but short in performance. In England the Wars of the Roses were over, but few expected the House of Tudor to last long. Only in the Iberian peninsula, in Portugal and Castile, were there signs of new life; but these kingdoms were too much on the periphery of Europe to alter the general picture of degeneracy and decay.

With the practical dissolution of the Empire and the Church's loss of moral leadership, Christians had nothing to which they might cling. The great principle of unity represented by emperor and pope was a dream of the past that had not come true. Belief in the institutions of their ancestors was wavering. It seemed as if the devil had adopted as his own the principle "divide and rule." Throughout Western Europe the general feeling was one of profound disillusion, cynical pessimism and black despair.

One may catch the prevailing mood by reading the final pages of the *Nuremberg Chronicle*. The colophon of this stately old folio, dated July 12, 1493, declares that it contains "the events most worthy of notice from the beginning of the world to the calamity of our time." Lest any reader feel an unjustified optimism, the Nuremberg chroniclers place 1493 in the Sixth or penultimate Age of the world, and leave six blank pages on which to record events from the date of printing to the Day of Judgment. Then begins a prophecy of the Seventh and final Age, "in comparison with which our age, in which iniquity and evil have increased to the highest pitch, may be regarded as happy and almost golden." Only the wicked will prosper, good men will fall into contempt and penury; there will be no faith, no law, no justice, no peace, no humanity, no shame and no truth. Gog and Magog "shall go out to deceive the nations which are in the four quarters of the earth . . . to gather them together to battle" (Revelation xx 8), war and civil tumults will spread over the whole world, neighboring

America that he accomplished with a maximum of faith and a minimum of technique, a bare sufficiency of equipment and a superabundance of stout-heartedness, gave Europe new confidence in herself, more than doubled the area of Christianity, enlarged indefinitely the scope for human thought and speculation, and "led the way to those fields of freedom which, planted with great seed, have now sprung up to the fructification of the world."

In his faith, his deductive methods of reasoning, his unquestioning acceptance of the current ethics, Columbus was a man of the Middle Ages, and in the best sense. In his readiness to translate thought into action, in lively curiosity and accurate observation of natural phenomena, in his joyous sense of adventure and desire to win wealth and recognition, he was a modern man. This dualism makes the character and career of Columbus a puzzle to the dull-witted, a delight to the discerning. It unlocks most of the so-called Columbus "mysteries," "questions" and "problems," which were neither mysteries, questions nor problems to his contemporaries, but recent creations of dull pedants without faith who never tasted the joy of sea adventure.

My main concern is with the Columbus of action, the Discoverer who held the key to the future in his hand, and knew in exactly which of a million possible keyholes it would turn the lock. I am content to leave his "psychology," his "motivation" and all that to others. Yet, as the caravels sail on tropic seas to new and ever more wonderful islands, and to high mountain-crested coasts of terra firma where the long surges of the trade winds eternally break and roar, I cannot forget the eternal faith that sent this man forth, to the benefit of all future ages. And so, writing in a day of tribulation both for Europe and for America, I venture to close my prologue by the prayer with which Columbus began his work: —

Jesus cum Maria
Sit nobis in via.

CHAPTER II

Genoa

1451–1473

"Et in fines mundi uerba eorum." Saltem temporibus nostris quibus mirabili ausu Christophori Columbi genuensis, alter pene orbis repertus est Christianorumque cetui aggregatus.

"And their words unto the ends of the world" (Psalm xix 4). At all events in our time, when by the marvelous daring of Christopher Columbus of Genoa, almost another world has been discovered and added to the company of Christians.

— GIUSTINIANI'S *Psalterium* of 1516

THERE is no mystery about the birth, family or race of Christopher Columbus. He was born in the ancient city of Genoa sometime between August 25 and the end of October, 1451, the son and grandson of woolen weavers who had been living in various towns of the Genoese Republic for at least three generations. As there was a good deal of moving about along the shores of the Mediterranean in the Middle Ages, some of the Discoverer's remote ancestors doubtless belonged to other races than the Italian. His long face, tall stature, ruddy complexion and red hair suggest a considerable share of "barbarian" rather than "Latin" blood, but do not prove anything; and he himself was conscious only of a Genoese origin. There is no more reason to doubt that Christopher Columbus was a Genoese-born Catholic Christian, steadfast in his faith and proud of his native city, than to doubt that George Washington was a Virginian-born Anglican of English race, proud of being an American.

This is not to say that Columbus was an Italian patriot in the modern sense. The people of proud Genoa, *Genova la Superba,* have always held themselves apart from other Italians. Columbus was so loyal a Genoese that he never became a naturalized Spaniard; but for him, "Italy" was a mere geographical expression. In the majorat or entail of his estate that he executed before departing on his Third Voyage to the New World, he charged his heirs "always to work for the honor, welfare and increase of the city of Genoa," and to maintain a house in Genoa for some member of the Colombo family, "so that he can live there honorably and have foot and root in that city as a native thereof . . . *because from it I came and in it I was born.*" And, "being as I was born in Genoa," his executors shall accumulate a fund in the famous Bank of St. George at Genoa, that "noble and powerful city by the sea."

Every contemporary Spaniard or Portuguese who wrote about Columbus and his discoveries calls him Genoese. Three contemporary Genoese chroniclers, and the commentator who is quoted at the head of this chapter, claim him as a compatriot. Every early map on which his nationality is recorded describes him as Genoese. Nobody in the Admiral's lifetime, or for three centuries after, had any doubt about his birthplace.

If, however, you suppose that these facts would settle the matter, you fortunately know little of the so-called "literature" on the "Columbus Question." By presenting farfetched hypotheses and sly innuendoes as facts, by attacking documents of proved authenticity as false, by fabricating others (such as the famous Pontevedra documents), and drawing unwarranted deductions from things that Columbus said or did, he has been presented as Castilian, Catalan, Corsican, Majorcan, Portuguese, French, German, English, Greek, and Armenian. It only remains for some American patrioteer to come forward and claim that Columbus was really an Indian, native to these shores, who was "blown across" (a favorite means of transportation in these fairy tales) and so knew his way home.

The history of Christopher's family and of his early life has to be pieced together from fifteen or twenty notarial records and municipal documents. When illiterate people, such as the Colombos were, made an agreement or settled a dispute or concluded an important business transaction, they went to a public notary, an educated gentleman who wrote down the essential facts and details in Latin. No signatures or marks were made; the notary put down who the witnesses were and what they said; his record was good in any court. Many of these records remained in the same notarial family for centuries, and some are still in private possession; but if the line died out they were deposited in the municipal archives, where most of those relating to the Columbus family have been found.

Giovanni Colombo, the Discoverer's paternal grandfather, was a weaver of woolen cloth from the village of Moconèsi in the Fontanabuona valley above Chiavari, a seaport about twenty miles east of Genoa. We first hear of him in 1429 in the town of Quinto, so called because located at the fifth milestone east of old Genoa. He was then apprenticing his son Domenico (Columbus's father), "aged about eleven," to a clothweaver from Brabant who lived in Genoa.

By 1440, several years after completing his apprenticeship, Domenico Colombo has become a master weaver, and hired a house just inside the Porta dell'Olivella, the eastern gate of Genoa. About 445 he marries Susanna Fontanarossa, daughter of a weaver who ved in the valley of the Bisagno River, which the Olivella gate overlooks. She brought Domenico a little dowry, and (unless this as another Domenico Colombo, which is quite possible) he was appointed warder of the Porta dell'Olivella, at a salary of 84 Genoese pounds a year (about $160 in gold), out of which he had to pay assistants. It must have been in this house near the gate, in a quarter so rebuilt that the site cannot now be definitely fixed, that Christopher was born in September or October of 1451. So Columbus's forty-first birthday fell during his great voyage of discovery. Very likely he did not remember the exact date, since boys and girls in Catholic countries celebrated the feast day of their patron saint rather than their own birthday. It would have been on June 25, the feast of Saint Christopher, that young Cristoforo attended Mass with his mother and received a little pocket money and a glass of wine from his father.

The story of Saint Christopher, familiar to every child in the Middle Ages, made Columbus's baptismal name far more significant to him than his patronymic. The famous saint was a great hulk of a pagan who, hearing of Christ, went forth in search of Him. A holy hermit said, "Perhaps Our Lord will show Himself to you if you fast and pray." "Fast I cannot," said Christopher, "and how to pray I know not; ask me something easier." So the hermit said, "Knowest thou that river without a bridge which can only be crossed at great peril of drowning?" "I do," said Christopher. "Very well, do thou who art so tall and strong take up thine abode by the hither bank, and assist poor travelers to cross; that will be very agreeable to Our Lord, and mayhap He will show Himself to thee." So Christopher built him a cabin by the riverbank and, with the aid of a tree trunk as staff, carried wayfarers across on his broad shoulders.

One night the big fellow was asleep in his cabin when he heard the voice of a Child cry, "Christopher! come and set me across." Out he came, staff in hand, and took the Infant on his shoulders. But as he waded through the river the Child's weight increased so that it became almost intolerable, and he had to call forth all his mighty strength to avoid falling and struggle through to the other bank. "Well now, my little fellow," said he, "thou hast put me in great danger, for thy burden waxed so great that had I borne the whole world on my back, it could have weighed no more than thou." "Marvel not, Christopher," replied the Child, "for thou hast borne upon thy back the whole world and Him who created it. I am the Christ whom thou servest in doing good; and as proof of my words, plant that staff near thy cabin, and tomorrow it shall be covered with flowers and fruit." The saint did as he was bid, and found his staff next day transformed into a beautiful date palm.

This story would certainly have gone home to the boy Christopher who was father to Columbus the man we know. He conceived it his destiny to carry the divine word of that Holy Child across the mighty ocean to countries steeped in heathen darkness. Many years elapsed and countless discouragements were surmounted before anyone would afford him means to take up the burden. Once assumed, it often became intolerable, and often he staggered under it; but never did he set it down until his appointed work was done. We may fairly say that the first step toward the discovery of America was taken by the parents of Columbus when they caused him to be baptized Cristoforo in some ancient church of Genoa, one day in the late summer or early fall of 1451.

As Domenico and Susanna had now been married six years, it is probable that Christopher was not the eldest child; but if he had any older brothers and sisters they died young. Bartholomew, the future Adelantado of the Indies, was at least a year or two younger than Christopher. There was a brother named Giovanni Pellegrino who died when a young man, and a sister named Bianchinetta about whom almost nothing is known. The youngest brother, Giacomo, must have been Christopher's junior by seventeen years; for there is record of his apprenticeship to a clothweaver in 1484 at the age of sixteen. Toward Giacomo, better known as Diego (the Spanish equivalent), Christopher felt the affection that an elder brother often does for the baby of the family. He took him on his Second Voyage, and after ascertaining the young man to be a failure as a seaman and a colonist, helped him to obtain holy orders, and made futile efforts to procure a Spanish bishopric for him from the Queen. Columbus's son Diego was probably named after this uncle.

In 1455, when Christopher was four years old, his parents removed to a house with a courtyard and garden near the Porta Sant' Andrea. A modern house on the same foundation is now marked as the *Casa di Colombo*.

Domenico Colombo was not a journeyman weaver dependent on wages, but a master clothier (to use the old English term), who owned one or more looms, bought his own wool, sold the finished cloth, and taught apprentice boys their trade. As a citizen of Genoa and member of the local gild of clothiers, he had a respectable position in the lower middle class. On ceremonial occasions, when the brethren marched to a corporate Mass in their own chapel of the Cathedral, he probably displayed the arms (blue bend on a gold field with red chief) which the Admiral afterwards quartered with the arms of Castile; members of trade gilds in the Italian cities often used just such a simple coat as this.

Christopher's mother is a shadowy figure, but the personality of his father emerges from the dry records. Domenico had his son's optimism, without his will. He was always making promises that he was unable to fulfill, buying goods for which he was unable to pay, starting sidelines like cheese and wine instead of sticking to his loom. We happen to know the name of the cheesemonger who married his daughter Bianchinetta, because he had to sue Domenico for the promised dowry. Although a poor provider for his family, Domenico must have been a popular and plausible sort of fellow to obtain so much property as he did on credit, and to be appointed on committees of his gild. He was the kind of father who would shut up shop when trade was poor and take the boys fishing; and the sort of wine seller who was his own best customer.

For fifteen years the records tell us nothing of the Colombos. Christopher grew tall and his red hair made him very conspicuous around his eighteenth birthday; Bartholomew was in his early teens. These two famous brothers were wool carders rather than weavers in their youth according to the Genoese chroniclers. Very likely they carded raw wool that their father bought, and their mother spun it into yarn, ready for the loom when properly dyed. Then, like as not, it was mother and boys who had to do the weaving, while Domenico sat drinking with boon companions.

Early in 1470 Domenico Colombo was placed on a committee by his gild to examine the rules and regulations of the master clothiers of Savona, with a view to adopting them in Genoa. Apparently this investigation convinced him that trade was better in Savona, since by the first of March he had removed thither with loom and family and an apprentice. We know that his side business there was retailing wine, for he is described in one document as *tabernarius*, and on October 31, 1470, son Christopher, "over 19 years of age," acknowledged a debt of over forty-eight Genoese pounds in settlement of a bill for wines delivered to him and his father. Christopher had attained his majority according to Genoese law, and as a hard-working, steady-going young man he was considered better security than his father.

The next traces of Christopher in the notarial records are on March 20, 1472, when he witnessed a will at Savona, and on August 26, 1472, when he and his father jointly contracted with a wool merchant to purchase a considerable quantity of wool, and pay for it in cloth. Possibly Christopher had been at sea in 1471; if so, he was now standing by at the parental loom. He certainly lived at Savona long enough to make one good friend in a superior class, Michele de Cuneo, who accompanied him on the Second Voyage; the island of Saona off Hispaniola is a record of their friendship.

On August 7, 1473, Christopher joined with both parents and his brother Giovanni Pellegrino in an agreement to sell the house near the Olivella gate at Genoa, and in 1474 "Dominicus de Quinto Ianue, habitator Savone, lanerius" leases land from the cathedral chapter of Savona. After that, we have no trace of the family for nine years. During the interval Susanna and Giovanni Pellegrino died, and Domenico moved back to Genoa with little Giacomo and Bianchinetta, taking up his residence in the Porta Sant' Andrea house. The old man, through with weaving, and living on remittances from his sons in Portugal, found the house was too big for him. So "Domenico Colombo son of Giovanni, citizen of Genoa, formerly clothweaver," leased the garden and most of the house to a shoemaker in 1483, reserving for himself the garret and some space on the ground floor. A few years later, Domenico's creditors put pressure on him to sell the house, which a certain cheesemonger offered to purchase for 250 Genoese pounds. But as Susanna had held the title, Christopher and his brothers had an interest in the property, and Domenico in his capacity as "father and legal administrator of Christopher, Bartholomew and Giacomo, sons to the said Domenico and heirs of the late Susanna their mother," was able to resist a sale on the ground that the price was insufficient. His name as witness to a document of September 30, 1494, is the last trace that we have of Christopher's father. Giacomo by that time had left home to follow his brother's fortune, Bianchinetta was married, and the old fellow probably died within a couple of years; for he is not mentioned in Christopher's majorat of 1498. But Domenico was not forgotten, for Christopher and Bartholomew named the new capital city of Santo Domingo after the patron saint of their father.

Besides these documents from which we may glean facts on Christopher's early life, there are others which identify the Discoverer as the son of Domenico the wool weaver, beyond the possibility of doubt. For instance, Domenico had a brother Antonio, like him a respectable member of the lower middle class in Genoa. Antonio had three sons: Matteo, Amigeto and Giovanni, who was generally known as Giannetto, the Genoese equivalent of "Johnny." Johnny like Christopher gave up a humdrum occupation to follow the sea. In 1496 the three brothers met in a notary's office at Genoa and agreed that Johnny should go to Spain and seek out his first cousin "Don Cristoforo de Colombo, Admiral of the King of Spain," each contributing one third of the traveling expenses. This quest for a job was highly successful. The Admiral gave Johnny command of a caravel on the Third Voyage to America, and entrusted him with confidential matters as well.

Such are the bare facts that we have of the life of Christopher Columbus to the age of twenty-two, and of his family. It gives us little on which to base conclusions as to his early home and character. Assuming that the boy whom we do not know was father to the man of recorded history, he was a proud and sensitive lad, faithful in his religious duties, following a humble trade in order to help support his parents, but eager for adventure and mystically assured of his high mission. We may picture him if we like as a poet did, a little fair-complexioned, red-haired boy dreaming the long thoughts of youth: —

> Now watching high on a mountain cornice,
> And steering now from a purple cove,
> Now pacing mute by ocean's rim.

Or we may imagine him as a leader in the rough-and-tumble street life of Genoa, and a flaming spark in his early twenties at Savona. One thing is certain, he had very little if any schooling.

Ferdinand's assertion that his father studied at the University of Pavia is disproved not only by the well-preserved matriculation records of that ancient foundation, but by the internal evidence of Christopher's Latin, which shows that it was learned after Spanish had become the language of his thought. The absence of Italian in the preserved writings of Columbus, excepting for a stray word or phrase, is a great talking point of the *Colón Español* sect. The earliest bit of writing that can possibly be his, a postil or marginal note dated 1481 on one of his books, is in bad Spanish mingled with Portuguese; all his letters, even those to Genoese friends and to the Bank of St. George, are in Spanish; and when he annotated an Italian translation of Pliny's *Natural History* in later life, all but one of his postils are Spanish translations of the Italian text; that one is in very bad Italian. None of the authors to whom he alludes wrote in Italian; the beauty of the *Divine Comedy*, with Ulysses' last voyage and the play of light on the ocean, apparently was unknown to Columbus.

Actually the lack of Italian in Columbus's writings is good evidence of a Genoese birth, rather than the contrary. The Genoese dialect of his day, even more than in ours (when a Genoese speaking it in a trial at Rome around 1910 had to have an Italian interpreter), was very different from Tuscan or classical Italian; even more than the Venetian and Neapolitan dialects. It was a language of common speech that was never written. A poor boy of Genoa would not have known Italian, unless he had learned it at school. Christopher undoubtedly left home almost if not completely illiterate, and when he finally learned to read and write used the Castilian language because it was that of his new associates. Many thousands of peasant Italian emigrants have done just that. Arriving in their New World home illiterate, they learn to read and write in English, Spanish or Portuguese, according to the country of their residence, and eventually forget the dialect which they were brought up to speak.

A careful analysis of Columbus's writings has recently been made by the most eminent living Spanish philologist, Ramón Menéndez Pidal. The Discoverer did not write Jewish-Spanish, or Italian-Spanish, but Portuguese-Spanish. To the end of his life, he wrote Castilian with Portuguese spellings, especially in the vowels, which prove that he spoke Portuguese before he learned Castilian. During the decade when he based his voyages on Lisbon, Castilian was the favorite language among the educated classes of Portugal, into which Columbus married; a little later Gil Vicente wrote his plays in Castilian, and even Camoëns used that language for his sonnets. So an ambitious young man such as we know Christopher to have been would naturally have chosen the more literary and widely expanded language. Possibly he wrote Portuguese as well; but only short notes of his have been preserved for the period before he went to Spain, and they are all in Castilian.

What effect if any did Christopher's residence of some twenty-two years on Genoese territory have on his future career? Genoa was certainly a place to give any active lad a hankering for sea adventure. The Ligurian Republic bathes her breasts in the sea, and spreads her arms to embrace it, one toward Savoy and the other toward Tuscany. *Genova la superba* looks southward to a clean horizon, drinking in the sun which circles seaward all winter and sets behind Monte Beguia at the summer solstice. The *libeccio* or southwest wind comes in freshened by a long journey across the Mediterranean, and gives the terraced hills above the coast sufficient moisture for tillage, vineyards and pastures. Shipbuilding went on in little coves and harbors all along the shore; great galleys and carracks were constantly clearing for and arriving from the

Aegean, the Levant and Northern Africa. Although the Republic had seen better days (as had most republics at that time), she cherished traditions of navigators like the Vivaldi who sought the ocean route to India by way of Africa as early as 1291, of Malocello, one of the discoverers of the Canaries; and Andrea Doria was not yet born. Genoa had a noted school of map makers who supplied portolan charts to half the Mediterranean, and to whom the Portuguese came when they wanted their new African possessions charted. One can well imagine young Christopher picking up the rudiments of map making in one of these shops, for he and his brother later plied that art in Lisbon. One may picture him looking wistfully out on the harbor from the weave-room in the Porta Sant' Andrea house, or letting his eyes linger on the broad sweep of Mediterranean from the home in Savona where he worked at a loathed trade. Here, too, he may even have conceived his grand enterprise; for the achievements of a great man are often but the fulfillment of his youthful dreams.

Such speculations are for the poet or novelist, not the historian. All we now know and all we shall probably ever know of Columbus's life to the age of twenty-two is that he helped his parents at Genoa and Savona in their respectable trade of woolen weaver, that he had no schooling and no privileges; yet his youth was neither so hard nor his life so bitter as to cause him to forsake allegiance to "that noble and powerful city by the sea."

CHAPTER III

Cheerfully at Sea

1473–1477

And cheerfully at sea
successe you still entise
to get the pearle and gould . . .
— MICHAEL DRAYTON *To the
Virginian Voyage* (1606)

WHEN did Christopher first go to sea? His own statements seem contradictory. "At a very tender age," he wrote to the Sovereigns about 1501, "I entered upon the sea sailing, and so have I continued to this day. That art [of navigation] inclines him who follows it to want to know the secrets of this world. Already 40 years have passed that I have been in this employment." In his Journal for December 21, 1492, he remarks, "I have followed the sea for 23 years without leaving it for any time worth reckoning." And in another place, according to Ferdinand, "he says that he began to sail at 14 years of age." Antonio Gallo, a Genoese chronicler who knew the Columbus family, says that Christopher and his brother Bart "puberes deinde facti" (which may mean anything from fourteen to twenty-one years old), "set forth on voyages after the manner of their people."

So, according to Columbus's own statements, he went to sea in 1461, 1465, or 1469–1470; according to Gallo's, at some date between 1465, when he was fourteen, and 1472, when he was twenty-one. Yet as we have seen, there is documentary evidence of his having been at Genoa on September 22 and October 31, 1470, at Savona on March 20 and August 26, 1472, and also on August 7, 1473. What about it?

Suppose we accept Madariaga's invitation for once, and "leave the dusty papers and come back to flesh and spirit." We are not to hold a seaman rigidly to these memorial additions and subtractions, or to assume that Christopher's foot never crossed a gunwale when he was a weaver. At what point would a seacoast-bred boy who eventually becomes a sailor, say that he first went to sea? When he began to play about with boats, made his first overnight sail, received his first pay for bearing a hand, or departed on his first long voyage? The writer might boast (and doubtless has) of having followed the sea "these forty year" if he counted back to his first cruise in a catboat around Mount Desert. But the forty years would have to be cut down to four, if his first real voyage in the wake of Columbus were meant. He recalls one old shellback in a Maine post office, reading aloud a postcard from a lad who had just left home in a coasting schooner. "Arrived safely in Boston," it said, "had a fine voyage." "Voyage!" snorted the old Cape Horner — "Two nights out!"

Christopher was living in a seafaring community, where every healthy boy took all the sailing he could get. Fishing trips, out at evening with the land breeze, net sardines all night by flaring torches under the stars, and race the fleet home at dawn with the fresh *libeccio* to be first to market with your catch. Short trips in a packet *fusta* eastward to Nervi, Portofino, Rapallo; westward to Cogoleto and Savona. Maybe a run over to Corsica and back; a great adventure, and his first taste of that lovely experience of seeing a high, jagged island rise above the ocean's rim like a row of little islands, watching them run together into one island, and the color change from blue to green, and the white specks on the shore become houses, and anchoring in a strange harbor where the men jabber at you in a weird dialect and (so Skipper says) are all pirates anyway if you give them a chance, and the wonderful girls ashore, so much more beautiful and outgoing than those of the old home town. ·

Most of the commerce along the Ligurian littoral was sea-borne; and if Christopher liked sailing, it would have been natural for his father to send him along the coast to buy wool, wine and cheeses, and sell his cloth. Perhaps Domenico kept at Savona and Christopher commanded a little lateen-rigged packet, which ran up to Genoa every week or two and carried freight for the neighbors. This kind of coastwise experience is not to be despised. Whoever can handle a small sailboat is on his way to command a great vessel; he who can cope with a sudden squall off the mountains is half prepared to meet a storm at sea.

Ferdinand, the Admiral's son, did not pretend to know when or under what circumstances his father first went to sea; for the Admiral died, says he, "before I made so bold as to ask him to give an account of such matters; or, to speak more truly, at that time I as a lad was far from being troubled by such thoughts." But in that *omnium gatherum*, his fourth chapter, Ferdinand quotes from a now lost letter to the Sovereigns, written from Hispaniola in January 1495. In order to illustrate the chances and errors of pilotage, Columbus says: —

"It happened to me that king René (whom God hath taken) sent me to Tunis to capture the galleass *Fernandina;* and being off the island of S. Pietro near Sardinia I was told there were two ships and a carrack with the said galleass, which disturbed my people, and they resolved to go no further, but to sail right back to Marseilles and pick up another ship and more people. I, seeing that nothing could be done against the force of their wills without some stratagem, yielded to their desires, and then, 'changing the feed' of the needle, made sail when night fell, and on the following day at sunup we found ourselves off Cape Carthage while all aboard were certain we were on our way to Marseilles."

To a mariner, this is one of the most intriguing passages in all the writings of Columbus. The Admiral declares that as a young captain he doctored the compass in some way so that when the card read NW by N (the course for Marseilles), his ship was really sailing SE by S (the course for Tunis). Is that possible? I should say it was, although there is no record in all marine literature, to my knowledge, of such a hoax being pulled on seamen; Columbus's "phony" reckoning on the First Voyage was nothing in comparison. Common seamen are very dumb about telling the stars, and the wind might have changed so that they would have noticed nothing wrong about the ship's direction with reference to the waves. On the dry-card compasses of that day the needle, fastened below, could be reversed; or the captain with his lodestone could have destroyed its polarity and remagnetized the other end.

Another difficulty is the distance. From S. Pietro Island to Cape Guardia, which the ship would have to pass before Cape Carthage, is 130 nautical miles; and from Toro Island south of S. Pietro to the nearest point of Africa in a southeasterly direction is 110 nautical miles. No ship of that day could have made Cape Carthage in a night's sail. But we may allow Columbus a little exaggeration; perhaps they did not raise the African coast until noon. One forgets these things after a few years. Always make an old sailor verify phenomenal day's runs and ocean passages from his log!

The story does fit in with the history of René d'Anjou, *le bon roi René* of happy memory. Although his troops were thrown out of Genoa in 1461, he continued to charter Genoese galleys for the defense of Provence against the Barbary corsairs, and for his various enterprises against Catalonia. Down to 1472 he was supporting a Catalan rebellion against Juan II of Aragon, whose throne was claimed by his son; and the name *Fernandina* of the galleass suggests that she was Aragonese. As we have seen in the previous chapter, there is no record of young Christopher between October 31, 1470, when he acknowledges a bill for wine in Genoa, and March 20, 1472. Again there is no record of him between August 26, 1472, and August 7, 1473. During the first interval of fifteen months, when René was still at war with the King of Aragon, Christopher could have made this voyage aboard a Genoese armed ship in the Angevin service. The one impossible circumstance is Columbus's claim to have been the captain. No young fellow of about twenty who had been carding and weaving wool most of his life could so quickly have risen to command. I suspect that Christopher was really a foremast hand on René's ship, and one of those who discovered the trick played on them when Cape

Carthage hove into sight. When relating the incident a quarter-century later in a letter to his Sovereigns, he promoted himself to captain, as more appropriate to his then dignity of Admiral.

If serving René afforded Columbus his first sea adventure, an expedition of his native city for the relief of Chios was the next. Twice on his First Voyage of Discovery, in Cuba and in Hispaniola, he describes the local gumbo-limbo tree (quite inaccurately) as the lentisk, "which I have seen in the island of Chios in the Archipelago," from which the profitable gum mastic was (and still is) extracted.

Chios had been captured in 1346 by a fleet of Genoese privateers, whose owners were compensated by the Republic with a monopoly of the land, trade and revenues of the island. These concessionaires formed a corporation called the Maona, which governed and exploited Chios exactly as the seventeenth-century joint-stock companies of France, England and the Netherlands exploited their several portions of North America. Control of Chios gave the Maona a virtual monopoly of mastic, which at that time, owing to its reputed medicinal qualities, was relatively far more valuable than today. The Maona made immense profits until the Turks appeared. Thereafter, what with tribute money and defense, the corporation had to borrow large sums from the Bank of St. George.

Three of the five Genoese individuals or families to whom Columbus made legacies in his last will and testament were Luis Centurione, "merchant of Genoa," his son-in-law Battista Spinola, and the heirs of Centurione's partner, Paolo di Negro. The house of Centurione was one of those merchant-banking concerns which were so important in the early development of finance. It had branches throughout the Mediterranean, in Spain and Portugal, and had even sent an expedition to the interior of Africa in search of gold. Columbus is known to have been employed by them in 1478–1479, and it seems likely that they took him to Chios. For in 1474 Gioffredo Spinola fitted out at Savona a ship named *Roxana* for trade with Chios and defense against the Turks; and her records, still preserved, mention that she carried besides seamen and soldiers a number of "workmen of Savona" including *tessitori,* weavers. Surely Columbus was one of these. How could he have passed up the chance? And in 1475 another and more formidable expedition, including ships of Nicolò Spinola and Paolo di Negro, left Genoa for Chios.

On one or the other of these voyages Columbus must have sailed. We may picture him in the crew of a Genoese carrack or galleass, passing Scylla and Charybdis in the Straits of Messina, stretching across the Ionian Sea to Cape Matapan and through the Cervi Channel behind Cythera, picking up the white columns of the Temple of Poseidon on Cape Sunium, negotiating the difficult currents in the D'Oro channel between Andros and Euboea, and then with luck catching a fresh norther for the last leg to Cape Mastika, Chios. It was on these voyages, if not under René, that he learned to "hand, reef and steer," to estimate distances by eye, to let go and weigh anchors properly, and all the other elements of seamanship. Christopher learned seamanship the old way, the hard way and the only way, in the school of experience. Book-larnin' such as arithmetic and a few notions of "astrology" would come later and ashore.

Not long after he had returned from Chios, Columbus joined a fleet that played into the hands of destiny by casting him up on the shore of Portugal. In May 1476, when most of the Mediterranean nations were at war, Genoa organized a big convoy in order to market a quantity of Chian mastic in Lisbon, England and Flanders. Three galleasses and a big armed ship, belonging to the Spinolas, Di Negro and one of their associates, made up the bulk of this fleet. A fifth vessel named *Bechalla,* a Flemish *urca* (the type the English called "cog"), manned largely by men of Savona, was probably the one on which Columbus sailed. His name is not found on the list of officers or passengers, so he must have been a common seaman. The fleet set sail from Noli on May 31, worked its way westward and passed safely through the Straits. On August 13, 1476, when they were off the southern coast of Portugal near

Lagos, not far from Cape St. Vincent, they were suddenly attacked by a Franco-Portuguese war fleet of thirteen or more vessels commanded by a famous naval hero, Guillaume de Casenove. Genoa and France were supposed to be at peace, but as *Bechalla* flew the flag of Burgundy with which Louis XI was at war, Casenove regarded the whole fleet as his legitimate booty. The Genoese proved no easy prey. Three ships grappled with their opposite numbers, the other two engaged the rest of the enemy, and all day the battle raged hot and heavy. By nightfall three Genoese ships and four of the enemy had gone down, hundreds of men were drowned, and the surviving vessels were glad to sheer off and seek the nearest friendly port for repairs. Columbus fought on one of the vessels, presumably the *Bechalla*, that went down; he leaped into the sea, grasped a sweep that floated free, and by pushing it ahead of him and resting on it when he was exhausted (for he had been wounded in the battle) he managed to reach the shore, over six miles distant. The people of Lagos treated the survivors kindly, and Columbus eventually made his way to Lisbon where he was taken in by some member of the local Genoese colony, and cured of his wounds.

One more adventurous voyage Christopher made before he entered a new career in the country on whose hospitality he had been so fortuitously cast. In one of the Admiral's notes, says Ferdinand, which he wrote to prove that the torrid and the arctic zones were inhabitable, he says: —

"I sailed in the year 1477, in the month of February, a hundred leagues beyond the island of *Tile*, whose northern part is in latitude 73° N and not 63° as some would have it be; nor does it lie on the meridian where Ptolemy says the west begins, but much further west. And to this island, which is as big as England, come English with their merchandise, especially they of Bristol. And at the season when I was there the sea was not frozen, but the tides were so great that in some places they rose 26 *braccia*,* and fell as much in depth."

* A Genoese *braccio* was equivalent to 22.9 inches.

Now, what are we to make out of this? Tile (Thule) meant Iceland, that is certain. Christopher, arriving penniless in Lisbon, would naturally have shipped at the first chance that offered. There is known to have been a lively trade between Lisbon, the Azores, Bristol and Iceland at that time. Latitude 63° 30′, not 73°, is right for the southern coast of Iceland; but Columbus never was much good at finding latitude, and presumably his captain on this voyage was no better. Cólumbus certainly visited Galway in Ireland, a natural port of call on Iceland voyages, for on the margin of his copy of Aeneas Sylvius's *Historia Rerum* he wrote, "Men of Cathay which is toward the Orient have come hither. We have seen many remarkable things, especially in Galway of Ireland, a man and a woman of extraordinary appearance in two boats adrift" — flat-faced Finns or Lapps, probably. "The author says that the northern ocean is neither frozen nor unnavigable."

The only incident in this Iceland voyage that sticks in one's crop is the 50-foot tides. Such can be found at only two or three places in the world; the spring range at Reykjavik is only 13 feet. It would be time and effort wasted to find an explanation of this. "They who go down to the sea in ships, and occupy their business in great waters" see many incredible "wonders in the deep." Old seafarers know that the psalmist spoke the truth. We do not talk about such things nowadays because we know they are just not so. In Columbus's day anything was possible, and every apparent monster or marvel was reported. There is no more reason to reject the Iceland voyage because of this "whopper" on the tides than to reject Columbus's third transatlantic voyage because he reported an enlarged polar distance of the North Star, as he was sailing over a breastlike swelling in mid-ocean.

One more question remains unanswered. Did Columbus gather any information in Iceland that was useful for his Great Enterprise? A new "Nordic" myth to that effect is now in the process of being built up. Columbus, it is hinted (then argued, finally asserted as a proved fact), obtained information in Iceland about Greenland and Leif Ericsson's Vinland; that was his "secret." Vinland, the Norsemen's land of wild grapes, was what he proposed to rediscover by cutting across the Atlantic.

Information about Vinland would certainly have been welcomed by Columbus; but any such would assuredly have been inserted by Ferdinand in his tenth chapter, where all the mythical and "reported" islands mentioned in his father's notes are thrown together. Since Vinland is not there, we may be sure that Columbus never heard of it. In other words, if we accept Ferdinand's positive evidence of the Iceland voyage, we must also accept his negative evidence that Columbus found no useful information there. The Vinland story was not likely to come his way, unless he had learned Icelandic and attended saga-telling parties ashore. Greenland, however, he would most probably have heard of, for Iceland had only recently lost touch with the Norse colony there, and there are a few mentions of it in pre-1492 literature. Part of the new "Nordic" build-up is to point out that Greenland is America, Greenland lies west of Iceland; so Greenland showed Columbus the way. But Greenland is always represented on pre-Columbian maps as a peninsula of Northwest Asia coming out over Iceland, and as such it had no significance for Columbus. Nor was he interested in Greenland's leading products, white falcons and walrus tusks. Consequently there is no reason to suppose that Columbus got anything out of his Iceland voyage but experience and adventure, plenty of both.

. Christopher had certainly not been idle since leaving the paternal loom. A voyage from Genoa to Marseilles and Tunis, one or two from Genoa to Chios, a voyage outside the Straits that ended in a sea fight and swimming ashore, and a voyage to Ireland, Iceland and parts north. He was now prepared for bigger things; perhaps the Great Enterprise was already simmering in his active brain.

CHAPTER IV

Lusitania

1477–1485

Eis aqui, quasi cume da cabeça
De Europa toda, o reino lusitano;
Onde a terra se acaba e o mar começa,
E onde Febo repousa no oceano.

Behold her seated here, both head and key
of Europe all, the Lusitanian queen;
where endeth land and where beginneth sea;
where Phoebus goeth down in ocean green.
— CAMOËNS *Lusiads* iii 20

BY THE SPRING of 1477 Columbus was back in Lisbon, where he had first arrived the previous fall, after drying his clothes and recovering from the sea fight off Cape St. Vincent.

This lucky landing in Portugal was the turning point in Christopher's career, for chance had washed him ashore in the world-center of oceanic voyaging and discovery. He was among people who could teach him everything he was eager to learn: Portuguese and Castilian, the languages of far-ranging seamen; Latin to read the geographical works of the past; mathematics and astronomy for celestial navigation; shipbuilding and rigging; and above all, discovery.

Portugal, the ancient Lusitania, was then the liveliest and most go-ahead country in Europe. She alone had been enlarging the bounds of the known world during this tag end of the Middle Ages. Portugal not only discovered and peopled the Azores, where no human beings had ever lived before; for almost half a century she had been sending vessels further and further south along the West African coast. *Os rudos marinheiros*, the rough mariners of

Camoëns, had proved that tropic seas were navigable and lands on the equator habitable. They had dispelled the myth of *mare tenebrosum*, the "green sea of gloom" of the Arabs. They were learning to find their way by the stars, and had acquired such confidence in ocean navigation that every few years a fresh attempt was made to discover new lands beyond the Azores.

INCIDENT IN A VOYAGE OF SAINT BRENDAN

From the Piri Reis Map of 1513

The Infante Dom Henrique * was the initiator of this forward movement. Men before him had the spirit of discovery; he organized discovery. His headquarters were on Cape St. Vincent, the southwestern promontory of Portugal and of Europe, only a few

---

* Prince Henry the Navigator to English writers, a title invented in the nineteenth century.

miles from where Columbus swam ashore. As the prevailing winds there are northerly, galleys and sailing vessels bound from Southern to Northern Europe used to anchor in Sagres roadstead just south of the cape, awaiting a favorable slant. On the desolate windblown cliffs overhanging Sagres Roads, a natural exchange post for marine information, the prince built himself a town that included everything needed to supply and attract seamen, including an information service that made this lonely settlement ancestor to every marine observatory and hydrographic office of today. D. Henrique procured all the charts and *roteiros* or sailing directions that he could find of the known world, mathematicians who encouraged seafarers to strike out from the shore into deep water, and pilots who were competent to find their way back. Young, daring and enterprising masters were encouraged to enter his service, and from the harbor of Lagos, a few miles down the coast, their ships were dispatched to destinations unknown.

On the Catalan and Majorcan maps that he procured, Prince Henry found a chain of islands well out in the ocean beyond Portugal. These represented nothing more definite than the legend of Saint Brendan, the seagoing Irish saint of the sixth century whose saga of ocean voyaging was one of the most popular stories of the Middle Ages. Much as Columbus stumbled on a New World when in search of the Indies, so the captains of the Infante, when searching for the mythical St. Brendan Isles, found the Azores. Seven of them had been discovered by 1439, and in 1452 far-flung Flores and Corvo, the latter only a little over a thousand miles from Labrador, were discovered by Diogo de Teive with a Spanish pilot who lived long enough to encourage Columbus. These beautiful and fertile islands, seven hundred to almost a thousand miles offshore, were promptly settled by Portuguese and Flemings. Madeira and the near-by Porto Santo, which had been discovered in the previous century, were colonized by order of the Infante in 1418; and the proprietor of the smaller island, Bartholomew Perestrello, was the father-in-law of Columbus. The Cape

Verde Islands were discovered by a Venetian and a Genoese in the service of the Prince between 1456 and 1459.

Even more closely integrated with the discovery of America were the African voyages made under Prince Henry's direction. For "above all," says his admiring chronicler Azurara, "was this prince bound to attempt the discovery of things which were hidden from other men, and secret." His first objective was to find out what lay around Cape Não or Nun on the western bulge of Africa; but that was no easy matter.

"Although many set out — and they were men who had won fair renown by their exploits in the trade of arms — none dared go beyond this cape. . . . And this, to tell the truth, was not by reason of any lack of courage or good will, *but because they had to do with a thing entirely novel*, which was yet mingled with ancient legends which had existed for generations among the mariners of the Spains.* And although these legends were deceitful, the idea of discovering if they were seemed full of menace; and it was doubtful who would be the first to be willing to risk his life in such an adventure."

Year after year vessels were dispatched by the Prince with orders to find what lay beyond Cape Nun; year after year they returned to Lagos with one excuse or another for not passing it. But "the Infante always welcomed with great patience the captains of the ships which he had sent to seek out these countries, never showing them any resentment, listening graciously to the tale of their adventures, and rewarding them as those who were serving him well. And immediately he sent them back again to make the same voyage." Princely persistence was finally rewarded when Gil

---

* A punning proverb of the Portuguese put it neatly: —

> *Quem passar o Cabo de Não*
> *Ou voltera ou não.*

> When old Cape Nun heaves into sight
> Turn back me lad, or else — good night!

This was not the modern Cape Nun, but either Cape Bojador, or the one next south of it. "The Spains," as used before 1500, meant all the kingdoms of the Iberian Peninsula.

Eannes rounded the cape in 1434, and found that the reputed terrors of the ocean south of 28° North Latitude did not exist. Within a few years ships had gone far enough to capture Negro slaves and trade for gold dust. The Portuguese erected a fort and trading factory on Arguin Island near latitude 20° N a few years later, and by 1460, when the Infante died, his caravels had passed the site of Dakar, and were within hailing distance of Sierra Leone, only ten degrees above the equator.

It is still a matter of controversy whether or not D. Henrique looked toward reaching India by circumnavigating Africa, and whether the Pope, when granting Portugal in 1456 exclusive jurisdiction over the coast of Guinea "and past that southern shore all the way to the Indians," meant the real India or only the "Hither India" of Prester John. That mythical Christian potentate was supposed to hold sway somewhere in Asia or Africa. The substance behind this legend was Abyssinia; but in the imagination of Europeans Prester John was a more wealthy and powerful monarch than any of their own princes, and contact with him was ardently desired in order to kindle a Christian backfire against the infidel Turk. Columbus once thought he was hot on the trail of Prester John in Cuba!

For almost a decade after Prince Henry's death the Portuguese made no further progress southward, except to settle the Cape Verde Islands. Then, in 1469, King Afonso V gave a Lisbon merchant named Fernão Gomes the monopoly of trading with the Guinea coast, on condition that he explore it a hundred leagues further every year. And there is no doubt that by this time the crown was seeking a southern sea route to India. Gomes's vessels promptly swung around the bulge and opened up the richest part of West Africa: the Gold and Ivory Coasts and Malagueta, where a variety of pepper almost as hot as the East Indian variety was found. By 1474 when his monopoly expired, Fernão Gomes had sent ships clean across the Gulf of Guinea and reached the island of Fernando Po on latitude 3° 30′ N, where the African coast again turns southward.

Commerce with Africa then became a crown monopoly, under the direction of the Infante D. João, who succeeded to the throne in 1481 as D. João II. So it was precisely at the moment when Columbus settled in Lisbon that Portuguese maritime enterprise was producing its richest fruits. Every spring fleets of lateen-rigged caravels, the type of vessel especially designed for this trade, were bringing into the Tagus bags of Malagueta pepper, cords of elephant tusks, coffles of Negro slaves, and chests of gold dust. In the autumn they set forth again with holds full of red caps, hawks' bells, Venetian beads and assorted trading truck that the Negroes bought for gold; and deckloads of horses, for which the native chiefs paid extravagant prices. Along the quays and in the narrow streets of the old town all the languages spoken from Iceland to the Cameroons could be heard; seamen from Scandinavia, England and Flanders jostled Spaniards, Genoese, Moors, Berbers and converted Negro potentates. From his palace windows on the Praça do Comércio Dom João could watch ships of a dozen different nations straining at their cables in the swift Tagus, while the royal nostrils were tickled with the odor of unloading spices, and the princely appetite was whetted by scents from the near-by ship-biscuit ovens. New churches and palaces were being built, Italian bankers and Jewish moneychangers had offices all around the square; Lisbon was enterprising, opulent and sanguine. All this in marked contrast to stagnant Genoa, whose possessions the Turks were plundering with impunity.

Lisbon, the *nobre Lisboa* of Camoëns, still the most beautiful of the world's greater seaports, was then the most stimulating place in all Europe for an ambitious young seaman like Columbus. Lisbon looked out and not in, forward to world dominion instead of backward to the glories of past centuries. From her quays there was no long and tedious sail to open water. Drop down the Tagus with the ebb tide, cross the bar with an east wind, and the whole western quadrant of 180 degrees lies open. Columbus and many others had sailed thence north, to Iceland and beyond. The Portuguese were sailing southward, along Africa. Why not try sailing west, to Japan, China and India?

What would prevent it? No flat-earth theory certainly; for of all the vulgar errors connected with Columbus, the most persistent and the most absurd is that he had to convince people "the world was round." Every educated man in his day believed the world to be a sphere, every European university so taught geography, and seamen, though they might doubt the practical possibility of sailing "down under" or holding on when you got there, knew perfectly well from seeing ships "hull-down" and "raising" mountains as they approached, that the surface of the globe was curved. Aristotle was reported to have written that you could cross the ocean from the Spains to the Indies *paucis diebus*, in comparatively few days; and Strabo, the Greek geographer who died about A.D. 25, hinted that it had actually been tried. "Those who have returned from an attempt to circumnavigate the earth do not say that they have been prevented from continuing their voyage by any opposing continent, for the sea remained perfectly open, but through want of resolution and the scarcity of provision."

Shortly before Columbus arrived in Portugal it occurred to King Afonso V that his people were perhaps seeking passage to India the hard way, that the Western Ocean route might prove shorter and less dangerous; and a Florentine scholar assured him that it would.

A canon of the Cathedral of Lisbon named Fernão Martins had met in Italy a Florentine physician and humanist named Paolo dal Pozzo Toscanelli. Physicians in the fifteenth century were apt to be good mathematicians and astronomers, since the stars helped their medicine to "take"; and from astronomy it was a short jump to geography and estimating the size of the globe. That happened to be Toscanelli's hobby.

Early in the fourteenth century Marco Polo and his elders had brought home their marvelous tale of the glories of the Grand Khan, of China, and of the island kingdom of Cipangu (Japan) which lay off the Chinese coast — 1500 miles off, said Marco; some wish he had been right. "The Book of Ser Marco Polo" spread around in countless manuscript copies before the invention of printing, and kindled the imagination of Columbus, among many others.

But the indoor geographers of the fifteenth century generally regarded Marco Polo as a liar, because he gave a far greater eastward extension to Asia than they found in the geography of Ptolemy. So great then was the veneration for the ancients that if any discovery conflicted with Ptolemy, so much the worse for the discoverer. American cartography for almost half a century after Columbus is marked by the amusing attempts of map makers to combine the new explorations with Ptolemaic Asia. Now, Toscanelli was one of the few men of science who accepted Marco Polo. Consequently he believed that the eastern edge of Asia lay much closer to Portugal than other men supposed. His friend Canon Martins broached this idea to the king of Portugal, who asked Martins to procure a letter from Toscanelli developing his views.

Toscanelli replied to the canon in a letter from Florence dated June 25, 1474, a copy of which was later obtained by Columbus and used as "exhibit A" in his "case." Paul the Physician is delighted to hear that the king is interested in a "shorter way of going by sea to the lands of spices, than that which you [the Portuguese] are making by Guinea." He has made a chart to demonstrate the course, with parallels of latitude and meridians of longitude, and sends it along for the king. On this chart he has marked divers landfalls that a ship sailing westward from Portugal might make, so that she may be able to identify the land and convince the natives that she "has some knowledge of that country, which will surely be no little pleasure to them" — a pleasure that Columbus was never in a position to afford. A course due west from Lisbon will take you in about 5000 nautical miles to Quinsay, capital of the Chinese province of Mangi. In the next province, Cathay, resides the Emperor of China, the Grand Khan, "which name in Latin means king of kings." (We shall hear more of this potentate later.) An alternate route to China passed by "the island of Antillia which is known to you," and after 2000 miles hits the "noble island of Cipangu" (Japan), "most fertile in gold, pearls and precious stones, and they cover the temples and the royal residences with solid gold." "Thus by the unknown ways there are no great spaces of the sea to be passed." Many more things Toscanelli might explain, but he expects that the king would rather work these out for himself.

Neither Afonso V nor his son did anything about this extraordinary letter, whose echoes we shall find in Columbus's journals of every major voyage. Portugal was content with her promising advance along West Africa, the immense profits that exploration in that direction was bringing to the crown, and the expectation that any day a southward-pressing caravel might open up the sea route to India.

Columbus's exact movements during the eight or nine years that he spent under the Portuguese flag can never be cleared up, for the Lisbon earthquake destroyed notarial and court documents where we might have found some trace of his activities. According to the contemporary Genoese chronicler, Antonio Gallo, Bartholomew Columbus established himself in Lisbon before Christopher, opened a chart-making establishment, took his elder brother into partnership, and imparted to him the ideas that led to the great discovery. Andrés Bernáldez of Seville, who knew Columbus well, describes him in his contemporary history as "a hawker of printed books, who carried on his trade in this land of Andalusia, . . . a man of great intelligence though with little book learning, very skilled in the art of cosmography and the mapping of the world." That Columbus was a skilled chartmaker is seen by the sure touch in his free-hand sketch of Northern Haiti, the only map indubitably his that has survived; but that Bartholomew taught him the art may be questioned. For, if Bartholomew's later statement about his age may be trusted, he was still in his teens when Christopher reached Lisbon. He had, to be sure, left home earlier than his elder brother, and might well have reached Lisbon first and, through the good offices of some Genoese compatriot there, gone through the apprentice stage of chart making before Christopher arrived. Or he may have learned the rudiments at one of the numerous ateliers of portolan charts in Genoa, and merely sought Lisbon as a promising opening. Men over fifty, like women over thirty, are apt to be forgetful about their birthdays; so it seems more likely that the Adelantado was nearer sixty than fifty years old in 1512, than that the Genoese chronicler got his facts wrong. Let us assume that Christopher did find Bartholomew, only a year or two younger than himself, already making charts at Lisbon in 1477, and that the two brothers became partners in providing articles for which the Portuguese maritime expansion created a great demand.

There was nothing new about Genoese working in Lisbon. Fifty years or more earlier, a group of them had offered to buy up the establishment of the Infante D. Henrique on Cape St. Vincent, "and the Genoese, as you know, are people who do not make employ of their money without great hope of gain," says Azurara. A number of Genoese captains like Usodimare and Antonio da Noli had entered the service of infante or king, and made important discoveries. There was even a *Rio de Ginoves* on the early map of West Africa. The contraction of Genoa's sphere of influence in the Levant forced many of her best seafarers and business men to emigrate. There were so many of them in Portugal that the Cortes in 1481 petitioned the king to exclude them from his dominions, alleging that they were good for nothing except to steal important secrets of the African and Western Island trade. Eventually the crown adopted a policy of exclusion as regards Africa; but when Columbus arrived in Lisbon the city had an important colony of Genoese. They cared for young Christopher when a castaway; and now, presumably, they patronized his chart-making business, and put him in the way of filling out his scanty education. We may suppose that it was in his first year or two in Portugal that Christopher learned to read and write Castilian, and that he began to get the hang of Latin. For Latin he must have if he wished to mingle with gentlemen and scholars; Latin alone could unlock the learning of the past.

How long Columbus stayed ashore we do not know; but he

was at sea again in the summer of 1478. Paolo di Negro, the associate of Centurione who had employed Christopher on the Chios voyages, engaged him at Lisbon to visit Madeira and purchase 2400 or more *arrobas* (about 60,000 pounds) of sugar for Centurione's account. Centurione had given Di Negro 1290 ducats for this purpose, but Di Negro gave Columbus only 103½ ducats. With this small portion of the purchase money in hand, Columbus took passage to Funchal and there made a contract for the full amount, to be shipped when the balance was paid. But by the time a vessel arrived to load the sugar, the balance had not been paid, and the Madeira merchants refused to deliver sugar on credit. So Columbus was forced to proceed to Genoa with a short consignment. This proved embarrassing to Ludovico Centurione, who perhaps had already contracted to deliver the whole; and on August 25, 1479, he had Columbus and other witnesses examined in court and the facts placed on record. Columbus, described by the notary as a citizen of Genoa, further declared his age ("27 or thereabouts"), admitted that he had 100 florins on him, and expressed his intention to depart for Lisbon the next morning.

Obviously this young man had won the confidence of his Genoese employers, to be entrusted with a business transaction involving several thousand dollars. And the next important event in his life, marriage to Dona Felipa Perestrello e Moniz, indicates that he was considered a good prospect by one of the first families of Portugal.

Christopher met his wife, according to Ferdinand, when attending Mass at the chapel of the Convento dos Santos in Lisbon. This convent belonged to the knights of the military order of St. Iago. Originally intended as a retreat for their womenfolk when the cavaliers were away fighting, it had by this time become a fashionable boarding school for daughters of the Portuguese aristocracy. In the convent, which overlooked the Tagus not far from Christopher and Bartholomew's chart-making establishment, there was a chapel to which the public were admitted, and where young men in search of a good match found it agreeable to perform their religious duties. How Christopher's wooing was managed we are not told. Presumably it was one of those sidewalk-to-window affairs; the process that the modern Spanish and Portuguese young men call "eating iron," or "gargling." The biographer merely says, "forasmuch as he behaved very honorably, and was a man of such fine presence, and withal so honest," Dona Felipa "held such converse and friendship with him that she became his wife." Date and place of the wedding we do not know; but as their son seems to have been born in 1480, we may assume that Christopher and Felipa were married in the latter part of 1479, after he returned from Madeira and Genoa, and in the chapel where they first met. It is quite possible, however, that the wedding took place earlier, and that Dona Felipa accompanied Columbus when he went to Madeira to buy the sugar.

To some writers this marriage appears to be a great mystery. How could a foreign chartmaker of low birth who had been literally "on the beach" a few years before, marry into one of the noble families of the kingdom? Dona Felipa was the daughter of D. Bartholomew Perestrello and of his third wife, Dona Isabel Moniz. Perestrello, son of a noble family of Piacenza that had emigrated to Lisbon in the previous century, accompanied the second colonizing expedition to Porto Santo and Madeira in 1425, received the hereditary captaincy of the smaller island from the Infante D. Henrique, and died there about 1457. Dona Isabel's father, Gil Ayres Moniz, belonged to one of the oldest families of the Algarve, and had fought with the Infante D. Henrique at Ceuta. After the death of her husband, Dona Isabel sold her widow's rights in the captaincy of Porto Santo to Pedro Correa da Cunha, husband of one of her stepdaughters, and retired to Lisbon. Her own son Bartholomew caused this act of cession to be annulled when he reached his majority, and himself took over the captaincy of Porto Santo in 1473. That left his mother with slender means to support her rank; and as Dona Felipa was the elder of two daughters, already about 25 years old when she caught young Christopher's roving eye, her mother was glad enough to have no more convent bills to pay, and as son-in-law to secure an up-and-coming young man of gentlemanly manners, who asked for no dowry.

Ferdinand Columbus, who was not the fruit of this marriage but of a later connection, informs us that Columbus lived for a time with his mother-in-law, who, observing his great interest in the sea, broke out the old yarns her late husband had spun. She told the amusing tale of how Dom Bartholomew had ruined Porto Santo for years by taking ashore on his first arrival a she-rabbit with her litter. The rabbits bred so fast that within a year they completely covered the island and ate up every green thing on it; the Portuguese had to shift to Madeira, and settlement of Porto Santo was postponed until the balance of nature was re-established. Since "these stories and voyages pleased the Admiral much," writes his son, Dona Isabel "gave him the writings and sea-charts left by her husband, by which the Admiral was the more excited, and he informed himself of the other voyages and navigations that the Portuguese were making."

Not the slightest hint has come down to us of the appearance or disposition of Columbus's only wife; Dona Felipa is as shadowy a figure as the Discoverer's mother. We do not even know when she died, only that it was before Columbus left Portugal in 1485, and that she was buried in the church of the Carmo, whose earthquake-shaken ruins still overlook the old city of Lisbon. Little definite information is preserved of Columbus's movements during the next few years. Apparently, after a short sojourn with Dona Isabel at Lisbon, he and his wife went to Porto Santo, where Dona Felipa's brother Bartholomew Perestrello II was captain and governor; their only child Diego Colón was born there about 1480.

Porto Santo, 30 miles northeast of Madeira, has the same high, jagged appearance as most of the Western Islands, and is visible from a great distance. Approaching Porto Santo from Cape Blanco in Africa, we sighted the island at 10.45 A.M., November 14, 1939; but although our sturdy cutter was doing her 5 knots in a fine NE trade wind, it was not until 4.45 P.M. that we came to an anchor in the roadstead off the town, Villa Baleira. Our hosts were quite certain that the charts and documents given to Columbus by his mother-in-law lie buried somewhere on the island, as that was what the people did with their valuables in the seventeenth century when raided by the Moors. The church where D. Diego must have been baptized is still standing, and a modest house near by, according to tradition, is where Columbus and Dona Felipa lived. I suspect, however, that the tradition was created for the benefit of an American who visited the island over fifty years ago looking for Columbian relics. Porto Santo is less beautiful close at hand than at a distance; it has the air of never having recovered from the depredations of Perestrello's rabbits.

Again probably (and no reader can be more tired than I am of these interminable probabilities), the Columbus couple spent most of the next few years in the island of Madeira. When he called at Funchal on his Third Voyage in 1498, Columbus wrote in his Journal (as paraphrased by Las Casas): "In the town he was given a very fine reception and much entertainment, for he was well known there, having been a resident thereof for some time." As Funchal was already a flourishing town of some fifty years' standing, rising proudly up the mountainside to the famous vineyards, Columbus must have located there as a merchant. With his Centurione connections and his new ones by marriage, he should have done well. Local tradition presents several candidates for the house where the couple lived.

In 1481 the old king died and was succeeded by his son D. João II, "the complete prince." Young and energetic, wise and learned, politic and ambitious, D. João was equal in ability to any prince of his age. Just before his accession, a long and fruitless war with Castile was concluded with the Treaty of Alcáçovas, in which Spain recognized Portugal's exclusive rights to the African coast and islands south of the Canaries, which were retained by Spain. D. João, who as infante had managed the crown monopoly of African trade, determined to build a castle or fortified trading factory on the Gold Coast, sufficiently strong to beat off any European rivals, and to keep the natives in order. A fleet of nine caravels and two *urcas* (cargo carriers like Columbus's ill-fated *Bechalla*) was fitted out at Lisbon, with several hundred soldiers, stonemasons and other artisans; the Pope conceded a full indulgence for their sins to all Christians who might die in this enterprise; and the fleet set sail from Lisbon late in 1481, under the command of D. Diogo d'Azambuja. On the Gold Coast the men worked hard and well that winter, erecting a great stone castle of medieval design, complete with turrets, moat, chapel, warehouse, and market court; and a garrison was left in charge. São Jorge da Mina (St. George of the Mine), as this castle was named, upheld Portuguese sovereignty and protected her trade on the Gold Coast as long as she remained independent. The site and the ruins today are called Cape Coast Castle.

Columbus either took part in D'Azambuja's expedition or made a voyage to Mina shortly after the castle was built. This is proved by the postils he jotted down on the margins of his favorite books. In his copy of Aeneas Sylvius' *Historia Rerum*, opposite a passage where Eratosthenes is quoted as to the climate below the equator being temperate, Columbus writes, "Perpendicularly under the equator is the castle of Mina of the most serene King of Portugal, which we have seen." With Pierre d'Ailly's statement that the Torrid Zone is uninhabitable because of excessive heat, Columbus disagrees: "It is not uninhabitable, for the Portuguese sail through it today, and it is even very populous, and under the equator is the castle of Mina of the most serene king of Portugal, which we have seen." Moreover, in his famous note to Pierre d'Ailly's speculations on the size of the Earth, Columbus says, "Note that often, in sailing from Lisbon to the southward into Guinea, I observed carefully the course . . ."

This word "often" has led some to infer that Columbus made more than one Guinea voyage; but it clearly refers to the frequency of taking sun sights, not to voyages. When was this Guinea voyage made? Nowhere does Columbus mention Diogo d'Azambuja, which presumably he would have done had he sailed under so distinguished a captain. I therefore conclude that he visited São Jorge da Mina in 1482–1483 or 1483–1484, perhaps both years, as master or officer of a trading expedition, or of royal ships sent to reinforce the garrison. An undated incident of Columbus's early voyages, when he had command of two ships and left one at Porto Santo while he proceeded to Lisbon with the other, would have fitted in perfectly with a return passage from the Gold Coast.

Columbus was much impressed by West Africa. In the journal of his First Voyage to America he frequently compares people and products of "The Indies" with those of Guinea; he is always talking about finding a "mine" in Hispaniola; and his Third Voyage had particular reference to the supposed latitude of Sierra Leone. The experience of a passage to the Gold Coast and back, in company with Portuguese pilots, must greatly have improved his seamanship, although it may be doubted whether it gave him any competence in celestial navigation.

Columbus learned many useful things from his Portuguese shipmates, who were the world's finest mariners of that era: how to handle a caravel in head wind and sea, how to claw off a lee shore, what kind of sea stores to take on a long voyage and how to stow them properly, and what sort of trading truck goes with primitive people. Every voyage that he sailed under the flag of Portugal made it more likely that he would succeed in the great enterprise that was already in his brain. Above all, he learned from the Portuguese confidence that with a good ship under him and God's assistance, the boundaries of the known world might be indefinitely enlarged; that the Age of Discovery had only just begun. From his own experience he had learned that the ancients did not know everything; the Torrid Zone *was* habitable; he, Christopher Columbus, had been in regions never seen by Roman or described by Greek.

By the time he was home from the Guinea voyage, Columbus was ready to make an amazing proposition to the king of Portugal.

CHAPTER V

The Man Columbus

*Christophoro Colombo Zenovese homo de alta et procera
statura rosso de grande ingegno et faza longa.*

Christopher Columbus, Genoese, a tall man and well built,
ruddy, of great creative talent, and with a long face.

— ANGELO TREVISAN

CHRISTOPHER COLUMBUS, thirty years old, an experienced seaman and trusted factor, having business connections
with one of the leading merchant-banker houses of Italy, related
by marriage with two important families of Portugal, had "arrived," according to the standards of the day. He needed but to
follow the upward curve of merchant shipping to be a success, if
that was what he wanted. Maybe at times his family and friends
wished that was all he wanted. Maybe Dona Felipa tried to persuade her husband to forget his youthful dreams and pay more
attention to business. You are a father, now, my lord, and should
settle down as my father did. A neat house and garden overlooking
the Tagus where you can watch the pretty ships come and go . . .
No! Never! Christopher I was baptized, and as Christoferens I
shall die.

So let us pause and find out if we can what manner of man was
this Columbus at the dangerous age of thirty — dangerous that is
to youthful ambition, to ideals and visions; the age that makes
rovers settle down, drains the fire from ardent youth, turns men
into tabby-cats content to sit by the fire. Hear what was said about
Columbus by men who knew him, and whose lives crossed his.

No description of Columbus at this precise period exists; we
have to work back from what people said of him after the great
achievement. Oviedo, who witnessed the Admiral's triumphant

entry into Barcelona in 1493, says this of him in a work that was printed forty years later: "A man of honest parents and life, of good stature and appearance, taller than the average and strongly limbed: the eyes lively and other parts of the face of good proportion, the hair very red, and the face somewhat ruddy and freckled; fair in speech, tactful and of a great creative talent; a nice Latinist and most learned cosmographer; gracious when he wished to be, irascible when annoyed."

Ferdinand Columbus, who was with his father constantly between the ages of twelve and eighteen, has this description in his biography: —

The Admiral was a well built man of more than medium stature, long visaged with cheeks somewhat high, but neither fat nor thin. He had an aquiline nose and his eyes were light in color; his complexion too was light, but kindling to a vivid red. In youth his hair was blond, but when he came to his thirtieth year it all turned white. In eating and drinking and the adornment of his person he was always continent and modest. Among strangers his conversation was affable, and with members of his household very pleasant, but with a modest and pleasing dignity. In matters of religion he was so strict that for fasting and saying all the canonical offices he might have been taken for a member of a religious order. And he was so great an enemy to cursing and swearing, that I swear I never heard him utter any other oath than "by San Fernando!" and when he was most angry with anyone, his reprimand was to say, "May God take you!" for doing or saying that. And when he had to write anything, he would not try the pen without first writing these words, *Jesus cum Maria sit nobis in via*, and in such fair letters that he might have gained his bread by them alone.

Las Casas, who saw the Admiral in Hispaniola in 1500, and whose father and uncle had been shipmates and colonists under him, amplifies Ferdinand's description in the *Historia de las Indias:* —

As regards his exterior person and bodily disposition, he was more than middling tall; face long and giving an air of authority; aquiline nose, blue eyes, complexion light and tending to bright red; beard and hair red when young but very soon turned gray from his labors; he was affable and cheerful in speaking, and, as says the abovesaid Portuguese history,[*] eloquent and boastful in his negotiations; he was serious in moderation, affable with strangers, and with members of his household gentle and pleasant, with modest gravity and discreet conversation; and so could easily incite those who saw him to love him. In fine, he was most impressive in his port and countenance, a person of great state and authority and worthy of all reverence. He was sober and moderate in eating, drinking, clothing and footwear; it was commonly said that he spoke cheerfully in familiar conversation, or with indignation when he gave reproof or was angry with somebody: "May God take you, don't you agree to this and that?" or "Why have you done this and that?" In matters of the Christian religion, without doubt he was a Catholic and of great devotion; for in everything he did and said or sought to begin, he always interposed "In the name of the Holy Trinity I will do this," or "launch this" or "this will come to pass." In whatever letter or other thing he wrote, he put at the head "Jesus and Mary be with us on the way," and of these writings of his in his own hand I have plenty now in my possession. His oath was sometimes, "I swear by San Fernando"; when he sought to affirm something of great importance in his letters on oath, especially in writing to the Sovereigns, he said, "I swear that this is true."

He observed the fasts of the Church most faithfully, confessed and made communion often, read the canonical offices like a churchman or member of a religious order, hated blasphemy and profane swearing, was most devoted to Our Lady and to the seraphic father St. Francis; seemed very grateful to God for benefits received from the divine hand, wherefore, as in the proverb, he hourly admitted that God had conferred upon him great mercies, as upon David. When gold or precious things were brought to him, he entered his cabin, knelt down, summoned the bystanders, and said, "Let us give thanks to Our Lord that he has thought us worthy to discover so many good things." He was extraordinarily zealous for the divine service; he desired and was eager for the conversion of these people [the Indians], and that in every region the faith of Jesus Christ be planted and enhanced. And he was especially affected and devoted to the idea that God should deem him

---

[*] João de Barros *Da Ásia* (1552), as we shall see.

worthy of aiding somewhat in recovering the Holy Sepulchre. . . .

He was a gentleman of great force of spirit, of lofty thoughts, naturally inclined (from what one may gather of his life, deeds, writings and conversation) to undertake worthy deeds and signal enterprises; patient and long-suffering (as later shall appear), and a forgiver of injuries, and wished nothing more than that those who offended against him should recognize their errors, and that the delinquents be reconciled with him; most constant and endowed with forbearance in the hardships and adversities which were always occurring and which were incredible and infinite; ever holding great confidence in divine providence. And verily, from what I have heard from him and from my own father, who was with him when he returned to colonize Hispaniola in 1493, and from others who accompanied and served him, he held and always kept on terms of intimate fidelity and devotion to the Sovereigns.

So Columbus appeared to those who knew him, and who took pains to study his character and set it down a few years after his death. The reader will have ample opportunity to judge the Discoverer's character for himself. Physical courage, which the early historians took for granted, he will find in plenty; and untiring persistence and unbreakable will. Certain defects will appear, especially lack of due appreciation for the labors of his subordinates; unwillingness to admit his shortcomings as a colonizer; a tendency to complain and be sorry for himself whenever the Sovereigns, owing to these shortcomings, withdrew some measure of their trust in him. These were the defects of the qualities that made him a great historical figure. For he was not, like a Washington, a Cromwell or a Bolivar, an instrument chosen by multitudes to express their wills and lead a cause; Columbus was a Man with a Mission, and such men are apt to be unreasonable and even disagreeable to those who cannot see the mission. There was no psalm-singing New Model, no Spirit of '76, no Army of Liberation with drums and trumpets behind Columbus. He was Man alone with God against human stupidity and depravity, against greedy conquistadors, cowardly seamen, even against nature and the sea.

Always with God, though; in that his biographers were right; for God is with men who for a good cause put their trust in Him. Men may doubt this, but there can be no doubt that the faith of Columbus was genuine and sincere, and that his frequent communion with forces unseen was a vital element in his achievement. It gave him confidence in his destiny, assurance that his performance would be equal to the promise of his name. This conviction that God destined him to be an instrument for spreading the faith was far more potent than the desire to win glory, wealth and worldly honors, to which he was certainly far from indifferent.

An incident of the Second Voyage proves how in the midst of active seafaring Columbus could be completely absorbed in worship. Off Portland Bay in Jamaica, one morning as *Niña* was ghosting along with the land breeze, the Admiral was praying in his cabin when a native cacique with a large retinue boarded the caravel. This must have created no small excitement on deck; but none of the loud talking and tumult disturbed the Admiral's prayers, and he finished his devotions with no suspicion that anything unusual was going on.

The physical description of Columbus shows that he was of a North Italian type frequently seen today in Genoa; tall and well-built, red-haired with a ruddy and freckled complexion, hawk-nosed and long of visage, blue-eyed and with high cheekbones. Unfortunately no portrait of him was painted in his lifetime, for the great age of Spanish portraiture was yet to come; there are no contemporary portraits of Ferdinand and Isabella except on coins. No less than seventy-one alleged original portraits of Columbus or copies were exhibited at the Chicago Exposition of 1893. They showed lean-faced, long-jowled Columbuses and fat-faced, pudgy Columbuses; blond Columbuses and swarthy, olive-tinted Columbuses; smooth-visaged Columbuses and Columbuses variously mustached, bearded and whiskered; Columbuses garbed in all manner of costume, lay and ecclesiastical, noble and vulgar, from the Franciscan robe to the courtier's dress, and in styles ranging over three centuries. Most of them tallied in no way with the contemporary descriptions, and the jury who examined them could find no satisfactory evidence that any one was authentic.

The portrait which has the greatest claim to authenticity is the so-called Giovio belonging to Count Alessandro Orchi. Count Orchi is a descendant of the humanist Paolo Giovio, who is known to have included Columbus in his portrait gallery of famous men, as early as 1550. But Giovio did not begin this collection until thirty years after Columbus's death, and the portrait is probably nothing more than a fancy posthumous sketch by some second-rate Italian painter who never saw the Admiral. Inscribed COLOM-BVS LYGVR NOVI ORBIS REPERTOR, it shows the head and shoulders of an elderly man with thin gray hair, downcast *brown* eyes, a round rather than a long face, and a somewhat dejected expression. His most prominent feature is an obstinate straight mouth, with a protruding lower lip. An engraving of the original Giovio portrait, published in 1577, is very different from the Orchi portrait, and even less convincing; for it shows a "Columbus" with an amiable and rather weak expression, looking straight at the observer.

Every biographer of Columbus finds among the eighty or more so-called portraits of the Admiral one that most appeals to him, and chooses that as "his" Columbus. An ideal portrait painted in the nineteenth century for the Naval Museum of Madrid follows closely the personal descriptions of Columbus, and gives an impression of force, dignity and integrity. This I have selected for the frontispiece to this volume.

Four early authorities on Columbus and his voyages will be quoted frequently in the course of this work: Ferdinand Columbus, Las Casas, Peter Martyr and Oviedo. These four I have relied upon probably more than any biographer of Columbus since Washington Irving; for the "scientific" historians of the last century tended to regard their predecessors either as hopeless amateurs or as incorrigible liars upon whom no dependence should be placed. My own experience in studying and writing history has impelled me almost to the opposite pole: to rely on contemporaries unless they are demonstrably false. *Contemporanea expositio fortissima est*, said the famous Justice Coke; the judgment of a man's peers may not be final, but it is based on a myriad of facts (and fancies too), on things both seen and heard that are now forever lost. Contemporary biographers and historians should be controlled by documents, if you have them, and discounted for bias, if bias can be detected. They are often irritatingly silent on questions that we moderns particularly wish to have answered. But for a body and background of knowledge about Columbus and his work, these four are as indispensable as the Discoverer's own writings and the Spanish documentary sources.

Ferdinand Columbus (Don Hernando Colón) was the son of the Discoverer and of Beatriz Enríquez de Harana, born at Cordova in August or September, 1488. At the age of ten he was appointed a page to the Queen; between the ages of twelve and sixteen he accompanied his father on the Fourth Voyage. Returning with him to Spain in order to continue his education, he went out to Santo Domingo with his half-brother D. Diego the second admiral in 1509, returned six months later, and thereafter led the life of a scholar, collector, traveler and man of letters. He inherited his father's tall stature and ruddy complexion, but grew extremely corpulent; an amiable disposition won him a host of friends.

Ferdinand was a man of wealth. He enjoyed several lucrative sinecures by royal appointment, and the revenue from four hundred slaves in Hispaniola, besides a share of the paternal estate. This enabled him to collect a library, and to travel extensively in Italy, France and the Low Countries, where he met Erasmus and received a presentation copy of one of his works. Learned men corresponded with Ferdinand and regarded him as one of themselves; he was the first European intellectual to bring fresh air from the New World into European letters. In 1525 "Don Hernando" settled down at Seville, in a house beside the river with a large garden that he planted with trees and shrubs from America. He accumulated a large and splendid library which numbered

over 15,000 volumes at the time of his death in 1539, and which
eventually went to the cathedral chapter of Seville. In their hands
it suffered a shameful neglect and dilapidation, so that not more
than 2000 of Ferdinand's own volumes remain. Yet this Biblioteca
Colombina, adjoining the great cathedral where the Admiral worshiped and where his sons lie buried, is today an inspiration for
every American scholar; an alembic as it were where a new civilization was distilled from classical scholarship, medieval piety and
modern science. There one may see books annotated in the Discoverer's own hand, his magazines of intellectual ammunition for
the Great Enterprise. There, too, one may read Seneca's famous
prophecy of the Discovery,* in an early edition of his Tragedies
that belonged to Ferdinand, and next it this simple but glorious an-
notation in the son's hand: —

*Haec profetia impleta est per patrem meum . . . almirantem
anno 1492.*
This prophecy was fulfilled by my father . . . the Admiral
in the year 1492.

How early Ferdinand began the biography we do not know,
but it was not finished until shortly before his death. The manuscript, which has since disappeared, was taken by D. Luis Colón
the Admiral's grandson to Italy in 1568, before any Spanish edition
had been printed; and the sole surviving text is an Italian translation
by Alfonso Ulloa printed at Venice in 1571. The title is so lengthy
that it is generally referred to by the first word, *Historie*.

Although the authenticity of the *Historie* was attacked by Harrisse, he lived to confess his error; even Vignaud the great icono-
clast admits that this work is "the most important of our sources
of information on the life of the discoverer of America." A first
printing in Italy was natural enough, for in Italy the keenest interest was shown in voyages and exploration, during the second
half of the sixteenth century, and Ulloa made faithful translations
of such works as Castanheda's *History of India*. Ferdinand's *His-*

* See head of next chapter.

torie needs no more discounting than does any biography of a distinguished father by a devoted son. It is particularly valuable for the First Voyage, and for the Fourth, in which Ferdinand took part.

Bartolomé de Las Casas wrote *Historia de las Indias*, the one book on the discovery of America that I should wish to preserve if all others were destroyed. This lengthy work was begun about 1527 in Hispaniola, but mostly composed between 1550 and 1563, after the author's return to Spain. It was not printed until 1875. Las Casas had all Columbus's papers at hand, including the Journals and the lost Spanish original of Ferdinand's biography; his room in the College of San Gregorio at Valladolid was reported to be so full of manuscripts that one could hardly get in and out.

Las Casas's father and uncle came to Hispaniola as colonists on Columbus's Second Voyage. He himself arrived there in 1500, a brisk young university graduate of 26 ready to make his fortune like the others. Conversion came instead, and in 1510 Las Casas was the first priest to be ordained in the New World. Out of his experience as a missionary in Cuba arose a passionate conviction that the Indians were men and brothers who should be converted and treated as fellow Christians; and he devoted the rest of his life to this cause. At all times he was the Indians' apostle, protector and friend; and at various times their advocate at court, governor on the Pearl Coast, and bishop of Chiapa in Mexico. The *Historia de las Indias*, written by a scholar and divine who was also a man of action over a wide field, is at once solid, spiritual and robust. Las Casas admired Columbus with reservations, and has no hesitation in reproving his policy towards the natives. His critical sense in the handling of texts is seen in his chapter on Vespucci; and although at times he is disappointingly vague on matters we are now eager to know, and not altogether reliable on subjects very close to his heart, such as the Indians, he left us a great and noble history of the discovery and first conquest of America.

Peter Martyr has the distinction of being the earliest historian of the New World. An Italian born on the shores of Lake Maggiore in 1457, he had a humanist education, and at the age of thirty went to Spain, where his learning and accomplishments made him a welcome member of the court. He lectured to enthusiastic students at Salamanca, took part in the war against the Moors, and with the court at Barcelona welcomed Columbus on his return from the New World. Peter Martyr was intensely curious about "The Indies," pumped Columbus and other shipmates for information, helped to spread the good news in his letters to Italian friends, and as early as 1494 decided to write a history of the discovery and conquest of the New World, a term coined by him. In this design he persisted, though diplomatic appointments and tutoring the young nobles of the court interrupted it constantly. He took holy orders in order to enable him to enjoy ecclesiastical revenues in absentia, including those of a monastery in Jamaica, and lived magnificently in Valladolid.

The first Decade *de Orbe Novo* came out in 1511, and the English translation by Richard Eden, first published in 1555, has all the freshness of our speech in the Elizabethan era. The value of Peter Martyr's letters and of his Decades is very great, for he had a keen and critical intelligence which pierced some of the cosmographical fancies of Columbus that the less erudite Las Casas was inclined to accept, and he gives us more information about the Second Voyage than any other contemporary historian. He never visited the New World, and apparently did not particularly admire Columbus, but gives a fair and straightforward account of his work.

El Capitán Gonzalo Fernández de Oviedo y Valdés, Oviedo for short, was a young hidalgo of fifteen in Barcelona when Columbus arrived there in 1493. An intimate friend of the Infante D. Juan, he fought in the war of Naples under Gonsalvo de Cordova, and after various adventures and employments sailed to America in 1513 with Pedrarias Dávila as comptroller of the gold diggings of Darien. Oviedo spent thirty-four years in different parts of the Caribbean. A brief description of America, which he wrote on a visit home in 1526, proved so good that he was made official chronicler of "The Indies," and in 1535 appeared the first volume of his *Historia General y Natural de las Indias*. Oviedo had uncommon powers of observation, and his descriptions of West Indian fauna and flora are illustrated by his own sketches. His chapters on navigation and the like are excellent. In narrative history he is inferior to Las Casas, but his account of Columbus's voyages, though somewhat meager, was written earlier than those of Ferdinand and Las Casas, and drew on oral sources to which they did not have access.

Thus we have four contemporary and fairly comprehensive accounts of Columbus and his voyages; one by a pious and scholarly son, one by the passionate Apostle to the Indians, one by a sophisticated Latinist and courtier, and the fourth by a *caballero*, artist and man of action. All four had seen Columbus, Ferdinand on terms of filial intimacy and as shipmate on a long voyage; all but Peter Martyr visited the New World, lived there for some years, and were familiar with the scenes of Columbus's exploits. In addition to what they and less important contemporaries wrote, a considerable body of Columbus's own letters, manuscripts and annotated books have been preserved, and the contemporary documents published by Navarrete and in the *Raccolta Colombiana* fill out the story. We still have but slender information about his life to the age of forty, but there is no excuse for regarding Columbus as a man of mystery. His life and voyages are better documented than those of any great navigator or discoverer previous to the seventeenth century.

CHAPTER VI

The Enterprise of the Indies
1474-1492

Venient annis
Secula seris, quibus Oceanus
Vincula rerum laxet, et ingens
Pateat telus tiphisque novos
Detegat orbes nec sit terris
Vltima tille.

An age will come after many years when the Ocean will loose the chains of things, and a huge land lie revealed; when Tiphys will disclose new worlds and Thule no more be the ultimate.

— SENECA, *Medea*

WE MUST now face the crucial question of what Columbus was trying to do, where he got the idea, and how he went about it.

La Empresa de las Indias, the Enterprise of the Indies, as Columbus called his undertaking in after years, was simply to reach "The Indies," that is, Asia, by sailing westward. That was the main idea to which everything else was subordinate. He expected to get gold, pearls and spices by trade or conquest when he reached "The Indies." He expected to find one or more islands on the way, which might prove convenient as ports of call, if not profitable in themselves. But he had no thought or intention of finding the continent which we call America; no suspicion of its existence. America was discovered wholly by accident, and only on his Third Voyage did Columbus admit that he had found a new continent.

These statements may seem too downright in the eyes of readers who have followed the so-called Columbus literature of the last fifty years; but they are made advisedly. Nobody doubted them until around the four hundredth anniversary of the discovery. They are derived from Columbus himself, from his son Ferdinand, from Las Casas, from Peter Martyr the first historian of the New World, Oviedo the first official historian of the Spanish Empire, and the Portuguese historian João de Barros. All these agree explicitly or implicitly; the Asiatic objective of Columbus was so taken for granted as to need no exposition or proof. It did not make sense otherwise. The whole gamut of historians from 1600 to 1892 — Benzoni, Herrera, Muñoz, Von Humboldt, Washington Irving, Henry Harrisse, Justin Winsor, Cesare de Lollis — agreed that Columbus was looking for some portion of "The Indies" such as Japan or China, or both, and hit America by chance.

Around 1900 men began to write about Columbus who were so bright as to "discover" what had been hidden for centuries; even though they had but a small fraction of the documentary evidence, and none of the oral and visual evidence available to Columbus's contemporaries. Henry Vignaud in two stout volumes and numerous pamphlets built up the hypothesis that Columbus was not looking for "The Indies," had no idea of sailing to China; he was simply searching for new Atlantic islands of whose existence he had secret information, in order to found a valuable estate for himself and his family. Having passed the position where he expected to find these lands, and made land much further west, he concluded that he had reached Asia. Then, with his son Ferdinand and Las Casas as fellow conspirators, Columbus falsified the Journal, forged the Toscanelli letter, even annotated the margins of his books, to prove that he had been looking for Asia all along!

No satisfactory motive has ever been alleged for this gigantic conspiracy to distort the truth, but the Vignaud hypothesis has been the theme of numerous "debunkers," and others have taken up the story where Vignaud left off.

It would require a larger volume than this to follow Vignaud and his successors point by point, and I am as eager as I hope the reader is to leave this stagnant harbor of idle speculation and get out into blue water. My interest is in what Columbus did rather than what he proposed to do. But I may say here that unless his enterprise had been to sail westward to Asia, no long sessions with experts and princes would have been necessary, no elaborate equipment would have been wanted, no honors and privileges demanded, no obstacles encountered, no objections raised. For forty years before 1492 the kings of Portugal had been granting undiscovered islands to specific explorers, if they could find them; and Columbus could have obtained a similar grant on the same simple conditions. Unless he proposed to do something more novel and important and eventually more profitable, there was no sense in his demanding three ships, hereditary titles, profits of trade and all that.

Whilst no valid ground exists to question the traditional concept that Columbus's purpose was to reach Asia by sailing west, there is plenty of room for argument as to where he got the idea, and when.

These questions can never be answered with any certainty; Columbus apparently never told anybody, and perhaps did not himself remember. Any philosopher or scientist who has built his life about one idea would be hard put to it to say when the first germ of it entered his mind. Sailing west to the Orient may have come to Columbus in childhood as he pondered the story of his namesake; or in youth at a season of fasting and prayer, which makes the mind receptive to inspiration; or in manhood as he watched a glorious sunset from the deck of a ship. It may have come silently, like the grace of God, or in a rush and tumult of passionate and emotional conviction.

Certainly the theory was not original with him. We have already seen what Aristotle was reputed to have said, and what Strabo did say, about the possibility of sailing west to the Orient. Since there was no doubt of the world being a sphere, almost everyone admitted that Columbus's theory was valid; his originality lay in proposing to do something about it. A concept of sailing west to China in 1480 was much like that of flying in 1900 or of reaching the moon today; theoretically sound, but impractical with existing means. And the people who opposed Columbus were in a sense more right than he; for nobody could have sailed west to Asia in 1492, even if America had not been in the way.

Among scholars, the favorite explanation of Columbus's great idea is that he read it in some book; for scholars find it difficult to imagine ideas coming in any other way. Ferdinand Columbus, who was a scholar and a collector, emphasized his father's study of ancient authors, such as Aristotle, Ptolemy, Marinus of Tyre, Strabo and Pliny. Certainly Columbus took much comfort from the ancient and medieval geographers (as we shall see in good time), most of whom he read in popular compilations; but it is much more likely that he used their words to support his theory, rather than deriving his theory from them. As one much addicted to prophecies, and who had already voyaged beyond Thule (Iceland), Columbus was much impressed by the passage in Seneca's *Medea* quoted at the head of this chapter. An age will come when the Ocean will break his chains, a huge land will lie revealed, Tiphys (Jason's pilot) will discover new worlds, and Thule no longer be the ultimate.

Ferdinand admits that "the third and last motive the Admiral had to undertake the discovery of the Indies was the hope of finding, before he arrived there, some island and land of great utility, whence he might the better pursue his principal design." From his father's notebooks, he completed a list of reputed islands and other evidence that seemed significant.

This search for more islands had been pursued by the Portuguese almost continuously since Prince Henry's time. It took them over twenty years to collect the nine Azores, and they had no reason to suppose that Corvo, discovered in 1452, would end the list; for on Corvo there was a natural rock statue of a horseman pointing westward. Columbus is said to have seen this on one of his early voyages, and to have taken it as meant for him. The rock formations on Corvo are fantastic indeed; as we sailed around the island in our *Capitana*, the early morning sun lighted up the figure of a grim crusader with visor down and arms resting on his sword. Grim enough for us, with Newfoundland only 1054 miles distant. *Absit omen!*

Diogo de Teive and his pilot Pedro Vasques sailed northeast from Corvo in 1452 to the latitude of Cape Clear, Ireland. They felt certain that land lay near to the westward of them, but turned back. Ten years later, Afonso V granted two of the mythical St. Brendan Isles, Lovo and Capraria, to one Vogado, if he could find them; and the same year an island was sighted WNW of the Canaries and Madeira. In 1473 San Borondon, the principal St. Brendan's isle, was searched for from the Canaries, and people went on sighting and losing it until the eighteenth century. Next year the king granted to one Teles "whatever islands he shall find," including Antillia or the Island of the Seven Cities.

Antillia, reputedly the largest of the mythical islands, whose existence Toscanelli took for granted and whose name is still on the map, was supposed to have been settled by seven Portuguese bishops with their followers who fled before the barbarian invasions of the eighth century. Columbus heard that a storm-driven Portuguese ship had landed there in the time of the Infante D. Henrique. The crew were welcomed ashore in good Portuguese and invited to stay; but, fearing foul play, made sail when the wind turned west. On their return voyage to Portugal, they found gold in the sand they had taken aboard for the firebox. Another island was sighted between Madeira and Terceira, and several fruitless searches were made for it. A Madeiran told Columbus about three islands that he had sighted west of Madeira; he thought they were only rocks, or floating islands such as Pliny mentioned, but Columbus believed that they must have been some of the St. Brendan chain. In England the men of Bristol began in 1480 to search for the mythical island of O'Brasil off Ireland, which people have sworn that they saw even in the last century.

Why did not some of these navigators reach America; or did they? Modern Portuguese historians have convinced themselves that they did. But there is no record of any of these voyagers finding anything, and there is no reason to suppose that they found anything. One and all struck out into the Atlantic at seasons and in latitudes where strong westerly winds, even today, make navigation full of danger and uncertainty for sailing vessels. Portuguese caravels were weatherly craft, but they could not cope with a head wind and a rough head sea. John Cabot was the first mariner to cross the Atlantic by the short northern route; yet in spite of taking off from Bristol, where he had a better chance for easterlies than from the Azores, and at the best time of year, he required almost eight weeks for the passage to Cape Breton Island; and Cabot sailed after Columbus had made two successful voyages. So it is no discredit to the Portuguese mariners that they turned back, discouraged by their buffetings, before reaching America. Even the islands that some of them imagined they saw encouraged Columbus; and if he succeeded where they failed, it was because he had the sense or the luck to follow a latitude where northeast trade winds prevailed.

As for the islands reported west of the Azores, only a person who has never been to sea would believe in their existence. Sighting phantom islands and disappearing coasts is a commonplace of ocean voyaging. A line of haze, a cloud on the horizon (especially at sunset) often looks so like an island as to deceive even experienced mariners who know that no land is there. In Columbus's day, when anything was possible, a shipmaster sighting an imaginary island at sunset would set a course for it if the wind served, and when day broke and no land appeared, he would conclude that by some compass or other error he had passed it in the night. Columbus made two such false landfalls on his First Voyage. Consult any terrestrial globe a century or more old, and you will find the Atlantic fairly peppered with imaginary islands, rocks and "reported breakers." Brazil Rock, last of these phantoms, was not removed from Admiralty charts until 1873. If every island were real that some mariner has thought he sighted during the last four centuries, they would be as close together as the Florida keys.

More substantial evidence of exotic lands to the westward was collected by Columbus during his residence in Portugal and the islands. A Portuguese pilot named Vicente picked up "a piece of wood ingeniously wrought, but not with iron," out beyond the Azores. Columbus's brother-in-law Pedro Correa da Cunha collected a similar piece of carved driftwood on Porto Santo, and canes so thick that each joint would hold a couple of quarts of wine; no such canes were known in Africa, and Columbus thought these must be the bamboo described (though not by that name) in Ptolemy. Two dead bodies had been cast up on Flores, not like Christians but broad-faced like the "Chinese" that Columbus had seen in Galway.

The driftwood was really a substantial clue. The Gulf Stream fans out so broadly northwest of the Azores that very little flotsam reaches them or the Madeiras, except objects of a low specific gravity which are helped across by the westerly winds. After every tempest the people in these islands pick up on their beaches specimens of the common horse-bean, which they call *fava do mar*, "sea bean." * This is the seed of *Entada gigas*, a woody climber related to the mimosa that grows all along the shores of the Caribbean. Its skin has the same color and texture as that of a horse chestnut, and inside there is a large median air space, which enables the bean to float long distances. Tropical rains carry them to streams and rivers, the Gulf Stream and the winds take them across the Atlantic and they have been picked up alongshore all the way from the Shetlands to Madeira. I was given a *fava do mar* by an Azorean fisherman, in which he had drilled a little hole so that it served him as a snuffbox; four months later, while searching for the site of Columbus's attempted settlement of Belén on

---

* In Porto Santo they are called *favas de Colom*, Columbus beans, for the people think that these are what gave him the clue.

the coast of Panama, I found hundreds of similar beans on the beach.

Large driftwood rarely comes ashore on the outer Azores, but an old gentleman recalled that after the great storm of 1869 he saw cast up on the beaches of São Miguel a number of tree trunks, "bluish, horizontally striped with black." These are easily identified as the Cuipo tree (*Cavanillesia platanifolia*) which grows in Central America; the wood is superlatively light so that it floats high and catches the wind.

Columbus, then, had definite physical clues of transatlantic lands with an exotic flora, as well as indefinite rumors of islands. Did he have any definite information? Not long after his great discovery a story began to circulate that Columbus was merely carrying out someone's sailing directions. As Oviedo, the first to publish this story of the Unknown Pilot (in 1535), says: —

Some say that a caravel that was sailing from Spain to England charged with merchandise and provisions, such as wine and other things which are usually shipped to that island . . . was subjected to such mighty and violent tempests and foul winds that she was forced to run westward for so many days that she picked up one or more of the islands of these regions and Indies; and [the pilot] went ashore and saw naked people . . . and when the winds moderated which had driven him thither against his will, he took on water and wood to return to his first course. They also say that the better part of the cargo which this vessel carried consisted of provisions and things to eat and wines, whereof they were able to sustain life on so long a voyage. . . .

But it took four or five months to return. Everyone but three or four mariners and the pilot died en route, and all save he arrived in so bad a condition that they died shortly after.

Moreover, it is said that this pilot was a very intimate friend of Christopher Columbus, and that he understood somewhat of the latitudes, and marked the land which he found, and in great secrecy shared it with Columbus, whom he asked to make a chart and indicate on it the land which he had seen. It is said that Columbus received him in his house as a friend and sought to cure him, as he too landed very weak; but that he died like the rest, and thus Columbus was informed of the land and navigation of those regions, and he alone knew the secret. Some say that this master or pilot was Andalusian, others have him Portuguese, others Basque; some say that Columbus was then in the island of Madeira and others in the Cape Verde Islands, and that there the aforesaid caravel came to harbor, and in this way Columbus learned of the land. Whether this was so or not, nobody can truly affirm; but so the story ran among the common people. As for me I hold it to be false; and as St. Augustine says, *Melius est dubitare de ocultis, quam litigare de incertis* — "Better to doubt what is obscure, than dispute about things uncertain."

Few later writers on Columbus took Augustine's excellent advice. Las Casas, who says that the story was current in Santo Domingo on his first arrival in 1500, repeats it in almost the same words as Oviedo. Other versions are given by Gomara (1553), the Inca chronicler Garcilaso de la Vega (1609), Orellana (1639) and later historians. Some name the unknown pilot Alonso Sánchez and give his home as Palos, Huelva, Galicia or Portugal; the fugitive caravel was engaged in commerce between the Peninsula and Madeira or the Canaries or the Gold Coast; she is "blown across" in 28 or 29 days by an "east wind of great fury and relentlessness" in 1484; she returns to Graciosa, Terceira, Madeira, Porto Santo or the Canaries, in each of which Columbus performs his well-rewarded act of charity.

Certain modern pundits, whose critical standards are so severe that they reject Columbus's sea journals as unauthentic, snap at this Tale of an Ancient Mariner and swallow it, hook, line and sinker. The real objection to the story is meteorological. It is impossible for a vessel to be "blown across" the North Atlantic from east to west: I challenge anyone to produce a single instance. She might drift across in the trades after a storm that blew all her sails to ribbons; but if she had any sails left there would have been no need to drift westward, she could have worked her way home after the storm subsided. In August–October, 1940, two boys, survivors of the torpedoed *Anglo-Saxon*, sailed in an eighteen-foot jolly-boat from a point about 800 miles SW by S of the Azores to Eleuthera in the Bahamas in 70 days; but they arrived half dead and could not possibly have returned unaided. Supposing the Unknown Pilot's ship had lost her sails in an easterly storm and then drifted to the Antilles. There she would have stayed, without means to make new sails. Never could she have worked her way north to the zone of westerlies and then home, unless by such supernatural aid as sent Coleridge's Ancient Mariner zooming along in a flat calm.

Why then did the story appear credible to so many people in the sixteenth century? Because, for one thing, the winds had not been charted, nor would they be until the nineteenth century; so, for aught anyone knew, there might have been a sufficient spell of easterly storm to blow a ship to hell or Hispaniola. Perhaps some aged and mysterious seaman did die in Columbus's house, and after the great discovery people whispered, "That old fellow must have told him the way!" More probably the Unknown Pilot tale was made up by some malcontent in Hispaniola, where Las Casas first heard it in 1500, and gained currency because of an unfortunate human tendency to pluck at the laurels of the great. As Von Humboldt cynically remarked, there are three stages in the popular attitude toward a great discovery: first men doubt its existence, next they deny its importance, and finally they give the credit to someone else.

Just when Columbus matured his plans to the point of doing something about them, it is impossible to say. The gathering of "evidence" must have gone on for some years, and the Toscanelli correspondence must have been concluded not later than 1481, for the Florentine died in May 1482. Somehow or other, Columbus got wind of the fact that Toscanelli had the same idea as he that a westward voyage from Spain to Asia was practicable. Obtaining an introduction to him from a Florentine at Lisbon named

Gerardi or Berardi, he wrote to the sage requesting particulars. Toscanelli replied enclosing a copy of his letter of 1474 to Fernão Martins, with this covering note: —

"To Cristóbal Columbo, Paul the Physician, greeting:

"I observe thy great and noble ambition to pass over to where the spices grow, Wherefore in reply to thy letter I send thee a copy of another letter which some time ago I wrote to a friend of mine, a servant of the most serene king of Portugal, before the wars of Castile, in answer to another which by command of his highness he wrote to me on this subject; and I send thee another sea-chart like the one which I sent to him, wherewith thy demands may be satisfied."

The letter enclosed to his friend Martins, we have already examined in Chapter IV. Although it and the chart (now irretrievably lost) gave Columbus the gist of the Florentine's ideas, he wanted more, and wrote again. Toscanelli's second letter to Columbus, also undated, exhibits some impatience at the young man's importunity, and merely repeats some of the observations in the 1474 letter to Martins. The concluding sentence, "I am not surprised that thou, who art of high courage, and the whole Portuguese nation who have always been noble men in all great enterprises, should be inflamed and desirous to prosecute the said voyage," indicates that Toscanelli supposed his correspondent to be Portuguese.

The important thing that Columbus obtained from Toscanelli, apart from the prestige of having an eminent scholar approve his enterprise, was the Florentine's approval of Marco Polo. For the Venetian traveler had added some 30° of longitude to the easternmost point of China described by Ptolemy. And beyond Mangi, Cathay, Quinsay and Zaitun, 1500 miles out to sea, Marco Polo placed the fabulously wealthy island of Cipangu (Japan) with its gold-roofed and gold-paved palaces. Even at that, Toscanelli predicted a sail of some 5000 nautical miles from Spain to China, although the voyage could be broken at the mythical island of Antillia ("well known to you," he wrote to Martins) and at Japan.

Columbus, however, thought he knew better, and that the ocean was even narrower than Toscanelli supposed.

The circumference of the globe can easily be figured out by multiplying the length of a degree by 360. But how long was a degree? That problem had been bothering mathematicians for at least eighteen centuries. Eratosthenes around 200 B.C. made a guess at it that was very nearly correct: 59.5 nautical miles instead of 60. Columbus, however, preferred the computation of Alfragan. That medieval Moslem geographer found the degree to be 56⅔ Arabic miles, which works out at 66.2 nautical miles; but Columbus, assuming that the short Roman or Italian mile of 1480 meters was used by Alfragan, upon that false basis computed that the degree measured only 45 nautical miles, roughly 75 per cent of its actual length, and the shortest estimate of the degree ever made. Arguing from this faulty premise, Columbus concluded that the world was 25 per cent smaller than Eratosthenes, 10 per cent smaller than Ptolemy, taught.

Not content with whittling down the degree by 25 per cent, Columbus stretched out Asia eastward until Japan almost kissed the Azores. The way he figured it was something like this; and you can follow him on any globe, however small. Ptolemy taught that the known world covered half the globe's circumference, 180° from the meridian of Cape St. Vincent (long. 9° W of Greenwich) to "Catigara" in Asia. That was already a 50 per cent overestimate, but Columbus insisted it was all too small. He preferred the estimate of Marinus of Tyre, who stretched out the known world to 225°. To that Columbus added an additional 28° for the discoveries of Marco Polo, and 30° for the reputed distance from eastern China to the east coast of Japan. The total width of Europe and "The Indies" thus measured 283°, and as Columbus proposes to start west from Ferro in the Canaries, which is 9° west of the "beginning of Europe" at Cape St. Vincent, he has only 68° of ocean to cross before hitting Japan.

Columbus, moreover, had two more corrections to be taken into account, and applied them in such a way as to give him all

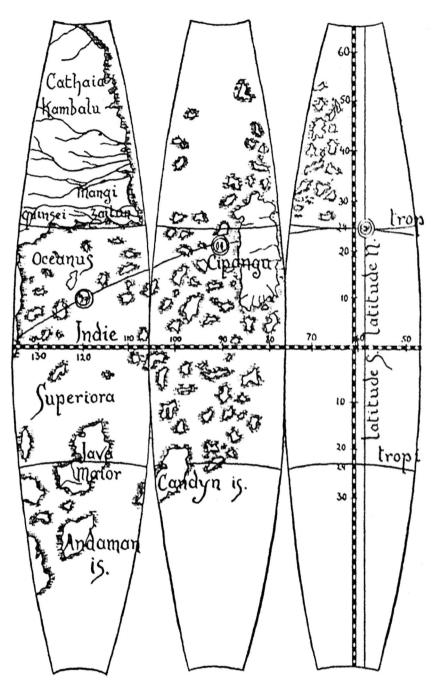

OCEAN SECTION OF MARTIN

Equator and Latitude Meridian as in

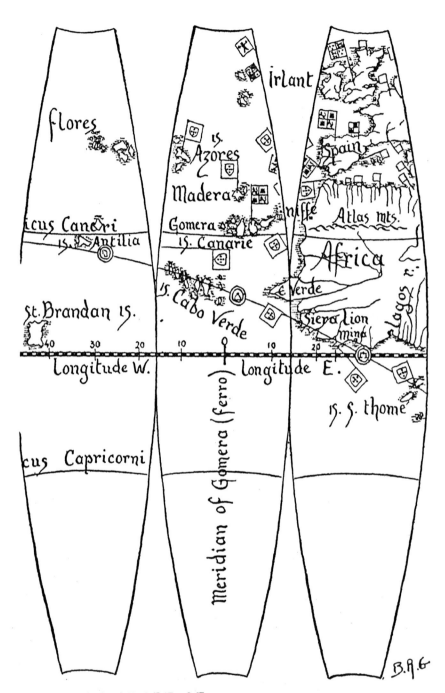

BEHAIM'S GLOBE OF 1492

Original. Degree Numbers Added.

the breaks. (1) Assuming that Marinus of Tyre's already exaggerated linear distance from Cape St. Vincent eastward to the end of Asia was correct, the distance in degrees was too small, because Marinus's degree (so Columbus thought) was oversize. So, instead of 68° of open water to be crossed between the Canaries and Japan, there were only 60° of longitude to cover. (2) As Columbus estimated a degree of longitude on the equator to be 45 nautical miles, it would measure only 40 miles on latitude 28°, which he proposed to follow for his ocean crossing. Therefore he had only 60 × 40 or 2400 nautical miles (750 leagues) to sail. As we shall see, he expected to hit land at exactly that distance from the Canaries on his First Voyage. In other words, his calculations placed Japan about on the meridian of the Anegada Passage, Virgin Islands.

A brief table will exhibit the colossal errors of these fifteenth-century optimists, the distances being reduced to nautical miles, and assuming Behaim's length of a degree to be the same as that of Columbus: —

	Toscanelli	Martin Behaim	Columbus	Actual air-line*
Canaries to Cipangu (Japan)	3000	3080	2400	10,600
Canaries to Quinsay (Hangchow) . . .	5000	4440	3550	11,766

Of course this calculation is not logical, but Columbus's mind was not logical. He *knew* he could make it, and the figures had to fit. To anticipate a bit, the Portuguese king's committee of mathematicians will have no difficulty in seeing the flaw in his reasoning; for even if he were right and Ptolemy wrong about the length of a degree (which they would hardly be disposed to admit), he had applied the corrections both ways in order to narrow down the ocean as much as possible. One can well imagine him explaining it, his eyes sparkling and his ruddy complexion flaming,

* Between the respective meridians, measured on latitude 28°.

with Bartholomew standing by to back him up; and one can anticipate the committee's reply. No bogy terrors of shoals and sea monsters, no flat-earth nonsense, but good solid arguments like this: —

Unfortunately, Captain Colombo, we deny the validity of your calculation of the globe, we suspect the accuracy of your compatriot Marco Polo, we doubt the existence of his Cipangu; Ptolemy mentioned no such place. According to the close calculations of our mathematical experts, who were already studying the heavens when you were plying the shuttle, it would be necessary to sail at least 10,000 nautical miles due west before reaching Catigara, the eastern verge of the known world. Master Paul, on your own showing, makes it 5000 miles to Quinsay, if such a place there be. Even assuming that you find favorable winds over that vast expanse of ocean (which we strongly doubt), and that you can sail an average of four knots, which is what our best caravels can do on long voyages, your passage would require a hundred days. Over fourteen weeks beyond sight of land! We should not feel justified in risking the money of the king our lord (whom God preserve), or the lives of his subjects, on so dubious an enterprise. . . . You may go.

Whether or not Columbus first tried to interest his native city in the Enterprise of the Indies, the first definite offer known to us is the one that he made to D. João II, king of Portugal.

These were busy years for the energetic young king and his navigators. In 1484 he appointed a *Junta dos Mathemáticos* or Maritime Advisory Committee to deal with matters of navigation and discovery. Its principal members were Diogo Ortiz de Vilhegas, a churchman high in the king's favor, and two learned Jewish physicians: Master Rodrigo the king's physician, and Master José Vizinho, a pupil of the famous Rabbi Abraham Zacuto who was professor of mathematics at Salamanca. Their first assignment was to provide instruments and tables by which navigators would ascertain their position in the low latitudes where the North Star was invisible. To this end Rodrigo simplified the astrologers' astrolabe and made it an effective instrument for taking a meridional altitude of the sun,* José Vizinho translated Zacuto's ephemerides and was sent by the king in 1485 to fix the latitude of important places in Africa. Columbus was present when he returned and reported that the Los Islands lay on latitude 5° N, a mistake of 4° 30'.

At home, D. João II was faced with privy conspiracy and rebellion. The Duke of Bragança was executed for treason in May 1483, and the Duke of Viseu, the Queen's brother, was personally assassinated by D. João II in August 1484. Now the king was ready to consider what Columbus had to offer, as the Spanish Sovereigns were after the conquest of Granada. We may assume that the Enterprise of the Indies was laid before him in the later months of 1484.

João de Barros, "the Portuguese Livy," is our first authority for the negotiations between Columbus and the king, and he had unusual means of information. In his *Decades of Asia*, begun in 1539 and first published in 1552, Barros says: —

As all men declare, *Christovão Colom* was of Genoese nation, a man expert, eloquent and good Latinist, and very boastful in his affairs. And since at that time the Genoese nation was one of the powers of Italy which navigated more by reason of their merchandise and commerce, he, following the custom of his country and his proper inclination, went a-sailing over these seas to the eastward for a very long time until he came to these regions of Spain, and gave himself to the navigation of the Ocean Sea, following the same profession. And, seeing that the king D. João frequently ordered the coast of Africa to be explored with the intention of going by that route to reach India, and as he was a Latinist and curious in matters of geography, and since he read a good deal in Marco Polo who spoke moderately [!] of Oriental matters of the kingdom of Cathay, and of the mighty Isle Cypango, he reached the conception that over this Western Ocean Sea one could sail to this Isle Cypango and other unknown lands. For, since in the time of the Infante D. Henrique the Azores were

* See illustration in Chapter XIII, below.

discovered, so there should be other islands and lands to the westward, since nature could not have made so disorderly a composition of the globe as to give the element of water preponderance over the land, destined for life and the creation of souls.* With these fancies, given to him by his continual voyaging and the conversation of men proficient therein, who in this kingdom were very knowing in past discoveries, he came to demand of the king D. João that he give him some vessels to go and discover the Isle Cypango by this Western Ocean, not confiding so much in what he had come to know (or rather dreamed) of some Western Islands, as in the experience he had that in these matters foreigners would be much accredited. . . .

Barros alludes to some of the foreigners like Antonio de Noli who had made discoveries for Portugal, and takes time out to refute what Cardan had written about the connection of Columbus's voyages with those of the Carthaginians. He then continues: —

The king, as he observed this *Christovão Colom* to be a big talker and boastful in setting forth his accomplishments, and full of fancy and imagination with his Isle Cypango than certain whereof he spoke, gave him small credit. However, by strength of his importunity it was ordered that he confer with D. Diogo Ortiz bishop of Ceuta and Master Rodrigo and Master José, to whom the king had committed these matters of cosmography and discovery, and they all considered the words of *Christovão Colom* as vain, simply founded on imagination, or things like that Isle Cypango of Marco Polo. . . .

Note the emphasis on Japan and on Marco Polo's story, which was the foundation of Columbus's ideas regarding the accessibility of Asia, and of the Toscanelli letter. Columbus's strongest point was the practical possibility of reaching gold-roofed Japan. And there must have been something mathematical about Columbus's proposition, or the king would not have submitted it to his maritime commission.

---

* That six sevenths of the globe were land was the favorite medieval geographical notion which Columbus shared, and referred for authority to the apocryphal Book of 2 Esdras vi 42, "six parts hast thou dried up."

Ferdinand hints that his father's price to the king of Portugal was too high. "For the Admiral," says he, "being a man of generous and lofty thoughts, would covenant to his great honor and advantage, in order to have his own reputation and the dignity of his house conform to the grandeur of his work and of his merits."

Las Casas, who wrote the *Historia de las Indias* after Barros's account had been published, repeats in substance what the Portuguese historian wrote, but adds considerable detail. Columbus proposed, he said, to sail to "the land of India and the great island of Cipango and the realms of the Grand Khan, which means in our vernacular Great King of Kings." And the materials and conditions he demanded were as follows: —

(1) That the king equip three caravels manned and provisioned for one year, and loaded with trading goods such as hawks' bells, brass basins, glass beads, red caps and colored cloth. (2) That the king make Columbus *caballero*, so that he and his descendants could be styled *Don;* that he create him "Great Admiral of the Ocean," with all rights and privileges appertaining to admirals of Castile; and appoint him perpetual Viceroy and Governor of all islands and mainlands that he might discover. (3) That Columbus retain a tenth part of all revenues and precious metals derived from these lands, and have the privilege of freighting an eighth part of all ships trading with the countries he discovers.

These are exactly the same conditions that Columbus later demanded and obtained from the Sovereigns of Castile. The almost word-for-word similarity arouses the suspicion that Las Casas simply read back into the Portuguese negotiations the known conditions of the Spanish "capitulations" of 1492. Especially suspect is the statement that Columbus demanded of the king of Portugal the rights of an admiral of Castile. Why of Castile? In Portugal the office of admiral was hereditary in the Genoese family of Pessagno or Pessanhas. Surely that would have been the obvious model for another would-be Genoese admiral. It looks very much as if Las Casas picked up from Ferdinand the hint that his father's negotiation with Portugal was wrecked by asking too much, and that he merely assumed that the same conditions were set as in 1492. I very much doubt whether his inference was correct. Columbus had doubtless observed that Diogo Cão, a man of the people like himself, was ennobled for merely discovering a big river and planting a stone column "furthest South." He may well have decided in his own mind that he must have something very substantial for making a far more original and significant discovery than that of the Congo. Son of a shiftless father in the lower middle classes, he had known poverty and struggle, the indifference of the great and the contempt of the secure; he would naturally have resolved to barter his enterprise for titles, honors, and riches which his descendants could inherit. But it is very doubtful whether he ever got to the point of stating these conditions to the king, and the question of rewards and honors was no business of the maritime committee.

Only this is certain about the Portuguese negotiations of 1484–1485: Columbus required the king to provide him with more than one ship, and Japan was his proposed destination. The proposition was rejected by a commission of experts on technical grounds. Now, Japan was oriental, a part of Asia or of "The Indies" as then commonly understood; Columbus's intention to reach "The Indies," and not merely to pick up Antillia or other reported islands, may then be considered proved. And we may fairly infer that the experts' objection to his enterprise was their knowledge that his estimate of the distance was impossibly small. How old Neptune must have laughed at this eager navigator and the skeptical experts, both in a sense right, yet both so completely wrong!

Yet Columbus had made an impression on the king. They parted friends, and very likely D. João encouraged him to call again, in case Diogo Cão's second voyage failed to round Africa.

In 1485 the king made a bargain with two of his own subjects to perform at least part of Columbus's and Toscanelli's project, the discovery of Antillia, which the Portuguese called the Island of the Seven Cities. Fernão Dulmo of Terceira, who applied for permission to sail in two caravels "to seek and find a great island or islands or mainland by its coast, which is presumed to be the Isle of the Seven Cities, and all this at his own proper charge and expense," was given a royal donation of anything he might discover. The king promised to confer on him, if successful, suitable "titles of honor"; a reflection, doubtless, of Diogo Cão's knighthood. Unable to swing it alone, Dulmo takes in João Estreito of Funchal as partner, and the king confirms the grant to both, with the interesting proviso that Dulmo shall command the fleet during the first forty days of their voyage from Terceira, and possess all lands discovered in that space of time, after which Estreito shall fly the commodore's pendant and keep everything discovered thereafter, until their return home. And, whilst the kings had contributed nothing to earlier Atlantic explorers, D. João now promises naval assistance in case the inhabitants of Antillia forcibly resist annexation to their former mother country.

So it is clear that D. João had become strongly interested in Atlantic exploration, if not in a western route to the Indies. Dulmo had given him a much better bargain than Columbus offered. The outfitting of Dulmo's fleet will not cost the crown a maravedi. Dulmo and Estreito agree to sail westward at least forty days, which they may have figured out to be the maximum time required to reach Cipangu. If they discover Antillia, why not continue to Cipangu? Portugal would then have an alternate route to the Indies. If not, the crown would lose nothing.

The date set for the start of this interesting voyage was March 1, 1487. Absolutely nothing about it can be found in Portuguese sources; but from an oblique reference of Ferdinand Columbus's to the land which Fernão Dulmo "sought to discover," and whose story he proposed (but forgot) to relate, Dulmo and Estreito evidently set sail. Their proposed starting point, Terceira in the Azores, is the key to their failure. Like earlier Portuguese explorers of the Atlantic, they had to buck the westerlies in high latitudes.

Had Columbus made the same mistake, we should probably know as little of him as we know of Dulmo and Estreito.

Columbus and D. João II, as we have said, parted friends after his enterprise had been rejected, and the possibility of their eventually coming to terms was held open. Columbus went to Spain in 1485; but he made very little progress there. Early in 1488 he wrote to D. João II from Seville expressing a desire to renew his application, and to visit Lisbon if he could have a safe-conduct from arrest; for he had probably left unpaid bills behind. The king replied in the most cordial terms, addressing Columbus as "our particular friend," lauding his "industry and good talent," urging and even begging him to come immediately, guaranteeing his freedom from arrest or detention for whatever cause, and assuring him that he would be highly grateful for his coming. What cause can be assigned for the king's amazing forthcoming-ness, save Dulmo's return empty-handed, and the lack of news from Bartholomew Dias, then searching for the African route to India?

Columbus proved a little less eager than the king, for he did not come to Portugal immediately. Possibly he expected a report from the Spanish committee that had had his proposition under advisement for over two years. But by December Columbus had reached Lisbon, in time to witness the dramatic conclusion of a great voyage.

Bartholomew Dias sailed from Portugal in the summer of 1487 with two caravels and a storeship, and India as his destination. Passing the furthest south of Diogo Cão's second voyage (22° south latitude), he felt his way along the coast, and at Christmas tide reached Angra Pequeña, a point south of Orange River at latitude 26° 38' S. There he left the storeship. As the wind was freshening from seaward the two caravels clawed offshore, and were overtaken by a heavy NW gale (a rarity in those latitudes) which drove them to the southward; and on January 6, 1488, Dias lost sight of land. When the wind moderated and shifted he turned east and, having failed in the course of several days to sight land, altered the course to the northward. On February 3, 1488, the lookouts reported land on the larboard bow. They were actually about 200 miles east of the Cape, at Mossel Bay. Dias followed the coast northward, about to the Great Fish River, where his seamen refused to go further, and he was forced to return. On the homeward passage Dias called at the Cape, which either he or D. João II named *Cabo de Boa Esperança*, Cape of Good Hope.

Columbus was in Lisbon in December 1488, when the Dias fleet came proudly sailing into the Tagus. In one of the postils written in his copy of Pierre d'Ailly's *Imago Mundi*, in order to refute Ptolemy's notion that only one sixth of the globe is land, he says: —

"Note that in this year '88 in the month of December arrived in Lisbon *Bartholomaeus Didacus* captain of three caravels which the most serene king of Portugal had sent to try out the land in Guinea. He reported . . . that he had reached a promontory which he called *Cabo de Boa Esperança*, which we believe to be in *Agesinba* (Abyssinia). He says that in this place he discovered by the astrolabe that he was 45° below the equator.* He has described his voyage and plotted it league by league on a marine chart in order to place it under the eyes of the said king. I was present in all of this."

Now that Africa had been circumnavigated and the eastern sea route to India was open, the king of Portugal had no more use for Columbus, who returned to Spain.

One more Portuguese postscript before we follow him thither. In 1484 there came to Lisbon a young Nuremberger named Martin Behaim, who by passing himself off as a pupil of the mathematician Regiomontanus managed to enter the most learned and courtly circles. D. João appointed him to the royal maritime commission (apparently he was absent when Columbus's scheme came

---

* The Cape is in latitude 34° 21' S, and Dias could not possibly have been below 37° S; another instance of the unreliability of celestial observations made in the era of Columbus.

up); he visited the Azores and married a daughter of the captain of Fayal, and received knighthood from the king in 1485. The next year he was proposed as a member of the Dulmo-Estreito voyage, but possibly did not go; in 1490 he returned to Nuremberg and there in 1492 constructed his famous globe, in time to receive complimentary mention in the *Nuremberg Chronicle.* The scale, the eastward extension of Asia, and the narrow ocean on this globe are so similar to the false geographical notions on which Columbus based his voyage, as to suggest that Columbus and Behaim were collaborators. But there is no positive evidence of their trails ever crossing.

Nevertheless, we have another strong connection between Behaim and Columbus, in an extraordinary letter from a German astronomer named Hieronymus Müntzer to D. João II. Müntzer writes from Nuremberg on July 14, 1493, in complete ignorance that Columbus had returned from "The Indies" four months earlier. He maintains that the East is very near the West by sea; numerous arguments demonstrate that by crossing the ocean, eastern Cathay can be reached in a few days. This is proved by the presence of elephants in Asia and in Africa, and by the canes that drift ashore in the Azores. Your Highness's seamen have proved that habitable land lies in the tropic zone of Africa; so it follows that similar land will be found on the same parallel in Asia. "You possess means and ample wealth; as also able mariners, eager to acquire immortality and fame. O what glory you would gain, if you made the habitable Orient known to the Occident, and what profits would its commerce give you, for you would make those islands of the Orient tributaries, and their kings amazed would quietly submit to your sovereignty!" And furthermore (here's what he is leading up to), our young man Martin Behaim is ready to take charge of such a voyage and set sail from the Azores whenever you say the word.

Here is Columbus's Enterprise of the Indies, complete even to the driftwood evidence and the naïve supposition that kings of the Orient will passively submit to the first European who reaches their coasts. It does not matter whether Behaim obtained this idea from Columbus, or worked it out independently from the same sources; Müntzer's letter is the last term of a cycle that began with the Toscanelli letter of 1474. Columbus's scheme of reaching the East by sailing West was in the air for eighteen years before he put it into execution; and if he had faltered or failed, another was ready to embark on the same bold adventure.

Martin Behaim, however, would have made the same old error of starting a transatlantic voyage from the Azores, in the teeth of westerly winds.

Note on the Toscanelli Correspondence

Readers who have followed Columbian controversial literature of the last forty years may be surprised that I accept as genuine Toscanelli's letters to Canon Martins and to Columbus, since Henry Vignaud devoted a whole volume and parts of several others to arguing that they were false. If any still accept the Vignaud hypothesis, they are referred to the able, scholarly and critical discussion of the Toscanelli question by Dr. Diego Luis Molinari in the University of Buenos Aires' co-operative *Historia de la Nacion Argentina* II (1937) 398–425. Dr. Molinari's chapter in that volume is the best account of the Grand Enterprise of Columbus that has appeared in any language.

CHAPTER VII

In Castile

1485–1490

Dimitte populum meum ut sacrificet mihi.

Let my people go, that they may serve me.
— EXODUS ix 1

ABOUT the middle of the year 1485 Christopher Columbus with his five-year-old son Diego took passage from Lisbon for the port of Palos in Andalusia, with the purpose of offering his Enterprise of the Indies to the Sovereigns of Castile. He left Lisbon furtively and in haste, probably because he feared arrest for debt. Living expenses during the many months of promotion in Lisbon, and the cost of giving Dona Felipa a burial commensurate with her rank, must have consumed all Columbus's savings from his Guinea voyage and his Funchal business. Bartholomew remained in Lisbon for at least three years, supporting himself by making and selling charts.

The ship that took Columbus and his little son from Lisbon rounded Cape St. Vincent, crossed the bar of Saltés and anchored off the town of Palos on the Rio Tinto. It was rather a melancholy region of Spain to which Columbus had come, by design or by chance. The ancient Condado de Niebla is an undulating coastal plain traversed by two tidal rivers, the Odiel and the Tinto, which unite a few miles from the sea to form the Saltés. Around the seaports there was a great waste of marshland. An even more optimistic temperament than that of Columbus would have felt a sinking of the heart on first viewing the sleepy little seaports of Huelva and Palos, comparing them with bright, brisk Lisbon or tidy Funchal surrounded by vineyards. Actually the stagnation of Huelva, Palos and Moguer was only temporary. The Niebla had been the center of Castile's African slave trade, and her men were only less skilled than the Portuguese in making long African voyages; but Castile had renounced her African trade in the treaty of 1481 and it was now forbidden. Columbus knew nobody in Spain except his Molyart brother- and sister-in-law, who lived at Huelva, but they were in no position to do anything for him.

When his ship rounded the promontory at the entrance to the Rio Tinto, Columbus noted on a bluff the buildings of the Franciscan friary of La Rábida. These suggested a solution of his first problem, what to do with Diego while he sought friends and ways and means. The Minorites were noted for their hospitality, and often conducted schools for young boys; perhaps this house would take charge of his son. Soon after landing at Palos, father and son set out for La Rábida.

On this occasion took place the pretty incident of the alms at the monastery door. García Fernández, physician of Huelva, testified at Palos in 1513 "that the said Admiral Don Cristóbal Colón with his son Don Diego now admiral, came on foot to La Rábida, a monastery of friars in this town, and asked the porter to give him bread and a drink of water for that little boy who was his son." No doubt this happened. It is a long and dusty walk to La Rábida from Palos, and the little fellow would have been hungry and thirsty. But Dr. Fernández places the incident about six years too late, implies that Columbus was down and out, and proceeds to tell how Fray Juan Pérez, who came to the gate, talked with the future Admiral, understood his project, and arranged an audience with the Queen. Hence this chance encounter and timely charity set the wheels rolling that led to the great discovery.

That part of the story belongs to 1491; Dr. Fernández combined two visits of Columbus to La Rábida in one. It is certain that Columbus left his boy at La Rábida very soon after landing in Spain; but the friar who helped him then was Antonio de Marchena, *custodio* of the Franciscan sub-province of Seville, a man of spirit and intelligence, and of high repute as an *astrólogo* (astronomer). Fray Juan Pérez, *guardian* or head of La Rábida, helped Columbus in 1491; on this first visit he perhaps sent Columbus to

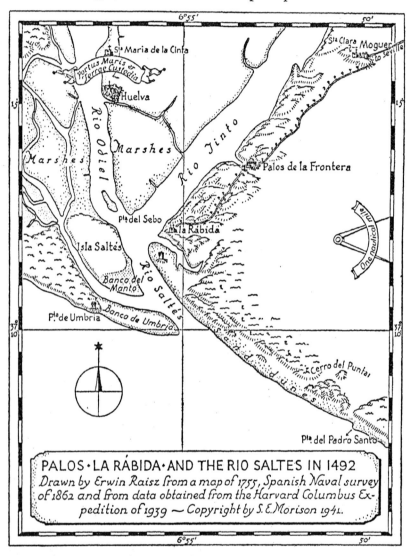

PALOS·LA RÁBIDA·AND THE RIO SALTES IN 1492
*Drawn by Erwin Raisz from a map of 1755, Spanish Naval survey
of 1862 and from data obtained from the Harvard Columbus Expedition of 1939 — Copyright by S.E.Morison 1941.*

Seville with a letter of introduction to Fray Antonio, or the *custodio* may have been visiting the friary when it received this unexpected visit from two future admirals of the Indies.

Antonio de Marchena was not so set in his ideas of the size of the globe as to be impervious to argument; Columbus later gave him credit for being one of the few Spaniards who believed he was right and furthered his enterprise. A man of imagination and human sympathy, he decided that Columbus had something, and became his advocate. On Fray Antonio's advice, application was first made to the very magnificent Don Enrique de Guzmán, Duke of Medina Sidonia, grandee of Spain and wealthiest subject of the Sovereigns. The duke became definitely interested, and was at the point of promising to equip a fleet for Columbus when, owing to an unseemly brawl with the Duke of Cadiz, the Sovereigns ordered him to leave Seville and the negotiations were broken off. Columbus then turned to Don Luis de la Cerda, Count of Medina Celi, who had a large establishment at Puerto Santa María and owned a merchant fleet.

At this point we have definite and contemporary evidence. A few days after the Admiral's return from his First Voyage, Medina Celi (who in the meantime had been created duke) wrote to the Grand Cardinal of Spain declaring that he had received Columbus on his first arrival from Portugal, and that he then decided to underwrite the Enterprise and provide the Genoese "with three or four well equipped caravels, for he asked no more." Thinking that royal permission was desirable for so important an affair, he applied to the Queen; she then ordered the man to come to court. After hearing Columbus, Isabella decided to submit his proposal to an advisory commission, but agreed that Medina Celi might outfit the fleet and invest in it if her decision was favorable. Later she decided to undertake the entire expense herself. In the meantime the duke had entertained Columbus for two years. Accordingly, on the ground that this great voyage was indirectly due to him, Medina Celi begs the cardinal to ask the Queen to permit him to send a few caravels annually to the newly discovered lands.

Most interesting is the statement that Columbus then demanded nothing more than three or four caravels, suitably equipped. Obviously a mere nobleman could not confer hereditary titles or offices or promise a tithe of the revenues and trade of the Indies. Following Portuguese precedent in the Western Islands, "The

Indies" if discovered by Columbus under ducal auspices would have been conferred by the Sovereigns on the duke, who might reward the discoverer with a hereditary captaincy, and whatever share of the revenues he saw fit. So, if Las Casas's account of the Portuguese negotiation of 1484–1485 is correct, Columbus had come down tremendously in his price. It seems much more likely that Las Casas made a mistake, and that Columbus never demanded titles, honors and revenues until 1491.

Columbus was so much the man of action, looked so constantly ahead and not astern, that the reminiscent passages in his writings are very few. One of these fixes the date of his arrival at the royal city of Cordova as January 20, 1486. He was too late to catch the King and Queen (they had left for Madrid at the end of 1485); but he always regarded himself as having been constantly in their service from the day of his arrival.

In that interval of waiting Columbus entered into relations with a young woman of Cordova named Beatriz Enríquez de Harana, who became the mother of his son Ferdinand in the late summer of 1488. Many and diverse have been the speculations about this girl, ranging all the way from a noble lady of Cordova down to chambermaid of the inn where Columbus stayed. Fortunately, the researches of my good friend D. José de la Torre, in the municipal archives of Cordova, have discovered exactly who Beatriz was, and how Columbus happened to meet her.

The Haranas were a family long established in Cordova and the vicinity as peasants, wine pressers and gardeners. Beatriz, daughter of a peasant named Pedro de Torquemada (a remote cousin of the grand inquisitor) and of Ana Núñez de Harana, was born about 1465 in the hamlet of Santa María de Trassiera up in the hills northwest of Cordova. Both her parents died when she was a child. With her elder brother, Pedro de Harana, who subsequently commanded a caravel on Columbus's Third Voyage, she went to live in Cordova with her mother's first cousin, Rodrigo Enríquez de Harana.

Rodrigo, though a wine presser by trade, was a man of culture and intelligence who married above his station and lived beyond his means. He had a son Diego de Harana, second cousin to Beatriz and subsequently marshal of the fleet on Columbus's First Voyage. These Haranas were friends and neighbors of Maestre Juan Sánchez, subsequently surgeon of the *Santa María*, and of a Genoese apothecary named Leonardo de Esbarraya whose shop was near the Puerto del Hierro of Cordova. In those days apothecary shops were informal clubs for physicians, surgeons and amateur scientists. Columbus probably drifted into the *botica* because it was kept by a compatriot, and frequented it as the place where local scientists foregathered. He made friends with Diego de Harana, a member of this informal club, was invited to his father's house, and there met the young orphan who became his mistress.

Although the sentimental and ecclesiastical biographers of Columbus insist that a clandestine marriage took place between him and Beatriz, nothing in his life is more certain than that he did *not* marry her, secretly or otherwise. Las Casas and Oviedo declare that Ferdinand was born out of wedlock. Columbus refers to Beatriz twice in his extant writings, in 1502 and 1506, and by her maiden name, not as his wife. She survived him fourteen years, and in sundry documents signs herself or is referred to by the notary as Beatriz Enríquez de Harana, never as Doña Beatriz Colón y Enríquez, or as widow of the great Admiral.

These documents prove incidentally that Beatriz knew how to read and write, but nothing is known of her appearance, personality or character. We do not even know how long Columbus lived with her; perhaps not after his First Voyage. But he had her on his mind all his life; for in 1502 he ordered his legitimate son Diego to give her the annuity of 10,000 maravedis which he took as reward for first sighting the New World, and in a testamentary codicil of 1506 he charged Diego to see that "Beatriz Enríquez, mother of Don Fernando my son, is put in a way to live honorably, as a person to whom I am in so great debt, and thus for discharge of my conscience, because it weigheth much on my mind."

Why he never married her, although his wife was dead, may easily be inferred. It was not to his advantage. Dona Felipa had been a lady of rank who helped him up in the world; if he married again, it must be to another lady of rank, like Doña Beatriz de Peraza, whom he is said to have wooed at Gomera. A peasant's daughter, unpresentable at court, would have been a bar to his ambition when still a suppliant, and an unsuitable match for an admiral and viceroy. The moral aspects of the relationship need not trouble us, since they did not bother his contemporaries. In an era when grandees, bishops and princes of the Church openly paraded their mistresses and procured honors and titles for their bastards, nobody criticized Columbus for not marrying the mother of his second son. Her family were evidently proud of the connection, since the cousin and the brother of Beatriz accepted responsible offices in the Admiral's fleets. Relations between them and the legitimate Colons remained intimate for at least three generations. D. Diego the second admiral of the Indies not only paid the annuity to Beatriz as his father had commanded, but remembered her in his will; and his widow, the Virreina Doña Maria de Colón y Toledo, made generous bequests to Beatriz's nephew Pedro de Harana and to Pedro's daughter Catalina. Moreover, it was Ferdinand, the son of this illicit union and biographer of the Admiral, who worked hard and successfully to protect the hereditary rights of his legitimate half-brother D. Diego.

·   ·   ·   ·   ·   ·   ·   ·   ·   ·   ·

In late April, which is almost summer in Andalusia, the Sovereigns again took up their residence in the Alcazar of Cordova, just over the Guadalquivir from the Moorish stone bridge and hard by the magnificent mosque, which had been rededicated as a cathedral church. For the first time Columbus was brought into the presence of Ferdinand and Isabella, to whose reign his achievements were destined to lend the brightest luster.

The marriage in 1469 of Isabella of Castile with Ferdinand of Aragon united modern Spain, the kingdom which became mistress of Europe in the next century through her own valor, implemented by the vast wealth that Columbus was now asking permission to pour into her lap. When he first appeared before *los Reyes Católicos*, "the Catholic Sovereigns," as Ferdinand and Isabella were generally called, they had been joint rulers of Castile, León and Aragon for twelve years. In this period they had curbed the power of the nobles and strengthened that of the crown, restored internal order, and " succeeded in arousing the economic energies of Castile in a variety of directions, and to an extent previously unknown." They had liquidated the secular struggle with Portugal by renouncing West Africa and securing the Canaries, whose conquest, a dress rehearsal for that of America, was already under way. Since the Canaries were Columbus's destined point of departure, that was all to the good; but a nearer conquest then being pressed, of the Moorish kingdom of Granada, was using so much energy and money as to hinder his chance of interesting the Sovereigns in an oceanic enterprise. It was as if a polar explorer had tried to interest Lincoln in the conquest of the Antarctic about the time of the Battle of Gettysburg.

Ferdinand of Aragon was not an agreeable person, and the contrast in this respect with the Queen has tended to obscure his abilities. His great and consuming interest was diplomacy: to deceive an old fool like Louis XII of France, which he boasted having done no less than ten times, was his greatest delight; and there was no league or combination of states on the continent in which he did not have a hand. His Catalan and Valencian kingdoms, bordering on the Mediterranean, had maritime interests and traditions, but looked eastward rather than westward. Columbus could not expect much from him.

Isabella of Castile was a strikingly handsome woman with regular features, a fresh, clear complexion, blue eyes and auburn hair; the coloring particularly admired in Spain because of its rarity. Her manners were gracious, dignified and affable, and she showed such tact in dealing with people as to gain an ascendancy over her turbulent subjects that no king of Castile could boast. She was simple in her tastes, temperate in her diet, and only tolerated frivolous entertainments at her court in the hope of weaning young ruffians of the nobility from their savage amusements. For the internal problems of Castile, which were many and complicated, she showed a statesman's grasp, and pursued a policy with tenacity and skill. When once she had given her confidence to a man, he could count on her unvarying support. Her piety and exemplary moral conduct were such that even in the corrupt court of her brother and predecessor, no scandal was ever breathed against her name. Unfortunately, too, she had the common defect of that quality, intolerance and bigotry; her expulsion of the Jews entailed a loss to her kingdoms that counterbalanced the gain from the conquest of Granada.

Christopher Columbus and Isabella the Catholic were of the same physical type, and very similar in character. She was his senior by only four or five months. Surely some spark of mutual comprehension and understanding passed between them when Columbus was first presented to her in the audience chamber of the Alcazar of Cordova, about the first day of May, 1486. She listened graciously to his ardent exposition of his desires. But before giving him further encouragement, several questions had to be settled. Did her counselors who were expert in such matters think a westward journey to the Indies practicable? Could the crown afford to underwrite it at that juncture? Or should Medina Celi be allowed to undertake it? In the meantime, she placed Columbus in charge of her comptroller of finances, Alonso de Quintanilla, who put him up at his house, and introduced him to the very magnificent Don Pedro Gonzales de Mendoza, Archbishop of Toledo, Grand Cardinal of Spain, first minister of the crown of Castile.

After this one burst of royal sunshine the clouds gathered once more, and the next five or six years were the hardest in Columbus's life. It would have been so much simpler had he been allowed to accept Medina Celi's offer. Las Casas says, "He began to sustain a terrible, continued, painful and prolonged battle; a material one of weapons would not have been so sharp and horrendous as that which he had to endure from informing so many people of no understanding, although they presumed to know all about it, and replying patiently to many people who did not know him nor had any respect for his person, receiving insulting speeches which afflicted his soul." For Columbus was not merely a mariner. He was proud and sensitive, he knew that he was right; and the clownish witticisms and crackpot jests of stupid and ignorant people were almost more than he could bear. Again and again in later life he alluded bitterly to those years, when almost everyone *fazen burla*, made game of him and his enterprise. Often, and most unwisely, he went out of his way to remind the Sovereigns and others how everyone had been wrong and he right.

Fray Hernando de Talavera, Prior del Prado (a Jeronymite monastery near Valladolid), the Queen's confessor and subsequently Archbishop of Granada, was chosen to organize a commission to examine Columbus's project. It first met at Cordova in the early summer of 1486, and adjourned to Salamanca where the court spent Christmas.

Salamanca was then a university of residential colleges, following the usual late-medieval organization that is now preserved only in Oxford and Cambridge. One of these colleges, that of St. Stephen, was presided over by the Dominican father Diego de Deza, later Bishop of Palencia and Archbishop of Seville. Columbus found in him one of his warmest and most useful advocates in Spain. In this college the Talavera commission sat. For, in 1515 a city councilor named Dr. Rodrigo Maldonado testified that he was there present when Talavera "with other wise and learned men and mariners, discussed with the said Admiral about his going to the said islands, and that all of them agreed that what the Admiral said could not possibly be true, and that contrary to what appeared to the most of them the Admiral persisted. . . ."

Obviously the thing that "could not possibly be true" was the Admiral's theory of a narrow ocean between Spain and the Indies. It was not true. Yet, owing to the feeling of Diego de Deza, perhaps also of Talavera, that there might be something in Columbus's project nevertheless, the commission postponed rendering a report.

What, then, becomes of the celebrated sessions of the University of Salamanca, before whose professors of mathematics, geography and astronomy Columbus argued his case, and was turned down because he could not convince them that the world was round? That is pure moonshine. Washington Irving, scenting his opportunity for a picturesque and moving scene, took a fictitious account of this nonexistent university council published 130 years after the event, elaborated on it, and let his imagination go completely. The result is that wonderful chapter where "an obscure navigator, a member of no learned society, destitute of all the trappings and circumstances which sometimes give oracular authority to dullness, and depending on the mere force of natural genius," sustains his thesis of a spherical globe against "pedantic bigotry" of flat-earth churchmen, fortified by texts from the Bible, Lactantius and Saint Augustine, until he began to feel nervous about the Inquisition. And how Columbus "met them upon their own ground, pouring forth those magnificent texts of Scripture, and those mysterious predictions of the prophets, which, in his enthusiastic moments, he considered as types and annunciations of the sublime discovery which he proposed." A gripping drama as Irving tells it, this has become one of the most popular Columbian myths; for we all love to hear of professors and experts being confounded by simple common sense.

Yet the whole story is misleading and mischievous nonsense. The University of Salamanca was not asked to decide. Columbus and Talavera merely held committee hearings in the College of St. Stephen, at which neither side was able to convince the other. The sphericity of the globe was not in question. The issue was the width of the ocean; and therein the opposition was right.

These informal conferences and hearings were presumably held around Christmastide 1486, when the court was at Salamanca. Not long after, Columbus was put on the royal payroll. The records of the treasury of Castile show that "Cristóbal Colomo, extrangero" (foreigner) was paid 3000 maravedis on May 5, 1487, the same amount on July 3, 4000 on August 27, 1487, "to go to the royal encampment" (then investing Malaga), the same on October 15, and 3000 maravedis on June 16, 1488. In other words he was given a retaining fee of about 12,000 maravedis a year, roughly eighty to ninety dollars, the pay of an able seaman. Not exactly princely, but enough for a man of his simple tastes to keep body and soul together.

Of Columbus's own movements this year we have no hint, except the payment to enable him to visit the royal camp before Malaga, the last important Spanish seaport held by the Moors. Malaga had capitulated on August 18, 1487, and Columbus doubtless expected that this would be an opportune juncture to interest the Sovereigns. If so, he failed; for there were still strong cities in the hands of the infidel. The Sovereigns' overwhelming interest in this war was an even greater obstacle to him than the doubts of scientists. Apparently the court lost interest in him the next year, for his retaining fee was not renewed after June 1488. In August or September of that year Beatriz gave birth to Ferdinand at Cordova. The Talavera committee had not yet reported, nor had Columbus been formally dismissed; but with his small income cut off he thought it wise to accept D. João's invitation and renew negotiations with Portugal.

These fell through, as we have seen, after Bartholomew Dias returned from the Cape of Good Hope; D. João II had found one ocean route to India and needed no other. Columbus then returned to Spain, and sent his brother Bartholomew to London.

The movements of Bartholomew are even more obscure than those of Christopher. He probably had stayed on in Lisbon after his elder brother's first departure in 1485, and did not leave until the return of Bartholomew Dias had spoiled the proposed deal with Portugal. The most meticulous research in English sources and archives has uncovered no trace of Bartholomew in England; but this is not surprising, for scarcely anything can be found about John Cabot. According to Ferdinand Columbus, his uncle obtained an interview with Henry VII and presented him with a world map containing an interesting but provokingly vague Latin inscription, to the effect that "you who wish to learn of the coasts of countries must learn by this map what Strabo, Ptolemy, Pliny and Isidore taught." Ferdinand adds that Henry VII became definitely interested, and was still dickering with Bartholomew in his parsimonious Tudor manner when news of the great discovery arrived; but Oviedo, who wrote earlier than Ferdinand, says that the proposition was rejected by the counselors of the king, who "made game of what Columbus said, and held his words to be vain."

Not later than 1490 Bartholomew proceeded to the court of France, where his proposition proved to be no more acceptable than in England. Again, we have the same provoking silence of the archives, but several statements from French sources of the next century say that Charles VIII thought no more of the Enterprise than did Henry VII. Bartholomew, however, found a protector and patroness in Anne de Beaujeu, the king's elder sister and regent during his minority. From her his hopes of French support must have been kept up, since Christopher himself was on the point of going to France in 1491. Bartholomew was still living at Fontainebleau as a retainer of Anne de Beaujeu, unhappily employed in making maps, when news of his brother's great discovery arrived.

Christopher Columbus, we may suppose, was back in Spain early in 1489, waiting, hoping and praying for a favorable report from the Talavera committee, and for a swift conclusion of the last campaign against Granada. He had two more years to wait. Until the latter part of 1491, when he reappears at La Rábida, his movements are purely conjectural. Presumably part of this time he put in at Cordova with Beatriz, who was bringing up their child Ferdinand; he certainly regarded Cordova as his home in 1493. He probably visited La Rábida from time to time to keep in touch with young Diego. Possibly he sold books and charts at Seville.

And, as the slender pittance from the Queen was cut short in June 1488, he may have been supported by the hospitable Duke of Medina Celi.

In any event, he had plenty of time for reading. Between 1485 and 1490 Columbus did some heavy combing through ancient and medieval authorities on geography in order to gather ammunition for his next bout with the experts. Let them throw Ptolemy at him, he would pay them back in their own coin and better. Four of these books that Columbus owned (three of them elaborately annotated) have been preserved: a 1485 Latin translation of the *Book of Ser Marco Polo;* an Italian translation of Pliny's *Natural History* printed in 1489; Pierre d'Ailly's *Imago Mundi* and minor treatises, all in Latin and printed at Louvain between 1480 and 1483; and a 1477 edition of the *Historia Rerum Ubique Gestarum* by Aeneas Sylvius (Pope Pius II).

Two in particular, the *Imago Mundi* and *Historia Rerum,* show by their multitude of postils or marginal notes, made with a variety of pens and inks with minor differences of handwriting, that Columbus and probably his brother Bartholomew also read them over and over again. The *Imago Mundi* seems to have been Christopher's bedside book for a number of years, and he used the blank leaves at the back of the *Historia Rerum* as a catch-all for miscellaneous observations. These postils have been studied by Columbus's biographers, beginning with Ferdinand and Las Casas. There has been much discussion by self-styled handwriting experts as to whether this or that note is by Christopher or Bartholomew. It really does not matter,* for the two brothers worked together with the same ideas and on the same project.

The *Imago Mundi* of Pierre d'Ailly, Cardinal of Cambrai, was a comprehensive world geography composed around the year 1410, before Ptolemy's *Geography* had been rediscovered by Western Europe. That is one reason why Columbus preferred D'Ailly to

---

* Excepting as regards the three relating to Bartholomew Dias and José Vizinho, which serve to date the Discoverer's (or his brother's) movements.

Ptolemy. The French cosmographer followed the system of Marinus of Tyre, who made Eurasia long and the Atlantic narrow. Incorporated in Columbus's copy of the *Imago Mundi* were two of the Cardinal's later cosmographical tracts, written after he had read Ptolemy; but they served Columbus even better, since D'Ailly ventures to disagree with the Alexandrian sage. For instance, he says, "The length of the land toward the Orient is much greater than Ptolemy admits . . . Arim * is not merely a distance of 90° from the [end of] the Orient, it is much farther, because the length of the habitable Earth on the side of the Orient is more than half the circuit of the globe. For, according to the philosophers and Pliny, the ocean which stretches between the extremity of further Spain (that is, Morocco) and the eastern edge of India is of no great width. *For it is evident that this sea is navigable in a very few days if the wind be fair*, whence it follows that the sea is not so great that it can cover three quarters of the globe, as certain people figure it." Heavy underscorings and long postil by Columbus; mental note to bring this up whenever anyone mentions Ptolemy's 180° of land.

Columbus notes every mention of the length of a degree, and sometimes writes in the margin, "Not so. A degree is 56⅔ Roman miles," or words to that effect. We have already cited the notes from his own experience in Africa, proving that the Torrid Zone is inhabitable. Any statement in the *Imago Mundi* about the narrowness of the ocean is eagerly picked up and copied or commented on by Columbus. For instance: —

The end of the habitable earth toward the Orient and the end of the habitable earth toward the Occident are near enough, and between them is a small sea.

Between the end of Spain and the beginning of India is no great width.

An arm of the sea extends between India and Spain.

India is near Spain.

---

* Aryim, the terrestrial umbilicus according to the ancients, should be halfway on Ptolemy's 180° length of the habitable world.

The beginnings of the Orient and of the Occident are close.

From the end of the Occident to the end of India by land is much greater than half the globe, viz. 180°.

Water runs from pole to pole between the end of Spain and the beginning of India.

Aristotle [says] between the end of Spain and the beginning of India is a small sea navigable in a few days . . . Esdras [says] six parts [of the globe] are habitable and the seventh is covered with water. Observe that the blessed Ambrose and Austin and many others considerҽd Esdras a prophet.

Julius [Solinus] teaches that the entire sea from India up to Spain behind (*per dorsum*) Africa is navigable.

The end of Spain and the beginning of India are not far distant but close, and it is evident *that this sea is navigable in a few days with a fair wind.*

As complement to the narrow ocean, Columbus grasps at every bit of "evidence" as to an excessive length of Asia.

Note that the king of Tarshish came to the Lord at Jerusalem and spent a year and 13 days on the way, as the blessed Jerome has it.

From a harbor of the Red Sea to India is a sail of one year. And Solomon took three years to make the round voyage. . . . From the end of the Occident (Portugal) to the end of the Orient (India) by land is a tremendous distance.

D'Ailly's chapter on India (Asia) is heavily annotated by Columbus. The mighty rivers, the gold, silver, pearls and precious stones, the elephants, parrots, gryphons and monsters excite him. One postil accompanied by an index finger calls attention to the innumerable islands around India, full of pearls and precious stones. Disappointed at the meager mention of Ophir in *Imago Mundi*, Columbus writes a postil so long as to be almost a supplement, referring to the third book of Kings and second of Chronicles for the movements of Solomon and Jehoshaphat. He adds, "See our maps on paper where the sphere is represented." Naturally a cartographer would have made maps to demonstrate his theory of the narrow ocean.

The *Historia Rerum Ubique Gestarum* (1477) of Aeneas Sylvius, although printed a few years earlier than the *Imago Mundi*, was written some thirty years later. Largely potted Ptolemy, it was more accurate and informing than *Imago Mundi*, but by the same token less acceptable to Columbus. Yet there was plenty in Ptolemy and the other ancient authors quoted by Aeneas Sylvius that Columbus could use.

Study and analyze as we will these "subtle shining secrecies, writ in the glassie margents of such bookes," * all point to one object and one only of the Great Enterprise: to reach the Orient by sailing west. Pierre d'Ailly's chapter "On the other celebrated islands of the Ocean" aroused no interest on Columbus's part, except to note that the Insulae Gorgades and Fortunatae were the modern Cape Verdes and Canaries, and that the terrestrial paradise was certainly not located there. Thus, the postils afford very cold comfort to those trying to prove that Columbus was seeking nothing more important than new Atlantic islands, that his interest in the Orient arose only when he missed Antillia. Writers of this description either ignore the unmistakable evidence in the postils or blandly assert that they were all made *after* the First Voyage either (1) to mislead posterity as to Columbus's real object, or (2) to gather material for the Book of Prophecies. The first charge is too frivolous to be worth a reply; the Book of Prophecies contains nothing but prophecies, mainly from the Bible, with only a few incidental gatherings from the *Imago Mundi*, *Historia Rerum* and Marco Polo. Three postils dated 1481 and "in hoc anno '88" prove that Columbus at least began reading the *Historia Rerum* well before 1490. These and others, as well as the detached postils preserved by Ferdinand, mention facts gathered from Christopher's experience on voyages to Africa, Ireland and Iceland, in order to refute something in the text.

Can anyone for a moment believe that Columbus could have made these annotations after 1492 and not inserted a single fact from his infinitely more marvelous experience in America?

---

* Shakespeare, *The Rape of Lucrece*.

CHAPTER VIII

The Queen Consents

1489–1492

Et erunt reges nutritij tui, et reginae nutrices tuae.

And kings shall be thy nursing fathers, and their queens thy nursing mothers.

— ISAIAH xlix 23

ONLY one certain trace of Columbus exists for the year 1489. On May 12 the Sovereigns furnished him with an open letter to all municipal and local officials, ordering them to furnish free board and lodging to "Cristóbal Colomo" who "has to come to this our court." The king was then directing the siege of Baza. A great fortified camp was built outside the Moorish city, the "flower of Spanish chivalry" were present, and everything was done in the most magnificent manner. Why the Sovereigns wished to see Columbus at this juncture we do not know. Possibly Talavera, who had not yet reported, suggested an interview; more likely Columbus himself, as soon as he returned from Portugal, renewed his application to the Queen, who graciously permitted him to come into her presence. And as he had no money, provision had to be made for his transportation.

How long Columbus stayed with the court in camp, and what if anything he accomplished, are unknown. He is said to have joined the army as a volunteer, and to have "given demonstration of the conspicuous valor which accompanied his wisdom and high desires." Considering his zeal against the crescent, he would naturally have welcomed an opportunity to strike a few blows for the cross; and a curious incident of this siege served to implement his highest desires. An embassy arrived from the Sultan of Egypt, who threatened to persecute the Christians in his dominions and raze the Holy Sepulchre unless Ferdinand and Isabella stopped fighting the Moslems of Spain. Columbus most certainly took occasion to point out to the Queen how precarious were the sacred places of Palestine under the infidel, and to beg her to send him westward in search of new sources of wealth for financing a crusade. But Isabella's attention could not be attracted to the Enterprise of the Indies while the Moorish kingdom of Granada still held out. When Baza capitulated, on December 4, 1489, Columbus was again turned out to grass.

This was the period when he suffered real distress; when, according to Bishop Geraldini, he applied to a Franciscan monastery near Marchena in Andalusia for hospitality. How did he manage to live, and where? Was he selling books and maps, as Andrés Bernáldez of Seville reported to be his occupation when first he met Columbus? Had he exhausted the hospitality of Medina Celi? Did he lodge with the Haranas in Cordova? Almost any conjecture is possible, since no facts have survived. It was not a period that Columbus cared to talk about in later years.

The court spent part of 1490 in Seville, and it was probably there late in the year that Talavera finally rendered a report. The committee "judged his promises and offers were impossible and vain and worthy of rejection," says Las Casas, and advised the Sovereigns "that it was not a proper object for their royal authority to favor an affair that rested on such weak foundations, and which appeared uncertain and impossible to any educated person, however little learning he might have." Ferdinand and Las Casas give six arguments used by Talavera to prove that Columbus was wrong. (1) A voyage to Asia would require three years. (2) The Western Ocean is infinite and perhaps unnavigable. (3) If he reached the Antipodes (the land on the other side of the globe from Europe) he could not get back. (4) There are no Antipodes because the greater part of the globe is covered with water, and because Saint Augustine says so. (According to Las Casas, *duda Sant' Agustin*, "Saint Augustine doubts," became a sort of refrain of the Talavera committee.) (5) Of the five zones, only three are habitable. (6) So many centuries after the Creation it was unlikely that anyone could find hitherto unknown lands of any value.

Although this set of reasons is denounced by Vignaud and others as frivolous and fabricated (for they help to prove Columbus's Asiatic objective, and are no great credit to the Spanish intellect of 1490), there seems no good reason to doubt Las Casas's word. They are exactly the sort of objections anyone would have made in 1490, in the then state of geographical knowledge in Castile, a country not so far advanced in such matters as Portugal. After all, the Portuguese had been merely pushing coastwise along a continent known to the ancients. Striking out westward to the Orient was a very different matter, novel, risky and uncertain. The postils in Columbus's books prove that he had been accumulating answers to the first five points, and Seneca's *Medea* was a sufficient answer to the sixth. It certainly did not take much learning to see that Columbus's 60° ocean was all wrong. Why then, we may ask, did the committee require four and a half years to report on it? Simply the custom of the country.

Ferdinand and Isabella neither accepted nor rejected the Talavera report. They caused Columbus to be informed, says Las Casas, that his Enterprise might again be brought to their attention at a more propitious moment, when the war with Granada was over.

Columbus waited another six to nine months, possibly at the house of Medina Celi. By the end of that time he swore "by San Fernando" he would wait no longer on the Queen's pleasure. He had had more than enough Castilian procrastination. Whether or not Bartholomew encouraged him from Fontainebleau we do not know; but Columbus determined to go to France and offer his Enterprise to Charles VIII.

In the summer of 1491 Columbus visited La Rábida to call for his son Diego, now ten or eleven years old. Perhaps the boy was unhappy with the friars, maybe Columbus wished to be under no further obligation to them; in any case he proposed to leave the lad at Huelva with his mother's sister, the wife of Miguel Molyart, before departing for France.

Now occurs the second half of the well-known La Rábida story. Fray Juan Pérez, head of the friary, deplored Columbus's intention to quit Spain forever. Dr. Fernández, who as a physician was the local authority on astronomy and cosmography, was called into consultation; as (in all probability) was Martín Alonso Pinzón, a leading shipowner of Palos. Fray Juan, who many years before had been confessor or comptroller to the Queen (perhaps both), promised to obtain for Columbus another royal audience if he would stay. The Queen was then at the fortified camp of Santa Fe, a city which was especially constructed in July 1491, in order to serve as Castilian headquarters during the siege of Granada. Fray Juan sent her a letter by Sebastián Rodríguez, a pilot of Lepe, and in two weeks' time received a favorable reply. Isabella commanded Fray Juan to come to court, to encourage Columbus, and tell him to await a summons of his own. The friar departed at once on a mule chartered for him by Columbus, and probably paid for by Martín Alonso Pinzón. Before long the Queen wrote directly to Columbus, commanding him to proceed to court. Either she recalled his shabby appearance on a former occasion, or Fray Juan excited her compassion by describing his state of extreme penury; for the Queen sent with her letter the sum of 20,000 maravedis in order that Columbus might procure some decent clothing and a mule.

Not before August, and probably somewhat later in the year 1491, Columbus in his new suit of clothes appeared before the Queen. And again his Enterprise was put in the hands of a committee; for Las Casas says that *astrólogos* (astronomers), mariners and pilots as well as *filósofos* were consulted. From this *ad hoc* committee (like the Ortiz one in Portugal and the Talavera one in Spain) which examined and reported on the technical aspects of the case, the Enterprise was referred to the Royal Council of Castile, composed of grandees and higher ecclesiastics. There, presumably, the technical aspects were reviewed. Bishop Geraldini, who was present, remembered the old "duda Sant' Agustin" being dragged out again; he observed to the Cardinal of Spain that, whilst Saint Augustine was undoubtedly a great theologian, navigators like Columbus who had sailed beyond the Line probably knew somewhat more about antipodean geography.

Columbus of course demonstrated his narrow ocean hypothesis with a *mappemonde*. We know that he had one or more among the "exhibits," and a keen search has been made in every depositary of old maps in Europe for one that might have been his. An entry in a library catalogue of 1629, "Declaratio chartae nauigatoriae Domini Almirantis," proved a false lead, as the last two words were a later interpolation. In the present century Charles de la Roncière thought he had found Columbus's very map among the collections of the Bibliothèque Nationale, and reproduced it in a sumptuous volume; but there is really nothing in this map to connect it with Columbus, for it does not demonstrate his Q.E.D., the narrow ocean and proximity of Asia to Spain.

Ferdinand and Las Casas both infer that the reason the Enterprise was rejected again was the enormous price Columbus demanded in honors, titles and revenues, as a reward for success. This suggests that the Enterprise was approved by the special committee and rejected by the Royal Council. For no committee of *astrólogos*, mariners and the like had any business to recommend what honors and titles their Sovereigns should accord to a successful discoverer. Their job was to report whether or not the project was feasible; and only if they favored it was there any need for the Council to take it up. The Council naturally would review the case, and decide whether to take the risk and pay the price. So, after sifting the various and conflicting statements by contemporaries, it seems probable that Columbus was now turned down for the third and last time, simply because his contingent demands were considered exorbitant.

This is the earliest occasion when we may be certain that Columbus stated his expected reward. Possibly he had settled in his own mind some years before what he intended to demand, but as yet there had been no occasion for him to let it out. The Ortiz commission in Portugal, the Talavera committee in Spain, were charged only with the technical aspects of Columbus's project. Las Casas does indeed say that Columbus's price to Portugal was the same as that which he demanded and obtained from Spain, but we suspect his accuracy. Columbus would certainly have retained enough peasant bargaining instinct to hold back what he expected in the way of titles and emoluments until his Enterprise was accepted in principle; his strategy was to have it pronounced scientifically correct, technically feasible, and likely to bring in money to the crown. Then and then only would he bring up the subject of rewards to King, Queen or Royal Council.

One may speculate endlessly as to when Columbus settled in his own mind that nobility and a coat of arms, a resounding title, high offices and substantial revenues should be his proper reward for success in the Enterprise of the Indies. Medina Celi's letter indicates that in 1485 his ambitions in this direction were still modest; and, in my opinion, the final schedule of honors and emoluments was not formulated before 1491. He had then made up his mind to go to France, and anticipated that Charles VIII would treat him handsomely (in which expectation he would certainly have been disappointed). He was under a sense of outrage and wrong over six wasted years in Spain. On a thousand occasions he had smarted under the insults which a "somebody" with no brains could inflict with impunity on a "nobody" with an idea. Columbus resented this treatment all his life long, frequently adverted to it bitterly. So, thought he, if those proud Castilians want my services after all, they will have to pay through the nose, God take them! I will not glorify Spain for nothing. If the Sovereigns will grant me appropriate titles and honors to found a noble family, and the means for my descendants to keep up their rank, well and good. If not, I go to France.

Granada capitulated on January 2, 1492, and Columbus had the joy of marching in the procession that entered the last stronghold of the Moslem in Catholic Spain. Then the axe fell for him.

Before many days he was informed that his Enterprise was absolutely and definitely rejected. The Sovereigns themselves confirmed this at an audience which they meant to be final, and in which they wished him *bon voyage*.

So that was the result of six and a half years' watching and waiting in Spain. "By San Fernando" he was through!

Columbus saddled his mule, packed the saddlebags with his spare shirt, world chart, *Imago Mundi* and *Historia Rerum*, and in company with the faithful Fray Juan set forth on the road to Cordova. He had saved enough of the Queen's present to take passage for France, no doubt. In any case, he could work his way.

Suddenly the whole picture changed. Columbus had made another friend at court, Luis de Santangel, *escribano de ración* (keeper of the privy purse) to King Ferdinand. The very day that Columbus departed from Santa Fe, Luis de Santangel "went to find the Queen, and with words which his keen desire to persuade her suggested, told her that he was astonished to see that her Highness, who had always shown a resolute spirit in matters of great pith and consequence, should lack it now for an enterprise of so little risk, yet which could prove of so great service to God and the exaltation of His Church, not to speak of very great increase and glory for her realms and crown; an enterprise of such nature that if any other prince should undertake what the Admiral offered to her, it would be a very great damage to her crown, and a grave reproach to her." If money were a consideration, Santangel would be glad to finance the fleet himself. Isabella, much impressed by his warmth and sincerity, said that she would reconsider the case as soon as she had a little breathing space; or, if there were any haste, pledge her jewels for the expenses, which Santangel assured her would be unnecessary. The Queen then sent a messenger for Columbus, who overtook him at the village of Pinos-Puente, about ten miles from Granada and four from Santa Fe, where the court was then residing.

Royal commands must be obeyed. The fellow travelers came about, and caught a fair wind that lasted to America.

Why this sudden change of mind? One may speculate that personality had much to do with it. The most impressive thing about Columbus's presentation of his case had not been the facts and the arguments, but the man. His dignity, sincerity and absolute certainty must have left their mark on the Queen. "When he had made up his mind," wrote Las Casas, "he was as sure he would discover what he did discover, and find what he did find, as if he held it in a chamber under lock and key."

His character was very similar to that of the Queen, and he reasoned much in the same way, from fixed ideas and religious preconceptions. So, if Isabella still hesitated when she sent for Columbus, his presence gave her confidence. Moreover, Santangel's reasoning was irresistible. So little risk for so vast a gain! What if the experts or some of them did laugh at the Enterprise and say that the geographical notions of this Genoese were absurd, impossible, ridiculous? How did they know, these closet cosmographers and Mediterranean mariners? The Queen had seen a good deal of experts in her reign of eighteen years, and realized that half the time they did not know what they were talking about. This man Colomo or Colón appealed not only to her reason, but to her instincts.

Let us give feminine intuition due credit, but not all. The King had to consent to everything the Queen did, Santangel was his official, not hers; and Santangel found at least half the money. Exact figures as to the expense of the First Voyage are not available; but from various hints and indications it seems to have cost around 2,000,000 maravedis (say $14,000) to fit out. Isabella had proposed to raise the money on her crown jewels, but this was not necessary; the fable that she actually pawned them for Columbus dates from the seventeenth century. Santangel and Francisco Pinelo, who were joint treasurers of the Santa Hermandad, an efficient police force that had its own endowment, borrowed from that treasury 1,400,000 maravedis, which was eventually repaid by the crown. Columbus himself invested 250,000 maravedis in the enterprise, which he must have borrowed from his friends and supporters, such as Juanoto Berardi the Florentine merchant-banker of Seville, or the Duke of Medina Celi. The balance was probably advanced by Santangel on his own account, or from the treasury of Aragon. This sum of two million maravedis did not include the payroll, which came to a quarter of a million monthly.

. . . .

Almost three months were required to negotiate with the Sovereigns after the Great Enterprise was accepted in principle; yet of these negotiations we have no information. We only know that Fray Juan Pérez acted as Columbus's attorney, and Juan de Coloma represented the Sovereigns. Very likely the delay was due to chancery red tape, copying and recopying documents, greasing the right palms, and all that. Crown officials must have been very busy liquidating the Moorish kingdom of Granada, demobilizing the army and preparing to expel the Jews — another and less happy enterprise that was under way at the time.

The main documents of the Great Enterprise are seven in number: the Capitulations or Articles of Agreement of April 17; the *Título* or Title of April 30, 1492 (sometimes called the Commission); the Letter of Credence to foreign potentates, dated April 30; the Passport, undated; and three Orders of the Sovereigns dated April 30 about fitting out the fleet.

The Capitulations of April 17 are in five articles, each signed "It pleaseth their Highnesses, Juan de Coloma," and the whole signed by the King and Queen. The preamble of the oldest copy we have, made in 1495, describes this document as "the things supplicated and which your highnesses give and grant to *Don Cristóbal de Colón* in some satisfaction for what he hath discovered [*que ha descubierto*] in the ocean seas and for the voyage which with God's help he is now about to make thereon." (The past tense has aroused no end of conjecture; but as it did not trouble contemporaries it need not trouble us.) Their Highnesses appoint the said Don Cristóbal Colón their Admiral in and over all islands and mainlands "which shall be discovered or acquired by his labor and industry," and that title with all rights and prerogatives appertaining thereunto shall be enjoyed by his heirs and successors perpetually. (2) The said *Don Cristóbal* is appointed Viceroy and Governor-General over all such mainlands and islands as he shall discover or acquire in the said seas, and he may nominate three candidates for each office, from whom the Sovereigns will select one. (3) He shall take and keep a tenth of all gold, silver, pearls, gems, spices and other merchandise produced or obtained by barter and mining within the limits of these domains, free of all taxes. (4) Any case involving such merchandise or products will be adjudicated by him or his deputy, as Admiral. (5) He is given the option of paying an eighth part of the total expense of any ship sailing to these new possessions, and taking an eighth of the profits.

The *Título* or Title of April 30 is a solemn but still contingent confirmation of the titles and offices: —

"Whereas you, *Cristóbal Colón*, are setting forth by our command . . . to discover and acquire certain islands and mainland in the ocean sea . . . it is just and reasonable that, since you are exposing yourself to this danger in our service, you be rewarded therefor, . . . it is our will and pleasure that you the said *Cristóbal Colón* after you have discovered and acquired the said islands and mainland . . . or any of them, shall be our Admiral of the said islands and mainland which you may thus discover and acquire, and shall be our Admiral and Viceroy and Governor therein, and shall be empowered henceforward to call and entitle yourself *Don Cristóbal Colón*, and his heirs and successors forever may be so entitled, and enjoy the offices of Admiral of the Ocean Sea, Viceroy and Governor of the said islands and mainland."

Now the extraordinary thing about these documents is their failure to refer to a route to the Indies, indeed to mention the

Indies in any manner whatsoever; they speak only of discovering and acquiring a mainland and islands in the Ocean Sea. On this negation was built the hypothesis of Vignaud that Columbus never thought of sailing to the Indies, never proposed or intended anything more than discovering hitherto unknown islands and mainlands, such as Antillia and the place touched at by the Unknown Pilot; that he shifted his whole emphasis and denatured his purpose when, having sailed past the supposed position of these islands, he found others at a longitude which he supposed to be that of China and Japan.

Yet the evidence of Columbus's oriental objective, as we have seen, is abundant, and the Sovereigns' intent to support that objective is unmistakable, despite the equivocal language of the agreement. The phrases "islands and mainlands of the Ocean Sea" meant Japan, China and neighboring islands. This is sufficiently proved by the fact that when Columbus returned in 1493, insisting that he had discovered Cipangu and certain outlying dominions of the Grand Khan, nobody contested his right to be Admiral, Governor and Viceroy thereof, and the Pope freely conceded Spanish sovereignty over them. Moreover, the agreement of April 17 mentions "pearls, precious stones, gold, silver and spices" among the products that the Admiral will be privileged to tithe, and these were of the Orient; there was no tradition or expectation that any such precious things were to be found in Atlantic islands. There is also a significant analogy to the letters-patent of John Cabot, whom we know positively to have been seeking a westward passage to India. His grant of 1496 from Henry VII was couched in terms very similar to the Columbus capitulations. The Indies are not mentioned by name, but the king confers on Cabot power to "conquer, occupy and possess" any "islands, countries, regions or provinces of heathens and infidels, in whatsoever part of the world placed, which before this time were unknown to all Christians."

Surely, the reader will ask, you do not suppose that Ferdinand and Isabella (and Henry VII) were so simple as to suppose that three small vessels (or one still smaller) with ninety (or eighteen) men could sail into a harbor of Japan or China and simply take over? The answer is, yes, they were as simple as that. Remember that letter of Dr. Müntzer to D. João II, which assumes that any and every oriental potentate will be only too glad to swear allegiance to the Christian monarch whose ship first appears in his territorial waters? * That is what had happened to the Portuguese in West and South Africa; and Europe envisaged the kings of the Orient as no better prepared to defend their possessions than the sable potentates of the Dark Continent. The information of the European chanceries about China was so out of date that they even alluded to the Emperor of China as the Grand Khan, a title that became extinct when the Tartar Dynasty fell in 1368.

Moreover, the oriental objective is proved by the next two documents with which the Sovereigns provided Columbus. The first, undated, was a brief Latin passport: —

"By these presents we dispatch the noble man Christoforus Colon with three equipped caravels over the Ocean Seas toward the regions of India [*ad partes Indie*] for certain reasons and purposes."

The other is the Letter of Credence. The record of it, which has been found in the registries of Aragon, may be translated in part as follows: —

"To the most serene prince
our very dear friend, Ferdinand and Isabella, King and Queen of Castile, Aragon, Leon, etc., greetings and increase of good fortune. We have learned with joy of your esteem and high regard for us and our nation and of your great eagerness to receive information concerning our successes. Wherefore we have resolved to dispatch our noble captain *Christopherus Colon* to you, with letters, from which you may learn of our good health and prosperity . . .

    I the King   I the Queen
done in triplicate"

Las Casas thus explains the blank, and the subscription "done in triplicate." Columbus carried "royal letters of recommendation for the Grand Khan, and for all the kings and lords of India and of any

---

* End of Chapter vi, above.

other region that he might find in the lands which he might discover." Probably in the blank space of one copy the engrosser inserted *Magno Cano*, and the other copies were left blank so that Rodrigo de Escobedo, secretary of the fleet, could insert the correct name and titles of the Emperor of Japan, the Lord of Mangi, or whatever potentate the fleet might encounter. The Grand Khan, moreover, is specifically mentioned in the prologue to Columbus's Journal of his First Voyage.

The alleged high regard of the Chinese Emperor for Spain, and his supposed eagerness to learn of her conquest of Granada, are based on the story of a mysterious oriental traveler, said to be from a Christian nation bordering on China, who visited Florence about 1445 and conversed through an interpreter with Toscanelli. Columbus inferred from the incidental reference to this strange personage in Toscanelli's famous letter, that he was an envoy of the Grand Khan, who was eager to conclude an alliance with Christian princes against the Moslems.

Practical matters of equipment did not enter into the formal agreement; they were probably settled by word of mouth between Columbus and some ministers of the crown before April 30, when the Sovereigns issued what they believed to be the necessary orders for chartering, equipping, provisioning and manning the fleet at Palos.

On May 12, 1492, Columbus left Granada and proceeded to the town where he had first set foot in Spain, and whence he was destined to depart on his great voyage of discovery.

CHAPTER IX

Niña, Pinta and Santa María

1492–1493

Ecce et naues . . .

Behold also the ships . . .

— JAMES iii 4

ARMED with his credentials and contracts, full of energy and eager to be off and away, Columbus arrived on May 22, 1492, at Palos de la Frontera. Why Palos? Seville or Cadiz, the principal ports of Andalusia, would seem to have been the logical places to prepare an important expedition; but Cadiz was out as a port of departure for Columbus, because it had been designated as the embarking place for the Jews who were then being forced into exile; 8000 families are said to have sailed from there in the summer of 1492. Palos very likely would have been chosen in any case, since it had a fleet of caravels and a seafaring population experienced in Guinea voyages. Palos, moreover, was the home of the friendly friars who had done so much to further the enterprise, and Palos had conveniently committed' some municipal misdemeanor for which the Sovereigns fined it the use of two caravels for a twelvemonth. If other reasons were good and sufficient, this last was conclusive.

On Wednesday, May 23, "in the Church of St. George of this town of Palos, in the presence of Fr. Juan Pérez" and of the mayor and councilors, "Cristóbal Colón gave and presented to the aforesaid this letter of their Highnesses, the which was read by me, Francisco Fernández, notary public of said town." So reads Francisco's endorsement on a letter of the Sovereigns dated April 30, the same day as the Capitulations and Titles: —

Ferdinand and Isabella, by the Grace of God King and Queen of Castile, León, Aragon, Sicily, etc., etc., to you Diego Rodríguez Prieto and all the other inhabitants of the town of Palos, greeting and grace.

Know ye that whereas for certain things done and committed by you to our disservice you were condemned and obligated by our Council to provide us for a twelvemonth with two equipped caravels at your own proper charge and expense. . . . And whereas we have now commanded Cristóbal Colón to go with three *carabelas de armada* as our Captain of the same, toward certain regions of the Ocean Sea, to perform certain things for our service, and we desire that he take with him the said two caravels with which you are thus required to serve us; therefore we command that within ten days of receiving this our letter . . . you have all ready and prepared two equipped caravels, as you are required by virtue of the said sentence, to depart with the said Cristóbal Colón whither we have commanded him to go, . . . and we have commanded him to give you advance pay for four months for the people who are to sail aboard the said caravels at the rate to be paid to the other people who are to be in the said three [*sic*] caravels, and in the other caravel that we have commanded him to take, whatever is commonly and customarily paid on this coast to the people who go to sea in a fleet, . . . and we forbid the said Cristóbal Colón or any others who sail in the said caravels to go to the Mine or engage in the trade thereof that the King of Portugal our brother holds. . . . Given in our City of Granada on the 30th day of April, year of Our Lord Jesus Christ 1492.

I THE KING   I THE QUEEN

Quite an order! There must have been some long breaths drawn, and significant looks exchanged among the town fathers of Palos when the public scrivener rolled out this royal command in the courtyard of the Church of St. George. And if Columbus imagined that caravels manned and equipped for an ocean voyage would be produced within ten days, he had plenty to learn about the difficulties and delays of fitting out ships in a far from enthusiastic community.

When arrangements were completed for furnishing *Niña* and *Pinta* and chartering *Santa María,* we do not know. The first two, as we have seen, were provided by the municipality at the tax-payers' expense. The letter above does not mean that Columbus was required to pay the wage bill; everyone in the fleet who had to do with working the ships was on the royal payroll. Columbus, perhaps after trying to argue the town fathers into providing a third caravel, himself chartered *Santa María* from her master-owner. Details of equipment and provisioning are wholly wanting,

SHIP WITH SAILS FURLED
From Juan de la Cosa Map of c. 1508

but they seem to have been done fairly efficiently since no complaints of carelessness and ship chandlers' dishonesty are recorded, as on later voyages. It took ten weeks instead of ten days to get ready for sea, but that was not excessive. The delay was fortunate; for if Columbus was lucky in escaping a West Indies hurricane with a September departure from the Canaries, he could not possibly have avoided some sort of "twister" with a June departure.

Three other royal letters of the same date, April 30, Columbus brought with him to Palos. All persons in Andalusia, especially timber merchants, carpenters, ship chandlers, bakers and provision dealers, were ordered to furnish Columbus with everything he required at reasonable prices. No customs or excises must be levied on said provisions, materials or equipment. All civil and criminal prosecutions must be suspended against anyone who agreed to ship with Columbus.

SQUARE–STERNED SHIP
SAILING FULL UNDER
FORE COURSE WITH
TWO BONNETS

From Piri Reis Map of 1513

My readers will be disappointed that I cannot furnish them with an authentic picture of the three famous vessels, whose preparations for the great voyage were now under way. But there are no data or documents from which it can honestly be done. Nobody knows what *Niña*, *Pinta* and *Santa María* really looked like. Every picture of them (including ours) is about 50 per cent fancy, and almost all are demonstrably inaccurate in some important respect. We have no contemporary painting or drawing of a single ship in which Columbus sailed. The woodcuts inserted in some of the editions of Columbus's published Letter on his First Voyage had already done duty in a work printed at Mainz in 1486. So-called models, replicas or reproductions of *Santa María* and her consorts are not models, replicas or reproductions, since no plans, drawings or dimensions of them exist; they merely represent what some naval architect, archeologist, artist or ship modeler thinks these vessels ought to have looked like. The best of these, representing an immense amount of research, are (1) Captain Ernesto D'Albertis's plans of 1892, from which models were made for the Marine Museum at Pegli, near Genoa; (2) *Niña II*, *Pinta II* and *Santa María II* constructed after plans made by Fernández Duro and Monléon for the Chicago Exposition of 1893; (3) D. Julio Guillén's *Santa María III*, constructed in 1927 for the Seville Exposition; (4) Mr. R. C. Anderson's miniature model of *Santa María* at the Addison Gallery of American Art, Andover, Massachusetts. My own description of the Columbus fleet is built on what few facts we can glean from the records, and illuminated by abundant data on contemporary vessels that these expert marine archeologists, D'Albertis, Fernández Duro, Guillén and Anderson, have brought to light.

Niña was the Admiral's favorite and so mine. "If she had not been very staunch and well found," he wrote after the February storm of 1493, "I should have been afraid of being lost." *Santa María*, which he never liked, ran aground off Hispaniola, and stayed there. *Pinta* returned home, and disappears from history. But *Niña* — there's a vessel to sing about! Built in the Ribera de Moguer, an estuary (now silted up) of the Rio Tinto, she made the entire First Voyage, bringing the Admiral safely home. She accompanied the grand fleet of the Second Voyage to Hispaniola, and Columbus selected her from seventeen sail for his flagship on an exploring voyage to Cuba, and purchased a half share in her. The only vessel in West Indian waters to survive the hurricane of 1495, she brought back the Admiral and over a hundred passengers to Spain in 1496, and after his return made an unauthorized voyage

from Cadiz to Rome, was captured by a pirate off Sardinia, recaptured by her master and crew, and returned to Cadiz in time
to sail for Hispaniola early in 1498, as advance guard of Columbus's
Third Voyage. She was lying at Santo Domingo in 1500, and we
last hear of her making a trading voyage to the Pearl Coast in
1501. Assuming that she reached Spain safely a third time, *Niña*
logged at least 25,000 miles under the Admiral's command. One
of the greatest little ships in the world's history.

Santa Clara she was named, after the patron saint of Moguer.
A Spanish vessel in those days had an official religious name, but
was generally known by a nickname, which might be the feminine
form of her owner's or master's patronymic, or of her home port
or some quality of sailing. Thus, a caravel owned by Gonzales
Bachiller was nicknamed *Bachillera;* ship *Santiago de Palos* was
called *Bermuda* after her master, Francisco Bermúdez; *Castilla* was
owned by one Castillo. In Southern Spain a Basque or Galician
ship might be nicknamed *La Vizcaína* or *La Gallega,* and Columbus's second *Santa María* earned the sobriquet *La Galante* by her
gallant sailing qualities. *Santa Clara* was always called *Niña* after
her master-owner, Juan Niño of Moguer.

Niña is the only one of the fleet of whose burthen we have
any record. Michele de Cuneo, who sailed in her to Cuba and
back in 1494, said she was of "about 60 tons," and on her unauthorized voyage to Rome in 1497 she carried a cargo of 51
tons. As the reason for chartering her on that voyage was the
shipping shortage, she presumably was loaded nearly to capacity.
We may therefore be certain that her tonnage was around 60; and
55 tons was a very common size for a caravel.

What did tonnage mean in 1492? Not weight or displacement
of the vessel, or her deadweight capacity; tonnage meant simply
her cubic capacity in terms of wine tuns. The Castilian *tonelada,*
or the Portuguese *tonel* (both of which I translate "ton"), was
really a tun of wine, a large cask equivalent in volume to two
pipas or pipes, the long, tapering hogsheads in which port wine is
still sold. As wine was a common cargo, and both pipe and tun of

Niña under Original Lateen Rig

Pinta (*Niña* Re-rigged Thus)

From the models after the D'Albertis plans in the Marine Museum, Pegli, Genoa

standard dimensions, a vessel's carrying capacity below decks in terms of *toneladas* became a rough-and-ready index of her size; and so a ship's tonnage in 1492 meant the number of tuns or twice the number of pipes of wine she could stow. The tun, *tonelada* or ton being roughly (very roughly) equivalent to 40 cubic feet, this last figure became in the course of time the unit of burthen (or tonnage or capacity) for English vessels, and was so used in America until the Civil War. From the seventeenth century on, it became customary in every country to fix a vessel's official tonnage by a formula composed of her length, breadth and depth, which gave a rough measurement of her capacity. But in 1492 tonnage meant simply the number of tuns of wine that the ship could stow, as estimated by the owner or verified by common report. It was not a constant but a variable.

Niña's tonnage then was around 60, rather less than more. The difficulty comes in translating the ancient capacity measure into linear dimensions. If we could only get one, we could deduce the others; for the classic proportion for caravels seems to have been, beam: length of keel: overall length = 1: 2: 3. Unfortunately I have been unable to find a single linear dimension of *Niña* to start with, and the formulas given by the marine archeologists for deducing them from tonnage do not inspire confidence. If my personal guess of what a 55- to 60-ton caravel of 1492 measured is any use, here it is: overall length (between perpendiculars) about 70 feet, length of keel about 50 feet, beam about 23 feet, depth of hold amidships about 9 feet. And from my own experience in the waters of Southern Cuba, I should say that *Niña's* draught could not have been over 6 feet.

Niña, like her two consorts, was a one-decker. The preposterous notion that the two caravels were open or half-decked boats was derived from Eden's bad translation in 1555 of Peter Martyr's Renaissance Latin. *Niña* must have had a raised quarter-deck on which was built a *toldilla* or house for the captain's and master's cabin. Her forecastle was relatively small and low, accommodating only the cables and the sail locker; perhaps also the bread room, and the *fogón* or firebox.

Now for *Niña's* rig. In the Genoa model and in every popular picture generally, she is represented as a three-masted lateener of the Portuguese type, the mainmast with the longest yard being almost amidships, and the other two aft. She probably was so masted when she set forth from Palos, although for aught we know she might have started as a two-sticker. But her rig was certainly altered to *vela redonda* (square rig) at the Grand Canary, so that (says Ferdinand) "she might follow the other vessels more quietly and with less danger." That was good judgment. Running down to the Canaries with the wind dead aft, *Niña* must have yawed badly, exhausting her helmsmen; and every time the wind shifted a little from port to starboard quarter or vice versa, she had to go through the complicated maneuver of throwing the great mainsail around the mast and lowering and hoisting again the other two. In the meantime, *Santa María* and *Pinta* were placidly scudding along under their main courses. Thus everyone was "sold" on square rig, and *Niña's* big lateen sails, efficient as they were for windward work, had to go.

Exactly how was she altered? When the Portuguese changed a *caravela latina* to *caravela redonda* they simply stepped a foremast right up in her bows, and crossed two yards on which to set course and topsail for running before the wind, when one or more of the lateen sails would be furled. This made an ugly but serviceable rig for the Cape passage. But there is no evidence that the Portuguese invented this rig before 1500, and Columbus's Journal proves that *Niña* had squaresails on two masts. In the storms of February and March, 1493, he several times mentions the *papahigo* or square main course, with its bonnet, and once mentions her *triquete*, which always means a square fore course. That sort of re-rigging required considerable resparring as well; old No. 2 lateen-rigged mast was probably stepped well forward to serve as the new foremast, and the old mainmast probably had to be moved a few feet aft. The two discarded lateen yards would have been cut down or replaced by two shorter yards for the courses. Columbus doubtless obtained assistance from shipyard workers at Las Palmas, and he had a week's time for the job. It was evidently well done, as the only other attention *Niña's* spars required was a new mizzenmast and yard, which the men cut and fitted from native pine in Cuba.

Thus rigged square, *Niña's* sail plan had the same general appearance as *Santa María's*, except that she had no top to her mainmast, carried no topmast or topsail, and no spritsail. Her sailing qualities even to windward were not seriously impaired, because square rig had been so improved in recent years that its effectiveness was approaching that of lateen. And for service downwind, as Columbus's fleet sailed most of the way across and at least half the passage home, square rig was infinitely superior. Sailing west before the trades, which often show a diurnal variation from ENE to ESE, a lateener would have been forced at least twice a day to perform the difficult maneuver of wearing; but in square rig, when the wind veers across your stern, all you need to do is trim the main course. Aboard our barkentine *Capitana* when rolling down to Trinidad in 1939, the only thing that gave us any trouble was gybing the fore-and-aft main and mizzen booms; and as the squaresails on the foremast did most of the pulling we eventually saved ourselves by furling both main and mizzen. No doubt Columbus's fleet furled their mizzens and fore courses, for the main course would have blanketed the fore when wind was dead aft, and the mizzen would have made steering difficult. As altered, *Niña* became the smartest sailer in the fleet out or home. Her rig, moreover, became the favorite one for Spanish caravels in transatlantic work; very few lateeners were ever taken out to the Indies.

Pinta is the vessel that we know the least about. She was a *caravela redonda* or square-rigged caravel of Palos, with the same rig that *Niña* received at Las Palmas. There is no reason to doubt that she was locally built, like *Niña*. Her owner, says Columbus, was Cristóbal Quintero of Palos, who sailed with the rating of seaman. What her real name was we do not know, and her nickname is not derived from Pinzón, the feminine of which was *Pinzona*. There was a Pinto family at Palos, which possibly had owned her before Quintero did; my conjecture is that Quintero, who seems to have been a mean sort of fellow, was married to a masterful Pinto, and the seamen called his ship *Pinta* as a joke on him. There is no certain clue to her tonnage, and she disappears from recorded history after successfully completing the great voyage of discovery. Quintero in 1495 or 1496 chartered to the crown a caravel of 55 tons carrying forty men as part of a naval fleet in the Neapolitan war, and this caravel may have been *Pinta;* but Quintero is known to have owned other vessels, and 55 tons was a very common size for a caravel. Tradition, based largely on the erroneous belief that *Niña* means "tiny," makes *Pinta* larger, and perhaps she was; but Las Casas says not. My guess would be to give her a tonnage of 55 to 60, overall length about 73–75 feet, beam about 25, and depth of hold about 11 feet.

Pinta proved herself a smart sailer, and Columbus became annoyed at a habit of Captain Pinzón in pressing on ahead when land was expected, in order to gain the reward. One of her men was first to sight the New World; she was the first to reach Hispaniola, and the first home to Spain. When both caravels were sailing on the wind during the return passage, *Niña* put it all over *Pinta*, but Columbus suggests that this was due to a sprung mizzenmast which Martín Alonso Pinzón had been too lazy (or busy looking for gold) to replace. This at least goes to show how important the lateen mizzen was in giving these square-rigged caravels good performance on the wind.

Santa María the flagship has been the subject of much more intensive study and idle speculation than the caravels. Unlike *Niña* and *Pinta*, which were home-town vessels, *Santa María* was built in Galicia, and for that reason was nicknamed *La Gallega*. Galicia was then the principal Spanish province for the building of large vessels, but *Santa María* was a small vessel for that period. We know nothing of her history before May 1492. She happened to be in the Rio Tinto on a trading voyage when Columbus was looking for ships, and as the Paleños could not be induced to furnish more than the two caravels that the Sovereigns had commanded, he chartered *Santa María* from her owner-master, Juan de la Cosa of Santoña. She became *capitana* or flagship because she was the largest of the fleet; but the Admiral disliked her for her dull sailing qualities, and because she drew too much water for his purposes. After she had been wrecked — through no fault of her own — he recorded in his Journal (December 26, 1492), "The ship was very heavy and not suitable for the business of discovery; and for taking such a ship the men of Palos were responsible, because they did not fulfil with the King and Queen what they had promised, to give vessels suitable for that voyage. . . ." If they made any such promise (which is improbable) it was a verbal one, for the most assiduous search of the archives has uncovered no such promise or contract, only the royal command that Palos furnish two caravels.

No record of *Santa María's* tonnage or any other dimension exists, to our knowledge. Somewhat on the principle of restoring the mammoth from a jawbone, Auguste Jal in 1840 proposed to work out *Santa María's* dimensions from the length of her boat, 5 fathoms, as supposedly given in Columbus's Journal; but unfortunately he picked the wrong jawbone. The 5 fathoms in that entry referred to the depth at the mouth of Baracoa harbor which was being sounded from the boat, not to the boat itself! Three out of four of *Santa María's* restorers built her up from that hypothetical 5-fathom boat; yet none seem able to agree. Fernández Duro made her tonnage 120 to 130; Monléon 127; D'Albertis (who did not use the boat) 150 to 200; and Guillén 120. Obviously there is not enough difference between these to fight about; but in my opinion she was smaller than any of these estimates, for the following reasons.

Las Casas says that *Santa María* was "somewhat," not "very much," bigger than the others. And there is also a hint that she was of about 100 tons in Columbus's Journal of the Third Voyage, as abstracted by Las Casas. One reason the Admiral went straight from Margarita to Hispaniola in 1498, he says, is "because the vessels he had were large for exploring, as the one was of more than 100 tons and the other more than 70, and only smaller ones are wanted for exploring; and because of the ship which he took on his First Voyage being large, he lost her in the harbor of Navidad." Now, that 1498 flagship (name unknown) of "more

SANTA MARÍA III AT ANCHOR

From a photograph

than 100 tons" drew approximately 6 feet of water, whilst the plans for Señor Guillén's 120-ton *Santa María III* call for a draught of 7.2 feet. Columbus says that his 100-plus tonner and his 70-plus tonner of 1498 were both too large for coastal exploration, and that *Santa María* was also too large. So what may we infer from his comparison? It looks to me as if *Santa María* had been a vessel of less than 100 tons, certainly smaller than *Santa María III*, or any other "models" or "replicas" of the original. If anyone wishes to build a fourth *Santa María*, he had better shoot at something that will carry about 100 tuns or 200 pipes of wine below hatches, and draw not more than 6½ feet aft when loaded.

Columbus's *Santa María* was a *nao* or ship, not a caravel. That is perfectly clear from his Journal. Repeatedly he speaks of *la nao* when he means the flagship, and *la carabela* or *las carabelas* when he refers to *Niña* or *Pinta* or both. Consequently we are safe in assuming that her model was round and chunky, like the carracks of Venice and other *naos* of the period. Perhaps because her northern builders had not incorporated the experience of African voyages, she was not so fast or weatherly as *Niña* and *Pinta*, nor

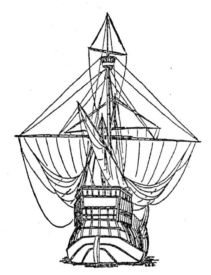

SANTA MARÍA *III* UNDER WAY,
WITH YARD HALF HOISTED

From a photograph

was her general appearance so graceful; the sheer (fore-and-aft curve) of her deck was broken by the castles. *Santa María III* has a sheer of 3 feet. Built on the assumption that the original was a caravel, she has no proper castle up forward, merely a half-deck almost level with the sheer of the bulwarks; *Santa María II* and the Genoa and Andover models have high triangular forecastles extending out over the bows, which I believe to be correct.* The

* The forecastle originally was just what the name implies, a forward castle for fighting purposes; but maritime conservatism has retained the name for crew's quarters wherever located. *Santa María II* has no more room under her forecastle than *Santa María III*, but the castle itself is quite a platform.

designer of *Santa María II* made a bad mistake in giving her a square stern; *Santa María III* and the Andover model both have a "round tuck," a neat finish formed by the planks meeting on the sternpost. *Santa María's* greatest breadth was on deck, not between wind and water as on later vessels. "Tumble-home" of topsides was introduced after 1500 in order to enable warships to bear the weight of their guns.

In the spar plan the most striking features of *Santa María* to a modern seaman would be the excessive height of mainmast and

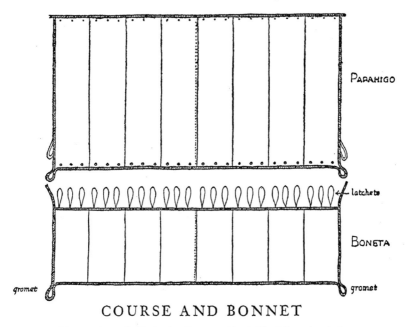

COURSE AND BONNET

From García Palacio, Instrución Náuthica (*1587*)

length of main yard in comparison with the others. The mainmast, all of one piece and stepped vertically in the middle of the keel, was higher than the ship was long, and the main yard was as long as the keel. Fore and mizzenmasts were only about one-third the height of mainmast, and sufficiently light to be stepped on the main deck; they had a pronounced rake. The bowsprit, too, was a very slender spar. Such a spar plan naturally looks very awkward to us, because square-riggers were just emerging from the medieval one-big-mast ship, and the main course with its bonnets was expected to do the driving; fore course and mizzen were mostly for balance on the wind. In order to spread enough sail to make the ship lively, the main yard had to be made of two big spars scarfed and woolded together. Lifts carried some of its weight when aloft, but it was hoisted by a single stout halyard rigged with triple purchase. Hoisting the main yard was a job that required all hands.

Santa María's sail plan is one of the few things we can bank on; since Columbus in his Journal for October 24, when he wished to make time, says "I set all the sails of the ship, main course with two bonnets, the fore course, spritsail, mizzen, topsail, and the boat's sail on the poop." Bonnets, which were used almost to our own day in lieu of rows of reef points, were narrow rectangular sails as long as the course, secured to it by a row of toggles and latchets, or by a lace line running through the latchets. When you shortened sail, you began by lowering the yard a bit, removing a bonnet, and re-reeving tacks and sheets. The topsail in 1492 was a little square "duster," with no more pull than a topgallant studdingsail of a later era; but trade-wind voyages soon demonstrated the possibilities of the topsail as a driver. It was first lengthened out on the foot like a trapezoid, then the topsail yard was lengthened, and by the seventeenth century Columbus's pocket handkerchief had evolved into the most important sail on a square-rigger. Not until even later did anyone have the wit to substitute a jib for the low-hanging spritsail, which had to be clewed up in rough weather; or to provide triangular staysails to fill the spaces between masts. *Santa María* could have done with a few; *Santa María II* when she crossed in 1893 was provided with jibs and a main staysail "to use in the solitude of the sea" where nobody would remark the anachronism.

We may now consider features that were common to all three vessels, or to any that Columbus sailed across the ocean; for we have very few details on his later ships. The experience of repeated ocean crossings enabled him to make improvements, and before the Fourth Voyage he hoped to have vessels of a new design especially constructed for him. But he was in no position to do that, and had to take what he could get.

Iron bolts were probably used for fastenings at points where the greatest strain was expected, but the 3- to 4-inch planking was fastened to the frames by wooden trunnels; that is why *Santa María* opened up so quickly when she grounded off Hispaniola.* All ships' bottoms were covered with a mixture of tallow and pitch in the hope of discouraging barnacles and teredos, and every few months a vessel had to be hove-down and graved on some convenient beach. This was done by careening her alternately on each side, cleaning off the marine growth, repitching the bottom and paying the seams. In order that the heaving-down process should not strain her, she had to be constructed with heavy wales and wide bilges and floor timbers; vertical skids were secured to the topsides in order to protect the planking. Some kind of dark preservative was applied to the topsides, probably a mixture of whale oil and pine tar, which the Niebla region produced.

Centuries elapsed before shipwrights learned to fasten outside ballast to the keel; and merchant vessels in Columbus's day (as almost to the other day) required no inside ballast if they carried a full cargo of some heavy substance like wine. If not, sufficient sand or shingle or cobblestones was taken in to ensure stability. Columbus's fleet sailed from the Canaries well laden with sea stores, but they must have had some ballast as well, for Columbus writes of a boy knocking down a sea bird with a stone; and where else but in the ballast could he have found a stone aboard ship? On the return passage *Niña*, as her depleted sea stores were consumed, became so crank that the men had to fill empty wine casks with sea water for ballast; and one of their first objects at the Azores was to procure stone or shingle before sailing for Spain.

Every wooden vessel will leak more or less under some conditions, and Columbus's vessels generally leaked more rather than

---

* "I have knowne a ship built, hath sailed to and againe over the maine Ocean, which had not so much as a naile of iron in her but onely one bolt in her keele." — Captain John Smith's *Sea Grammar* (1627).

less. A fixed wooden pump, operated by the morning watch until it sucked, was supposed to take care of the daily leakage; but no pump of that sort could keep a ship completely dry, and as she rolled and pitched, bilge water sloshed about the hold among the bales and barrels and ballast. As the men threw most of their slops into the bilge, it became a happy refuge for the seaman's inevitable companion, the *cucaracha* or cockroach: —

> *Ai! que mi piqua*
> *Ai! que mi araña*
> *Con sus patitas*
> *La cucaracha*

as an old song goes. Every landsman who went to sea in the era of discovery complained of the vermin, and of the horrible stench that arose from the bilges, especially when the pump was working. When these "funkes," as Elizabethan seamen called them, became unbearably foul the ship was "rummaged." She was run into shoal water, the stores and cargo hoisted out on deck, the ballast (if any) hove overboard, casks and bilges scraped clean and sprinkled with vinegar, and new ballast taken in.

On Columbus's ships the white sails were painted with crosses, and possibly other heraldic or religious devices. Both running and standing rigging was of hemp rope; wire would not make its appearance aboard ship for 350 years. The blocks (pulleys to landsmen) were blocks indeed; chunks of hardwood carved to an oval or almond shape, hollowed out to admit the sheave, and pierced at one end for the pendant, but not stropped. Double- and triple-purchase blocks were used on halyards. It is a matter of dispute whether block-and-tackle or deadeye-and-lanyard was used to secure and set up the shrouds that stayed the masts. Ratlines were possible only on the latter rig; on the former, as shown in the Andover model, a Jacob's ladder on the after side of the mast, such as pilots use to come over a vessel's side today, was the means of going aloft.

Details of running rigging are so difficult to describe in anything but technical language that anyone really interested had better inspect the models at Andover or Cambridge, or examine the clear drawings in Señor Guillén's book. Sufficient here to say that almost all the lines of a modern square-rigger were already employed: halyards, lifts and braces to hoist, support and adjust the yards; tacks and sheets to trim the sails; clewlines, buntlines and martnets to spill the wind and prepare them for furling; bowlines to stretch their leaches (vertical edges) taut when sailing on the

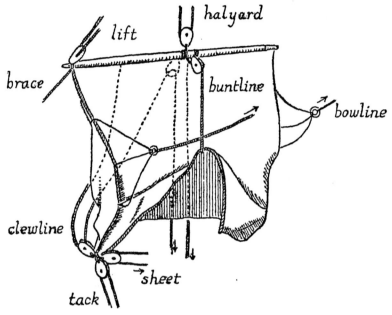

RIGGING OF YARD AND SQUARESAIL ON
CARAVELS OF 1492

From Julio Guillén, La Carabela Santa María

wind. *Santa María III* has a stout pinrail at the foot of the great mast to make fast all the main running rigging; the Andover model uses belaying pins spaced along the bulwarks for everything but the main halyard.

In Columbus's day the great majority of anchorages in the Atlantic islands and on the West Coast of Africa were open roadsteads exposed to considerable swell and only partially protected from winds. Vessels commonly moored with two bowers and a stern anchor, and expected to lose one or more in the course of a long voyage. Usually seven anchors were carried: four bowers, two of which were kept constantly ready on the bows, a stream anchor to keep her headed into the swell, a kedge anchor for hauling her ahead in shoal water, and a big sheet anchor (called by the Spaniards *la esperanza* or *ancla de salvación*) which was stowed with its cable in the hold and only let go as a last resort. The two bowers were lashed to catheads forward when at sea. Their cables led through hawse-holes in the bows to a horizontal Spanish windlass, located either under the forecastle or in the waist forward of the main hatch.

All vessels of that period were steered by an outboard rudder and a great wooden tiller, to the forward end of which relieving tackles were attached. The after end was mortised directly to the rudderpost. This junction required a large open port aft, which could not be closed, since there had to be room for the tiller to work. Consequently when the ship was running before a heavy sea, every following wave must have sloshed water into the steerage. On the caravels, with their comparatively short poop decks, the helmsman might have been able to watch the weather clew of the main course, but on *Santa María III* the quarter- or poop-deck over his head (and he had to be a short man not to stoop) completely obscured his view of sea or sails. Captain Concas of *Santa María II* insisted on rigging a steering wheel on the poop deck before he made the ocean crossing. The Andover model affords her miniature helmsman a sight of sails and sky by cutting away a portion of the poop deck; but this consideration was unnecessary, for until the eighteenth century, when the steering wheel was invented, helmsmen were not supposed to see anything. They steered by compass and the feel of the ship, and by instructions shouted down to them by the officer of the watch.

The more you learn about vessels of the Columbian period, the more you have to admire their seaworthiness, and what is now called their "functional" features; but the living arrangements were so primitive that one would suppose shipbuilders were still assuming everyone would go ashore for the night, as in ancient Greece. The only means of cooking was an open firebox provided with a back to screen it from the wind; on the floor of the box sand was spread, and a wood fire built on that. The builder of *Santa María III* could provide no sleeping accommodations above deck for anyone but the Admiral. The *toldilla* (what we should call a "dog house") on the poop deck afforded him a roomy cabin; but there was no space below the forecastle for anything but the cables, firebox and spare gear. A forward space in the hold below is partitioned off on *Santa María III* and called "Juan de la Cosa's cabin," but it seems incredible that the master would have slept in the stinking hold among the rats and cockroaches. There must have been bunks somewhere for the pilot, master, marshal, comptroller, interpreter and other swells of the afterguard; even *Niña* provided bunks for her Portuguese visitors at the Azores. Probably on the actual vessels the *toldilla* was larger than those of the reconstructions, giving the captain a snug stateroom and a general cabin for the other officers. Or else the steerage was higher, and cabins were installed around its sides. No sleeping place was provided on ships of that era for able seamen, gromets, and soldiers. They simply lay down anywhere — in the forecastle, the steerage, or on deck in fair weather.

Like all vessels of the day, *Santa María's* deck beams were arched, so that the decks had considerable camber,* and the only flat place on deck was the main hatch amidships. That this was a favorite sleeping place appears in an incident of the Fourth Voyage. When *Capitana* was anchored off the Rio Belén some Indian captives, confined below, pried the hatch off, tumbled its sleeping occupants into the scuppers, and jumped overboard. Eventually the Indians' hammocks, first observed in 1492, solved the shipboard sleeping problem for seamen of all nations. The crew of *Santa María II* slung hammocks in the hold, which must have been kept sweeter and cleaner than that of the original.

The low place on the profile of these vessels between mainmast and foremast was called the *combes* or waist. This space was closed

* Latitudinal convexity.

in time of battle by waistcloths to protect the men from arrows, and on gala days a ship spread these waistcloths and hung outboard a row of shields bearing the arms of the *caballeros* in her company. On such occasions, too, the royal ensign of Castile and León was hoisted at the main truck. Columbus had a special banner for his fleet, consisting of a green cross on a white field, with a crown on each arm of the cross, one over an *F* for Fernando and the other over a *Y* for Ysabel; on later voyages he doubtless displayed his own arms on a jackstaff forward. A variety of gaily colored pendants, bannerols and flags was carried to be run up on mastheads and yardarms on great church festivals if the vessel were in port; and these banners were much larger in comparison with the ship's length than is considered proper today. At sea (popular illustrations to the contrary notwithstanding) no flags were flown, because they soon wore out.

All vessels of that era were provided with a number of long ash sweeps, which were worked through ports in the bulwarks and used to give the vessels steerageway in a calm, or to keep them from drifting ashore with a current in light airs. We tried one of those on *Santa María III*, were impressed with its excellent balance and surprised how easily one could shove along so beamy and heavy a vessel. If the ship's boat were used in addition to tow her, Columbus's *Santa María* could probably have made 2 knots in smooth water with an "ash breeze." Each vessel carried but one boat, which took up the entire port or starboard gangway in the waist. It was a stout, heavy yawl boat, so difficult to hoist aboard that when once in the water they towed it as long as wind and sea were moderate.

Artillery was carried by all three vessels: iron "lombards" of about 9-cm. caliber which threw a stone cannon ball, mounted in carriages on deck; and small breech-loading swivel guns called "falconets," of about 4.5-cm. caliber, which were charged with odd bits of ironmongery to repel boarders, and were mounted on the bulwarks. The only small arms mentioned by Columbus on the First Voyage are crossbows and *espingardas*, primitive muskets made of a tube of bronze or iron secured to a wooden stock.

After *Niña II*, *Pinta II* and *Santa María II* were built in Spain in 1892, the first two at the cost of the United States and the last by the Spanish government, the two caravels were towed across. But the Spanish navy, to its great honor and credit, took *Santa María II* from the Canaries to Cuba under her own sail. She departed from Santa Cruz de Tenerife on February 22, 1893. Trade winds were unsteady that year and *Santa María II* had a much tougher passage than her original. For several days, while the wind blew from the W of N, she "rolled badly" and "pitched furiously," records her commander; even articles lashed down broke loose, while hull and masts worked and groaned so that nobody could sleep.* Squally days came in mid-March around latitude 21° N, oilbags were set to windward, and for a time the mainsail was furled. The trades never seemed to last on this voyage for more than two days at a time, and when they blew on the stern it was very difficult to steer, even with a modern wheel. In a fairly high sea *Santa María II* yawed as much as 7 and 8 points. Setting jibs and staysails which her captain had smuggled aboard in defiance of marine archeology, and raising the weather clew of the mainsail, helped steady her a bit; but throughout the voyage steering gave the most trouble. To the great relief of all hands, Virgin Gorda was sighted on March 28, thirty-four days out. This was just one day less than Columbus's ocean crossing, but his route was several hundred miles longer. On March 30 *Santa María* entered the harbor of San Juan de Puerto Rico. The best day's run of the passage was 139 miles; the worst 11. It is evident that *Santa María II* was neither so fast nor so well-balanced as the original of 1492. The constructional features that made her pitch and roll so badly were her short keel and round bilges, which were characteristic of seagoing sailing vessels in the fifteenth century.

Santa María III was also designed to be sailed across the At-

---

* An American seaman who sailed north in her from Havana when she was being towed is said to have reported that "she jumped about like a Bowery 'hoor.'"

lantic, but political conditions prevented. She made five short voyages under sail, attained a speed of 8 knots, and with wind abaft the beam steered easily and answered her helm readily. She rolled abominably, though not dangerously, behaving "like a barrel in a surf." The great length of her main yard and lack of ballast probably enhanced the tendency of any vessel with round bilges to roll.

These vicissitudes of the models are suggestive, but by no means conclusive as to the actual performance of the original *Niña*, *Pinta* and *Santa María*. They, constructed by shipwrights who had centuries of experience behind them, under the supervision of men who had been on African voyages, were probably better ships in all essential respects than the so-called replicas and reconstructions made by archeologists on the basis of such scanty data as they could cull from the records of the past. The one essential defect in *Santa María II* and *III*, their tendency to pitch and roll, was due to the shortness of their keels in relation to overall length, and to the roundness of their bilges. Columbus complained of the original *Santa María* pitching and taking in water forward the first day out from the Canaries, but that was probably remedied by restowing her stores, as there were no further complaints of that sort. From all that we can learn about the caravels, *Niña* and *Pinta* were sweet little vessels, seaworthy and sea-kindly, the sort that seamen become attached to. Columbus, when he had the pick of the whole merchant marine, took *Niña* on his Second Voyage, and selected her as his flagship on the Cuban reconnaissance.

Anyone could design better seagoing vessels and rig them better today; but the gain would be largely in comfort, labor saving and safety, not in speed. *Niña*, *Pinta* and *Santa María* were well built, well rigged, well equipped and well manned; *muy aptos para semejante fecho*, "well suited for such an enterprise," as the Admiral himself wrote in the prologue to his Journal. They were fine ships, competent for their allotted tasks. So let us hear no more chatter about Columbus setting forth in "tubs," "crates," or "cockleshells."

NOTES ON SAILING

Although the principles of sailing are the same now as in 1492, I propose to give here a short explanation of them for the benefit of non-nautical readers.

The appended diagram will help to explain the *points of sailing*. Here is a compass rose containing the 32 points of the compass. The wind is Northeast. A ship in Columbus's day could not sail nearer to the wind than five compass points (56°), even with a smooth sea. That is what the two ships headed N by W and E by S are doing; the one on the *starboard tack* (because the wind is blowing on her starboard side), the other on the port tack. The whole shaded quadrant is closed to them by the NE wind. If their destination lies in a north-easterly direction they must *come about* (either by luffing through the eye of the wind, or by *wearing*, i.e., turning away from the wind and then heading up), and sail a zigzag course. That is called *tacking*, or beating to windward. In a high sea, or with a current running in the same direction as the wind, it is impossible to gain anything beating to windward.

The ships in the diagram headed NW and SE have the wind *abeam*, i.e., at right angles to their hull. Those sailing W and S have the wind *on the quarter*. During most of his first outward voyage, Columbus was sailing W with a NE wind, like the ship in the diagram. That is generally a ship's fastest point of sailing. He would not have considered the wind *fair* for any course between WNW around by N to SSE. The ship headed SW is *running* (or *scudding*) *before the wind*. In such a position her foresail was blanketed and her mizzen furled; the mainsail (or main course) and main topsail, if any, did all the work.

Windward means toward the wind; i.e., on the present diagram, with the wind NE, any direction from NW to SE, clockwise. *Leeward* means away from the wind, i.e., any direction from SE to NW, clockwise.

A *lee shore* is a coastline upon which the wind is blowing. If a ship suddenly finds herself on a lee shore, as happened to Columbus when approaching the coast of Portugal in 1493, her only means of saving herself is to *claw off*, i.e., to trim her yards and alter her direction to windward. You cannot anchor in safety off a lee shore. You must anchor in a spot where the wind blows off the land.

Suppose night overtakes a sailing vessel in strange waters off sound-

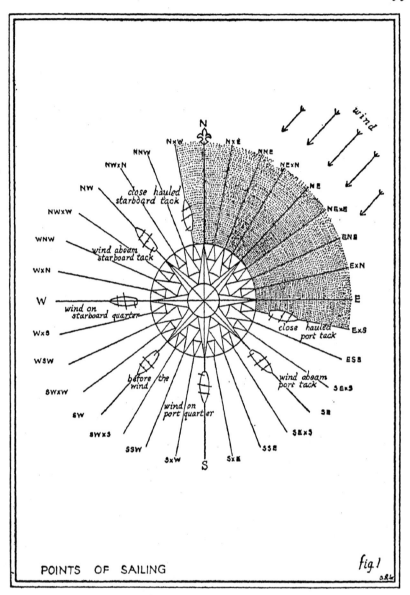

POINTS OF SAILING

fig. 1

ings, and she fears to proceed further. She then has a choice between *heaving-to* and *jogging off-and-on*. In heaving-to the vessel is headed fairly close to the wind, and her sails adjusted so that she drifts slowly sideways, also surging ahead a little. In such a position she is said to be *hove-to*, or, as seamen say, *laying-to*. Columbus frequently used this maneuver when he was in unknown waters near the land and did not think it safe to sail at night. The same thing happened to us in *Capitana* off the Gulf of Darien on New Year's Eve, 1939. Approaching the coast with a head wind, we sighted land at 4 P.M. but lost it again in a black squall that came over the mountains, and were unable to verify our position. The dipsey lead yielded no bottom, so we lay her to for the night under main and fore staysails, a night black with heavy clouds through which lightning shot, and saw the New Year in with 16 bells. Laying-to is a peculiar sensation after a long voyage. Everything is unnaturally quiet; there is no sound of waters rushing by the ship or of wind whistling in the rigging. You roll and pitch a little but the motion is different, and the hull makes curious creaks and groans that you do not hear when sailing. Without the familiar noises and routine (for there is nothing to do, not even to steer) your ship seems curiously lonely and cut off from the world; it is a relief to make sail in the morning and fill away on your course again.

Jogging off-and-on means taking short tacks with sail reduced and wind abeam, so that the vessel sails up and down about over the same course. Columbus did that after his first landfall, until day broke.

CHAPTER X

Officers and Men

1492–1493

Habitatores Sidonis et Aradij fuerunt remiges tui: sapientes tui, Tyre, facti sunt gubernatores tui. Senes Giblij, et prudentes eius, habuerunt nautas ad ministerium variae supellectilis tuae.

The inhabitants of Sidon and Ärvad were thy mariners; thy wise men O Tyrus . . . were thy pilots. The ancients of Gebal and the wise men thereof were in thee thy calkers.
— EZEKIEL xxvii 8, 9

THE business of recruiting officers and men for the Great Enterprise was fully as important as the ships themselves. Fortunately, owing to the fact that everyone's wages were paid by the crown, we have almost a complete payroll and crew list of the First Voyage. Unfortunately the voyage gave rise to a controversy between Columbus and the Pinzón family which has broken all count of chancery records; for it dragged along for fifty years, and is still being debated (with more heat than light) by historians.

The object of these *pleitos* (pleadings) *de Colón* was to defend or annul the hereditary privileges of Columbus's descendants. His family summoned witnesses to sustain the common report that the First Voyage was the conception of Columbus, carried out under his leadership, and against the advice and wishes of most people; the crown tried to prove by another set of witnesses that Columbus was only the nominal head of an enterprise which was set on foot and brought to a successful conclusion by the energy, courage and maritime skill of Martín Alonso Pinzón. Survivors of the

First and subsequent voyages and people present when the fleet was being fitted out or when the two caravels returned home were located in various parts of the Spanish empire, doubtless well coached, asked a series of leading questions, and their answers taken down by a notary without cross-examination; so each separate inquest was either pro-Columbus or anti-Columbus.

Common sense tells us that evidence taken under such circumstances and so long after the event should be used only to support or fill out contemporary evidence, and that much of it must be worthless. But a number of writers, eager to defame Columbus, rely on the pro-Pinzón *pleitos* while they ignore the pro-Columbus ones and reject other documents of his time as prejudiced and falsified. Yet we may not discount these *pleitos* completely; and there is much even in the pro-Pinzón testimony that fits in with and supplements the evidence in Columbus's own Journal.

Martín Alonso Pinzón, the head of a middle-class seafaring family of Palos, was between forty-six and fifty years old in 1492. García Fernández, steward of *Pinta*, declared, "Martín Alonso was a very valiant man, and of great courage, and he knows that without his giving the two ships to the Admiral he would not have been where he was, nor would he have found people, because nobody [in Palos] knew the said Admiral, and that by reason of the said Martín Alonso and through giving him the said ships, the said Admiral made the said voyage."

A very judicious statement. Columbus, a comparatively unknown man in Palos and a foreigner to boot, could hardly have induced mariners (proverbially suspicious of any new enterprise) to embark with him on a voyage of dubious safety and improbable success, unless some person of local standing came forward and showed his own faith in it. Martín Alonso took command of *Pinta*, with his younger brother Francisco Martín as her master, while Vicente Yáñez Pinzón, younger than Martín Alonso but older than Francisco, took command of *Niña*, and Diego Pinzón, a cousin of theirs called *el viejo* ("the old boy"), shipped as mariner on *Pinta*. The Pinzons owned neither *Pinta* nor *Niña*; but it must

have reconciled somewhat the owners of these expropriated caravels to have prominent Paleños take over their command.

At the inquest held at Seville in 1515, two leading questions
were asked by the fiscal, who corresponded more or less to our
district attorney: "(1). Whether you know that when the Admiral went to discover those regions, Martín Alonso Pinzón of
Palos was about to seek them out at his own charge with two of his
own vessels, and had certain knowledge and writings of the land,
which he had seen in Rome in the library of Pope Innocent VIII
in the year that he came from Rome, and had begun to talk of
going to discover them, and encouraged him, etc.?" "(2). Whether
you know that the said Martín Alonso Pinzón gave information
to the said Admiral D. Cristóbal Colón about the land and discussed with him the aforesaid writing, in which it was said it was
an opinion of the time of Solomon that the Queen of Sheba had
sailed by the Mediterranean Sea to the end of Spain and that there,
95° to the westward, by an easy passage, he would find between
north and south a land of *sypanso* (Japan) which is so fertile and
abundant and whose extent surpasses Africa and Europe?"

Whatever the truth of this story, it was evidently current in
Andalusia in 1515. Several of the hand-picked witnesses, one of
whom claimed he had sailed with Martín Alonso on the Roman
voyage, simply said yes, they had heard the tale, or knew it to
be true; but Martín Alonso's son Arias Pérez, who declared that
he had been with his father on that Roman voyage, said a good
deal more. One of Martín Alonso's friends, it seems, was a cosmographer employed in the Vatican Library, whom he visited at
Rome. One day this man lent him a document from the papal
library describing a Sheban transatlantic voyage to Japan, and
the story of this mythical marine enterprise so impressed Martín
Alonso that he determined to try such a voyage himself. When he
was casting about for ways and means, Columbus called at
La Rábida for the purpose of removing his son, and intending
to leave for France. Martín Alonso encouraged him by reading the
document, and persuaded him to visit the court once more. But,

after returning to Palos with his royal authority and his contract, Columbus tried for two months to engage men and procure caravels before joining forces with Pinzón, who put the enterprise on its feet.

Can one dismiss Arias Pérez' tale as a cock-and-bull story, created by family pride, jealousy and resentment? I think not. The "document" on the Queen of Sheba's marvelous voyage has never been found or identified, but there may well have been such a legend of the seagoing queen in some Hebrew codex in the Vatican Library. What gives the tale verisimilitude is the evidence in Columbus's own journal of Pinzón's particular interest in discovering Japan, and in finding other islands in the Atlantic. But among the numerous false leads that encouraged Columbus, no such heartening story as a westward voyage by the Queen of Sheba to Japan is mentioned by Ferdinand and Las Casas.

The substratum of truth in the Pinzón story seems to be that Martín Alonso picked up a yarn of some mythical transatlantic voyage which led him to suppose that Marco Polo's Cipangu could be reached that way, and consequently lent his support to Columbus. No doubt his example and influence were useful in recruiting men, but his conduct on the voyage was such that Columbus failed to make what the Pinzón family regarded as suitable acknowledgment.

A Pinzón myth began to take shape aboard *Pinta* on the homeward passage, and after the death of Martín Alonso his friends and family inflated it to the point where the captain of *Pinta* appeared to be the real source and leader of the First Voyage, while Columbus was relegated to the role of a mere window dresser who had influence at court. Jean Charcot, who had plenty of experience of that sort of thing, noted the tendency "common to Latin countries" to depreciate a great leader who wins popular applause. "Subordinates often feel this jealousy; if they do not attack openly, their still more eloquent insinuations and reticences are quickly picked up and interpreted by those who hope to inflate themselves by diminishing others." By no means confined to Latin countries!

Whatever one may think of Martín Alonso, his younger brother Vicente Yáñez, captain of *Niña* and about thirty years old in 1492, proved to be a first-class seaman, and unlike his brother obeyed orders. Vicente's discovery of the Amazon on an independent voyage in 1499–1500 entitles him to the first rank among discoverers native to Spain. Of Francisco Martín, the youngest brother, nothing is known after the First Voyage; but their cousin Diego, "the old boy," accompanied Columbus to Paria in 1498, and made the Amazon voyage with Vicente Yáñez the following year.

No contemporary record gives the Pinzons of Palos any special position in the Great Enterprise, or proves that they lent it more influence and gave it more aid than another seafaring family of the Niebla region, the Niños, whose social and economic status in the near-by town of Moguer was equivalent to that of the Pinzón family in Palos. At least three Niños went on the First Voyage. Juan, eldest of four brothers, owned *Niña* and sailed on her as master. Peralonso, the second brother, who was about twenty-four years old in 1492, sailed as pilot of *Santa María*, took some supply ships to Hispaniola and back in 1496, was appointed the first *piloto mayor* of Castile, made an independent voyage to the Pearl Coast in 1499–1500, and died soon after. Francisco, the next brother, about nineteen years old, shipped as gromet on the First Voyage, became *Niña's* pilot on the Second, and also made the Fourth Voyage with the Admiral. Several other members of the family went with him on his last three voyages; and their testimony in the *pleitos* was uniformly loyal to the Admiral. In these Niños one recognizes that competent and loyal type of seaman and officer whose work is essential to the success of any voyage; men who never lay claim to more than their deserts, or talk against their captain behind his back. Juan Niño was Columbus's favorite shipmate, whom he took with him to his triumph at Barcelona. As the Niños neither attempted to chisel away Columbus's fame, nor became the favorite sons of a local or patriotic build-up, they are less known than the Pinzons; but I suspect that they did quite as much as anyone to obtain seamen and put the voyage through.

Related to the Niños were the Quinteros of Moguer, two of whom shipped with Columbus. Cristóbal Quintero, owner of *Pinta*, relinquished her command to Pinzón, but became master of Columbus's flagship on the Third Voyage. Juan Quintero, *Pinta's* boatswain, is the only man besides the Admiral who is known to have sailed on all four voyages.

According to the testimony in the *pleitos*, the local seamen were held back less by fear than by skepticism. "All thought that the enterprise was vain" is the phrase constantly repeated, and at least two of the witnesses gave a very interesting reason why they thought so — because many Portuguese had "gone to discover" in the Western Ocean, and found nothing. A Portuguese who accompanied Columbus on the Second Voyage but not the First admitted that he had considered the enterprise "to be a vain thing, and thought that they would not have fallen in with land," because he "knew that the king of Portugal had fitted out once or twice and they returned without finding land."

That being so, it was lucky for Columbus that there happened to be living in Palos an ancient mariner called Pedro Vasques de la Frontera who in 1452 had made a voyage of discovery with a Madeiran named Diogo de Teive, under orders from the Infante D. Henrique. Sailing southwesterly from Fayal in the Azores, Vasques had run into the Sargasso Sea (which, incidentally, he warned Columbus not to fear), then turned northeastward, discovered the two westernmost Azores, Flores and Corvo, continued on that course in search of the mythical island of Brazil and reached the latitude of Cape Clear, Ireland. Although morally certain that they were near an undiscovered island, they turned back. Forty years later Pedro Vasques came forward and told Columbus and Pinzón "that he had information of the land of the Indies," and (says another witness in 1535) "encouraged the people and told them publicly that all should go on that voyage, and they would find a very rich land, . . . and said it publicly in the plazas."

How vivid it all is! The grizzled pilot, who believed he had just missed something big forty years before, becomes greatly excited at Columbus's preparations, confers with him and with Pinzón, and, warmly approving their enterprise, undertakes to beat up recruits for them in the plaza of Palos, where the unemployed hung about just as they do now. One can imagine the talk: Sign on with Master Christopher, you swabs, and he will make you rich for life, I know there's something big out there! Voice from the crowd: Did you ever *see* anything, skipper? — Sure thing, and if I was twenty years younger, I'd sail with you. Why, when I piloted Don Diogo we saw one day a big island with gold shining on the rocks . . . — So what? — Well, the fog closed in, and when it lifted we couldn't find the island, and it got cold, and Don Diogo wanted to go home to his wife (you know how it is), and so we lost it; but if I was twenty years younger and had half the chance of you mugs . . .

Unfortunately Pedro Vasques did not live to learn that his enthusiasm was justified. He was murdered before Columbus returned to Palos.

Now let us see who took his advice. The thoroughgoing researches of Miss Alice Bache Gould have made it possible to give the names of 87 out of 90 men and boys who sailed on this first voyage of discovery to the New World, with most of their wages and ratings and a few biographical details. A few of the names are in Columbus's own Journal, others were obtained from the later *pleitos*, but most of them are found on payrolls in the Spanish archives and elsewhere, owing to their wages being paid by the crown.

The number of men left behind at Navidad, 39, presumably represents very nearly the crew of the wrecked *Santa María*, although some of the garrison were from *Niña*, and some of the *Santa María's* men took their places. Of the remaining 51 more than half can be assigned to *Pinta*. Of the 87 whose names we know, only four besides Columbus were not Spaniards: Juan Arias of Tavira in Portugal, Jácome el Rico of Genoa, Antón Calabrés (presumably a Calabrian), and Juan Veçano (probably a Venetian). English and Irish national pride have been flattered by the idea that a man of each nation accompanied the fleet; but there was no Englishman or Irishman or other North European aboard.

The royal order suspending all civil and criminal processes against men who signed on with Columbus gave rise to the notion, repeated *ad nauseam*, that the Admiral's crews were composed of desperate characters, criminals and jailbirds. The grain of truth is this. Not long before Columbus came to Palos, one Bartolomé de Torres of that town had been found guilty of killing a man in a quarrel, and sentenced to death. When awaiting execution he was rescued from jail by three of his friends, Alonso Clavijo, Juan de Moguer, and Pedro Yzquierdo. In accordance with a curious law of Castile these three also were condemned to death. All four, when still at large, took advantage of the royal offer to enlist under Columbus, and at their return each received a pardon "because to serve us you ventured your person and underwent much danger with D. Cristóbal Colón our Admiral of the Ocean Sea to discover the Islands of the Indies." Even these four were not in the ordinary sense jailbirds, and at least three of them made good. Bartolomé de Torres shipped on the Second Voyage as a crossbowman; Columbus took Juan de Moguer as able seaman aboard his flagship on the Second Voyage, and Juan later became a pilot under Aguado.

Apart from the few foreigners, one man from Murcia, and ten northerners (who were probably of *Santa María's* original crew), all Columbus's men hailed either from some town or village in the Niebla (Palos, Moguer, Huelva, Lepe) or from other towns in Andalusia such as Cadiz, Seville, Cordova, Jeres, Puerto Santa María. There were at least three family groups besides the Niños, Quinteros and Pinzons: Gil Pérez and his nephew Alvaro on *Pinta;* Pedro Arráez and his son Juan on *Niña,* and the Medel brothers aboard *Pinta.* Far from being manned by criminals, cutthroats and desperadoes, Columbus's vessels were what we used to call in New England "home-town ships," manned by the local boys and their neighbors and friends from near-by seaports. They doubtless represented the pick of the seafaring population, active young seamen whose sporting sense was aroused by the novelty of the enterprise, and the hope of gain. Apart from their pardonable apprehension at the length of the outward voyage, these men behaved well while under the Admiral's command; and the bad actions of those left behind at Navidad, which aroused the natives' hostility and caused their death, were probably no worse than what any group of sailors would have done under the circumstances. All in all, it seems to me that Columbus's ship-mates were "good guys," hardy, competent and loyal to their commander. No one but real seamen could have sailed *Niña* and *Pinta* home safely; and a considerable number of them are known to have accompanied Columbus on his later voyages.

The total monthly payroll of the expedition was 250,180 maravedis; but except for the advance pay, this was allowed to accumulate and the men were paid off when they returned. Masters and pilots received 2000 maravedis a month; *marineros* (the able seamen), 1000; *grumetes* (gromets, ordinary seamen or ship's boys), 666 maravedis a month or 22 a day. This was the usual pay for long voyages, as the royal order of April 30 specified; Columbus paid exactly the same wages on his Fourth Voyage in 1502–1504.

What these sums were equivalent to in modern terms is difficult to say. A thousand maravedis, if paid in gold (as these men seem to have been paid), were equivalent to $6.95 in gold dollars of before 1934. If paid in silver, they were worth only half. Whatever way you figure it, a maravedi was less than a cent in specie value, but its purchasing power was much greater. Twelve maravedis a day were allowed by the crown for feeding each seaman in the navy. A bushel of wheat in 1493 cost 73 maravedis. Sancho Panza's wages from Don Quixote were 26 maravedis a day and found, a little better than that of Columbus's gromets.

The men were not provided with clothing, and when paid off after the voyage there were no deductions from their wages for "slops." Seamen in those days generally wore what they had. The only distinctive sailor's garments were a hooded smock or parka, and the *gorro*, a red woolen stocking-cap, similar to those worn by Portuguese fishermen today. Everyone went barefoot, and let his beard grow, for there were no shaving facilities aboard ship.

Turning from the forecastle to the afterguard, the officers of Columbus's vessels (as in all Spanish ships in the age of discovery) were the captain, master and pilot. The captain was the commanding officer, responsible for everything and everybody on board; and Columbus, beside being captain of *Santa María*, was captain general of the fleet. García Palacio, who published the first Spanish seafaring manual in 1587, says that the captain should be a good Christian, "very fearful of God," possessed of all manly virtues, of a cheerful disposition to keep his people happy and contented, zealous to see that everyone did his duty, and above all things vigilant. He did not necessarily have to be a seaman, because the master had immediate command of all the mariners, and full responsibility for getting under way, stowing the cargo, managing the ship under sail, and anchoring. The master "above all things, must be a good seaman."

The owner of a vessel, when chartered to the crown or to others, normally acted as her master. Thus Juan Niño, owner of *Niña*, was her master as well; and Columbus's second in command on *Santa María* was her owner, Juan de la Cosa. But Martín Alonso Pinzón took his younger brother Francisco as master of *Pinta*, whose owner, Cristóbal Quintero, rated as able seaman.

Juan de la Cosa, master of *Santa María*, is commonly supposed to be the man of the same name who made the famous world map and later explored the Spanish Main; but these were two different persons. The confusion is natural, since both were Basques, the one from a ward or parish of Santoña called Santa María del Puerto, and the other shifted his residence to a town on the Bay of Cadiz called Puerto Santa María. Juan de la Cosa of the First

Voyage disgraced himself when his ship grounded, and never again was mentioned by the Admiral; Juan de la Cosa the map maker shipped aboard *Niña* in 1493 as able seaman, and made the Cuban voyage with Columbus. While the Second Voyage was under way the first Juan de la Cosa, having procured another ship in Spain, applied to the crown for permission to carry 200 *cahizes* of wheat from Andalusia to Guipuzcoa; and this privilege was granted by Ferdinand and Isabella on February 28, 1494 (when the second Juan de la Cosa was in Hispaniola), on the express ground that he had lost his ship in the Indies.

The pilot on Spanish vessels of that era corresponded to the first mate or first officer of English and American ships. Second to the master in command over the seamen, he also had to take charge of the navigation, keeping the reckoning and pricking off the estimated daily positions on the chart. García Palacio declares that this officer should be a man of considerable age and experience, vigilant and weather-wise, knowing when to take in sail and acquainted with astronomy. Columbus's pilots were good men and true, and on the outward passage Peralonso Niño, pilot of *Santa María*, was more accurate than the Admiral; but none knew celestial navigation, and on the return voyage Columbus kept the better dead-reckoning. Cristóbal García Sarmiento (or Xalmiento) piloted *Pinta;* and Sancho Ruiz de Gama, *Niña.* Bartolomé Roldán also did some "making points" aboard *Niña.* He and Sarmiento sailed on the Second Voyage, and Roldán also on the Third, as well as making voyages with Aguado, Hojeda and Lepe. Eventually he settled down and became a leading citizen of Santo Domingo. Pilots were paid 2000 maravedis a month, twice the seaman's pay, and the same as masters.

Besides the ships' officers, there were a number of landsmen in the fleet with particular duties. Luis de Torres, a *converso* or converted Jew, was taken along as interpreter because he knew Hebrew and a little Arabic. It was then commonly supposed that Arabic was the mother of all languages, so Torres was expected to make shift at conversing with the Grand Khan and other oriental potentates. Diego de Harana, cousin of Columbus's Cordovan mistress, shipped as *alguacil de la armada*, marshal of the fleet. The same office existed in English ships into the seventeenth century. Captain John Smith says, "The Marshall is to punish offenders, and to see justice executed according to directions; as ducking at the yards arme, haling under the keel, bound to the capsterne or maine-mast with a bucket of shot about his necke, setting in the bilbowes." Diego de Harana sailed on *Santa María*; *Pinta* and *Niña* each had her own marshal.

Rodrigo de Escobedo was *escribano de toda la armada*, secretary of the fleet. He had nothing to do with keeping the journal, but wrote up proceedings when possession was taken of any island in the name of the Sovereigns. He would probably have been called upon for diplomatic correspondence if the Indians had been able to read and write.

Two royal officials were aboard *Santa María*. Rodrigo Sánchez de Segovia, *veedor real* or comptroller, came to keep track of expenditures, and to see that the crown got its share of gold and precious stones. Pedro Gutiérrez is referred to as *repostero de estrados del rey*, butler of the king's dais. He appears to have been a gentleman volunteer, for Columbus had a personal steward (Pedro de Terreros, who rose to command a caravel on a later voyage) and a page-boy.

Each vessel carried her own surgeon. Maestre Juan Sánchez of *Santa María* belonged to the Haranas' circle of friends in Cordova; Maestre Alonso of Moguer took care of *Niña*, and Maestre Diego of *Pinta*. There was so little for them to do aboard this healthy fleet that the first two were allowed to stay at Navidad; Alonso's heirs were paid 11,688 maravedis for his services.

Among the petty officers and men of *Santa María* were nine northerners, Basques and Galicians, probably the only members of her original ship's company who could be induced to remain. They formed a clique under Juan de la Cosa, and five of them, greatly to the relief of the Andalusians, elected to remain at Navidad. Chachu (Basque for Juanito), boatswain of *Santa María*,

was the leader of this gang. The boatswain then as now had special charge of the gear. It was his duty to lead the seamen in carrying out the master's or pilot's orders, to direct the stowage of
cargo, to watch the spars for weakness and the rigging for chafe,
to see that the cables were kept dry at sea, that the coils of the
running rigging were properly made up, that the pump was kept
clear, that the galley fire was extinguished every night, that the
ship's boat was kept clean and properly fitted, and that the rats
were prevented from eating the sails in port. He must have been
the busiest man aboard. Juan Quintero, the one who accompanied Columbus on all four voyages, was Chachu's opposite
number on *Pinta*, and Bartolomé García was boatswain of *Niña*.
These two were paid 1500 maravedis a month, and Chachu somewhat more — a bonus perhaps to induce him to stay with the
ship. Even today it is easier to procure a good captain than a good
boatswain.

The *despensero* or steward was another important petty officer.
He had entire charge of the water, wine and food, of firewood,
and of some of the chandlery; he trimmed the lamps and fed the
fire on the galley hearth; and he also saw that the boys learned to
box the compass and say the proper ditties when the glass was
turned and the watch relieved. García Fernández was steward
of *Pinta;* we do not know the names of the other two.

Below the boatswains and stewards were a group of petty officers known as *oficiales* who received able seaman's pay, but had
special duties, such as carpenter, cooper and caulker. "Chips" had
the same duties as today, except that *calafate* the caulker took
charge of the pump, as well as seeing that the decks, topsides, and
bottom (when she was hove-down) were kept properly caulked
and payed with pitch and tallow. He also saw to it that the gromets
employed their spare time making up caulking stuff instead of
skylarking. *Tonelero* the cooper "is to looke to the caske, hoopes
and twigs, to stave or repaire the buckets, baricos, cans, steepe
tubs, runlets, hogsheads, pipes, buts, etc. for wine . . . fresh
water, or any liquor." *Pinta* carried a painter, and one gromet

aboard *Santa María* had the resounding title of "silversmith, assayer of minerals and washer of gold."

The total complement was about 24 men aboard *Niña;* 26 aboard *Pinta;* 40 aboard *Santa María.*

According to contemporary standards, this was an unusually well-organized fleet for discovery and exploration. There were no "idlers" except the royal butler, secretary and interpreter, and these might have been useful if Columbus had had occasion to entertain the governor of a Chinese province. Popular illustrations usually show men-at-arms complete with pike and morion stalking about *Santa María's* deck, apparently as a marine guard; but Columbus shipped no men-at-arms on this voyage, not even cannoneers or crossbowmen. He was not equipped for fighting or conquering but for just one thing, discovery. The three caravels were provisioned for at least a year, which suggests that Columbus expected to be home in much less time than that. He was not planning so long a voyage as Bartholomew Dias had already made to South Africa.

Columbus did not once mention in his writings a tragic movement that was under way at the same time as his preparations, one which must in some measure have hampered his efforts and delayed his departure. This was the expulsion of the Jews from Spain. On March 30, 1492, one month before concluding their agreements with Columbus, Ferdinand and Isabella signed the fateful decree giving the Jews four months to accept baptism or leave a country where many thousands of them had made their home for centuries, and to whose intellectual life they had contributed in a degree far beyond their numbers. As Columbus journeyed from Granada to Palos he must have been witness to heart-rending scenes similar to those which modern fanaticism has revived in the Europe of today. Swarms of refugees, who had sold for a trifle property accumulated over years of toil, crowded the roads that led seaward, on foot and leading donkeys and carts piled high with such household goods as could be transported. Rabbis read the sacred scrolls and others played the traditional chants on pipe and tabor to keep their spirits up; but it was a melancholy procession at best, what with weeping and lamenting, and the old and sick crawling into the fields to die. When they arrived at Puerto Santa María and for the first time beheld the ocean, the Jews raised loud cries and invocations, hoping that Jehovah would part the waters and lead them dry-shod to some new promised land. Camping where they could find room or crowded aboard vessels that the richer Jews chartered, they forlornly awaited the order to leave; finally word came from the Sovereigns that every Jew-bearing ship must leave port on August 2, 1492, the day before Columbus set sail from Palos. Perhaps that is why he waited until the following day; but even then he did not avoid sailing in unwanted company. Sixty years later an old man deposed in Guatemala that he had been gromet on a ship of the great migration that dropped down the Rio Saltés on the same tide with the Columbian fleet; and by a curious coincidence, when his ship was sailing back to Northern Spain after discharging her cargo of human misery in the Levant, she spoke *Pinta* returning from the great discovery, and heard news that in due time would give fresh life to this persecuted race.

Of the many difficulties that Columbus and the Pinzons had to surmount in order to get their people aboard and the vessels ready for sea, no details have survived; all have been swallowed up in the surpassing interest of the voyage itself. Tradition designates a fountain near the Church of St. George at Palos, connected by a Roman aqueduct with a spring of sweet water in the hills, where the water casks of the fleet were filled. Last thing of all, every man and boy had to confess his sins, receive absolution, and make his communion. Columbus, after making his confession (writes the first historian of the Indies), "received the very holy sacrament of the Eucharist on the very day that he entered upon the sea; and in the name of Jesus ordered the sails to be set and left the harbor of Palos for the river of Saltés and the Ocean Sea with three equipped caravels, giving the commencement to the First Voyage and Discovery of the Indies."

THE FIRST VOYAGE TO AMERICA

CHAPTER XI

Bound Away

August 3–September 9, 1492

Et turbabuntur insulae in mari, eo quod nullus egrediatur ex te.

Yea, the isles that are in the sea shall be troubled at thy departure.

— EZEKIEL xxvi 18

COLUMBUS began his Book of the First Navigation and Discovery of the Indies, commonly called the Journal of his First Voyage, with a preamble characteristic both of the Admiral and of his times: —

IN THE NAME OF OUR LORD JESUS CHRIST

BECAUSE, most Christian and very exalted excellent and mighty Princes, King and Queen of the Spains and of the islands in the Sea, our Lord and Lady, in this present year 1492, after Your Highnesses had made an end to the war with the Moors who ruled in Europe, and had concluded the war in the very great city of Granada, where in the present year, on the second day of the month of January, by force of arms I saw the royal standards of Your Highnesses placed on the towers of Alhambra (which is the citadel of the said city), and I saw the Moorish King come forth to the gates of the city and kiss the royal hands of Your Highnesses and of the Prince my lord, and soon after in that same month, through the information that I had given to Your Highnesses concerning the lands of India, and of a prince who is called "Grand Khan" which is to say in our vernacular "King of Kings," how many times he and his ancestors had sent to Rome to seek doctors in our Holy Faith to instruct him therein,* and that never had the Holy Father provided them, and thus were lost so

---

* Note similarity of language to that of the Toscanelli letter.

many people through lapsing into idolatries and receiving doctrines of perdition;

AND Your Highnesses, as Catholic Christians and Princes devoted to the Holy Christian Faith and the propagators thereof, and enemies of the sect of Mahomet and of all idolatries and heresies, resolved to send me Christopher Columbus to the said regions of India, to see the said princes and peoples and lands and [to observe] the disposition of them and of all, and the manner in which may be undertaken their conversion to our Holy Faith, and ordained that I should not go by land (the usual way) to the Orient, but by the route of the Occident, by which no one to this day knows for sure that anyone has gone; —

THEREFORE, after all the Jews had been exiled from your realms and dominions, in the same month of January Your Highnesses commanded me that with a sufficient fleet I should go to the said regions of India, and for this granted me many rewards, and ennobled me so that henceforth I might call myself by a noble title and be Admiral-in-Chief of the Ocean Sea and Viceroy and Perpetual Governor of all the islands and mainlands that I should discover and win, or that henceforth might be discovered and won in the Ocean Sea, and that my eldest son should succeed me, and thus from rank to rank for ever.

AND I departed from the city of Granada on the 12th day of the month of May of the same year 1492, on a Saturday, and came to the town of Palos, which is a seaport, where I fitted for sea three ships well suited for such an undertaking, and I departed from the said harbor well furnished with much provision and many seamen, on the third day of the month of August of the said year, on a Friday, at half an hour before sunrise, and took the route for the Canary Islands of Your Highnesses, which are in the said Ocean, that I might thence take my course and sail until I should reach the Indies, and give the letters of Your Highnesses to those princes, and thus comply with what you had commanded.

AND for this I thought to write down upon this voyage in great detail from day to day all that I should do and see, and encounter, as hereinafter shall be seen. In addition, Lord Princes, to noting down each night what that day had brought forth, and each day what was sailed by night, I have the intention to make a new chart of navigation, upon which I shall place the whole sea and lands of the Ocean Sea in their proper positions under their bearings, and further to compose a book, and set down everything as in a real picture, by latitude north of the equator and longitude west; and above all it is very important that I forget sleep and labor much at navigation because it is necessary. All of which will be great labor.

So begins the most detailed, the most interesting and the most entrancing sea journal of any voyage in history. And it is, furthermore, the source of about 98 per cent of our information about the actual discovery of America. Columbus's Journal, as I shall call it in deference to long usage, although it is much more than an ordinary sea journal, contains not only the navigator's "day's work" of courses steered, and distances covered, objects sighted at sea and lands discovered, but long descriptions of people, places, fauna and flora, and the Admiral's reflections and conclusions on cosmography, on future colonial policy and on many other subjects.

The original manuscript of the Journal has long since disappeared. It was sent or presented in person by Columbus to the Sovereigns at Barcelona, where it doubtless found its way into the ever-perambulating royal archives, and so was lost or thrown away before one of the frequent moving days. Fortunately, one or more fair copies were made shortly after the Journal was received at Barcelona. One was in the possession of Las Casas, who made an abstract for his own use, quoting long passages of the original. The same or another was used by Ferdinand Columbus in writing the *Historie*, wherein he preserved in direct quotation some parts that Las Casas merely abstracted, and which prove that the bishop did his work honestly and well. Las Casas's abstract of the Journal, in his own hand, is still preserved in the National Library at Madrid; and that is the text we have today.

This Journal, as Las Casas abstracted it, has been the target of every writer with a peculiar theory. Those who pretend that Columbus was never seeking "The Indies," the advocates of someone else having discovered them first, or of his having been there before under another name; those who insist that Colón the discoverer was a different person from Colombo the Genoese, patriotic Spaniards who wish to give Martín Alonso Pinzón the credit; Scandinavians who assert that Columbus deliberately concealed important information gleaned in Iceland — all these and others with even wilder theories which the text of the Journal proves to be preposterous must do their best to discredit the document. Vignaud and Carbia in particular have built up a case for the abstract Journal having been truncated, garbled, falsified, and rewritten by Las Casas or Ferdinand or others in order to prove what they call the exploded tradition that one Christopher Columbus, a Genoese, discovered America on October 12, 1492, when searching for a western route to the Indies.

The scribe who copied the Journal made common errors such as writing "east" for "west," which are shown up when you plot the fleet's course. Las Casas doubtless omitted some nautical detail that we should wish to have, and interpolated some stupid remarks of his own that are easily detected. But the charge that he or anyone else garbled the Journal is false. My shipmates and I, who have probably given the Journal the most intensive study to which it has ever been subjected, will go even further. We say that nobody not a seaman, and no seaman who did not follow Columbus's route, could possibly have faked this document, so accurate are the bearings, the courses and the observations; and any such navigator would have needed the aid of the cleverest of literary forgers to complete the work, so closely are woven into it Columbus's ardent quest for the Indies, and the wonder and surprise at completely new experiences. Columbus did not even take the trouble to expunge the numerous mistakes that he made in navigation, and which he knew to be mistakes a few days later.

The Preamble that we quoted at the head of this chapter has been the particular target of the critics, because of its mention of the "lands of India" and the Grand Khan. All the "debunkers" insist that this was written after the voyage was over, and Columbus was making the best of a bad failure. It is indeed probable that the Preamble was not written on the opening day of the voyage, when Columbus was busy with other things, but at the Canaries. That it could not have been written much later is shown by the promise in the last paragraph that was not performed: to set down all the "sea and lands of the Ocean Sea in their proper positions under their bearings," with latitude and longitude. This Columbus did not do because he had not the science. Like other navigators, he probably thought he could "work it up at sea"; but we have only three latitudes (all wrong) and no longitude for the entire voyage. This gap between promise and performance did not escape the eyes of the Sovereigns, who invited him rather pointedly to supply the missing data before his Second Voyage began. They would hardly have asked him to do what no navigator of that period had sufficient skill to do, had they not noted his rash promise in the Preamble.

Columbus's plan for the voyage was to sail first to the Canaries, and thence due west to the Indies. And about this simple plan have been spun fancy webs of theory. It seems clear enough why he chose that route. A direct westerly course from Spain was ruled out by the experience of the Portuguese, who so many times had bucked the westerlies of the North Atlantic in vain. But the Canaries were within the zone of the northeast trade winds, and to reach the Canaries there was assurance, at that season, of favorable northerlies. There is no hint in the Journal or elsewhere that Columbus knew that the northeast trade wind would carry him across; but he must have observed on his African voyage that a westward course from the Canaries would enjoy a fair wind as soon as you pass out of the Canary calms. It was merely his good fortune that the same wind carried his fleet all the way to America.

There was another and compelling reason for choosing the Canaries as the point of departure. They lay on the same parallel of latitude as Cipangu or Japan. Turn back to glance at our sketch of Martin Behaim's Globe, completed the year that Columbus sailed, and note how the route that he chose was the simplest and shortest to the Indies, in the light of the geographical misinformation then current. It has always been the plan of simple dead-reckoning navigators to get on the presumed latitude of their destination, and run their easting or westing down until they reach it. The Orient most nearly approached the Occident on the parallel of the Canaries, in Columbus's estimation. The winds at the Canaries generally blew from the eastward. So what could be more sensible than to make these islands his point of departure? Moreover, a break in the voyage made the first leg of it a sort of "shake-down cruise," highly useful to test the quality of his ships and the temper of his men.

The Captain General, as we should style Columbus on the out-ward-bound passage, made his communion at St. George's, Palos, in the small hours of the morning Friday, August 3, went aboard his flagship before dawn, and "in the name of Jesus" gave the command to get under way. Cheerful chanteys accompanied the creak of the windlasses, and at half an hour before sunrise (which at that date and latitude came about a quarter past five) the anchors were aboard *Santa María*, *Pinta* and *Niña*. It was one of those gray, calm days that herald the coming of autumn, when the sea is like a mirror of burnished steel, and the spectacular cloud masses of Castile (such as El Greco alone could paint) seem to pause in their endless change; a halcyon day, when not a leaf stirs ashore, and but for the outward flow of tide one could imagine that time stood still. Lack of wind mattered not to the fleet, for their departure was timed at the beginning of the ebb, which had sufficient strength to take them over the bar before the water fell too low for *Santa María's* draught. The sweeps were manned to give steerageway, and with sails hanging limp and no sound but the slow plash of the long oars and their rattle and creak in the ports, the fleet dropped down-river. A mile and a half from Palos on the port hand they passed the buildings of La Rábida close aboard; it was the hour of prime, and the friars were chanting their ancient liturgical hymn for that office: —

> *Iam lucis orto sidere*
> *Deum precemur supplices,*
> *ut in diurnis artibus*
> *nos servet a nocentibus.*

The Captain General, who often had joined in that hymn during his stay at La Rábida, removes his hat; seamen who are not working follow his example; all cross themselves and many kneel as the last stanza comes out over the water: —

> *Deo Patri sit gloria,*
> *eiusque soli Filio,*
> *cum Spiritu Paraclito*
> *et nunc et in perpetuum.*

"Evermore and evermore." This modest armada was setting forth on a conquest for the Cross that would outlast all worldly empires.

A few hundred yards beyond La Rábida the course was altered to port and the fleet entered the Rio Odiel, then called the Saltés. With ebb current and the lightest of airs they floated between pine-clad sand dunes of the mainland and the isle of Saltés, then turned 50 degrees to starboard, and at eight in the morning crossed the bar. There the sails caught a "strong sea breeze" which would not permit them to steer nearer the wind than due south, or to make better speed than four knots. Until sunset they were within sight of land. The wind then backed to the north and they steered south-west to get a good offing. Sometime during the night, when he was sufficiently offshore, the Admiral set the course for the Canaries: *Sur cuarta del sudoeste* — South and by West.

Although nothing is said about it in the Journal, Columbus must have devised or adopted from his Portuguese instructors a system of signals to keep the fleet together. In the iron cresset or brazier which hung over the stern, it was possible to make a fire by night or smoke by day, and to smother it with a swatch of wet canvas. Thus two, three or even four *fuegos* or *fumos* could be made in succession, as orders to change course, make or strike sail, or draw up to the flagship for instructions. A *farol* or torch of pitch pine could be used in combination with the brazier. For weighty occasions such as a landfall, the Journal informs us that a gun was fired. The natural course for any fleet of sailing vessels is to draw apart, as we see in ocean yacht races today; but the object of Columbus was to keep his fleet together. That was no easy task, as the flagship was a slower sailer than *Pinta* and *Niña*. So the two caravels had constantly to restrict their speed by reducing sail, in order not to drop the flagship astern.

The ocean between Spain and the Canaries is a rough bit of water, which the Spaniards generally required eight or ten days to cover. They called it *el Golfo de las Yeguas* (the Sea of the Mares) because so many brood mares being shipped to the Canaries died on board; "and might as well have called it *el Golfo de las Vacas*," says Oviedo, "because no fewer cows than mares died in the same manner." Columbus's fleet was lucky to raise the Grand Canary only six days out, but he did not make it without accident. On August 6 the big outboard rudder of *Pinta* jumped its gudgeons. She made the usual distress signal, the flagship drew near and Columbus went aboard. Martín Alonso Pinzón confided to Columbus that in his opinion this was the result of dirty work by the caravel's owner, Cristóbal Quintero, who hated having his ship commandeered for this voyage, and had been grousing and grumbling ever since the start. The sea was too heavy for *Santa María* to go alongside and lend her tackle to ship the heavy rudder, but Columbus "reflected that Martín Alonso Pinzón was a man of energy and ingenuity," and could manage alone.

This was the first and last compliment to Pinzón recorded in the Admiral's Journal. But I have special reasons for not being favorably impressed by Pinzón's hint of foul play, knowing by personal experience that these waters are hard on steering gear. *Mary Otis's* rudder worked loose from the post as we were beating to windward from Cadiz toward Madeira on November 4, 1939; and when we put in at Casablanca for repairs, there was an English cutter with a big outboard rudder like *Pinta's* which had become unshipped off the African coast. Moreover, if Quintero had wished to put *Pinta* out of commission in order to escape the dangers of the deep, the place for such trickery was in the Canaries. Deliberately to tamper with steering gear on the high seas would endanger his life as well as his vessel.

By the next day, August 7, *Pinta's* rudder was secured for the time being, and the fleet filled away for Lanzarote. This drifting about spoiled the reckoning, and on the eighth the pilots could not agree as to their position; Columbus's reckoning proved the nearest to the truth, he admits. (The commanding officer is always right.) *Pinta's* rudder gave trouble again, and she began to leak. So Columbus changed course for the Grand Canary, with the idea of exchanging *Pinta* there for some other vessel; or, if that were impossible, repairing her at a place where there were facilities

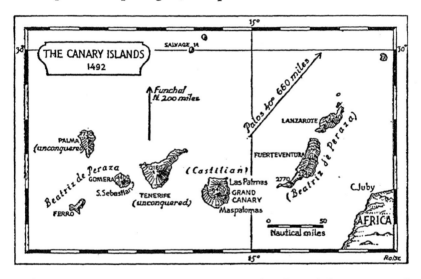

for forging iron. At dawn on August 9 the Grand Canary was in sight, but the fleet ran into a flat calm. Neither that day nor the two following could they reach the island. Consequently, in order to save time, and to have a double chance of encountering a suitable vessel that could be bought or chartered, Columbus, when a breeze sprang up on the third night, left Martín Alonso to take *Pinta* into Las Palmas, while he with *Santa María* and *Niña* proceeded to Gomera.

As yet the Canaries were only in part conquered by Spain from their warlike and vigorous native inhabitants the Guanches; the story of their conquest, as Roger Merriman points out, was a microcosm of the early history of America. Columbus might have read a prophecy of his own fate, and that of the Indians, in current events that he must have heard discussed. Two Spanish conquistadors had been falsely accused, seized and sent home in chains. The Guanches had been overcome by a combination of cruelty and treachery, forcibly converted to the Catholic faith, and reduced to slavery. The conquest of the island of Palma was being pursued that very summer, and Tenerife was still completely in the hands of the natives.

Columbus, passing the northern coast of the Grand Canary and the south coast of Tenerife, islands so lofty and beautiful that we sometimes wonder at his enthusiasm for the Bahamas, anchored in the roadstead of San Sebastián, Gomera, on the evening of August 12.

That island, one of the first of the Canaries to be conquered, was an hereditary captaincy held by the Herrera y Peraza family under the crown of Castile. In 1492 the virtual captain was a young, energetic and beautiful widow, Doña Beatriz de Peraza y Bobadilla, who was governing the island as guardian of her minor son Guillén, later the first Count of Gomera. It was perhaps fortunate for the success of the enterprise that she was then absent, although daily expected from Lanzarote in a vessel of 40 tons, which Columbus hoped might prove a fit substitute for *Pinta*.

San Sebastián, a small town fronting the best roadstead in Gomera, at the mouth of a river that flows down from the mountainous interior through a deep *barranca* (ravine), preserves its fifteenth-century aspect better than any other Old World town associated with Columbus. The stone castle where Columbus was entertained is still standing, a house is shown where he is said to have lodged, and the Church of the Assumption, where he certainly worshiped, has remained virtually unchanged. Gomera afforded the best of meats, breadstuffs and cheeses, a river of excellent water flowed past San Sebastián, and the heights were well forested. So Columbus sent gangs of men to procure more wood and water, and purchased more provisions. The caravels carried a number of knocked-down water butts which the coopers set up and the men filled; and if they had no salt for preserving meat, jerked beef could be made in a few days under the hot Canary sun. On August 14 Columbus sent one of his best men aboard a small island coaster bound for Las Palmas in order to tell Martín Alonso where he was, and to help him repair *Pinta's* rudder.

Nine days slipped by, and no ship bearing Doña Beatriz appeared. Finally Columbus felt he could wait no longer, and decided to join Martín Alonso at Las Palmas. On the way he overtook the coaster that had sailed nine days earlier, and took his man aboard again. That night he sailed close under Tenerife, whose superb volcano, rising 12,000 feet above sea level, was belching forth fire and smoke. On August 25 Columbus arrived at Las Palmas to find that *Pinta* had arrived only the previous day, after drifting about for two weeks. Her steering gear must indeed have been in a bad way. And Doña Beatriz had sailed five days earlier for Gomera. So Columbus decided not to play hide-and-seek with her any longer, and to make the best job he could of repairing *Pinta*.

The Grand Canary had been "pacified" in 1483, and by the time of Columbus's visit the chief settlement of Las Palmas had already become, as it still is, the metropolis of the Canaries; a brisk and busy little settlement of merchants and planters who were prospering from the incredibly rich soil and marvelous climate. Sugar cane had been brought over from Morocco, grapevines from Spain, and slaves from Africa; as many as four crops a year of grass or grain could be reaped in some favored localities. Las Palmas was the best place to have *Pinta's* rudder rebuilt; near the waterfront is the *Herrería* or blacksmiths' quarter, where her new pintles and gudgeons and bolts and straps were forged under the eye of Martín Alonso.

At the same time, "that she might follow the other vessels with more tranquillity and less danger" *Niña's* lateen rig was altered to square by crossing yards on main and foremast and recutting the great triangular sails. Columbus and the Pinzons evidently agreed that the big, unwieldy lateen mainsail of the Portuguese-style caravel was a hazard on the high seas, especially in a following wind. One careless gybe, and your mast and gear would be gone. The great virtue of the lateen rig, its ability to take a vessel close to the wind, would have been little use, since there was no point in having *Niña* outfoot the fleet on a beat to windward; the change of rig more nearly equated her speed and performance with her larger consorts.

From the list of personnel in Columbus's fleet, which is fairly complete, it is clear that there were no desertions in the Canaries, although one new hand may have been shipped there. Knowing the propensity of seamen to become dissatisfied and take a "pier-head jump" at the first port of call, this fact speaks well for the confidence that Columbus and the Pinzons inspired in their men.

On Friday, September 1, in the afternoon the fleet sailed from Las Palmas, and on the following day made San Sebastián. There at last Columbus met the fair if somewhat formidable ruler of Gomera, Doña Beatriz de Peraza. Born Beatriz de Bobadilla, and first cousin once removed of the Marquesa de Moya, when a beautiful young girl she was appointed maid of honor to Queen Isabella, and attracted the amorous attentions of King Ferdinand. At the time when Isabella noticed this and was wondering what to do about it, Hernán Peraza the Captain of Gomera appeared at court, to answer charges of having murdered a rival conquistador in the Canaries. He was pardoned in return for marrying Beatriz and taking her back to Gomera, an arrangement that pleased everyone but the King. Hernán was so arbitrary, despotic and cruel that his seduction of a native girl touched off an uprising in which he was killed. Beatriz, besieged with her two children in the castle of San Sebastián, managed to get word to Pedro de Vera, Governor of the Grand Canary, who came to her rescue. That act of gallantry did not save Pedro's son, Hernando, from later being captured by Beatriz in the hope of regaining Isabella's favor, there being a price on his head for having written libelous verses against the Queen. Fortunately he made good his escape.

At the time of Columbus's visit this energetic widow was still under thirty, and very beautiful; and we have it on good authority that he fell in love with her. Why not? His own Beatriz was far away, and Doña Beatriz, belonging to one of the first families of Castile, would have made a very suitable match for him. That she returned his admiration, if not his love, is evident by the splendid reception she gave him on his next visit, in 1493; but this nascent romance did not delay the Great Enterprise.

Doña Beatriz must have entertained Columbus in the old stone castle at San Sebastián, a part of which, the Torre del Conde, still stands. And we read in his Journal, "many honorable Spanish gentlemen who were at Gomera with Doña Inés [*sic*] Peraza, mother of Guillén Peraza, who was afterwards the first Count of Gomera, and who were natives of the island of Ferro, declared that every year they saw land to the west of the Canaries; and others, native of Gomera, affirmed the same on oath."

This land was the mythical St. Brendan's Isle, or *San Borondon*, the most persistent phantom island of the Atlantic. Martin Behaim's Globe of 1492 depicts it just above the equator, and the Canary Islanders were still searching for it in the eighteenth century. Probably you could find aged fishermen in Ferro or Gomera today who would claim they had seen San Borondon, just as old fishermen of Galway still believe that they catch sight of O'Brasil now and then.

Columbus did not take much time out for dalliance with Doña Beatriz; he did not even wait for the night of the full moon (September 6). His men who were left behind in the previous call had not been idle, and within four days' time the caravels were loaded to the gunwales with additional ships' stores, water casks secured on deck, and piles of firewood lashed down on every bit of vacant space. In the early hours of September 6, Columbus heard his last Mass in the Church of the Assumption, where we of the Harvard Columbus Expedition attended an impressive memorial service in 1939. Then, saying farewell (a tender one, we hope) to Doña Beatriz, the future Admiral of the Ocean Sea went aboard, and anchors were weighed for the last time in the Old World.

All that day and night the winds came faint and variable, and on the morning of September 7 the fleet found itself between Gomera and Tenerife. At 3 A.M. Saturday, September 8, "the NE wind began to blow, and he made his way and course to the West," leaving Gomera well to starboard. *Santa María* plunged heavily, taking in water over her bows and so retarding the fleet's progress that for the next twenty-seven hours they made an average speed of less than one knot. By sunrise on Sunday the ninth this fault, due probably to stowing the last of the provisions and water too far forward, had been remedied, and for the next twenty-four hours the fleet made a good run of 130 miles.

Before leaving San Sebastián Columbus had been warned by a caravel that arrived from Ferro that three Portuguese vessels were cruising off that island "with the object of taking him." Probably they had been sent by D. João II merely to observe the Castilian fleet, and to warn them from making discoveries south of the Canaries and west of Africa, a section of the ocean which the king of Portugal regarded as his own sphere of influence. Whether or not the report was true, Columbus saw nothing of this Portuguese squadron; it might however have been lying under the island's lee as he passed some 12 miles to windward of Ferro.

During the morning and early afternoon of September 9 the coast of Ferro lay abeam and the peak of Tenerife was still visible astern. By nightfall every trace of land had disappeared, and the three ships had an uncharted ocean to themselves.

CHAPTER XII

A Day at Sea

Qui nauigant mare enarrent pericula eius, et audientes auribus nostris admirabimur.

They that sail on the sea tell of the danger thereof, and when we hear it with our ears, we marvel thereat.

— ECCLESIASTICUS xliii 26

A DECENT formality has always been observed aboard ships at sea, even to our own day. The wheel is relieved in a certain manner, the watches are changed according to formula, solar and stellar observations are made at fixed hours; and any departure from the settled custom is resented by mariners. In Columbus's ships these formalities were observed with a quasi-religious ritual, which lent them a certain beauty, and reminded the seamen every half hour of the day and night that their ship depended for safety not only on her staunchness and their own skill, but on the grace of God.

In Columbus's day, and until the late sixteenth century, the only ship's clock available was the *ampolleta* or *reloj de arena* (sand clock), a half-hour glass containing enough sand to run from the upper to the lower section in exactly thirty minutes.* Made in Venice, these glasses were so fragile that a large number of spares were carried — Magellan had eighteen on his flagship. It was the duty of a gromet or ship's boy in each watch to mind the *ampolleta*, and reverse it promptly when the sand ran out. A very rough sea might retard the running of the sand, or the

* Cf. Shakespeare's *Tempest*, V i 265: "Our Ship, which but three glasses since, we gave out split . . . " The British navy kept time by glasses of half an hour each until 1839.

gromet might go to sleep; Columbus on one occasion expresses in his Journal the fear that the boys were slack about it. As a ship gains time sailing east and loses it sailing west, even the most modern ship's clock has to be corrected daily by wireless. The only way Columbus could do this with his hour-glass clock was to erect a pin or gnomon on the center of his compass card, and watch for the exact moment of noon when the sun's shadow touched the fleur-de-lis that marked the north, and then turn the glass. But that could hardly be counted on to give him true noon nearer than 15 or 20 minutes, and he did not do it very often; for it is evident from some of his log entries that his "ship's time" was as much as half an hour slow by the sun.

The *marineros*, *grumetes* and *oficiales* of the ship's company — the able seamen, gromets (ordinary seamen and boys) and ratings such as caulker and cooper — were divided into two watches (called by Columbus *cuartos* or *guardias*) of four hours each. Each watch was headed by an officer. Aboard *Santa María*, Master Juan de la Cosa, having the greater dignity, would have taken starboard watch, and pilot Peralonso the port watch. From sundry entries in Columbus's Journal, it is clear that watches were set at 3, 7, and 11 o'clock. These hours seem odd to a modern seaman, who by immemorial usage expects watches to change at 4, 8, and 12. Possibly changing watch at 3, 7, 11 was the usual practice in Columbus's day. Perhaps it was left to the captain's discretion, and Columbus set the night watch on his first day out at 7 P.M., the approximate hour of sunset, and kept up the four-hour intervals on that basis. Presumably the afternoon watch was "dogged" as we still do today in order that the men may change their hours nightly. Suppose, for instance, the port watch comes on at 3 P.M. It goes off at 5, and is on again from 7 to 11. The men then have four hours' sleep, until 3 A.M. They go below again at 7 A.M., and take the noon watch from 11 A.M. to 3 P.M. They then come on deck for the second dogwatch, 5 to 7 P.M., which gives them from 7 to 11 P.M. below on the second night. Aboard many modern steamships the watches are no longer "dogged," only the hours are changed at each fresh departure; for in short runs there is little inconvenience in having the same hours on and off every day and night. But on a sailing vessel that might be many weeks or even months at sea, it was fairer all around to "dog" the watches daily, so that each man would have the unpopular "graveyard watch" from midnight to 4 A.M. (or from 11 to 3) on alternate nights.

Seamen did not think of time in terms of hours, but of *ampolletas* and *guardias*, glasses and watches, eight glasses to a watch. The system of half-hourly ship's bells that we are familiar with was simply a means of accenting the turning of the glass. No ship's bell is mentioned in any of the sea journals of the sixteenth century that I have seen, and García Palacio's *Instrución Náuthica* (Mexico 1587), the Spanish seamen's first Bowditch, says nothing of them.

At night, whenever the weather was clear and the latitude not too low, Columbus could tell approximate clock time from the Guards of the North Star. The Little Bear or Little Dipper swings around Polaris once every 24 hours sidereal time. The two brightest stars of that constellation, β (Kochab) and γ, which mark the edge of the dipper farthest from the North Star, were called the Guards; and if you knew where Kochab the principal Guard was stationed at midnight every two weeks of the year, you could tell time from it as from a clock hand. The early navigators constructed a diagram of a little man with Polaris in his middle, his forearms pointing E and W, and his shoulders NE and NW. That gave eight positions for Kochab: Head, West Shoulder, West Arm, Line under West Arm, Feet, Line under East Arm, East Arm, and East Shoulder. As Kochab moved from one position to another in three hours, you could tell time at night if you knew the relative position of Kochab at midnight on that date. Around 1500, Kochab was at "Head" at midnight April 15, at "West Arm" at midnight July 15, at "Feet" at midnight October 15, and at "East Arm" at midnight January 15. Thus, if you found this natural clock hand to be at the "East Shoulder" position on January 15, you knew it was 3 A.M. and time to call the watch.

Columbus shows his familiarity with this method by an entry in his Journal for September 30, 1492. He probably had a simple

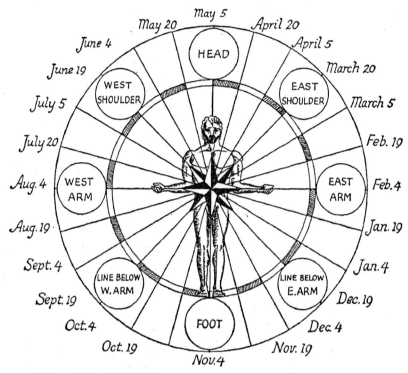

DIAGRAM FOR TELLING TIME FROM
POLARIS, 1942

Kochab (β Ursae Minoris) moves counter-clockwise one line per hour. Its position relative to Polaris at midnight is indicated for each date

instrument, the nocturnal, with which you sighted Polaris through a hole in the center, and then turned a movable arm representing the constellation until it hit Kochab. That gave you the exact position, and so the time. With a little practice, anyone on a long voyage can learn to tell time by this method within a quarter-hour.

Occasionally in his Journal Columbus mentions clock time in such terms as "the first hour of the night" (1 A.M.); but more often he times events by the changing of the watch, or by tierce, vespers and compline, three of the canonical hours of prayer. As a pious Christian, faithful in his religious duties, Columbus kept a book of hours in his cabin, and whenever possible said his prayers in private at the appointed hours, as he had learned to do when staying at La Rábida. But what hours in clock time did he mean by tierce, vespers and compline? That is a difficult question, for there was then no uniformity in usage. Tierce might be said anywhere between 8 and 9 A.M., vespers anywhere from 2 P.M. to dark, and compline between 6 and 9 P.M. A careful comparison of the liturgical authorities with Columbus's journals indicates that he said the office of tierce at 9 A.M. midway in the morning watch; vespers at 2 or 3 P.M., and compline immediately after the *Salve Regina* was sung, at 7 or a little after. For it is the essence of compline to be the last office of the day — *completas*, a fulfillment and conclusion. It includes the hymn *Te lucis ante terminum*, and that noble Psalm xci of faith and confidence: —

Qui habitat in adiutorio Altissimi, in protectione Dei caeli commorabitur.

Whoso dwelleth under the defense of the Most High, shall abide under the shadow of the Almighty.

These canonical hours or offices that Columbus read were private devotions, which he said in his own cabin. Public prayers were a different matter.

In the great days of sail, before man's inventions and gadgets had given him false confidence in his power to conquer the ocean, seamen were the most religious of all workers on land or sea. The mariner's philosophy he took from the 107th Psalm: "They that go down to the sea in ships and occupy their business in great waters; these men see the works of the Lord, and his wonders in the deep. For at his word the stormy wind ariseth, which lifteth up the winds thereof . . ." It behooved seamen to obey the injunction of the psalmist, "O that men would therefore praise the Lord for his goodness, and declare the wonders that he doeth for the children of men!" That is just what they did, after their own fashion. Even the Protestant Reformation did not change the old customs of shipboard piety: as Captain John Smith wrote in 1627, "they may first goe to prayer, then to supper, and at six a-clocke sing a Psalme, say a Prayer, and the Master with his side begins the watch, then all the rest may doe what they will till midnight; and then his Mate with his Larboord men with a Psalm and a prayer releeves them until foure in the morning."

These religious observances which marked almost every half-hour of the day were led or performed by the youngest lads aboard, the *pajes de escober* ("pages of the broom") if any there were. This I suppose was on the same principle as having family grace said by the youngest child; God would be better pleased by the voice of innocence. On Columbus's first fleet there was no rating of page, but this duty was performed by the youngest gromets, probably those who were also called *criados* (servants), and who received slightly better pay than their mates.

Of the public prayers or hymns, Columbus's Journal mentions only the most important, when at sunset the Blessed Virgin was saluted with her ancient canticle, *Salve Regina*. But we have an account of a voyage from Spain to Santo Domingo in 1573 by a humorous Spanish official named Eugenio de Salazar, which gives every detail. Assuming that a pious commander like Columbus, venturing on unknown seas where the divine protection was imperatively needed, would have omitted nothing of these traditional observances, I have repeated them just as Salazar reports them, with a translation.

Daybreak was saluted by a young gromet of the dawn watch with this ditty: —

Bendita sea la luz,	Blessed be the light of day
y la Santa Veracruz	and the Holy Cross, we say;
y el Señor de la Verdad,	and the Lord of Veritie
y la Santa Trinidad;	and the Holy Trinity.
bendita sea el alma,	Blessed be th'immortal soul
y el Señor que nos la manda;	and the Lord who keeps it whole,
bendito sea el día	blessed be the light of day
y el Señor que nos lo envía.	and He who sends the night away.

The gromet then recites *Pater Noster* and *Ave Maria*, and adds: —

Dios nos dé buenos días; buen viaje; buen pasaje haga la nao, señor Capitán y maestre y buena compaña, amén; así faza buen viaje, faza: muy buenos días dé Dios a vuestras mercedes, señores de popa y proa.

God give us good days, good voyage, good passage to the ship, sir captain and master and good company, so let there be, let there be a good voyage; many good days may God grant your graces, gentlemen of the afterguard and gentlemen forward.

Before being relieved the dawn watch was supposed to have the decks well scrubbed down with salt water hauled up in buckets, and stiff besoms made of twigs. At 6:30 the *ampolleta* is turned up for the seventh and last time on that watch, and the gromet who has charge of it sings out: —

Buena es la que va,	Good is that which passeth,
mejor es la que viene;	better that which cometh,
siete es pasada y en ocho muele,	seven is past and eight floweth,
mas molerá si Dios quisiere,	more shall flow if God willeth,
cuenta y pasa, que buen viaje faza.	count and pass makes voyage fast.

As soon as the sands of the eighth successive glass run out, at 7 o'clock, the gromet in turning it up says, instead of his usual ditty: —

Al cuarto, al cuarto, señores marineros de buena parte, al cuarto, al cuarto en buena hora de la guardia del señor piloto, que ya es hora; leva, leva, leva.

On deck, on deck, Mr. mariners of the right side,* on deck in good time, you of Mr. Pilot's watch, for it's already time; shake a leg!

There is no need to give the new watch time to dress, for nobody has undressed; when they "went below" at 3 A.M. each man simply sought out his favorite soft plank, anywhere that he could

---

* Meaning the watch, port or starboard, that is due on deck.

brace himself against the rolling and pitching. They are soon awake, rubbing their eyes and grumbling, and each man grabs a ship biscuit, with some garlic cloves, a bit of cheese, a pickled sardine or what-have-you for breakfast and shuffles aft to the break in the poop. The helmsman gives the course to the master who is captain of his watch, Juan de la Cosa repeats it to the pilot who is captain of the new watch, he repeats it and gives it to the new helmsman, and he repeats it again. No chance for error! And most of the time on this outward passage the course is simply

Oeste: nada del noroeste, nada del sudoeste.

West: nothing to the northward, nothing to the southward.

A lookout is posted forward, another in the round-top, the off-going master transfers his reckoning from slate to logbook and a gromet wipes the slate clean for the pilot, Chips the carpenter (or *calafate* the caulker if it is his watch) primes the pump, and if the ship has made water during the night two or three hands pump her dry. The off-going watch eat whatever is on for breakfast, and curl up somewhere out of the sun to sleep.

Now the decks are dry, the sun is yardarm high, and the caravel is dancing along before the trades with a bone in her teeth. Columbus, whose servant has brought him a bucket of sea water, a cup of fresh water and a bit of breakfast in his cabin, comes on deck, looks all around the horizon, ejaculates a pious *gracias á Dios* for good weather, and chats with the pilot.

Each watch is responsible for the entire work of the ship during its hours of duty, except in case of tempest or accident, when all hands are called. The usual duties are keeping the decks both clear and clean, making and setting sail as required, trimming sheets and braces; and when there is nothing else to do, scrubbing the rails, making spun yarn and chafing gear out of old rope, and overhauling the gear. In this morning watch, as soon as the running rigging has dried from the night dews, it has to be swayed up, and every few days the lanyards or tackles that hold the shrouds must be taken up taut.

On large ships the master's or pilot's orders were transmitted to the men through the *contramestre* or boatswain, who carried a pipe or whistle on a lanyard around his neck and on it played a variety of piping signals. But there is no mention of one on Columbus's ships. The captain of the watch gives all orders himself, as on the ship of Salazar, who said he had never seen an officer so well and promptly obeyed by his soldiers as the pilot by his watch. Let him but cry *Ah! de proa* (Hey! up forward), they all come aft on the run "like conjured demons" awaiting his pleasure. Here are some samples of the orders: —

dejad las chafaldetas	well the clewlines
alzá aquel briol	heave on that buntline
empalomadle la boneta	lace on the bonnet
tomad aquel puño	lay hold of that clew
entren esas badasas aprisa por esos ollaos	pass them toggles through the latchets quick
levá el papahigo	hoist the main course
izá el trinquete	raise the foresail
dad vuelta	put your back into it
enmará un poco la cebadera	give the spritsail a little sheet
desencapillá la mesana	unbend the mizzen
ligá la tricia al guindaste	belay the halyard on the bitts
tirá de los escotines de gabia	haul in on the topsail sheets
suban dos á los penoles	two of you up on the yardarm
untá los vertellos	grease the parral trucks
amarrá aquellas burdas	belay them backstays
zafá los embornales	clear the scuppers
juegue el guimbalete para que la bomba achique	work that pump brake till she sucks

Nautical Castilian, like nautical English of the last century, had a word for everything in a ship's gear and a verb for every action; good strong expressive words that could not be misunderstood when bawled out in a gale.

For any lengthy operation like winding in the anchor cable or hoisting a yard, the seamen had an appropriate *saloma* or chantey, and of these Salazar gives an example which it is useless to translate.

The chanteyman sung or shouted the first half of each line, the men hauled away on the "o" and joined in on the second half, while they got a new hold on the halyard: —

> *Bu izá*
> *o dio — ayuta noy*
> *o que somo — servi soy*
> *o voleamo — ben servir*
> *o la fede — mantenir*
> *o la fede — de cristiano*
> *o malmeta — lo pagano*
> *sconfondi — y sarrahin*
> *torchi y mori — gran mastín*
> *o fillioli — dabrahin*
> *o non credono — que ben sia*
> *o non credono — la fe santa*
> *en la santa — fe di Roma*
> *o di Roma — está el perdón*
> *o San Pedro — gran varón*
> *o San Pablo — son compañón*
> *o que ruegue — a Dio por nos*
> *o por nosotros — navegantes*
> *en este mundo — somo tantes*
> *o ponente — digo levante*
> *o levante — se leva el sol*
> *o ponente — resplandor*
> *fantineta — viva lli amor*
> *o joven home — gauditor*

And so on, improvising, until the halyard is "two-blocks," when the captain of the watch commands *dejad la driza, amarrá* (well the halyard, belay!).

When he was not ordering the men about, the captain of the watch kept his station on the poop, conning the helmsman through a hatch in the deck just forward of the binnacle. The helmsman had a compass to steer by, but he could not see the sails, and consequently had to be an expert at the feel of the ship to keep her on her course. Salazar gives us some specimens of the pilot's orders to the helmsman: —

botá a babor	port your helm
no boteis	steady
arriba	up helm *
governá la ueste cuarta al sueste	steer W by S

Besides a nautical language, a nautical slang had developed. Just as modern seamen with mock contempt speak of "this wagon" or "the old crate," a Spaniard called his ship *rocín de madera* (wooden jade) or *pájaro puerco* (flying pig). The nickname for the firebox meant "pot island." People on board got in the habit of using nautical phrases for other things; Salazar for instance says, "When I want a pot of jam I say *saca la cebadera*, break out the spritsail; if I want a table-napkin I say *daca el pañol*, lead me to the sail-locker. If I wish to eat or drink in form I say *pon la mesana*, set the mizzen. When a mariner upsets a jug he says *¡oh! cómo achicais*, oh how she sucks. When one breaks wind, as often happens, someone is sure to cry *¡ah! de popa*, hey there, aft!"

Naturally there was a good deal of joking about the seats that were hung over the rail forward and aft, for the seamen and afterguard to ease themselves. These were called *jardines*, perhaps in memory of the usual location of the family privy. Salazar writes in mock sentiment of the lovely views they afforded of moon and planets, and of the impromptu washings that he there obtained from the waves. A later voyager, Antonio de Guevara, complained of the indecency of thus exposing a Very Reverend Lord Bishop to the full view of the ship's company, and adverts bitterly to the tarred rope end which performed a function assigned by American folklore to the corncob.

Apparently the seamen on Columbus's ships had only one hot meal a day. This would naturally have come around 11 A.M., so that the watch below could get theirs before coming on deck, and the watch relieved could eat after them.

---

* Or, as we should say nowadays, "keep her off."

Who did the cooking? I do not know. There was no rating of cook on any of Columbus's ships, or on Magellan's. The *Instrución Náuthica* of 1587, which gives all ratings and tells everyone's duties, has neither cook nor cooker, although the steward, it says, has charge of the fire. Probably the hard-worked gromets did the cooking, except that the captain's servant would naturally have taken care of him and perhaps of any gentlemen volunteers who made up the afterguard. Columbus when visited by the cacique at Port de Paix, Haiti, was dining in his cabin, apparently alone. Aboard the big galleons described by García Palacio a table was set for the men forward, the boatswain presided and the pages served and cleared away. Aboard *Santa María*, *Pinta* and *Niña* it is more likely that foremast hands took their share in a wooden bowl, and ate it with their fingers wherever they could find room. How the little *fogón* or open firebox could take care of food for 125 people on a small caravel, as it must have on *Niña's* voyage home in 1496, staggers the imagination.

The only drinks mentioned in Columbus's Journal and in his orders for supplies are water and wine, both of which were kept in casks; for Vasco da Gama first learned from the Arabs to construct wooden watertanks below decks. It was the cooper's job to see that these casks kept tight and were stowed or lashed so that they would not roll. Coffee and tea had not been introduced, and Spaniards did not care for beer.

The staff of life for Spanish seamen was wine, olive oil and bread in the form of sea biscuit or hardtack, baked ashore from wheat flour and stowed in the dryest part of the ship. Columbus's ideas of the proper provisioning of vessels on an American voyage are given in a letter to the Sovereigns of about 1498–1500: "Victualling them should be done in this manner: the third part of [the breadstuff to be] good biscuit, well seasoned and not old, or the major portion will be wasted; a third part of salted flour, salted at the time of milling; and a third part of wheat. Further there will be wanted wine, salt meat, oil, vinegar, cheese, chickpeas, lentils, beans, salt fish and fishing tackle, honey, rice, almonds and raisins." Olive oil, carried in huge earthenware jars, was used for cooking the fish, meat and legumes. Salted flour could be made into unleavened bread and cooked in the ashes, as the Arab seamen do today. Barreled salt sardines and anchovies are frequently mentioned among ships' stores of the time, and garlic would certainly not have been forgotten. It is probable that Columbus's seamen fared quite as well as peasants or workers ashore, except during a storm, or weather so rough that a fire could not be kept.

Dinner for the afterguard was announced by a gromet in this wise: —

Tabla, tabla, señor capitán y maestre y buena compaña, tabla puesta; vianda presta; agua usada para el señor capitán y maestre y buena compaña. Viva, viva el Rey de Castilla por mar y por tierra! Quien le diere guerra que le corten la cabeza; quien no dijere amén, que no le den á beber. Tabla en buena hora, quien no viniere que no coma.

Table, table, sir captain and master and good company, table ready; meat ready; water as usual for sir captain and master and good company. Long live the King of Castile by land and sea! Who says to him war, off with his head; who won't say amen, gets nothing to drink. Table is set, who don't come won't eat.

Salazar describes how the pages would slam on the table a great wooden dish of ill-cooked stringy salt meat, when everyone would grab his share and attack it with a sheath knife as if he were a practitioner of anatomy; and how every bone was left "clean as ivory." The table conversation, he says, was mostly sighing for what you couldn't have — "O how I'd like a bunch of white grapes of Guadalajara — I could eat a few turnips of Somo Sierra — If we only had aboard a plate of Ilescas berries!"

Dinner over, we may assume that Columbus retires to his cabin and indulges in a little shut-eye until it is time to say vespers.

At 3 the first dogwatch is set. The day's work of scrubbing, splicing, seizing and making repairs is now over; and if the wind is such that the gear needs no handling, as was almost always the case on this outward passage, the men sit about talking and spinning yarns, tending a fishline, washing as well as they could in salt water. These Spanish seamen were a cleanly lot; at least twice on the First Voyage Columbus mentions their going swimming, and they never missed a chance to wash themselves and their clothes upon landing near a river.

In the second dogwatch, just after sunset and before the first night watch is set, all hands are called to evening prayers. The ceremony begins by a gromet trimming the binnacle lamp: and as he brings it aft along the deck he sings out: —

Amén y Dios nos dé buenas noches, buen viaje, buen pasaje haga la nao, señor capitán y maestre y buena compaña.

Amen and God give us a good night and good sailing; may the ship make a good passage, sir captain and master and good company.

The gromets then lead the ship's company in what was technically called *la doctrina cristiana*. All hands say the *Pater Noster*, *Ave Maria* and *Credo*, and sing the *Salve Regina*. This beautiful hymn, one of the oldest Benedictine chants, was a fitting close to the day. The music of it has come down to us, so that we can in some measure re-create that ancient hymn of praise to the Queen of Heaven that floated over uncharted waters every evening, as the caravels slipped along.

We are not to suppose that the seamen kept very close to this music. Columbus once refers to the "*Salve Regina*, which seamen sing or say after their own fashion," and Salazar wrote his friend: "Presently begins the *Salve*, and we are all singers, for we all have a throat . . . For as mariners are great friends of divisions, and divide the four winds into thirty-two, so the eight tones of music they distribute into thirty-two other and different tones, perverse, resonant and very dissonant, as if we had today in the singing of the *Salve* and Litany a tempest of hurricanes of music, so that if God and his glorious Mother and the Saints to whom we pray should look down upon our tones and voices and not on our hearts and spirits, it would not do to beseech mercy with such a confusion of bawlings!"

The boatswain or boatswain's mate, whichever is on watch, ex-

SALVE REGINA

tinguishes the galley fire before the first night watch is set at seven o'clock. As the *ampolleta* is turned up, the gromet chorister sings: —

Bendita la hora en que Dios nació,	Blessed be the hour in which God was born
Santa María que le parió,	Saint Mary who bore Him
San Juan que le bautizó.	Saint John who baptized Him.
La guarda es tomada,	The watch is called,
La ampolleta muele,	the glass floweth;
buen viaje haremos	we shall make a good voyage
si Dios quisiere.	if God willeth.

On sail the caravels through the soft tropic night. Every half hour the gromet turns his *ampolleta* and sings his little ditty: —

Una va pasada	One glass is gone
y en dos muele;	and now the second floweth;
más molerá	more shall run down
si mi Dios querrá,	if my God willeth.
á mi Dios pidamos,	To my God let's pray
que bien viaje hagamos;	to give us a good voyage;
y á la que es Madre de Dios y abogada nuestra,	and through His blessed Mother our advocate on high,
que nos libre de agua de bomba y tormenta.	protect us from the waterspout and send no tempest nigh.

Then he calls to the lookout forward: —

¡Ah! de proa, alerta, buena guardia.

Hey you! forward, look alive, keep good watch.

At which the lookout was supposed to make a shout or grunt to prove that he was awake (like our "Lights burning brightly, sir!"). Every hour the helm and the lookout are relieved, but the captain of the watch keeps the quarter-deck for the whole watch, pacing up and down and peering into the binnacle to see if the helmsman is keeping his course. If the night is quiet, all members of the watch not on lookout or at the helm lean over the forecastle rail, watching entranced the phosphorescent sea, dreaming of epic morrows.

CHAPTER XIII

How Columbus Navigated
1492–1504

Tria sunt difficilia mihi . . . Viam aquilae in caelo, viam colubri super petram, viam nauis in medio mari . . .

There be three things which are too wonderful for me . . . the way of an eagle in the air; the way of a serpent upon a rock; the way of a ship in the midst of the sea . . .
— PROVERBS XXX 18, 19

MANY have applied this to Columbus. Granted that he had to hit land if he kept on going, how did he get back to Spain, and what's more, how did he find "The Indies" again? In other words, how did Columbus know where he was on the surface of the globe?

There are two main methods of keeping track of "the way of a ship in the midst of the sea": celestial navigation and dead-reckoning. Celestial navigation means plotting your position on the earth's surface by observing the motions of the heavenly bodies, which (fortunately for mariners) can be predicted to a split hair. When practised with instruments of precision (which Columbus did not have), celestial navigation is most accurate, and every ship's officer must now learn it. But in Columbus's day the art was in its infancy, and neither he nor his shipmates knew very much about it.

The Admiral liked to pose as an expert in celestial navigation, which (he well said) was a mystery to the uninitiated, like prophetic vision. In forty years at sea, off and on (so he wrote in 1501), he had acquired sufficient "astrology" (that is, astronomy), geometry and arithmetic, as well as practical knowledge, for the purposes of maritime discovery. In a postil of uncertain date he talks of "taking

the sun" on his Guinea voyage. Yet the testimony of his own
journals proves that the simple method of finding latitude from a
meridional observation of the sun, long used by Arabs in "camel
navigation" of the desert, was unknown to Columbus. Polaris observations for latitude he made not infrequently on his last two
voyages, but these observations, though "not too bad," were of no

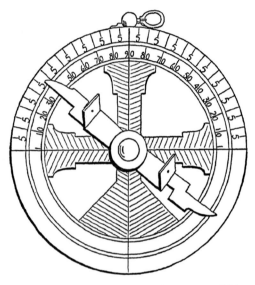

MARINER'S ASTROLABE

*From García Palacio. The Altitude is
read from the upper pointer of the
Alidade*

use to his navigation, because he never knew the proper corrections to apply. It has been stated that the invention of the astrolabe
enabled Columbus to discover America; but his Journal proves
that he was unable to use the astrolabe on his First Voyage, and
there is no evidence of his taking such an instrument on any other.
The picture books also show Columbus taking solar or stellar altitudes with a cross staff. That simple instrument would have been
more useful to him than a quadrant for shooting Polaris in low
latitudes; but he never had one, and probably never saw one.

The common quadrant (not to be confused with Hadley's quad-

rant or any other reflecting instrument) was the only instrument
of celestial navigation that Columbus ever employed. This was a
simple quarter-circle of hardwood, with sights along one edge
through which the heavenly body could be lined up, a plummet attached to the apex by a silk cord, and a scale of 90° on the arc,
from which the altitude could be read as cut by the cord at the
moment when sun or star was lined up through the sights. On a

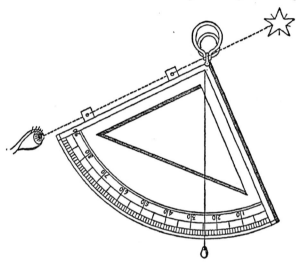

MARINE QUADRANT OF 1492

*Altitude is read from the point where
thread cuts Arc*

rolling and pitching ship it was very difficult to keep the plane of
the quadrant perpendicular and at the same time catch your star
through the pin holes. When you did, you hallooed to the other
fellow to mark the degree on the arc cut by the cord; but the cord
just then might be doing a big swing. Columbus never managed
to do any accurate work with his quadrant until he had a whole
year ashore at Jamaica.

The only known method of ascertaining longitude in Columbus's
day was by timing an eclipse. Regiomontanus's *Ephemerides* and
Zacuto's *Almanach Perpetuum* gave the predicted hours of total
eclipses at Nuremberg and Salamanca respectively, and if you com-

pared those with the observed hour of the eclipse by local sun time, wherever you were, and multiplied by fifteen to convert time into arc,* there was your longitude west of the almanac maker's meridian. Sounds simple enough, but Columbus with two opportunities (1494 and 1503) muffed both, as did almost everyone else for a century. At Mexico City in 1541 a mighty effort was made by the intelligentsia to determine the longitude of that place by timing two eclipses of the moon. The imposing result was 8h 2m 32s (= 120° 38′) W of Toledo; but the correct difference of longitude between the two places is 95° 12′; so the Mexican savants made an error of about 25½ degrees, or 1450 miles! Even in the eighteenth century, Père Labat, the earliest writer (to my knowledge) who gives the position of Hispaniola correctly, adds this caveat: "I only report the longitude to warn the reader that nothing is more uncertain, and that no method used up to the present to find longitude has produced anything fixed and certain."

So many indoor geographers and armchair admirals have adduced Columbus's ignorance of celestial navigation as evidence that he was no seaman that I must rub in two points.

1. Celestial navigation formed no part of the professional pilot's or master's training in Columbus's day, or for long after his death. It was practised only by men of learning such as mathematicians, astrologers and physicians, or by gentlemen of education like Antonio Pigafetta who accompanied Magellan, or D. João de Castro, who on India voyages in the 1530's and '40's had everyone down to the ship's caulker taking meridional altitudes of the sun. Mathematics was so little taught in common schools of that era, and the existing ephemerides (compiled largely for astrologers) were so complicated, that even the best professional seamen could do nothing with them. So simple an operation as applying declination to altitude and subtracting the result from 90° was quite beyond their powers. The great Portuguese-Jewish mathematician Pero Nunes (Nonnius), who discovered the vernier, wrote some forty-five years after Columbus's discovery, "Why do we put up with these pilots, with their bad language and barbarous manners; they

* One hour of time is equivalent to 15 degrees of longitude.

know neither sun, moon nor stars, nor their courses, movements or declinations; or how they rise, how they set and to what part of the horizon they are inclined; neither latitude nor longitude of the places on the globe, nor astrolabes, quadrants, cross staffs or watches, nor years common or bissextile, equinoxes or solstices?"

2. Celestial observations were not used in Columbus's day, even by the Portuguese, to find one's way about the ocean; but to determine latitudes of newly discovered coasts and islands in order to chart them correctly. Vasco da Gama on his great voyage of 1497–1499 to India was far better equipped than Columbus for celestial navigation, but he always disembarked and hung his astrolabe on a tree or a tripod to take the altitude of the sun, as the poet Camoëns describes him doing.

So, in order to determine his daily positions at sea, and trace his course across the unknown stretches of the Western Ocean, Columbus was dependent on *dead-reckoning* (D.R.), which means simply laying down your compass courses and estimated distances on a chart. That is not so easy as it sounds. In the previous chapter we have seen how he kept track of time with the *ampolleta* or half-hour glass. How did he know his course, and estimate distance?

Columbus took the course off his mariner's compass, which was the most reliable and the one indispensable instrument of navigation aboard. We do not know when the magnetic needle was first used for purposes of navigation, but it had been so used for at least three centuries before Columbus, and practical improvements in the mounting of the needle must have been worked out by the Portuguese for their African voyages. Columbus's instrument was similar to the dry-card dory compasses that could be purchased in ship chandlers' shops until the other day. A circular card, on which diamonds, lozenges and lines marked the 32 compass points, was mounted on a pivot in a circular bowl, so that it could turn freely in any direction with the motion of the ship.* Its virtue was derived from a magnetized needle or wire fixed on the underside, between

---

* Gimbals had been invented by 1545, and possibly were used by Columbus. Without a gimbal mounting of the bowl, the card must have jammed on every steep pitch or heavy roll of the ship.

the north and south marks. Whenever this needle showed any disinclination to "seek the north" it was remagnetized with a bit of lodestone that the captain guarded as his life; and plenty of spare needles were taken — Magellan had thirty-five on his flagship. At the forward edge of the bowl a black vertical line (the "lubber line") was drawn. As the needle always sought magnetic north, the point on the floating card that touched the lubber line indicated the direction in which the ship was heading, provided the diameter of the bowl that passed through the lubber line was kept parallel to the ship's keel. That was done by keeping the compass in a fixed position in the *bitácora* or binnacle, a rectangular box fastened with wooden pins and secured to the deck, provided with a hood to protect the compass from the weather and with a little copper oil lamp to illuminate the card at night. This binnacle, containing what we should call the "standard" compass, was on the quarter-deck where the captain or officer of the watch could keep an eye on it; on the main deck close to the great tiller was another for the helmsman to steer by. The officer of the watch gave the course to the helmsman, and checked him by keeping an eye on the standard compass. He communicated with the helmsman through an open hatch in the quarter-deck.

Modern compass cards have abbreviations for the points or degrees, or both, printed on them, but those that Columbus used had neither; nor would letters have done any good, as few seamen could read. They simply distinguished between points by the length, shape or color of the diamonds and lozenges; except that North was marked by the fleur-de-lis then as now. In 1939 we shipped aboard *Capitana* at São Miguel an illiterate Azorean who proved to be the best helmsman among us. Those who spoke English only had to indicate with their finger the point on the card by which he must steer; but when I said *Leste cuarta del Sudeste* (E by S) he understood perfectly, and held her close to that point. Literacy has helped seamanship very little indeed.

Spaniards, like other seafarers at the time, did not think of direction in terms of degrees as we do, or of compass points as our immediate forbears did, but in terms of winds, *los vientos.** Although the ancients recognized twelve winds, and wind roses on medieval maps followed this system, by Columbus's time the winds had been reduced to eight: N, NE, E, SE, S, SW, W, NW. The intermediate points (NNE, ENE, ESE, SSE, SSW, WSW, WNW, NNW) were called *los medios vientos*, the half-winds; and what we call the "by" points (N by E, NE by N, and so on) they called *las cuartas,*

COMPASS CARD OF
THE SIXTEENTH
CENTURY

(*García Palacio*)

MODERN COMPASS
CARD

*Courtesy Kelvin & Wilfrid O.
White Company*

the quarter-winds; consequently *una cuarta* was their name for a compass point (11¼°). Thus, if Columbus wished to give the course that we should call West by South, he would call it *Oeste cuarta del Sudoeste*, literally "West, one quarter of the Southwest wind."

How about compass variation, the difference between a magnetic and a true course? We shall find Columbus wrestling with that problem on his first three voyages, and, if not solving it, at least recognizing its existence. Fortunately his routes seldom crossed a region where the compass variation was more than 6° or half a point, and a good part of the time in the West Indies he was in

* The Portuguese still call the compass card *a rosa dos ventos*, the wind rose.

the zone of no variation. Deviation, the variation caused by local attraction, did not bother him because his vessels contained only negligible quantities of iron.

It was an easy matter for the captain of the watch to keep reckoning. He simply wrote the course steered on a slate that hung against a bulkhead on the poop deck, and indicated by a stroke every half hour that she sailed on that course. But he also had to estimate the third factor in dead-reckoning, the rate of speed.

In the sixteenth century there was invented the chip log, a billet of wood weighted and flanged so it would float without moving in the water, attached by a light line in which knots were so spaced that the number of knots paid out over the rail in half a minute, which was measured by a special log glass, equaled the number of nautical miles per hour the ship was making. Hence our term "knots" for speed at sea. You "hove the log" every watch, or whenever the ship picked up or lost speed, and recorded the rate. That, multiplied by time, gave distance. But this simple device for finding speed was unknown to Columbus. He or the officer of the watch simply estimated by eye the speed that *Santa María* was making, in Roman miles per hour, by watching the bubbles or the gulfweed float by.

Any seaman of good judgment and experience can estimate the speed of a vessel by this primitive method within a knot, or even a half-knot if he is used to her. But, just as modern dead-reckoning at sea can be checked by daily sights, so a modern estimate of speed can be checked by patent log, or a measured mile. Columbus had no such check, yardstick or other fixed standard. He estimated speed in Roman miles per hour, and distance in leagues of 4 Roman miles each, his league being equivalent to 3.18 nautical miles. But with no standard save experience, and no check, Columbus was not accurate. A careful plotting of his ocean crossing in 1492 proves that he overestimated the distance run at sea on the average 9 per cent, and he came very close to that overestimate on crossings such as Crooked Island Passage and the Windward Passage. In other words, by crediting *Santa María* with too much speed, the league that he actually used measured only 2.89 nautical miles. Moreover, when sailing within sight of land, Columbus either used a different league, or, by fixing his eyes on objects ashore instead of on flotsam, made an even greater overestimate; for when you check the alongshore distances recorded in his Journal by actual distances, it appears that his alongshore league was roughly equivalent to but 1.5 nautical miles. This error was so constant that I am inclined to believe he was consciously using a different "land" league. He never knew exactly how fast his vessel was sailing, because he had no fixed standard and no check.

The one thing everyone knows about Columbus's navigation of the First Voyage is that he kept the "accurate" reckoning to himself, and made a reduced or "phony" one for the crew, so that they would not complain of being taken so far from home. But, owing to his overestimate of distance, the "phony" reckoning was nearer the truth than the "accurate" day's work!

So much for computation of time, speed and distance. The next indispensable aid to navigation that Columbus used was a collection of sea charts. These were big sheepskins on which the coasts of Spain, Portugal and North Africa, and the Azores, Madeira and the Canaries were sketched in fairly accurately, hypothetical islands such as Antillia were laid down by guess, Cipangu and Cathay drawn in where Columbus thought they should be according to Marinus of Tyre and Marco Polo. The surface of the chart was crisscrossed by rhumb (that is, straight) lines, which radiated from a number of wind roses placed at convenient intervals out in the ocean. Every chart had a scale of leagues, but no latitude and longitude grid. Columbus did not think in terms of latitude, but of the Ptolemaic "climates," arbitrary parallel belts laid down by the Alexandrian geographer; he had copied a table of them into his *Imago Mundi*. Instead of longitude, he thought in terms of "hours" west of Cadiz, 15° of longitude to one hour.

Columbus began "making points" for the big jump by taking a simple departure from the place where he lay becalmed between Gomera and Tenerife on the night of September 7–8, 1492. It was only two or three days after full moon, so he could see both islands, take their bearings by squinting across the compass card, and estimate their distance. He pricked the corresponding point on his chart, and that was his point of departure. He then set the course due W for the Indies. On Sunday, September 9, at sunrise he reckoned that they had made 9 leagues from the point of departure. So he took his ruler, laid its edge on that point and parallel to the nearest W rhumb line on the chart, laid off 9 leagues with his divider, and pricked a new point. This process was called by the Spaniards *fazer* or *echar punto* (to make, or apply the point), or simply *cartear* (do the chart); and in English it used to be called "pricking the chart," or "pricking her off." One's progress on the chart was traced by a series of small holes punched by the points of the dividers.

Columbus did not do this all himself; on one occasion he mentions the pilots and mariners looking on and giving advice while he pricked off the course. It seems odd to us that Columbus should let in mariners even on his "phony" navigation; but apparently that was the rule in his day. García Palacio says (1587) that able seamen should be able to "make point," and he advises the pilot, if he gets into difficulties with his navigation, to consult with the captain and master and some good able seamen, giving and taking counsel, and to be gracious about it. I feel sure, however, that Columbus allowed no discussion about the speed, and that he came on deck frequently to see that the officer of the watch used his standard and no other for logging speed.

"Making points" on the chart was simple enough when you did not often change course, as on most of Columbus's outward passage; but when you had to beat to windward, as in the first month of the homeward passage, the error involved in laying down a multitude of very short courses on an ocean chart would be serious. Under such conditions a dead-reckoning navigator resorts to a traverse table; and there is evidence in Columbus's Journal that he had one and knew how to work it. The principle of the traverse table is to transform any number of diagonal courses into one big right angle: so many miles east or west (departure), and so many miles north or south (difference of latitude). The principle may be compared with finding your way about in New York City. Suppose you wish to walk from 53rd Street and First Avenue to 58th Street and Fifth Avenue. You may make it by a series of north and west "tacks," according as the traffic lights make you "come about," occasionally catching a "fair wind" to cross diagonally a block that is an open park. But if you can manage to find a native New Yorker and ask him the way, he will say "five blocks north and six west." He has transformed the short tacks by his mental traverse table into "diff. lat." and departure. So by a very simple computation Columbus could transform any number of tacks or changes of course into one big right angle. This he applied to the chart and made a point for the resulting position. He then measured on the chart the course and distance between the two points, and noted in his Journal, "we made good 13 leagues NE," or whatever the result was.

As a former map maker Columbus was well equipped to chart his own discoveries, and undoubtedly he entered every new island and sketched in every coastline on a blank chart as he sailed along. Twice on the Second Voyage we find references to his entering even the smallest islands on a chart that he was preparing; Hojeda's voyage of 1499 was admittedly based on a chart of the mainland that the Admiral had sent home; a witness in the *pleitos* of 1514 said that all later discoverers of the mainland "went by the charts that the Admiral had made, because he alone made charts of all that he discovered." As the new lands were more minutely explored, new charts were made and the Admiral's destroyed, all save one rough sketch of Northern Haiti. This has a sureness of touch that fully sustains his reputation as a cartographer, and gives us a keen sense of our loss in having none of the larger charts that he presented to the Sovereigns.

Like all good practical navigators Columbus made frequent use of the sounding lead when approaching the coast, or when he thought he was near land. The standard length of lead line for small vessels in those days, and for centuries after, was 40 fathoms; but each of Columbus's fleet carried a dipsey (deep sea) lead line of 100 fathoms, and on one occasion he bent two together to make a 200-fathom sounding. We may smile at his trying to sound in mid-ocean, where the modern chart reports a depth of some 2400 fathoms; but the leadsman reporting "No bottom, sir," after repeated casts through heavy mats of gulfweed was far more reassuring as to the safety of the Sargasso Sea than any amount of speculation. Sounding in a breeze is troublesome, as a vessel has to back some of her sails in order to check her way and give the lead a chance to reach bottom. For that reason this elementary precaution when approaching a coast is often forgotten, and more vessels go ashore through neglect to heave the lead than from any other cause.* Columbus was very punctilious about sounding until he found by experience that the outer Bahamas were so steep and the water so clear that you could find no bottom until it was visible. Then he too grew careless, and so lost his flagship on Christmas eve.

Columbus's only aids to navigation, then, were the mariner's compass and dividers, quadrant and lead line, sea chart and ruler, traverse table and ordinary multiplication table, and one of the recent Ephemerides of Johannes Müller (Regiomontanus) designed more for astrologers than for navigators. There is no evidence that he added to this equipment on any later voyage; indeed the astrolabe that he had on the First Voyage and was unable to use seems to have been left behind. Two mariners who were with him on the Third Voyage later testified that he carried "charts, quadrants, tables, sphere, and other things." So, to all intents and purposes, he was a dead-reckoning navigator pure and simple.

This is not to say that Columbus was a poor navigator; far from it. Dead-reckoning was about 99 per cent of the navigator's art in 1492, and in high latitudes there are long periods of overcast or stormy weather when celestial observations are impossible. Dead-

---

* Several groundings of large steamships in recent years have been caused by too confident reliance on electrical sounding devices. Yachtsmen are just as bad.

reckoning is still the foundation of navigation. On the navigating table of every ocean liner or battleship today you will find the ship's "D.R." laid down on a chart, and the most modern systems of celestial navigation are worked out by assuming your D.R. position and correcting it by celestial observation. Columbus's few recorded celestial observations before 1504 were of the most cock-eyed description — as we shall see when we come to them; but like every good dead-reckoning navigator he had the common sense to throw them out. That is done nowadays more often than you think. What navigator has not heard a shipmate say, after a prolonged bout of figuring, "Well, that can't be right; my D.R. shows . . ."? A New London–Bermuda race in recent years was lost because the navigator trusted a celestial observation rather than his D.R. and altered course accordingly — excusing himself because it was an observation of Venus's lower limb!

It must be remembered, however, that the modern navigator checks his D.R. daily (if weather permits) by latitude or longitude sights or both, which Columbus never learned to do. And, as an error of half a point in your course will mean an error of about 250 miles in landfall on an ocean crossing, it is evident that Columbus's D.R. was extraordinarily careful and accurate. Possibly he was not much more skillful than his better contemporaries, although the bad guesses of the pilots on the First Voyage home, and their surprise at Columbus's excellent landfall in 1496, would seem to show the contrary. Andrés Bernáldez, who had his information directly from the Admiral after that event, wrote, "No one considers himself a good pilot and master who, although he has to pass from one land to another very distant without sighting any other land, makes an error of 10 leagues, even in a crossing of 1000 leagues, unless the force of the tempest forces him and deprives him of the use of his skill." No such dead-reckoning navigators exist today; no man alive, limited to the instruments and means at Columbus's disposal, could obtain anything near the accuracy of his results.

Judged therefore not simply by what he did, but by how he

did it, Columbus was a great navigator. He took his fleet to sea not as an amateur possessed of one big idea, but as a captain experienced in *el arte de marear*. He was well, though not superlatively well, equipped with such navigational aids and instruments as the age had produced. Modestly conscious of his own imperfections, he wrote to the Sovereigns before his last voyage predicting that "with the perfecting of instruments and the equipment of vessels, those who are to traffic and trade with the discovered islands will have better knowledge" than was vouchsafed to him. Over and above his amazing competence as a dead-reckoning navigator, he had what a great French seaman, Jean Charcot, recognized and named *le sens marin*, that intangible and unteachable God-given gift of knowing how to direct and plot "the way of a ship in the midst of the sea."

CHAPTER XIV

Atlantic Crossing

September 9–30, 1492

Cumque extendisset Moyses manum contra mare, reuersum
est primo diluculo ad priorem locum. . . .

And Moses stretched forth his hand over the sea, and the
sea returned to his strength when the morning appeared.
— EXODUS xiv 27

THIS most momentous voyage in modern history was also
one of the easiest, from the nautical point of view. Columbus's greatest difficulty, that of obtaining ships and men and
securing royal authorization, was over when he sailed from Palos.
The vessels were in fine shape after their "shake-down cruise" to
the Canaries and the repairing and re-rigging at Las Palmas; they
had water, wine, provisions and stores enough to last a year; the
officers and men had had five weeks to get used to each other and to
their ships. Now that the Canaries had dropped below the eastern
horizon, no Portuguese warships had materialized, and "wind
come fair," Columbus was serene and confident of success. He
knew, for he had read it in great works on geography, that the sea
was narrow between Spain and the Indies and could be traversed
easily *paucis diebus*, in a few days. And, if we insert "West" before
"Indies," was he not right? Thirty-three days from departure to
landfall was a few days, as traveling was counted in that era; it
was less time than a Roman needed to reach Britain, or than a pilgrim from Northern France required for a sea voyage to the
Holy Land. The only question was, whether these "few days"
would not be too many for the men, whether their fears would
not force Columbus to turn back when the goal was just over the

horizon, as had happened to Bartholomew Dias, and doubtless to other brave captains.

In other words, the difficulties ahead of Columbus on this voyage were entirely of a moral or (if you will) psychological nature. Practical difficulties there were none; no storms or prolonged calms, no foul winds or heavy seas, no shortage of victual or drink, nothing to bother a well-built, properly equipped and well-found ocean-going fleet, as this was. If Columbus had died in the West Indies before the fleet returned to Spain, there might be some reason to suspect that he was merely a competent mariner with an idea, but no great navigator. His opportunities to prove seamanship of the highest order occurred on the homeward passage in 1493, and on the other three voyages.

Lord Dunraven, the English yachtsman who made a study of Columbus's navigation of this First Voyage, declared that if a modern sailing vessel wished to make a voyage from Palos to the Bahamas and back, she "could not follow a better course out and home than that adopted by Columbus." And George Nunn, in his study of the First Voyage, concluded that Columbus knew everything essential about ocean winds and currents, "and understood them so thoroughly that he did not make a single false move in the entire voyage." Both these judgments need considerable qualification. A westerly course from the Canaries runs out of the trade-wind belt into the "horse latitudes" of calms and variables. Moreover the northern limit of the northeast trades for October (and September 22 in the Julian Calendar is October 1 in ours) dips south of his course after he was a few days out, and runs approximately along latitude 26° N, so that he only re-entered the trade-wind zone on the last few days of the passage. This northern limit of the trades is variable, and the variations are unpredictable. Some years you catch them further north, as Columbus did, and in others further south; our *Mary Otis* did not find them until she was below latitude 20° S in November 1937, and averaged less than 2 knots in waters where Columbus's fleet did better than 5. Any sailing vessel proceeding from Spain to the

West Indies today, whether or not calling at the Canaries, would be well advised to drop down almost to latitude 15°, 500 miles south of Tenerife, before straightening out on a westerly course. Even the recommended trade-wind sailing route for September from Northern Europe to New York swings away down below latitude 24° N, some 250 miles south of the parallel of Ferro. So Columbus did not take the best route, even for the position — 750 leagues west of the Canaries — where he supposed Cipangu to be; and his course was not the correct one for making such a voyage. He had what we Yankees call "a mighty good chance," skirting as he did the horse latitudes in the hurricane season. Not a single day of storm, not one day of flat calm, only a few days of variables did he experience. He had all the "breaks" you may say; but fortune always favors the brave.

September 9, the day that Columbus passed Ferro, "he decided to reckon less than he made, so that if the voyage were long the people would not be frightened and dismayed." It was easy enough for him to practise this deception, because nobody ever ventures to check up on a commanding officer's arithmetic. The stratagem was entirely proper and ethical, considering the sort of people with whom he had to deal. Mariners are an odd tribe, little understood by landsmen. The same man who is capable of the highest courage in going aloft in a gale, or manning a boat to save a shipmate, will be frightened as a high-strung horse at anything outside his experience. And if his code of superstition has been violated by something like sailing on Friday, he will be uneasy the entire voyage. It has always been difficult to recruit common seamen for exploring expeditions, at least down to this age of publicized sea dogs. Columbus knew very well that the time would come when his men would clamor to return; and he wished to be in a position to quiet them by telling the boys they weren't so very far from home, they had sailed further than that on voyages to Africa, hadn't they? But the amusing thing is that Columbus overestimated speed and distance in his own mind by almost the same amount that he underestimated it for the ignorant seamen; so that his "phony" reckoning was nearer the truth than his "true" one! The pilots kept independent reckonings as well; and on the one occasion when the four reckonings were compared, Peralonso Niño of *Santa María* came nearest the truth.

Those whose knowledge of the sea is confined to modern high-powered vessels, which constantly tend to fall off their courses, may question the accuracy of Columbus's courses as given in the Journal. But it is usually easier to keep a square-rigger on her course than a steamship. In a steady wind the helmsman soon gets the feel of a well-balanced sailing vessel, and only glances at the compass now and then to check himself. Columbus's helmsmen were carefully conned by the officer of the watch, who had his eye on the standard compass in the binnacle. In the Journal for September 9, Columbus says, "The seamen steered badly, letting her run up to the W by N, and even WNW, for which the Admiral scolded them many times." (One can imagine sarcastic inquiries if they thought they were steering a ferryboat across the River of Seville, whether they had a girl in the Azores, and so on.) It would not be considered a serious offense today on a sailing vessel the size of the *Santa María* if the helmsman let her run up a point or two scudding before a brisk trade and a rising sea, provided that he compensated for it by letting her fall off a corresponding amount to leeward. The steering of *Santa María* and her consorts must have been watched with very great care. And there are no further complaints of bad helmsmanship in the Journal.

During the first ten days (September 9–18 inclusive) the trade wind blew as steadily as it ever does, the westerly course was constantly followed, and the fleet made 1163 nautical miles. The least twenty-four hours' run was 60 miles, and the best 174, which for sailing vessels of their burthen was very good sailing indeed.* That was the honeymoon period of the voyage, the sort of sailing that old salts dream of. Wind and sea on the stern gave the caravels a regular lift and roll that sea legs take in their stride; no

---

* All distances quoted are net, after deducting the 9 per cent average overestimate from the distances logged by Columbus.

making and setting of sail or hauling on sheets and braces; seascape of surpassing beauty (and don't imagine, you esthetic snobs, that common seamen don't appreciate it), brightest of blue seas, fat puffy trade-wind clouds constantly rising up from astern, deliberately passing overhead, and setting under the western horizon; weather warm and balmy but always fresh from the blessed trades. Nothing to do but keep the vessels clean, observe ship routine, watch for birds and flying fishes, and spend the gold you are going to pick up in Cipangu.

"The Admiral says here," abstracts Las Casas for September 16, *que era plazer grande el gusto de las mañanas,* "that the savor of the mornings was a great delight." What memories that phrase evokes! A fragrant cool freshness of daybreak in the trades, the false dawn shooting up a pyramid of grayish-white light, the paling stars, the navigators bustling about to shoot their favorites in the brief morning twilight of the tropics, rosy lights on the clouds as sunrise approaches, sudden transformation of the square-sails from dark gray to ruddy gold, smell of dew drying from the deck, the general feeling of God's in his Heaven and all's right with the world. "The weather was like April in Andalusia," said Columbus; "the only thing wanting was to hear nightingales." Well, you landsmen can have the nightingales, I'll take the flashing boatswain-birds screaming overhead, and the downy little petrels skimming the seas in wide circles about the ship, softly chirping as they dabble for plankton in the vessel's wash or wake.

There was no lack of these or of the tropic birds, *rabo de juncos,* "reed-tails," as Columbus called them; old-time seamen call them boatswain-birds "because they carry a marlinspike in their tails." Two came aboard our *Capitana* in mid-ocean. Columbus and his men, who were no ornithologists, thought that the appearance of these and of some birds that he calls *garaxaos* (probably the small Arctic tern, or a young boatswain-bird) indicated land; but the nearest land that day (September 14) was Santa Maria in the Azores, some 570 miles to the NNE.

On Sunday, September 16, when they crossed 33° west longitude, they saw their first sargassum, or gulfweed — "many bunches of very green weed, which had a short time (as it seemed) been torn from land; whereby all judged that they were near some island, but not the mainland according to the Admiral, who says 'because I make the mainland to be further on.'" Next day they picked up more of it, and found therein a live crab, the little green *Nautilus grapsus minutus*, about as big as a thumbnail. They were entering the Sargasso Sea, that great oval-shaped area of the Western Ocean that extends roughly from longitude 32° W to the Bahamas, and from the Gulf Stream down to latitude 18° N. It is probable that nobody aboard had noticed gulfweed before, because one seldom encounters it within a day's run west of the Azores, and almost never on a voyage between Spain or Portugal and Africa. But Columbus had been warned about it by our old friend Pedro de Velasco, and advised to keep on a straight course when he struck the weed. Ferdinand relates that the men were alarmed on September 21–22 when the ocean was one great meadow of the green and yellow weed, and the caravels wasted time trying to find open water, fearing lest they be "frozen" in sargassum. Actually, gulfweed is no hindrance to navigation; for even when it forms an almost continuous mat on the surface it is never more than half an inch thick, and parts readily to admit a vessel's prow. Within a few days everyone was used to the gulfweed, and *vieron muchas yerbas*, "saw plenty weed," became an almost daily notation in Columbus's Journal. But the superstition of getting stuck in the Sargasso Sea is still alive.

Columbus's serene plunge into the Sargasso Sea, about which only vague, contradictory and alarming data were hitherto known, was sufficient to make this voyage one of the most important in maritime history. His theory that the weed grew on rocks or submarine ledges not far from the Azores, from which it was wrenched by storms, died very hard; for similar weed does grow on rocks along the tropical shores of America. Columbus's theory was still held by scientists such as the great Von Humboldt a century ago, and has even been seriously maintained in the present century. The *Challenger* expedition of 1873, by disproving the existence of any such oceanic banks, gave this idea a blow; and the report of the Danish scientist Winge on the Danish Oceanographical Expedition of 1908–1910 leaves no doubt that gulfweed is a pelagic perennial, the descendant of algae torn loose in prehistoric times. It propagates itself by partition, the plants constantly growing the fresh greenish shoots (that Columbus noted) at one end, and withering to a brown color at the other. The *como fruta* ("sort of fruit") that Columbus noted are the little berrylike globules filled with air that keep the weed afloat.

The only phenomenon that caused any dismay during these ten days of ideal sailing was an apparent variation of the compass needles. On September 13 Columbus reported that at the beginning of night the needles varied to the NW of the polestar, and in the morning to the NE. Again, on the seventeenth the pilots "took the north, in order to mark it." That ancient custom, the traditional gesture which used to be called the "pilot's blessing," consisted in raising the arm with flattened palm between the eyes, pointing at the North Star, and bringing the palm straight down on the compass card, to see if the needle varied from true north. On this occasion they found that the needles "varied to the NW a full point, and the mariners took fright and were troubled and did not say why." They were familiar with easterly variation, but none of them had ever been in the zone of westerly variation, into which the fleet had crossed on the fourteenth. "The Admiral knew," continues the Journal for September 17, "and ordered that the North be marked again at dawn, and found that the needles were true. The cause was that the star appeared to move and not the needles."

Columbus was right. Polaris in 1492 described a radius of about 3° 27′ about the celestial pole, as against a 1° radius or polar distance today. At nightfall in mid-September 1492 Polaris lay at this full distance east of the pole. Consequently, on the thirteenth, when there was no variation, the needle pointed about 3½° west of the star just after dusk, and about the same small angle east of the star just before dawn. It is astonishing that this small variation should have been observed on compass cards graduated only to full points of 11¼° each. On September 17, when the fleet had entered the zone of 2° westerly variation, the needle varied about 5½° at dusk, less than half a full point, but the "pilot's blessing" method was hardly accurate; whilst just before dawn, Polaris having moved over, star and needles were only a little over one degree apart. To anticipate a bit, on September 30, when the fleet had reached the isogonic line of 7° westerly variation, Columbus observed that at nightfall the needles varied a full point to the westward. Polaris then lay some 3° 20′ east of the celestial pole, and that angle plus the real variation of 7° falls little short of a compass point (11¼°). At dawn, says Columbus, they were "right on the Star." Polaris having moved over, the actual 7° westerly variation was cut down to about 3½°, as observed by the compass needle, and on this occasion the small difference was not observed. Eventually Columbus realized that he had observed a westerly variation of the compass, and no doubt he was the first to report it. But during the voyage he was at some pains to deny a phenomenon so novel and disturbing to the mariners. What he then discovered for himself was the diurnal rotation of Polaris, a fact which many late medieval and renaissance astronomers had denied. Practical seamen had assumed for centuries that the North Star marked true north.

September 18, when the fleet made a twenty-four-hour run of 159 miles, was the last good sailing day that month. Columbus's course was taking him out of the trades; he was very lucky to have carried them to longitude 40°, sailing as he did along the 28th parallel of latitude. On the nineteenth "it fell calm," and they made only 72 miles' westing. The gradually flattening sea, a more or less stationary cloudbank, a drizzle of rain, visits from boobies and other sea fowl such as the small Arctic tern (which Columbus did not recognize and supposed to be land birds), a westward flight of petrels, a tuna fish that was caught from *Niña*, even the crab in the gulfweed, were so many signs of land to these innocent mariners on their first ocean crossing. The chart that Columbus had aboard, "compiled from the most reliable sources" as all the worst modern charts claim, showed islands on both sides of them at this position. Everyone was very cheerful, and the caravels sailed gaily ahead of the flagship, hoping to win the prize for first landfall. Columbus, however, ordered the bonnet unlaced from *Santa María's* main course, as the wind at that moment was freshening.

On the nineteenth the three pilots totted up their position. Peralonso Niño of *Santa María* made it 400 leagues west of the Canaries, which was according to the "phony" reckoning handed out by Columbus — and was very nearly correct! Cristóbal García Sarmiento of *Pinta* made it 420, and Sancho Ruiz of *Niña*, 440, which was very near Columbus's own reckoning from the place where the wind came up on September 8. The actual distance was about 396 leagues or 1261 nautical miles. Columbus observed that he "did not wish to delay matters by beating to windward to ascertain if there was land," although he felt certain that they were "going through between" islands, "because his desire was to follow right along to the Indies. 'And the weather is favorable; wherefore on the return passage, please God, all will be seen.' These are his words." Actually the nearest land at that time was Flores in the Azores, some 850 miles to the northeastward. They were not yet halfway across to America.

Next day, September 20, they ran out of the trades and had to change course: "sailed this day to the W by N and WNW because the winds were very variable." Several birds came aboard — some of them mistaken for warblers — and hopes ran high of an early landfall. In a flat calm Columbus ordered the dipsey lead hove. No bottom at 200 fathoms. (The nearest sounding to that point on the modern ocean chart is 2292 fathoms!) The fleet made 57 miles in the next two days, for they were in that section of the North Atlantic that has the largest percentage of calms, light airs and variables in September, and were lucky to have any wind whatsoever. At dawn on the twenty-first the sea was covered with

weed, "very smooth like a river, and the air the best in the world."
That night at sundown they saw the new moon.

Columbus was sorry to lose the trades, but he always found
consolation in contrarieties. In his Journal for September 22, when
the fleet could do no better than WNW, he noted, "This contrary wind was of much use to me, because my people were all
worked up, thinking that no winds blew in these waters for returning to Spain." They had had too much of a good thing. But
seamen can always find something to beef about. Next day, when
the wind dropped, "the people grumbled, saying that since there
was no heavy sea, that proved it would never blow hard enough
to return to Spain." All right boys, just wait a few hours, the Old
Man knows his stuff. "Afterwards the sea made up considerably,
and without wind, which astonished them." There must have been
a hurricane far to the southwestward, for it was now the season
for a Line gale. Columbus's stock went up several points: "Thus
very useful to me was the high sea, a sign such as had not appeared save in the time of the Jews when they came up out of
Egypt and grumbled against Moses who delivered them out of
captivity."

Columbus always loved to apply the Sacred Scriptures to his
own life and adventures; it is ridiculous to read into this passage
a secret admission of Jewish blood, or an ambition to provide a
new home for a persecuted race. The really significant thing about
these entries for September 22–23, as Charcot pointed out, was
the men's uneasiness over scudding free for so many days on end,
which proves that they had no previous experience of the trade
winds. Columbus knew little if anything more than they; his
serenity came from an inward assurance and confidence in God,
not from superior knowledge. And the "very useful to me" passage
is one in which a seaman speaks to seamen. No mariner in a small
sailing vessel welcomes rough water, which renders navigation
more difficult and dangerous. He accepts foul weather or heavy sea,
but never likes it, and is not afraid to say so. Columbus explains
that he welcomes the high sea merely because it enhances his

reputation among the men. And when he has smooth water, he ejaculates "Thanks be to God!" It is the nautical bluffers who pretend to glory in stormy weather and rough water, and affect to find smooth-water sailing dull.

It was dull enough to be sure that week of the autumnal equinox — 234 miles in five days. The men even went in swimming. During these calms and light airs, it was easy for the crews to exchange banter and for their officers to consult. In the smooth sea the caravels could be shoved along with their sweeps whenever the Captain General gave the signal; and in the absence of whistling wind and rushing waves, conversations from ship to ship were not difficult. On September 25 *Pinta* came close alongside the flagship in order to discuss with Columbus a chart containing mythical islands, which he had lent Martín Alonso three days before. Pinzón, whose particular interest in discovering islands is evident, wished to spend more time looking for them, because he said they must be somewhere about. Columbus "replied that so it appeared to him; but since they had not fallen in with them, the currents must have . . . set the ships all the while to the NE, and they had not gone so far as the pilots said." Martín Alonso sent the chart over to the flagship on a line, and Columbus "began to plot their position on it with his pilot and mariners."

While the plotting was going on, just at sunset on the twenty-fifth, Martín Alonso suddenly rushed up on *Pinta's* poop and joyfully shouted, *"Tierra! tierra! señor, albricias!"* — Land, land, sir! I claim the reward! There was a general scramble up the rigging on all three vessels, and everyone declared he saw land, about 25 leagues to the southwestward. Columbus fell on his knees to thank God, *Gloria in excelsis Deo* was sung by all hands, the course was altered to SW, and "all continued during the night declaring it to be land." They supposed it to be a high mountain like Tenerife, which is visible over 100 miles in clear weather.

At dawn no land was visible. Columbus continued the same course until the afternoon, when he decided "that what had been supposed to be land was not, but sky." False landfalls are a common sea phenomenon. A cloud on the horizon at sunset, as this seems to have been, is often mistaken for land, especially when people on board are eagerly searching for it; and man is so suggestible that if one sees it all see it. Such was the origin of the phantom islands of the Atlantic, which Columbus thought would make good ports of call on the passage to India.

Columbus was not greatly disturbed by this false alarm, because at the time he reckoned they had sailed only 533 leagues, a little over two thirds of the way to "The Indies." Twice he states that since the main object of this voyage is to reach the Indies, he does not care to delay by looking up odd islands. His Journal reflects nothing but confidence, serenity, and joy at the beauty of the ocean. "The sea was like a river," he noted on September 26, "the air sweet and very soft." The wind was so light, and so near were they to the northern edge of the trades, that no sea made up; one often sees such summer days in the North Atlantic. But the people, says Ferdinand, saw the westerly course resumed with heaviness of heart. Day after day they had "wind on the stern," but little of it, and the ships sailed slowly west. In six days (September 26–October 1) they made only 382 miles. There was nothing to keep the men busy, nothing to do but keep the vessels clean and the gear in good shape, troll for fish (and they caught some savory *dorado* or dolphin, that tastes like salmon) and watch the birds.

Under these circumstances the usual grumbling began to assume the proportions of incipient mutiny. This Genoese, in his mad fantasy, is trying to make himself a great lord at the expense of our lives, someone suggested. To follow this westerly course much longer will be our ruin. Food and water will give out, for it never rains in this desert waste of salt water. (It seldom does rain on the northern edge of the northeast trades.) After all, he is a foreigner, wouldn't it be a sound plan to heave him overboard, and to pretend that when observing the stars he had fallen in by accident? Isn't that the only means for our safe return?

Columbus must have known what was going on. No Spanish

seaman can hold a poker face very long; and the sour looks, the violent gestures (with sidelong glances at himself) when a group of mariners got together for a game, told him that something very evil was stewing. Indeed he showed that he knew it, for when some of the officers remonstrated and said he should turn back, Columbus remarked they might kill him if they would, he and his servants were too few to resist; but it would do them no good, the Sovereigns would have the whole lot hanged if they returned without him. His usual policy, however, was to use *palabras dulces*, "soft words," as Oviedo says. As anxiety increased among the common seamen, the more serene and confident appeared their Captain General, the more he flattered them with prospects of oriental wealth, and of the favors that they would receive from their Sovereigns after a successful voyage.

It became more and more difficult to maintain morale. The fleet had now been three weeks without sight of land; probably no man aboard had ever equaled that record. Only those who have experienced it, know what wear and tear shipmates inflict on each other's tempers during a long sea voyage. Ashore you may hate your boss or despise your fellow workers, but you are with them only from nine to five. Even in a boys' school or military training camp, there are some means to gain privacy for short intervals. But on a vessel like these caravels, where men even had to ease themselves in public, it is impossible to get away from your mates except by sleep; and even then they fall over you or wake you up to ask silly questions, such as, where did you leave that marlin-spike last watch? In a really long voyage such as this, which is full of anxiety and disappointment, especially if there is no stiff weather to keep them busy, the men invariably form gangs and cliques, work up hatreds against each other and their officers, brood over imaginary wrongs and unintended slights, and fancy that they are shipmates with some of the world's worst scoundrels. Warm friendships are formed as well, and the finest loyalty and sacrifice are brought out at sea; but simply seeing the same faces and hearing the same voices day after day and week after week, with no chance to shake it off even for an hour, wears many a man ragged. There is no reason to suppose that these human relationships were any worse aboard *Santa María*, *Pinta* and *Niña* than on other ships of the time; these people, to judge by the record, were pretty good fellows: but by the time September changed to October they were not only working up a mighty fear of the unknown, but getting in each other's hair. Columbus and the Pinzons needed all their moral force and prestige to prevent outbreaks or even mutiny.

CHAPTER XV

Adelante! Adelante!
October 1–11, 1492

Tonet mare, et plenitudo eius.

Let the sea roar, and the fulness thereof.
— I CHRONICLES xvi 32

AT DAWN October 1, last day of the stretch of variable winds, pilot Peralonso Niño of *Santa María* figured out the distance they had sailed from Ferro as 578 leagues. "The lesser reckoning that the Admiral showed to the people was 584 leagues; but the true one that the Admiral found and kept back, was 707." According to Captain McElroy's reckoning, Peralonso was right again, for the correct figure was 575 leagues. But the actual westing made, what really counted, was only 1794 miles or 564 leagues. Consequently Columbus's "phony" reckoning was much nearer the truth than his real one. Since he had predicted land at 750 leagues west of the Canaries, he must have been getting anxious at this point; but in order to make time and reach land before anything boiled up among the men forward, and because the moon was nearing full, he continued to carry on day and night.

And how they did sail, that first week of October! An average of 142 miles every twenty-four hours for five days (October 2–6), including the best day's run, 182 miles, of the outward passage; almost 8 knots. The magnetic course was still due west, but owing to the unsuspected variation of the compass the fleet was slowly (and fortunately as it turned out) trending southward. Rumblings of revolt were again heard forward, but flocks of petrels and other birds came to the rescue of authority on October 3 and 4, raising new hopes of land. The seamen still had much to learn about the habits of petrels; but Columbus by this time had decided that petrels were pelagic. For on October 3 he believed that they had left astern the islands depicted on his chart. "The Admiral here says that he did not care to delay by beating to windward last week and on those days when they had so many signs of land, although he had information of certain islands in this region, so as not to delay; because his object was to reach the Indies, and if he had delayed, he says, it would not have been good sense." His repetition of this remark is interesting, and not only as additional proof of his oriental objective. Columbus evidently feared that on his return he would be accused of having missed something; and he wished to make it clear to the Sovereigns why he pressed on.

Martín Alonso Pinzón put in a plea for altering the course to SW by W on October 6, when the fleet had passed the 65th meridian of longitude and lay directly north of Puerto Rico. Columbus observed that it seemed to him "that Martín Alonso did not say (that is, mean) this for the island of Japan, and the Admiral saw that if they were going wrong, they would be unable to reach land so soon, and that it was better to go at once to the mainland, and later to the Islands."

This, as to Columbus's route and intentions, is one of the most significant entries in his Journal. It proves by a circumstantial and somewhat involved statement that no faker could possibly have invented, that Columbus's plan was to make due west for Japan. Reading between the lines of the sea journal, one can guess what happened. By dawn October 6 the fleet has sailed so much further than the expected 750 leagues that everyone who has kept a reckoning is asking the question, supposing we have missed Japan? *Pinta* shoots under the flagship's stern, and Martín Alonso shouts something like *sudoeste cuarta del oeste, señor; sudoeste cuarta del oeste . . . Cipango* — "SW by W, sir, SW by W, . . . Japan." His explanation of why he wants this change of course, and the connection of it with Japan, is lost in the sound of rushing waters; but Columbus, who is anxious enough himself, assumes that Martín Alonso believes that they have passed Japan hull-down, and advises a SW by W course in order to reach China. Or, may be the captain of *Pinta* thinks Japan lies SW by W. In any case, Columbus decides that even if they have missed Japan, a due west course will take them to land quicker than a more southerly rhumb, which might miss the southeast cape of China, where Martin Behaim located Zaitun. It would be best to make sure of land first, and visit Japan on the way home.

At sunrise on Sunday, October 7, when the fleet was about 370 miles from the nearest land (Turks Island), came the second false landfall. *Niña*, ranging ahead of her consorts contrary to Columbus's orders, in the hope of winning the reward, broke out a flag at her masthead and fired a gun, the signal for land dead ahead. People aboard the flagship had seen this "land" earlier, but dared not sing out; for the Captain General was so fed up with false landfalls that he gave orders to the effect that anyone who raised another false cry of *tierra* would be disqualified for the reward, even though he should sight the true land later. (By the same token, Columbus should later have disqualified himself!)

By sunset, when they had run 67 miles and no land had materialized, Columbus ordered the course to be changed to WSW (one point more westerly than Martín Alonso had recommended) because great flocks of birds were passing overhead to the southwestward. He remembered that the Portuguese had discovered the outermost Azores by attending to the flight of birds. This judgment was good, for the fall migration of North American birds to the West Indies via Bermuda was in full flight, and Columbus's decision to follow these feathered pilots rather than his inaccurate man-made chart was vital for the whole future of Spanish colonization. For when Columbus determined to follow the birds, his fleet was on latitude 25° 40' and fast approaching the area of zero compass variation. Had the due west course been maintained from that point, the voyage would have taken at least a day longer, and the landfall, provided Columbus had managed to keep down mutiny another day, would have been Eleuthera Island or Hole-in-the-Wall on Great Abaco. What then? Except for the unlikely contingency of the local Indians piloting Columbus south through Tongue of the Ocean, the fleet would have sailed through Providence Channel slap into the Gulf Stream; and once involved in that mighty current, the caravels could never have made any southing. The fleet would have touched (and perhaps more than touched — gone ashore) on the coast of Florida somewhere between Jupiter Inlet and Cape Canaveral; and then, provided they survived that ocean graveyard, have been swept along the coast of Georgia and the Carolinas, returning to Spain (if they managed to return) by the westerlies north of Hatteras and Bermuda.

Obviously the results of any such voyage, considering what Columbus was after and what his Sovereigns wanted, would have been highly disappointing to everyone, and it is questionable how soon if ever he would have been allowed to try again. For it was the gold of Hispaniola, and nothing else, that attracted Spaniards to the New World. A great deal was made of this change of course in post-mortems on the voyage, and rightly so; but most of the witnesses attributed it to Pinzón's advice. The Journal shows that the birds of North America deserve the credit.

During the eighth day of October, when " 'Thanks be to God' says the Admiral 'the air is soft as in April in Seville, and it's a pleasure to be in it, so fragrant it is,' " the WSW course was maintained. On the ninth a shift of wind forced them W by N for 43 miles, but on the tenth a fine run of 171 miles was made to the WSW. Moon came full on the fifth, consequently there was no risk of overrunning the land. And all night October 9–10 the men could hear flocks of birds flying overhead to the southwestward, and sometimes could see them against the moon. Martín Alonso Pinzón remarked to his men, "Those birds know their business."

Notwithstanding this encouraging sign, October 10 was the most critical day of the entire voyage, when the enterprise came nearest to failure through the stubborn conservatism of the men. It is unfair to present the issue between Columbus and his crew as one between a brave man and cowards. Nor was it one between knowledge and ignorance, education and superstition: for if Columbus had had a university education, or listened attentively to the best opinions of his day, he would never have expected Japan to lie 750 leagues west of the Canaries. It was, rather, the inevitable conflict between a man of one great, compelling idea and those who did not share it in anything like the same degree. Look back at the events of the voyage, think of the two false landfalls, the innumerable "signs of land" that failed to make good; glance at the fleet's position October 10, on a modern chart with America blotted out, and reflect that thirty days out, they had doubled all previous records for ocean navigation, that they had long passed the position where Columbus predicted land would be found, and that the men knew it; no "phony" reckoning could conceal that fact from the pilots, who were as keen as any to turn back, and communicated their fears to the people. So can we fairly blame the men? Their issue with their commander was the eternal one between imagination and doubt, between the spirit that creates and the spirit that denies. Oftentimes the doubters are right, for mankind has a hundred foolish notions for ᵉvery sound one; it is at times of crisis, when unpredictable forces are dissolving society, that the do-nothings are tragically wrong. There are tides in the affairs of men, and this was one of them.

And so, on October 10, when the fleet was steering straight for the Bahamas, and the nearest land was less than 200 miles ahead, all the smoldering discontent of the men flared up into open mutiny. They had done enough and more than enough; the ships should and must turn back. This mutiny, so far as we have any record, was confined to the flagship, although the crews of *Niña* and *Pinta* were as eager to return. Aboard *Santa María* there was a clique of stubborn, know-it-all Basques and Galicians, and to all her crew the Captain General was a foreigner. What Columbus noted down (and Las Casas abstracted) is short and to the point, and not ungenerous to the men: —

"Here the people could stand it no longer, complained of the long voyage; but the Admiral cheered them as best he could, holding out good hope of the advantages they might have; and he added that it was useless to complain, since he had come to go to the Indies, and so had to continue until he found them, with the help of Our Lord."

Perhaps what the Captain General said was not quite so dramatic; for it was later stated, as a matter of common report, that he promised the men to turn back if they did not sight land within two or three days. He would certainly have pointed out that, with a fresh easterly trade wind and rising sea, the ships could do nothing anyway on a course for home, and so might as well carry on until the next soft spot in the weather. In any case, the mutiny was quelled.

Although we may dismiss as incredible the Pinzón yarn about Columbus being frightened at the gulfweed early in the voyage, we cannot ignore the damaging testimony brought out in the protracted lawsuit of 1514-1536 to the effect that at some time during this second week of October the Admiral either lost confidence or, frightened by the attitude of his men, proposed to turn back; and that the Pinzons dissuaded him.

Although all this testimony was taken down at least twenty-two years after, and some of it forty-four years after the event, illiterate men in simple social surroundings, where they are not continually assailed by newspapers, loud-speakers and the like, have good memories; and the First Voyage of Columbus was one that a man would not readily forget. On the other hand, Martín Alonso was a man with a grievance, and for almost four months (November–March) *Pinta* was sailing alone, or without any communication with the flagship. Pinzón, then, had plenty of time to create a sort of *Pinta* myth of the discovery, and inculcate it among his relatives and other men of Palos aboard his ship.

This testimony was evoked by a leading question propounded by the *fiscal* or crown attorney to picked witnesses in various Andalusian seaports, in 1515: —

"Whether you know that . . . they had run 800 leagues westward from the island of Ferro, and that during this time, 200 leagues

before the Admiral sighted land, and when he did not know where
to go and thought he would make no discovery, he went aboard the
ship of Martín Alonso and asked what he thought they should do,
for they had already gone 200 leagues beyond what he expected
and should by now have reached land?

"Also whether you know that the said Martín Alonso said,
'*Adelante! Adelante!* this is a fleet and mission of such great princes
as the Sovereigns our lords of Spain, . . . but if you, sir, wish to
turn back I am determined to go on until land is found or never
return to Spain,' and that because of his efforts and counsel they
went forward?"

A number of the witnesses said what was expected of them,
and played up to these leading questions, with suitable trimmings.
For instance, Francisco García Vallejo, seaman aboard *Pinta*, declared that on October 6, with 800 leagues gone and 200 to go,
Columbus held a conference of all the captains, and said, " 'What
shall we do, captains; my people are complaining; what, sirs, do you
think we should do?' And then said Vicente Yáñez, 'Let's proceed,
sir, up to 2000 leagues, and if there we don't find what we set
out to find we'll turn back'; and then replied Martín Alonso
Pinzón, who was the senior captain, 'Come, sir, when we have
scarcely left Palos, your honor is displeased; go forward, sir, for
God will give us success in discovering land, for God would not
wish us to turn back so shamefully.' Then replied the said Admiral
Don Cristóbal Colón, 'Good luck to you,' and so because of Martín
Alonso Pinzón they went on. . . ." And Martín Alonso advised
him to steer a course SW for land, and Columbus replied "so be
it."

The legend of the timid landsman Colombo being bucked up
by the hearty seafaring Pinzons improved and enlarged with age
as this sixteenth-century case of Jarndyce *v.* Jarndyce dragged on
its weary way. In 1536 an octogenarian cousin of the Pinzons who
pretended to have been on the voyage (which was not true) declared that seven days before they made land, Columbus called a
conference, disclosed the mutinous state of his crew, and asked his

captains' advice; and Martín Alonso replied, " 'Sir, let your honor string up half a dozen of 'em or heave 'em overboard, and if you don't dare to, I and my brothers will board you and do it; a fleet like this under the orders of such high princes can't return without good news.' And with this, all cheered up. Don Cristóbal Colón said, 'Martín Alonso, let's fix these fellows and carry on for some days, and if we don't find land we shall consult further what we ought to do.' And so they sailed seven more days. . . ."

On the other hand, the greater part of the witnesses simply gave a formal "yes" to the leading questions, or said *no sé;* and some came out unexpectedly with a very different version. Manuel de Valdovinos, who sailed with Vicente Yáñez Pinzón on his Amazon voyage, heard from him and the other Palenos aboard Vicente's flagship that it was the Pinzón brothers who wanted to turn back. They represented to Columbus, "Sir, where are we going now that we have run 800 leagues and not found land, and these people say that they are going to be lost?" And Columbus replied, "Martín Alonso, do me this favor, to stay with me this day and night, and if I don't bring you to land before day, . . . cut off my head and you shall return." The Pinzons then gave in, and next morning land was sighted.

The heirs of Columbus asked just as leading questions in the hearings held under their auspices. For instance, "Whether it is known, believed and is public and notorious that . . . many people and mariners wished to turn back without finding land, saying that they would be lost?" Neither Columbus nor his heirs (so far as we have record) accused the Pinzons of being in this cabal, but Francisco Morales, who had made the Second Voyage on the *Niña* under her former master Juan Niño, reported him as having said that "in mid-ocean or somewhat further, the masters of the three ships which composed the First Voyage joined forces and proceeded to request the Admiral to return to Castile, because, on account of the easterly winds prevailing in the ocean, they did not believe that if they went any further they could return to Spain, and that the Admiral replied that he cared not for that, for God

who gave them this weather would give them other to return, . . .
and that they would not gain their end, because in killing him and
his servants, who were few, they would not accomplish much,
. . . but that they might do one thing: they might set him a
limit of three or four days and hold to the course they were
following and if they did not sight land within that time, they
might turn back, as they wished; and that with this agreement they
went ahead on their voyage, and within that limit saw land."

The only thing common to all these depositions is that at some
date very close to the landfall a conference of captains was held,
that Columbus (or the Pinzons) wanted to turn back, and that
the Pinzons (or Columbus) agreed to go on a few days more.
Now, it is no easy matter to hold such a conference at sea; impossible to do so when a high sea is running, and a strong wind blowing. Unlashing and lowering with crude tackle a heavy boat, and
rowing men from two of the ships and boarding a third, is both
difficult and dangerous. And you cannot hold conversations such
as these deponents describe by bellowing back and forth from ship
to ship, at sufficient distance to avoid collision. If a shipboard
conference occurred shortly before the landfall, it must have been
on October 9 when the wind was variable and the fleet made only
58 miles, or the previous day when they made only 33 miles. It
could not possibly have been on October 10, which both Columbus and Oviedo declare to be the day of greatest danger of
mutiny, because that day a run of 171 miles was made, and the sea
was making up fast. To insist in 1941 on a new interpretation of
documents that were known four hundred years ago, and known
in their original setting with all the attendant circumstances that
enabled some tales to be discounted and others accepted, seems to
me highly presumptuous. Yet historians like Fernández Duro,
Vignaud, and Carbia have not hesitated to declare that Columbus's
Journal is false, that Las Casas and Ferdinand are liars, and the
"real truth" is told by pro-Pinzón *pleitos* taken down between
sixteen and forty-five years after the event.

Ferdinand's version (and he makes no accusations against the

Pinzons, but declares his father handled the mutiny himself) we may perhaps discount as over loyal. There is less reason to do this with Las Casas; but let us pass him over. A really impartial authority on the First Voyage is Fernández de Oviedo, the first official historian of the Indies, who had every temptation to adopt the crown's official theory, but did not; and who knew and talked with Vicente Yáñez Pinzón and Hernán Pérez Mateos, the author of the "throw 'em overboard" story. Oviedo says categorically that by tactful and cheering words Columbus "moved the courage of the weakened minds of those who were about to resort to something shameful, *especially the three brother captains I have mentioned*, and they agreed to do what he commanded and sail three days and no more," within which space of time land was discovered. Oviedo pays his respect to the Pinzón theory in these words: "Some say the contrary of what has been said here of the steadfastness of Columbus, they even declare he would have turned back voluntarily from the course and would not have finished it, if the brothers Pinzón had not made him go forward; and they say more, that because of them the discovery was made, and that Columbus already weakened and wanted to come about. This would be better referred to a long suit between the Admiral and the royal *fiscal*, where many things are alleged pro and con, and in which I do not intervene, for since they are matters of *justicia* and by it are to be determined they should take the course that they will. . . . The reader may take that which his judgment dictates." There is no doubt, then, that Oviedo was well apprised of the Pinzón version, and that he discarded it as false.

Here is what I believe happened. On October 9, when the course was altered to W by N by reason of a southerly shift in the wind, a wind so moderate that the average speed was only a trifle over 2 knots, Martín Alonso and Vicente Yáñez came aboard the flagship, held a more or less stormy conference with Columbus in his cabin, demanded that the search for land be abandoned, and that advantage be taken of the southerly breeze to start home. But Columbus (supported by the birds) succeeded in persuading the brothers to carry on three more days, and they returned to their respective vessels. Then, at sunrise October 10, the trade wind made up fresh, sending the fleet along at a speed of 7 knots, which reawakened the fears of *Santa María's* crew that they would never be able to return. Hence the flare-up of mutiny that day. Columbus made the same promise to his men that he had to the Pinzons, and by nightfall the last danger of abandoning the Great Enterprise on the brink of success, was over.

All day Thursday, October 11, the trade wind still blew a gale, the sea rose higher than at any time on the voyage, and the fleet ran 78 miles between sunrise and sunset, an average speed of 6.7 knots. But signs of land were so many and so frequent that "everyone breathed more freely and grew cheerful." *Niña* picked up a green branch with a little flower that resembled the dog roses on hedges in Castile. *Pinta* gathered quite a collection: a cane and a stick, a piece of board, a land plant, and "another little stick fashioned, as it appeared, with iron," doubtless carved by an Indian with a stone chisel. These objects must have floated up from the Lesser Antilles or even South America; but they served their purpose of stopping complaints, and preparing every man aboard for a speedy end to this first Atlantic crossing.*

* Summary of the First Voyage Outward: —

	Columbus		McElroy
	leagues	n. miles	n. miles
Distance logged from Ferro September 9 to landfall October 12	1072	3409	3066
Add distance from departure 3 A.M. September 8 to Ferro	18	57	51
Total	1090	3466	3117

Capt. John W. McElroy, chief navigating officer of the Harvard Columbus Expedition, made the detailed study of the navigation of Columbus's First Voyage that appeared in *American Neptune* I (1941) 209-40.

CHAPTER XVI

Landfall

October 11–14, 1492

Et potestas eius a mari usque ad mare, et a fluminibus usque ad fines terrae.

And his dominion shall be from sea even to sea, and from the river even to the ends of the earth.

— ZECHARIAH ix 10

SUN set under a clear horizon about 5.30, every man in the fleet watching for a silhouette of land against its red disk; but no land was there. All hands were summoned as usual, and after they had said their evening prayers and sung the *Salve Regina* "which all seamen are accustomed to say and sing in their own fashion," Columbus from the sterncastle made his men a little speech, reminding them of the grace Our Lord had shown them in conducting them so safely and prosperously with fair winds and a clear course, and in comforting them with signs of better things to come; and he urged the night watch to keep a particularly sharp lookout on the forecastle, reminding them that although he had given orders to do no night sailing after reaching a point 700 leagues from the Canaries, the great desire of all to see land had decided him to carry on that night. Hence all must make amends for this temerity by keeping a particularly good watch, and looking sharp for land; and to him who first sighted it he would then and there give a silk doublet, in addition to the annuity of 10,000 maravedis that the Sovereigns had promised. The gromet then sang his little ditty for changing the watch and turned the *ampolleta*, boatswain Chachu bellowed out the Castilian

equivalent to "Watch below lay belo-o-w!" and the men took their
stations with eyes well peeled.

During the eleven and a half hours since sunrise, with a brisk
trade wind and the heaviest following sea of the entire voyage,
the fleet had made 78 miles, an average of almost 7 knots. At sunset it breezed up to gale force, until the vessels were tearing along
at 9 knots. At the same time Columbus ordered the course changed
from WSW back to the original West. Why he did this, nobody
has explained. I suspect that it was simply a desire to prove that
he was right. He had begun the voyage by steering a course due
west for Japan, and so he wished to pick up land on a due west
course. I have known commanders, good seamen too, who are like
that. Or the change may have been just a hunch. If so, it was a
good one, for the WSW course would have missed Guanahaní,
and put the fleet next day in a dangerous position with the long
shelterless shore of Long Island under its lee. Common prudence
would have made Columbus heave-to for the night, since shoals
and rocks invisible by moonlight might lie ahead. *María's* pilot,
Peralonso Niño, is said to have so advised him; but the Captain
General felt that this was no time for common prudence. He had
promised the men to turn back if land were not made within three
days, and he intended to make all possible westing in this gale of
wind. So the signal was made for *oeste!*

Anyone who has come onto the land under sail at night from an
uncertain position knows how tense the atmosphere aboard ship
can be. And this night of October 11–12 was one big with destiny
for the human race, the most momentous ever experienced aboard
any ship in any sea. Some of the boys doubtless slept, but nobody
else. Juan de la Cosa and the Pinzons are pacing the high poops
of their respective vessels, frequently calling down to the men at
the tiller a testy order — keep her off damn your eyes must I go
below and take the stick myself? — pausing at the break to peer
under the main course and sweep the western horizon, then resting their eyes by looking up at the stars. Consultation as to whether
or not to shorten sail; Martín Alonso perhaps confiding to pilot

Cristóbal García that he doesn't like carrying sail this way in a gale of wind with possible shoals ahead, but if that crazy Genoese can carry sail we can carry sail; *Pinta* can stand it better than that Galician tub, and heave-to quicker if anything shows up, and I want one of you men of Palos to win that *albricias*, d'ye see? Lookouts on the forecastles and in the round-tops talking low to each other — Hear anything? Sounds like breakers to me — nothing but the bow wave you fool — I tell you we won't sight land till Saturday, I dreamt it, and my dreams — you and your dreams, here's a hundred maravedis says we raise it by daylight. . . . They tell each other how they would have conducted the fleet — The Old Man should never have set that spritsail, she'll run her bow under — if he'd asked my advice, and I was making my third voyage when he was playing in the streets of Genoa, I'd have told him. . . . Under such circumstances, with everyone's nerves taut as the weather braces, there was almost certain to be a false alarm of land.

An hour before moonrise, at 10 P.M., it came. Columbus, standing on the sterncastle, thought he saw a light, "so uncertain a thing that he did not wish to declare that it was land," but called Pedro Gutiérrez to have a look, and he thought he saw it too. Rodrigo Sánchez was then appealed to, "but he saw nothing because he was not in a position where he could see anything." One guesses that Rodrigo was fed up with false alarms, and merely stuck his head out of the companionway to remark discouragingly that he didn't see nothing; no, not a thing. The light, Columbus said, "was like a little wax candle rising and falling," and he saw it only once or twice after speaking to Gutiérrez.

At this juncture one of the seamen named Pedro Yzquierdo, a native of Lepe, thought he saw a light and sung out, *"Lumbre! tierra!"* Pedro de Salcedo, Columbus's page-boy, piped up with "It's already been seen by my master," and Columbus, who heard the cry, snubbed the man with, "I saw and spoke of that light, which is on land, some time ago."

What was this feeble light resembling a wax candle rising and falling, which Columbus admits that only a few besides himself ever saw? It cannot have been a fire or other light on San Salvador, or any other island; for, as the real landfall four hours later proves, the fleet at 10 P.M. was at least 35 miles off shore. The 400,000 candlepower light now on San Salvador, 170 feet above sea level, is not visible nearly so far. One writer has advanced the theory that the light was made by Indians torching for fish — why not lighting a cigar? — but Indians do not go fishing in 3000 fathoms of water 35 miles offshore at night in a gale of wind. The sentimental school of thought would have this light supernatural, sent by the Almighty to guide and encourage Columbus; but of all moments in the voyage, this is the one when he least needed encouragement, and he had laid his course straight for the nearest land. I agree heartily with Admiral Murdock, "the light was due to the imagination of Columbus, wrought up to a high pitch by the numerous signs of land encountered that day." Columbus admitted that only a few even thought they saw it. Anyone who has had much experience trying to make night landfalls with a sea running knows how easy it is to be deceived, especially when you are very anxious to pick up a light. Often two or three shipmates will agree that they see "it," then "it" disappears, and you realize that it was just another illusion. There is no need to criticize Columbus's seamanship because he sighted an imaginary light; but it is not easy to defend the fact that for this false landfall, which he must have known the next day to have been imaginary, he demanded and obtained the annuity of 10,000 maravedis promised by the Sovereigns to the man who first sighted land. The best we can say in extenuation is to point out that glory rather than greed prompted this act of injustice to a seaman; Columbus could not bear to think that anyone but himself sighted land first. That form of male vanity is by no means absent from the seafaring tribe today.

At 2 A.M. October 12 the moon, past full, was riding about 70° high over Orion on the port quarter, just the position to illuminate anything ahead of the ships. Jupiter was rising in the east; Saturn had just set, and Deneb was nearing the western horizon, toward which all waking eyes were directed. There hung the Square of Pegasus, and a little higher and to the northward Cassiopeia's Chair. The Guards of Polaris, at 15° beyond "feet," told the pilots that it was two hours after midnight. On speed the three ships, *Pinta* in the lead, their sails silver in the moonlight. A brave trade wind is blowing and the caravels are rolling, plunging and throwing spray as they cut down the last invisible barrier between the Old World and the New. Only a few moments now, and an era that began in remotest antiquity will end.

Rodrigo de Triana, lookout on *Pinta's* forecastle, sees something like a white sand cliff gleaming in the moonlight on the western horizon, then another, and a dark line of land connecting them. "*Tierra! tierra!*" he shouts, and this time land it is.

Martín Alonso Pinzón, after a quick verification, causes a lombard already loaded and primed to be fired as the agreed signal, and shortens sail in order to wait for the flagship. As soon as *Santa María* approached (remembered *Pinta's* steward many years later) Columbus called out, "Señor Martín Alonso, you have found land!" and Pinzón replied, "Sir, my reward is not lost," and Columbus called back, "I give you five thousand maravedis as a present!"

By Columbus's reckoning the land was distant about 6 miles. The fleet had made 65 miles in the eight and a half hours since sunset, an average better than 7½ knots; according to our reckoning they were very near latitude 24° N, longitude 74° 20' W when Rodrigo sang out.

As the fleet was heading straight for a lee shore, Columbus wisely ordered all sail to be lowered except the *papahigo*, which as Las Casas explains was the main course without bonnets; and with the main yard braced sharp and port tacks aboard, *Santa María*, *Pinta* and *Niña* jogged off-and-on until daylight. When they appeared to be losing the land they wore around to the starboard tack, so the net result was a southerly drift at a safe distance from the breakers, during the remaining two and a half hours of

SAN SALVADOR (GUANAHANI) OR WATLINGS ISLAND

Drawn by Erwin Raisz from U.S. Hydrographic Office chart N° 2805, data furnished by George B. Massey and reconnaissance by the Harvard Columbus Expedition 1940 ~ Copyright 1941 by Samuel E. Morison

moonlit night. The windward side of the island today is strewn with the wrecks of vessels that neglected this precaution.

This first land of the Western Hemisphere sighted by Columbus, or by any European since the voyages of the Northmen, was the eastern coast of one of the Bahamas now officially named "San Salvador or Watlings Island." Other candidates there have been for this honor: the Grand Turk, Cat Island, Rum Cay, Samana Cay and Mayaguana. But there is no longer any doubt that the island called Guanahaní, which Columbus renamed after Our Lord and Saviour, was the present San Salvador or Watlings. That alone of any island in the Bahamas, Turks or Caicos groups, fits Columbus's description. The position of San Salvador and of no other island fits the course laid down in his Journal, if we work it backward from Cuba.

San Salvador is a coral island about 13 miles long by 6 wide; the 24th parallel of latitude and the meridian of 74° 30′ West of Greenwich cross near its center. The entire island, except for a space of about 1¾ miles on the west or leeward side, is surrounded by dangerous reefs. By daylight Columbus's fleet must have drifted to a point near the Hinchinbrooke Rocks off the southeastern point. Making sail and filling away, they sought an opening through the reef barrier where they might safely anchor and send boats ashore. And the first gap that they could have discovered, one easy to pick out with a heavy sea running, was on the western shore about 5 miles north of Southwest Point. Here, rounding a prominent breaking ledge now called Gardiner Reef, the caravels braced their yards sharp and entered a shallow bay (Long or Fernandez), protected from winds between N by E around to S by W. Off a curving beach of gleaming coral sand, they found sheltered anchorage in 5 fathoms of water.

Somewhere on this beach of Long or Fernandez Bay took place the famous Landing of Columbus, often depicted by artists, but never with any respect for the actual topography. Las Casas's abstract of the Journal, and Ferdinand Columbus, who had the Journal before him when he wrote the biography of his father, are the unique sources for this incident. Fitting together the two, we have this description: —

Presently they saw naked people, and the Admiral went ashore in the armed ship's boat with the royal standard displayed. So did the captains of *Pinta* and *Niña*, Martín Alonso Pinzón and Vicente Yáñez his brother, in their boats, with the banners of the Expedition, on which were depicted a green cross with an F on one arm and a Y on the other, and over each his or her crown. And, all having rendered thanks to Our Lord kneeling on the ground, embracing it with tears of joy for the immeasurable mercy of having reached it, the Admiral arose and gave this island the name *San Salvador*. Thereupon he summoned to him the two captains, Rodrigo de Escobedo secretary of the armada and Rodrigo Sánchez of Segovia, and all others who came ashore, as witnesses; and in the presence of many natives of that land assembled together, took possession of that island in the name of the Catholic Sovereigns with appropriate words and ceremony. And all this is set forth at large in the testimonies there set down in writing. Forthwith the Christians hailed him as Admiral and Viceroy and swore to obey him as one who represented Their Highnesses, with as much joy and pleasure as if the victory had been all theirs, all begging his pardon for the injuries that through fear and inconstancy they had done him. Many Indians having come together for that ceremony and rejoicing, the Admiral, seeing that they were a gentle and peaceful people and of great simplicity, gave them some little red caps and glass beads which they hung around their necks, and other things of slight worth, which they all valued at the highest price.

At this point Las Casas begins to quote the *palabras formales* (exact words) of the Admiral, as we may now fairly style Columbus. So we may gather, as well as words can convey, the impression made by this branch of the American Indians on the vanguard of the race that would shortly reduce them to slavery, and exterminate them: —

In order that we might win good friendship, because I knew that they were a people who could better be freed and converted to our Holy Faith by love than by force, I gave to some of them red caps and to some glass beads, which they hung on their necks, and many other things of slight value, in which they took much pleasure; they remained so much our friends that it was a marvel; and later they came swimming to the ships' boats in which we were, and brought us parrots and cotton thread in skeins and darts and many other things, and we swopped them for other things that we gave them, such as little glass beads and hawks' bells. Finally they swopped and gave everything they had, with good will; but it appeared to us that these people were very poor in everything. They go quite naked as their mothers bore them; and also the women, although I didn't see more than one really young girl. All that I saw were young men, none of them more than 30 years old, very well made, of very handsome bodies and very good faces; the hair coarse almost as the hair of a horse's tail and short; the hair they wear over their eyebrows, except for a hank behind that they wear long and never cut. Some of them paint themselves black (and they are of the color of the Canary Islanders, neither black nor white), and some paint themselves white, and others red, and others with what they have. Some paint their faces, others the whole body, others the eyes only, others only the nose. They bear no arms, nor know thereof; for I showed them swords and they grasped them by the blade and cut themselves through ignorance; they have no iron. Their darts are a kind of rod without iron, and some have at the end a fish's tooth and others, other things. They are generally fairly tall and good looking, well made. I saw some who had marks of wounds on their bodies, and made signs to them to ask what it was, and they showed me how people of other islands which are near came there and wished to capture them, and they defended themselves. And I believed and now believe that people do come here from the mainland to take them as slaves. They ought to be good servants and of good skill, for I see that they repeat very quickly all that is said to them; and I believe that they would easily be made Christians, because it seemed to me that they belonged to no religion. I, please Our Lord, will carry off six of them at my departure to Your Highnesses, so that they may learn to speak. I saw no beast of any kind except parrots in this island.

Saturday October 13: At daybreak there came to the beach many of these men, all young men as I have said, and all of good stature, very handsome people. Their hair is not kinky but loose and coarse like horsehair; and the whole forehead and head is very broad, more so than any other race that I have seen, and the eyes very handsome and not small, and themselves not at all black, but of the color of the Canary Islanders; nor should anything else be expected, because this is on the same latitude with the island of Ferro in the Canaries. Their legs are very straight, all in a line; and no belly, but very well built. They came to the ship in dugouts which are fashioned like a long boat from the bole of a tree, and all in one piece, and wonderfully made (considering the country), and so big that in some came 40 or 45 men, and others smaller, down to the size that held but a single man. They row with a thing like a baker's peel and go wonderfully [fast], and if they capsize all begin to swim and right it and bail it out with calabashes that they carry. They brought skeins of spun cotton, and parrots and darts and other trifles that would be tedious to describe, and gave all for whatever was given to them.

In his Letter to the Sovereigns, which was promptly printed at Barcelona and widely distributed throughout Europe in a Latin translation, Columbus lays stress on the gentleness and generosity of the natives: —

They are so ingenuous and free with all they have, that no one would believe it who has not seen it; of anything that they possess, if it be asked of them, they never say no; on the contrary, they invite you to share it and show as much love as if their hearts went with it, and they are content with whatever trifle be given them, whether it be a thing of value or of petty worth. I forbade that they be given things so worthless as bits of broken crockery and of green glass and lace-points, although when they could get them, they thought they had the best jewel in the world.

Unfortunately this guilelessness and generosity of the simple savage aroused the worst traits of cupidity and brutality in the average European. Even the Admiral's humanity seems to have been merely political, as a means to eventual enslavement and exploitation. But to the intellectuals of Europe it seemed that Columbus had stepped back several millennia, and encountered people living in the Golden Age, that bright morning of humanity which existed only in the imagination of poets. Columbus's discovery enabled Europeans to see their own ancestors, as it were, in a "state of nature," before Pandora's box was opened. The "virtuous savage" myth, which reached its height in the eighteenth century, began at Guanahaní on October 12, 1492. As Peter Martyr, who first gave it currency, wrote of these Indians, and as Richard Eden translated him in 1555: —

And surely if they had receaued owre religion, I wolde thinke their life moste happye of all men, if they might therwith enioye their aunciente libertie. A fewe thinges contente them, hauinge no delite in such superfluites, for the which in other places men take infinite paynes and commit manie vnlawfull actes, and yet are neuer satisfied, whereas many haue to muche, and none inowgh. But emonge these simple sowles, a fewe clothes serue the naked: weightes and measures are not needefull to such as can not skyll of crafte and deceyte and haue not the vse of pestiferous monye, the seede of innumerable myscheues. So that if we shall not be ashamed to confesse the truthe, they seeme to lyue in that goulden worlde of the whiche owlde wryters speake so much: wherin men lyued simplye and innocentlye without inforcement of lawes, without quarrellinge Iudges and libelles, contente onely to satisfie nature, without further vexation for knowelege of thinges to come.

These Indians of the Bahamas, and indeed all whom Columbus encountered on his First Voyage, belonged to the so-called Taino culture of the Arawak language group. Their ancestors had emigrated to the Antilles from the mainland of South America, and within a century of Columbus's voyage had branched out from Haiti, overrunning Cuba, Jamaica, and the Bahamas, pushing back or enslaving an earlier and more primitive tribe known as the Siboney. The Tainos were fairly advanced in civilization, growing corn, yams and other roots, making cassava bread from yucca, spinning and weaving cotton, making a fine brown pottery adorned with grotesque heads, and various ornaments and utensils of shell, living in huts made of a wooden frame and palm thatch. The broad, low forehead that Columbus remarked was due to a process of artificially flattening the skulls of infants, by pressing them between boards.

Columbus's frame of reference, it is interesting to note, was partly African and partly classical. He expected to find kinky-haired blacks such as he had encountered on the coast of Guinea, because Aristotle taught that people and products on the same latitude were similar; but he reflected that being on the same latitude as Ferro — a mistake of 3° 41′ — it was not surprising to find them of the same brown color as the Guanches, the primitive inhabitants of the Canaries. The word that he used for their canoes, *almadias*, was what the Portuguese used for the dugouts of West Africa; and the trading goods that he brought, Venetian glass beads, brass rings, red caps, and the small round bronze bells used in falconry, were exactly what the Portuguese had found to be in most demand among the Negroes.

Although the Tainos had driven back the primitive hunter folk, their only weapon, a short spear or dart with a fish-tooth or fire-hardened wooden point, was insufficient to cope with the Caribs, who occasionally raided them from the Caribbee Islands. Much less were they prepared to resist domination by the Spaniards. And it is clear from the concluding sentences of Columbus's Journal for October 12 that on the very day of discovery the dark thought crossed his mind that these people could very easily be enslaved. On October 14 he noted, "These people are very unskilled in arms, . . . with fifty men they could all be subjected and made to do all that one wished." It is sad but significant that the only Indians of the Caribbean who have survived are those who proved both willing and able to defend themselves. The Tainos, whom Columbus found so gentle and handsome and hospitable, are long since extinct.

Guanahaní, the native name of this island, means the *iguana*, a reptile now extinct there. Columbus described it as "very big and very level and the trees very green, and many bodies of water, and a very big lake in the middle, but no mountain, and the whole of it so green that it is a pleasure to gaze upon." The island is honeycombed with salt lagoons, the largest of which is only a few hundred yards from the beach where Columbus landed; and the highest hill on the island is only 140 feet above sea level. Later, after exploring the northern part, Columbus noted groves of trees, the most beautiful he had ever seen, "and as green and leafy as those of Castile in the months of April and May." Visitors to San Salvador and the other Bahamian Islands find Columbus's descriptions of nature extravagant, and are inclined to accuse him of laying it on thick to impress the Sovereigns.

Any land looks good to seamen after a long and perilous voyage, and every woman fair; but Columbus's description of the Bahamas was not extravagant for 1492. At that time they were highly fertile and covered with a dense growth of tropical hardwood, which the Indians had cleared but slightly to plant gardens. In the late eighteenth century, the English colonists (many of them loyalist refugees from the United States) caused a large part of the forest to be cut down in order to grow sea-island cotton. This exhausted the soil, and hurricanes stripped the island at not infrequent intervals. When cotton culture ceased to pay, the fields were abandoned, and today such parts of the islands as the Negroes do not use for their potato patches and pasturage are covered with a scrubby second growth and ruins of old plantation houses. Large trees for making dugout canoes of the size that Columbus described no longer exist. Near an inland lagoon of San Salvador we were shown a surviving grove of primeval forest which for lushness and beauty merits Columbus's praise, and this grove harbors a variety of tropical woodpecker that must once have had a wider forest range. Skeletal remains of other birds which could only have lived among dense foliage have been discovered on the island by naturalists.

All day Saturday, October 13, the caravels lay at anchor in Long Bay with a swarm of canoes passing back and forth, while the Spaniards in turn took shore leave, wandered into the natives' huts, did a little private trading for the curios that all seamen love, and doubtless ascertained that the girls of Guanahaní were much like others they had known. Columbus, who ever had an eye for "improvements," reported that he found "a quarry of stones naturally shaped, very fair for church edifices or other public uses." Three centuries elapsed before anyone thought to build a church at San Salvador, and then it was found easier to fashion the soft coral rock into rectangular blocks; the outcrop that Columbus saw at Hall's Landing just north of his landing place, partly under water and curiously split into squares like flagstones, is still unquarried.

The Admiral was busy gathering such information as he could from signs and gestures; his Arabic interpreter was of no use in this neck of the Indies. On Saturday night he decided that no time must be lost, he must press on to Japan. But first San Salvador must be explored. On Sunday morning the three ships' boats took the Admiral north along the leeward coast "to see the other side, which was the eastern side, what was there, and also to see the villages; and soon I saw two or three, and the people all came to the beach, shouting and giving thanks to God. Some brought us water; others, things to eat. Others, when they saw that I did not care to go ashore, plunged into the sea swimming and came aboard, and we understood that they asked us if we had come from Heaven. And one old man got into the boat, and others shouted in loud voices to all, men and women, 'Come and see the men who come from Heaven, bring them food and drink.' Many came and many women, each with something, giving thanks to God, throwing themselves flat and raising their hands to Heaven, and then shouting to us to come ashore; but I was afraid to, from seeing a great reef of rocks which surrounded the whole of this island, but inside it was deep and a harbor to hold all the ships in Christendom, and the entrance of it very narrow."

This was the place now known as Grahams Harbor, formed by the reefs that surround the island coming together in an inverted V. At three or four places the reefs rise high enough to form cays, and beside one of these on the western side, Green Cay, is a good boat channel with 7 feet of water. Here, rather than the alternate High Reef channel, which is difficult for a stranger to find, was probably where the boats entered. "Inside there are some shoal spots," Columbus correctly observed, "but the sea moves no more than within a well." The smooth water inside these coral-reef harbors is always a pleasant surprise to mariners.

Glenn Stewart's yacht lay quietly and safely in Grahams Harbor during a heavy norther in January 1930.

Columbus's boats rowed across the harbor, about two miles to the eastward, where they found a rocky peninsula that thrusts out from the northern side of San Salvador, half of it almost an island, and "which in two days could be made an island," suitable for a fortress. Since Columbus's visit the sea has here broken a narrow channel that one can wade across at low water. Someone, probably the English, took up Columbus's suggestion that the place was a natural fortress, for Dr. Cronau found an iron cannon there in 1891. After inspecting the harbor the boats returned to the vessels at their anchorage in Long Bay, a row of some twenty miles going and coming; and in the early afternoon the fleet made sail for Cipangu.

So ended forty-eight hours of the most wonderful experience that perhaps any seamen have ever had. Other discoveries there have been more spectacular than that of this small, flat sandy island that rides out ahead of the American continent, breasting the trade winds. But it was there that the Ocean for the first time "loosed the chains of things" as Seneca had prophesied, gave up the secret that had baffled Europeans since they began to inquire what lay beyond the western horizon's rim. Stranger people than the gentle Tainos, more exotic plants than the green verdure of Guanahaní have been discovered, even by the Portuguese before Columbus; but the discovery of Africa was but an unfolding of a continent already glimpsed, whilst San Salvador, rising from the sea at the end of a thirty-three-day westward sail, was a clean break with past experience. Every tree, every plant that the Spaniards saw was strange to them, and the natives were not only strange but completely unexpected, speaking an unknown tongue and resembling no race of which even the most educated of the explorers had read in the tales of travelers from Herodotus to Marco Polo. Never again may mortal men hope to recapture the amazement, the wonder, the delight of those October days in 1492 when the New World gracefully yielded her virginity to the conquering Castilians.

CHAPTER XVII

The Quest for Japan

October 14–28, 1492

Rex insule palacium magnum habet auro optimo supratectum sicut apud nos ecclesie operiuntur plumbo. Fenestre ipsius palacij omnes auro ornate sunt; pauimentum aularum atque camerarum multarum aureis tabulis est coopertum, que quidem auree tabule duorum digitorum mensuram in grossitudine pertinent. Ibi sunt margarite in copia maxima. . . .

The king of the Island [Japan] hath a mighty palace all roofed with finest gold, just as our churches are roofed with lead. The windows of that palace are all decorated with gold; the floors of the halls and of many chambers are paved with golden plates, each plate a good two fingers thick. There are pearls in the greatest abundance. . . .
— COLUMBUS'S OWN COPY OF *Marco Polo* fol. 57

WAS this island really of the Indies? That must have been the first question Columbus asked himself on reaching Guanahaní, and the last question that he asked himself about all his discoveries, when sailing for home. Or was it but an island in the Atlantic like Antillia? One may say that all the Admiral's voyaging for the next six years was a search for evidence that would enable him to answer that second, teasing question with a thumping "No!" San Salvador must be of the Indies, for it was where the Indies should be; and the definite clue that fairly shouted "Indies!" at every man in the fleet was gold. Not much of it to be sure, only little pieces of gold "hanging from a thing like a needle-case which they wear in the nose," but certainly gold, and so of the Indies. — Do you not remember, my Lord Admiral, that the Portuguese who reported Antillia to Prince Henry brought back gold? — Ah no, this cannot be Antillia, it is too far away, and the people are not Portuguese; it must not be Antillia. — Yet this Guanahaní cannot be Japan, great golden Cipangu, inhabited by white and civilized people, Cipangu of the royal palaces roofed, paved, and pierced with gold? — Granted, but who said that Cipangu was the only island in the Indies?

On two world maps of the fifteenth century that show Cipangu, the Genoese of 1457 and the Behaim Globe of 1492, it lies (for so Marco Polo had reported) some 1500 miles off the coast of China. North of it is an archipelago of islands large and small. Columbus wished to believe and did believe that he had reached the edge of this archipelago, through which his fleet might sail in a southwesterly direction to strike Cipangu; if Japan were missed, they must fetch up on the coast of China. It was clear that the little gold ornaments displayed by the natives of Guanahaní came from somewhere else. The names *Cipangu, Cathay, Gran Can* rang no bell in the simple minds of the savages, eager as they were to please; but by signs they gave the Admiral to understand that other islands, perhaps a continent, lay all around the horizon arc between northwest and south. Somewhere in that direction must be Cipangu. So Columbus concluded his Journal for October 13, "I intend to go and see if I can find the Island of Japan." All the rest of his First Voyage was, in fact, a search for gold and Cipangu, Cathay and the Grand Khan; but gold in any event. In all else he might fail, but gold he must bring home in order to prove *la empresa* a success.

So it was in quest of Japan that the fleet sailed SW from San Salvador on the afternoon of October 14. Columbus was a bit puzzled what course to take, for the six Indians whom he had detained as guides and future interpreters swept their arms in a wide arc around the western and southern horizon, "and called by their names more than a hundred" islands. Southwest was evidently the average course that Columbus selected from these swivel-like indications. Under easy sail the fleet jogged along before a moderate trade. In the later afternoon, when about 15 miles from San Salvador, they sighted what appeared to be a string of six islands, and the Admiral gave orders to steer for the biggest. As they approached nearer, the six parts seemed to join, for they were all hillocks of a single island. Unable to reach this six-in-one island before dark, the fleet lay-to that night, filled away at dawn, and at noon made land. Columbus named this second island of his discovery *Santa María de la Concepción* after a doctrine to which he was devoted, the Immaculate Conception of the Virgin. The modern name is Rum Cay.

Columbus describes this island as ten leagues long and five leagues wide. This is the first instance of what we shall find numerous examples of his using, when sailing alongshore, a different league from the sea league of 3.18 nautical miles. Whenever Columbus estimated distances run at sea, he was usually accurate within 10 per cent. But when he was estimating the length of a coastline, he used, consciously or unconsciously, a league of about 1½ nautical miles.

Monday, October 15, must have been an unusually clear day since from off the southeast point of Rum Cay Columbus "saw another bigger one to the west." That was Long Island, distant 22 miles. Columbus coasted along the south shore of Rum Cay, and about sunset anchored under Sandy Point, at the southwest end. It certainly did not look much like Cipangu; but as Columbus had gathered from his unwilling guides that the people ashore sported heavy gold armlets and anklets, the island had to be investigated. On Tuesday morning at daybreak the Admiral went ashore with the boats, and ascertained that the natives were numerous, naked, and in all respects like those of San Salvador. They "let us go over the island and gave us what we asked for." Gold armlets and anklets there were none; that story was evidently "all humbug"; the San Salvadoreans merely wished him to anchor at Rum Cay "in order to escape." One of them had swum ashore the previous night; and while the Admiral was ashore another Guanahaní boy jumped into a Rum Cay canoe that came alongside. Her crew paddled away much too fast for the Spaniards to catch them in their heavy ship's boat. The pursuit continued ashore, but "they all ran away like chickens" says Columbus. While this exciting chase was under way, a small canoe from another cape of the island came alongside *Niña*, with a single native who wished to sell a skein of cotton. The sailors seized him as a substitute for the escaped Salvadorean; but the Admiral, observing this from the poop of *Santa María*, ordered him to be brought aboard the flagship, presented him with the standard red cap, glass beads and hawks' bells, and sent him ashore happy. "For this reason I used him thus," wrote Columbus, "in order that they might hold us in such esteem that on another occasion when your Highnesses send men back here again, they [the natives] may not make bad company." Unfortunately the Admiral's kindly acts to the Indians only rendered them less prepared to cope with the kidnapers who followed him. The next Spaniard that came to these parts was Alonso de Hojeda on a slaving raid.

These alarums and excursions came fairly early in the morning of October 16. The Indian guides, in no wise discomfited because their previous information was incorrect, now cheerfully assured Columbus that in the island already sighted to the westward "there is a lot of gold, and they wear it in the form of bracelets on the arms, legs, ears, nose and neck." In the forenoon the wind shifted to the SE and veered southerly, making the Rum Cay anchorage untenable, so Columbus ordered anchors aweigh. All day the fleet ghosted westward in light southerly airs. In mid-channel the flagship picked up a native in a single canoe, who evidently came from San Salvador, as he had a string of glass beads and two small coins in a native basket; he also carried "a lump of bright red earth powdered and then kneaded," doubtless body paint, "and some dry leaves which must be something much valued by them, since they offered me some at San Salvador as a gift." Tobacco leaves, almost certainly; but the Spaniards did not observe anyone smoking until they reached Cuba. This native was fed and given a free ride to the next island, where he was released.

Columbus named this island *Fernandina* after the King of Castile and Aragon. That regal derivative has long since disappeared in favor of the common appellation Long Island, which fits this island better than most of that name, for it is 60 miles long and in no place more than 4 miles wide. Columbus reported Fernandina to be "very level, without any mountains like those of San Salvador and Santa María"; but to us, approaching it from the same angle, it presented the same appearance of a disconnected chain of small, hilly islands. The Admiral accurately described the windward shore as "all beach without boulders" except for "some rocks under water near the shore, for which you must keep your eyes peeled when you wish to anchor, and not anchor very near the shore, although the water is always very clear and you see the bottom . . . for here it is necessary to take great care in order not to lose the anchors." Columbus was making the acquaintance of that bane of Bahamian navigators, the pinnacle of coral rock that rises unexpectedly from a clean bottom. These "nigger heads" shear off any anchor cable that fouls them, and punch holes in any wooden vessel so unfortunate as to run upon them. "And among all these islands," he justly adds, "at a distance of two lombard shots * off shore there is so much depth that you can't find bottom." His dipsey lead line, as we have seen, measured 100 fathoms, but the windward shore of Long Island drops off so sharply that the hydrographers have not bothered to sound along it, and the channel between Long Island and Rum Cay runs to 1400 fathoms, over a mile and a half deep.

Off a village somewhere near the present Burnt Ground the fleet closed with the Long Island shore, but was unable to come to an anchorage by daylight, and lay-to for the night. Columbus sent ashore the wayfarer, who gave Long Island natives such a good account of these "men from Heaven" that a fleet of canoes at once came out with "water and what they had." Water is an article of value in the Bahamas because there is not a single river

---

* Comparing Columbus's frequent measurements by lombard shots, the distance. that his larger cannon could fire, this unit seems to have varied between 500 and 1000 yards.

or stream in the entire archipelago — not even Ponce de León's fountain of youth; fresh water can only be had by collecting rain water or digging wells. The volunteer water carriers were given beads, brass tambourine jingles and lace points (the metal tips of the laces then used instead of buttons on men's clothing); and those who came aboard were treated to molasses. It is difficult now to imagine that there ever was a time when molasses was a curiosity in the West Indies; but many years elapsed before the Spaniards brought the sugar cane from Africa, and the only sweetening that the Tainos had was wild honey.

At nine the next morning (October 17) the flagship's boat was sent ashore for water, and the natives led the seamen to the wells and obligingly carried the full casks to the boats. These helpful acts on the part of the Indians, which occurred in most places where the Spaniards landed, were unfortunate for the Indians. Columbus himself remarked before the end of the voyage, "Nothing was lacking but to know the language and to give them orders, because every order that was given to them they would obey without opposition." Every man in the fleet from servant boy to Admiral was convinced that no Christian need do a hand's turn of work in the Indies; and before them opened the delightful vision of growing rich by exploiting the labor of docile natives.

Columbus noted the absence on Long Island of sheep, goats, or any animal life except birds; and the absence of mammals is one of the features of West Indian fauna. He viewed for the first time a patch of Indian corn, which he supposed to be a kind of panic grass; and marveled at the brightly colored fishes that swam about the flagship, easily visible in the clear water. He observed that the natives wore short cloaks of woven cotton, and that unlike those of San Salvador, they had some idea of driving a bargain. Perhaps the released canoeman had given them the tip that "men from Heaven" were more cheerful receivers than givers. The anticipated gold armlets and anklets did not appear. They were always at the next island.

As a result of his shore visit, Columbus reported an extraordinary sort of tree that had "branches of different kinds, all on one trunk, and one twig is of one kind and another of another, and so unlike that it is the greatest wonder in the world. . . . For instance, one branch has leaves like a cane, other like mastic; and thus on one tree five or six kinds, and all so different." Of course no plant even approaches this polymorphy; Columbus must have observed a tree full of the different parasites that are common in the West Indies. Apart from this tall story, his reports of natural phenomena are objective and accurate. And that they were so is to be commended; for Marco Polo, Sir John Mandeville and their imitators had made Europeans expect any traveler returning from unknown parts to report marvels and monsters, such as fish growing on trees, tailed men, and headless people with eyes in their bellies. Columbus knew perfectly well what was expected, indeed hoped to see such things; but he invented nothing, and only rarely was tempted to twist or exaggerate a bit in order to satisfy his Sovereigns' thirst for the marvelous.

Since the previous evening the fleet had been standing off-and-on, as the lee shore was so steep-to as to make anchoring unsafe. At noon October 17 the fleet got under way with a light offshore wind, intending to steer SE for Crooked Island, which the Indians called *Saomete*. But Martín Alonso boarded the flagship insisting that the shortest way to Saomete was to sail around Long Island to the NNW, so one of the captives had given him to understand. Very bad advice, or a misunderstanding, since nothing larger than a boat can pass around the leeward side of Long Island. Nevertheless Columbus decided to try it, as the wind was fair for this course and foul for the other. "And when I was distant from the island cape [Cape St. Maria] 2 leagues, I discovered a very wonderful harbor with . . . two mouths, for it has an islet in the middle, and both are very narrow, and within it is wide enough for a hundred ships, if it were deep" — which unfortunately it was not. But "there seemed good reason to look it over well and take soundings, so I anchored outside and went in with all the ships' boats, and saw that there was no depth."

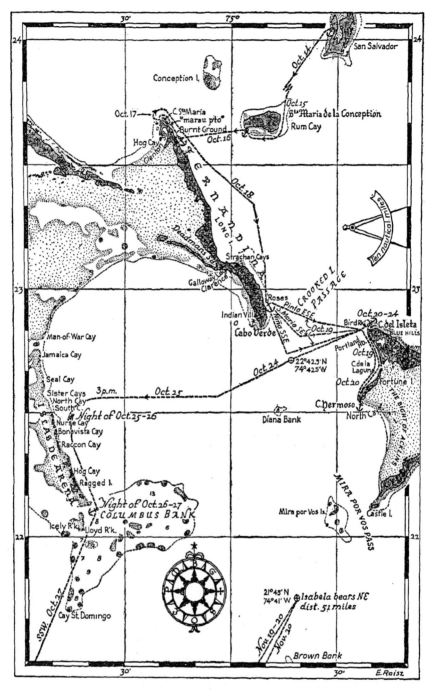

COURSE OF COLUMBUS'S FLEET
THROUGH THE BAHAMAS

This *maravilloso puerto* is not shown on modern charts, but is easily identified by those who have sailed there. It is a harbor with two entrances, one each side of an island called Newtor Cay, and with a maximum depth of about a fathom. Columbus rather stupidly assumed this shallow harbor to be the mouth of a great river, and sent the boats within for more water, which they obtained at a village well.

The watering party visited in several natives' houses, and reported that "their beds and furnishings were like nets of cotton." "These," comments Las Casas, "are here in Hispaniola called *hamacas*, which are in the form of slings, not woven like nets with the threads going zigzag, but the lengthwise threads are so loose that you can insert the hand and fingers, and at a hand's breadth more or less they are crossed with other close-woven threads like well made lace-trimmings, in the manner of the sieves which in Seville are made of esparto-grass. These hammocks are a good *estado* * in fullness or length, and the two ends are finished off in many loops of the same threads, in each of which are inserted some delicate threads of another substance stouter than cotton, like hemp; and each of these is a fathom long. And at the head all these loops are joined together as in a sword hilt, which at each end is attached to the posts of the houses, and thus the hammocks are off the ground and swing in the air; and as the good ones are three and four *varas* † and more in width one opens them when they swing as we should open a very big sling, putting oneself in diagonally as in an angle; and thus there is the rest of the hammock with which to cover oneself, and that is sufficient because it is never cold. It is very restful to sleep in."

Every successive navigator in the West Indies noted and admired the hammock. The Spaniards, first to experience its convenience in a hot climate, were the first to introduce it aboard ship; the hammock is just going out in the United States navy. Big family hammocks woven in several colors as Las Casas describes are still used

---

* Five and a half feet.
† Eight to eleven feet.

by the natives of Yucatán and elsewhere in Central America.

While the watering party was away Columbus wandered about the shores of this marvelous harbor (which no Spaniard to our knowledge ever revisited) and made some observations of his own. The native dwellings he compared in shape to Moorish tents "very high and with good chimneys," these being a sort of open cupola to let the smoke out. His men reported them to be "very simple and clean inside," a reflection of the contrary quality in Castilian hovels. The natives were much the same as those already encountered; "the married women wore clouts of cotton, the wenches nothing." They kept pet dogs — the barkless kind, of which more anon — and one man wore a big gold nose-plug which Columbus was eager to possess because it seemed to have letters which he suspected to be the inscription on a Japanese or Chinese coin. But the fellow would not part with it, and Columbus was too scrupulous to take it by force. The vegetation of Fernandina aroused the Admiral's enthusiasm; he assured the Sovereigns that it was "the best and most fertile and temperate and level and goodly land that there is in the world." Poor Long Island! Nobody has praised you like that since 1492; most of your visitors nowadays are glad to leave your shallow harbors, arid soil, impoverished pastures and scrubby vegetation.

"After taking on water," says Columbus, "I returned to the ship and made sail, and sailed to the NW until I had explored all that part of the island along the coast which runs east-west." In other words, he rounded the Aeolian limestone cliffs of Cape St. Maria, and sailed far enough to see the coast of Long Island falling away to the southwestward. The wind now veered to WNW, and the fickle or misunderstood Indian guides now insisted that the shortest route to Saometè lay in the contrary direction, which was correct. So the fleet came about at nightfall, and all that night, an oppressive and rainy one, steered E, ESE and SE in order to keep clear of the land. "There was little wind, and it did not permit me to approach the land to anchor." "And all these days since I've been in the Indies it has rained more or less," says the Admiral. This little sentence is significant on two counts. It is the first place in his Journal since the landfall that Columbus uses the term "Indies" for the Bahamas; and it is the first meteorological report of the New World. The rainy season had set in.

Daybreak October 18 found the fleet "at the SE cape of the island, where I hope to anchor until it clears off, to see the other islands to which I have to go." By the southeast cape he must have meant the southerly third of Long Island, from the Strachan Cays onward. "After it cleared up I followed the wind and went around the island as far as I could, and anchored in weather such that I could no longer sail; but I did not go ashore." This anchorage must have been off or very near the village of Roses.

At daybreak on the nineteenth, about 5 A.M., Columbus ordered the anchors broken out, and dispatched his fleet fanwise in search of Saomete: *Pinta* to the ESE, *Niña* to the SSE, and *Santa María* between them to the SE. The caravels had orders to proceed on their respective courses until noon, when they should converge on the flagship, unless land were sighted earlier. Wind came fresh out of the north. At about 8 A.M. *Pinta*, having made 14 or 15 miles from the Long Island anchorage, sighted the Blue Hills of Crooked Island (elevation 200 feet) bearing about E by S, distant 20 miles. *Santa María* was about 5 miles to leeward, and *Niña* as far again; but Columbus had a system of signaling by gunfire, so they were able to communicate. All three altered course for Saomete, which Columbus named *Isabela* after his royal patroness. Before noon the fleet made rendezvous off the islet now called Bird Rock, and which now supports a high and powerful lighthouse to guide vessels through Crooked Island Passage.

This passage, which Columbus had just crossed, is now one of the world's most frequented waterways, through which steamers from North Atlantic ports of the United States pass on their way to Eastern Cuba, Southern Hispaniola, Jamaica, and the mainland from Costa Rica to Venezuela. While we in the *Mary Otis* were hove-to in the passage on the night of June 10–11, 1940, within the orbit of Bird Rock Light's split-second flash (for we failed to

time our departure as Columbus did), the running lights of steamers
kept our watch on the alert. But we shared one delight with the
men of 1492. The wind that night was offshore, and "there came
so fair and sweet a smell of flowers or trees from the land, that it
was the sweetest thing in the world," as Columbus observed.

Santa María and *Pinta* paused off Bird Rock only long enough
for *Niña* to catch up; fortunately the wind held north, so she was
able to fetch. The fleet then squared their yards and coasted along
the curve of Crooked and Fortune Islands, a distance of about 18
miles, to the southern point of Fortune, which to Columbus
seemed so exceptionally beautiful that he named it Cabo Hermoso.
"And it is indeed handsome," says the Admiral, "round and low-
lying, with no shoals offshore . . . and here I anchored this night
Friday until morning." The south end of Fortune Island is bold,
and the anchorage there is still recommended for its excellent holding ground — it is amazing how often Columbus found the best
anchorages. But nobody would call that end of Fortune Island
hermoso today. Low cliffs of dark, weathered Aeolian limestone,
which is far from a beautiful rock, interspersed with a few small
sand beaches, support a plateau that is covered with scrubby trees
and bushes. The hill on Fortune Island, which Columbus praised
as "a thing that beautifies the rest — not that it can be called a
mountain," is green and shapely; but both island and cape must
have been covered with an exceptionally fine growth of tropical
hardwood in 1492 to have aroused such enthusiasm on the part of
Columbus. Fortune Island "is the most beautiful thing that I have
seen," he wrote, "nor can I tire my eyes looking at such handsome
verdure, so very different from ours. And I believe that there are
in it many plants and many trees which are worth a lot in Spain
for dyes, and for medicines of spicery; but I do not recognize
them, which gives me great grief." Columbus often wished that
he had shipped a botanist instead of a Hebrew interpreter on this
voyage. But his guess about the dye wood was correct. The Bahamas were once rich in logwood; a shipload of it from Eleuthera
in 1641 paid for a house and lot in the Harvard College Yard.

From his anchorage off the south cape of Fortune Island (which he did not name although he noted that it was separated from Crooked Island) Columbus looked into the great protected sound now known as the Bight of Acklins, but could find no channel to enter. The Bight is very shoal. So at sunrise on Saturday, October 20, the fleet weighed and proceeded to the anchorage (still recommended in official Sailing Directions) off the gap between Crooked and Fortune Islands. Columbus hoped to enter the Bight of Acklins at this point, which he named *Cabo de la Laguna*, and to proceed across the lagoon to Acklin Island, where his pressed guides said he would find the king who owned so many golden vessels. But there was even less water here than at Cabo Hermoso, so the Admiral decided to try and sail around Crooked Island by its outer coast. Before dark the fleet put to sea again. The wind flattened out, and *Santa María* lay-to that night; the caravels misunderstood the Admiral's signals and anchored close to the shore. Sunday morning the twenty-first at 10 o'clock the whole fleet arrived at the Cape of the Islet, as Columbus named the northwestern cape of Crooked Island, and anchored in Portland Harbor, the small and well-protected anchorage between the cape and Bird Rock. Wind had veered to the eastward, so there was no use trying to proceed further in that direction.

Here the Admiral and his captains made a shore excursion. They saw marvelous verdure, grass like springtime in Andalusia, air full of birdsong, flocks of parrots that "obscured the sun," and a great salt lagoon, on the edge of which they hunted and killed a large iguana. The only plant that Columbus thought he recognized was aloes; but as aloes was not introduced into America until the following century he must have seen one of the agaves, such as the Bahama Century Plant. All natives fled from the only village that the explorers encountered. One native, bolder than the rest, approached to receive the usual handout of beads and bells, and then showed the Christians where to fill their ever-empty water casks.

After a good day's work this Sunday, Columbus sat down and wrote exactly what he intended to do next.

"I here propose to leave to circumnavigate this island until I may have speech with this king and see if I can obtain from him the gold that I heard he has, and afterwards to depart for another much larger island which I believe must be Japan according to the descriptions of these Indians whom I carry, and which they call *Colba*, in which they say that there are ships and sailors both many and great; and beyond this is another island which they call *Bofio*, which also they say is very big; and the others which are between we shall see as we pass, and according as I shall find a collection of gold or spicery, I shall decide what I have to do. But in any case I am determined to go to the mainland and to the city of Quinsay, and to present your Highnesses' letters to the Grand Khan, and to beg a reply and come home with it."

It is clear that by now the captive guides had grasped that gold was what the men from Heaven were after. Very likely their former false directions had been due to a misunderstanding. Having observed the Christians taking specimens of plants and going over everything in the native houses in search of gold, the simple savages perhaps thought that they were collecting leaves, earthenware and hammocks, of which there were plenty everywhere. Now the Indians decided to take their inexplicable captors to "Colba" (Cuba) by the regular canoe route; and from Cuba they could visit Haiti, where there really was gold, plenty of it. The word *bofio* or *bohio*, which Columbus later identified with Haiti, was really, as Las Casas explains, the Arawak word for "house" or "home"; the palm-thatched huts of the peasantry are still called *bohios* in Cuba. Columbus's guide-interpreters were either trying to say that in Haiti there were big *bohios*, or were endeavoring to convey the idea that Haiti was their mother country. Columbus, from their gestures and misunderstood phrases, believed Colba to be Japan, and Bohío to be another big island unknown to Marco Polo. He proposed, after visiting them both, to go on to Quinsay (Hangchow), the "City of Heaven" that Marco Polo described in such glowing terms that for Europe it had become a symbol of the fabulous wealth of the Indies. Quinsay, located on Martin Behaim's Globe just around the corner from Zaitun, would be easy to hit if the fleet missed Cipangu. Unfortunately they had wested only 56° of longitude since leaving Ferro, and had 186° to go before making Quinsay, with America between.

Having decided on this course, Columbus made no attempt to buck the trades and circumnavigate the Crooked-Acklin group. The fleet lay in Portland Harbor over Sunday and Monday, October 21 and 22, "waiting to see if the king here or other people would bring gold or anything substantial." A crowd of natives paddled out, and a few gold nose-plugs were swopped for a hawk's bell or a handful of beads; "but there's so little that it amounts to nothing at all," wrote Columbus. Martín Alonso killed another big iguana, and the men cut a load of useless agave under the impression that it was valuable lignum aloes.

Columbus was ready to sail Tuesday the twenty-third, but there was a dead calm with rain. At midnight a breeze sprang up, and "I weighed anchors from the island of Isabela, Cape of the Islet, which is on the northern side where I was lying, to go to the island of Cuba, which I heard from this people is of very great extent and trade, and has gold, spices, big ships and merchants, and they showed me that to the WSW would lead to it. And to my course I held, for I believe that . . . it is the island of Japan, of which are related marvellous things; and on the globes that I saw,* and in the delineations on the world-map it is in this region. And so I sailed until day to the WSW."

It was now October 24, and again he was crossing Crooked Island Passage. At daybreak the wind dropped flat, and only revived at noon, very feebly. As *Santa María* in a light breeze was at a disadvantage compared with the caravels, Columbus like a true seaman set every sail he had: main course with two bonnets, maintopsail, fore course, spritsail under the bowsprit, lateen mizzen, and even a bonaventure mizzen on the poop, contrived out

---

* An interesting admission that Columbus had seen a globe which must have resembled Martin Behaim's.

of the boat's mast and sail. But by nightfall, when Columbus reported "Cabo Verde of the island of Fernandina, which is at the western point of the southern end," bearing NW distant 7 leagues, the fleet had made only 21 miles from Bird Rock.

Columbus then signaled the fleet to strike all sail except the fore courses; and later, when the wind freshened, stripped down to bare poles. He explained for the Sovereigns' benefit what all good seamen knew, that it would have been imprudent to carry sail at night "because all these islands are very steep-to, with no bottom around them except within two lombard shots, and this all patchy, a bit of rock and another of sand, for which reason it is not possible to anchor safely except by eyesight." The hunters' moon was only four days old, affording little light and setting early. That night "we did not make two leagues," he says.

At sunrise October 25 the fleet made sail and resumed the WSW course. At 9 A.M., presumably on the advice of his Indian guides who were anxious to pick up the line of cays that marked their canoe route to Cuba, the Admiral changed course to West. The trade wind blew fresh that day, so that at 3 P.M., after logging 32 miles, "they sighted land, and there were seven or eight islands strung out north to south." These were the line of cays (Seal, Sister, North, South, Nurse) that mark the eastern edge of the Great Bahama Bank. Columbus named them *Las Islas de Arena*, the Sandy Isles, which is just what they are. Approaching the nearest, he either hove-to or jogged along during the night, and on the twenty-sixth sailed slowly along the line of islands until he found himself in shoal water to the southward of the last of them, Little Ragged Island. At this point the Great Bahama Bank makes a fluke-like salient to the south and east, which has appropriately been named Columbus Bank after the Discoverer. It was now the afternoon of Friday, October 26. The Indians aboard said that from there to Cuba was a journey of a day and a half in their canoes; Columbus figured that his fleet could do it in less, but as he wished to cross the bank in daylight he decided to anchor there and make a fresh start at sunrise. "Departed thence for

Cuba," reads the Journal, "because from the signs that the Indians made of its greatness and of its gold and pearls, he thought it was Japan."

If this seems a peculiar course to take for Cuba, the explanation came to us readily enough when we followed it in the *Mary Otis*. Columbus was in the hands of his pressed Indian guides, who only knew the way from cay to cay, making the shortest possible jump over blue water. At sunrise on Saturday, October 27, the Admiral, following their pointed arms, set the course SSW. By eight o'clock the trade wind freshened, and the fleet fairly tore over Columbus Bank for 16 or 17 miles at 6 knots, leaving Icely and Lloyd's rocks close aboard and passing into deep water by Santo Domingo Cay, most southerly outpost of the Bahamas, a scant 30 miles from the Cuban coast. The wind moderated in the afternoon, and the Admiral was just able to sight the Cuban mountains by nightfall.

That night he jogged off-and-on, taking short tacks to windward in order to hold his position and avoid possible shoals. At sunrise on Sunday the twenty-eighth the fleet resumed the SSW course, which took them "into a river very beautiful and without danger of shoals or other impediments, and the whole coast that he came upon in that direction was very steep-to and clear up to the shore. The mouth of the river has 12 fathoms, and is wide enough to beat in. He anchored inside."

"The Admiral says that he never beheld so fair a thing; trees all along the river, beautiful and green and different from ours, with flowers and fruits each according to their kind, and little birds which sing very sweetly." But no ivory and alabaster cities rose golden-crowned from the strand, no gentlemen of Japan in gold-stiffened brocade awaited the Christians on marble jetties, no lords and ladies advanced in screened palanquins over curved stone bridges, no temple bells clanged, no silver trumpets brayed, no dragon-mouthed bronze cannon roared. Certainly this was not Japan, unless Marco Polo was a liar.

Could it be Cathay, and was the "City of Heaven" around the next cape?

CHAPTER XVIII

Pursuit of the Grand Khan

October 28–November 20, 1492

Beati oculi qui vident quae vos videtis. Dico enim vobis,
quod multi prophetae et reges voluerunt videre quae vos
videtis, et non viderunt. . . .

Blessed are the eyes which see the things that ye see: For
I tell you, that many prophets and kings have desired to see
those things which ye see, and have not seen them. . . .

— LUKE X 23, 24

AS Columbus had named the two larger islands of the Bahamas
after Ferdinand and Isabella, so he christened *Juana* this
land that the Indians called Cuba, after the heir to the throne of
Castile and Aragon, the Infante Don Juan.

Almost every town and village of the beautiful Oriente Province
of Cuba from Baracoa to Puerto Padre, as well as Nuevitas in the
Province of Camagüey, claims to be the San Salvador that Columbus entered on October 28, 1492. There is no doubt in our
minds, after following his SSW course from the Ragged Islands,
that San Salvador was Bahía Bariay. As Columbus says, that harbor
is approached "without danger of shoals or other impediments."
It is wide enough — three quarters of a mile — to tack in, and the
curve of 12 *brazas* (11 of our fathoms), which Columbus gives
as the depth, swings well within the two headlands. Mangrove
trees cover the beaches inside as Columbus observed, and mountains rise from the country behind. One of these reminded him
of the Peña de los Enamorados in the kingdom of Granada, the
Lovers' Leap whence Christian Manuel and Moorish Laila leapt
to their death when pursued by angry father. Another mountain,
unmistakable as a landmark for Bahía Bariay, "has on its summit

another little peak like a pretty little mosque" (*una hermosa mezquita*). The Spanish pioneers of Cuba, with more homely realism and less poetry than Columbus, named it *La Teta de Bariay*. There is not another such mountain east of Baracoa.

After the impressed Indian pilots, no doubt unintentionally, had filled the Admiral with high hopes of encountering Chinese junks at anchor off a great stone city of the Grand Khan, the reality of Bahía Bariay was a bit depressing. Columbus went ashore in the first

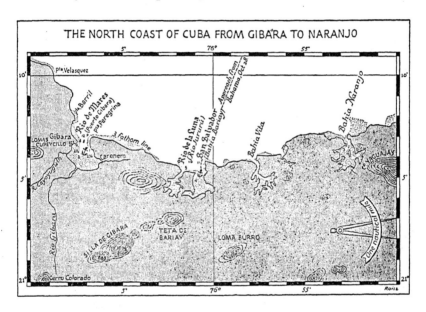

THE NORTH COAST OF CUBA FROM GIBARA TO NARANJO

boat, but found no trace of human beings except some fishermen's palm-thatched *bohíos* containing palm-fiber nets, bone fishhooks and harpoons, and "a dog that didn't bark." These small dumb dogs, which the Spaniards observed throughout the Antilles, were not a special breed of canine, but common yellow "hound dogs" that the Tainos domesticated largely for eating purposes. They gave a sort of grunt instead of a proper bark, and were completely useless as guardians of the home. Michele de Cuneo, the Genoese gentleman who accompanied Columbus on his Second Voyage, said that roast barkless dog was "none too good"; but Oviedo declares that the *perros mudos* became extinct because the Spaniards liked their flavor only too well. Some escaped to the forest, reverted to species and became such a nuisance to farmers that they were hunted down in the last century.

Columbus had the men row him up the river where "the grass was as high as in Andalusia in April and May," and he saw purslane and amaranth and palms unlike those of Africa, and it was "a great pleasure to see those green things and groves of trees, and to hear the birds sing," so that he could hardly bear to turn back. But natural beauty was nothing he could take home. So on Monday, October 29, the fleet weighed and sailed westward for the City of Quinsay. It was almost noon when they got under way, and the wind was light. After passing a river "not so wide at the entrance" which the Admiral named Rio de la Luna, they reached "at the hour of vespers," "another river much greater than the others," on the shores of which was a large village. Columbus named this bay *Rio de Mares*. It was the best harbor he had yet seen in the Indies, and he predicted — this time correctly — that it would become a place of importance for trade. Rio de Mares, "River of Seas," was undoubtedly Puerto Gibara.

On the western shore of this harbor was a large Indian village, the huts reminding the Spaniards of tents in a Moorish camp; and these were eagerly searched by the first landing party in quest of gold. None was found. Columbus does not mention finding a single gold object in Cuba, nor have any been excavated; it is a wonder he still believed anything that his Indians said. But they were useful as interpreters, for the same language prevailed in Cuba and Haiti as in the Bahamas. One in particular, who lived to reach Spain (where he was baptized Diego Colón) and who made the whole Second Voyage with the Admiral, became indispensable. As yet Diego had not picked up enough Castilian to be a two-way interpreter; but he could assure the natives that his captors were good people, and had an interesting line of trading goods. That was sufficient.

The westward search for the Grand Khan did not last long. An easy day's sail from Puerto Gibara took the fleet to a cape covered with palms, undoubtedly Punta Uvero which is conspicuous for palms today. The wind then unseasonably backed to the westward. All night October 30–31 the fleet beat to windward, and on the next day, still close-hauled, saw "an inlet or bay where small vessels could lie" and an outjutting cape, either Punta Cobarrubia or Punta Brava. By morning the wind had veered to the northward and the temperature dropped; a typical Caribbean winter norther was making up. And so, because it was impossible with a north wind to sail along a coast trending NNW, and dangerous to attempt it, Columbus ordered the fleet to come about and scud back to the Rio de Mares. A night sail over waters traversed before, especially with a moon past first quarter, offered no difficulty. They arrived at Puerto Gibara about dawn on November 1, and there remained for eleven days.

Columbus's first object was to acquire the confidence of the natives, in the hope of finding out where gold could be had and the Grand Khan located. After Diego the interpreter had reassured the local Tainos, a brisk exchange began of trading truck for food, cotton and hammocks. The natives, eager to please, unwittingly fed Columbus's delusion that he was hot on the trail of the Chinese emperor, not far from the "noble city of Zaitun" and Quinsay, the City of Heaven. Las Casas has a plausible explanation of how the Admiral was misled by his helpful hosts. A district in the interior of Cuba where a limited quantity of gold existed was called by the natives *Cubanacan* (mid-Cuba). Whenever Columbus produced a gold object and asked where more could be found, the natives pronounced this word, which he mistook for *El Gran Can*. Perhaps they simply mistook the Spaniards' dumb-show of imperial majesty for a desire to meet their cacique, who resided near the present town of Holguín, about 25 miles from Gibara up the pretty valley of the Cacoyuguin.

So the Admiral prepared with pathetic punctilio an embassy to visit the Emperor of China at Holguín. The official interpreter Luis de Torres, a converted Jew "who knew Hebrew and Aramaic and even some Arabic," was made the head of it; and to him were intrusted all the diplomatic paraphernalia: Latin passport, Latin letter of credence from Ferdinand and Isabella, and a royal gift, the nature of which unfortunately we do not know. He was accompanied by Rodrigo de Xeres, who had visited a Negro king in Guinea, by a local Indian and one from Guanahaní; samples of spicery were taken to compare with local products, and strings of Venetian glass beads to exchange for food. The "embassy" was instructed to return within six days.

· While the two Spaniards and their eager guides were plodding up the Cacoyuguin valley, the Admiral was not idle — he never was. On the night of November 2, two days before full moon, he endeavored to establish his position by taking the altitude of the North Star with his wooden quadrant. After applying the slight correction he decided that Puerto Gibara, actually in latitude 21° 06′ N, was in 42° N, the latitude of Cape Cod! And by his dead-reckoning he figured that he had wested 1142 leagues, that is, 3630 nautical miles, since his departure from Ferro in the Canaries. In other words, his fleet had made over 90 degrees of westing; ample distance, according to his underestimate of the globe and overestimate of the length of Asia, to place him in China. He therefore decided that Cuba was not Japan, but the Asiatic mainland.

Given Columbus's faulty geographical premises, his conclusion as to his longitude was inevitable. But why the faulty latitude, exactly double the true one? When at sea in about the same latitude on November 21, he tried the old quadrant once more, and obtained the same result. The reasons for this colossal error have much exercised the pundits. Navarrete postulated an imaginary, nonexistent quadrant that read double. Magnaghi argued that Columbus was trying to throw the Portuguese and others off the scent. Las Casas believed that the scribe copied "21" as "42." The real explanation is simple: Columbus picked the wrong star. He was "shooting" Alfirk (β Cephei), which in November bore due north at dusk; mistaking her for Polaris, whose familiar "pointers" were below the horizon. Columbus knew perfectly well that latitude 42° N was fantastically wrong. He had earlier noted in the Journal that Guanahaní was on the same parallel as the Canaries; and in his printed Letter on the First Voyage he gives the mean latitude of his new discoveries as 26° N. But, as he remarked rather plaintively in his Journal, "The North Star" (that is, Alfirk) "looks as high as in Castile."

One day was spent exploring the Rio Gibara in a boat. Martín Alonso Pinzón brought in specimens of the native creole pepper, and something he thought to be cinnamon, which raised hopes of a lucrative trade in spicery. Columbus had his first taste of sweet potatoes — or were they yams? — with "the flavor of chestnuts" and of cultivated American beans; he saw the wild cotton growing, with flowers and open bolls on the same bush. The boatswain of *Niña* brought in resin from the gumbo-limbo, which the Admiral thought he recognized as the mastic he had seen in Chios on one of his early voyages. Some Indians "yessed" the Spaniards when they inquired about the one-eyed and dog-headed men of Sir John Mandeville; others accurately pointed eastward toward Haiti when asked where gold came from.

Until the last day of his stay, Columbus kept the confidence of the natives, because he maintained good discipline among his men, and the natives had no gold to tempt their cupidity. There must have been considerable sporting between the seamen and the Indian girls, for the habits of the Tainos were completely promiscuous. But Columbus says nothing of that, since his Journal was intended for the eyes of a modest queen. Instead, he dwells on the Indians' docility and imitativeness; when they heard their visitors saying the *Ave Maria* and singing *Salve Regina* at sundown they tried to join in, and readily imitated the sign of the cross. His own words about the natives of Puerto Gibara are directly quoted by Las Casas: —

They are a people very guileless and unwarlike, all naked, men and women, as their mothers bore them. It is true that the women wear merely a piece of cotton big enough to cover their genitals but no more, and they are very handsome, not very black, less so than the Canary Islanders. I maintain, Most Serene Princes, that if they had access to devout religious persons knowing the language, they would all turn Christian, and so I hope in Our Lord that Your Highnesses will do something about it with much care, in order to turn to the Church so numerous a people, and to convert them, as you have destroyed those who would not confess the Father, Son, and Holy Ghost. And after your days (for we are all mortal) you will leave your realms in a very tranquil state, and free from heresy and wickedness, and will be well received before the eternal Creator, whom may it please to grant you long life and great increase of greater realms and lordships, and both will and disposition to increase the holy Christian religion, as hitherto you have done. Amen.

On the night of November 5 the embassy returned from Holguín with a most discouraging report. They had walked up the valley, past fields cultivated with sweet potatoes, beans and maize; they observed many kinds of birds, including the Hispaniola mocking-bird that they took for a nightingale; but they had pricked the Grand Khan bubble. Instead of visiting the imperial court of Cathay where Luis de Torres expected to air his Arabic, they received a primitive welcome in a village of fifty palm-thatched huts and a few hundred inhabitants. They had been treated with great dignity, "chaired" into the principal house, and seated on one of the carved seats or *metates* that Taino caciques used, well described by Ferdinand as "made of one piece, in a strange shape, and almost like some animal which had short legs and arms and the tail, which is no less broad than the seat, lifted up for conveniency to lean against; with a head in front and the eyes and ears of gold. These seats are called *duchi.*" Rodrigo the mariner doubtless enjoyed it, but Torres felt humiliated in having to call upon the interpreter from Guanahaní to make a speech to the men. After that was over the women and children were allowed in to see the "men from Heaven," whose hands and feet they adoringly kissed. They pressed their visitors to spend a week or two; but the Spaniards, seeing "nothing that resembled a city," returned next day, in company with the cacique and his son. These were entertained aboard one of the caravels, since *Santa María* was then high and dry.

If the embassy missed meeting the King of Kings, they nevertheless encountered a more pervasive sovereign, My Lady Nicotine. "The two Christians met on the way many people who were going to their villages, women and men, with a firebrand in the hand, and herbs to drink the smoke thereof as they are accustomed." The tobacco pipe of the North American Indians was unknown to the Tainos, who rolled cigars which (as in Cuba today) they called *tobacos*. Inserting one end in a nostril, they lit the other from a firebrand and inhaled the smoke twice or thrice, after which the cigar was handed to a friend or allowed to go out. When a party of Tainos went on a journey, as Rodrigo and Luis de Torres observed them, small boys were charged to keep one or more firebrands glowing in readiness for anyone who wanted a light; and by halting every hour or so for a good "drag" all around, Indians were able to travel great distances. Las Casas, commenting on this passage some forty years later, says that the Spaniards of Hispaniola were then beginning to take up smoking, "although I know not what taste or profit they find in it." Apparently the bishop never got beyond his first cigar. Within a century of his writing this, the use of tobacco had spread throughout the Western World, to men and women alike, despite the opposition of kings and clerics. As a gift from the New World to the Old it proved far more valuable than gold.

On the morning of November 5, in a bight of Puerto Gibara that is still used for that purpose, the Admiral had *Santa María* careened and her bottom cleaned, a seamanlike precaution against teredos. The next day she floated, and plans were made to sail on the eighth; but strong easterly trades kept the fleet in harbor four days more. Possibly this opportunity was taken to careen *Pinta* and *Niña*, but there is no mention of it in the Journal. Samples were taken of the gumbo-limbo resin, which Columbus supposed to be mastic, and of the agave which he mistook for aloes. As a final reward to these nonresistant Indians of the Golden

Age "without knowledge of what is evil, . . . and so timid that a hundred of them flee before one of ours," the Admiral kidnaped five young men who came aboard for a farewell visit, and then sent his boat ashore to bag "seven head of women, large and small, and three boys." The husbands and fathers of some came out and begged to join them, which was granted. Columbus explained that he wanted the youths to train as interpreters, and the women to keep them from getting spoiled; for he had already observed when voyaging for Portugal that the Negroes brought home from Guinea in order to learn the language received so much attention in Portugal that they were no good when returned to Africa. Two of the young men escaped at Tánamo Bay; none of the rest survived the voyage to Spain.

"At the relieving of the dawn watch" on Monday, November 12, the fleet left Puerto Gibara "to visit an island which many of the Indians aboard declare to be called *Babeque* where, the Indians aboard declare by signs, the people gather gold on the beach by candles at night, and then make bars of it with a hammer." "Babeque" undoubtedly was Great Inagua Island; for the Indians gave the correct course for it, and *Pinta* actually went there.

All that day the wind held fair, but very light. Columbus set a straight course, E ½N, for Punta Cañete, noted but did not examine Puerto Naranjo, noted Puerto Sama and named it *Rio del Sol,* River of the Sun. He excused himself for not exploring these inlets because they looked too shoal for his ships (as indeed they were), and because the wind was fair for Babeque. On his next Cuban voyage the Admiral took *Niña* as flagship and two smaller caravels; and even they drew too much water for coastal work. You cannot sail into narrow, uncharted harbors and rivers with a vessel drawing more than 6 feet, except by running undue risks. The lookout can see bottom up to 6 feet, and even deeper in clear weather with the sun abaft.

By sunset the fleet had made a scant 30 miles. It was off Punta Lucrecia, which Columbus named *Cabo de Cuba* because he thought it was the easternmost promontory of the island. One looking south from that point toward Nipe Bay, sees the lowlands of the Mayarí valley below the horizon, and the high mountains to the eastward look as if they belonged to another island. This Columbus supposed to be "Bohío," that is, Haiti. All night he stood off-and-on in order to hold his position, and at daylight November 13 steered toward the land, passing Punta Mulas. But the weather was overcast, and the atmosphere thick, so that even then Columbus could not see that Cuba and Bohío were contiguous. Another norther was making up. So with the object of making Babeque and avoiding the danger of being driven onto a lee shore with a strong north wind, Columbus ordered the course set due east. With the wind abeam, the fleet logged 31 miles by sunset.

After another night during which the fleet cautiously stood off-and-on (moon was in last quarter and sky overcast), wind veered to NE, making the easterly course for Babeque no longer possible. So, after jogging awhile to the E by S, the Admiral decided to make for a harbor somewhere along the coast of Bohío. A southerly course took him to a point somewhat near the eastern entrance to Puerto Cayo Moa, which he dared not enter through the gap in the breakers with a high sea running; so he ran along shore northwesterly, looking for a safe opening. After coasting some 30 or 35 miles, he came upon a bottleneck entrance a little over 200 yards wide. A boat sent forward to sound reported no bottom at 40 fathoms in the fairway, and the fleet sailed boldly in. There was an elbow in the fairway, requiring three changes of course, but a following wind made these possible, and the Admiral's courage was rewarded when this twisty passage opened into a great bay studded with high, picturesque islands. This was the Bahía Tánamo. Columbus named it *La Mar de Nuestra Señora*, the Sea of Our Lady, and the first harbor just inside the entrance (probably Bahía Jucaro), which he did not stop to investigate, he called *Puerto del Príncipe* after the Infante Don Juan. It was now Wednesday evening, November 14.

Along this coast of Oriente the Admiral's descriptions are so accurate that one can identify his harbors even from the air. Following his course in *Mary Otis*, drawing 7 ½ feet (about the same as *Santa María*), we were impressed with his courage in sailing near enough to the shore to spy out the numerous openings in the many-harbored Oriente, and with his good judgment in the places that he selected for anchoring and detailed exploration.

Martín Alonso Pinzón considered Columbus to be reckless and foolhardy; but unless an explorer is willing to take risks that merchant captains avoid, he does not discover much that is worth while. Thus, Captain Robert Gray of the Boston ship *Columbia*, named after the Great Admiral, was sharply criticized by his officers for standing too close inshore, and occasionally running aground. But it was Captain Gray's willingness to take risks that sent *Columbia* across the breaking bar of the great river that bears her name, where no earlier explorer had dared enter. Columbus, to be sure, had missed Nipe Bay, one of the best harbors in the world; but anyone who has experienced a norther in those waters will not blame him for then seeking sea room.

Tánamo Bay with its cluster of wooded islands running up "like diamond points" and others flat-topped "like tables," as Columbus said, and a lofty sierra arising from all around the scalloped shore, well deserved the Admiral's enthusiasm. There was good soft bottom everywhere, "which the seamen like very much," says Las Casas, "because rocks cut the ships' anchor cables." Columbus was rowed all around the bay in the ship's boat, and on the windward point of the entrance he found two big trees which *Santa María's* carpenter fashioned into a great cross, and there set up. It was the Admiral's custom to leave a cross standing at every place where he anchored. He found Indians fishing for "large snails" (conchs), and made his people dive for oysters in the hope of finding pearls; they caught a curious trunkfish which the Admiral salted down to show the Sovereigns. The seamen found their first *hutía*, the Cuban quadruped resembling a large rat, which still furnishes food to the natives. The most interesting new flora observed about Tánamo Bay were "big nuts of the same kind as those of India." Columbus had read of *nueces de India* (coconuts) in

Marco Polo, and supposed that these were they; but they cannot have been, because the coconut palm was introduced to the Caribbean by later Spaniards. Furthermore, Columbus does not say that these *nueces* grew on a palm tree — nor does Marco Polo. What he probably saw was the local nut called *nogal del país* (*Juglans insularis*), which was formerly very abundant in Oriente Province.

Although it was not new moon until November 19, the day after Columbus left Tánamo, he there made a remarkable lunitidal observation. In his day the tidal establishment of each port was determined by the bearing of the moon at low water. "The tide is the reverse of ours in Spain," says he, "because here when the moon bears SW by S, it is low tide in that position." The waning moon bore SW by S at Tánamo about noon November 15, when Columbus could have observed her in a clear sky. Bowditch gives the mean high-water lunitidal interval at Huelva in Spain as 1h 40m and at Tánamo as 7h 51m, a difference of 6h 11m. So, as the mean interval between high and low water is 6h 13m, it was low water at Tánamo *at almost the exact hour and minute* by local time when it would have been high water at Huelva. And, as the mean range of tide on the north coast of Cuba is a trifle under two feet, the Admiral here proved himself to be an observer of almost uncanny accuracy.

There was no gold in this lovely bay, no hint of Asia except the mistaken coconuts, no large village of natives, nothing of profit to the Spaniards. Only Columbus's love of natural beauty, a trait unusual in that era and still uncommon among navigators, kept him there five days. He even excuses himself for not departing on the fourth day because it was Sunday. But mere scenery was not getting him anywhere; another attempt must be made to reach Babeque.

Before sunrise November 19 the fleet departed with a light land breeze. Columbus was learning the technique for leaving these northern harbors of the greater Antilles under sail; you must catch the offshore wind at night or in early morning, for the trades that come up with the sun draw right in as through a funnel. That day the trade wind came from due E, and the fleet sailed NNE, 6 points off the wind. At sunset, when the entrance to Tánamo bore SSW, distant 20 miles, Columbus thought he sighted Babeque bearing due east. Actually Great Inagua was over 80 miles distant from that point, and could not possibly have been seen. Probably the Indians, seeing a cloud making up over the horizon at sunset, pointed to it and shouted "Babeque!" and Columbus believed them. From sunset November 19 to 10 o'clock the next morning the fleet made good 52 miles to the NE by N, which took them to the approximate position of latitude 21° 45′ N, longitude 74° 41′ W.

This course was fast leading them away from the presumed position of Babeque; so when the wind turned ESE and the sea began to make up from the eastward, Columbus decided to return to Tánamo. The alternative, he wrote, was to maintain the northeasterly course to Isabela (Crooked Island) which he believed lay 12 leagues ahead. Sixteen leagues was the correct distance if I have plotted his course accurately; and it was one month and a day since he had left Cabo Hermoso of Isabela. Few modern navigators by dead-reckoning could hope to do better than that.

Columbus turned back toward Cuba, he says, for two reasons. He feared lest the Indians from Guanahaní escape at Isabela. And, second, he sighted two islands to the southward that he wished to investigate. These were clouds, not islands, as he must have ascertained within an hour or two; but that entry in his Journal stood. It is a great temptation to any shipmaster, when he makes an entry that proves to be mistaken, to alter or erase it with a stroke of the pen; but Columbus always let his mistakes stand; and a shipmate on the Second Voyage observed how careful he was to log any accident. Crackpot critics of Columbus always base their theories on a presumed going-over of the Journal by Columbus or Las Casas to iron out inconsistencies and play up "The Indies." But Las Casas's abstract reveals plenty of errors by the Admiral, as well as kidnaping episodes of which the editor thoroughly disapproved.

CHAPTER XIX

Oriente

November 20–December 5, 1492

Vidimus enim stellam eius in oriente, et venimus adorare eum.

We have seen his star in the east, and are come to worship him.

— MATTHEW ii 2

RETURNING to Tánamo was easier decided than done; and the next few days were full of such disappointment and vexations as beset all mariners in sail. Tánamo lay about SSW, 8 points off the wind; but the distance was too great (some 71 miles) for the fleet to cover that day, and the current carried it to leeward. So at nightfall November 20, when within sight of land, Columbus decided to make another try for Babeque. He ordered the fleet about, and for a time sailed NE with a stiff ESE wind. At the third night watch (about 3 A.M. November 21) the wind moderated and became variable between S and SE, so that an easterly course could be sailed. At sunrise November 21 Tánamo bore SW westerly, distant about 35 miles. Although the wind held south during the day, the sea was so heavy as to check the easterly progress of the caravels; and up to vespers (about 3 P.M.) they had made only 15 to 18 miles to the eastward. The wind then backed to the E, forcing the fleet S by E.

As soon as the North Star appeared that evening, and when, according to my plotting of his dead-reckoning he was in latitude 20° 52′ N, Columbus broke out his quadrant and tried a little celestial navigation. He reached the same deplorable result of

latitude 42° that he had obtained on November 2, and for the same
reason: mistaking Alfirk for Polaris. The Admiral himself was
puzzled, and "here says that he has had the quadrant hung up until
he reaches land, to repair it, since it seemed to him that he could
not be so far distant" from the equator. Many better navigators
than he, even in our own century, have given up star sights with
disgust, to rely on "good old dead-reckoning." The truth is, Columbus was not conscious of the stars, even from an esthetic point
of view. Many times in the course of his four voyages he comments
on the beauty of tropical landscapes, sometimes when off soundings
he adverts to the glory of the sea; but never does he remark on
the splendor of the stars in the tropics. Not once does he mention
the Southern Cross, or the enormous constellation of the ship Argo
or brilliant Canopus, which he must have seen for the first time since
his African voyages. His eyes were not turned upward, at least not
above the clouds that carried messages of wind and rain; he had
enough to do to watch them, and the compass card and the surface
of the ocean, and to keep his reckoning and constantly to run his
eyes over sails and gear for signs of weakness or chafe. Almost any
old-time shipmaster can construct an accurate model of a vessel
for which he has once been responsible, with every spar, block and
line in place; but only a trained celestial navigator can identify
the stars without consulting a sidereal chart, and between voyages
that sort of lore is quickly forgotten. Columbus, we repeat, was a
dead-reckoning and not a celestial navigator.

The defection of Martín Alonso Pinzón worried the Admiral
much more than did his screwy latitude sights. During the dawn
watch (3 to 7 A.M.) November 22 the wind backed to NNE, and
the Admiral kept on to the southward in the hope of reaching land.
Niña dutifully followed, but Martín Alonso "without the permission or desire of the Admiral" took advantage of the change of
wind to alter *Pinta's* course to the eastward. It was not until the
second week of the New Year that Columbus saw him again, at
Monte Cristi. The one reason for Martín Alonso's insubordination,
says Columbus, was his cupidity; an Indian guide aboard *Pinta* had

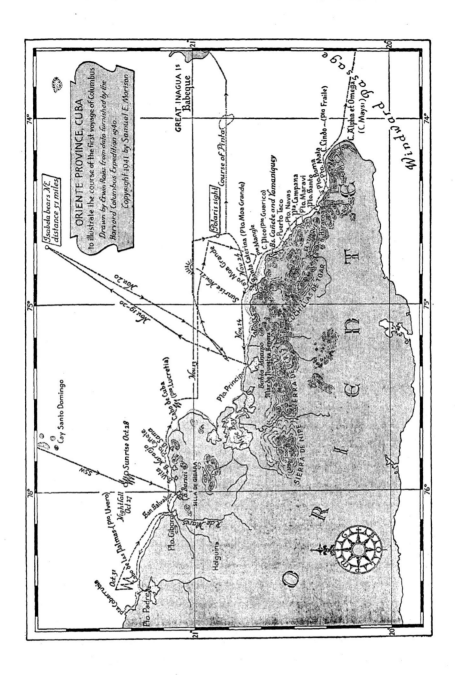

ORIENTE PROVINCE, CUBA
to illustrate the course of the first voyage of Columbus
Drawn by Erwin Raisz from data furnished by the
Harvard Columbus Expedition 1940.
Copyright 1941 by Samuel E. Morison

filled him up with tales of the gold at Babeque, and he wished to get there first.

Although this is the earliest indication in the Journal of unpleasantness between the Admiral and his senior captain, clearly it was not the first. "Many other things he had done and said to me," concludes the day's work for November 21. Martín Alonso died shortly after the voyage ended, and in the long *pleitos* that began in 1512, the only explanation of this gross breach of discipline offered by his friends and partisans was the feeble one that the Admiral got lost, while Pinzón went on. One therefore assumes that he had no case, and that the greedy motive assigned to him by Columbus was correct. Yet one may imagine other motives as well. *Pinta* was a smarter sailer than *Santa María*, especially in the conditions of light wind and heavy head swell that prevailed on November 21; and very likely Pinzón was exasperated at continually having to shorten sail in order not to outdistance the flagship. When the wind turned fair for Babeque on November 22, and the Admiral continued on his course for Cuba instead of turning east, it was too much for Martín Alonso. He'd be damned if he'd follow that Genoese upstart any longer! The proper thing to do, in his way of thinking, was to go after the gold. And although he found not a grain of it at Great Inagua, he did discover Haiti and had first whack at the gold of the Cibao.

Columbus's "many other things he had done and said to me" suggests a good deal. Friction between these two strong men was inevitable. Martín Alonso's local influence had been essential for manning the expedition. Possibly Columbus failed to give him due credit for these practical details. There had been, as we have seen, dissension just before the Bahamian landfall, and Columbus, by rubbing in the fact that he was right, may have irritated Martín Alonso into saying and doing those unmentioned things. Men of genius are not always easy on their subordinates. But in contrast to the insubordination of Martín Alonso, note the loyalty of his brother Vicente Yáñez, who had the same temptation to put off for Babeque, but dutifully steered *Niña* where his Admiral commanded.

The wind was so light on November 22 that *Pinta* was in sight of the others all day, and they made little progress. Friday the twenty-third was about the same, the westerly-setting current taking *Santa María* and *Niña* to leeward faster than they could sail south. The Indian guides were terrified because they thought that the land ahead belonged to the people "called *Canibales*," the Caribs who were accustomed to make slave raids on the Tainos. Finally at 9 A.M. on the twenty-fourth the reduced fleet of two made land at "the flat island," Cayo Moa Grande. When they passed it ten days before, the sea was breaking so heavily that the Admiral dared not enter the harbor. We do not blame him; the entrance to Puerto Cayo Moa through a gap in the breakers looks pretty tough, even when you have a chart.

After three days of light wind, the sea had calmed down so that the entrance now did not seem so bad. *Santa María's* boat, sent in ahead to sound, reported 20 fathoms in the fairway and 6 fathoms with good clean sand bottom inside, as today. In sailed the caravels "turning the bow to the SW and then to the W, keeping the flat island to the northward close aboard" (directions which we found useful in June 1940, all buoys then being absent), and found themselves within "a lagoon in which all the ships of Spain could lie and be safe without cables from all winds." It was the morning of November 24, and the most unprofitable leg of the First Voyage was over. In five days *Santa María* and *Niña* had logged about 200 miles and made good 25.

Puerto Cayo Moa is unlike any other harbor in the Oriente province of Cuba. About 8½ miles long by 1½ wide, it runs along the base of a mountain range, protection from the north being given by the "flat island" (Cayo Moa Grande) and "a reef the length of the mountain, like a bar." Through this reef there are two entrances, sailing directions for both of which Columbus noted in his Journal. Several streams flow down the sierra, forming short deltas and a bar where they empty into the harbor; but, as Columbus observed, the salt water does not back up into their lower courses, as into the Rio Gibara. The Admiral had the men row him up the Rio Moa, in whose bed and on whose banks he detected signs of valuable minerals — stones the color of iron, others that someone associated with silver, iron pyrites which glittered for so many explorers, but were never gold; "and he recollected that gold is found at the mouth of the Tagus." While Columbus and the officers were prospecting, "the gromets sung out that they saw pine trees; he looked toward the sierra and saw many great and such marvellous ones that he could not exaggerate their height and straightness, like spindles, thick and elongated, whence he realized that ships could be had, and planks without number, and masts for the best ships of Spain." Today the descendants of these *pinus cubenses* are being sawed into boards and planks by a mill run by the mountain stream whose distant roar the Admiral heard on that far-off Sunday in 1492. He caused a new mizzenmast and a yard to be cut and shaped for *Niña;* but the great shipbuilding industry that he planned for this place, and described "in great style to the Sovereigns," has never materialized. Except for a few fishermen's cabins on the shore, and a few lumbermen's clearings among the pine groves on the sierra, the aspect of the harbor is still clean of human touch.

Columbus the poet appreciated Puerto Cayo Moa as well as Columbus the seaman. "The land and the air are milder than hitherto, owing to the height and beauty of the sierra." Words failed him, as they do us, to describe the peculiar beauty of this harbor, resting so placidly between austere mountains and the arc of hissing reefs. "Finally, he says," reports Las Casas, "that if he who sees it is so full of wonder, how much more will it be for him who hears of it, and that nobody can believe it without seeing."

At sunrise November 26 they reluctantly weighed anchors from Puerto Cayo Moa, and sailed slowly along with a light SW wind to Punta Guarico, which the Admiral called *Cabo del Pico.* There the coast makes a turn to the southward. Soon he sighted the most prominent headland in this part of Oriente, and named it *Cabo Campana*, "Cape Bell." It has a smooth, curved surface, which was probably cultivated by the Indians in 1492. Between these two capes "he noted and marked nine very remarkable harbors which all the seamen considered wonderful, and five great rivers; because he always sailed close along shore, in order to see everything well." He certainly sailed closer than we cared to do in a vessel of like draught, for we could make out only seven harbors and rivers, including Bahías Cañete and Yamanigue, which the Admiral particularly described. But we were near enough to agree with him that "all this country has very high and beautiful mountains, not dry and rocky but all accessible, and most beautiful valleys; and the valleys like the mountains were thick with high and leafy trees, which 'twas glorious to see."

As the wind left him that evening when off Cabo Campana, and the weather was clear, Columbus decided not to attempt entering any one of these numerous harbors, but hove-to and drifted. When day broke on the twenty-seventh he was so far offshore, and the clouds hung so low, that the country behind Baracoa seemed to be an inlet of the sea, with "a mountain lofty and square, that looked like an island" standing out in the middle. This was El Yunque, the anvil-shaped mountain that can be seen 50 miles away, a landmark known to everyone who navigates these waters. With a land breeze from the SW blowing on the port side, the fleet returned to Cape Campana in order to resume exploring the coast. The wind then veered to the N, and the caravels sailed gaily along close inshore, noting eight little basin-shaped harbors and V-shaped river mouths. Foothills bright green with guinea grass and bristling with royal palms rise from a rim of white surf; above them high, wooded mountains in tumbled irregular shapes thrust up into the trade-wind clouds which are constantly piling up in nubilous traffic jams, and then dissolving into showers. By the time he reached a point off Puerto Maraví at the end of this string of little harbors, the Admiral found that the supposed inlet "was only a great bay."

Throughout this scenic cruise along the north shore of Oriente,

Columbus's Taino passengers were shaking with terror at the thought of landing on the so-called Island of Bohío, which they supposed to be the land whence their Carib enemies came. "After they saw that he was shaping a course for that land, they couldn't speak for fear lest they (the Caribs) make a meal of them, nor could he quiet their fears; and they said that these people had but one eye and dogs' faces. The Admiral believed that they were lying" — why, when he himself had suggested these monsters out of Mandeville? — and thought that the Caribs "must really be subjects of the Grand Khan" — in other words, Chinese soldiers! The Admiral was further off than the simple natives.

These had a very pronounced attack of Caribphobia when the fleet sighted a big village beyond Puerto Maraví, "and saw countless people come to the seashore making great shouts, all naked and with darts in hand." At this horrid sight, all Indians aboard promptly retired below hatches, and became so useless from sheer funk that no effort was made to take them ashore as interpreters. The fleet came to an anchor, and Columbus sent both boats ashore with orders to placate the yelling natives with trading truck. The boats' crews landed on the Playa de Duaba (just west of Baracoa), crying out some appeasing phrase that they had picked up from their Taino shipmates; but the entire native population took to flight.

At noon on November 27 the two vessels made sail from their anchorage off this now deserted beach, and steered eastward for Cape Maisi. They had not gone two miles when there opened up, a short distance to the southward, "a most singular harbor" (Puerto Baracoa), surrounded by open country and big villages, and Columbus decided to call. Entering by the 300-yard-wide fairway, avoiding the rock just off the windward point, *Santa María* and *Niña* found themselves in a harbor round "like a little porringer," and separated by a narrow beach from a river "of such depth that a galley could enter." Columbus promptly decided that this harbor, which he named *Puerto Santo*, was the best he had yet seen for building a city and fortress — "good water, good land, good surroundings, and much wood"; and on the strength of his recom-

mendation it was pitched upon for the first Spanish settlement in
Cuba, in 1512. Baracoa today is the largest town located on the
route of Columbus's First Voyage, a lively little city with a thriving export trade of bananas and coconuts. Native sloops and
lighters still unload in the river "that a galley could enter," which
flows around the harbor's rim, behind the beach.

Bad weather kept *Santa María* and *Niña* at Baracoa for a week.
The people went ashore and washed their clothes in the river, as
seamen love to do. Other parties wandered about the interior,
found the land well cultivated with yams, maize and pumpkins,
visited many Taino villages from which all natives fled on their
approach, and reported finding "a man's head in a basket, covered
with another basket and hanging to a post" in a house. "The Admiral believed the heads must have been those of some ancestors of
the family." An old Guinea custom, perhaps? The Tainos are not
known to have preserved their ancestors' skulls, nor were they
head-hunters; one suspects that the seamen enjoyed pulling their
Admiral's leg. Several immense dugout canoes were seen, neatly
moored under palm-thatched boathouses; one was over 70 feet
in length and big enough to hold 150 people. The men raised a
great cross on the windward point of Baracoa Harbor, where now
there is a ruined fort.

Unfavorable winds gave Columbus an excuse to tarry, and opportunity to explore by boat the next bay east of Baracoa. There
he entered the mouth of the Rio Miel with a fathom's depth over
the bar, and found inside a lagoon where the whole Spanish navy
might ride. Rowing upstream, he found five large canoes in a
backwater, with a thatched boathouse to protect them, and, leaving his boats, climbed the hillside until he reached a plain with
cultivated fields of pumpkins, and many huts. Here he managed at
last to make contact with the natives of Baracoa by sending
"Diego" ahead with a supply of brass rings, glass beads and hawks'
bells. They proved willing to do business, but had nothing to
exchange except their wooden darts with fire-hardened points. Returning to his boats, Columbus sent another party of seamen up the

hillside to investigate a collection of huts that he mistook for bee-hives; and while they were gone, large numbers of natives flocked around the Spaniards, and "one of them went into the river next the stern of the boat and made a great speech, which the Admiral didn't understand, except that from time to time the other Indians raised their hands to Heaven and gave a great shout. The Admiral thought that they were reassuring him and that his coming pleased them; but he saw the face of the Indian whom he took with him change color and become yellow as wax, and he trembled much, saying by signs that the Admiral had better leave the river, that they sought to kill them. And he went up to a Christian who held a loaded crossbow and showed it to the Indians, and the Admiral understood that he told them that they would all be killed, because that crossbow shot far and to kill. Also he took a sword and drew it from its scabbard, brandishing it, saying the same; the which when they heard, all took to flight, the said Indian trembling from cowardice and slight courage, and he was a man of good stature and strong."

In the meantime other Tainos had gathered on the opposite bank of the Rio Miel, to which the Admiral crossed. "They were very many, all painted red and naked as their mothers bore them, and some with feathers on the head and others plumes, all with their bundles of darts." These darts, too, were handed over in return for the usual trading truck, and for bits of the shell of a turtle that the gromets had killed. Columbus came away filled with admiration for the workmanship of the canoes and the native huts, but disappointed at the total absence of "gold and spicery," and contemptuous of the natives' courage. "Ten men could put to flight ten thousand, so cowardly and timid are they." If a relatively humane Columbus reacted thus, it is no wonder that the common seamen regarded the Tainos as despicable, fit only to be slaves.

On December 4 *Santa María* and *Niña* left Baracoa with a light but favorable wind, skirting the coast and looking in at Puerto Boma, a narrow V-shaped harbor with high banks, and at Puerto

Mata, one of the round bottlenecked harbors common on that coast. By sunset they were off the Punta del Fraile (which Columbus named *Cabo Lindo*, "Pretty Cape") of Cape Maisí, and within sight of the Windward Passage between Cuba and Hispaniola. Having twice been fooled by bays that he mistook for passages, the Admiral at first thought this was merely another bay, and did not discover his error until the morning after a night spent hove-to off Punta del Fraile. At sunrise December 5 he sighted the tip of Cape Maisí, from which the land trended south, and then southwest; and in that direction he saw a dark, high cape, Punta Negra. So he decided that this was a passage after all, and named the easternmost extremity of Cuba "Cape Alpha and Omega," to indicate that it was the beginning or end of the Eurasian continent, corresponding to Cape St. Vincent in Europe.

Up to the morning of December 5 Columbus planned to make Great Inagua (Babeque) his next stop after finishing with Cuba; for it was high time that he should be collecting some gold before Martín Alonso got it all into the hold of *Pinta*. But that morning the trade wind came up from the northeast, which the Indian guides, quite correctly, indicated as the course for Babeque. And when *Santa María* was steering close-hauled on the port tack, headed about ESE, the Admiral sighted land on the starboard bow, "and it was a very great island, of which he already had information from the Indians, that they called it 'Bohío.'" This was Haiti; a sight welcome to the Spaniards as it was a disappointment to the Guanahaní and Gibara guides, who, having successfully escaped being killed and eaten at Baracoa, were trying to divert the Admiral to the Great Inagua, inhabited by their own kind. If, as seems probable from their calling Haiti by the name for "home," they had retained the tradition of its being their mother country, they also believed that the Caribs had since moved in, and were hungry for Taino meat.

Columbus now made a quick change of plan, which was uncommon for him, and decided to use the favorable wind for Haiti, instead of beating up to Great Inagua. Steering SE by E, in order to keep a little to windward of the course (for he had noted the diurnal variation of the trade wind from NE to SE), he crossed the Windward Passage that day and arrived off the mouth of a great harbor "like the Bay of Cadiz" at nightfall December 5, vigil of the feast of Saint Nicholas. *Port Saint Nicolas* it still is; the first of Columbus's New World names that has never been altered.

As he left Cuba and crossed the Windward Passage, Columbus must have wondered how he, in his fumbling Castilian and with such poor evidence as he had picked up, could convince the Sovereigns that this beautiful coastline along which he had been sailing for five weeks really belonged to the semi-fabulous Cathay. No Grand Khan, no potentates or mandarins in silk brocade had he encountered, but naked savages with cotton clouts; no towering Chinese junks, but dugout canoes; no teeming cities of a thousand bridges, but villages of palm-thatched huts; not one grain of gold or other precious metal, but artifacts of wood, bone and shell; no merchantable spicery, but poor substitutes for cinnamon and pepper; no monsters of humankind or marvels of the vegetable kingdom, but a few odd nuts and a trunkfish in pickle. We who have benefited from Columbus's voyage can hardly imagine what a disappointment it had been, after the first wonder and delight at San Salvador had worn off. But for the visit to Haiti, where gold was discovered, this voyage would undoubtedly have been written off by the Sovereigns as a curious adventure but a costly failure. That, obviously, is what the Pinzons and most of Columbus's shipmates thought it to be, on December 5, 1492. But the Admiral's faith that God had sent him forth for His glory and for the benefit of mankind made him see the bright side of things; and, in a significant passage entered in his Journal during the delay at Baracoa, point out that even if he had not found a western route to Asia, he had lifted the veil from a New World of opportunity.

I do not write how great will be the benefit to be derived hence. It's certain, Lord Princes, that where there are such lands there should be profitable things without number; but I tarried not in any harbor, because I sought to see as many countries as I could, to give the story of them to Your Highnesses, and also I knew not the language, and the people of these lands did not understand me nor I them, nor anyone aboard. And these Indians aboard I often misunderstood taking one thing for the opposite, and I don't trust them much, for many times they have tried to escape. But now, please Our Lord, I will see the most that I can, and little by little I shall come to understand and know, and I will have this language learned by people of my household, because I see that all so far have one language. And afterwards the benefits will be known, and it will be attempted to make all these folk Christians, for that will easily be done, since they have no religion; nor are they idolaters.

And Your Highnesses will command a city and fortress to be built in these parts, and these countries converted; and I certify to Your Highnesses that it seems to me that there could never be under the sun [lands] superior in fertility, in mildness of cold and heat, in abundance of good and pure water; and the rivers are not like those of Guinea, which are all pestilential. For, praise be to Our Lord, up to the present among all my people nobody has even had a headache or taken to his bed through sickness; except one old man with pain of gravel, from which he has suffered all his life, and he was well at the end of two days. This applies to all three vessels. So may it please God that Your Highnesses send here . . . learned men, who will ascertain the truth of all. .. . . And I say that Your Highnesses ought not to consent that any foreigner do business or set foot here, except Christian Catholics, since this was the end and the beginning of the enterprise, that it should be for the enhancement and glory of the Christian religion, nor should anyone who is not a good Christian come to these parts.

Thus, before he had been seven weeks in the New World, Columbus sketched in outline the colonial policy of Spain that has left a permanent impress on America, foretold "the profitable things without number" that Europeans would find therein, and predicted the vast extension of Christianity that his discovery made possible.

CHAPTER XX

La Isla Española

December 6–24, 1492

A son arrivée "dans un nouveau monde et sous un nouveau ciel," il observe attentivement la configuration des contrées, la physionomie des formes végétales, les mœurs des animaux, la distribution de la chaleur et les variations du magnétisme terrestre. Tout en s'efforçant de découvrir les épiceries de l'Inde et la rhubarbe, rendue déjà si célèbre par les médecins arabes et juifs, par Rubruquis et les voyageurs italiens, il observait avec un soin scrupuleux les racines, les fruits et les feuilles des plantes.

— VON HUMBOLDT *Cosmos* II 320

DURING the night of December 5, while *Niña* was comfortably anchored in Port St. Nicolas, and beacon fires of the Indians flared from the surrounding hills, *Santa María* sailed to the NNE with the land breeze, in order to be in a good position to coast down-wind to her first Haitian harbor next morning.

At daylight Columbus took a set of bearings so accurate that we can confidently place *Santa María* 12 miles N by E from Cape St. Nicolas Môle, which is the exact distance given by the Admiral himself. Anyone who has tried to take bearings without pelorus or other sighting apparatus, merely by squinting across a small compass card, will share my surprise that four out of five of Columbus's bearings actually converge at a point on the modern chart. From that position, latitude 20° 03' N, longitude 73° 24' W, he sighted and named from its resemblance to a turtle the famous buccaneer island of Tortuga; the northwestern point of Haiti, which he called the *Cape of the Star;* Pointe Jean Rabel, which he named *Cabo Cinquín;* and the Haut Piton mountain with its northern slope, which he called *Cabo del Elefante.* Haut Piton does suggest

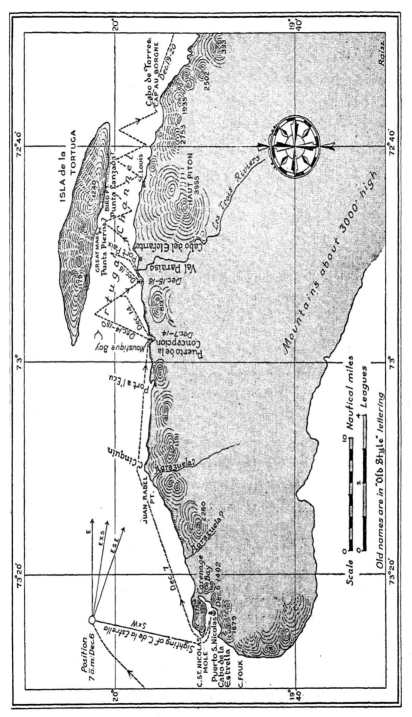

NORTHWEST COAST OF HISPANIOLA

a huge elephant coming down to the Tortuga channel to drink, but Columbus had never seen an elephant. The association was probably a literary one, with Aristotle's remark that the presence of elephants both in Africa and in India proves that fauna are similar on the same parallels of latitude. Doubtless the Admiral expected that very day to see elephants sporting among the forests of Hispaniola.

As the wind was light December 6, it took *Santa María* all the morning and part of the afternoon to reach *Puerto de San Nicolás*, as Columbus named the harbor because it was the feast of the patron saint of children. It was much the finest seaport he had yet discovered; deep with clean bottom and good holding ground, and at the head of it an inner and completely landlocked harbor (the modern Carénage) where a ship could moor close enough to the shore to lay her gangplank on the grass. He noted a fine beach and a river, and trees "of a thousand kinds, all laden with fruit which the Admiral believed to be spiceries and nutmegs — but they were not ripe and he did not recognize them." He proposed that the narrow isthmus at the head of the inner harbor be pierced to make a second channel, and predicted a great future for the place. Port St. Nicolas Môle, as we call it today, is so fine a harbor, and lies so close to the Windward Passage, that it seems destined to become a naval base. The eighteenth-century fortifications have fallen into decay, and the harbor today is deserted except for a poor village and a few fishing boats.

Every Indian fled at the fleet's approach, so the Admiral did not see fit to tarry. "At the relieving of the dawn watch" on Friday morning, December 7, *Santa María* and *Niña* got under way with the land breeze. Outside the harbor they were fortunate to catch a SW wind that whipped them around Cape St. Nicolas Môle and sent them scudding along the coast to the eastward. At what Columbus calls *un' agrezuela* (a craggy spot), a fertile valley opened up inland, but no inhabitants were visible. Off Pointe Jean Rabel they noted an isolated rock that is marked on eighteenth-century charts, but has since been undermined by the sea. They passed

Port à l'Écu without entering, and at 1 P.M. anchored in a harbor between the hills that Columbus named *Puerto de la Concepción*, because it was the vigil of the Conception of the Virgin. For more practical reasons, the Spaniards soon renamed it *Bahía de los Mosquitos*, now Moustique Bay.

Here, although the anchorage was only fair, he was detained five days by rain and easterly winds; and here, according to Las Casas, "seeing the grandeur and beauty of this island, and its resemblance to the land of Spain, although much superior, and that they caught fish similar to . . . those of Castile, and for other and similar reasons, the Admiral decided on Sunday, December 9, being in this Puerto de la Concepción, to name and call this island *La Isla Española*, as it is called today." *Hispaniola* (as Peter Martyr latinized it) is still the name of this great and beautiful island, the scene of the first European colony in the New World, of Columbus's trials and of his bitterest humiliation, and the final resting place of his ashes.

The Indian guides whom "every day we understand better, and they us," convinced Columbus that this land was insular, and that beyond it lay a continent called *Caribata*, the land of the *Caniba* or Caribs. Eager as ever to establish an oriental connection, Columbus jumped to the conclusion that these *Caniba* must be subjects of *El Gran Can*, and that the miscreants who made slave raids on his gentle Tainos were Chinese pirates or sea raiders.

On December 12 Columbus raised a great cross on the western cape of Moustique Bay, and took formal possession of Hispaniola for Ferdinand and Isabella. On the same day his men made their first contact with the people of Haiti. Three seamen who were exploring the fertile valley at the head of the harbor pursued a crowd of fleeing natives, and captured a "very young and beautiful woman" clad only in a gold nose-plug. They brought her aboard *Santa María*, where she conversed with the captives from Cuba. They must have given her a good account of their usage by the Spaniards, for when the Admiral "sent her ashore very honorably," decently covered with some of the sailors' cast-offs and bedecked with jingly trading truck, she declared that she would rather stay with the "men from Heaven," whose godlike attributes evidently impressed her. It was deemed more useful, however, that she serve as a sort of decoy.

On the following day the Admiral sent nine men with an Indian interpreter upcountry in the hope that the restored damsel would have allayed the people's fears. The seamen followed a well-beaten trail which took them to the valley of Trois Rivières, where they came upon an immense village of a thousand huts, from which all the inhabitants fled. The Spaniards gave chase, their Indian guides calling out reassuringly that these "were not from Caniba but from Heaven," and to such good purpose that the delegation was soon surrounded by a curious though fearful crowd of some two thousand natives, who conducted them in triumph to the village. There the natives offered their guests cassava bread and fish, and satisfied their other wants. Understanding that seamen liked parrots, they presented them with a whole flock of the birds, which doubtless began their education in nautical Castilian forthwith. The Spaniards reported these natives to be handsomer than those of Cuba, "and among them they saw two wenches as white as they can be in Spain." The land, too, was fertile and beautiful, better than the plains of Cordova; there was a wide path up the valley; the Hispaniola mockingbird sang by day like the nightingales of Spain, crickets chirped and frogs croaked in a homelike manner at night, "the fishes were as in Spain," and "it was the greatest delight in the world" to be there. Columbus's only disappointment was their failure to find gold. Even the beautiful girl's nose-plug appeared to be exceptional, as she was a cacique's daughter.

At Moustique Bay Columbus made another celestial observation, the only one recorded in Haiti. He found the latitude to be 34° N, which is about that of Wilmington, N. C.; Moustique Bay is on latitude 19° 55′. He had mistaken for Polaris a star (Er Rai) of the constellation Cepheus.

Columbus still intended to visit Babeque, not knowing that Martín Alonso had already taken *Pinta* there and found no gold whatsoever. The Indian guides believed that it lay to the northeastward of Tortuga. So on December 14 with the wind due E, *Santa María* and *Niña* sailed NNE for Tortuga. They approached near enough to ascertain that it was a high and well-cultivated tableland "like the plain of Cordova," and to name three promontories. But as the wind was contrary for the presumed course to Babeque, they returned to Moustique Bay that night. Making a fresh start on December 15, they beat up the Tortuga Channel to the mouth of Trois Rivières, a clear river that flows over a pebbly bottom to the sea. Columbus, proposing to visit the great village that his men had seen on the thirteenth, had the people row him in *Santa María's* boat over the bar, and then, finding the current swift, had them haul the boat upstream by a hawser. That did not take him very far, for Trois Rivières is a mountain stream, quite unlike the drowned river valleys of Northern Cuba. It was far enough, however, for him to see "lands fit for crops and cattle of all sorts (of which they have none), for orchards, and for everything in the world that man can want."

On January 15, 1939, I visited the spot where the Admiral's boat journey ended, and can testify that this river valley, opening up the country for miles inland, and lined with wooded mountains and banana groves, is one of the loveliest of the Antilles. Columbus well named it *Valle del Paraíso* (Valley of Paradise), and the river the Guadalquivir, because it reminded him of that famous Andalusian river at Cordova. "This island throughout is a terrestrial paradise," commented Las Casas, "and as for Tortuga, near to which I lived some years, its beauty is a thing incredible." They say that no one who has not had a wild-boar hunt on Tortuga knows the ultimate joys of good hunting.

Columbus on his voyages seldom made protracted land excursions himself; he usually sent some of the men, while he stayed near or aboard the ships. I do not know whether this was owing to some constitutional defect that made walking difficult and painful to him, or whether he felt that an admiral should remain afloat. When it appeared that the great village on this new Guadalquivir could

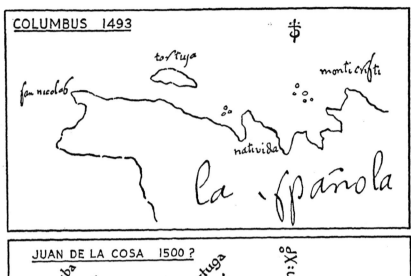

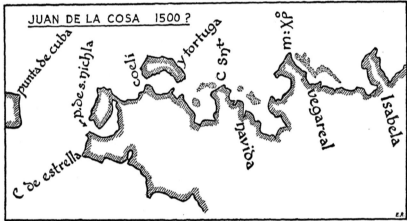

COLUMBUS'S SKETCH OF NORTHERN HAITI
COMPARED WITH LA COSA'S MAP

not be reached by boat, he gave up the attempt and remained aboard that night, wondering at the Indians' beacon fires that gleamed from the mountains, and from the heights of Tortuga. "This folk must be hunted hard by someone" he correctly inferred.

Progress in the Tortuga Channel had proved so difficult against head wind, sea and current that Columbus made sail from the Valle del Paraiso at midnight with the land breeze, hoping to get clear of Tortuga before the trade wind sprang up. "At the hour of tierce," about 9 A.M., "the wind came east." In mid-channel

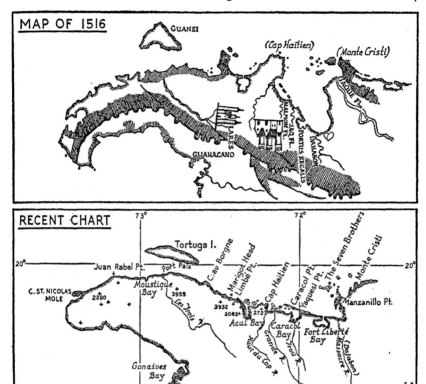

BOLOGNA MAP AND MODERN CHART
OF HAITI

where the sea was roughest they encountered a solitary Indian in so small a canoe that the men wondered how he could keep it afloat in that rough sea. They hoisted him and canoe aboard, presented him with beads, bells and rings, and set him ashore at a village of newly built huts on a beach of the Hispaniola coast. This settlement was probably on the site of Port de Paix, a pretty little town founded by the French in 1664.

The solitary Indian made an excellent ambassador, and at this place the Spaniards made their first satisfactory contact with the Tainos of Haiti. About five hundred people came down to the beach accompanied by their "king," a youth of about twenty-one years to whom they showed much reverence. "This king and all the others went naked as their mothers bore them, and so the women without any shame; and they are the most handsome men and women he had found hitherto; so white that if they went clothed and protected themselves from the sun and air they would be as white as in Spain." Nowadays, we who sail Caribbean waters dress as near to the Indians as decency will permit and acquire all the sunburn we can; but the Spaniards were strongly of the opinion that too much sun was unhealthy, and a tanned body undignified.

Several of the common people came out to the ships, and Columbus sent ashore his marshal Diego de Harana accompanied by an interpreter, to present the king with a gift, and inquire about gold and Babeque. The monarch supplied the desired sailing directions and came aboard that evening (December 16). Columbus "showed him due honor" and offered him Castilian food, of which he ate a mouthful, and passed the rest along to some aged men of his suite whom Columbus took to be his tutors and counselors.

What cheered Columbus more than anything else was a relative abundance of gold ornaments worn by the natives of this village. The next day, when men were sent ashore to trade, they encountered a cacique (the first time that Columbus uses this word) whom they took to be a "governor of a province," and who showed a remarkably acute trading sense with a piece of gold leaf that he owned, as big as a man's hand. Instead of handing it over and accepting whatever was offered in exchange, the cacique kept this piece of gold in his hut so that the Spaniards could not see how much he had, and peddled it out in little bits, one at a time. Naturally the men bid against each other in eagerness to get their share. He declared that there was plenty of gold in Tortuga, but evidently did not welcome competition from that quarter; for when a canoe with forty men came over from that island, the cacique threw pebbles in the water until they sheered off. Columbus tarried at this anchorage two days, hoping that the promised gold would arrive.

On December 18, the feast of the Annunciation, "Santa María de la O" as the Spaniards called it because the proper anthems of the day began with an invocation, *Santa María* and *Niña* dressed ship. Every banner aboard was displayed, armorial escutcheons were hung along bulwarks and waist, and salutes were fired with the lombards. Gunpowder evidently failed to frighten the natives, for at the hour of tierce the youthful cacique appeared on the beach, and not long after came aboard *Santa María* with his attendants. Las Casas has preserved for us the Admiral's own vivid account of this state visit:—

Without doubt his dignity and the respect in which all hold him would appear well to Your Highnesses, although they are all naked. He, when he came aboard, found that I was dining at the table below the stern castle, and at a quick walk he came to sit down beside me, nor would he let me rise to meet him or get up from the table, but begged that I should eat. I thought that he would like to eat our viands and gave orders that he should straightway be brought some. And when he entered below the castle, he made signs with the hand that all his suite should stay outside, and so they did with the greatest readiness and respect in the world, and they all seated themselves on the deck, except two men of mature age, whom I took to be his counselors and tutor, who came and seated themselves at his feet. And of the viands which were placed before him he took of each as much as one would take for a pregustation, and then sent the most part to his suite, and all ate of it; and so he did with the drink, which he simply raised to his lips and then gave to the others, and all with a wonderful dignity and very few words, and those that he said, according to what I could understand, were well arranged and sensible. . . . After dinner a squire brought a belt which is like those of Castile in shape but of different workmanship, which he took and gave me, and two pieces of worked gold which were very thin, so that I believe that here they obtain little of it, although I hold that they are very near to where it comes from and much exists. I saw that a tester which I had over my bed pleased him; I gave it to him, and some very good amber beads which I wore at my neck, and some red shoes, and a bottle of orange water, with which he took such satisfaction that it was marvellous. And he and his tutor and counselors were much troubled because they understood not me nor I them. Withal I recognized that he said that if anything here pleased me, the whole island was mine to command. I sent for some more beads, among which for a symbol I had a gold *excelente* on which are portrayed Your Highnesses, and showed it to him, and told him again as yesterday that Your Highnesses ruled and were lords over the best part of the world, and that there were none such great princes; and showed him the royal banners and the others with the cross. With this he was much impressed and said before his counselors what great lords Your Highnesses must be, since they had sent me without fear from so far and from Heaven. And many other things were said, but I understood not, except that I saw well that he held everything in great admiration.

It will be recalled that Columbus had already received aboard a cacique from the village near Holguín, Cuba; but the port and state of this young Haitian king, who was only a subordinate chief to the cacique Guacanagarí, impressed him as indicating a state of culture far superior to that of the sister island. He had the naked but dignified young savage piped over the side in proper naval style, and gave him "numerous lombard shots," the equivalent of our twenty-one guns, as he was being rowed ashore. There the cacique mounted a litter and was carried off by retainers to his residence, which lay some miles inland.

Although Columbus might treat a visiting cacique with dignity and even honor, his real thoughts, as he recorded them in his Journal for the eyes of his Sovereigns, indicate that he meant to take full advantage of the Tainos' weakness and good nature. "Your Highnesses may believe . . . that this island and all the others are as much yours as Castile, that here is wanting nothing save a settlement, and to command them to do what you will. For I with these people aboard, who are not many, could overrun all these islands without opposition; for already I have seen but three of these mariners go ashore where there was a multitude of these Indians, and all fled without their seeking to do them ill. They bear no arms, and are all unprotected and so very cowardly that a thousand would not face three; so they are fit to be ordered about and made to work, to sow and do aught else that may be needed, and you may build towns and teach them to go clothed and to adopt our customs."

There never crossed the mind of Columbus, or his fellow discoverers and conquistadors, any other notion of relations between Spaniard and American Indian save that of master and slave. It was a conception founded on the Spanish enslavement of Guanches in the Canaries, and on the Portuguese enslavement of Negroes in Africa, which Columbus had observed and taken for granted, and which the Church condoned. It never occurred to him that there was anything wrong in this pattern of race relations, begun and sanctioned by that devout Christian prince, D. Henrique of Portugal. But Las Casas, who spent the better part of a noble life vainly invoking the words and example of Jesus against the cruel and inordinate greed of Castilian Christians, comments on these words of the Admiral in stern and measured words: —

"Note here, that the natural, simple and kind gentleness and humble condition of the Indians, and want of arms or protection, gave the Spaniards the insolence to hold them of little account, and to impose on them the harshest tasks that they could, and to become glutted with oppression and destruction. And sure it is that here the Admiral enlarged himself in speech more than he should, and that what he here conceived and set forth from his lips, was the beginning of the ill usage he afterwards inflicted upon them."

If gold or something else of great and immediate value had not been discovered, the conquest of the New World might have been a brighter page in the history of Christianity. But Columbus was now nearing the gold-bearing regions of Hispaniola. On Monday, he was still talking of Babeque; on Tuesday "the Admiral learned from an old man that there were many neighboring islands within a hundred leagues or more . . . in which much gold was produced; he even told him of an island that was all gold, and in the others so great a quantity that they gather it and sift it as in a sieve, and smelt it and make bars and a thousand works of art; he showed the work by signs. This old man indicated to the Admiral the route and the position where it was; the Admiral determined to go there, and said that if the old man had not been so important a subject of that king, he would have detained him and taken him along, or, if he had known the language, he would have invited him; . . . but there was no sense in irritating them, so he decided to let him go." Without any sense of incongruity, Columbus follows this revelation of his covetousness by an account of raising a cross in the Indian village, at which ceremony the Indians exhibited such proper respect that "he hopes in Our Lord that all these islands will be converted."

Whether the old man had some knowledge of far-off Costa Rica where the Indians really did smelt gold and copper, or whether Columbus misunderstood his gestures, does not matter; the point is that the Admiral was now convinced that the gold-bearing regions lay toward the east; and to the eastward he got under way with the land breeze that very night.

"With the coming of day the wind turned east, with which all this day he could not get clear of the channel between those two islands, and at night he could not make a harbor that showed up there." But from mid-channel he could look far to the eastward, where cape after cape jutted out, a new mountain range showed up, and a high island (as it first appeared) which he called *Monte Caribata*, for he thought that this was the land of the Caribs. It was the mountainous Cape Haitien. That evening the new moon first appeared and soon set; but in the bright tropical starlight Columbus ventured to use the land breeze to make easting.

Sunrise December 20 discovered to the south of them a bay so beautiful that Columbus completely ran out of adjectives, and wished he had not used them all up on earlier harbors and bays. "He excuses himself," abstracts Las Casas, "saying that he has praised the former ones so much that he knows not how to extol this one, and that he fears that he will be supposed to have exaggerated it excessively; but . . . ancient mariners say and will say the same." In twenty-three years' following the sea, and sailing from the Levant to England and south to Guinea, he had seen nothing like it.

La Mar de Sancto Thomé (or *Santo Tomás*) as Columbus called this bay, because it was the vigil of Saint Thomas the Apostle,

Acul Bay, as it is now called after a lady once loved by many sailors, is indeed one of the world's loveliest harbors. It offers such perfect protection in all weathers as to wring admiration from the most hard-boiled mariners. The mountains "which appear to reach the sky," wrote Columbus, "so that the Peak of Tenerife is nothing in comparison," compose like a landscape of Claude Lorrain, about the conical "Bonnet de l'Evêque" that King Henri Christophe crowned with a great stone citadel. But the entrance to Acul Bay is forbidding by reason of the outlying reefs, and Columbus had to feel his way in by lead line and the sharp eyes of boys posted aloft. He left exact directions which are still good today; you line up a little wooded island with the head of the harbor and steer straight for it, favoring the eastward side of the channel, and passing within a lombard shot of the island, which Columbus named *La Amiga*.

That day the wind was very light, the shoaler and more lively *Niña* sailed ahead; and while waiting for *Santa María* to catch up, Vicente Yáñez sent a boat ashore on the friendly little island, where the men dug up some roots that he and the Admiral took to be medicinal rhubarb, the Chinese drug that was imported into Spain over the caravan routes. So excited was Columbus at this evidence of being in Cathay that he later sent a boat 30 miles to obtain more of the plants, which turned out to be only a false rhubarb after all.

At sunset the vessels anchored in the inner harbor, which the Spaniards later called Lombardo Cove, doubtless because it is about half a mile, a "lombard shot," across the mouth. It is so protected, the Admiral says, "that one could moor with the ship's most ancient cable." The American yacht *Alice* proved the truth of this a few years ago, when she rode out a heavy norther in Lombardo Cove without even straightening her anchor chain.

Next morning, December 21, Columbus explored the harbor in the boats and landed and sent two men up a mountain to look for signs of a village. He knew that there must be one near by, from a canoe that had visited the flagship the night before. The men reported a village not far from the sea (the Tainos seldom built right on the seashore for fear of Carib raids), and the boats rowed to the nearest landing, where "so many came, men, women and children, that they covered the shore." As the visitors the previous night had been treated well, these Indians brought cassava bread and water in calabashes and earthenware vessels, and everything that they had. " 'And it should not be said that they gave it freely because it was worth little,' says the Admiral, 'for those who had pieces of gold gave them just as freely as those who gave a calabash of water; and it is easy to recognize,' says the Admiral, 'when something is given with a real heart to give.' "

These Acul Bay people were in an even more pristine state of innocence than elsewhere, for the women did not even wear the customary cotton clout; and whilst "in the other places all the men try to conceal their women from the Christians out of jealousy, here they do not, and the women have very pretty bodies, and they were the first to give thanks to Heaven and to bring what they had, especially things to eat, bread made of yams, and shrivelled quinces, and five or six kinds of fruit," which Columbus tried to preserve in order to exhibit them to the Queen. It is feared that none of his specimens reached Barcelona.

The Admiral remained with the boats, as was his custom, while six men were sent to view the Indian settlement. During their absence some canoes came from the "lords" of other villages on the bay, pressing the Admiral to visit them. This he did later in the day, and the same scenes of cheerful giving and profitable barter were repeated.

At daybreak on the twenty-second the fleet made sail with the land breeze, but found so strong an easterly wind outside that they returned to an anchorage near the mouth of the bay. There Columbus received messengers from Guacanagarí, the cacique who held sway over all northwestern Haiti, and whose seat was on the other side of Cape Haitien. The cacique's messenger brought as a gift the finest work of art that Columbus had yet seen in "The Indies." Las Casas describes it as a cotton girdle embroidered with white and red fishbones interspersed "in the same manner that the embroiderers make the orphreys on the chasubles in Castile." It was four fingers wide, and so stiff and strong that a shot from an arquebus could not penetrate it. In the center was a mask with the ears, tongue and nose of hammered gold.

It was late that day before the messengers managed to convey their invitation, for the Indian interpreters did not understand them very well. Columbus then decided to accept, but to send a boat piloted by the native canoe, to report on the route. In the afternoon he sent six men to another village upcountry, accompanied by Rodrigo de Escobedo the secretary, in order to see that the Indians were not imposed upon; the entire population escorted this embassy back to the ship, carrying the Spaniards pick-a-back across rivers and through swamps, and bearing fat tree ducks, skeins of cotton, and some little pieces of gold. That night and the next the Spaniards were kept awake entertaining visitors; Columbus reckoned that a thousand natives boarded *Santa María* in canoes, each bringing some gift, and that five hundred more came out swimming for want of canoes, although she was anchored almost a league from the shore. Everyone who appeared to enjoy some authority was questioned through the interpreters about gold, and the Admiral wrote, "Our Lord in his goodness guide me that I may find this gold, I mean their mine, for many here say they have knowledge of it." Columbus had high hopes of finding a rich gold-bearing region, like La Mina which he had visited on the coast of Guinea.

Sunday evening, December 23, the boat returned from Guacanagarí's village, reporting multitudes of people so eager to see the Admiral that "if the feast of the Nativity could be held in that harbor, all the people of that island, which he now guessed to be bigger than England, would come to see them." They brought basketfuls of presents for the Admiral, including pieces of gold and live parrots, as well as promises of lavish hospitality. The men who manned the boat reported that the course was clear to the royal residence, and recommended it as the perfect place to keep Christmas.

A merry enough Christmas might have been spent in Acul Bay;

the real pull of Guacanagarí's invitation was the report of one of his subjects who came back with the boat, "concerning *Çipango,* which they called *Çybao.*" Cipangu, it will be recalled, was Marco Polo's name for Japan; and although he intended the initial "Ci" to be pronounced in the Italian manner *chi,* the Spaniards pronounced it after their manner, *Sipango.* So, when the Indians spoke of the *Cibao,* as central Hispaniola is still called to this day, and "declared that there was a great quantity of gold there," which was in a measure true, "and that the cacique bore banners of beaten gold," which was not, Columbus concluded that at last he was on the road to the fabulous Cipangu of the gold-roofed palaces.

So, after inditing another tribute to the kindness, generosity and "singularly loving behavior" of the Indians whom he was planning to enslave, Columbus took his departure from Acul Bay before sunrise on December 24, planning to spend a merry Christmas with Guacanagarí in Japan. He was heading for his first serious accident.

CHAPTER XXI

La Navidad
December 24, 1492–January 16, 1493

Qui autem in praesidiis et speluncis sunt, peste morientur.

And they that be in the forts and in the caves shall die.
— EZEKIEL xxxiii 27

IN DUE COURSE the trade wind blew up from the eastward — in Northern Hispaniola it generally runs parallel to the coast — and the two vessels had a tiresome day beating to windward, taking long tacks off shore, and making little progress because the wind was light and the current set westerly. Columbus took the opportunity to note down sailing directions for Acul Bay, and to write the words in praise of the natives that we have already quoted. Nightfall Christmas eve found *Santa María* and *Niña* off a high, rocky headland that he named *Punta Santa* in reference to the approaching festival, and which is now called Cape Haitien. At 11 P.M. when the watch was changed, *Santa María* had progressed only a league beyond the cape. The wind had died away until only occasional light airs ruffled the calm surface of the bay, and no sound was heard but a far-off swish of surf on the coral ledges of Cape Haitien harbor and the barrier reef that encloses Caracol Bay from the ocean. It was just such a night as Milton tells preceded the day of Christ's Nativity, when

> The winds, with wonder whist
> Smoothly the waters kist,
> Whispering new joys to the mild ocean,
> Who now hath quite forgot to rave,
> While birds of calm sit brooding on the charmed wave.

The middle watch was very loath to be routed out, for it had been impossible to sleep aboard on the two previous nights with curious savages swarming all over the flagship. The course to their destination seemed perfectly clear, for it had already been studied by the men who made the journey in the ship's boat; this was in fact the first night's sail on the entire voyage whose course had in some measure been charted before. *Niña* as usual was showing the way, and in the faint light of a setting five-day-old moon her spars and limp sails could be dimly seen. Yet the moon was too young and low to reveal any ruffle of white water where the ground swell was breaking lazily on three coral reefs, almost dead ahead. A feeling of complete security, the most fatal delusion that a seaman can entertain, stole like an opiate over the sleepy men aboard *Santa María*. The great majority of accidents at sea are not due to violence of the elements or defects in the ship, but to ignorance and over-confidence as to the ship's position.

Eleven o'clock, one hour before Christmas. The gromet on duty turns the *ampolleta* and sings his ditty,

> *Siete va pasada*
> *y en ocho muele;*
> *mas molera*
> *si mi Dios quería,*
> *a mi Dios pidamos,*
> *que bien viaje hagamos . . .*

The pilot scratches on his slate the few miles he reckoned *Santa María* had made during the last four hours, the helm is relieved, and everyone off duty curls up in the steerage or along the bulwarks, and soon falls fast asleep. Columbus paces the quarter-deck for a few minutes, exchanges a few inconsequential remarks with Juan de la Cosa, the new officer of the watch, and retires to his cabin. He thanks God for another day's safe sailing, and for sending His only begotten Son to redeem the world. For a few moments he ponders on that scene in the stable at Bethlehem, then says an *Ave Maria* and falls into a deep sleep, his first in over forty-eight hours.

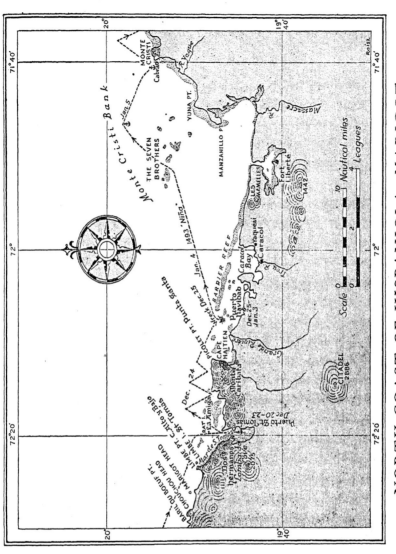

NORTH COAST OF HISPANIOLA, MARIGOT
TO MONTE CRISTI

As soon as the Old Man is out of sight, the lookouts, boys and other members of the middle watch select soft spots on the deck to indulge in a bit of "shut-eye" themselves. Juan de la Cosa paces the quarter-deck a few times, yawning heavily, looks all around the horizon and sees no sign of wind, notes *Niña* leading the way, orders the helmsman (whom it was his duty to con) to steer by a star and call him if there is any change in wind or weather, and lies below to resume his own sleep. And pretty soon the helmsman, who had dozed off once or twice already, decides he can bear it no longer, kicks awake the gromet whose duty it is to turn the *ampolleta*, gives him charge of the huge, unwieldy tiller (which Columbus had forbidden under all circumstances) and curls up to sleep in the steerage. So of forty men and boys (not counting Indian captives) aboard the flagship, nobody was awake but one little gromet. *Niña* was invisible to him. He could see nothing out of the dark, low steerage. The creaking of the great rudder on its gudgeons, and the groans and squeaks and slats and rattles that any sailing ship makes in a calm, shut out the sound of surf from his ears.

Just as the sand in the *ampolleta* ran out for the second time that watch, indicating that Christmas Day had begun, *Santa María* slid onto a shelving coral reef in Caracol Bay, so gently that nobody was awakened. The sleepy boy was brought to attention by feeling the rudder ground, then he heard the ground swell breaking close aboard, and "gave tongue," says Columbus. The Admiral was first on deck, then Juan de la Cosa ran out of his cabin, and before many moments elapsed the deck was full of men and the calm night was broken with shouts, orders, curses and imprecations.

Columbus promptly sized up the situation. *Santa María* had grounded gently, bow on; and as she drew more water aft than forward, the best chance to float her was to warp an anchor out into deep water, lead the cable through the tiller-port to the big windlass forward, and kedge her off stern first.

He ordered the master to haul in the ship's boat that was towing astern, take the anchor and cable aboard, and go to it. Instead of executing this proper seamanlike order, Juan de la Cosa with some of his Basque pals piled into the boat and pulled away to *Niña* in order to save their own skins. And *Santa María* had but the one boat. Vicente Yáñez very properly refused to allow these cowardly refugees aboard, and ordered them back, having previously sent over *Niña's* boat well manned to do what they could to help the Admiral.

In the meantime, *Santa María* was being driven higher and higher on the reef by the long swells that came in from seaward, her stern swung around so that she lay athwart the seas, each surge lifted her up and let her down with a thump on the rock; and coral rock can punch holes in a wooden ship faster than any other kind. So Columbus ordered the heavy mainmast cut away in order to lighten her. By the time *Niña's* boat came alongside it was too late to kedge her off and presently the seams had opened with the pounding, and the hull was filling with water. Seeing he could do no more, Columbus allowed himself and his crew to be ferried to *Niña*, and stood by until daylight.

Since this was one of the notable shipwrecks of history, we may pause a moment to comment. There is no allusion to it in the prolonged lawsuit between the heirs of Columbus and the crown, in which every effort was made to cast dirt on the departed Admiral. Hence it is natural to conclude that his own account of it is correct. The major blame attaches to Juan de la Cosa, who was not only master and part owner of *Santa María*, but officer of the middle watch that night. It was his responsibility to see that proper discipline was maintained, and he had no business to turn in and leave the deck in charge of a gromet. When the ship struck he showed gross insubordination and want of common seamanship in disobeying the Admiral's orders; pulling away to *Niña* and leaving *Santa María* to her fate was mutinous. Was it cowardice? Columbus himself calls the action of the master and his pals *traición* — treachery, making no charge of *cobardía* or poltroonery; and pure treachery I think it was. For men who had made the first ocean crossing, a gentle grounding on a calm night a few miles from shore was no occasion for funk. Reading between the lines, it seems that Juan de la

Cosa was one of that contemptible breed of mariners who are jealous of their superior officer, and who make factions among the crew. Perhaps he thought himself a better seaman than Columbus, and his pride had been hurt by frequent overriding of his orders; for men of genius, imbued with one idea, are not always considerate of their inferiors. Perhaps there had been some wrangle between them about the very course they were sailing that night. Hence, I imagine, Juan de la Cosa's first thought on waking up and finding his ship aground was "damn him, he got her on and he can get her off," and he obeyed a disloyal impulse to save his particular cronies and leave the Castilians to get off as best they could. So singular an action on the part of a shipmaster and shipowner can hardly be explained except by some grave defect in his character.

The first Christmas to be celebrated in the New World was marked not by Masses and carols or feasting and sports, but by unremitting hard labor to float *Santa María* and salvage her stores, cargo and equipment. At daybreak Columbus sent ashore Diego de Harana and Pedro Gutiérrez to ask Guacanagarí's assistance, while he in the other boat made directly for the ship from behind the line of reef. By the time the sun was high Guacanagarí had sent out all his canoes and many of his people to discharge the ship, and that heavy task was almost completed on Christmas day. The cacique and his brothers kept careful watch both aboard and ashore to see that none of the cargo or the gear was stolen; and Columbus records that not so much as a lace point, a board or a nail was pilfered, although holes had to be chopped in the deck and topsides in order to get at some of the cargo. "From time to time," the cacique "sent one of his relatives to the weeping Admiral to console him, telling him that he must not be troubled or annoyed; that he would give him whatever he had." At sunrise December 26 Guacanagarí came aboard *Niña*, to which the Admiral had transferred his flag, "and almost weeping said that he must not show grief, that he would give him all he had, and that he had given the Christians who were ashore two very big houses, and would give more if necessary. . . . 'To such extent,' says the Admiral, 'are they loyal and without greed for the property of others, and that king was virtuous above all.' "

Gold dried more tears than sympathy. Even as he was receiving this early morning consolation from Guacanagarí a canoe from another place came alongside, the paddlers so eager for hawks' bells that they stood up, showing bits of gold and shouting "*Chuque! chuque!*" to imitate the sound of the little tinkly bells which they were mad to possess. Guacanagarí stood by in dignified silence until this unseemly barter was concluded, and then let fall that if the Admiral would keep one hawk's bell for him, he would pay for it "four pieces of gold as big as the hand. The Admiral rejoiced to hear this, and later a seaman who came from shore said to the Admiral that it was marvellous the pieces of gold that the Christians ashore bartered for nothing; for a lace-point they gave pieces of gold worth more than two castellanos, and that this was nothing in respect to what it would be after a month. The king rejoiced to see the Admiral merry, and understood that he desired much gold, and said by signs that he knew a place near at hand where there was plenty of it in great abundance, and that he should be of good cheer, that he would give him as much gold as he wanted, . . . and especially that in *Çipango*, which they call *Çybao*, there was such a lot of it that they hold it for naught."

After giving this welcome information the cacique was presented with a shirt and a pair of gloves which pleased him immensely; thus clothed he was invited to dinner aboard *Niña*, which was probably not so pleasant. After that was over Guacanagarí treated the Admiral to what he considered a real dinner ashore. Columbus partook of "two or three kinds of *ajes*" (yams or sweet potatoes), of roast hutía and lobsters, and "their bread that they call *caçabí*," cassava bread. The cacique ate so cleanly and decently, even washing his hands and rubbing them with herbs after the meal, that Columbus regarded him as one of nature's gentlemen. After dinner Guacanagarí led his guest to the *playa*, the strip of level white sand between his village and the mangrove swamps that fringe Caracol Bay; and when he began to talk of the dreadful

Caribs and their bows and arrows which so terrified the Tainos, Columbus said, "I'll show you," and had one of his men put on an archery exhibit with a Turkish bow and arrows saved from the wreck. This was followed up by some lombard and musket shots, which terrified the natives and convinced Guacanagarí that his visitors were allies worth having. He presented to the Admiral, apparently without ironical intent, a great mask that had golden ears and eyes.

In no entry of Columbus's Journal are the workings of his mind so clear as on this day after his first Christmas in the New World. He now concluded that the shipwreck was the predestined will of God, in order to enable him to discover the Cibao gold mine and make a settlement. As Las Casas quotes his exact words, "So many things came to hand that in truth it was no disaster but great luck; for it is certain that if I had not run aground I should have kept to sea without anchoring in this place, because it is situated within a great bay, . . . nor on this voyage could I have left people here, or, had I desired to leave them, could I have given them good equipment, or so many weapons or supplies." Even poor mishandled *Santa María* is now written off the Admiral's books, because she was "very heavy and not suitable for the business of discovery." He concludes this day's work with the pious hope that the men he is leaving behind will obtain a barrel of gold by barter and also find "the mine of gold and the spicery," from whose products the Sovereigns will be able "to go and conquer the Holy Sepulchre" within three years. For, says he, "I declared to Your Highnesses that all the gain of this my Enterprise should be spent in the conquest of Jerusalem, and Your Highnesses smiled and said that it pleased you, and that even without this you had that strong desire." Smile if you will; but there can be no doubt of Columbus's sincerity in this matter. Even in such a crisis of the voyage his thoughts ran to Jerusalem regained.

Before the shipwreck Columbus had no intention of founding a settlement on this voyage of discovery, for he had only enough men to work his vessels. Now, making a settlement answered the question what to do with *Santa María's* people. There was no knowing what had become of *Pinta*, and the forty men from *Santa María* overcrowded little *Niña* with her crew of twenty-two. Guacanagarí was friendly, even affectionate; Cipangu-Cibao lay near, and the Spaniards were begging their Admiral for permission to remain behind, in order to get first whack at the gold, before all Castile came flocking over to buy castellanos at two a penny. So Columbus gave orders that a "tower and fortress" be erected ashore, and named it *La Navidad* in honor of the day of disaster that had so unexpectedly been turned to advantage — as he thought.

The shallow bay where fate decreed that this first, ill-fated European settlement in the New World should be attempted still remains nameless, although in the eighteenth century it was one of the richest localities in all America. About twelve miles long by three wide, it is bounded by the rocky peninsula of Cape Haitien (Columbus's Punta Santa), where the French later built their gay "Paris of the Antilles," by a rich alluvial plain, a tangle of mangrove swamp, and a barrier reef pierced by the broad channel where *Santa María* sailed her last sail. This reef protects the bay from the sea. A little behind the shore of the eastern section of this bay, which the Spaniards named *Caracol* because of the snail-like boat channels through the mangrove swamp, was Guacanagarí's village.

Facing the reef where *Santa María* was wrecked, near the middle of the bay and about two miles to the southward, is a long sand beach; and somewhere near its eastern end Columbus selected the site for Navidad.

Here the French founded an *embarcadère* for the wealthy alluvial parish of Limonade, which on the eve of the Revolution had thirty-seven sugar mills with an annual production of eight million pounds, and numerous coffee plantations, indigo works, and rum distilleries. All that is now ruined; but there is a small Haitian fishing village, Limonade Bord-de-Mer, very near the point on the beach where Columbus founded his fort; and in the Admiral's *Puerto de la Navidad* the fishermen moor their small craft today, except when a norther compels them to haul out. Columbus would have done better to have pitched this first American colony on Cape Haitien Harbor; but the convenience of having it near the wreck was obvious, and the misconduct of the garrison would have brought the same result, wherever located.

Navidad fort was built largely of *Santa María's* planks, timbers and fastenings, and provided with a "great cellar" for storage of wine, biscuit and other stores salvaged from the flagship. Seeds for sowing crops and a supply of trading truck to barter for gold were also left. Thirty-nine men picked from the two caravels were placed under the command of Diego de Harana, the marshal of the fleet, and cousin to the Admiral's mistress. Juan de Medina the tailor, Lope the ship-caulker, Alonso Morales, "chips" of *Niña*, Domingo Vizcaino the cooper, Chachu the Basque boatswain, Diego Pérez the ship's painter, "a gunner who was a man of good skill," Luis de Torres the converted Jewish interpreter, Rodrigo de Escobedo the secretary, Maestre Juan and Maestre Alonso the two ships' surgeons, and Pedro Gutiérrez the former butler of the king's dais, were among the volunteers who deemed themselves lucky to be chosen to man the fort. Columbus left *Santa María's* boat with the garrison, so that they could explore the coast, discover the gold mine, and find a better harbor than Navidad for a permanent settlement.

Several days elapsed while the men worked on the fort, with helpful Indians doing the lighterage and heavy lifting. Columbus exchanged daily visits, banquets and presents with Guacanagarí and his subject caciques. On the twenty-seventh some Indians arrived with news that *Pinta* was lying in a river two days' sail to the eastward. Guacanagarí furnished a canoe to bear a messenger and a "loving letter" from Columbus, who tactfully concealed his displeasure at the desertion, and begged Martín Alonso to return, "since Our Lord had shown them all so much favor." For Columbus did not wish to explore that unknown coast without a consort; one more grounding might be fatal. The canoe turned back without delivering the letter, but the messenger reported having seen a "king" with two great plates of gold on his head. On the thirtieth another Indian from the eastward declared that he had seen *Pinta;* and although some believed he was lying, the Admiral thought it best to make haste in that direction.

A choice item in the collection of mendacious stories that were circulated about Columbus after his death is this. Columbus lost himself on the way to Hispaniola, and only by virtue of letters and pilots sent by Martín Alonso did he manage to find the island and join *Pinta.*

On January 2, 1493, Guacanagarí and Columbus had a farewell party. The Admiral staged a sham fight and had *Niña* fire lombard shots through the grounded hull of *Santa María* in order to impress the natives. "The cacique showed the Admiral much love and great grief at his parting, especially when he saw him embark." After final embraces, and protestations of mutual love and esteem, Columbus was rowed aboard his new flagship *Niña*, intending to weigh anchors at once; but the wind in the meantime had turned east, and the sea was reported rough outside. So he remained in harbor that night and all next day, and also a second night because some of the Indians were still missing, and he wished to give them another chance to come aboard. How typical of exploring voyages was this delay to await the pleasure of dilatory, drunk or unwilling shipmates! Finally on the morning of Friday, January 4, "at sunrise he weighed anchors with a light wind, and the boat led the caravel out on a NW course, to get clear of the reef."

Columbus intended to shape a course directly for Spain, fearing lest Martín Alonso beat him home with the news and escape "the punishment that he deserved for having done so ill by parting company without permission." Once outside the reefs he sighted to the eastward what appeared to be an island "in the shape of a very fine tent, to which he gave the name Monte Cristi," a name it bears to this day. The peninsula, as it proved to be, looks exactly like a great yellow tent with a ridgepole, when one sights it at sea. You do not see its connection with the shore until about halfway from Cape Haitien.

Owing to light wind, *Niña* could not make Monte Cristi that day. She passed among the islets called the Seven Brothers and anchored on the edge of the bank, well out to sea. On the fifth she made the natural harbor between Monte Cristi and Isla Cabra, a harbor "sheltered from all winds except the N and NW, and he says that they seldom blow in that country." Oh! don't they? Las Casas, who knew better, interpolates here, "The Admiral had never experienced the fury of these two winds."

On the morning of January 6, sailing on a Sunday as he was so eager to get along, the Admiral did a good stretch eastward with the land breeze. At noon the trade wind blew up fresh, forcing *Niña* to take a leg offshore, near some shoals where the Comte de Grasse's great flagship *Ville de Paris* touched in 1781 when she was hastening to Chesapeake Bay. Columbus sent a seaman aloft to spy out the deep spots, when whom should he see but *Pinta* scudding down-wind towards them. And as there was no anchorage near, *Niña* put about and sailed back to the Isla Cabra anchorage in her company.

Martín Alonso came aboard the flagship that evening "to excuse himself, alleging that he had left him against his will, giving reasons for it. But the Admiral says that they were all false, and that with much insolence and greed he had separated that night that he parted from him, and that he knew not (says the Admiral) whence came the insolence and disloyalty that he had shown him on that voyage, which the Admiral wished to forget, in order not to help the evil works of Satan, who sought to hinder that voyage." It appeared that *Pinta* had called at Babeque (Great Inagua) and found no gold, thence proceeded eastward to Monte Cristi, and for three weeks had been in a harbor to the eastward — probably Puerto Blanco — where she had found plenty. According to his son Arias Pérez, who joined *Pinta* at Bayona and heard the story of this voyage from his father's lips, Martín Alonso made an excursion upcountry from the harbor, reached the territory of the powerful Caonabó, and brought back much gold. If this be true, and not merely part of the Pinzón "build-up," Martín Alonso was first to reach the Cibao, the gold-bearing region which had been Columbus's objective in Hispaniola.

Martín Alonso, it seems, had heard from the Indians of *Santa María's* shipwreck, and was sailing down-wind to join the others when he met *Niña*. Both Admiral and captain must have been relieved at finding a consort for the homeward passage, and Columbus decided that he could now afford to explore the rest of Northern Hispaniola before taking off for Spain. But, owing to the manner in which they had parted, the meeting must have been unpleasant. Vicente Yáñez showed a tendency to gang up with the rest of the Pinzón family against Columbus, "and did not obey his orders, but did and said many improper things against him . . . and they were very undisciplined people," and "a mutinous lot." So the Admiral determined "to make the greatest possible haste" home. "I will not suffer," he says, "the deeds of lewd fellows devoid of virtue, who contrary to him who conferred honor upon them, presume to do their own will with slight respect."

Two days wind-bound at Monte Cristi were employed in caulking *Niña*, taking on wood and water, and exploring the lower course of the Rio Yaque del Norte. Columbus reported it to be so full of gold that grains of the fine metal adhered to the barrel hoops when they filled the casks with river water, and some of these grains were as large as lentils. Las Casas comments marginally, "I think that most of it would have been fool's gold, because there's much of it in that place, and the Admiral was much too inclined to think that all's gold that glitters." Perhaps so; but this Rio Yaque drains the Cibao, principal source of gold in Hispaniola, and on its upper waters in 1494 Columbus built his first interior fort. Even today there is gold in the valley of the Yaque; the country women pan it out and collect the grains in quills of turkey feathers, which they take to the market towns as currency. So I think that here the Spaniards found their first virgin gold in the New World.

On the way to this Rio del Oro, as Columbus called the Yaque del Norte, "he saw three *serenas* (mermaids) who rose very high from the sea, but they were not as beautiful as they are painted, although to some extent they have a human appearance in the face. He said that he had seen some in Guinea on the coast of Malagueta." These last were the West African dugong; the Haitian "mermaids" were the Caribbean manatee or sea cow whose articulated head and armlike fore limbs have an uncanny human appearance. They are certainly not beautiful, but stuffed manatee used to be a staple of our country fairs as "gen-u-wine mermaids." Columbus's habit of accurate and honest observation is proved by resisting the temptation to engraft these sea cows onto the classical myth. What a good story it would have made for the Sovereigns, to have the Spaniards conducted to their first River of Gold by lovely and seductive mermaids!

Eager to get on with the voyage, and break up the Pinzón cabal, Columbus ordered sail to be made at midnight January 8 despite a SE wind, and took an ENE leg out to sea. Coming about during the day, the two vessels made anchorage that night in the shelter of a cape that Columbus named *Punta Roja;* it was probably the modern Punta Rucía. The rich hinterland and wooded mountains tempted him to stay, but he pressed on. On January 10 the caravels made Puerto Blanco, where *Pinta* had traded so profitably on her own. Martín Alonso had named it after himself; but Columbus, annoyed at this presumption on the part of his disloyal subordinate, changed the name to Rio de Gracia, River of Grace. This indicated that Martín Alonso was pardoned, but had better behave himself in future. "His wickedness was notorious," notes Columbus, "for he had kept half the gold obtained for himself, and had taken by force four Indian men and two wenches," whom the Admiral caused to be set ashore. Apparently it was immoral for anyone but himself to kidnap Indians.

Next day, the fleet sighted the Loma Isabela de Torres, which Columbus named *Monte Plata*, because of the silver clouds that covered its summit; he looked into the harbor at its foot (Puerto Plata), but did not tarry. Many capes and harbors were discovered that day, and the night was spent jogging off-and-on outside Escocesa Bay, for fear of shoals to the eastward. At dawn January 12 the two caravels made sail and went boiling along before a fresh westerly, skipping several tempting bays and harbors because of the good chance to make easting. That evening they rounded Cape Samaná, which Columbus well said looked like Cape St. Vincent, but he romantically named it *Cabo del Enamorado* (of the Lover), probably because it suggested some "lovers' leap" that he had seen in Spain. They continued along the coast southwesterly around Punta Balandra, and came to an anchor in 12 fathoms near the mouth of Samaná Bay, between Cayo Levantado (which Columbus described as *una isleta pequeñuela*, "a tiny little island") and the northern shore.

Here, on a pretty beach just east of a point that is still called Las Flechas (The Arrows), Columbus came as close as he ever did on this voyage to a dangerous encounter with the Indians. Samaná Bay, according to Las Casas, was inhabited by a tribe called the Ciguayos, Arawaks who had either received an infiltration of Caribs, or who in self-defense adopted Carib weapons. When the boat went ashore to obtain a few yams — for Columbus had been overgenerous with supplies for Navidad, and wished to stock up for the homeward passage — his people encountered some very ugly natives whose faces were stained with charcoal instead of painted in bright Taino colors, and whose long coarse hair was gathered behind into nets of parrots' feathers. And, what was more significant, they were carrying bows and arrows, the first that the Spaniards had seen in the Indies. Columbus had passed Escocesa Bay so far offshore that he could see no land at the head of it, consequently he believed that Cape Samaná and Balandra Head belonged to a separate island, and that these ill-favored fellows were the dreaded Caribs. He questioned one of them through an interpreter, who, as Las Casas comments, did not understand the language; for when inquiry was made about gold the interpreter picked up the word *guanin*. This was an alloy of gold and copper that the Indians smelted on the mainland, but the Spaniards took it to be the name of an island where gold was to be found. After this quiz the Indian was brought aboard to be suitably entertained as a decoy for the others, and later sent ashore with an assortment of trinkets and bits of colored cloth; but the usual impression made by these free samples was not produced.

When *Niña's* boat landed over fifty naked Indians armed with bows and arrows and palm-tree cudgels were encountered. At

ANCHORAGE OF *NINA* AND *PINTA* IN SAMANA BAY

the instance of the shore-going native they laid aside their weapons, which the Spaniards endeavored to buy; but after two bows had been sold, the Indians ran back to their deposit of weapons as if to pick them up and attack. "The Christians being prepared, as always the Admiral advised them to be, fell upon them, and gave an Indian a great slash on the buttocks and wounded another in the breast with an arrow. Seeing that they could gain little, although the Christians were not more than seven and they fifty and more, they turned in flight, until not one remained, one leaving his arms here, and another his bows there." Plenty of souvenirs were obtained by the landing party.

Next day, January 14, a cacique came down to the beach without weapons and was entertained aboard and sent away "content," biscuits and honey inside, and a red cap and beads outside. He promised a gold crown in return; and the crown was duly sent aboard on the fifteenth, together with some skeins of cotton.

Both caravels were leaking badly (owing, says the Admiral, to scamped work by the Palos shipyards), and he and Pinzón were eager to find a suitable beach for careening and caulking them before the long voyage home. But there was something so odd and sinister about these Ciguayos that the men were uneasy and eager to be off. Columbus had planned, he says, to stay over the seventeenth, in order to observe a conjunction of Mars with Mercury, and an opposition of Jupiter with the sun that was predicted in his Regiomontanus *Ephemerides*. But he dared not risk a longer stay; and when the wind came west on Wednesday, January 16, he decided to leave this "Bay of the Arrows." It was the last anchorage of *Pinta* and *Niña* in the New World.

CHAPTER XXII

Homeward Passage

January 16–February 11, 1493

Et cum anchoras sustulissent, committebant se mari, . . .
et leuato artemone secundum aurae flatum . . .

And when they had taken up the anchors, they committed
themselves unto the sea . . . and hoisted up the mainsail
to the wind. . . .

— ACTS xxvii 40

IN THE DARK of the moon, three hours before daybreak on
Wednesday, January 16, 1493, the Admiral "departed from
the gulf which he called *el Golfo de las Flechas* (of the Arrows)
with the land breeze, afterwards with the wind West, turning the
prow East and by North." So begins his Journal of the first homeward passage from America to Europe. It proved to be a far more
difficult feat of navigation than the outward passage of discovery,
for no soft trade winds would serve to blow the two caravels gently
back to Spain. Columbus must get them out of the trade-wind
area and into the zone of westerlies; and it was the winter season
when westerlies in the North Atlantic are strong and boisterous,
accompanied by heavy rain and high seas. The Admiral would need
all his resources of seamanship to cope with the weather, and all
his native wit to deal with the Portuguese, before he could report
his discovery to the Sovereigns of Spain. And he must accomplish
this without *Santa María.* The homeward passage is a fascinating
story of a man of genius, with the greatest geographical secret of
all time locked in his breast, fighting against human depravity and
winter weather for the privilege of making known his glad tidings.

When *Niña* and *Pinta* passed Balandra Head, Bay of Samaná, before daybreak on January 16, it was not supposed that the voyage of discovery was over. From the Indians of Hispaniola, particularly four youths who boarded *Niña* at Samaná and were promptly impressed, Columbus learned of an *Isla de Carib* (probably Puerto Rico), visible "from there." The Admiral was curious to see those dreadful man-eating Caribs, of whose incredible exploits he had been told by the timid Tainos; and he was even more eager to check their tale of an island named *Matinino*, "wholly inhabited by women without men." Later conquistadores connected this with the classical myth of the Amazons, and so named the world's greatest river; but Columbus was looking for oriental evidence. He had read in Marco Polo of the Islands Masculina and Feminea in the Indian Ocean, the one exclusively inhabited by men and the other only by women. Every year the men visited the female island and stayed three months, after which the women threw them out, along with the small boys who were growing up. This tale seemed such an amusing and practical solution to the eternal war between the sexes that it became one of the most popular of Marco Polo's yarns.

Now, curiously enough, the Arawaks had a very similar myth. Their culture-hero Guagugiona set forth with a chosen band of shipmates and women passengers from the cave Cacibagiagua in which all mankind hitherto had lived, in order to discover new lands for *Lebensraum*. He left all the women on an island called Matinino, where they had lived an Amazon-like existence ever since, receiving the annual male visitation and all that, just as Marco Polo had described on the Female Island in the Indian Ocean. Columbus's eagerness to see this Isle of Women came not only from a natural male curiosity, and the desire to relate a genuine marvel, but because it would furnish that incontrovertible evidence of being in the Indies which he still lacked. And he wished, as he wrote, "to bring five or six" of the women "to the Sovereigns." So the Admiral's plan was to touch at the Carib Isle, visit Matinino, and then head for Spain.

Niña and *Pinta* passed out of Samaná Bay on January 16, 1493, with a westerly wind (which was exceptional for that season), and steered E by N, which the impressed Indians indicated to be the course for the Isle of Women. Actually that course took the fleet out to sea. Before they had sailed 40 miles the Indians began to make signs that the Amazon Isle lay to the southeastward. Assuming that they meant the actual island of Martinique, this was correct. Columbus changed course accordingly, and very shortly changed his plan too. As the Journal says: —

"After he had gone two leagues the wind freshened, very good to go to Spain. He observed among the people that they began to be downhearted because they were deviating from the direct course, because of the considerable water that both caravels were making, and they had no remedy save in God. He had to abandon the course that he thought led to the island, and turned to the direct course for Spain, NE by E, and proceeded thus until sunset 48 Roman miles which are 12 leagues."

This is one of the few quick changes of plan that Columbus made, and certainly it was wise. On the return passage of his Second Voyage, in the winter season of 1496, it took *Niña* a month to beat from Isabela in Northern Hispaniola to Guadeloupe, which is nearer than Martinique. The chance of collecting a few women, some oriental evidence and a tall tale, was not worth the delay.

The key to Columbus's plan for the homeward passage is that sentence in his Journal for January 16 on the change of course: *bolvió al derecho de España, nordeste quarta del leste,* "he turned to the direct course for Spain, Northeast and by East." He was grossly mistaken if he supposed this to be the direct course for Spain. It would have missed even the British Isles, and fetched up somewhere in the Arctic. Yet, just as his colossal underestimate of the width of the Ocean led him to discover America, so this equally gross error in the course for home enabled him to get there. For, as the experience of later voyages proved, the fastest route for a sailing vessel from Hispaniola to Europe was to work northward, close-hauled on the trade wind, to the latitude of Bermuda, and there catch the prevailing westerlies for Spain. Columbus, of course, did not know this. He apparently expected a convenient westerly turn of wind, in the latitude where he then was. Actually the trade wind never did allow him to steer NE by E; yet, by clinging as close as he could to that course, sailing anywhere from N by E to NE by N on the starboard tack, coming about and heading from E to SE on the port tack when the wind headed him, he made northing pretty steadily, toward the latitude of Bermuda where the brave winter westerlies would send the caravels rolling home before the wind.

Columbus had a very good chance for his homeward as for his outward passage, and the caravels did very well on this long beat to windward; their performance inspires respect for their weatherly qualities. Although most of the twenty-four-hour runs were less than 100 miles, *Niña* (with *Pinta* holding her back) logged 127 on January 21 and 138 on January 19, this last being an average of 5.7 knots, and on four different courses; very nice sailing indeed.* As yet the trade wind had not raised enough head sea to bother them. " 'The air,' says the Admiral, 'very soft and sweet as in Seville during April and May,' and 'the sea,' says he, 'many thanks be to God, always very smooth.' " Next day, having reached latitude 25°, the air was notably cooler. After you become used to the tropics, a drop of five degrees Fahrenheit seems terrible.

On the first day out they entered the Sargasso Sea, on the evening of the third they saw the new moon, and every day boatswain-birds, boobies and petrels were about; the man-o'-war birds followed them for 200 miles from the islands. Columbus, observing one of these that circled the caravel "and later made off to the SSE," inferred "that in that quarter there were some islands," which gave him an idea for the Second Voyage. A welcome sight was a school of tunny fish, with which Spaniards were familiar at home. As they sped away northeasterly the Admiral joked with the men, saying that the tunnies must be bound for the Duke of Cadiz's

---

* Distances quoted are all net, after deducting the 15 per cent average over-estimate in the Journal for the homeward passage.

tuna-meat factory at Conil near Cape Trafalgar; too bad we can't throw them a line!

Shortly before midnight of January 22, *Niña* and *Pinta* crossed the route of the outward passage, and entered a wide stretch of the North Atlantic where no ship had sailed before. Seamen used to call this zone the "horse latitudes" from the long calms fatal to livestock, but Columbus fortunately knew nothing about that. On January 25, when he crossed latitude 28° and sailed but 49 miles, "the seamen killed a porpoise and a tremendous shark; and he says that they had good need of them, because they had nothing left to eat but bread and wine and *ajes* of the Indies." A pretty grim prospect for grub, to be sure.

From noon January 27 to sunrise January 30 the fleet ran ENE with a light southerly breeze, and in sixty-six hours footed only 112 miles. They were lucky to do so well. Fish were caught and birds and gulfweed were sighted every day. During the last two days of January the wind picked up a little, and by sunset January 31, according to Captain McElroy's plotting of the Admiral's dead-reckoning, they had reached latitude 31° 46' N, very near that of Bermuda (32° 15'), which lay about 450 miles to the westward. This was the point where, as the Spaniards learned a few years later, one might expect to catch the westerlies, and straighten out for the run home; and that is what happened to Columbus. From sunrise January 31 until sunset February 3, "with the same wind aft" and "the sea very smooth, thank God," the caravels made 358 miles to the ENE: "sea so covered with weed that if they hadn't seen it before they would have been afraid of shoals." They were right in the midst of the Sargasso Sea. February 1 was the night of full moon, and the effect of moonlight on a sargassum-covered ocean with a fresh and favoring wind impelling your ships through the undulating meadow at a high rate of speed, the weed making a peculiar soft swishing sound as it brushes by, has a strange and magical beauty.

Undoubtedly Columbus had set the new course ENE, one point south of his "direct" course for Spain, because he deemed it necessary to compensate for the many days that he had been forced to sail to the northward. But how far north of that direct course was he? With changes of course almost every day it had been difficult to plot the dead-reckoning, and Columbus was none too sure that this ENE course would lead to Spain. Actually it would have led him somewhere between Scotland and Iceland. Accordingly on the night of February 2–3, the much-abused quadrant and a hitherto unmentioned astrolabe were brought on deck for the Admiral to try another shot at Polaris. But he was out of practice and had waited too long. Three days of westerlies had raised quite a swell, and *Niña* was rolling and pitching too heavily for these crude instruments to catch a luminous pinpoint in the heavens. Too bad, for this time Columbus made no mistake in the identity of Polaris. He remarked "the North Star appeared very high, as on Cape St. Vincent," which is on latitude 37° N. According to our interpretation of Columbus's dead-reckoning, at sunset February 2 he was crossing latitude 33° 36', and at sunrise the third had reached 34° 15'. Consequently his calculation was not less than 165 and not more than 200 miles out; not bad for a naked-eye star shot.

Columbus's belief that he was approaching latitude 37° N was confirmed by a change of weather on the night of February 3. "The sky was very overcast and rainy, and it was rather cold, because of which he knew he had not reached the height of the Azores." This statement seems a *non sequitur*, for the Azores are notably cold and rainy in winter. But he evidently believed that *Niña* had made sufficient northing, for at sunrise on February 4 he set his course due East.

Niña and *Pinta*, according to our plotting of Columbus's dead-reckoning, were now in latitude 35° 30' N, and so about 100 miles south of the parallel of Santa Maria, most southerly of the Azores. A 90° (true) course from this point would have missed the Azores and fetched up on Cape Spartel, but for two circumstances. The caravels were crossing the isogonic lines of 7° and 10° westerly variation of the compass, and consequently a magnetic E course worked out at 80° to 83° true, which constantly took them a little further north. The other was a storm that drove *Niña* northeasterly just in time to fetch up at Santa Maria.

A winter northwest gale was now blowing the two caravels home at steamboat speed. During the four days February 4–7 they did the fastest sailing of the entire voyage out or home, making 598 miles, an average of almost 150 a day. From sunset February 5 to sunset on the sixth, *Niña* and *Pinta* made the magnificent run of 198 miles, and at times approached a speed of 11 knots.

Suppose we luff up a minute and consider what this means. With the wind on their port quarters, fore and main courses set, in a rough, breaking sea of cobalt blue under a brilliant winter sky, these caravels of 1493 were making a speed that any ocean-going sailing yacht of today might envy. Whenever a modern schooner or ketch of the approximate length of *Niña* makes a 200-mile run, her owner's friends hear about it. In ocean races, yachts built only for speed, equipped with wire rigging and a cloud of light sails, tuned up to a high pitch and driven by a crew of tough young Corinthians, often surpass the performance of *Pinta* and *Niña;* but old-fashioned gaff-headed schooners and brigs do not often equal it.

Speed under sail, because of the beauty of the ship herself, the music of wind and water, and also because of some deep, unfathomable sentiment in the soul of a seaman, yields even today an acute sensation of speed, comparable only to skiing or riding a fast horse in a steeplechase. Motorized travel afloat or ashore, or even in the air (unless in the latest fighting planes of which I have no experience), is slow and tame in comparison. Imagine then if you can what a glorious experience those seamen were having aboard *Niña* and *Pinta.* Unless any of them had ridden a racehorse, 11 knots was a greater absolute speed than they had ever known. They were homeward bound after the greatest sea adventure in the history of mankind, bursting with stories of a world unknown even to the boldest sea rovers of antiquity, a world untouched by a Rome in the days of her greatest glory, undivined by the subtle Arabs. Their Admiral knew the way, and all the saints in Heaven were conspiring to send him fair winds, clear weather and following seas. But this was the domain of the pagan gods Neptune and Aeolus, who were getting ready to uncork something very nasty.

On February 6, in the midst of this gorgeous and long-sustained burst of speed, there was an interesting discussion aboard *Niña* about her position; the wind was blowing too hard to take the opinion of navigators aboard *Pinta*. Captain Vicente Yáñez Pinzón declared that on the morning of February 6 Flores in the Azores bore due N, and Madeira due East. Bartolomé Roldán, who had been studying pilotage on the voyage, said that Fayal bore NE and Porto Santo, East. Both were very wrong indeed, but the amateur less so than the professional. Roldán's position was about 375 miles SE by E, and Pinzón's about 600 miles ESE of the true position, as plotted from Columbus's dead-reckoning.

On February 7 another pilot, Peralonso Niño, declared that *Niña* was already between the meridians of Terceira and of Santa Maria and would pass 38 miles north of Madeira; he was only 200 miles out in latitude and 600 miles in longitude! Columbus himself placed the fleet 75 leagues south of the parallel of Flores, an overestimate of about 65 miles. He wisely did not commit himself about longitude at this point.

Disagreements of this sort among navigators were to be expected in days of primitive instruments and rule-of-thumb plotting; and they are by no means absent today when we have instruments of precision and scientific methods. Eugenio de Salazar, who crossed from the Canaries to Hispaniola in 1573, exclaimed in one of his letters home, "O! how God in his omnipotence can have placed this subtle and so important art of navigation in wit so dull and hands so clumsy as those of these pilots! And to see them inquire, one of the other, 'how many degrees hath your honor found?' One says 'sixteen,' another 'a scant twenty,' and another, 'thirteen and a half.' Presently they ask, 'how doth your honor find himself with respect to the land?' One says 'I find myself 40 leagues from land,' another 'I say 150,' another says

'I find myself this morning 92 leagues away.' And be it three or three hundred, nobody agrees with anyone else, or with the truth."

By nightfall February 7 the fresh northwesterly gale was spent, and during the next two days the fleet experienced "soft and variable winds," according to Las Casas. In an E wind they made 75 miles to the SSE, which pulled them further from an Azorean landfall, but before dawn of the ninth the wind veered to ESE, so starboard tacks were boarded and the caravels steered NE. Columbus did not intend to call at the Azores, but he was probably now hoping to pick up one of them in order to check his position. At ten in the morning of February 9 the fleet straightened out again on an easterly course, but made only 24 miles by sunset. The brave west winds then returned; and during the next twenty-four hours *Niña* and *Pinta* made a fine run of 154 miles.

That day, February 10, there was more anxious plotting of the reckoning. Vicente Yáñez, Peralonso Niño, Sancho Ruiz and the amateur Roldán agreed that they had reached a meridian 5 leagues east of Santa Maria in the Azores, and were about on the latitude of Madeira and Porto Santo. This was about 500 miles E by S ½S of their true position. Columbus reckoned that at the end of this day's run, when the fleet according to our calculation was in latitude 35° 58' N, longitude 33° 15' W, the island of Flores bore due north. He also figured out that Nafe (Casablanca in Morocco) bore due east. In other words, he put the fleet 175 miles SE ¾S of its true position — supposing he knew the correct positions of Flores and of Casablanca.

Yet in comparison with the pilots' reckoning, and assuming that they all agreed on the relative positions of the Azores, Madeira and Casablanca, Columbus was about 30 miles nearer the true latitude and 340 miles nearer the true longitude than anyone else.

It must have been during these three weeks of good weather and serviceable if not always fair winds that Columbus composed the famous Letter on his First Voyage, often called the Letter to

Santangel or to Sánchez. This letter, not addressed to any particular person, but intended as a public announcement of his voyage, was enclosed in one to the Sovereigns that has been lost. They had a number of manuscript copies made for different court officials, and one of these, endorsed to Luis de Santangel, was printed (very badly) at Barcelona in the summer of 1493 as a four-page folio pamphlet, the unique surviving example of which is in the New York Public Library. From a better copy than the Barcelona printer used, a Latin translation was made by Leandro de Cosco, which passed through nine editions (Rome, Paris, Basle, Antwerp) in 1493–1494; this was promptly turned into Italian verse, of which three editions were printed before the end of 1493. Some editions of *De Insulis inuentis* (the earliest Latin title) were liberally illustrated by woodcuts taken from other books, having no relation whatsoever to Columbus, his ships, or the West Indies. The letter is dated February 15 *en la caravela, sobre las yslas de Canaria,* "aboard the caravel, off the Canaries," but it must have been composed before February 12, not in the storm that followed; and for "Canaries" read "Azores," within sight of which Columbus was on the fifteenth. He probably completed and signed the letter a few days later aboard *Niña* when at anchor off Santa Maria, hoping to forward it thence by way of Portugal in case anything should happen to him on the last leg of the voyage; but the attitude of the Azorean authorities, as we shall see, was such that the Admiral decided to be his own postman.

Everything important or calculated to interest the Sovereigns and invite support for a second voyage is cited in the Letter; but courses and distances are omitted, lest interlopers gather forbidden fruit. The loss of *Santa María* is not told; Columbus deceptively remarks that he left one of the vessels with his men at Navidad. On the whole, the Letter is an excellent précis of the Journal, and proves that Columbus had developed considerable skill in exposition.

CHAPTER XXIII

Azorean Agony

February 12–24, 1493

*Turbati sunt, et moti sunt sicut ebrius: et omnis sapientia
eorum deuorata est. Et clamauerunt ad Dominum cum tribularentur, et de necessitatibus eorum eduxit eos.*

They reel to and fro, and stagger like a drunken man,
and are at their wit's end. Then they cry unto the Lord in
their trouble, and he bringeth them out of their distress.
— PSALM cvi 27–28

THE WINTER of 1492–1493 was unusually cold and tem-
pestuous in Southern Europe. Even the harbor of Genoa was
frozen over on Christmas day, so that small vessels could not enter
or clear, and ships lay wind-bound at Lisbon for months. *Niña*
and *Pinta* had been lucky so far, but they were headed right into
one of the stormiest regions of the North Atlantic.

On Monday, February 12, after another fine day's run of 150
miles to the eastward, the fleet ran into dirty weather, the first
experienced this voyage. Columbus's account of the next few days
is exceedingly interesting, for it is one of the earliest, if not the
first detailed description of an actual storm at sea. The data in his
Journal when examined in the light of modern meteorology show
that this was no ordinary cyclonic storm, but a disturbance marked
by well-developed "fronts," dividing radial areas where a cold air
mass moving south from the Arctic comes up against a warm air
mass moving north from the tropics.

Storms of this character are not uncommon in the region of the
Azores, and their importance for shipping and flying is so great
that in recent years they have been intensively studied. Among

existing descriptions of such storms during the last five years there
are at least two which fit in almost every detail those that Columbus
experienced. We can see that the disturbance which brought so
much agony to *Pinta* and *Niña* was caused by an intense low-
pressure area the center of which was passing north of the Azores,
with SW to W winds of "strong" or "full gale" strength (9 or 10
on Beaufort scale) in its southern and southwestern sectors. The
isobaric system was probably elongated in a WSW to ENE direction, which by bringing different winds near one another was
responsible for the terrible cross seas that almost overwhelmed
Niña. Three distinct air masses, separated by one warm and two
cold fronts, seem to have been involved in the circulation; and the
passage from one air mass to another through the front separating
them gave the caravels their worst beating.

At daylight February 12 Columbus "began to have heavy seas
and tempest, and, says he, if the caravel had not been very staunch
and well found, he would have been afraid of being lost." From
sunrise to sunset, wind SW and force 7 to 8, she ran about 35 miles
"with much toil and peril" under bare poles — "dry tree" the Spaniards called it. That night *Niña* labored heavily. Lightning flashed
thrice to the NNE, direction of the low center. In the morning
of February 13 the wind moderated a little, since they were skirting the southern edge of the disturbance; and *Niña* made a little
sail. In the afternoon the wind increased again, "the ocean made
up something terrible," with a cross sea that caused the caravels
to labor heavily. They rolled and pitched in an alarming manner,
and everything that was not lashed down went tumbling about
the decks and cabins. A westerly swell kicked up by another sector
of the storm was coming through and crossing the wave crests
raised by the strong SW wind.

At nightfall February 13 the wind blew yet harder, and the
cross seas formed dangerous pyramidical waves that stopped the
caravels' headway with a menacing shiver, and then broke on
their decks in torrents of green water and white foam. These
seas were all the more dangerous to *Niña* because she was under-

ballasted. Columbus explains that she sailed from Hispaniola in that condition because so much of her heavy stores and provisions had been consumed, and he had intended to replace them with water and native edibles at the Isle of Women, but the change of plan prevented. During the voyage the men had done their best to restore her stability by filling empty wine casks with salt water; but these were a poor substitute for good rock ballast, well secured, covering the bottom of the hold.

All attempts to steer a compass course were now abandoned. The helmsmen were ordered to let her scud before it in a general northeasterly direction, while the officer of the watch scanned each oncoming wave and gave quick orders that the caravel might take it at the best angle. Without extreme watchfulness and expert handling, *Niña* would have broached-to and filled, which would have been fatal to all; *Pinta* had no means of picking up survivors. For sail *Niña* carried only her *papahigo*, a small main course with the bonnet off, on a yard slung as low as possible in order to take the strain off the mast. A modern vessel, provided with a "North Atlantic Directory," a Bowditch, and hydrographic office charts, would have hove-to on the starboard tack, in order to drift as far as possible from the storm center; but Columbus knew nothing of the law of storms. Even if he had, scudding before the wind was the only proper course, for in that heavy, breaking cross sea any attempt to heave-to might have swamped a vessel so low in the water as *Niña*. These high-pooped caravels did pretty well scudding in heavy sea, since there was small chance of their being pooped by a following wave. But every big one swashed in through the rudder port, drenching the helmsmen, and it was all they could do to keep her before it and prevent a fatal broaching-to.

Pinta, with whom no hails had been exchanged during the strong wind of the previous week, paid off and scudded before the tempest at the same time as *Niña*. In the night of February 13–14 the Admiral "made flares and the other replied," until they were too far apart to exchange signals, and by morning they had lost sight of each other. *Pinta* missed the Azores, and the two caravels did not meet again until a month later, in the harbor of Palos.

The same conditions continued all day February 14, when the first of the two successive cold fronts overtook *Niña*. She was still scudding with main course and yard slung low, and a horrible cross swell, due apparently to a north wind beyond the second cold front not far to the north. Her company now called celestial power to their aid, in a manner typical of the age; and the way of their doing it, under the Admiral's direction, had the further merit of keeping the men busy and in a sense amused. Three successive lotteries were arranged to decide which man should represent the ship in going on a certain pilgrimage if she were saved alive. As many chick-peas as there were men aboard (excluding Indians not baptized, we presume), one pea cut with a cross, were placed in a seaman's cap; and he who drew the crossed pea must perform a pilgrimage to Santa María de Guadalupe in the mountains of Estremadura. Columbus put in his hand first, and drew the marked pea; and "henceforth regarded himself as a pilgrim and bound to fulfil the vow." As the wind and sea showed no sign of abating, the peas were shaken up again, this time for the privilege of representing *Niña* on a pilgrimage to the shrine of Santa Maria de Loreto in far-off Ancona. Pedro de Villa, a seaman of Puerto Santa María, drew the crossed pea, and the Admiral promised to pay his traveling expenses. Again, no sign that the heavenly host were paying any attention to these poor storm-tossed mariners. So a third vow was made, to watch all one night and pay for a Mass at the church of Santa Clara de Moguer, near Palos. Once more the Admiral drew the cross — is it possible that some expert gambler among the men juggled the peas against him? And still no sign of better weather. Perhaps Our Lady did not appreciate this method of playing "beano" for her favor. So all made a vow "to go in procession in their shirts" to the first shrine of the Virgin they should encounter, and say their prayers. And in addition "everyone made his special vow, because nobody expected to escape, considering themselves all lost." And after that (on February

14) the storm abated. The first cold front had crossed *Niña's* course with showers and squalls, wind changed to due W, and *Niña* scudded NE.

Columbus was man enough to admit that he was as frightened as anyone. Jotting down his impression of these terrible days of tempest, after *Niña* was safely anchored, he admitted that he should never have wavered as he did in trusting divine providence, which already had brought him safe through so many perils and tribulations, and afforded him the glory of discovering a western route to the Indies. God must have intended that discovery to be of some use to the world. But, "my weakness and anxiety would not allow my spirit to be soothed," he confessed. His greatest fear was not for loss of the discovery, since there was a good chance that *Pinta* would come through if *Niña* went down; but for the future of his lad Diego and for little Ferdinand, both of whom he had left at school in Cordova. For if he were drowned and Martín Alonso reached home with the news, they would be left orphans in a strange land with nobody to care for them, since the Pinzons undoubtedly would reap all the glory of the discovery.

So, in his cabin on that pitching and rolling vessel the Admiral got out vellum, quill and inkhorn, wrote a brief account of the voyage and of his discoveries, wrapped the parchment in a waxed cloth, ordered it to be headed up in a great wooden barrel, and cast into the sea. No more was heard of this "manuscript in a bottle" until 1892, when a fly-by-night London publisher had the impudence to claim that he had secured it, as recently picked up by a fisherman off the coast of Wales! It was written in English, he explained, because the Admiral thought that the manuscript would stand a better chance of being understood if couched in that universal maritime language. A "facsimile edition," printed in Germany in imitation script on imitation vellum, entitled "My Secrete Log Boke" and suitably adorned with genuine barnacles and seaweed, found many credulous purchasers, several of whom have tried to unload their unhappy acquisitions on the present writer.

After sunset February 14, the day of the three vows, "the sky began to show clear in the west, showing that the wind intended to blow from that quarter" — a very bad guess. But the wind moderated, the sea began to go down, and Columbus ordered the bonnet to be laced on *Niña's* course, equivalent to shaking out a reef. She continued to sail ENE at a speed of only three knots. Shortly after sunrise on Friday, February 15, a seaman named Ruy García sighted land dead ahead. The wildest conjectures were made as to what land it was. Some believed it to be Castile; others, the Rock of Sintra near Lisbon; others, Madeira. Columbus alone insisted that it was one of the Azores, and as usual he was right. It was Santa Maria, southernmost of the group, and one of the smallest. Seventy-two hours elapsed before *Niña* came to an anchor there.

During the night of relatively moderate wind, when the ship was about 16 miles distant from the island, as they calculated, the wind whipped around to the ENE. The second cold front had passed over *Niña*, leaving her on the edge of the high-pressure area; but the sea continued high from the westward. The reason for this strange phenomenon must have been that the front, with the west winds beyond it, lay not far south in a general east and west direction. Fortunately *Niña* was a weatherly little caravel, and had sustained no important damage. So the Admiral sailed her on the wind, which veered to E February 16, and then to ESE. At sunrise February 16, just as she was coming about, they caught sight of the larger island of São Miguel over the stern, distant about 25 miles. All that day and the following night *Niña* with a fresh easterly wind was clawing her way toward the elusive Santa Maria, hidden by a great cloud rack. Columbus had his first sleep in three or four days, "and he was much crippled in the legs from always being exposed to cold and to water, and from eating little." The arthritis that the Admiral contracted on this passage stayed with him all his life, and grew more painful with advancing age.

At sunrise February 17, having overshot Santa Maria to the eastward, *Niña* took a SSW course with wind ESE, and by nightfall reached the island; but owing to the "great cloudmass" that obscured its upper slopes, the "Admiral could not recognize which island it was." After dark he came to an anchor off some houses, in the hope of hailing someone to tell him where they were; but the cable presently chafed through on the sharp rocks and parted. So the weary mariners, robbed of the quiet night's rest they anticipated, made sail and stood off-and-on all night. It had never been Columbus's intention to call at the Azores on the way home — all Portuguese islands he had carefully avoided; but ship and seamen had taken such a beating that he decided to take a chance in the hope of obtaining wood, water, fresh provisions, and a bit of rest.

Santa Maria, earliest of the Azores to be settled by the Portuguese, is only ten miles long by five wide. Mountainous, rising to 1870 feet, it contains many fertile valleys and tiny plains suitable for stock raising, but no natural harbor and only a few anchorages, none of which are tenable when the wind blows onshore.

After sunrise on Monday, February 18, Columbus again searched the northern side of the island, "and where it seemed fit anchored with one anchor and sent the boat ashore and had speech with the people, and found that it was the island of Santa Maria, one of the Azores, and they indicated the anchorage where he should moor the caravel, and the people of the island said that never had they seen such a tempest as there had been these 15 days past, and they wondered how he had escaped; and they gave many thanks to God and showed much joy at the news which they heard, that the Admiral had discovered the Indies."*

At this point, where Columbus's men first went ashore after leaving Hispaniola, the rugged mountains of Santa Maria fall away to a green coastal plain about half a mile wide. On the edge of it, where a small sand beach makes a good boat landing and a mountain stream affords fresh water, the first settlers of Santa Maria had disembarked over fifty years before Columbus's visit. Their village was called Nossa Senhora dos Anjos (Our Lady of the Angels) because the Virgin surrounded by angels had appeared

---

* "Appears fictitious this joy that the Portuguese showed," comments Las Casas sourly on the margin of the Journal for February 18.

to a fisherman on a rock awash at low tide; and a little chapel or hermitage dedicated to her had been built near the spot. The anchorage chosen by *Niña* off Anjos being far from safe, she shifted her position as the villagers advised to the eastward, on the other side of a high rocky cape called Punta Frades. There, in a bay open to the northeast, rimmed by high volcanic cliffs and lonely as any

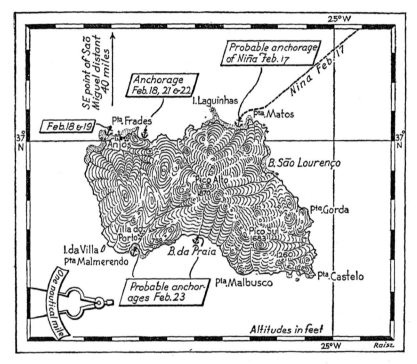

SANTA MARIA IN THE AZORES

anchorage in the West Indies, *Niña* lay secure as long as the wind held southerly. Three men were left ashore at Anjos, a mile and a half away, in order to obtain fresh provisions and water.

All that afternoon *Niña* rode at anchor in this lonely bay, out of sight of the village, and without communication from shore. After sunset three islanders appeared on the cliff and hailed. Columbus "sent them the boat, in which they came aboard." Fortunately it was Shrovetide, so they brought fresh bread and chickens "and other things that were sent by the captain of the island, who was called João de Castanheira, saying that he knew him (the Admiral) very well, and that as it was night he did not come to call, but at daybreak he would come and bring more refreshments with the three men of the caravel who remained there, whom he did not then send back because of the great pleasure that he had with them, hearing about events of his voyage." The messengers who came aboard were given bunks for the night, as it was a long row home.

Informed by these men of a "little shrine like a hermitage which was near the sea" and dedicated to Our Lady, Columbus decided that this was the proper occasion to fulfill vow number three made at the tempest's height. This chapel, although enlarged and rebuilt in the seventeenth century, is still very small and severe in style, so that one can easily reconstruct in imagination the serio-comic scene that followed. At daybreak on Tuesday, February 19, Columbus sent half the crew ashore in *Niña's* one boat, asking the messengers who returned with them to hunt up the village priest to say Mass; after which the men should come aboard again and act as shipkeepers while Columbus with the other half of the crew performed their vows.

The padre was routed out, and *Niña's* shore party, divesting themselves of shoes, hose and all nether garments, marched in procession, clad only in their shirts (the proper penitential garb), into the tiny chapel. As they were saying prayers of thanksgiving before the old Flemish triptych that still adorns the altar, "the whole town on horseback and afoot fell upon them and took them all prisoners"; for with nothing on but shirts, how could they resist? As Washington Irving observes, "such was the first reception of the Admiral on his return to the Old World, an earnest of the crosses and troubles with which he was to be requited through life, for one of the greatest benefits that ever man conferred upon his fellow beings."

The local official who ordered this cowardly capture of ten trouserless seamen at prayers was not the ruling captain of the island, who was absent, but his *locum tenens*, a young man named

João de Castanheira. He boasted, and Columbus believed, that he had received orders from the king of Portugal to arrest him. It may be doubted whether Castanheira had any such orders, or he would have been more persistent in carrying them out; for he had already been rebuked for allowing a prisoner to escape. The Portuguese had been much troubled by Castilians poaching on the Guinea coast, contrary to the Treaty of Alcáçovas; and as the Azores were natural places of call for vessels returning from Guinea to the Peninsula, it seems probable that Castanheira suspected Columbus and his men of having been on an illicit Guinea voyage, which they were endeavoring to cover by tall tales of "The Indies."

About eleven in the morning Columbus, anxiously awaiting the return of his boat from the village that he was unable to see, decided that either the boat had been stove on the rocks or the people detained. Weighing anchor, he sailed *Niña* around Punta Frades, "and saw many horsemen who dismounted and entered the boat armed, and came out to the caravel," commanded by Castanheira. Their obvious intention was to arrest the Admiral. A parley followed between ship and boat, amusing enough for us but trying enough to Columbus. He tried to lure Castanheira aboard in order to hold him as hostage, while the Portuguese endeavored to inveigle Columbus into the boat, in order to clap him into prison with the pious pilgrims. Columbus exhibited his passport and credentials over the bulwarks, but refused to allow the Portuguese near enough to read them. High words were exchanged; Columbus "said that he was the Admiral of the Ocean Sea and Viceroy of the Indies which belong to Their Highnesses" (one can imagine Castanheira exclaiming derisively "In that little caravel!") and that he would return to Castile with half his crew if the others were not released, and see that offending Portuguese were suitably punished. Captain Castanheira replied that he knew nothing of the Sovereigns of Castile and cared less, that this was Portugal and be damned to him. Columbus then lost his temper and swore by San Fernando he would not leave until he had depopulated Santa Maria and captured a hundred Portuguese to carry home as slaves, God take them. "And so he returned to anchor in the harbor where he first lay, because wind and weather were very bad for doing anything else."

This anchorage was evidently the one off the village against which Columbus had been warned, for on the twentieth, when he was employing his remaining crew in filling casks with sea water for ballast, the cables parted and Columbus made sail for São Miguel. "Although in none of the Azores is there a good harbor in the weather that they then had, . . . he had no other recourse but to escape to sea." São Miguel is visible from Santa Maria in fair weather, but the weather was now exceedingly foul, and *Niña* was unable to make the island by nightfall. It was very difficult to handle her because of the crew left aboard only three were seamen, the rest being soldiers, landsmen or Indians who had not managed to pick up enough seamanship to be useful in a pinch. That night *Niña* lay-to "with a severe tempest and in great peril and toil," fortunately with "the sea and waves from one direction only." At sunrise on February 21, wind N and São Miguel not yet in sight, Columbus decided to bear away for Santa Maria and see what diplomacy could effect. By late afternoon he was moored by his two remaining anchors in the bay east of Punta Frades.

There, his first greeting was a defiant shout from the cliff by an officious villager. Presently, however, *Niña's* own boat came around the point, bearing five of the captured seamen, two clerics and a notary public. After such evening's entertainment aboard as the Admiral could offer, and passing the night, the priests and scribe scrutinized the Admiral's credentials, expressed themselves satisfied, and granted free entry and pratique. Castanheira had apparently repented of his rashness, and perhaps had failed to extract any evidence of poaching on the Guinea coast after giving his prisoners some sort of third degree. The boat went ashore and returned with the rest of *Niña's* crew, who said that the real reason for their release was Castanheira's failure to capture Columbus. He cared nothing for small game.

With her full crew restored *Niña* left this uneasy anchorage for the last time on February 23, and sailed around Santa Maria to the westward in search of a good place to take on wood and stone ballast. By the hour of compline (6 P.M.) she came to an anchor, in either Bahia Villa do Porto or Bahia da Praia on the southern shore of the island, there being a good landing beach and plenty of loose rocks in each. But at the passing of the first night watch (11 P.M.) the wind began to blow W, backed to SW, and as "in these islands . . . in blowing SW it presently comes S," said Columbus, and a south wind would render his anchorage untenable, it was necessary to put to sea. Columbus ordered anchors aweigh, made sail, and shaped an easterly course to steer clear of the island.

It was now Sunday, February 24. Ten days had been spent in and around Santa Maria, two or three anchors had been lost, and Columbus had nothing to show for the delay but fresh water, a few provisions, and a diplomatic victory over João de Castanheira.

CHAPTER XXIV

In Portuguese Power
February 24–March 13, 1493

Quoniam probasti nos Deus: igne nos examinasti, sicut examinatur argentum . . . Transiuimus per ignem et aquam: et eduxisti nos in refrigerium.

For thou, O God, hast proved us; thou hast tried us, as silver is tried. . . . We went through fire and through water: but thou broughtest us out into a wealthy place.
— PSALM lxvi 10, 12

AT THE ZERO HOUR of Sunday, February 24, Columbus, "seeing it was favorable weather to go to Castile, gave up taking on wood and water, and gave orders that they lay a course to the East." Before daylight *Niña* was well beyond the inhospitable island. This easterly course was well chosen, for Santa Maria lies upon the same parallel as Cape St. Vincent, the proper landfall for a vessel approaching Palos from the westward. The distance, about 800 miles, under ordinary circumstances would not have required more than a week's sailing, for the prevailing wind at that season is north. But this stretch of water between the Azores and Portugal is a stormy one in the winter months; wind velocity beyond 100 miles per hour was reported at Lisbon in February 1941. Low-pressure areas show a tendency to "stall" in this area, along a slowly moving polar front. This means that violent storms may come close together, and may last a long time.

Another formidable tempest overtook *Niña* when she was about 250 miles out from Santa Maria; and it stayed with her right up to the bar of the Tagus. Again, the data in Columbus's Journal form a remarkable meteorological record. They show that this storm was a large well-developed cyclone, apparently with an open sector of warm air thrusting up from the tropics into cold air masses from the higher latitudes. The two whirling air masses were probably moving slowly eastward or northeastward, say at 10 knots, and took six days to pass Columbus, who was sailing along with them. This cyclone was even more of a trial to *Niña* than the storm west of the Azores, because the center passed nearer, perhaps only 150 miles or so to the northward.

The first sign of trouble came on the morning of February 26, when the zone of brisk to strong winds in the advance cold sector of the storm overtook *Niña*. Wind shifted to the SE, forcing her to head ENE, two points off her course to Cape St. Vincent. Next day the wind increased from the SE and S, the sea rose, and again Columbus could not lay his course. "It was very painful," he observed, "to have such a tempest when they were already at the doors of home." That day (February 27) Columbus "found himself 125 leagues from Cape St. Vincent and 80 from Madeira and 106 from Santa Maria." He or Vicente Yáñez or Peralonso Niño had a fairly accurate knowledge of this neck of the ocean, for if we lay off those three distances from their respective points of reference, without any deduction for overestimate, we place *Niña* on latitude 37° 05′ N, between longitudes 17° 30′ and 18° W. According to my plotting of Columbus's dead-reckoning, the longitude was about right, but the latitude, after the northing that *Niña* had been forced to make, must have been around 38° N. Madeira was probably placed too far north on Columbus's chart, which would account for his mistake in one of the three estimated distances.

On February 28 wind came SE to S with heavy seas; it was impossible to steer nearer the course than NE and ENE. So it continued for the next two days, March 1 and 2, while the slowly moving cyclone passed over *Niña*. That night the warm front of the cyclone apparently overtook her, and she entered the tropical sector of the storm. Wind shifted to SW, and it was possible to scud E by N. On the night of March 2 to 3, fifth of the storm, the cold front overtook *Niña* with a violent squall "which split all the sails, and he found himself in great peril." She could hardly have been under more than one lower course at the time; the squall must have blown the other course and mizzen out of their gaskets and stripped them off the yards.

On she drove under bare poles, rolling and pitching frightfully in a dangerous cross sea. Peas were shaken up in a cap for another shirt-clad pilgrimage, this time to the church of Santa María de la Cinta near Huelva, and as usual Columbus drew the marked pea. The seamen then vowed to spend their first Saturday night ashore fasting on bread and water, instead of feasting and carousing. A desperate state of things, indeed!

March 3 was the worst day of the entire voyage. The cold front, the squall line which *Niña* had crossed, seems to have extended almost parallel to and southward of her course, so it was almost as if she had a hostile fleet firing at her from just under the horizon. Wind rose to at least force 10 on Beaufort scale, and (in Dr. Brooks's opinion) to hurricane strength in the squalls. It was some consolation that it blew from the NW, so *Niña* drove ahead to the eastward; but the coast was coming dangerously near, and there was the same terrible cross sea as in the earlier tempest. As the dark afternoon waned, anxiety became intense; for Columbus knew by his dead-reckoning and the look of things that he was very near the land, driving toward the ironbound coast of Portugal.

Sun set at six on March 3, and shortly afterward the cyclone delivered her last tail-lashing. The wind rose to "so terrible a tempest that they thought they were lost from the seas that came aboard from two directions, and the winds which seemed to raise the caravel into the air, and the water from the sky and lightning flashes in many directions." Fortunately it was the night of full moon, which sent enough light through the storm clouds so that at 7 P.M., when the first night watch was set, the seamen sighted land dead ahead. That was a moment for quick thinking. "In order not to approach the land until he had recognized it, to see if he could pick up some port or roadstead where he could save himself," Columbus set a spare fore course that had escaped destruction in the sail locker, and clawed offshore on the starboard tack, wind NW. "And so God preserved them until day, which was accomplished with infinite toil and terror." Only one little sail to save them from crashing on Cabo da Roca, which would have meant certain death for all hands. A gallant little vessel was *Niña*, and superbly handled. Not every modern sailing ship would have come through under such conditions.

"At daybreak (March 4) he recognized the land which was the Rock of Sintra, which is next the River of Lisbon, where he decided to enter, because he could do nothing else." This Rock of Sintra is the mountainous peninsula, now studded with palaces and villas, that juts out from Portugal north of the Tagus, and makes a perfect landmark for entering Lisbon. Steep cliffs, rimmed with foam, showed the seamen what they had avoided.

Columbus, when he reached Spain, was meanly accused of having visited Lisbon with the express purpose of selling out his discovery to the king of Portugal, and a number of modern writers have repeated the ungenerous and preposterous charge. It should be clear to anyone, seaman or not, that after the cyclone had driven *Niña* north of the parallel of Cape St. Vincent, stripped her of every sail but one, and whipped around to W and NW, driving her toward a lee shore, Columbus must have entered the Tagus, as he says himself, "because he could do nothing else." Any attempt to sail 225 miles north to Galicia or south and east to Palos with his single square of canvas would have been unseamanlike and probably suicidal.

Shortly after sunrise *Niña* rounded Cabo Raso into the Tagus estuary, passed the village of Cascais, where the fishing folk were so astonished at seeing this tiny caravel come scudding in from seaward, and so alarmed for her safety, that they "spent all that morning making prayers for them." In this unusually stormy winter many vessels of the Flanders fleet had been lost, and some ships had been lying four months wind-bound in the Tagus.

Niña sailed close alongshore, safely crossed the northern channel over the bar of Lisbon, and after passing the island where D. Manuel a few years later erected the gothic Castle of Belem, came to an anchor at 9 A.M. on Monday, March 4, off Restello. This place, whose name was later changed to Belem, was the outer port of Lisbon, about four miles below the city. *Niña's* anchorage, now covered by filled-in land, was off the site of the Jeronymos Convent where lie buried Columbus's great contemporary Vasco da Gama and the poet Camoëns, who sang his praises in noble verse.

Columbus was now in a very hot spot, completely within the power of his Sovereigns' principal rival and recent enemy D. João II. His experience at Santa Maria suggested what the king's attitude might be. Powerless to resist capture or ill usage, the Admiral had to rely on his native wit and diplomacy.

Learning that the king was in the country, he dispatched a messenger with a letter requesting permission to proceed upstream to Lisbon, because he feared an attack from certain ruffians "thinking that he carried much gold," in that lonely anchorage where he was. He cited his credentials from Ferdinand and Isabella, and informed the monarch "that he came not from Guinea, but from the Indies." That was what he had to prove.

Having written to the king, Columbus wrote a postscript to the letter announcing to Ferdinand and Isabella the results of his voyage, that he had composed at sea and dated at Santa Maria.

"After having written this, and being in the Sea of Castile, there rose upon me so great a wind from the S and SE that I had to ease the ships. But today, which was the greatest wonder in the world, I made this harbor of Lisbon, whence I decided to write to Their Highnesses. In all the Indies I have always found weather as in May; thither I went in 33 days, and had returned in 28, but for those tempests which detained me 14 days running through this sea. All mariners here say that never has there been so bad a winter or so many losses of ships.

"Done on the 4th day of March."

Trouble was never far away from Columbus, whether afloat or at anchor. Moored near *Niña* was a great Portuguese man-of-war, the pride of the king's navy, equipped with sufficient artillery to blow a little caravel out of the water. Presently her master, who was none other than Bartholomew Dias, discoverer of the Cape of Good Hope, came aboard *Niña* in an armed boat and ordered Columbus to return with him and give an account of himself to the captain. Columbus stood on his dignity as Admiral of the Ocean Sea, and replied that he would not come unless by force of arms. Dias thought it would be all right with the captain if Vicente Yáñez Pinzón were sent aboard with the ship's papers. Columbus replied that neither his captain nor anyone else should go unless compelled by *force majeure;* that it was the tradition for Admirals of Castile to die before they yielded themselves or their people. Dias then asked to see his papers, which Columbus was only too glad to exhibit. The boat returned to the great ship, Dias told his story to his captain, Álvaro Damão, who then came aboard *Niña* "in great state, with drums, trumpets and pipes, making a great celebration of it," paid a visit of courtesy to the new Admiral of the Ocean Sea, and "offered to do all he commanded."

Round one for the Admiral.

All that day and the next *Niña* was receiving visitors from shore, including, no doubt, some of Columbus's old friends. The people were immensely impressed with the stories they heard and the captive Indians that they saw; there was much thanking God "for so great good and increase of Christianity that Our Lord had given to the Sovereigns of Castile." That was just like the kindly Portuguese. Devoid of the touchy pride and haughty jealousy of the Castilians, they seem as genuinely delighted at the good fortune of others as if it were their own. But it remained to be seen if the king would react like his subjects.

On Friday, March 8, Martin de Noronha, a young gentleman of the king's court, brought out a letter from D. João himself inviting the Admiral to come and visit him, "since the weather was not favorable for departing with the caravel." Evidently the wind still held westerly. And the king gave orders to his agents to supply *Niña* with provisions and ship chandlery at his own expense. Columbus decided to accept the invitation in order "to disarm suspicion, although he did not wish to go." Either he feared foul play, or he suspected that the purpose of his visit might be misconstrued, as it was. Mules were provided by D. Martin, a few gold noseplugs and other souvenirs of the Indies were doubtless packed in the saddlebags, and as undeniable evidence that he had been to an undiscovered country, Columbus selected some of the healthiest specimens of his ten captive Indians to share the royal week end. After being subjected to the terrors of the deep, these poor creatures were now to experience the horrors of muleback navigation in Portugal; unless, as is likely, they were required to trudge barefoot in the mud, and to be stroked and pinched by curious crowds in the streets of Lisbon. A "great pestilence" was then raging along the lower Tagus, but *Niña's* company, both white and red, fortunately escaped contamination.

What memories and thoughts must have passed through the mind of Columbus as his cavalcade threaded the narrow ways and close-built *praças* of Lisbon! His route led past the chapel of the Convento dos Santos where he had first met his wife, and below the great church of the Carmo where she had been buried in the Moniz family chapel. Perhaps he took time out to visit the tomb of Dona Felipa and say a prayer for her soul. He may even have passed the shop where Bartholomew and he had made charts for a living, while they planned the great enterprise now so brilliantly concluded. As he left the city and passed between high-walled vineyards along the road that led north by the right bank of the Tagus, Columbus must have thought out very carefully what he would say to the king, and with what fair words he might appease the monarch's irritation at his entering the service of another prince. Nightfall overtook the party at Sacavem, a pretty town on the Tagus about twelve miles from Lisbon; and there they spent the night. Next day, Saturday, March 9, the country roads were in such an execrable state after the heavy rains that it took them all day to reach the king's residence, a distance that one can now cover by car in about three quarters of an hour.

The royal house of Aviz, not provided with numerous palaces like their successors of the Bragança line, were accustomed to put up at the wealthy monasteries of their kingdom, thus saving their subjects much expense and profitably depleting the swollen ecclesiastical revenues. At that moment D. João was making a prolonged stay, to escape the pestilence, at the monastery of Santa Maria das Virtudes, situated in a pinewood at the foot of the Valle do Paraiso, a rich farming region about thirty miles from Lisbon. There is little left of that great monastery today except a large roofless gothic church, with apartments over the west end of the nave, whence royal guests could observe the celebration of Mass in privacy and seclusion. Marks on the masonry indicate that other apartments were built against the north side of the church adjoining those occupied by the king. One of these may well have been allotted to Columbus.

The meeting of king and admiral, men of high courage and inflexible will, must have been dramatic. Columbus was forty-two years old, D. João thirty-eight. Columbus had first seen him as a suitor, and then been rejected; summoned to court in 1488, he had again been dismissed. Columbus well knew that only fear of offending the Sovereigns of Castile would prevent D. João from doing him ill; and there was always the uncomfortable feeling that *Pinta* might already have reached Spain with the news, so that Ferdinand and Isabella might not greatly care if some "accident" should cut short his inconvenient privileges of admiral, governor and viceroy.

It must have been a relief to be graciously received at Virtudes. Columbus's account of the meeting is in his Journal for March 9: —

"The king ordered him to be received very honorably by the principal officers of his household, and the king also received him with much honor and showed him much favor, and bade him be seated, and spoke very fair, offering to command all to be done freely which might be of use to the Sovereigns of Castile and for their service completely, and more than for his own, and showed that he was very pleased in the voyage having ended so favorably and having been accomplished."

Fortunately we have another account of this meeting from the pen of Rui de Pina, who as court chronicler may well have been present. According to him the king's expression of pleasure at the Admiral's success was insincere; he was irritated and inwardly enraged "because the said Admiral was somewhat elevated above his condition and in telling his tale always exceeded the bounds of truth and made the tale of gold, silver and riches much greater than it was." Moreover, the king "believed that this discovery was made within the seas and boundaries of his Lordship of Guinea; which was prohibited." He did not mean to impute that Columbus had been poaching off the West African Coast; nothing so crude as that. What the king did claim, as his subsequent diplomacy proved, was the "Ocean Sea" south of the Canaries and west of Africa as his sphere of influence, reserved exclusively for Portuguese discovery. He believed that Ferdinand and Isabella had expressly recognized this in the Treaty of Alcáçovas, which had been confirmed by the papal bull *Aeterni Regis* in 1481. D. João remarked to Columbus that if the new discovery was correctly described, "he understood from the treaty that he had with the Sovereigns, that that acquisition belonged to him." To which the Admiral replied in a placating manner that he had not seen the treaty, but the Sovereigns had ordered him "not to go to Mina or to any part of Guinea," and he had obeyed. D. João kept his poker face, said he was confident all could be amicably arranged, and handed his guest over to the Grand Prior of Crato, "who was the most eminent person there, and from whom the Admiral received many courtesies and favors."

After this first interview the courtiers, reading their king's real sentiments, crowded around and urged him to have this upstart and boastful Admiral assassinated forthwith, since "the prosecution of this enterprise by the Sovereigns of Castile would cease with the death of the Discoverer; and that this could be done discreetly if he consented and ordered it, for inasmuch as Colombo was discourteous and elated they could fix it so that any one of his shortcomings would seem to be the cause of his death. But the king like the God-fearing prince that he was, not only forbade that, but on the contrary showed him honor and much kindness."

The chronicler's tribute to his sovereign's forbearance is amusing, in view of the fact that D. João had personally assassinated his brother-in-law; but the Admiral's attitude and the king's irritation are convincing. Columbus was no longer a suppliant but a successful discoverer. Very likely he allowed himself to be carried away by pride, as was his wont, tactlessly reminded the king how he had been laughed at and told that it could never be done. Yet even the bare unvarnished truth about his First Voyage would have seemed wild and extravagant boasting to a prince whose discoveries had been made bit by bit, not in a single spectacular expedition.

Sunday morning after Mass the king "conversed long with the Admiral about his voyage, and always caused him to be seated and showed him much honor," asking all manner of questions and hearing all sorts of details, "dissimulating the chagrin that he had in his breast." The whole neighborhood flocked to view the strange people, and agreed that nothing like them had been seen in the whole world. And as Columbus boasted to the king that his Indians were intelligent, D. João arranged a test. He caused to be brought a bowl of dried beans which he scattered on a table, and ordered an Indian to arrange them so as to make a rough map of the lands that the Admiral claimed to have discovered. One of them did so promptly, indicating which group of beans was Hispaniola and which Cuba, while single beans represented the Bahamas and the Lesser Antilles. The king, observing this geographical game with a gloomy countenance, as if by inadvertence disarranged what the man had set forth, and commanded another Indian to play map maker with the scrambled beans. The second Indian — surely the clever "Diego Colón" — reassembled the bean chart of the Antilles, and "added many more islands and lands, giving us an explanation of all that he had depicted and indicated in his own tongue, although nobody understood it. Whereupon the king, clearly apprehending the extent of the lands discovered, and the wealth that he already imagined to be in them, could no longer conceal the great chagrin, which so far he had dissembled, over the

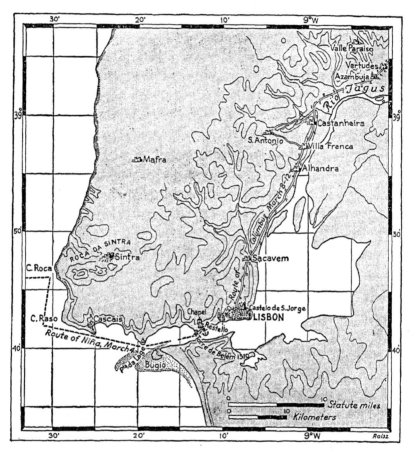

SINTRA, LISBON AND THE LOWER
TAGUS VALLEY IN 1493

loss of things so inestimable, which by his own fault he had let slip from his hands; and in a wave of passion smote his breast and cried in a loud voice, 'O man of little comprehension!' and 'Why did I let slip an enterprise of so great importance?' — these or similar words.'' But he graciously concluded the scene by presenting the Arawak cartographers with some scarlet-colored clothes.

Rui de Pina introduces his account of this interview with a curious remark to the effect that "*Christovam Colombo* an Italian came from the discovery of the islands of Japan and of Antillia." Antillia, it will be recalled, was the mythical Island of the Seven Cities that so many Portuguese navigators had sought in vain. Columbus doubtless claimed that Hispaniola was Japan. He may have told the king that he had discovered Antillia, either to mislead him or to "put one over" on the Portuguese. Or, Rui de Pina may merely have reflected the king's opinion of what Columbus found, rather than the Discoverer's own claim. For it was the Portuguese who affixed the generic name *as Antilhas*, the Antilles, to the West Indies.

So with smoldering anger D. João heard a first-hand account of a voyage that gave his Castilian rivals the greatest empire in the world's history; one to which his own kingdom and all her African and Indian possessions were destined to be annexed when the seed of Aviz ran out.

This tense and exciting week end was soon over. On Monday, March 11, D. João gave Columbus certain messages for Ferdinand and Isabella, and bade him farewell, "showing him always much affection." After dinner the Admiral departed, escorted by D. Martin de Noronha and a troop of *cavaleiros*. They made a detour from the direct route for Lisbon, in order that Columbus might pay his respects to the Queen.

Dona Leonor, as her subjects addressed her, was staying at a monastery some 15 or 20 miles from Virtudes, for it was too great a strain on one establishment to entertain king and queen at the same time. News of the king's extraordinary visitors had reached her; and, as it is the privilege of royalty to hear travelers' tales from their own lips instead of waiting to read their books, Dona Leonor sent word that Columbus must not leave Portugal before calling on her.

The Convento de São Antonio de Castanheira where the queen was staying is one of the loveliest places in Portugal. The old monks chose a level plateau on the western slope of the Tagus valley, in a region evenly divided between vineyard, tillage and pasture, in order to provide themselves with every human need from their own soil. And that even fish might not be wanting, they contrived a pond between their main building and the break of the slope, edged with the *azulejos* or colored tiles that the Portuguese learned to make from the Moors. So well provided with amenities of every sort were the monks that when Portugal secularized her monasteries over a century ago, São Antonio made a perfect country estate, where a gentleman might live on his own in a land of quiet beauty. The great gothic abbey church with its elaborately sculptured tombs and chapels has been turned into a wine lodge, the choir and aisles are occupied by enormous tuns and presses, and the odor of fresh grape and fermenting wine has long since driven out the perfume of wax and incense. But the fish pond has been made into a swimming pool; and the patio where Dona Leonor took her exercise under the cloister has been preserved as on the day of the Admiral's visit.

In this cloister, or perhaps in the great hall if that March day was cold and blustery, Columbus with his suite of naked Indians knelt before Dona Leonor, kissed her hand, and "received much courtesy." With her, he says, were the father of his guide, D. Pedro de Noronha, Marquez de Villa Real, and the Queen's brother D. Manuel, Duque de Bejar and heir to the throne. If the Admiral's audience at São Antonio was small, it was interested; for the young duke, who succeeded D. João in 1495, pushed overseas enterprise with more vigor and success than any prince of that era. By D. Manuel's command Vasco da Gama sailed on a voyage more difficult in execution than that just completed by command of the Spanish Sovereigns.

Columbus did not tarry long at São Antonio. That evening he took leave of Dona Leonor, "and went to sleep at Alhandra," a town on the Tagus about 22 miles above Lisbon. The Admiral was feeling very chafed and sore after spending the better part of a third day in the saddle, and decided to charter one of the river *fregatas* the next day and be rowed or sailed down to Restello.

Next morning (March 12) occurred a curious episode. Columbus, in his lodgings at Alhandra, was making arrangements about the boat when he was called upon by an *escudero* or squire of D. João, who offered on the king's behalf that, if Columbus "wished to go to Castile by land he would go with him to see to the lodging and order animals and all that he might want." Why was not this offer made at Virtudes? Had the would-be assassins won the king over, and was this a trap? It would have been easy, in the mountains between Elvas and Badajoz, to arrange an "attack by brigands" in which this boastful upstart Admiral would be "accidentally" murdered; it might even be managed on the Castilian side of the frontier, so that Portugal could evade responsibility. Or was this offer simply a belated act of courtesy? Columbus did not know, but he took no chances. What made this invitation the more suspicious was the fact that "D. João's squire ordered the Admiral to be given a mule, and presented another to his pilot, . . . and to the pilot he gave a tip of twenty *espadines*," equivalent to about fifty gold dollars. Was this messenger endeavoring to suborn the pilot? Nobody can tell. D. João had no motive but personal resentment for assassinating Columbus. Even if *Pinta* had gone down, *Niña* would have reported the discovery in Castile. Indeed the news was already on its way overland from Lisbon. But it is a privilege of tyrants to slay the bearers of ill tidings. Columbus evidently feared the worst, for, immediately after mentioning in his Journal the offer and the tips, "he says that all was told so that the Sovereigns might know of it."

At all events, Columbus refused to put his head in the bag, had himself and his suite conveyed down the Tagus, and went aboard *Niña* that night. The following morning (March 13) at eight, *Niña* got her anchors aboard, and with a swift ebb tide and a fair NNW wind passed out over the bar of Lisbon.

Now Columbus was out of Portuguese power for good and all.

CHAPTER XXV

Home Is the Sailor
March 13–April 20, 1493

Et deduxit eos in portum voluntatis eorum.

And so he bringeth them into the haven where they
would be.

— PSALM cvi 30

URING the Admiral's absence the men of *Niña* had not
been idle. Indeed there was not much for them to do but
work. They had vowed to spend their first Saturday night fasting on
bread and water; and after the experience at Santa Maria, they
had no desire to see the inside of another Portuguese clink. *Niña*
wanted a new suit of sails and running rigging, not to speak of
paint and carpenter work, but with a blank check that the king
had given them on the royal shipyards, everything was quickly
effected. The filthy hold was scraped and disinfected with vinegar,
new caulking applied where she leaked, new stone ballast obtained
from the opposite shore of the Tagus; by the time the Admiral
came aboard she was all "shipshape and Bristol fashion." The
whole ship's company, Christian and Indian, was aboard Tuesday
night and ready to sail.

Niña sailed from Restello at 8 A.M. Wednesday, March 13.
Slow progress was made that day, and it was not until after sunset
that she was far enough out to sea to shape a southerly course for
Cape St. Vincent. Well abaft, out of sight under the northern
horizon, *Pinta* was sailing the same course.

Martín Alonso, who had parted from his Admiral the stormy
night of February 13, did not sight the Azores. *Pinta* made port at
Bayona near Vigo, just north of the Portuguese boundary, some

450 miles from Palos and over 5 degrees of latitude north of Cape St. Vincent. Obviously Martín Alonso shared the conviction of his brother that the caravels were near Madeira when the storm hit them on September 13, and after it was over he set a north-easterly course which missed his intended destination by several hundred miles. The date of his arrival is not recorded; but as *Pinta* was sailing while *Niña* wasted time at Santa Maria, she must have escaped the cyclone that overtook her consort on February 26, and made her unexpected Galician haven some time in the last week of February. This was another pennant for *Pinta;* first to sight America, first to reach Haiti, and first home with the news.

Columbus had always been afraid that Martín Alonso would try to beat him to the Sovereigns with the glad tidings; and that is exactly what *Pinta's* captain had in mind. He sent a message across the entire width of Spain to Ferdinand and Isabella at Barcelona, begging permission to proceed thither and acquaint Their Highnesses with the news of the discovery. The Sovereigns replied with a complete snub, declaring that they chose to hear the news from the Admiral himself. So Martín Alonso set sail from Bayona with his tail between his legs, as it were, and doubtless torn between the hope that *Niña* had gone down and fear for the safety of his brother.

In the meantime, during the night of March 13–14, refitted *Niña* was rolling southward before the "Portygee trades," covering the 85 miles between Cape Espichel and Cape St. Vincent in her usual gallant manner. Before sunrise the dark profile of the Sacred Promontory loomed up on the port bow. As Columbus wore ship, turned eastward under the lee of the cliffs, and fired the traditional salute, he must have thought of the Infante Dom Henrique, and wished that he could have reported his discovery to a sailor prince who would appreciate his dangers and difficulties. In any case, he sighted the beach where he had swum ashore with an oar seventeen years before. Wind came light on March 14, and sunset found *Niña* off Faro, southernmost harbor of the Algarves. *Pinta* must then have been rounding Cape St. Vincent.

At sunrise on the fifteenth day of March the Admiral "found himself off Saltés," took his bearings on the pine-clad summit of the Cerro del Puntal, stood off-and-on until the ebb was spent, "and at midday with a flood tide entered by the bar of Saltés within the harbor whence he had departed on August 3 the preceding year." The round voyage was completed in exactly thirty-two weeks.

" 'Of this voyage I observe,' says the Admiral, 'that it hath miraculously been shown . . . by the many signal miracles that He hath shown on the voyage and for me, who for so great a time was in the court of Your Highnesses with the opposition and against the opinion of so many high personages of your household, who were all against me, alleging this undertaking to be folly, which I hope in Our Lord will be to the greater glory of Christianity, which to some slight extent already has occurred.' These are the last words of the Admiral Don Christopher Columbus concerning his First Voyage to the Indies and their discovery."

So Columbus concluded his Journal of the First Voyage, when *Niña* was fairly anchored in the Rio Tinto off the town of Palos.

Close in her wake sailed *Pinta;* the same tide took both caravels across the bar and up the river. As *Pinta* rounded the promontory where Nuestra Señora de la Rábida stands guard, and Martín Alonso was straining his tired eyes for the first sight of his native town, someone forward pointed ahead and shouted *La Niña, señor Capitán!* And, by St. Iago, there she was, snugged down as pretty as you please, might have been there a month. Thought we had shaken off that Genoese upstart forever near the Azores; but he beat us home with the news after all. Queen Isabella's blue-eyed boy — probably kissing her hand now.

That finished poor old Martín Alonso. Already a sick man from the hardships and exposure of the voyage, mortified by his snub from the Sovereigns, he could bear no more. Without waiting for *Pinta's* sails to be furled, without reporting to the flagship, or so much as hailing Vicente Yáñez, Martín Alonso Pinzón had himself rowed ashore, went to his country house near Palos, crawled into bed, and died.

Both caravels and their passengers and crews were the objects of much admiring curiosity on the part of the people of Palos, Moguer and Huelva. Many years later a citizen recalled how he had visited *Niña* with a committee of inquisitors who at that time were combing Palos for Jews and heretics; how they saw the Indians aboard, to whom doubtless the inquisitors would have given the "third degree" had they been able to make themselves understood; how the Admiral had shown him some of the gold masks presented by Guacanagarí, and taken a knife and cut off a bit of pure gold and presented it to him. A highly tactful way to treat inquisitors! The Niños returned to their home town of Moguer, and many years later one Juan Roldán remembered well the *bodas y banquetes*, the parties and banquets, that were held there in honor of the heroes.

Columbus, who had already dispatched the Letter on the First Voyage to his Sovereigns overland from Lisbon, now sent another copy by way of Seville, where there was an official courier who spent his time traveling back and forth from Seville to the court. A special messenger delivered letters to the Admiral's family at Cordova, which he now considered his native city, together with a letter to the *cabildo* or municipality "concerning the islands that he had found." The city fathers were so pleased with this attention that they tipped the messenger 3351 maravedis — but unfortunately for us they lost the letter.

The Sovereigns were holding court at Barcelona diagonally across the peninsula, an overland journey of some 800 miles. Columbus, with painful memories of muleback riding in Portugal, at first intended to go there by sea. But the arrival of Martín Alonso the same afternoon put a different complexion on the matter. Haste was a consideration. Yet he could not start by land until a messenger returned from Barcelona with the desired permission to proceed. Accordingly in his letter to the Sovereigns, which was dispatched immediately, Columbus requested that the reply be sent to Seville. After performing his vows at Santa Clara de Moguer and Santa María de la Cinta at Huelva, and spending almost two weeks with Fray Juan Pérez and his other friends at La Rábida, Columbus proceeded with ten Indian captives to Seville. He entered the city "with much honor on the 31st day of March, Palm Sunday, having fully realized his object, and there was very well received." The Indians were lodged near the Gate of the Imágines, where Bartolomé de las Casas remembered staring at them as a boy; the Admiral probably put up at the Monastery of Las Cuevas, where he always stayed on subsequent visits to Seville.

Holy Week in Seville, with its alternation of abject humility and superb pride, penance and pardon, death and victory, seemed at once a symbol and a fitting conclusion to his great adventure. The daily processions of the brotherhoods with their gorgeously bedecked statues of saints, the ancient ceremonies in the Cathedral — rending of the temple veil, knocking at the great door, candles on the great *tenebrario* extinguished until only the one representing the Light of the World remained, the washing of feet on Maundy Thursday, the supreme Passion on Good Friday when the clacking of the *matraca* replaced the cheerful bells, the consecration of the paschal candle, and the supreme ecstasy of Easter morning — all that moved Columbus as no worldly honors could, and strengthened the conviction that his own toils and triumphs fitted the framework of the Passion. And it was pleasant to receive the congratulations of old friends (we always knew you would make it, old man!), to be presented to nobles and bishops, to dine with the alcalde and the archbishop and the Duke of Medina Sidonia, and to be pointed out in the crowd as the man who had sailed to the Indies and back; to have choice young *caballeros* introduced by their fathers in order to plead with Señor Almirante to take them to the Indies, and they would scrub decks or do anything he asked.

What the Indian captives thought of it all we are not told.

On or shortly after Easter Sunday, which fell on April 7, Columbus's cup of happiness overflowed on receiving this letter from the Sovereigns, addressed to "Don Cristóbal Colón, their Admiral of the Ocean Sea, Viceroy and Governor of the Islands that he hath discovered in the Indies." No quibbling about titles, no proofs

of discovery required, but all that had been promised, promptly
and generously conceded: —

We have seen your letters and we have taken much pleasure in
learning whereof you write, and that God gave so good a result to
your labors, and well guided you in what you commenced, whereof He
will be well served and we also, and our realms receive so much advantage. It will please God that, beyond that wherein you serve Him, you
should receive from us many favors, . . . Inasmuch as we will that that
which you have commenced with the aid of God be continued and
furthered, and we desire that you come here forthwith, therefore for
our service make the best haste you can in your coming, so that you
may be timely provided with everything you need; and because as you
see the summer has begun, and you must not delay in going back there,
see if something cannot be prepared in Seville or in other districts for
your returning to the land which you have discovered. And write us
at once in this mail which departs presently, so that things may be provided as well as may be, while you are coming and returning, in such
manner that when you return hence, all will be ready. From Barcelona
on the 30th day of March 1493.

I THE KING   I THE QUEEN
By order of the King and of the Queen, *Fernando Alvarez.*

That was short and to the point, with not a word too much
or too little; titles and privileges confirmed, royal command to
attend court, and an order to prepare a new expedition to the
Indies.

Immediately after receiving this, Columbus drew up a memorial
to the Sovereigns containing his ideas of how the colonization of
Hispaniola should be effected and managed. This document is of
the highest interest, as it shows the Admiral in a new role, that of
pioneer lawgiver to the New World.

Volunteer settlers up to the number of two thousand should be
accepted, and these on arrival at Hispaniola should be distributed
among three or four towns to be founded at convenient places,
each with an alcalde, a clerk, a church and sufficient priests or
friars "for the administration of the sacraments, and for divine wor-

ship and the conversion of the Indians." Nobody should be allowed
to collect gold except bona fide settlers who build houses in these
towns and receive a license to do so from the governor or alcalde;
and since "extreme eagerness of the colonists to gather gold may
induce them to neglect all other business" (as abundantly proved
to be true) there should be a close season on gold hunting during
a part of every year. The licensed gold gatherers must hand over
their takings to the town clerk, to be melted down, weighed and
stamped, and half to be taken by the colony treasurer for the
crown, and 1 per cent of the whole to be reserved for the support
of religion; all gold not so melted and stamped to be forfeited.
All trade between Spain and Hispaniola should be conducted between Cadiz and a selected port or ports in the island, with due
regulations to see that the crown's share is not pilfered on the way
home. Anyone who wishes to make further discoveries should be
allowed to do so — a liberal concession, not required in his original
contract with the Sovereigns, which Columbus later regretted.
This document, highly realistic in so far as it recognized that gold
was the only object to draw colonists to Hispaniola, but suggesting regulations that proved in practice impossible to enforce, was
signed

· S ·

S · A · S

X   M   Υ

:X͠ρο FERENS. /

Some forty-five or fifty of these signatures of Columbus have
been preserved, each with the pyramid of letters arranged in exactly
the same way, but the last line occasionally reading *el Almirante*,
and on at least two, Virey, the Viceroy. Columbus attached great
significance to it, and in his *mayorazgo* or entail instructed his heirs
to continue to "sign with my signature which I now employ which
is a X with an S over it and an M with a Roman A over it and
over that an S and then a Greek Y with an S over it, preserving
the relation of the lines and points." The heirs did not follow his
instructions, and he never revealed the meaning, which has aroused

endless speculation. The problem has particularly interested those endeavoring to prove that Columbus was a Jew, a Portuguese, a Freemason, or what not; for by inverting it or reading it backward, or in some other odd manner the monogram can be twisted into almost any meaning you like. Thacher gives eight possible expansions of the initials. The third line is probably an invocation to Christ Jesus and Mary (Christe, Maria, Yesu), or to Christ, Mary and Joseph, Columbus having confused a "Greek Y" with the Greek I that begins the name of Our Lord, and of Saint Joseph. The first four letters lend themselves to almost infinite combinations, of which the simplest and most reasonable is

Servus Sum Altissimi Salvatoris
Servant I am of the Most High Saviour

The final signature, Xр̃о Ferens, is simply a Graeco-Latin form of his given name, a reminder that by baptism he was consecrated to the task of carrying the word of God overseas to heathen lands.

Speculate as we may, it is unlikely that any certain solution of the cipher will be found; the exact meaning was a secret that Columbus took to his grave.

Sending this letter ahead by a swift courier, the Admiral set forth from Seville clad in the garments, and using the state, suitable to his rank. With him traveled at least one of his officers, a few men whom he had engaged as servants, and six Indians. They carried brightly colored parrots in cages, and wore their native *guayças,* ornaments and belts studded with polished fish bones "fashioned with admirable art, together with a great quantity and samples of finest gold, and many other things never before seen or heard tell of in Spain." The rumor had gone before that Columbus had discovered new lands called "Las Indias" with a strange heathen people and new things; so all along the way to Barcelona the people flocked from far and near to see the show. Nobody — not even an Irishman — loves a parade as does a Spaniard; so the Admiral did not lack popular attention and applause to enliven his long journey. In early April, moreover, Andalusia is at her fairest, with trees in full leaf, fruit in blossom, the fields green with young grain, and the pastures fresh with young grass.

Traversing the great rolling plain of Andalusia, over which Columbus had traveled on his first journey to court, the cortege on the second or third day entered Cordova by the great Moorish stone bridge over the Guadalquivir. Here Columbus saw his two sons Diego and Ferdinand, visited his mistress Beatriz Enríquez de Harana and his old friends of the apothecary-shop club; here too doubtless he was entertained by the municipality, especially informed of the discovery. The cavalcade then crossed the Sierra Morena into Murcia, reached the coast at Valencia, and followed the coastal road through Tarragona to Barcelona, where it arrived between April 15 and 20. "All the court and the city came out" to meet the Admiral, says his son.

Next day Columbus was publicly received in the Alcazar with great pomp and solemnity by the King and Queen. He entered the hall where the Sovereigns held court with a multitude of caballeros and nobles; and among the best blood of Spain his fine stature and air of authority, his noble countenance and gray hair, gave him the appearance of a Roman Senator, as he advanced with a modest smile to make his obeisance. As he approached Ferdinand and Isabella they arose from their thrones, and when he knelt to kiss their hands they graciously bade him rise and be seated beside them and the Infante Don Juan. An hour or more passed quickly while the Sovereigns examined his plunder and the Indians and their trappings, asked him a multitude of questions about the islands, and discussed plans for the next expedition. Then all adjourned to the chapel royal where the *Te Deum* was chanted in honor of the Great Discovery, while tears of joy streamed from the Sovereigns' and the Admiral's eyes. At the close of the service, Columbus was ceremoniously conducted as a royal guest to the lodgings that had been provided for him.

This was the height of his fortunes. Never again would he know such glory, receive such praise, enjoy such favor from his Sovereigns. A more subtle man, one who worked only for material reward, would have taken it forthwith and retired, leaving others to colonize. But Columbus was not that sort of man, or he would not have made his discovery. He must hold the islands gained for Spain, extend his discoveries, meet the Grand Khan, find the mines of gold, begin the work of conversion. The task that God intended him to perform had only begun.

NOTE ON THE ORIGIN OF SYPHILIS

No problem on Columbus's voyages has been so widely discussed as the question whether he did or did not import the syphilitic spirillum from America to Europe. Evidence that syphilis existed in a mild endemic form among the American Indians before 1492 is abundant. No certain evidence of syphilis in Europe exists before 1494, although certain medical historians assert the contrary. In any case, the disease appeared in a most virulent form in Italy in 1494, and spread rapidly. By 1520 it was generally believed in Europe that syphilis came from America, because a reputed cure for it, the guaiacum or lignum vitae, had been discovered there (doctrine of specifics). In view of the excellent health aboard homecoming *Niña* in 1493, and the absence of evidence to the contrary on *Pinta*, it seems highly improbable that Columbus's crews had then contracted the disease. But Las Casas states positively that the Indians gave it to the Spaniards, Oviedo definitely assigns the European importation to the Second Voyage, and Ruy Díaz de Isla, a Spanish physician whose book on syphilis appeared in 1539, assigns it to the First Voyage. He asserts that the disease was first observed at Barcelona in 1493, and that he treated some of the victims.

Two hypotheses are tenable. (1) Syphilis existed in both America and Europe in endemic form, and was stirred up by like events on both sides of the Atlantic, simultaneously: (a) the invasion of Italy by the French army under Charles VIII in 1494–1495, (b) the Spaniards roving and raping all over Hispaniola in 1494–1496. (2) The spirillum was brought to Europe in the bloodstream of Columbus's captive Indians in 1493, and by them transmitted to public women in Barcelona, whence it crossed the Pyrenees and the Mediterranean.

The subject is discussed at length in the two-volume edition of this work, II 193–218.

CHAPTER XXVI

Diplomatic Interlude
1493–1494

Ecce dies Domini veniunt, dicit Dominus, et diuidentur spolia tua in medio tui.

Behold, the day of the Lord cometh, and thy spoil shall be divided in the midst of thee.

— ZECHARIAH xiv I

FOR five or six weeks Columbus remained with the court at Barcelona, taking a prominent part in the great festivals of Whitsuntide, Trinity Sunday and Corpus Christi, attending state dinners, receiving people who wished to go to the Indies, advising the Sovereigns on diplomatic matters, and making plans for the Second Voyage. Unique and memorable was the ceremony of baptizing the six Indians. King, Queen and Infante D. Juan acted as godparents; to the Indian first in rank, a relation of the cacique Guacanagarí, they gave the name Fernando de Aragon; to another, Don Juan de Castilla, and to a third (the clever interpreter), Don Diego Colón. "Don Juan" remained attached to the royal household, "where he was as well behaved and circumspect," says Oviedo, "as if he had been the son of an important caballero"; but he died in two years' time. The others accompanied Columbus on his Second Voyage, but only two survived it.

The most important man in the kingdom after Ferdinand was D. Pedro Gonzales de Mendoza, Archbishop of Toledo and Grand Cardinal of Spain. Las Casas extols his wisdom and ability, his warm and generous nature, the splendor and munificence of his state, and the favor that he enjoyed with the Sovereigns; indeed his character was such that no one was jealous of his power, and it was said "that the Cardinal carried the court with him; for when he was in the court, court was held, and when he was absent there was no court." At a banquet given by this great man Columbus was allotted the place of honor, and treated with the ceremony of the *salva*, usually reserved for royalty; which meant that every dish offered to him was first tasted by the host, and then served covered. To this ceremonial occasion was attributed the famous egg story, the only anecdote about Columbus that everybody knows. We may as well translate the "original source" of it, Benzoni's *Historia del Mondo Nuovo*, the first Italian history of the New World, which came out in 1565: —

Columbus being at a party with many noble Spaniards, where, as was customary, the subject of the conversation was the Indies: one of them undertook to say: — "Señor Cristóbal, even if you had not undertaken this great enterprise, we should not have lacked a man who would have made the same discovery that you did, here in our own country of Spain, as it is full of great men clever in cosmography and literature." Columbus made no reply, but took an egg and had it placed on the table saying: "Gentlemen, you make it stand here, not with crumbs, salt, etc. (for anyone knows how to do it with meal or sand), but naked and without anything at all, as I will, who was the first to discover the Indies." They all tried, and no one succeeded in making it stand up. When the egg came round to the hands of Columbus, by beating it down on the table he fixed it, having thus crushed a little of one end; wherefore all remained confused, understanding what he meant: that after the deed is done, everybody knows how to do it; that they ought first to have sought for the Indies, and not laugh at him who had sought for them first.

"The universal popularity of this anecdote is a proof of its merit," says Washington Irving. Unfortunately the egg story had already done duty in several Italian biographies of other characters, including the architect Brunelleschi. Moreover, a Spanish courtier, unless very drunk, would hardly dare address an insolent query to the guest of honor of the Grand Cardinal of Spain; and a self-made admiral at his first gastronomic dinner would probably have found something better to do than juggle a hard-boiled egg.

Columbus as a newly created nobleman required a grant of arms as outward and visible sign of his rank; and on May 20, 1493, the Sovereigns issued letters patent conferring the right to bear arms on him and his descendants. In this document they declare: —

"You may place above your arms a castle and a lion that we grant you for arms, viz. the gold castle on a green field in the upper quarter of the shield of your arms on the dexter hand and in the other upper quarter on the sinister hand a purple lion rampant with green tongue on a white field, and in the other quarter below on the dexter hand some gold islands in waves of the sea, and in the other quarter below on the sinister hand your own arms which you are accustomed to bear." No crest or motto, and no blazon of the alleged Colombo family arms.

It was a signal honor of the Sovereigns to allow Columbus to augment his arms with the gold castle of Castile and the purple lion of León; but as there was a difference in the fields, these were not, strictly speaking, the royal arms. Thus, Henry VIII of England in granting the Seymours an augmentation consisting of the lilies of France and the leopards of England, prescribed a somewhat different arrangement from that of the royal arms.

No Columbus coat of the exact description quoted above has come down to us, although doubtless every vessel on the Second Voyage had these arms of the Admiral emblazoned on her banners and waistcloths. By 1502, when Columbus compiled a Book of Privileges for the benefit of his descendants, he had made some important alterations in the blazon. The chief he made identical with the royal arms by placing the gold castle on a red field, and bringing the lion rampant in accord with the lion of León. In the lower dexter quarter there is an emerging continent as well as a cluster of islands, for by that time Columbus had discovered terra firma. A new sinister quarter is introduced, consisting of five gold anchors placed horizontally on a blue field, presumably to represent the office of Admiral of the Ocean Sea; and the family arms, blazoned as a blue bend on a gold field with a red chief, are relegated to an arched point in the base, between the third and fourth quarters. There is no particular significance in the alterations, which Columbus according to continental usage had a perfect right

ARMS OF COLUMBUS

From Oviedo

to make. Few people in those days adhered strictly to their original blazon.

Oviedo, in the first edition of his *Historia General de las Indias* (Seville 1535), further augmented the Columbus arms by a crest representing a globe surmounted by a red cross, and by a white motto-ribbon encircling the shield, containing the words: —

Por Castilla y por Leon: Nuevo Mundo hallo Colom
For Castile and for León: a New World found Colón.

Both crest and motto may well have been added by the second admiral, D. Diego Colón.

An immense amount of research has been expended by heraldic

experts and others on the "family arms" of the 1502 shield in the hope that they would explain one of the numerous "secrets" or "mysteries" of Columbus invented by writers of the last century. Nothing exactly resembling them has ever been found. A dove is the feature common to all known arms of patrician Colombos of Italy, Colons of Castile and Coloms of Aragon; and none of the ingenious promoters of Portuguese, Jewish, Catalan, French and Polish "real Columbuses" has been able to show that his favorite bore a blue bend on a gold field under a red chief. Very likely Columbus's father did use this coat; for quite humble citizens of European communes in the fifteenth century could and often did bear arms, especially when they were members of a trade gild. At least half the continental coats that have come down to us were borne by middle-class families. And this device of Columbus was a typical middle-class coat. Any freeman had a right to assume simple arms like these; if Columbus had been trying to pretend a noble origin, he would have used a flock of doves, or something more pretentious.

At the same time that they conferred the original grant of arms, the Sovereigns made the Admiral's two brothers, Bartholomew the future Adelantado and Diego whom he sent for from Genoa, "*nobles y caballeros*, and gave them the faculty and privilege of being addressed as *Don*."

It was also necessary, from Columbus's point of view, that the rights and privileges granted him conditionally at Granada on April 30, 1492, should be expressly and formally confirmed, now that the conditions had been fulfilled. The text of this confirmation, issued on May 28, does not prove anything (as Vignaud imagined it did) about the Sovereigns' opinion of exactly what Columbus had found, because it simply repeats the phrases "islands and mainland" used in the original document signed at Granada the previous year. That document is repeated word for word in the confirmation, which then proceeds: —

And now, forasmuch as it has pleased Our Lord that you discover many of the said islands, and as we hope with his aid that you will find and discover other islands and mainland in the said ocean sea in the said region of the Indies . . . We do by these presents confirm to you and to your children, descendants and successors, one after the other, now and forever, the said offices of Admiral of the said Ocean Sea, Viceroy and Governor of the said islands and mainland that you have found and discovered, and of the other islands and mainland that shall by you or your industry be found and discovered henceforward in the said region of the Indies.

Columbus is confirmed in his right to appoint and remove all judges and other officials in the Indies; to hear, judge and determine all suits civil or criminal, and to enjoy all other things properly appertaining to the offices of viceroy and governor including the obedience of all persons living within the said islands and terra firma; whilst all who sail upon the Ocean Sea, which is defined as all the ocean west and south of a line drawn from the Azores to the Cape Verde Islands, are required to obey him as Admiral.

This matter of the admiralty was made much more explicit in the confirmation than in the capitulations; and as Columbus preferred the sea title to those of Governor and Viceroy, and was always referred to as "The Admiral" by contemporaries, we may well inquire what it meant. *Almirante* was a title of Moorish origin, meaning simply "the sea lord," by which the medieval kings of Castile used to designate a great officer of state whose business it was to administer the royal fleets and dockyards, and to exercise what is still known as admiralty jurisdiction. It was his duty to settle disputes among fishermen and in the merchant marine between owners, mariners and merchants, and to take cognizance of piracy, mutiny and all other crimes committed on the high seas or on tidal rivers. All these matters, for the narrow seas and the Canaries, were exercised by the Admiral of Castile or High Admiral (*Almirante Mayor*), who held court at Seville, and who at that time was one Don Alfonso Enríquez. What Columbus wanted was jurisdiction over his own discoveries and the route thither, where he did not wish the Admiral of Castile to interfere.

The *Almirantazgo* or office of admiral was as necessary for the control of men afloat as the viceroyalty for the government of men ashore. That is why Columbus was created Admiral "of the Ocean Sea" or "of the Indies" — both titles were used in official documents. At a line drawn from the Azores to the Cape Verdes, where the High Admiral's jurisdiction ended, that of Columbus began. I imagine that whenever the fleet crossed that meridian outward bound on the three last voyages, Columbus caused a gun to be fired and had some officer tell the seamen that they'd better behave themselves, since the Admiral now had power of life and death over them.

The office and title of Admiral had no implication of commanding a fleet. This is proved by the fact that on May 28, the same day that the privileges of Columbus were confirmed and his title defined, the Sovereigns issued letters patent appointing D. *Cristóbal Colón nuestro Almirante del Mar Océano*, also *Capitán General de la Armada*, Captain General of the fleet, which was then being prepared for the Second Voyage to the Indies.

His office of Admiral of the Ocean Sea, then, gave Columbus jurisdiction over Spanish ships bound to or from the Indies, as soon as they passed the meridian of the westernmost Azores. He also claimed, by analogy with the rights and perquisites of the Admiral of Castile (which he carefully compiled and inserted in his Book of Privileges), the exclusive right to issue letters of marque and reprisal within his jurisdiction, and a one-third rake-off on the trade to the Indies, over and above what had been promised him by the Capitulations; but he never made that pretension good. While his privileges were still intact, Columbus doubtless appointed his brother or some other officer a judge of admiralty at Isabela and Santo Domingo, and even himself heard cases involving admiralty law, such as seamen's wage disputes, mutiny and piracy. But after Bobadilla came out to Hispaniola, Columbus was so effectually prevented from exercising admiralty jurisdiction that, as he bitterly complained, he could not even punish mutineers on his own exploring fleet, once it had reached shore. He always retained the title Admiral of the Ocean Sea, but after 1500 it was a mere title and nothing more.

. . . .

Columbus would have been more than human if he did not relish the favor of the Sovereigns, the friendship of the great and the admiration of lesser people at Barcelona. But he did not tarry there merely to bask in social sunshine, to have his privileges confirmed, and to indulge in his unpopular habit of saying "I told you!" to the courtiers who had made fun of the Great Enterprise. Ferdinand and Isabella wanted him on hand in order to give information and advice on a very delicate diplomatic negotiation with Portugal and with the Holy See in order to secure their title to his discoveries, and to whatever future discoveries he or others might make in the same "region of the Indies."

Even before Columbus arrived at Barcelona in mid-April, the Spanish Sovereigns, warned by their ambassador at the court of Portugal that D. João II was equipping a fleet whose rumored destination was the new discoveries, began the necessary diplomatic *démarches* at Rome to secure their exclusive title. This was in accordance with usage. The public law of Europe recognized the Pope's right to allot temporal sovereignty to any lands not possessed by a Christian prince, and the kings of Portugal had obtained a series of bulls confirming their rights to the coast of Africa "as far as the Indians who are said to worship Christ," that is, to the kingdom of Prester John. Columbus's Letter on his First Voyage, the first printed edition of which may have appeared before he arrived at Barcelona, was certainly known at Rome a few days before April 18, and a Latin translation of it by Leandro de Cosco, completed April 29, was printed at Rome very shortly. Extracts from it were included in the first bull on the subject issued by the Pope on May 3.

His Holiness Alexander VI (Rodrigo Borgia) was a Spaniard who owed his recent election as well as many earlier favors to the influence of Ferdinand and Isabella. Ferdinand had allowed him to enjoy three Aragonese bishoprics at the same time, had conferred the dukedom of Gandia on his natural son Pedro, had legitimized Pedro's more famous brother Cesare Borgia and nominated him to the bishoprics of Pampeluna and Valencia. Despite these favors the new Pope had been flirting with a group of powers on the opposite side of the balance from Spain. Eager to square himself with his royal patrons, he practically let them dictate a series of papal bulls on the new discoveries, without considering the just claims of Portugal. These four bulls were not arbitral decisions. They were acts of papal sovereignty in favor of Castile based on the Holy Father's presumed right to dispose of newly discovered lands and heathen peoples not hitherto possessed or governed by any Christian prince.

The first bull *Inter caetera*, dated May 3, 1493, declared that whereas *dilectus filius Christophorus Colon* had sailed "toward the Indians" (*versus Indos*) and discovered "certain very distant islands and even mainlands hitherto undiscovered by others, wherein dwell very many people living peaceably, going naked and not eating flesh, . . . well disposed to embrace the Christian faith," each and every island and country discovered or to be discovered by the envoys of the Sovereigns of Castile and their successors, provided they have never been in the possession of any Christian prince, are confirmed to the said monarchs and their successors in full sovereignty. This first *Inter caetera* bull was sent to Spain on May 17, and doubtless arrived before the end of the month.

By this time an ambassador from Portugal had arrived at Barcelona, to assert the claim of D. João to anything discovered west of Africa, and southward of the Canaries. We know from a subsequent remark of Columbus in the Journal of his Third Voyage that the king of Portugal predicted the existence "of mainland to the south," and he now wished to insure that the South Atlantic be explicitly reserved to him as a field of discovery, as implicitly it had been in the bull *Aeterni Regis* of 1481. In that bull the Pope confirmed Portuguese sovereignty "over whatever islands shall be found or acquired from beyond [south of] the Canaries, and on this side [west] of and in the vicinity of Guinea." Whatever the former pope's intention may have been, D. João believed that *Aeterni Regis* gave Portugal a horizontal line of demarcation running through the Canaries. He was prepared to dispute Spanish claims to anything discovered south of that latitude, no matter

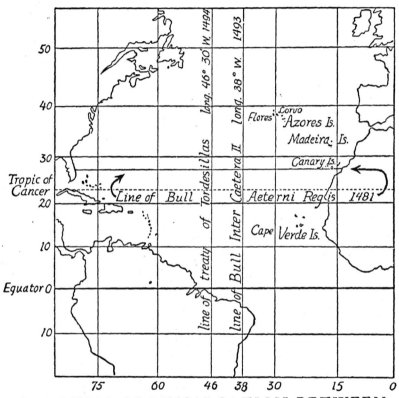

THE LINES OF DEMARCATION BETWEEN
SPAIN AND PORTUGAL

how far west of Africa. In view of this Portuguese claim, the dispositions of the bull of May 3, although clearly recognizing the Spanish title to Cuba, Hispaniola and the Bahamas, were unsatisfactory as to future discoveries; and Columbus intended to take a more southerly course on his next voyage. Accordingly a fresh application was made to Rome by Ferdinand and Isabella.

On its way to Spain, the May 3 bull *Inter caetera* crossed a special mission from Spain to Rome. The Archbishop of Toledo and Don Diego López de Haro were on their way to the Holy See, for the double purpose of confirming Ferdinand's and Isabella's filial obedience to the newly elevated Supreme Pontiff, and of insuring his loyalty to their cousin and ally, the king of Naples. The embassy made a solemn entry into Rome on May 25. At a consistory on June 12, López de Haro, in the name of his Sovereigns, addressed very strong language to the Pope, reproaching him for a foreign policy which had the effect of keeping Italy in a continual state of war, for the venality of his curia, the scandalous auction of benefices, and even with harboring in his territory Moors expelled from Spain. The Roman diarists who recorded these bold words said nothing of any allusion to the Indies. But the Great Discovery was mentioned in a sermon preached on June 19 by the Spanish ambassador to Rome, Bernardino de Carvajal; and this sermon was promptly printed. By way of reminding the Pope of what he and the Church owe to the Sovereigns, Carvajal says, "Christ has subjected under them the Fortunate [Canary] Islands, whose fertility has been proved marvellous; and he has lately given them other unknown islands toward the Indians (*versus Indos*), which may be fully regarded as the most precious things in the whole world, and it is expected that they will shortly be prepared for Christ by royal messengers."

Carvajal's warning, it is reasonable to suppose, "put the heat on" Alexander VI, who promptly issued a bull more satisfactory to Spain. It was after and not before this speech that the Pope issued two predated bulls: *Eximiae devotionis* which repeated the earlier concession in more emphatic terms, and a second *Inter caetera* which confirmed both the others and drew the famous demarcation line. The line is described as drawn from the North to the South Pole, "one hundred leagues towards the west and south from any of the islands commonly known as the Azores and Cape Verdes." West of it all future discoveries of lands not previously possessed by a Christian prince shall belong to Castile.

Columbus undoubtedly suggested this demarcation line. In the

Journal of his Third Voyage, as abstracted by Las Casas, "he remembered that when he came to these Indies in past voyages,
always when he reached 100 leagues toward the west from the
position of the islands of the Azores, he found a change from the
temperature of the north to [that of] the south." And in his Letter
to the Sovereigns on the Third Voyage, Columbus says, "When
I sailed from Spain to the Indies, I found straightway on passing
100 leagues to the west of the Azores a very great change in the
sky, the stars, the air temperature and in the ocean; and I used much
care in verifying this. I found that from North to South, in passing
the said meridian of 100 leagues beyond those islands, the compass needles that formerly northeasted, now northwested a full
point. And on reaching that line it is as if you had put a hill below
the horizon. And also I found the sea there full of weed . . .
and up to this meridian not a single spray of it was encountered. I
also found the sea, on arriving there, to be very soft and smooth,
it never made up even when the wind was stiff. Also I found
beyond the said meridian toward the west, the temperature of the
air to be very mild, and no change winter or summer."

In other words, the meridian 100 leagues west of the Azores
marked the division between European and American conditions,
between boisterous winds with high seas and gentle trades blowing
over a "sea like the river of Seville," between cold weather and
perpetual springtime. This letter to be sure was written in 1500,
after Columbus had had much more experience; but that he had
already reached the same conclusion on his First Voyage may be
seen in his Journal. So, the second *Inter caetera* bull, prompted
by Columbus, took an imaginary physical or meteorological
boundary and made it a political one.

According to Las Casas, it was an entomological boundary as
well. Speaking of the fauna of the Indies, he remarks on the absence of lice and fleas. "As a general rule the ships and people who
follow the sea are so crawling with this 'fruit,' that for him who
goeth to sea for the first time it is no small anxiety and travail;
but for the Indies voyage we have a singular thing to remark: that

up to the Canaries and 100 leagues beyond, or in the region of the
Azores, many are the lice that breed; but from there on they all
commence to die, so that upon raising the first islands [of the
Indies] there be no man that breedeth or seeth one. On the homeward passage to Castile, every ship and person proceedeth clean
of these creatures, until they attain the aforesaid region of the
ocean, whenceforward, as if they waited upon us, they presently
return in great and disturbing numbers." Undoubtedly it was
an advantage to leave this "fruit" on the Portuguese side of the
line. My own marine experiences indicate that the seaman's little
companions which Fernández Duro humorously terms *animalejos
navigantes* have since overcome their prejudice against a voyage
to the Indies.

Returning to matters of deep diplomacy, Columbus left Barcelona in early June, before the last two papal bulls were executed;
but the negotiations were not yet over. Evidently the Sovereigns
showed the line-of-demarcation bull to the Portuguese ambassadors
who arrived at Barcelona in August, and who declared themselves
dissatisfied, on the ground that their royal master expected to discover lands and a continent "very profitable and richer than all
the others" between this demarcation line and Africa. This news
disquieted Ferdinand and Isabella, and on September 5 they wrote
to Columbus at Cadiz inquiring what he thought of the rumor,
and suggesting that "the bull be amended" if he thought it advisable, in order to secure these lands for Spain. In the same letter
they asked for the chart of the new regions that he had promised
them, and for their courses and latitudes. Columbus's reply has not
been preserved, but the bull was amended. On September 26,
1493, the day after Columbus sailed from Cadiz, the Pope issued
a fourth bull entitled *Dudum siquidem,* which augmented the
previous grants in these words: —

"Since it may happen that your envoys and captains or subjects,
while voyaging to the west or south, might land in eastern regions
and there discover islands and mainlands that belong to India (*que
Indie essent*) . . . we amplify and extend our aforesaid gift . . .

to all islands and mainlands whatsoever, found and to be found,
. . . in sailing or travelling toward the west or south, whether
they be in regions occidental or meridional and oriental and of
India." It further declared that all grants previously made to the
regions in question, "Whether to kings, princes, infantes, religious
or military orders" – Prince Henry of Portugal and his Order of
Christ being obviously intended – are null and void, even if there
had been previous possession.

It was now the turn of Portugal to be alarmed. This "Bull of
Extension," so people called the last papal grant, was grossly unfair to her. To Spain it threw open the eastern route to the Indies,
which the Portuguese had been pursuing for at least a generation.
Columbus might sail around the world and plant the standard of
Castile on Ceylon and Madagascar; might discover lands to the
southward within striking distance of the West African coast, and
assert Spanish sovereignty over them. D. João II, evidently concluding it hopeless to do business with a Spanish pope, pushed a
direct negotiation with Ferdinand and Isabella for a modification
of the demarcation line that would more narrowly delimit the
Spanish sphere of influence. The Spanish Sovereigns were in no
position to stand stiffly on their rights. They had a healthy respect
for the powerful and ruthless D. João, and well knew that his navy
and merchant marine, bigger and better than theirs, could render
their communications with "The Indies" insecure if the two countries came to blows. Consequently, in the treaty concluded with
Portugal at Tordesillas on June 7, 1494, Ferdinand and Isabella
consented that the line of demarcation be moved to the meridian
370 leagues west of the Cape Verde Islands. East of this meridian
all discoveries, even if made by Spanish ships, should belong to
Portugal; and west of it all discoveries, even if made by the Portuguese, should belong to Spain.

How great a relief this was to the Sovereigns may be judged
by a letter of theirs to Columbus at Hispaniola, dated August 16,
1494. They propose to establish a monthly packet service between
Cadiz and Hispaniola, "since the affairs of Portugal are arranged,

and vessels will be able to go back and forth in safety." They had already sent him a copy of the treaty, and now suggested that he come home and help them to establish the new line of demarcation.

In the treaty of Tordesillas it was provided that each country appoint a commission of "pilots, astrologers, seamen and others," who should meet at the Grand Canary and there begin a joint cruise to the Cape Verde Islands. Thence each in its own caravel should sail due west until both parties struck land, or agreed that the correct meridian had been reached. Having decided that point, at a mid-ocean conference, they should sail due south and set up a pillar at the first land they encountered on the meridian. Considering the differences of opinion as to a ship's position among the pilots of Columbus's fleet, the impossibility of determining longitude, and the lack of knowledge of compass variation, the failure of this joint cruise to come off is a sad loss to the humors of maritime history. Instead, Spain and Portugal agreed by an exchange of notes in 1495 that this procedure would be "unprofitable," and that each would simply keep the other informed as to new discoveries and their reputed positions. That was done; and it was by virtue of the Treaty of Tordesillas, and not the papal line of demarcation, that Portugal obtained title to Brazil. Implemented by a series of royal marriages, this treaty preserved peace and friendship between the two great colonizing powers until Magellan's circumnavigation intruded on the sphere that Portugal rightly believed to be hers. Never in modern history has so vast a colonial expansion been carried out with so little friction between rivals.

CHAPTER XXVII

Spreading the News
¹493–¹494

Epistola Cristoferi Colom (cui etas nostra multum debet: de Insulis in mari Indico nuper inuentis. Ad quas perquirendas octauo antea mense: auspicijs et ere Inuictissimi Fernandi Hispaniarum Regis missus fuerat) ad Magnificum dominum Raphaelem Sanxis: eiusdem serenissimi Regis Thesaurarium missa. quam nobilis ac litteratus vir Aliander de Cosco: ab Hispano ydeomate in latinum conuertit: tercio kalendas Maij. M.cccc.xciij. Pontificatus Alexandri Sexti Anno Primo.

Letter of Christopher Columbus (to whom our era oweth much, concerning the Islands newly discovered in the Indian Ocean, for the discovery whereof eight months before he had been sent under the auspices and in the pay of the most unconquerable Ferdinand King of the Spains), sent to the magnificent Don Raphael Sánchez Treasurer of the said most serene king. The which a noble man of letters Leandro Cosco hath turned into Latin from the Spanish on the 29th of April 1493, in the first year of the Pontificate of Alexander VI.

— Introduction to First Latin Edition of COLUMBUS LETTER

H IGHLY entertaining and significant are the traces of how the news of Columbus's discovery spread, and what people thought about it. For Columbus gave a new world not only to Castile and to León, but to European curiosity.

Earliest evidence that the news had reached Spain is the Duke of Medina Celi's letter of March 19, 1493, written from his castle about fifty miles northeast of Madrid, and stating that Columbus had arrived in Lisbon, after finding all that he went to seek. This is the only private letter about the First Voyage by a Spaniard that we have. The duke must have received word from Lisbon, where Columbus arrived March 6, and not from Palos, where the voyage ended on March 15.

Many Italians were then established in Spain as merchants, diplomats or churchmen, and a number of their letters written to their friends and patrons in Italy mentioning the Great Discovery have been preserved. As early as the last week of March, 1493, according to a contemporary chronicler named Tribaldo de Rossi, the Signory of Florence received a letter from Spain stating that certain youths with three caravels had gone in search of new countries "not already seen by the King of Portugal," and had discovered a very great island inhabited by naked people "wearing certain leaves about their genitals but nothing more," and using spears "tipped with porcupine quills instead of iron, of which they had no knowledge." The discoverers found considerable gold and a river whose sand was mixed with it, as well as cotton, pines, cypress trees and spicery.

The earliest Italian letter about Columbus to be preserved intact was written by a Barcelona merchant named Hannibal Zenaro or Januarius to his brother at Milan on April 9, 1493: —

Last August these Lord Sovereigns, on the plea of a certain *Colomba*, were content that the aforesaid should equip four caravels, because he said he wanted to pass over the Great Sea and sail directly to the west, in order to reach the Orient; since, the world being spherical, he would have to turn and find the oriental region. And so he did; the said caravels were accordingly equipped and the westward course was taken from outside the Straits, according to the letter which he wrote and which I have seen. In 34 days he arrived at a great island inhabited by naked people of olive complexion without any skill in fighting and very timorous. And, some having landed, they took some by force, so as to have knowledge of them, and to learn their language, in order that they might understand. [The natives] having thus lost their fear, for they were men of intelligence, [Columbus and his men] accomplished their object, and by signs and other means it was learned that they were among islands of India. And so the said captives went through the houses and towns of their neighbors, saying that there had come into that region a man sent from God. And, therefore, all these people, being of good faith, contracted warm friendship and amity with the said *Collomba* and his men. From this island they then passed on to other islands, so far that in taking that course they have found a great number of islands, two of which are each of greater extent than England or Scotland, and the other greater than all Spain. The aforesaid *Colomba* has left there some of his men. And before departing he built a fort furnished with victual and artillery, and carried off thence six men who are learning our language. In that island they say they have found pepper, lignum aloes, and a mine of gold in the rivers, i.e., a river, which has sand with many grains of gold. And the people there, it is said, navigate with *canne* which are so big that the largest hold 70 and 80 men. *Collomba* aforesaid has returned directly and made land in Lisbon, and has written this to the Lord King, who has written to him to come here at once. I expect to have a copy of that letter which he has written, and shall send it to you, and when he has come and I learn anything further I shall let you know. And this is regarded as certain in this court; and, as I have said, I have seen the letter which says, furthermore, that he has not observed among those people any law or religion, except that they believe that all things come from Heaven, and that there is the creator of all things; whence cometh hope of their easy conversion to the Holy Catholic Faith. He says further that he was afterwards in a province where men are born with a tail.

Including the last item, which was a slight exaggeration of Columbus's hearsay report that Sir John Mandeville's tailed men grew in the Province of Havana, Zenaro's information was derived from Columbus's Letter on the First Voyage, either a manuscript copy or the first printed edition. The recipient of Zenaro's letter gave a copy of it to Jacome Trotti, the Ferraran envoy at Milan, who sent it on April 21 to his master the duke. This was none other than the famous Ercole d'Este, who was keenly interested in voyages and discoveries. He replied promptly, demanding more detail; and on May 10 Trotti wrote again enclosing another "letter come from Spain," probably the copy of Columbus's Letter that

Zenaro had promised to procure. As the court of Ercole d'Este was a center of scientific inquiry as well as of humanist learning, we may be certain that news of the discovery spread fast among the *cognoscenti* of Northern Italy.

A copy of Columbus's own Letter on the First Voyage reached Rome a few days before April 18, as it is mentioned in a Venetian chronicle on that day. On the twenty-seventh the Milanese envoy at Venice sends a copy of the Letter to his master, the famous Ludovico il Moro. On April 22 an architect named Luca Fancelli writes from Florence about the discovery to his patron, the Marquis of Mantua. Fancelli does not mention the name of Columbus. He says that in sixteen (!) days vessels of the King of Spain "discovered certain islands, among others a very large island toward the Orient which had very great rivers and terrible mountains and a most fertile country, inhabited by handsome men and women, but they all go naked, except that some wear a leaf of cotton over their genitals, . . . the country is most abounding in gold, . . . from it one sees neither the Arctic nor the Antarctic Pole." Allegretto Allegretti, a Sienese diarist, noted on April 25 that he had heard "from many letters of our merchants in Spain, and from the lips of many people," that *Cristoforo Colombo* (the first time his name is given correctly) had found islands with gold, spicery, and people of strange customs, and had left a garrison of eighty men on one island; "they consider our men as gods." And he has heard that a second voyage is already being planned. The Duke of Milan's agent at Bologna reported on June 17 that *Columbo* had found some "southern islands in the crossing of the Indian Ocean" inhabited by "simple and naked people whom they tried to capture, treating them with liberality and humanity." Battista Fregoso, a former doge of Genoa, noted in his "Chronicle of Memorable Words and Deeds" for 1493 that *Christophorus Columbus natione Genuensis* had safely returned from India, having reached it in 31 days from Cadiz, as he proposed to do.

Columbus's Letter on the First Voyage (the one usually described as "to Santangel" or "to Sanxis") must have been printed at Barcelona as early as April 1, before Columbus came to court, to circulate so quickly. The first Latin translation, dated April 29, made by a Catalan named Leandro de Cosco, was printed at Rome in May in news-letter form, as a pamphlet of eight pages, entitled *De Insulis inuentis. Epistola Cristoferi Colom.* This became a "best seller"; it ran through three Roman editions in 1493, and six different editions were printed at Paris, Basle and Antwerp in 1493–1494. Giuliano Dati, a Florentine theologian and poet who was living in Rome, translated the Latin Letter into Tuscan verse, a poem of sixty-eight stanzas which was printed at Rome on June 15, and at Florence twice in 1493. A German translation was printed at Strassburg in 1497, and the second Spanish edition appeared at Valladolid about the same time.

News of the First Voyage must have reached Northern Europe slowly. The great *Nuremberg Chronicle* was printed on July 12, 1493, without any mention of the discovery; and two days later a Nuremberg scientist wrote to D. João II, urging him to undertake a western voyage to the Indies, in complete ignorance that Columbus had taken the trick. As for England, the earliest evidence that anyone there had heard about Columbus's First Voyage is in a letter from Ferdinand and Isabella of March 28, 1496, to their ambassador at London, referring to news from him that "one like Columbus" (John Cabot) was trying to persuade the king "to enter upon another undertaking like that of the Indies." One would suppose that Ferdinand and Isabella would have seen that copies of the Pope's bulls reached the kings of every seafaring nation; but no copies of any such communications have been found in the archives of any European state except Portugal.

It is clear, then, that news of the Great Discovery traveled very quickly from Spain to Italy, partly through private letters of Italian merchants and partly through the efforts of Ferdinand and Isabella to secure their title from the Pope. But beyond the Alps and the Pyrenees it traveled very slowly indeed; three months after it was known at Rome and in Northern Italy, almost four months after it was known at Barcelona, the *Gelehrten* of Nuremberg, center of geographical studies in Northern Europe, had no word of Columbus's First Voyage. Indeed the news seems to have aroused very little interest outside Italy and the Iberian peninsula. Not until after a colony had been planted in the New World did the learned people in France, the Low Countries, Germany and England take notice that something important had happened. And the first nation after Spain to seek a western route to the Indies did so on the initiative of another Genoese, John Cabot.

From such letters and chronicles as we have quoted, and the few others that have been discovered, it is clear that Columbus's discovery struck the European imagination as a unique combination of the marvelous united to the truth. Scientific and literary curiosity were equally aroused. The points in Columbus's discovery that chiefly interested people were the new things that recalled something very old, like Adam and Eve in the garden of Eden. The one touch of nature that made all newsmongers kin was the naked natives, especially the women who wore nothing but a leaf. Naked women were much less common in 1493 than today. All Europeans of that era were overdressed, according to our notions; and women were not accustomed to strip or bathe in public. Completely naked Negroes had been seen by the Portuguese discoverers in equatorial Africa; but whatever the Portuguese saw in the Dark Continent they did not tell. So Columbus's story of men and women going winter and summer without clothes was news indeed. Another group of facts that aroused comment were the lack of religion among these natives, their timid and generous nature, and ignorance of lethal weapons; these characteristics, combined with their prelapsarian innocence, suggested to anyone with a classical education that the Golden Age still existed in far-off corners of the globe. Fascinating to all was Columbus's statement that "most of the rivers" in Hispaniola "yield gold," for everyone knew the legend of King Midas and the River Pactolus, for which the Portuguese had been vainly searching the west coast of Africa. Europe was short of specie, and any new gold strike, as in our own day, made a story of universal appeal. The exact location of these marvelous discoveries apparently interested nobody; and the possibility that Columbus had opened up a new sea route to the Indies, and thus damaged the commerce of Italian seaports, did not occur to any letter writer of that nation.

One minor reaction to the news is an interesting illustration of the adage that the truth does not matter so much as "who has the telling of it." Owing to the news being broadcast from the capital of Aragon, and to a Catalan making the first Latin translation of the Columbus Letter, King Ferdinand gained all the credit that should have gone to the Queen. Cosco prefaced his edition with an introductory paragraph stating that *Colom* (the Catalan form of the name) had sailed by command of "the unconquerable Ferdinand King of the Spains," and the illustrated editions have a woodcut of *Fernandus rex hyspania[rum]* clad in armor, bearing the pomegranates of Aragon on one arm and the castle and lion of Castile and León on the other. Queen Isabella receives a credit line in later editions; but in the Italian letters we have quoted, the Voyage is represented as a purely Aragonese enterprise.

To what extent did public opinion support Columbus's own view of his discoveries? As the news spread largely through copies, digests and translations of the Letter, his own claim that he had really reached "The Indies" was generally accepted. Ferdinand and Isabella adopted it officially, as it was their interest to do; and the Pope accepted their claim at its face value. The Admiral's great delusion is perpetuated by the name "Indian," by which we still call the natives of the New World. Until the latter half of the eighteenth century Spain officially called her overseas empire "The Indies." With the qualification "West" this name still persists. Yet there were skeptics even from the first. The king of Portugal, first European of any importance to whom Columbus communicated his news, refused to believe that the Genoese had discovered anything but islands in the ocean like the fabled Antillia; and the West Indies were always called "Las Antilhas" in Portugal and "Les Antilles" in France. Indeed any learned man who had read Ptolemy and accepted his approximately correct idea of the size of the globe must have concluded that Columbus could not possibly have reached Asia in thirty-three days' sailing from the Canaries. Either that, or Ptolemy was wrong — a proposition difficult for any man of learning to entertain.

This dilemma, which was not solved until the conclusion of Magellan's circumnavigation in 1521, is first seen in the letters of Peter Martyr d'Anghiera. That young Italian humanist in the Spanish service was with the court at Barcelona when Columbus arrived there in April 1493. He was not very prompt to inform his correspondents about Columbus, but gradually became more and more interested, and within a year decided to write a history of the discoveries. On May 14, 1493, at least seven weeks after the news reached Barcelona, Martyr wrote to his friend Count Borromeo: —

A few days afterward there returned from the western antipodes a certain *Christophorus Colonus* of Genoa who had with difficulty obtained from my Sovereigns three ships [to visit] this province, for they considered what he said fabulous; he has returned and brought proofs of many precious things, especially of gold, which these regions naturally produce.

So far, Peter Martyr does not question Columbus's claim that he had reached the "antipodes," meaning Asia. And in a letter dated September 13 to Count Tendilla and the Archbishop of Granada, he writes: —

Listen, you two very wise old gentlemen, and consider a new discovery. You remember how *Colonus* the Genoese, in camp with the Sovereigns, demanded permission to pass over to a new hemisphere by the western antipodes; you certainly should. Because in some measure it is owing to you. Nor without your advice, so I think, did he undertake the thing. He has returned safe and sound and declares that he has discovered marvels.

There then follows an accurate digest of Columbus's Letter on the First Voyage. Peter Martyr's letter of the same date, September 13, to Cardinal Ascanio Sforza, also declares that " a certain *Christophorus Colonus* Genoese" had reached the Antipodes. By October 1, Peter Martyr begins to be doubtful. In a letter of that date to the Archbishop of Braga he writes: —

A certain *Colonus* has sailed to the western antipodes, even to the Indian coast, as he believes. He has discovered many islands which are thought to be those of which mention is made by cosmographers, beyond the eastern ocean and adjacent to India. I do not wholly deny this, *although the size of the globe seems to suggest otherwise*, for there are not wanting those who think the Indian coast to be a short distance from the end of Spain. . . . Enough for us that the hidden half of the globe is brought to light, and the Portuguese daily go farther and farther beyond the equator. Thus shores hitherto unknown will soon become accessible. For one in emulation of another sets forth on labors and mighty perils.

One month later Peter Martyr seems at first glance to have decided that Columbus had *not* reached the Indies; for in a letter to Cardinal Sforza of November 1, 1493, he speaks of *Colonus ille Novi Orbis repertor*, "that famous Columbus the discoverer of a New World." This is the first recorded mention of the discoveries as constituting a new world. But in Peter Martyr's mind *novus orbis* was not incompatible with "The Indies." For, in a letter to Count Giovanni Borromeo, written late in 1494 after the first news of the Second Voyage to Cuba had arrived, he says: —

Daily more and more marvels from the New World are reported through that Genoese *Colonus* the Admiral. . . . He says that he has run over the globe so far from Hispaniola toward the west that he has reached the Golden Chersonese, which is the furthest extremity of the known globe in the east. He thinks he has left behind only two hours of the four and twenty in which the Sun in its course encircles the universe. . . . I have begun to write books about this great discovery.

The Golden Chersonese was the Ptolemaic name for the Malay Peninsula. Consequently Peter Martyr, when describing Columbus's discoveries as a new world, means to suggest that they were new-found islands lying off Asia, in much the same position as the

Moluccas. This mistake is important, for Columbus made the same error and obstinately adhered to it all his life. We are so used to considering the Americas as the New World that we find it hard to understand how educated men could consider outlying parts of Asia as a new world; but so almost everyone thought in Columbus's lifetime, and many continued in that opinion until Magellan's circumnavigation proved that Ptolemy and not Columbus was right about the extent of the globe. Columbus himself, in his Letter on the Third Voyage, employed *otro mundo* ("an other world") in exactly the same sense as Peter Martyr did *novus orbis:* a hitherto undiscovered appendage of Asia. Amerigo Vespucci, in his "Medici" letter which was printed in 1503 or 1504 under the title *Mundus Novus*, declares that the South American coasts which he had sailed along in 1501 "we may rightly call a new world because our ancestors had no knowledge of them, and it will be a matter wholly new to all those who hear about them." Yet even he probably conceived of South America as having much the same relation to Southeastern Asia as Australia has. Vespucci's admirer Waldseemüller announced in 1508 that Amerigo had discovered a "fourth part of the world" which therefore should be named *America;* but it was some years before the new name and the new geographical conception were accepted. Alessandro Geraldini, writing reminiscently in 1522 of Columbus's original project which he had heard discussed in court, speaks on the same sentence of the Admiral's proposition "for discovering a new world" and his belief that by crossing the ocean he could reach "the Antipodes" of Eastern Asia. He saw no incompatibility between a new world and the Indies. All the learned quibbling of modern historians over the phrase *mundus novus*, as though it necessarily meant America, is a waste of words.

Columbus's discoveries, then, were taken at his own valuation; he had discovered a new world of islands "in" or "toward" the Indies, and everyone expected that on the next voyage something definitely Asiatic as described by Ptolemy or Marco Polo would be reached. Neither he nor anyone else suspected in 1493 or 1494 that the prophecy of Seneca had been fulfilled, and a vast continent lay revealed. Before Peter Martyr had finished the history *de Orbe Novo* that he told his friend had already been begun, he well knew that it was a new world indeed; but Columbus was not so easily convinced. The very pertinacity which had made him push his Grand Enterprise during ten discouraging years, the serene confidence that kept him steadfast, prevented him from ever altering his conviction that he had discovered a western route to Asia. In his cosmographical ideas Columbus remained stubbornly and obstinately, to the end of his life, absolutely and completely wrong.

THE SECOND VOYAGE TO AMERICA

CHAPTER XXVIII

The Grand Fleet

May–October, 1493

Et convertet faciem suam ad insulas, et capiet multas.

After this shall he turn his face unto the isles, and shall
take many.

— DANIEL xi 18

COLUMBUS planned a Second Voyage before the First was
over, and the Sovereigns ordered him to begin preparations
as early as March 30, 1493. Little if anything was done before the
Admiral left Seville for Barcelona, where the general plan, purpose
and scope of the voyage were discussed by him with the Sovereigns,
the Cardinal of Spain and other important persons. On May 20
he was appointed Captain General of the fleet, and on the twenty-
third, very likely at his suggestion, the Sovereigns made Don Juan
de Fonseca, Archdeacon of Seville and nephew of the Archbishop,
jointly responsible with Columbus for the preparations. Las Casas,
who in later years had a row with Fonseca (then Bishop of Burgos)
about the treatment of Indians, admits grudgingly that he was
a good business man and organizer, especially in the matter of
equipping fleets *que era más oficio de vizcaínos que de obispos,*
"which was a more appropriate job for Basques than for Bishops."

Be it so, Fonseca on this occasion did an excellent job. Within
five months, and in a country where the most rapid transit was by
mule, he managed to assemble a fleet of seventeen vessels, and to
equip them with sea stores, spare gear, ship chandlery and arms
for a round voyage of six months; to accumulate the necessary
food and much of the equipment for twelve to fifteen hundred
men; to recruit the essential workmen and artisans and collect the

necessary seeds, plants, domestic animals, tools and implements for founding a mining-agricultural colony, and transplanting Spanish civilization to the Indies.

No European nation had ever undertaken an overseas colonizing expedition on anything approaching this scale. The nearest thing to it had been São Jorge da Mina, the fortified trading factory that the Portuguese built on the Gold Coast in 1482. Columbus, as we have seen, had made a voyage or two to "The Mine," and his experience there taught him that Europeans transplanted to another country and climate could not depend on native food. He demanded enough Spanish provisions such as flour and biscuit, salt meat and molasses, oil, vinegar and wine to sustain his colony for many months. Failure to provide that was his one real ground of complaint against Fonseca as purveyor. Of course there was a certain amount of cheating by the land sharks; but that is expected by seafarers great and small, and Don Juan could not oversee every little detail. The wine contractor furnished secondhand or defective casks, which failed to stand up in the tropic heat and let down much of the precious wine into the bilges. Columbus was particularly annoyed at the horse-trading done by a cavalry troop of twenty lancers that the Sovereign sent with him to the Indies. These caballeros made a fine showing at a parade in Seville, but they sold their blooded barbs at Cadiz and substituted a herd of sorry hacks, pocketing the difference. No doubt they needed money to live like gentlemen before embarking, and figured out that a cheap "plug" was more likely to stand the voyage than a thoroughbred — and no doubt they were right.

Many orders about the voyage were issued by the Sovereigns in May. The officials of all cities, towns and villages in Andalusia were to grant every facility for purchasing provisions and other sea stores, forbidden to assess any tax or duty, and required to punish profiteering. The Alcaide of Malaga was ordered to furnish fifty cuirasses, and as many crossbows and *espingardas*, the standard muskets of that era; a like number were ordered from the Alhambra. Powder and other military stores were furnished by the major-domo of the royal artillery. Juanoto Berardi, Florentine merchant at Seville and friend of Columbus, was ordered to purchase a vessel not over 200 tons burthen for the flagship. Columbus and Fonseca were given power to purchase or charter whatever ships, caravels or *fustas* they needed, and at prices they thought proper, and to take full charge and responsibility for equipping them and engaging the personnel, seamen, soldiers and artisans, "the which will be paid the reasonable wages or salary that they ought to receive." And all other vessels not so chartered or attached to the fleet were forbidden "to sail to the said islands and mainland of the Indies without our license and command."

As an example of the manner in which a fleet was equipped in that day of petty business, accounts have been preserved of payments to twenty-five persons in the neighborhood of Jerez de la Frontera for amounts of wheat varying from 2 to 10 *cahizes* (36 to 180 bushels) at the uniform rate of 1320 maravedis a *cahiz* or 73 maravedis a bushel; and of payments to others for grinding it into flour and baking ship's biscuit. This ship's bread department was placed in charge of an official of the Holy Inquisition. We may be certain that his orders were promptly and honestly filled.

The Sovereigns' formal instructions to the Admiral were dated at Barcelona on May 29, 1493. Their declared prime object of this voyage was the conversion of the natives, for which purpose Fray Buil "with other *religiosos*" was sent out in the fleet. Columbus must see to it that the Indians "are treated very well and lovingly." He must promote friendly relations between the Indians and the newcomers, punish anyone who maltreats the natives, and give the Indians some of the goods sent out by Their Highnesses for barter. The second object is to establish a crown trading colony. All trade is to be conducted with goods provided by the government; one eighth of the net profits will go to the Admiral, and the rest to the crown; private trading is prohibited. Everything sent home from the Indies must be landed in Cadiz, as Columbus had already recommended. A number of details about the accounting are added, in order to prevent leakage and ensure that the Sovereigns obtain their just profits; but Columbus is given a free hand as to methods of administering the colony, procuring gold, and attempting further discoveries. Las Casas says that the Sovereigns further commanded and charged the Admiral as soon as possible to explore Cuba, "to see whether it were an island or mainland as he believed and declared it was, for the Sovereigns sagely suspected and the Admiral declared that a mainland should contain greater good things, riches, and more secrets, than any one of the islands."

This wide liberty of action accorded to Columbus is in marked contrast to the minute instructions issued to overseas servants of the crown in a later era. Ferdinand and Isabella recognized that he must be governed by circumstances; but they made it perfectly clear that their two main interests in the voyage were religious and fiscal. The first European colony in America was conceived of as a means of converting infidels and acquiring gold; in practice the higher object became completely submerged by the lower. Apparently the Sovereigns had lost all desire to exchange compliments with the Grand Khan. Perhaps they figured out that he would not be too well pleased with the mining and missionary game.

In June 1493, when all necessary orders for the Second Voyage had been issued, and the Sovereigns felt that the negotiations with Portugal and the Holy See were so well advanced that they could spare the Admiral's presence, they gave him leave to depart from Barcelona. Several servants of the royal household accompanied him to act as officials in Hispaniola, and many more sought in vain for the privilege. Five of the six baptized Indians followed the Admiral.

Columbus took a different and longer route to Seville than the one by which he had come, in order to fulfill his vow of a pilgrimage to Guadalupe made aboard *Niña* in the great storm. He crossed the great plain of the Ebro to Saragossa, followed the castle-studded highway across the eastern spurs of the Sierra Guadarrama into the high plains of New Castile, passed Cogollado the seat of his patron the Duke of Medina Celi, and entered Madrid. Thence he took the road to Portugal over which the news of his discovery had first reached Castile. Leaving this much-traveled way at Talavera de la Reina, the Admiral's cortege crossed the Tagus by a great stone bridge and followed a road that led through the foothills of the Sierra de Estremadura. One of his nights in that poor, barren country must have been spent in the town of Trujillo, where a thirteen-year-old swineherd's son named Francisco Pizarro would certainly have turned out to see the Indians; perhaps then and there he caught that flame of ambition which led him to the conquest of Peru.

Columbus passed along the pilgrims' way through defiles in the sierra, constantly ascending, and in about three days reached a high tableland of sheep pastures. On its southerly slope, half surrounded by high mountains, rose the crenellated walls of the mighty Jeronymite monastery of Guadalupe. Around the walls clustered the hovels of a poor village that lived by exploiting the pilgrims; within were a great gothic church, vast conventual buildings, cloisters separated from green gardens and fountains by delicate gothic tracery or Mudejar colonnades, sacristies whose presses were crammed full of gold-embroidered copes, dalmatics and chasubles, a treasury containing some of the richest goldsmiths' work in Spain — and, what Columbus had come to see, Nuestra Señora de Guadalupe. This ancient image of the Virgin, said to have been carved by Saint Luke himself, had such a reputation for saving soldiers from death and sailors from drowning, and protecting rulers from the consequences of their evil deeds, that her shrine had become the most venerated and wealthy in all the Spains. Even kings and princes made the long journey to pray before the Virgin of Guadalupe, and some of these chose a chapel of the great church for their last resting place. The monks were much interested in seeing the first converts of a race hitherto untouched by Christianity; they asked the Admiral on his next voyage to name an island after their sacred city, and this he did. Through later conquistadors, very many of whom came from Estremadura, the fame of Santa María de Guadalupe was carried to all parts of the Indies, and new Guadalupes arose in Mexico, Peru and other regions of Spanish America.

Descending the Sierra by its southern slope to the valley of the Guadiana, Columbus crossed that river to the little town of Medellín, where a small and delicate boy named Hernán Cortés must have seen him pass. Cortés in later years prayed for nine consecutive days before the miraculous image in the hope of expiating his sins committed in the conquest of Mexico; and it was at New Guadalupe, near the city of his conquest, that the Virgin deigned to appear to a poor native boy in 1531, creating a shrine no less venerated by Indians than was the parent in Estremadura by Spaniards. Columbus, after a ride of another 130 to 150 miles, reached Cordova, where again he said farewell to Beatriz Enríquez de Harana, and where both his sons joined the company. Thence he proceeded to Seville. By this time it must have been the end of June, or early July.

Seville was the headquarters of Don Juan de Fonseca, who in Columbus's absence had taken full charge of assembling and equipping the fleet. The two men did not hit it off well. Las Casas says that they fell out because Fonseca refused to allow Columbus the number of body servants that he considered right and proper to maintain his rank and dignity of Admiral, and because Columbus went over his head and obtained an order from the Sovereigns allowing him five servants. No doubt there were other and more important sources of friction. The organization of a maritime expedition requires a special sort of talent, for which a man of natural business ability such as Fonseca is far more apt than a man of genius. Columbus proceeded after a few days to Cadiz where the grand fleet was being assembled, and was chagrined at finding it far from ready. He had hoped to be able to sail by mid-August at the latest, in order to be certain of the same fair weather that he had enjoyed on the First Voyage. He found fault with the vessels that had been chartered, the men who had been engaged, and the provisions and ships' stores that were in the course of delivery;

and Fonseca resented fault-finding and interference on the part
of a man who, though Captain General of the fleet, had been bask-
ing in royal sunshine at Barcelona and indulging in a pious pilgrimage while he had borne the heat and burden of organization.

The complete armada included seventeen sail. Unfortunately
we know very little about the vessels or their crews. Three were
naos or ships, including the Admiral's *capitana*, which like that
of the First Voyage was named *Santa María*. Her nickname, referring probably to her gallant ways at sea, was *Mariagalante*. We
do not know her tonnage, but Columbus had been authorized to
procure a flagship of 200 tons, and she was certainly larger than
the old *Santa María*, affording quarters for the Admiral suitable
to his rank. Antonio de Torres, brother of the *aya* or governess of
the Infante D. Juan, was her master and owner. Two other large
ships were named *Colina* and *La Gallega*, the latter presumably of
Galician build or ownership. That leaves fourteen to account for.
Twelve of these were square-rigged caravels, but gallant *Santa
Clara* (*Niña*) is the only one that we can name.

Columbus had found the fleet on the First Voyage too deep
of draught to enter small rivers and inlets. He insisted on a certain
number of seagoing craft that were small enough to sail close
alongshore and enter shoal waters, for Nicolò Syllacio of Milan,
in a little pamphlet on the Second Voyage printed in 1494, says
that many of the vessels were "very light and called *barchias can-
tabricas* (Cantabrian barques) . . . to which were added some
others especially equipped for exploring the Indians' islands."
San Juan and *Cardera*, the two small lateen-rigged caravels that
Columbus took to Cuba in 1494, were among those so equipped.
The bulk of the fleet consisted of *caravelas redondas* like *Niña*,
caravels square-rigged on fore and mainmast, lateen on mizzen.

Personnel was more carefully selected than on the First Voyage,
since the Admiral and Fonseca were overwhelmed with volunteers.
A considerable number of Columbus's former shipmates continued
with him. The payrolls and crew lists have never been found,
and we know the names of very few of the men. There were four

faithful Niños of Moguer — Juan the master and Francisco the pilot of *Niña*, Cristóbal Pérez Niño, master of *Cardera*, and Juan's nephew Francisco who shipped as a gromet. If the crew lists of *Niña*, *San Juan* and *Cardera*, the only ones we have, are representative, the fleet contained a fair number of Genoese mariners, and a sprinkling of Basques; but most of the people were from Palos, Moguer, Huelva and Lepe. This indicates, despite the conspicuous absence of any member of the Pinzón family, that Columbus had retained the confidence of seafaring folk in the Niebla region. Among the captains of vessels were Juan Aguado; Pedro Fernández Coronel, who later took the advance fleet of the Third Voyage to the Indies; Alonso Sánchez de Carvajal, mayor of Baeza, a municipality which was required to pay him his full salary while at sea; Ginés de Gorbalán; and Alonso de Hojeda. Other members of the expedition of whom much would be heard in future were Juan de la Cosa, second of that name, a chartmaker of Puerto Santa María who shipped as mariner aboard *Niña*; Ponce de León the future discoverer of Tierra Florida and conquistador of Puerto Rico; Pedro de Terreros (the Admiral's personal steward), who commanded a caravel on the Fourth Voyage; and Diego Tristán, gentleman volunteer, who lost his life on that voyage in the fight at Belén. The commander of the armed forces was Francisco de Peñalosa, a servant of the Queen and uncle to the historian Bartolomé de las Casas, whose father, Pedro, also shipped on this voyage. Another soldier, Mosén Pedro Margarit, commanded the first fort in the interior of Hispaniola, and went home in a huff because the local council tried to control him in the Admiral's absence. Other landsmen who made the voyage in one capacity or another were Melchior Maldonado, a former envoy to the Holy See from whom Peter Martyr derived much of his information; Dr. Diego Alvarez Chanca, a physician of Seville who left us the most detailed account, and Michele de Cuneo of Savona near Genoa, a childhood friend of the Admiral who wrote the most sprightly narrative of this voyage. In contrast to the First Voyage, there were a number of ecclesiastics, of whom the most important was a Benedictine called Fray Buil, to whom the Sovereigns particularly entrusted the work of conversion. Another, Fray Ramón Pane of the Jeronymite order, is remembered for having compiled the first collection of Indian folklore. The three others were Franciscans, natives of Picardy and Burgundy. They brought out complete equipment for the first church in the New World, a gift of the Queen.

The total complement of seamen, colonists, officials and ecclesiastics reached twelve to fifteen hundred men, according to various authorities; the former number is the more probable, because even that meant an average of seventy men to a ship, and many of the vessels were very small. All were on the royal payroll except about two hundred gentlemen volunteers, but everyone's pay was allowed to accumulate at home, and many did not touch a maravedi of it before 1500. Of course there would have been no sense in paying the men off in Hispaniola where there was nothing to spend money on; all of it would have fallen into the hands of the most skillful gamblers.

Not a single woman was taken aboard the fleet, nor can I find clear evidence of Spanish women being sent to Hispaniola before 1498, when Columbus was allowed to recruit one for every ten emigrants.

Although Columbus now enjoyed great authority and reputation by reason of his discovery, and had a number of veteran shipmates under his command, he still suffered from being a foreigner, and from having few officers on whose personal friendship and loyalty he could rely. The only man in this great company to whom he could give his whole mind was his youngest brother, Diego, whom Las Casas describes as "a virtuous person, very discreet, peaceable and simple, and of good disposition, neither artful nor mischievous, who went very modestly clothed in a sort of clerical garb." As the historian suspected, Columbus was grooming his brother for a bishopric, which he never received because of his foreign birth. Don Diego was not up to the responsibilities that the Admiral thrust upon him. Unfortunately his much more energetic and capable brother Bartholomew did not return from France in time to ship with this fleet.

In a royal letter of September 5, probably the last that Columbus received before sailing, the Sovereigns advised him to ship a competent *astrólogo* (astronomer) such as his old friend Fray Antonio de Marchena. One gathers from the letter that the Portuguese ambassadors at Barcelona had been asking inconvenient questions about the latitude and longitude of the new discoveries, which Columbus had been unable to ascertain, and that the Sovereigns wanted more definite information. The suggestion was sound; keeping track of a ship's position at sea and ascertaining that of her successive landfalls is a full-time job. Why Marchena was not engaged we are not told. Perhaps he refused to go, and possibly nobody else was available with enough mathematical knowledge to apply declination to a meridional altitude of the sun. But I rather suspect that Columbus, like sundry other captains I have known, wanted no rival navigator aboard. Maybe his latitudes were not so good, but he had complete confidence in finding anything he wanted by dead-reckoning. Anyway, no *astrólogo* was engaged.

Unfortunately the Admiral was unwell on the sailing day, September 25; loving pageantry as he did, one hopes he was able to keep the deck and view this brave sight. The breeze was light and the caravels, with every stitch of their bright-painted sails spread, dressed ship as they sailed. Gorgeous royal standards of Castile were hoisted at their mainstaffs, waistcloths emblazoned with the arms of the gentlemen volunteers closed the spaces between fore and stern castles, and so many other colors were displayed that they became entangled in the rigging. Cannon roared, trumpets brayed, harps twanged, and a fleet of gay Venetian galleys escorted the Admiral's armada from white-walled Cadiz to the open sea. His sons Diego and Ferdinand were there to see them off, and watched the fleet out of sight from the Castle of Santa Catalina.

"This fleet so united and handsome," as Columbus proudly called it, made straight for the Canaries. A Spanish naval squadron was ordered to keep watch off Lisbon for any hostile preparations by the Portuguese, and Columbus was warned to look out for enemy caravels and keep away from Portuguese possessions.

On October 2, the fleet made the Grand Canary, and sailed again at midnight. Passing the yet unconquered Tenerife without calling, they anchored on the fifth at San Sebastián, Gomera, where Doña Beatriz de Peraza, "with whom our Admiral in other times had fallen in love," says Cuneo, received them with salvos of cannon and showers of fireworks. Unfortunately we have no further details of this second meeting of Columbus with Doña Beatriz. If he did offer his hand and heart to the handsome and vigorous young widow, they were declined; for she wanted a husband who would stay at home and take care of her and her son's four islands. Perhaps it was just as well that Doña Beatriz did not become the Admiral's wife; for if half the stories that are told of her are true, she was as cruel as she was beautiful. An inhabitant of San Sebastián who was rumored to have questioned her chastity during her widowhood was invited by Doña Beatriz to call on her in the castle and talk it over. After he had said all she cared to hear, she gave a signal, a gang of her servants seized him, and hanged him on a rafter in the castle hall. Doña Beatriz, after watching his expiring agonies, had his body rehanged outside his residence, as a warning to male gossips. She finally married Don Alonso de Lugo, conquistador and adelantado mayor of the Grand Canary; a very proper husband for her.

At Gomera the fleet took on fresh supplies for the voyage, and live animals in order to start flocks and herds in Hispaniola. These like the horses must have been penned up on the decks of the larger vessels, for no animals could have survived below hatches. At some time between October 7 and 10 (no two chroniclers agree), all seventeen vessels set sail from San Sebastián. They ran into the usual Canary calms, and it was not until Sunday, October 13, that the fleet took a final departure from Ferro. Every captain had sealed instructions what to do if the fleet were separated. The Admiral set the course for all, *Oeste cuarta del sudoeste*, West and by South.

CHAPTER XXIX

Many Marys
October 13–November 11, 1493

Me enim insule expectant, . . . ut adducam filios tuos de longe.

Surely the isles of the sea shall wait for me, . . . to bring thy sons from far.

— ISAIAH lx 9

WHEN Columbus set his course W by S he did not intend to sail directly to Hispaniola, but to discover new islands en route. When leaving Samaná Bay in January he intended to visit "Matinino," the Amazon isle to the southeastward, but had reluctantly given that plan up when the wind came fair for Spain. His Indian guides told him about the beautiful arc of Caribbee islands that were flung out to the east and south of Hispaniola, and he had observed man-o'-war birds flying in that direction. So on this voyage the Admiral (wrote Dr. Chanca the flagship's surgeon) "rectified his course to discover them, because they were nearer to Spain, and the route thence to Hispaniola was direct." Excellent judgment, for this new course shortened the ocean passage by at least a week. And "to those islands, by the goodness of God and the *buen saber* (good knowledge) of the Admiral, we came as straight as if we had been following a well known and customary course." How about it, writers who assert that Columbus was no navigator? How about it, Pinzón partisans? No Martín Alonso to "show him the way," this voyage!

Columbus's Indian captives, as we know from the story of the map-making party at Virtudes, were no mean geographers. The Admiral, by careful and persistent questioning, had roughly plotted the position of these still undiscovered islands on his ocean chart, and stretched a string from Ferro to the nearest. The direction he figured out to be West by South.

Here we run into a minor problem of Columbus's navigation. The course from a position south of and within sight of Ferro to the north end of Dominica was not W by S but W by S ½S. The W by S course would have taken the fleet to the northward of the Lesser Antilles. Yet Columbus must have made his landfall after steering W by S all the way across, because that was the course he gave to the vessels bound to Dominica in 1498, and they made it all right. He was crossing the ocean in latitudes where the current is negligible. In a fleet of seventeen sail any local deviation of the flagship's compass would certainly have been noted.

So how may we explain the mistake of half a point? Only one answer is possible. Columbus must have been using Flemish compasses, which were adjusted for one-half point of easterly variation. In the zone of zero variation the fleur-de-lis on a compass card so adjusted would point to N ½W true, and when the W by S diamond of the card was on the lubber line of the compass bowl, the ship would be heading 253° or West by South half South.

Of the ocean passage we have few details because it was uneventful; and that was because it began so late in the year. If the fleet had left the Canaries by September 1, as Columbus hoped to do, it could have hardly avoided a hurricane before reaching the islands, for the good luck of 1492 was too much to expect a second time. Leaving as it did on October 13, the fleet reached the Lesser Antilles after the hurricane season was over. Don Juan de Fonseca deserved a vote of thanks for the delay! As it was, they had one stiff little duster on the eve of SS. Simon and Jude (October 26), when about two thirds of the way across. It was not a hurricane, but a thundersquall of considerable violence that struck them in the night, split a number of sails and broke a few spars before the vessels snugged down. The weather was so thick that no one ship could see another's light, and the landsmen thought their end had come. After the ghostly electrical discharges that seamen called corposants or St. Elmo's fires had appeared on the topmasts, the wind began to moderate, and the sun rose on a sea "smooth as polished marble." This storm lasted only four hours, and the damage was comparatively slight.

Otherwise there was nothing to record. "In the space of these twenty-one days" from land to land, said Peter Martyr, "they thynke that they sayled 820 leagues, the NNE wynde was so full with them, and so fresshely folowed the sterne of theyr shyppes." This proves that they kept excellent dead-reckoning, for the rhumb-line course W by S ½S from Gomera to Dominica measures 820 leagues or 2608 nautical miles. The trades were indeed "full with them" to send the fleet along at this average speed of 5.2 knots; and they could have done better, says Dr. Chanca, "if the flagship had been as good a sailer as the other vessels, for on many occasions the others had to shorten sail because they were leaving us far behind." By taking a more southerly rhumb than on the First Voyage, Columbus profited by the full force of the trades. Any fleet of modern yachts would feel proud to cross that stretch of ocean today in twenty-one days.

This second outward passage must have been very near to the mariner's dream of perfect sailing. Running before the trades is a glorious sensation even when you are alone on the ocean; and on this voyage the beauty of deep blue water, flashing flying fish, curling wave crests and changing cloud formations, was enhanced by seeing sixteen other white-winged ships spread out over the face of the sea. At the hour of the *Salve*, towards sundown, the faster vessels shortened sail and drew near to the flagship like homing birds. All night they sailed as near as possible in formation, their stern lanterns pricking the black surface of the water like fallen stars. Most of the voyage they had a waxing moon, and on the days near full moon (October 24), when hulls and sails reflected her silver light, there was no need to kindle the cressets. At dawn Fray Buil or one of the Franciscans celebrated a "dry Mass" on *Mariagalante's* quarter-deck, while on the other ships men watched for the elevation of the host to kneel and cross themselves. Then a hymn was sung, the watch was relieved, and every ship cracked on sail and raced her sisters during the gorgeous sunlit hours. Except for the one storm on St. Simon's eve it was a downhill coast all the way from the Old World to the New; not one day of calm or head wind after dropping Tenerife. But there was grumbling and grousing for all that, since most of the people were making their first ocean crossing, and the rest were sailors who can always find something to "beef" about. Dr. Chanca says that by late October most of them were "so wearied with bad living and pumping water, that they all sighed with much longing for land," and they sighed not long in vain.

On All Saints' Day the Admiral was so confident of making land within three days that he issued an extra allowance of water aboard the flagship. At sundown November 2, he was certain that land was near from the look of the sea, the flight of birds, and an unmistakable piling up of clouds ahead, indicating a mountainous island. He ordered the fleet to shorten sail lest they overrun in the darkness. We may be sure it was a nervous night, with the dipsey lead hove frequently, the young and inexperienced imagining that they saw lights and heard breakers, the officers testy and irritable, and the Admiral keeping watch. He knew that with proper vigilance and good seamanship on his part God would save the fleet from harm. Was he not *Christoferens*, the chosen instrument of divine providence to illuminate these dark heathen countries with the Light of the World?

At a quarter to four on Sunday morning, November 3, a gibbous moon rises, five days past last quarter. About five o'clock, when her light is reinforced by the first faint gray of approaching dawn, an ancient pilot stationed in the forechains of *Mariagalante* sees a black cone on the horizon ahead pricking up into the dome of paling stars. He climbs to the round-top to make certain, and sings out *Albricias! que tenemos tierra!* — "The reward! We have land!" Cries of *Tierra! Tierra!* spread from ship to ship, and everyone strains his eyes to see more, in the quickly breaking dawn of a tropical winter. A cock crows, and everyone laughs. Horses catch the general excitement and a whiff of the land, and begin tossing their heads and pawing and neighing. The watch below is routed out, and the Admiral, as soon as he is certain that it is land indeed, summons "all hands to prayer on the quarter-deck, where they sing the *Salve* and other prayers and hymns very devoutly, rendering thanks to Our Lord" for so short and safe a voyage.

By this time a high and mountainous island on the port bow was taking the rose of morning. Columbus named it *Dominica* from the Sabbath landfall. The native name was *Caire*. Shortly after sunrise there appeared on the starboard hand a flat and heavily wooded island, which Columbus named *Santa María la Galante* (says Cuneo) "for love of the ship in which he sailed." And the name Mariegalante still records a great seaman's love for his gallant ship, finest of his four *capitanas*. As more light appeared and the fleet sailed on, four other islands, Guadeloupe, Désirade and Les Saintes, came up over the horizon.

The marvelous thing about this landfall is that Columbus made it at almost the exact spot in the Leeward Islands recommended by the writers of sailing directions during the next four hundred years. Vessels bound for any part of the West Indies north of Barbados were advised to make for Désirade, the small high island that rides out to windward of Guadeloupe. *Deseada* (the Desired), as the Spaniards named it, was the goal of the great colonial *flotas* of merchant vessels bound from Spain to Vera Cruz, Porto Bello, Puerto Rico, Santo Domingo and Cuba; of French fleets bound for the Iles sous le Vent and Saint-Domingue, of Englishmen destined for the Caribbee Isles, Jamaica and Virginia. For, if you try to sail north of the Leeward Islands, you are apt to miss the strong trades; and if you try to hit one of the passages between Antigua and Sombrero, the dangerous reefs around Barbuda and Anguilla may pick you up. But the passages on either side of Désirade, one of which Columbus hit right in the middle, lead safely to protected waters; and they are so placed with reference to the prevailing winds that one can scud free to any point of the

Caribbean, the Gulf of Mexico or Florida. So on his Second Voyage Columbus discovered the shortest and best route from Europe to the West Indies. Put it down to luck, seamanship or the finger of God, as you will; it was marvelous.

He also had the good fortune to make his landfall on one of the loveliest islands of the New World. Dominica, wrote Syllacio, "is remarkable for the beauty of its mountains and the amenity of its verdure, and must be seen to be believed; in many places huge trees come down to the shore, as in Thessalian Tempe." All were impressed by the lush verdure of this Sabbath-day island, at a season when Andalusia was brown and parched. The fleet continued on its course; and the Admiral, as yet ignorant of the iron-bound windward coasts of the Lesser Antilles, searched in vain for a harbor along the eastern shore of Dominica. He then decided to try the island Mariegalante, but detached one vessel to round the Capucin rock off Dominica's northern cape and explore the leeward side. She discovered Prince Rupert's bay, the best roadstead on Dominica, and rejoined the fleet at Mariegalante.

Just as well, perhaps, that the Spaniards did not call at Dominica. The Caribs there in the next century made a practice of killing and eating anyone who ventured ashore. On one occasion the natives were made so violently sick by eating a friar that thereafter anyone in ecclesiastical garb was let strictly alone. When Spaniards were forced to call at Dominica for water, they either sent a friar ashore or rigged up the boat's crew with sacking and the like to fool the natives. How they managed the tonsure we are not told.

Mariegalante is almost round and has no harbor, but Columbus found good enough anchorage for one night in one of the roadsteads on the lee side. He went ashore with the royal standard displayed and took possession for his Sovereigns in proper legal form, all noted down and attested by the secretary of the fleet with witnesses and seals. While some of the men raised a cross at the landing place, others went in search of wood and water. They noted the spice tree whose leaves when crushed give forth the odor of cloves, and a noxious tree, whose very boughs dripped poison, and whose touch and taste made the men's tongues and faces swell up and burn. This was the *manzanillo* or manchineel, from whose fruit the Caribs made the poison for their arrowheads. No natives appeared, although everyone was looking for them.

Before daylight November 4 the fleet weighed anchors and steered toward the high island to the westward. On the port hand they sighted a group of four small islands which Columbus named *Todos los Santos* after All Saints' Day just past; the French still call them *Les Saintes*. The mountainous island ahead, which the natives called *Kerkeria*, Columbus named *Santa María de Guadalupe* after the famous Virgin of Estremadura, as the monks had asked him to do on his recent pilgrimage. His approach to Guadeloupe was spectacular. A high volcanic peak (La Soufrière) rose into the clouds, and from its wooded slopes in that rainy season "flowed many streams in different directions." As the fleet drew near, he sighted a waterfall that seemed to leap from the lowest clouds, a sight so strange that the seamen laid bets as to what it might be — a series of white rocks, a ravine full of snow, a broad white road or a river. "It was the fairest thing in the world," noted Dr. Chanca, "to see from what height it fell and how so small a place gave rise to so great a fall of water." These are the falls of the Grand Carbet River, which from the sea look slender as a silver thread, and when the clouds hang low on La Soufrière the thread appears to hang directly from them.

Making the shore of Guadeloupe near the present village of Capesterre, the fleet coasted south and west looking for a suitable anchorage, Caribs fleeing from their villages at the strange sight of ships. Late in the evening of November 4 the fleet anchored in a cove now called Grande Anse, sheltered from the northeast trades but otherwise open to the sea. There they remained six days.

That they stayed so long was owing to a shore party's losing itself in the forest. Diego Marquez of Seville, *veedor* of the new colony, took a company of ten men "for purposes of plunder" says Cuneo, struck into the interior, and promptly got lost; "and this in spite of the fact that they were all seamen and looked for the sun, which they could not well see because of the thick and dense forest." When they did not return the next day, Columbus sent out four search parties of fifty men each, "with trumpets, horns and lanterns, and for all this they could not find them, and there were times when we were in more doubt about the two hundred than for the first ones. But it pleased God that the two hundred came back very tired and hungry. We thought," adds Cuneo, that the Diego Marquez party "had been eaten by the aforesaid Caribs who are accustomed to do it."

The searching party found plentiful evidence of these unpleasant Carib habits which were responsible for a new word — *cannibal* — in European languages. In the huts deserted by the warriors, who ungallantly fled, they found large cuts and joints of human flesh, shin bones set aside to make arrows of, caponized Arawak boy captives who were being fattened for the griddle, and girl captives who were mainly used to produce babies, which the Caribs regarded as a particularly toothsome morsel. The search party brought in about twenty of these captives, and others made their way down to the shore and gave themselves up voluntarily; also a few Caribs were captured by force. One could tell a Carib from an Arawak, said Dr. Chanca, because the former bound their legs tightly with cotton below the knee and above the ankle in order to make their calves bulge. Much as the Spaniards abhorred the Caribs' habits, they were forced to admire their cotton rugs, "so well woven that they owed nothing to those of our country," and their earthenware vessels. But no trace of gold was found.

Apart from the lack of gold, the Spaniards enjoyed this high and beautiful island, clothed with tall, heavy-leaved hardwoods up to its volcanic cones. They were impressed by the flocks of brightly colored parrots "as numerous as sparrows or other little birds with us" and with the fine headdresses that the natives made of their feathers, green, red, black and yellow. Here for the first time Europeans tasted the pineapple, and those new to America had their first cassava bread, roast yam and sweet potatoes. One shore party viewed with interest a piece of ship timber which they supposed to have come from the wreck of *Santa María* on the First Voyage; but it must rather have belonged to a Portuguese caravel, and floated over from Africa in the equatorial current.

This enforced stay at Guadeloupe enabled Columbus to get a better idea of the shape of the island than he acquired of the other Caribbee Isles. Juan de la Cosa the map maker was in the

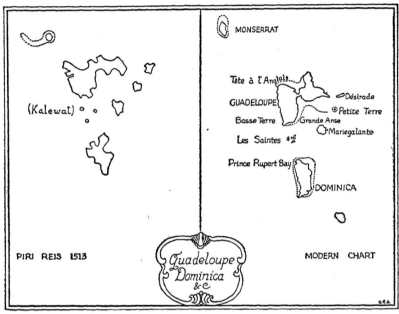

GUADELOUPE AND NEARBY ISLANDS
ON PIRI REIS MAP COMPARED
WITH MODERN CHART

fleet, but one would never know it from the shape and disposition of the Lesser Antilles on his famous world map. From various entries in Dr. Chanca's letter, it is clear that the Admiral was compiling a chart as he sailed along; but this, like all but one of Columbus's autograph maps, has been lost. A few years ago there turned up at Constantinople a Turkish world map made in 1513 by an Ottoman cartographer named Piri Reis, on which an inscription states that the Antillean portion was copied from a chart by "The Genoese infidel Colombo," taken off a ship captured by the Turks, and with the aid of information furnished by a captive who had sailed on three voyages with said distinguished infidel. Most of the New World portion of this map is so fantastically incorrect that it cannot possibly have been copied from a chart of Columbus; and on a string of conventionalized Caribbee Isles the Columbian names are all misplaced. But one group of eight islands, here reproduced, is so nearly an accurate representation of Guadeloupe and her satellites as to suggest that Piri did have a copy of a chart made by Columbus on this voyage. The name *Vadluk*, which was probably as near as Piri could get to *Guadalupe*, is attached to an island in the position of Nevis, whilst the real Guadeloupe he calls *Kalevut*, which may be a rather farfetched corruption of the Carib name *Kalucaera, Kerkeria* or *Quiqueri.*

At the end of four days spent in the woods the lost Spaniards built a fire on top of a mountain peak, which their shipmates saw from the anchorage. A boat was then sent to the nearest place on the shore, but even then the strays could not have been found unless an old native woman had shown the rescue party the way. Apparently Spaniards were then very deficient in boy-scout lore. This rescue took place just in time, for the Admiral had determined to sail the next day, whether the men turned up or not.

Columbus ordered all the dugout canoes that his people could lay hands on to be destroyed, in order to stop slaving raids on his Arawak friends to the westward. The fleet took aboard "twelve very beautiful and plump girls from 15 to 16 years old," says Cuneo, together with two mutilated boys of the same age, some older Arawak captives redeemed from the Caribs, and a few Caribs as well.

At daybreak November 10 all seventeen vessels made sail. Most of that day they lay becalmed under the lee of Guadeloupe, and lay-to for the night not far from its steep wooded slopes. At noon November 11 they reached a not very big island which the girls aboard said had been depopulated by the Caribs. So Columbus decided not to lose time by calling there. He was anxious about his friends at Navidad and exceedingly vexed with the unnecessary delay at Guadeloupe; so all shore leave was stopped.

The Admiral named this island *Santa María de Monserrate* from the famous monastery of Monserrat near Barcelona, where thirty years later Ignatius Loyola dedicated his life to the Virgin. Monserrat in the early seventeenth century was occupied by the English, at the same time that the Frenchman D'Esnambuc took possession of Guadeloupe; for the Spaniards never colonized any of the islands east of Santa Cruz that Columbus discovered on this voyage.

From the northern end of Monserrat, Columbus sighted a large island to the northeastward, but did not care to beat up to it against the trade wind. He named it *Santa María la Antigua* after a famous miracle-working Virgin in Seville Cathedral, before whom he is said to have prayed a few days before this voyage began. Antigua has retained her name through good fortune and bad, in three centuries of British occupancy.

Proceeding in a general northwesterly direction, the fleet passed a small, steep and rounded but inaccessible rock less than a mile long, which Columbus named *Santa María la Redonda,* "St. Mary the Rotund." Redonda retains her name and her importance as a sea mark to this day; but she has never been worth inhabiting. Finding no anchorage near Redonda, the fleet continued on its way, and for the night of November 11–12 found fair shelter and anchorage in the lee of a much larger island. As Columbus had already named five islands after the Virgin, and it was the vigil of the feast of a popular saint, Saint Martin of Tours, he named this one *San Martín.* Early in the next century the name St. Martin was transferred to another island about 60 miles to the northwestward, and the Virgin received the credit after all. For Columbus's San Martín shortly came to be known as *Nuestra Señora de las Nieves,* Our Lady of the Snows.* English since 1630, and famous as the birthplace of Alexander Hamilton, this island is still called Nevis.

---

* Not because of any fancied resemblance of the clouds to snow, but in reference to the pleasant legend of the Virgin causing snow to fall on the Esquiline in August, as a direction to a pious Roman couple who wished to found a church in her honor. At Santa Maria Maggiore, the basilica so founded, a feature of the commemorative Mass on August 5 is an imitation snowstorm.

You must follow Columbus's course along this range of islands, and under sail, to appreciate what a marvelous voyage he and his gallant company were enjoying. No "tropical languor" here; the water is still warm in November, but there's a zip and sparkle in the air like August in Maine with an offshore breeze. The experience of approaching and passing each island that the Admiral discovered in those brave days of 1493 leaves an impression of stately beauty, comparable only to high mountain peaks set in an ocean that varies from the most vivid sapphire to a luminous smaragdine. At the first gleam of dawn the island ahead appears as a vague shadow, blotting out a small sector of the star-studded celestial sphere. With the swift advance of light and of one's own progress, literally "on the wings of the morning," the land begins to take form, substance, and finally color. By the time that sunrise enflames the mountain pinnacles the lower slopes are already shading from gray to green, and from green to a blue that is only a shade lighter than the sea. As the sun rises higher the trade wind blows more briskly; clouds form and pile up on the slopes even if there are none to seaward. In the noon calm under the land's lee the sea becomes a trembling mirror, broken only by flying fish and their enemies. Afternoon brings a series of showers; and as the eye passes ahead to the next island, the clouds crushed down over its summit reflect orange from the declining sun, which as it dips under a clear horizon shoots up in a split second a brilliant emerald flash.

Many in the Admiral's fleet must have promised themselves to revisit these enchanting islands, once their appointed tasks at Hispaniola were fulfilled; but other duties called the leaders, and the gold of Cibao held their shipmates. Except for a call at Guadeloupe on the return voyage, and a brief visit in 1502, Columbus was destined never again to set foot on the Leeward Islands, which were left for English, French and Netherlanders to fight over during the better part of two centuries.

CHAPTER XXX

Saints and Virgins

November 12, 1493–January 2, 1494

*Universi habitatores insularum obstupuerunt super te; et
reges earum omnes tempestate percussi mutaverunt vultus.*

All the inhabitants of the isles shall be astonished at thee,
and their kings shall be sore afraid, they shall be troubled in
their countenance.

— EZEKIEL xxvii 35

FROM his anchorage in the lee of Nevis, Columbus could see
three lofty islands, St. Kitts, Statia and Saba, stretching in a
northwesterly direction. These would have set his course even if
the captives had not assured him that the direct route to Hispaniola
lay that way.

Unfortunately the literary-minded gentlemen who wrote letters
home about this Second Voyage tell us nothing substantial about
these islands. Dr. Chanca was probably too busy attending men
who had been overindulging in tropical fruits at Guadeloupe to
pay much attention to geography; and by the time Cuneo and the
others put down their impressions so many things had happened
that the lesser Caribbees were forgotten.

After comparing all the sources, it is my opinion that Columbus
named St. Kitts *San Jorge*, but the sailors nicknamed it *La Isla
Gorda* (the Fat Island); for the northern portion, as one approaches
it from the southward, resembles the belly of a fat man floating
on the water. The next island to the northward was named by the
Admiral after the virgin martyr Saint Anastasia, and that name
appears on several maps of the sixteenth century; but Alonso de

Santa Cruz (1541) refers to it as "*Sant Estacio* which formerly was called *Sancta Anastasia*," and the Dutch, who took possession in the seventeenth century, stabilized the name as St. Eustatius. The third island was named *San Cristóbal* because of its pick-a-back

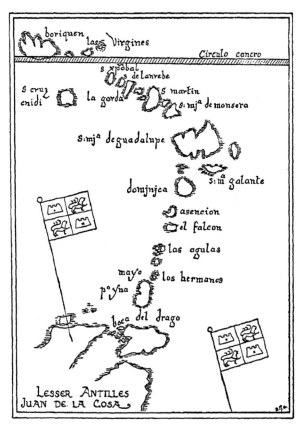

THE CARIBBEE ISLES ON JUAN
DE LA COSA'S MAP

appearance; but that name was transferred by later explorers and map makers to the original San Jorge, and San Cristóbal became Saba. The marked resemblance of Saba to the figure of his patron saint carrying the Christ Child must have persuaded the Admiral to depart from his rule of never naming anything after himself or his family connections.

Nobody was allowed ashore at any island between Guadeloupe and St. Croix. On November 12, when the fleet got under way from Nevis, some of the anchor flukes brought up pieces of red coral, a rarity in those regions. They passed to leeward of St. Kitts, Statia and Saba that day, and hove-to for the night. Cuneo says that there was no night sailing on this leg of the voyage; "when we did not anchor we kept the ship hove-to and this in order not to make any way, and from fear of running foul of the islands."

One wishes that some chronicler of this voyage had told us the technique of laying-to a fleet of seventeen vessels for the night. Every ship has her own manner of doing that. Some lay up almost into the wind's eye, and others no nigher than seven points; all drift to leeward at a greater or less speed. Constant watchfulness and no small skill must have been required to prevent the caravels from fouling each other; for the four-days'-old moon was not much help. A fine sight it must have been from *Mariagalante's* quarter-deck: dark shapes of hulls, spars pricking up into the dome of brilliant stars, lights flaring from the cressets aft and twinkling on the water. By the morning the fleet would have been widely scattered, some even hull-down. The Admiral collected them as they made sail, and the fleet stretched out towards an island to the westward, which the native guides called *Ayay*.

Wind came light that day (November 13), and when darkness set in they had not raised the island, so the fleet lay-to a second night. On the morning of the fourteenth, shortly after the westerly course was resumed, they sighted Ayay, which Columbus named *Santa Cruz* after the Holy Cross. After many changes of owners the French form of the name, St. Croix, became affixed to this island; but even today, when it has become a possession of the United States, seamen call it Santa Cruz.

St. Croix is shaped like a slipper with its toe pointing into the trade wind. Consequently it parts the trades, which pass westward along either shore; the short western coast is normally the only lee outside Christiansted Harbor. But on this occasion the wind seems to have been following the clock around by way of south, so the northern side was a lee and Columbus ranged it. His men were much more pleased with St. Croix than with the other islands they had seen because it was cultivated like a great garden; the Carib population was comparatively dense. Passing the entrance to

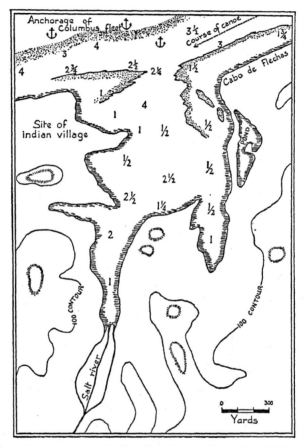

SALT RIVER BAY, ST. CROIX

Soundings in Fathoms

the modern Christiansted Harbor, which is so well protected by a barrier of breaking reefs as to seem inaccessible to explorers, the fleet reached the mouth of a small estuary now called Salt River Bay, which by its shape suggested that a stream of fresh water could be found at the head.

Here the Spaniards had their first recorded fight with natives of the New World, first of a long series of battles and encounters that ended only when the Araucana Indians of Chile were finally subdued in the nineteenth century.

"At the hour of eating," presumably about 11 A.M., the fleet came to an anchor. Most of the vessels must have remained outside the entrance to Salt River, which is narrow and not deep. Columbus, wishing to have speech with the natives and to take on water, sent an armed pulling boat to the head of the harbor, where he saw a few huts. As the men landed the natives fled. Part of the boat's party marched inland, found a village from which most of the inhabitants had escaped to the woods, and captured some of their Arawak slaves, girls and boys. As the boat's party was about to return to the flagship, a canoe containing four native men, two women and a boy, came down the coast, and within full sight of the fleet. Stupefied at the sight of these strange vessels with their lofty masts and high bulwarks, so utterly foreign to their experience and comprehension, the natives stopped paddling and stared open-mouthed. The shore party took advantage of their stupor to place the boat in such a position as to cut off the canoe's escape. When the Caribs recovered their senses they saw that flight was useless, and "with great courage they took up their bows, the women as well as the men," says Dr. Chanca, "and I say with great courage because they were no more than four men and two women, and ours were more than 25, of whom they wounded two," one mortally; more Christians would have been winged but for the shields that they carried. Even after the ship's boat had rammed and upset the canoe, the Caribs swam to a rock awash, and "fought manfully until they were overcome and taken. When they were brought aboard the Admiral's ship," says Peter Martyr, "they did no more put off their fierceness and cruel countenances than do the lions of Libya when they perceive themselves to be bound in chains. There is no man able to behold them, but he shall feel his bowels grate with a certain horror, nature hath endowed them with so terrible, menacing and cruel aspect."

One of these captives, who had been shot up until his intestines hung out, was pronounced by Dr. Chanca to be so far gone that the seamen threw him overboard. Yet he swam toward the shore, holding his guts in place with one hand. The Arawaks aboard persuaded the Spaniards to pursue and dispatch this tough warrior, lest he arouse his fellows to vengeance. So the Carib was recaptured, bound hand and foot, and again thrown into the sea. Nevertheless he managed to free himself from his bonds and to swim; so "this resolute barbarian," as Peter Martyr calls him, was shot through and through with arrows until he died. "Scarcely had this happened, when the *Canaballi* came running in great numbers to the shore, dark in complexion and of fierce and horrible aspect, painted red and in various colors to increase their ferocious appearance; one side of their heads was shorn and the other covered with long black hair." But they had no weapons that could reach the ships. Several of their Arawak captives took advantage of the excitement to swim out and join the Spaniards, for anything was better than being a slave of the Caribs.

The Spaniards were much impressed by the stout courage of the Caribs, whom Columbus ever after held to be implacable enemies of his Sovereigns and of their Arawak subjects. Even more surprising was the conduct of a "very beautiful Carib girl," whom Michele de Cuneo captured personally in the fight, and whom Columbus let him keep as a slave. "Having taken her into my cabin," writes Cuneo, "she being naked according to their custom, I conceived a desire to take pleasure. I wanted to put my desire into execution but she did not want it and treated me with her finger nails in such a manner that I wished I had never begun. But seeing that (to tell you the end of it all), I took a rope and thrashed her well, for which she raised such unheard of screams that you would not have believed your ears. Finally we came to an agreement in such manner that I can tell you that she seemed to have been brought up in a school of harlots."

From the menacing attitude of the Caribs it was certain that the fleet had run into a very hot spot. So, after naming the most prominent point *Cabo de la Flecha* (Cape of the Arrow), Columbus ordered anchors aweigh. Northward of St. Croix, about 35 miles from his anchorage, he could see the rounded tops of the Virgin Islands rising above the horizon, and decided to make for them. In view of his anxiety to reach Navidad, and the fact that it took two days to reach the Virgins, this detour can only be explained by the assumption that the wind had veered around the compass so that the fleet could only sail to the eastward without beating. It probably blew hard and they were hove-to most of the time, for it was not until the evening of November 16 that they closed with the land. That night also they lay-to; and if our guess at the wind's direction is correct, they must have been by this time somewhere to the E or SE of Virgin Gorda.

From his Bahamian experience Columbus expected all the separate hills that he sighted from St. Croix to pull together as he approached, and make one big island. But instead, the nearer he approached, the more islands appeared. So, with singular appropriateness, the Admiral named the archipelago after Saint Ursula and her companions, the eleven thousand seagoing Virgins.

According to this legend, Ursula was the daughter of Dionotus, king of Cornwall, who promised her in marriage to the pagan king of Brittany; but she, desiring to remain a virgin and a Christian, prevailed on the old man to grant her three years' grace for a pleasure voyage with some of her friends. She first selected ten young virgins of noble birth and maritime proclivities; but so many Cornish lasses wished to prolong their maidenhood and improve their minds by travel, and Ursula was so hospitable, that what with one thing and another, by the time the final list of guests was made up, 10,999 virgins besides Ursula had been promised a three years' cruise! This was rather more than the king had bargained for, but, true to his word, he furnished eleven of the largest ships in the royal navy of Cornwall, and off sailed the Eleven Thousand Virgins. One of their numerous ports of call was Rome, where they were received by the pope, who was a Welshman from somewhere about Holyhead; and Ursula's account of their adventures gave His Holiness such an irresistible call to the sea that he abdicated the papal chair and joined the cruise.

By and by, as the close of the third year drew near, the Eleven Thousand Virgins with their unique male passenger directed their course towards Cornwall. King Dionotus naturally expected that after three years at sea his daughter and her companions would be prepared to marry anybody, pagan or Christian. But the nearer they approached Cornwall, the more repulsive to these seafaring Virgins was the thought of settling down to married life ashore. What the ex-pope thought about it is not stated; but apparently he joined his prayers to those of the Virgins, since before they reached land a great gale made up from the westward and blew them straight through the English Channel to the mouths of the Rhine. There, as the wind held foul for England, Saint Ursula decided that they might as well sail up-river and see Cologne. The fleet negotiated the river nicely; but it was a bad moment to visit Cologne. Attila and the Huns were attacking the city.

A painting at Lisbon by Gregório Lopes, a contemporary of Columbus, illustrates the tragic ending to this feminine Odyssey. Saint Ursula and Saint Cyriacus are entertaining the clergy of Cologne aboard a fleet of splendid ships and caravels. Some of the vessels are lying at anchor dressed in Sunday colors, yards square and all a-taunto; others are cleverly beating about in the river, which looks more like the Tagus than the Rhine. Unfortunately, the Huns chose just that day to break through the defenses of Cologne. At left center the guests are being taken aboard, and everything is bright and merry. In the middle the party is fully under way. But on the right hand the Virgins are setting their guests ashore (ex-pope and archbishop in the stern sheets), only to be cut down by the swords of a brutal and licentious soldiery, dressed in Turkish costume. And that was the end of Saint Ursula and the Eleven Thousand Virgins, except that they became objects of great veneration at Cologne, and among sailors generally.

To return to Columbus's Second Voyage: weather cleared up and the trade winds returned at daybreak November 17, when the fleet was hove-to E or SE of Virgin Gorda. Here was a chance at

last to use the Cantabrian barques and other light-draught vessels
brought along for exploration. So while *Mariagalante, Gallega,
Colina* and the bulk of the fleet jogged along south of Virgin Gorda,
Salt, Peter and Norman Islands and St. John and St. Thomas, keeping "clear in the maine sea for fear of reefs," the barques and
lighter caravels fetched through Necker Island Passage to have
a look at Anegada, then squared away before the trades down the
Sir Francis Drake Channel, high and handsome islands on either
hand. These Eleven Thousand Virgins (they actually counted
forty-six) "marvellously differed one from another," and many
were fantastically colored; "some shewed purple colors on the
naked rocks" from the stone locally known as blue bit; others
shone "dazzling white" from marl or marble; some were mere
barren rocks; others were muffled in trees and herbage and bordered by pink coral beaches. Today one can climb to a lookout
point above the charming town of Charlotte Amalie in St. Thomas,
look eastward up the Sir Francis Drake Channel, and imagine half
a dozen little barques and caravels, some square and others lateen-
rigged, romping through this superb seaway before the northeast
trades. Then you may turn your gaze southward and think of
Mariagalante and her nine or ten consorts crossing the harbor
mouth of St. Thomas. Not until Sir Francis Drake came that way
on his last voyage in 1595, hoping to take San Juan de Puerto
Rico by surprise, was there a braver fleet of sail in the luminous
waters that wash the Virgin Islands.

Outside St. Thomas the small caravels joined the main fleet,
toward nightfall November 17 or the next morning. On the
eighteenth Columbus discovered Vieques, one of the Passage
Islands, so fair with its covering of green verdure that he named it
Gratiosa after the mother of his friend Alessandro Geraldini. Gratiosa Geraldini, according to her son, was "famous for her high
birth, holiness, old-fashioned manners, great learning, and manifest
piety towards God. I rejoiced because the Admiral had remained
loyal to his friendship with me from the time that I gave him aid in
undertaking this great expedition on the wide ocean; for when I

praised my mother very highly, he replied, though I did not press him, that he would bestow her illustrious name upon some noble island." When Alessandro came out to the Indies in 1522 as Bishop of Santo Domingo he made a point of calling at this island. "I stayed there about two days," he writes, and "during this time, the dear bosom of my mother, the ancient memory of her who bore me, her adored and boundless caresses, and her joyful countenance as I recalled it from boyhood, never left me." Unfortunately the name Gratiosa, recording manly friendship and filial piety, did not last.

Passing Vieques, probably laying-to off shore for the night of November 18–19, the fleet reached a large island that the Indians called *Boriquen, Buriquen* or *Burenquen,* and which the Admiral named *San Juan Bautista;* for Saint John the Baptist's relics were an object of particular veneration in Genoa. Early in the next century his shipmate Ponce de León founded the city of San Juan on a superb harbor of the northern coast. This city became known as San Juan de Puerto Rico, and the last two words gradually replaced San Juan Bautista as the name of the entire island.

All day November 19 the fleet sailed along the spectacular southern coast of Puerto Rico, outside the line of reefs, with so fresh a wind that the Admiral did not stop to investigate the harbors. The Spaniards estimated the island to be as big as Sicily, but Dr. Chanca's statement that it was 30 leagues long is correct; no need for 9 per cent reduction here. Covering the whole distance 'twixt dawn and dark, they lay-to for the night off Cape Rojo, made sail on the morning of November 20, and beat into the spacious Boqueron Bay. There they spent the better part of two days in order to procure fresh water and provisions. The natives fled at their approach, so there was no opportunity to trade; but many of the seamen and passengers went fishing, and made an excellent haul. Shore parties saw birds that they mistook for falcons, and wild grapevines, the common sea grape of the Antilles. Others who wandered inland found a deserted village of twelve well-built huts placed around a plaza, together with one great house that had wattled turrets roofed with verdure, like garden arbors in Valencia. This they naïvely supposed to be a Carib summer resort.

At daybreak November 22 the fleet took its departure from Puerto Rico, the last important island newly discovered on this outward passage, and steered a northwesterly course for Hispaniola as indicated by the Arawak guides. After sighting the little island later named *Mona* by the Admiral, and from which the Mona Passage is called, they steered northwesterly; and before nightfall, after a good run of about 65 miles, made a "low and very flat" landfall. The Indians insisted that this was their native "Haiti," but there was considerable doubt about it among the Admiral's veterans of the First Voyage, since every part of Hispaniola known to them was mountainous. It turned out that the natives were right. The landfall was the flat, wooded easternmost promontory of Hispaniola, whose distant mountains were probably obscured by haze. Columbus named it *Cabo San Rafael* after the archangel; but the Spaniards soon renamed it *Cabo Engaño*, "Cape Mistake."

The fleet lay-to for the night. On the morning of November 23 they proceeded along the coast northwesterly, and soon picked up Balandra Head of Samaná Bay, whence *Niña* and *Pinta* had taken their departure the previous January 16. Around noon they put into the bay in order to return one of the two Indians who had survived from the considerable number of captives taken on the First Voyage. Well clothed and provided with trading goods and presents, he was set ashore at Las Flechas whence he had been taken, in the hope that he would persuade the somewhat belligerent tribe of Ciguayos that the Christians were their friends. On the same day the Basque seaman who had been wounded in the skirmish at St. Croix died, and was given a Christian burial ashore, while two caravels hovered near the land ready to let fly with their ordnance in case the Ciguayos started anything; but this first funeral in the New World passed off peaceably. Some of the native onlookers were received aboard *Mariagalante*, and a certain amount of trading was done; but Columbus excused himself from calling on the Ciguayo cacique on account of his anxiety to reach Navidad.

From Samaná Bay the fleet ranged the north coast of Hispaniola before the trades as far as Monte Cristi, covering about 170 miles in two days. At Monte Cristi, while looking for a settlement site more convenient than Navidad, they began to find ghastly evidence of what had happened to the men left in the garrison last Christmas. A shore party found on the banks of the Rio Yaque two dead bodies bound with ropes, and on the next day two more, all so decomposed as to be unrecognizable; but on one were the remnants of a heavy beard that strongly suggested his Spanish race. With this macabre discovery the gay and adventurous portion of the Second Voyage ended abruptly.

On November 27 the fleet weighed from the harbor inside Isla Cabra, Monte Cristi, and made all possible speed toward Cape Haitien and Navidad. Twilight came before they could enter Caracol Pass, and Columbus, in view of what had happened to his first *Santa María* on Christmas eve, refused to attempt entering in the dark. So as soon as they reached soundings the fleet anchored. Flares were made aboard the fleet, but no answering fire was seen where Navidad should be; cannon were fired, but there was no answering salute. Then, says Syllacio, sadness and "the most acute grief took possession of their hearts, suspecting what really had happened, that the shipmates whom they had left there were totally extinct." At 10 P.M. a canoe which they had earlier seen hovering about approached from the shore, the paddlers calling "Almirante! Almirante!" Directed to the flagship, they refused to come aboard until a torch was brought so that they could recognize Columbus. The leader of the party was a cousin of Guacanagarí, who sent his greetings to the Admiral with two golden masks, one for him and the other for "a captain who had been with him on the other voyage." They assured Columbus that the Christians at Navidad were well, except that some had died of sickness and others had been killed in a quarrel; they excused Guacanagarí for not coming out because he had been wounded in a fight with another cacique named Caonabó. During the three hours that the

Indians remained aboard, Diego Colón the interpreter got the truth out of them and told it to his master; but Columbus would not believe it. Surely some of the garrison must be alive. These timid, defenseless Indians could not have wiped out forty seamen, soldiers and gentlemen of Spain.

Next day (November 28) the fleet moved to an anchorage off Navidad, but no edifice was visible, nor any sign of human life. A shore party found the fortress burned to the ground, with clouts and refuse lying about. Such few Indians as did appear, says Dr. Chanca, went about *muy cabareños* (very stealthily), and ran away when the Spaniards approached. Bad, very bad indeed. Guacanagarí's cousin was induced to come aboard and submit to questioning, by the irresistible bait of hawks' bells. He admitted that every single Christian had been killed by the warriors of Caonabó, and declared that Guacanagarí had been wounded defending them and his own village. The cousin was given more presents, his paddlers were treated to wine, and they were sent ashore with a message to the cacique that the Admiral commanded him to report on board and give an account of himself.

Another day passed, and no Indians appeared. It looked as if treachery must be added to tragedy. Another search was made of the fort site, without finding any further evidence. Columbus and Dr. Chanca then walked along the beach to the mouth of Grande Rivière, where they found a village of mean and mouldy huts from which all the natives fled on their approach. Inside them the search party found many articles plundered from the fort, including stockings, a Moorish scarf in its original package, and one of *Santa María's* anchors. When they returned to the site of Navidad, some Indians who were bartering with the men casually showed them eleven bodies of Christians lying where they had fallen near the fort. They insisted that Caonabó and his ally Mayrení had killed them; "but at once began to complain that the Christians had taken three or four women apiece, whence we believed that the evil which had befallen them was out of jealousy."

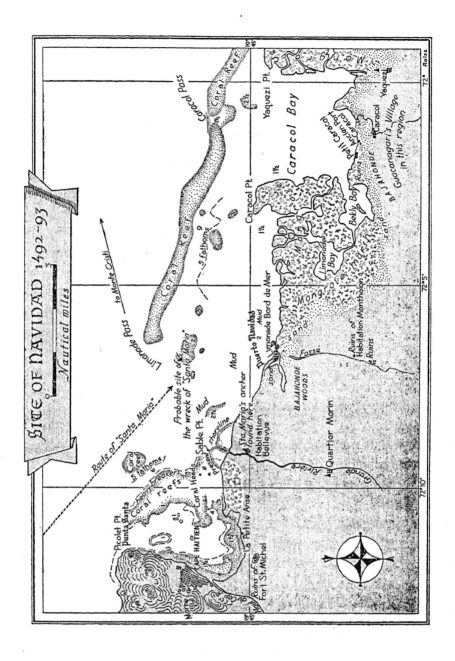

Before getting to the bottom of this affair, Columbus sent one light caravel to the westward and another to the eastward to search out a proper site for his permanent colony. The one returned after examining Cape Haitien harbor, on the shores of which a French city was built in the eighteenth century; but Columbus decided that it was too far from the "mine" of Cibao. The other caravel, commanded by Melchior Maldonado, sailed through a bottleneck entrance into the present Fort Liberté Bay, where they anchored and received a message from Guacanagarí to come and call. The cacique was found stretched out in a hammock nursing an injured thigh, and apparently eager to see his good friend the Admiral. He confirmed the story that Caonabó had killed the Christians.

When Columbus heard this story from Maldonado he decided to make the cacique a state visit in force. More than a hundred of his principal officers and men, "so richly attired as would have appeared well in a leading city," formed in battle array and marching to the music of pipe and drum, escorted him to the squalid village of the cacique of Marien. Guacanagarí persisted in his story, but Columbus on pretense of giving expert medical treatment had Dr. Chanca unroll the bandage from his leg, which was found to be unmarred by any wound, "although he was foxy and pretended that it hurt him greatly." Guacanagarí was certainly well enough to return the Admiral's visit that very evening, take supper aboard *Mariagalante*, and have the surprise of his life when he saw his first horse.

After the cacique had gone ashore the Admiral held a council as to what should be done about the murder. Fray Buil and a number of others jumped to the conclusion that Guacanagarí was guilty, and demanded that he be seized and put to death as a warning to his countrymen. Columbus trusted human nature better than did the reverend father. Although the sham wound aroused suspicion, he had sized up the cacique's character and doubted his guilt. He decided to dissemble until more knowledge was obtained, when it would be possible to obtain reparation if the guilt could be ascertained. After all, the Christians were not so numerous that they could afford to execute a friend on mere suspicion.

As the Spaniards and Tainos got to know each other's language better, the story got out bit by bit, and was pieced together by Las Casas and Ferdinand. Guacanagarí told the truth. The Navidad garrison had not long been left to their own devices when the men began to quarrel over women and gold; Rodrigo de Escobedo the secretary and Pedro Gutiérrez the royal butler killed Jacome the Genoese gromet, and made up a gang that roved the island in search of more gold and women. On their travels they encountered Caonabó. This stout cacique of Mayguana, said to have been of Carib stock, would stand for no nonsense in his territory. He put the Gutiérrez gang to death, and promptly descended on Navidad with a strong force to wipe out the source of trouble. In the meantime most of the other Spaniards had split up into predatory gangs, and only ten men were left under Diego de Harana to guard the fort; they were residing in huts with five women apiece and no sufficient guard. Caonabó attacked them at night, killed three, and chased the rest into the sea, where they were drowned. The others wandering about the interior were killed off by the Indians whom they had robbed or otherwise wronged. It was true that Guacanagarí tried to help Diego de Harana; that was proved by the fact that some of his men had been wounded by fish-bone spearheads, which were Caonabó's especial weapons. But he felt responsible to Columbus for the safety of the Spaniards, and feared being blamed for their death; hence his sham wound and equivocal attitude. And in after years, despite numerous provocations, Guacanagarí remained so steadfastly loyal to the Admiral that we may be certain that Navidad would have been unmolested as long as the Spaniards behaved themselves.

The rank and file of Spaniards did not draw this conclusion. For them the outstanding fact was the death of their comrades. Columbus had exaggerated the timidity and defenselessness of the Tainos. Evidently they were men after all, and could defend themselves if treated with too much indignity. Could the Admiral restrain his own men from taking vengeance, and restore the "golden age" of Hispanic-Indian relations?

Now that Navidad was wiped out, the question arose where to pitch the new settlement. Dr. Chanca, observing signs of river floods and spring tides in the native huts, ruled out all the low, damp shores of Caracol Bay. They could have found a dry and healthy site inland, or where the future city of Cape Haitien was built. But Columbus was looking for gold, not planting. So, since Navidad was finished, he decided to beat back to the eastward and locate near the reputed gold mines of the Cibao.

That was easier decided than done. On December 7 the wind gave the fleet a good slant toward Monte Cristi, which they reached the next day. Then there set in an uninterrupted run of easterly trade wind. "The weather was so contrary," reports Dr. Chanca, "that it was more trouble for us to sail thirty leagues up-wind than to come all the way from Castile." Anyone who has tried beating against the trade winds along the north coast of Hispaniola will sympathize with the doctor. Nobody thought it worth while to record the details of this uphill struggle, and probably many days were spent in port waiting in vain hope that the wind would change. It took twenty-five days to make good about 32 miles to windward!

On January 2, 1494, the fleet anchored in the lee of a wooded peninsula that afforded shelter from the wind, and contained a small plain that seemed a fair site for a city. The livestock were dying; the people, falling sick and worn-out with shifting sail, were begging the Admiral to go no further. So he selected this unsuitable spot for a permanent settlement, and named it *Isabela* after the Queen.

Here for the time being discovery ended, as happiness had already ended for Columbus when he discovered the fate of Navidad. Yet he must have derived great satisfaction from this voyage to Hispaniola. Unusually favored by wind and weather, he had conducted across the Atlantic seventeen vessels, many of them very small, made a perfect landfall, and continued through a chain of uncharted islands, with no accident serious enough to be recorded. He had discovered twenty large islands and over two-score small ones, upon which the eyes of no European had rested before. Over the biggest fleet that had yet crossed deep water, bearing twelve hundred seamen, colonists and men-at-arms, he had kept discipline during a voyage that lasted fourteen weeks. In a region inhabited by fierce man-eating Caribs, he had avoided conflict save for one brief skirmish, and lost but a single man. Plenty of trouble was awaiting the Admiral when he left the deck of *Mariagalante* for dry land, and exchanged the office of sea lord for that of colony builder. The turn in his fortunes was sharp, and it came quickly. In the years to come, when suffering in mind and body from the evil nature of man, the ingratitude of princes and the frowns of providence, Columbus may have sought consolation in the memory of those bright November days of 1493, the fleet gaily coasting along the lofty, verdure-clad Antilles with trade-wind clouds piling up over their summits and rainbows bridging their deep-cleft valleys; of the nights spent hove-to with his gallant fleet all about, stars of incredible brightness overhead, and hearty voices joining in the evening hymn to the Blessed Mother of God.

CHAPTER XXXI

Cibao

January 2–April 24, 1494

Reges Tharsis et insule munera offerent; reges Arabum
et Sabba dona adducent.

The Kings of Tarshish and of the isles shall bring presents;
the kings of Sheba and Seba shall offer gifts.

— PSALM lxxi 10

GREAT discoverers and explorers seldom make successful colonists, and pioneer colonial expeditions almost never select
a suitable site. Jamestown in Virginia and the first French settlement on the St. Croix River are cases to the point; even the
clever Dutch did not pitch upon Manhattan Island until they had
been active in North American waters for many years. The maps
of Central and South America are studded with sites of settlements made by the conquistadors and abandoned by their more
practical successors. Isabela was the first of these unfortunate
choices, and the most excusable, since nobody aboard the Castilian
fleet had any experience in colonization. Dr. Chanca piously records, "It pleased Our Lord that through the foulness of the
weather which would not let us go farther, we had to land on the
best site and lay-out that we were able to select, where there is
a very good harbor and fine fishing, of which we stood in great
need owing to the lack of meat."

Fishing is good anywhere along that coast, but harbor at Isabela
there was none. The roadstead is sheltered from the trade winds,
but open to the north and northwest, rendering the anchorage untenable during a winter norther. Holding ground is good enough,
but the larger vessels of Columbus's fleet could not anchor nearer

than half a mile from the shore. Good drinking water could be had only from the Rio Bajabonico about a mile to the southwestward, and that river was not navigable. Doubtless the fleet needed rest and refreshment; but it is hard to understand why Columbus, after a short stay, did not press on to the Rio de Gracia only nine miles to the eastward, and where *Pinta* had lain in safety for two or three weeks the year before, or to the landlocked Puerto Plata, twice as far again, which had been seen on the First Voyage. Instead, he made a quick decision in favor of Isabela, and at once began disembarking men and animals, planting seeds, and laying the foundations of a city that he expected to last for all time.

Probably it was the Admiral's extreme anxiety to procure a substantial quantity of gold that decided him to proceed no further. For, instead of having a barrel or two of precious metal collected by the garrison of Navidad, all ready to send home, he had nothing whatsoever; and he well knew what the Sovereigns would say if this large fleet returned without anything to show for the expense and the expectation. He had already wasted a month looking for a site which the Navidad garrison should already have selected; and the Sovereigns would be highly displeased if he kept seventeen vessels on the royal payroll any longer than necessary. The fleet must be sent home soon, and with enough gold to prove that it really had reached "The Indies." At Isabela the natives declared that the long-sought mines of Cibao were near by, and offered to guide the Spaniards thither. That was reason enough to stay. Without further loss of time Columbus organized an inland expedition, headed by Alonso de Hojeda, with Ginés de Gorbalán as second in command.

Hojeda was one of those agile, wiry, hot-tempered little men who make excellent soldiers, explorers and football quarterbacks, but are rather trying as shipmates or subordinates. Las Casas tells us: "He was slight of body but very well proportioned and comely, handsome in bearing, his face good-looking and his eyes very large, one of the swiftest men . . . who came in the fleet and who remained in Hispaniola. All the bodily perfections that a man could have, seemed to have been united in him. . . . He was very devoted to Our Lady, and his oath was *devodo de la Virgen María*. . . . He was always the first to draw blood wherever there was a war or a quarrel." A client of the Duke of Medina Celi, Columbus's patron, he had called attention to himself when the Queen was residing in Seville. During one of the popular festivals that center around the Cathedral, young Alonso walked out on a beam that projected from the Giralda some 250 feet above the street, and pirouetted on one foot. Then, after descending safely, he threw an orange so far in the air that people said it reached the top. Fonseca decided that Hojeda was just the man for the Second Voyage, and gave him command over a caravel. At Guadeloupe he proved able to take care of himself in the forest; so Columbus selected him to conduct this first inland exploring expedition.

The Admiral's eagerness to make contact with the Cibao is shown by the fact that Hojeda started four days after the fleet reached Isabela. On the Feast of the Epiphany, January 6, 1494, all hands attended a Mass administered by Fray Buil, in the temporary church, the first Mass ever celebrated on the soil of the New World. As soon as it was over, Hojeda and Gorbalán with somewhere between fifteen and thirty men and a number of native guides set forth from Isabela, crossed the Cordillera Setentrional into the great central valley of Hispaniola, forded the Rio Yaque, and near the present village of Janico came on a network of mountain streams that brought down gold from the high range which the natives called Cibao. The weather then turned bad, and a swollen river — either the Boa or the Janico — seemed too wide and swift to cross in safety. Hojeda decided to go no farther. He turned back to the nearest village, where the natives assured him that there really was gold in vast quantities on the upper slopes of the Cibao, and as proof of it presented him with three great nuggets, one worth nine, one twelve, and the biggest fifteen castellanos. So, as soon as the weather cleared up, and after he had recruited a corps of native porters to carry the specimens and other gifts,

Hojeda turned north toward the coast, and arrived at Isabela on January 20.

At the river which baulked the impatient Hojeda, Gorbalán with some of the men waited until the Indians brought a large dugout canoe. In this the Castilians crossed, the natives pushing it through the swift flood waters by swimming. "Having crossed the river, they were treated with many marks of respect by the benevolent Indians, and conducted on their way by courteous caciques." One of them introduced Gorbalán to a native goldsmith, who was beating the metal into thin leaf on a polished cylindrical stone, just as a European gold beater would do. He reached a district called by the natives *Niti,* well within the kingdom of Caonabó, and there found more abundant evidence and samples of gold than further down the valley. Indeed the strike was so good that he relinquished his intention to visit Caonabó (which was probably a good thing for him) and hastened north, reaching Isabela on January 21, one day later than Hojeda.

With the news and the specimens that the captains brought, Columbus "and all of us made merry, not caring any longer about any sort of spicery but only for this blessed gold," says Cuneo. Some of the nuggets were distributed among the exploring party, most of whom doubtless had collected a private store as well. "The Lord Admiral wrote to the King that he was hoping to be able shortly to give him as much gold as the iron mines of Biscay." But the Admiral was not yet ready to send the fleet back; for from the tales that he had told in Spain the Sovereigns were expecting something more than a new line of samples. Would it not be better to wait until after the systematic exploitation of the Cibao had begun, so that the gold dispatched to Spain could be measured by the pound rather than the ounce?

That was what Columbus first intended; but as the days elapsed he saw that it would be impossible. Discontent was rife in Isabela, and worse. In contrast to the excellent health that everyone enjoyed on the First Voyage, three or four hundred men fell sick within a week after their landing, so Dr. Chanca reported. Some of Hojeda's hidalgos returned sick from the Cibao, to find half the population of Isabela incapacitated. Dr. Chanca, so devoted that he tasted every new variety of fish before allowing the men to eat it, was worn ragged attending to their wants; and the medicaments gave out. Some may see in this wholesale illness the deadly work of the "sinister shepherd"; * but there is no reason to go behind Dr. Chanca's diagnosis that change of climate, diet and occupation was responsible. The history of American colonization proves that you cannot land a body of men after a long ocean voyage, subject them to hard labor with inadequate housing in torrential rains, expose them to mosquitoes full of germs with which their systems are unprepared to cope, and feed them on fish, maize, yams and cassava instead of beef, pork, wheat bread and wine, without excessive sickness and great mortality. Columbus quickly concluded what every subsequent discoverer for over a century had to learn from experience, "that, under God the preservation of their health depends on these people being provided with the provisions they are used to in Spain." Wheat, barley and other seeds had already been sown, but it would be some months before a harvest could be gathered; rattoons (the roots of the sugar cane) and grapevines had been set out, but when would they come into bearing? So the Admiral's first consideration for the good of his colony was to send the fleet home immediately so that there might be some chance of relief arriving within four months.

Accordingly twelve of the seventeen sail were dispatched home under Antonio de Torres on February 2, 1494. Our only information on their voyage, the second return passage from the New World to the Old, is derived from letters of Italian merchants who were at Cadiz and Seville when the fleet arrived. Torres evidently followed Columbus's example; he worked along the north shore of Hispaniola and then northward until he caught the westerlies, arriving at Cadiz on March 7, 1494, after a fast land-to-land passage of twenty-five days. The principal part of his return cargo was reported to be 30,000 ducats' worth of gold. In addition he brought

* See note at end of Chapter XXV above.

"cinnamon enough, but white like bad ginger, pepper in shells like beans, very strong but not with the flavor of that of the Levant; wood said to be sandalwood but white, . . . sixty parrots of different colors, eight of them being big as falcons and the fairest species of fowl that fly in the air." What interested these Italians the most were twenty-six Indians "of different islands and languages, . . . three of them *Canibali* who live on human flesh." Evidently most of the Carib captives had died on the voyage.

Columbus retained only five vessels at Isabela: flagship *Mariagalante* and ship *Gallega*, stout little *Niña* and two smaller caravels, *San Juan* and *Cardera*. Of the flagship he purchased a three-eighths share from her master-owner, and the caravels he bought outright, in order to save the crown the expense of charter money. The two ships he wanted for the protection that their artillery afforded, not only from a possible attack by Indians, but from a probable mutiny of the Spaniards; the caravels were needed for coastal exploration.

In addition to letters to the Sovereigns from the Admiral, Fray Buil and treasurer Villacorta, which have long since disappeared, Torres bore the Admiral's memorandum of what he should relate personally to Ferdinand and Isabella; and that document has fortunately been preserved with the Sovereigns' comments. Columbus gave the reasons we have already quoted for dispatching the fleet home with so little gold aboard. He begged that three or four caravels be sent back immediately, laden with salt meat and wheat, wine, oil and vinegar, sugar and molasses, for general subsistence, with medicaments for the sick, and with almonds, raisins, honey and rice for the convalescent. He particularly commended Hojeda, Dr. Chanca, Margarit, Aguado, Coronel and other officers, and asked that their pay be increased. Although the Admiral had already been troubled by grumbling, sabotage and attempted mutiny, he complained of nobody except the troopers, who declined to do any labor that could not be performed on horseback; and when laid up with the prevalent sickness refused anyone else permission to use their horses. He suggested, however, that the two hundred gentlemen volunteers not on the payroll should be put on it at once as a means of controlling them. He needed a supply of shoes, clothing and cloth; mules or other beasts of burden to take the heaviest labor from men's shoulders; two hundred cuirasses, one hundred arquebuses and one hundred crossbows. Apparently the colony had about all the artisans it could employ; but in the expectation of finding a gold mine in the Cibao, Columbus asked that some expert miners be recruited in the Estremadura and sent out in the next ship. The Carib captives were sent home to be turned into good Christians and interpreters; and some of them seem to have survived.

Ferdinand and Isabella were evidently pleased with this work-manlike objective and straightforward report; for they gave orders that everything the Admiral needed should be provided, and that almost everything he proposed should be done; and against the first paragraph of the memorandum, in which he reported the explorations of Gorbalán and Hojeda, they caused to be written: —

"Their Highnesses give many thanks to God for this, and they regard as a very signal service of the Admiral all that he has done and is doing herein, for they appreciate that next to God it is to him that they are indebted for all that they have had and will have herein, and since they are writing him hereof more at length, to their letter they refer him."

The letter, dated April 13, was almost fulsome: "Rely upon it that we consider ourselves well served and obliged by you, so that we shall confer upon you favors, honors and advancement as your great services require and deserve." Columbus must have reread this letter rather ruefully when including it in his Book of Privileges of 1502. Far from conferring on him further honors and advancements (for he had not yet been admitted to any order of knighthood, or been created count or duke, or given a castle or estate in Spain), the Sovereigns began shortly after to strip from him in fact though not in name the honors and privileges that he already had, until he ended his life almost as naked of privilege as he had entered it.

One clause of the Sovereigns' letter Columbus must have enjoyed almost as much as the promises — the permission to send Bernal de Pisa home. This man, the *contador* or comptroller appointed by the crown to keep count of the gold, had been making trouble from the first. Shortly after Torres sailed, a paper of his full of false charges against the Admiral and outlining a plan to seize some of the caravels and return to Spain was discovered in an anchor buoy. Columbus had him arrested, and for better precaution placed all the arms and most valuable gear of the fleet aboard the flagship with his brother Don Diego in command. That done, he prepared to send an expedition into the Cibao.

Hojeda's journey had been a mere reconnaissance; of far greater importance was this expedition in force that the Admiral led south from Isabela on March 12, 1494. It was the first of those overland marches of the conquistadors that make the story of Spain in the New World so gorgeous a pageant. Short as it was, this march into the Cibao set the pattern followed by Vasco Nuñes de Balboa, Cortés, Pizarro, Coronado, De Soto, Orellana and countless others who never ceased their labors until the American continent had been crossed at every possible pass between latitudes 40° north and 50° south.

All able-bodied Christians who were not required to garrison Isabela were taken. For protection the Admiral had crossbowmen, the cavalry troop, and hidalgos on foot armed with swords and arquebuses. For artisans, there were carpenters, axe men, masons and ditch diggers, with tools and implements suitable to mine gold and build a fort. In military formation, with banners displayed and trumpets sounding, this first of a long line of Castilian cavalcades set forth from Isabela on March 12, 1494. Fording the Rio Bajabonico, they crossed a dry plain covered with dense scrub, and camped that night at the foot of the Cordillera Setentrional, whose jagged, razor-edged peaks rise about 2500 feet above sea level. A crew of hidalgos and workmen had been sent ahead to widen the Indian trail which Hojeda used. After a breath-taking climb the path reached a pass which Columbus named after the

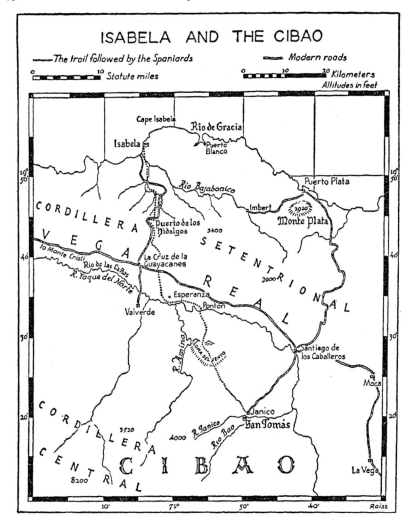

ISABELA AND THE CIBAO

......*The trail followed by the Spaniards* ≡≡≡ *Modern roads*

0 ━━━━━━ 10 *Statute miles*   0 ━━━━━ 10 ━━━━ 20 *Kilometers*
Altitudes in feet

trail makers *El Puerto de los Hidalgos*, the Pass of the Gentlemen.
The narrow way suddenly turned east through a split in the range,
passed a cold spring in a glen overshadowed by great palms and
mahogany trees, and came into full view of a broad, fertile valley.
Las Casas did not exaggerate when he described this vast valley,
which runs clear through from Monte Cristi to Samaná Bay, as
"one of the most admirable things in the world, . . . a place that
ought to call forth blessings and infinite thanks to the Creator

. . . of such perfection, grace and beauty; . . . so fresh, so green, so open, of such color and altogether so full of beauty, that as soon as they saw it they felt that they had arrived in some part of Paradise; . . . and the Admiral, who was profoundly moved by all these things, gave great thanks to God and named it *Vega Real,* the Royal Plain." My own first view of this Vega Real, at a season when the *madre de cacao* trees put forth their pink blossoms, is one of the most memorable sights in my long wanderings over the routes of Columbus.

As the hidalgos descended, they found themselves in a different soil and climate from that of the arid coast; rich, black earth, big silk-cotton, mahogany and ebony trees with shiny dark green leaves, and little streams of water. Large flocks of brightly colored parrots screamed at them from the trees, and the Hispaniola mockingbird sang sweetly as nightingales in Castile. As they approached the Rio Yaque, they passed native villages of palm-thatched huts whence the chief men came out bearing gifts of food and little packages of gold dust, which they had learned from Hojeda was what the Christians liked best. Hojeda had well prepared this reception for his Admiral. The Spaniards entered the huts and helped themselves to anything they liked, "with much pleasure to the owners," who in turn tried to lift odd trifles of the Castilians' equipment; but they were promptly and emphatically informed that these communistic customs did not prevail in Castile. Las Casas could not omit a sigh of regret over what perfect material these natives were to be made Christians and "imbued with all the virtues" (for virtue there could be none without knowledge of the true God), "if we Christians had acted as we should."

The whole valley was one great garden. Reaching the Rio Yaque del Norte, which they found to be as big as the Ebro or the Guadalquivir, Columbus, not identifying it with the "Rio del Oro" whose mouth he had explored on the First Voyage, called it Rio de las Cañas, after the canebrakes that lined its banks. There they camped for the night, everyone bathing and splashing about in high spirits at finding so fertile and lovely a region. Guided by Hojeda they ascended the valley to a spot, still appropriately called *Pontón,* where the Indians were accustomed to cross. It was too deep for any but the horsemen to ford; some crossed in canoes and rafts, others swam; "those who did not know how to swim," wrote Cuneo, "had two Indians who carried them swimming; the same, out of friendship and for a few trifles that we gave them, carried across on top of their heads our clothes, arms, and everything else there was to be carried."

From this crossing the little army struck south toward the other wall of the valley, rugged mountains of the Cordillera Central where Hojeda reported the gold was to be found. The natives on this side of the valley, frightened doubtless by frequent discharges of muskets, fled before the Spaniards' approach, barring their flimsy huts with bolts of cane, which the Admiral ordered to be respected. The land was still rich and fertile, and crossed by many *arroyos;* but Cuneo says that nobody in the army managed to find a nugget or to pan out any gold dust himself. When they reached a sizable stream, the Rio Janico, Columbus decided it was time to call a halt. This was probably the limit of Hojeda's exploration the previous month.

High in the hills to the southwest of the present village of Janico there is a small group of huts which on the official map of the Dominican Republic bears the proud name of *Fortaleza,* recording the site of the first inland fortress erected by Europeans in the New World. Two or three hundred yards beyond this little *finca* is a bend in the river. Within that bend, for about a hundred yards from the bank, there is a level field, beyond which rises a little mesa about twenty feet high, which is used for grazing. This, beyond any reasonable doubt, is where Columbus established his Fort of Santo Tomás, so named as a jovial reproof to a doubting hidalgo who refused to believe that the island produced gold until he had actually touched it.

It was now Sunday, March 16. Columbus laid out a plan for

the fort, oversaw the beginning of the work, and left over fifty men under Mosén Pedro Margarit to dig the ditches, raise a wooden palisade and garrison the fort. A number of horses were left with Margarit, since the Indians were so afraid of them that they dared not even enter a building where a horse was — a great annoyance to the caballeros, who had to be their own grooms. Columbus planned the fort not only as a shelter and protection for the garrison, but as a center for mining operations in the Cibao. This, he now learned, was not Cipangu, but the native name of the Cordillera Central, in whose rocks and sands were the greatest gold deposits on the island. During the five days that Columbus remained there, Juan de Luxán was sent further into the mountains and reported more gold. Santo Tomás in the meantime was visited by hordes of natives who flocked to see the *Guamiquina* or "great lord" of the Christians, as they styled the Admiral. Eagerly they pressed food and gold nuggets on him and his men. Some two thousand castellanos' worth of gold was collected officially, including nuggets that weighed twenty-four castellanos; "and besides the above dealings . . . there was also exchanged in secret, against the rules and our own agreement, to a value of one thousand castellanos," recorded Michele de Cuneo. "For as you know, the devil makes you do wrong and then lets your wrong be discovered; moreover, as long as Spain is Spain traitors will never be wanting. One betrayed the other so that almost all of them were betrayed, and whoever got caught was well whipped; some had their ears slit and some the nose, which was very pitiful to see."

On March 21 the cavalcade marched northward again. Weather turned wet, the streams were swollen, and provisions gave out; consequently many of the hidalgos and common people had their first reluctant meals of cassava bread and yam. "On that trip, between going, staying and returning, we spent 29 days with terrible weather, bad food and worse drink," wrote Cuneo; "nevertheless, out of covetousness for that gold, we all kept strong and lusty." The Yaque was again crossed, the Puerto de los Hidalgos passed once more, and on March 29 the army, not quite so smart and well groomed as on the day they left, marched into Isabela to the sound of trumpets and musket shots.

Crops had done well in their absence. Melons and cucumbers were ripe, and next day the first ears of wheat were harvested; both sugar canes and grapevines were coming on.

Nevertheless the morale at Isabela was very low. Of the sick who had been left behind a good many had died; the wine and ship biscuit, last of the Spanish provisions, were almost spent, and everyone was eager to return to Spain. The day after Columbus arrived, on April 1, a messenger came from Margarit at St. Thomas saying that the friendly Indians had fled, after informing him that the cacique Caonabó, reputed murderer of the Navidad garrison, was about to attack. So Columbus sent seventy men with provisions and ammunition to help Margarit defend the fort.

Reading between the lines of the Torres Memorandum, it seems that Isabela up to early February was a settlement of wattled huts; two hundred of them, according to Cuneo, "small like our hunting cabins and roofed with thatch." Columbus was eager to make it into a proper walled town, with plaza, church, fort, stone-walled houses, and a governor's palace, by the time the next fleet arrived from Spain. He even embarked on more ambitious works: digging a canal to the river, both in order to give the settlement a better supply of water than it could obtain from wells, and to provide power for a gristmill. So many of the workmen and artisans fell sick that hidalgos had to be drafted for the menial work, which caused them the greatest indignation; but Columbus enforced his orders by stern and (as the victims claimed) cruel punishments. After all, these men had not come out to be ditchers and masons, but to get rich; and apart from the gold illicitly acquired on the march to the Cibao, nobody as yet had any plunder to show for a three months' voyage and three months ashore. It became a question whether the Admiral and his officers could keep seven or eight hundred men in hand until the relief fleet came.

A bright idea occurred to Columbus: to place four hundred of the people, including the lustier fellows and the trouble-makers, under the command of Alonso de Hojeda and send them up to the fort of St. Thomas. There Hojeda would relieve Margarit, who should take the bulk of the force on an exploring expedition, living off the country. That, Columbus figured, would solve several problems: keep the men busy and off his hands, habituate them to native food, relieve the restive Margarit from garrison duty, and acquire more information about the island. Hojeda had acted with courage and circumspection on both the reconnaissance and the exploration; Columbus trusted him. But Hojeda, it seems, had been holding onto himself with great difficulty.

This second expeditionary force left Isabela on April 9, crossed into the Vega Real by the Puerto de los Hidalgos, and came to the large Indian village at Pontón, the ford of the Yaque. There one rash act of Hojeda broke the peace which so far on this Voyage had been maintained with the natives. Hearing that three Spaniards returning to the coast from Santo Tomás had been robbed of some of their clothes by the natives who carried them across the river, and that the cacique of Pontón had appropriated the garments, Hojeda cut off the ears of one of the cacique's men, and sent the chief with his brother and nephew in chains under guard to Isabela. "This," says Las Casas, "was the first injustice, with vain and erroneous pretension of doing justice, that was committed in these Indies against the Indians, and the beginning of the shedding of blood, which has since flowed so copiously in this island." But by his own showing, the Admiral shares Hojeda's guilt, since on the latter's say-so he condemned the cacique and his two relatives to be beheaded in the plaza at Isabela, merely for the stealing of a few old clothes by natives who always gave the Spaniards everything they had. Fortunately another cacique who had done the Admiral a service accompanied the prisoners to plead for them; and his tearful entreaties persuaded Columbus to release the intended victims. But irreparable harm had been done. Despite the disappearance of the Navidad garrison, and the many opportunities for friction that occurred in the two marches upcountry, relations between Spaniards and Indians had been marked by a condescending kindliness on the one hand and a desire to please on the other. There was no reason why, if Columbus continued to keep his men in hand, this relation should not long have endured. The old-clothes incident was the first break, and before long an age of iron had succeeded to the "golden age" that Peter Martyr inferred from the Admiral's account of the First Voyage.

Columbus now decided it was time for him to resume the more congenial work of maritime discovery. If Cibao was not equivalent to Cipangu, it might well be Sheba, whence the famous Queen came; Syllacio said as much in his letter on the Second Voyage, and the fact that Columbus included Psalm lxxi 10 in his Book of Prophecies indicates that he thought so too. Hispaniola was certainly an island, all the natives admitted that; it was advisable to discover the continent of Asia without further delay, and have something to report when the relief fleet arrived. So, appointing a council consisting of his brother Don Diego as president, together with Fray Buil, Captain Coronel, Alonso Sánchez de Carvajal and Juan de Luxán, to govern the island in his absence, Columbus had the three caravels re-equipped from the arsenal aboard *Mariagalante*, and on April 24, put to sea.

CHAPTER XXXII

Cuba and Jamaica
April 24-May 14, 1494

Si quis mihi ministrat, me sequatur: et ubi sum ego, illic et minister meus erit.

If any man serve me, let him follow me; and where I am, there shall also my servant be.

— JOHN xii 26

HAVING arranged all matters in the colony to his satisfaction, Columbus set forth from Isabela "to explore the mainland of the Indies" with three caravels. He had left Cuba sixteen months earlier, hoping rather than believing it to be a peninsula of Asia. Now the idea was to follow the coast until definite proof of its continental character was obtained, and if possible to make contact with the elusive Grand Khan.

Well-tried *Niña*, of which Columbus was now half owner, served as flagship; the other two were *San Juan* and *Cardera*, of which he may also have owned a half share. These were the two Portuguese-style lateeners in the original fleet, which Columbus had selected for coastwise exploration. *Niña's* tonnage was about 60, and Cuneo says that *San Juan* and *Cardera* were "much smaller." Judging by the size of their crews, each was under 40 tons burthen. *Niña* was piloted by Francisco Niño of the family who formerly owned her; Alonso Medel of Palos sailed as her master, and Juan de la Cosa the chartmaker shipped as able seaman. The boatswain was Pedro de Terreros, ex-steward on the First Voyage, and on his way up to a command. Diego Tristán, also slated for promotion, and another gentleman of Seville, served as volunteers. There were sixteen able seamen and gromets, two of them Genoese, one a

Venetian, and most of the remainder from Palos and the neighborhood; also a servant to the Admiral and a public notary; total, twenty-five. *San Juan* had Alonso Pérez Roldán for master, a pilot, and boatswain, seven able seamen (one of them the cooper) and five gromets, all Castilians except one Portuguese; total ship's company, fifteen. *Cardera's* master was Cristóbal Pérez of Palos. She carried a Genoese boatswain named Fernerin, seven able seamen and five gromets, one a Genoese and the rest Castilian; total fourteen. Including five persons known to have been aboard but not mentioned in the list of names, the total roll comes to about sixty men and boys.

The fleet sailed from Isabela on April 24, 1494. That is the fairest season of the year for navigating the Greater Antilles, when the trade wind can be counted upon to blow steadily by day, and a light breeze off the land may be expected from midnight until well into the forenoon; a season when there is no danger of squalls or hurricanes, or excessive heat. But the voyage was prolonged along a hot coast in a torrid summer, and the vessels had to beat home in a squally August and September.

After calling at Monte Cristi and the site of Navidad, where Guacanagarí prudently made himself scarce, the fleet fell becalmed in the Tortuga Channel, anchored one night off the mouth of Trois Rivières, and on the twenty-eighth reached Port St. Nicolas at the northwest tip of Hispaniola, whence Cuba could be just sighted, 45 miles to the WNW. It was an easy day's sail across the Windward Passage to Cape Maisi, the eastern extremity of Cuba. On his First Voyage Columbus had named this Cape Alpha and Omega, but Bernáldez, owing perhaps to the Admiral's inadequacy in Greek, calls it *Cabo de Alfa et O.*

On Cape Maisi, probably at the point now called Pintado where the reefs break off, Columbus went ashore, set up a column surmounted by a cross, and took formal possession of Juana (as he had named Cuba) for the Sovereigns. He had already done this at Puerto Tánamo and other Cuban ports on his First Voyage, but doubtless wished to reaffirm Spanish dominion at this cape which he considered to be the beginning of the Asiatic mainland. "For you should know," says Andrés Bernáldez, "that this is the extreme headland of terra firma, corresponding to Cape St. Vincent in Portugal at the West; between these two Capes is contained all the world's population, so that if one should set forth by land from Cape St. Vincent one could always go eastward without crossing any part of the Ocean Sea, until one arrived at Cape Alfa et O, and from Alfa et O on the contrary route with God's aid one could reach Cape St. Vincent by dry land." It was many years before anyone was in a position to correct him.

Having duly asserted Spanish dominion, the Admiral called a council of his pilots, officers and gentleman adventurers "to discuss which way we should turn," says Cuneo. Should it be the north coast, some 150 miles of which the Admiral had already explored, or the unknown south coast? If Cuba was a peninsula of Asia, as Columbus hoped and prayed it might prove to be, either would do. But the south coast received the unanimous vote of the Council, not because it was terra incognita, but for a reason typical of the era: "because should there be anything good it would rather be to the southward than to the northward." That was the orthodox geographical theory of the day. So, after standing off-and-on during the hours of darkness, the fleet on the morning of April 30 put the land to starboard, and began to range the southern coast of Cuba.

From the lofty Punta Negra 8 miles to the southwest, which the Admiral had glimpsed on his First Voyage, he entered upon new discoveries. An ironbound coast consisting of a series of limestone terraces, backed by a sierra that rises to 4000 feet, runs thence almost in a straight line W by S for 50 miles. Although rugged and picturesque, this southern coast of the province of Oriente is much less interesting than the northern, whose mountains condense most of the moisture in the trade winds; the southern coast is relatively arid, and lacks the palm groves, the lush vegetation and the small river-mouth harbors which lend such charm to its northern counterpart. The vegetation is what botanists call xerophytic, with numerous agaves, cacti, and leguminous trees that are able to conserve moisture; but in the spring of the year there was moisture enough to give the land breeze a delicious smell of growing things. As the fleet sailed westward, notes Bernáldez, "there was wafted out to sea a very delicate odor." That same delicious scent of cactus flowers and sea grape, mingled with the smoke from charcoal-burning fires, came out to us in the dawn watch on June 21, 1940, as we followed Columbus's course in *Mary Otis*. There flashed into one's memory that superb sonnet of the poet José Maria de Heredia, when a whiff of gorse and wild rose on the Breton coast recalled the scent of his native Cuba.

> *C'est de trois mille lieues*
> *Qu'il vient, de l'Ouest, là-bas, où les Antilles bleues*
> *Se pâment sous l'ardeur de l'astre occidentale.*

Unless it be in the Aegean, where nature is inseparable from the memories of ancient Hellas, there is no other shore line comparable with that of the islands which Columbus first revealed to the Western World. Sea of the deepest blue or emerald or opal, rugged coastline bordered by a white line of surf, mountain slopes clothed in tropical verdure, flowering trees of a bold brilliance unknown to the temperate zones; all these, whether steeped in the hot sunshine of a summer noon, or lashed with a tropical rainstorm, or unseen in a spring night but exhaling a sweet humid fragrance, fairly drench the mariner with sensuous satisfaction.

Fifty miles from Punta Negra, near the end of the last day of April, the fleet entered a harbor described as "in the form of a sickle, shut in on both sides by promontories that break the waves; and it is large and of great depth." This harbor, which Columbus named Puerto Grande, is Guantanamo Bay, where at the tip of the sickle, invisible from seaward, the United States has established one of her most important naval stations. It is shown very clearly in Juan de la Cosa's map. But the Spaniards saw only two huts, instead of the large settlement that they expected to find in so great a harbor. Going ashore they found a large quantity of fish, some *hutías*, and two gigantic iguanas being cooked on spits in the open, guarded by one dumb dog. Other large iguanas, which the Spaniards thought the most ugly and disgusting creatures they had ever seen, were "tied with ropes like monkeys," awaiting their turn. Peter Martyr thought from the description that these harmless edible reptiles must have been crocodiles, another proof of land connection between Egypt and Cuba!

After helping themselves to a good fish dinner, the men in the flagship's boat began to search for inhabitants. On the crest of a hill appeared a crowd of naked Indians, making friendly gestures. Columbus's interpreter Diego Colón found that he could understand their language well enough. Through him they informed the Admiral that they were on a fishing and hunting expedition at the command of their cacique, who was preparing a great feast in honor of a visiting potentate; the fish had to be cooked or smoked in order to prevent spoiling. Columbus handed around a few hawks' bells and other trifles which the Indians were glad to exchange for fish, of which they could catch more that night. But they were greatly relieved that no iguanas had been taken, as these were difficult to capture, and it would go hard with the hunters if they failed to provide the cacique with his anticipated *plat du jour*. Roast iguana is a delicious meat, as travelers off the beaten track in the West Indies may ascertain today. But the Spaniards were not so bold as that hero who ate the first oyster.

Leaving Guantanamo Bay with the land breeze on May day morning before sunrise, the fleet sailed westward in waters covered with gulfweed. They kept the shore close aboard, for this southern coast of Oriente province shelves off so rapidly that the 100-fathom line is often but a ship's length offshore. Today that section of the coast has hardly a hut or a clearing to relieve the steep wooded slopes of the Sierra Maestra; but in 1494 as Columbus sailed along, multitudes of Indians old and young flocked to the water's edge or paddled out in canoes, offering cassava bread and calabashes filled with water, crying in their language, "Eat and drink, men from Heaven!" The Admiral graciously accepted these simple gifts, but ordered them all paid for out of the trading truck.

Forty miles from Guantanamo the fleet found a break in the Sierra, where a channel only 180 yards wide leads between steep cliffs into the great Bay of Santiago de Cuba. Here "there were an infinite number of villages, and the lands and fields were such that all appeared to be the loveliest gardens in the world, and all the lands high and mountainous. They anchored within, and straightway the people of the neighborhood came and brought them bread and water and fish." This was the Indian village of Bagatiquirí, a site so favorable for trade and farming that Diego de Velásquez chose it in 1514 for the second city of Cuba, Santiago. The Indians had no gold, but they taught Michele de Cuneo a good camp method of broiling fish. You split a stick of wood, place the fish in the cleft, balance the stick across two stones, and light a fire underneath. If inserted in a green stick the fish will be cooked before the wood burns through.

Departing at dawn on May 2, *Niña, San Juan* and *Cardera* ranged the ironbound coast where on July 3, 1898, the battle fleet of Admiral Cervera was forced ashore. By nightfall, supposing the wind blew fresh that day, the Columbian fleet was off Punta Turquino, 50 miles to the westward. That is where the Admiral's namesake, the cruiser *Cristóbal Colón*, last of Cervera's squadron to surrender, ended her gallant, desperate fight, and wrote a last and glorious sentence to the history of Spanish dominion in the New World.

Columbus, anticipating no change in the character of the coast, kept his fleet sailing westward all night, and on Saturday, May 3, the day of the Discovery of the True Cross, reached a prominent cape that he named *Cabo de Cruz*. This is the only name given by Columbus to any part of Cuba that has survived to this day.

As the Cuban coast turns around Cape Cruz to the northeastward, this seemed the obvious point for Columbus to leave it for a visit to Jamaica. He had been told of this important island by the

Indians at Santiago, who named it correctly but declared incorrectly that it was the source of "the blessed gold," according to Cuneo. Columbus now thought he was at last on the track of that elusive golden island of the First Voyage that the Bahamian Indians called Babeque. Babeque — Jameque, it sounded much the same.

On the afternoon of Saturday, May 3, the fleet set a course a little S of SE for Jamaica. That course, if made good, would have cleared the eastern point of the island; actually they made land about the middle of the north coast, 95 miles on a straight rhumb from Cape Cruz, after a sail of forty-eight hours. Cuneo records that the weather was terrible, and the fleet most of the time was under bare poles. Undoubtedly what hit them was a NE trade wind so strong that the caravels, after running before it, hove-to in order not to be swept to leeward of Jamaica altogether. While hove-to all hands on the flagship went below for a much needed rest; the Admiral, first on deck as usual, noted that the weather was moderating and set about making sail himself in order not to disturb his weary shipmates.

On May 5 Jamaica rose sheer and dark green from the sea against the westing sun, and the fleet steered for St. Ann's Bay, which Columbus named *Santa Gloria* "on account of the extreme beauty of its country." Bernáldez communicates to us the Admiral's well-justified enthusiasm over Jamaica: —

It is the fairest island that eyes have beheld; mountainous and the land seems to touch the sky; very large, bigger than Sicily, has a circumference of 800 leagues (I mean miles), and all full of valleys and fields and plains; it is very strong and extraordinarily populous; even on the edge of the sea as well as inland it is full of very big villages very near together, about four leagues apart. They have more canoes than elsewhere in these parts, and the biggest that have yet been seen, all made each of a single tree-trunk; and in all these parts every cacique has a great canoe for himself in which he takes pride as a Castilian gentleman is proud of possessing a fine, big ship. They have their canoes carved and painted both bow and stern with ornaments so that their beauty is marvellous; one of these big ones that the Admiral measured was 96 feet in length and 8 foot beam.

Canoes of that length have not been made since the Indians were exterminated, but the modern Jamaicans inherited the art. Their dugouts, made of the silk-cotton tree and holding as many as fifteen paddlers and considerable freight, are the largest in the Caribbean today. With sand ballast and a homemade sail, a Jamaican canoe can make a speed as high as 15 knots on her way to the fishing banks.

Although the Jamaica Indians belonged to the same Arawak language group and showed the same Taino culture as those of Cuba and Hispaniola, they were more warlike; and when the Columbian fleet approached the coast it looked as if they would have to fight a naval battle. Just as the Admiral was sending the boats away to sound, sixty or seventy canoes full of shouting and gesticulating warriors paddled out from St. Ann's Bay. The fleet calmly continued its course, and fired a blank salvo from the lombards, which scattered the natives. Diego Colón was then sent ahead in a boat to try to appease them, which he accomplished to such good purpose that one canoe came alongside the flagship, and received a handout of old clothes and trading truck.

At Santa Gloria, where his Fourth Voyage was destined to end ingloriously ten years later, Columbus spent only one night. On May 6 he sailed 15 miles westward to a harbor "shaped like a horseshoe" which he named *Puerto Bueno,* and which has the unique distinction among Jamaican ports of having kept its Columbian name. Here the Indians, wearing feather headdresses and palm-leaf corselets, made another hostile demonstration, even hurling their wooden spears at the caravels, and throwing stones at the Spaniards when they tried to land. As the fleet needed wood, water and a chance to do a bit of caulking, the Admiral decided to make the Indians "acquainted with the arms of Castile." This was easily effected by sending the ships' boats ahead with crossbowmen who "pricked them well and killed a number"; and when

the survivors landed, the Spaniards let loose on them a big dog "who bit them and did them great hurt, for a dog is worth ten men against Indians." Next day, six Indians came down to the shore with propitiatory gifts of cassava, fruit and fish, which the Admiral graciously accepted; and during the rest of their stay at Puerto Bueno the Spaniards were well furnished with provisions, and the Indians with trading truck. Here, as elsewhere in Jamaica and in Cuba, the Admiral was much disappointed at finding no gold ornaments among the natives' apparel, or any trace of the precious metal.

On May 9, after completing the necessary caulking and repairs, the fleet sailed 34 miles westward to *El Golfo de Bien Tiempo* (Fair Weather Gulf), now called Montego Bay. It is always improvident for a seaman to affront the gods with a name like that! When the fleet was ready to continue its course westerly, on May 13, the wind unseasonably turned foul. So, after taking aboard an Indian volunteer despite the weeping protests of his wife and children, the fleet set sail for Cuba again, and made Cape Cruz on May 14.

CHAPTER XXXIII

The Queen's Garden
May 14–June 12, 1494

Fons hortorum: puteus aquarum viuentium, quae fluunt impetu de Libano.

A fountain of gardens, a well of living water, and streams from Lebanon.
— SONG OF SOLOMON iv 15

JUST inside Cape Cruz Columbus found an Indian village, where to his great surprise he was both known and expected. The local cacique had talked with the chieftains of Northern Oriente who had met Columbus on his First Voyage; he even knew all about the converted interpreter Diego Colón. It was a relief to the Spaniards to be among friendly people again after their hot reception in Jamaica.

On May 14 the fleet steered northeasterly, following the Cuban coast, and passed through Balandras Channel into the Gulf of Guacanayabo. At vespers, when over 40 miles from Cape Cruz, they saw ahead that the coast turned west again, and cut the corner. "Next day at sunrise they looked out from the masthead and saw the sea full of islands in all four quarters, and all green and full of trees, the fairest that eyes beheld; the Admiral wished to pass to the southward and leave these islands to starboard, but, remembering that he had read that all that sea is full of islands and that Sir John Mandeville says that there are more than five thousand islands in the Indies, he decided to go forward, and to follow and not lose sight of the terra firma of Juana, and to see for certain whether it was an island or not. And the farther he went the more islands they discovered, and on one day he caused to be noted 164 islands.

God always sent him fair weather for sailing among them, and the vessels ran through those waters as if they were flying."

Although Sir John Mandeville, that prince of lying travelers, was not the best authority on Cuba, Columbus chose the proper route for detailed exploration. These islands, which he named collectively *El Jardín de la Reina*, The Queen's Garden, extend for over 150 miles from the Gulf of Guacanayabo to Trinidad, and to a distance of 20 to 50 miles off the south shore of Cuba. The channels among these hundreds of cays are so few that we can easily infer the course of *Niña*, *San Juan* and *Cardera*. Sunrise on May 15 found the fleet near the northeast corner of the Gulf of Guacanayabo, within sight of the cays that compose the Buena Esperanza bank. Sailing westward between this group and the Cuban shore, the caravels entered the archipelago near the present town of Santa Cruz del Sur, passed through the Bergantine or another parallel channel, and then through the Rancho Viejo and Pingue channels into the gulf behind the chain of outer cays now known as the Laberinto de Doze Leguas. It was a marvel to us, as we navigated these same waters in 1940 with the aid of modern charts and a local pilot, that the Columbian fleet passed through safely; and we frankly do not believe Bernáldez' statement that they threaded this labyrinth at flying speed. Any careful navigator would frequently have anchored or jogged off-and-on while a ship's boat went ahead to sound a doubtful channel.

The daily afternoon thundersqualls which bothered us in those waters in June 1940, were equally embarrassing to Columbus in May 1494. Horrible black clouds made up from the eastward every evening without fail, and brought a squall of wind and rain that lasted until moonrise (it was full moon May 19). Sometimes the fleet was caught in a narrow channel, where the Admiral had to make a quick decision between striking sail, and thus losing control of his ships to the peril of running aground, or carrying on with the possibility of losing gear — and then running aground. The caravels touched bottom frequently, and *Niña* once stuck in the mud for several hours, but no important damage was done. We are inclined to agree with Las Casas that the Admiral's escape from disaster was little short of miraculous. Or, to express it in other words, the sleepless attention that Columbus gave to the details of navigation was almost superhuman.

It was a loyal and a gallant thought of Columbus to name this archipelago the Garden of his Sovereign Lady the Queen; for in 1494 these cays must have been very beautiful. Some were cultivated by the natives, the rest were covered with handsome verdure such as royal palms and calabash trees. Time has not dealt kindly with the Jardín de la Reina, which is now the sorriest, raggedest looking archipelago in the seven seas, quite unworthy of being a seagoing queen's garden. By the present century the monotonous mangrove had crowded out all other trees or plants, and the hurricane of 1932, by destroying the soil, killed even that. Now the cays are largely covered with bare, bristling dead limbs, relieved by a few tufts of green where the mangrove has regained a foothold. So melancholy was the sight and so difficult the navigation that we in *Mary Otis* were glad to turn southward, as Columbus had first intended, and to continue our Cuban periplus outside the Laberinto de Doze Leguas.

For Columbus and his men, however, the Jardín was full of marvels. Frequently they encountered "birds like cranes, but bright red." Las Casas explains from his own experience that these were not really cranes, although of the same shape and stature; the chicks are white, but gradually they turn red, and when half-grown a flock of them looks like a herd of ocher-colored sheep; and they cannot live without salt water. The Indians, he says, make pets of them, and keep them with no food but a little cassava and a pot of salt water to drink. These strange long-legged birds were flamingoes.

Behind the Jardín de la Reina the fleet came upon a river so hot "that a man could scarcely bear his hand in it." Only a slight exaggeration; several rivers along this swampy coast empty into the sea through shallow lagoons which reach a high temperature under the sun's rays. On the day after discovering this river, the Spaniards encountered the first natives they had seen since leaving the village near Cabo Cruz. These Indians had come in a canoe to hunt turtle with a fish hound, a method which they obligingly demonstrated for their distinguished visitors. The pilot fish, *Echeneis naucrates*, the kind with a sucker on its head that attaches himself to sharks, was caught young by the Indians and fed until big enough to go hunting. When large manatee or turtles were about, the pilot fish's master encouraged him with kind words, and sent him away just as hounds are cast off by a huntsman, except that a cord of vegetable fiber was tied to his tail. Presently he attached his head to the quarry, which with him was drawn to the boat, the fisherman winding in the line on a primitive reel. As soon as the manatee or turtle was gaffed, the fish hound was released, politely thanked, and rewarded with gobbets of the kill. The Spaniards were fascinated by this pleasant sport, and the Indian huntsmen presented them with four turtles that were captured in their presence.

Westward the fleet continued among the islands, as close to the Cuban shore as the Admiral dared sail. On May 22 they came upon "a large island, at the end of which was a large village." All the natives had fled, leaving behind about forty of the non-barking native dogs, which were killed and eaten. Such Spaniards as were bold enough to try the new dish declared that Roast Jardín de la Reina Barkless Dog was tasty as Castilian kid. Only the fastidious Genoese gentleman Cuneo reported that they were "not too good."

After visiting another and larger island, the fleet put out to sea by the Boca Grande to get away from the shoals. From Cayo Breton Columbus shaped his course for some lofty mountains that seemed to be 14 leagues distant. "Continuing his route towards the west, the Admiral arrived . . . in the neighborhood of a very lofty mountain, where, because of the fertility of the soil, there were many inhabitants." This mountain must have been the Sierra de Trinidad, which rises boldly from the coast between Casilda and Cienfuegos; for that is the westernmost point on the south coast of Cuba where high mountains come close to the sea. The fleet approached the shore as night was coming on and found it full of shoals — the same shoals that make access to Casilda so difficult today — and prudently decided to let the land breeze waft them out to deep water. There, probably at some distance to the southwestward of Tunas de Zaza, they lay-to during a lazy night memorable for sweet odors from the land. Next morning they closed with the coast, and entered one of the drowned river mouths that occur there, probably the Rio San Juan, which Columbus revisited on the return voyage and then named *Rio de las Misas*, River of the Masses. Crowds of natives assembled, and brought out bread, *hutías*, birds and cotton wound in skeins.

This part of Cuba, Columbus learned, was called *Ornofay*, and beyond lay *Magón*, where (reports Bernáldez) "all the people had tails, like beasts." On the First Voyage it had been the province of Havana where the men-monkeys lived, but now it was "Magón." That name suggested to Bernáldez Sir John Mandeville's mythical land of *Moré* where the tailed people lived. But to Columbus *Magón* was obviously the same as Mangi, the province of southeast China described by Marco Polo, and in after years he always referred to Cuba as Mangi, to express his intense conviction that it was a peninsula of Asia. Very likely he inquired about the ape-men through his interpreter, and the Indians, ever eager to please, cheerfully agreed to everything he said. They also confirmed what he wished to believe, that the coast of Cuba had no end, because they knew nothing about it. But they were accurate in warning him that innumerable islets with slight depth between them lay to the westward.

As the fleet sailed on along the bold fringe of the Sierra de Trinidad, they sighted villages innumerable from which the people came out bearing gifts and "singing for joy, believing that the people and ships came from Heaven." Diego the interpreter tried to discourage this notion and inform them about Castile, but "they believed that Castile was Heaven, and that the King and Queen, lords of those ships, dwelt in Heaven." A short distance west of the Rio San Juan the fleet must have cut away from the shore,

which there trends more northerly than westerly; for they missed the entrance to Jagua Bay, where Cienfuegos is located. Columbus, with all his good luck, missed the two greatest harbors in Cuba, which are also two of the world's finest: Nipe Bay on the First Voyage, and Jagua Bay on the Second. The next important bay that they encountered was the Gulf of Cochinos, which thrusts a thumblike shape some 15 miles up into the land. Some thought it to be a channel between Cuba and Asia, being unable at first to see land at the head or to find bottom at the mouth; but after sailing within, they found land all around. The northeastern shore of this gulf is noted for the subterranean streams that flow down through the limestone and break out under the sea not far from the shore, welling forth such a volume of sweet water that swarms of manatee are attracted to quench their thirst, and seamen may fill water casks without the trouble of going ashore. Columbus told Bernáldez that "on the edge of the sea, close by a great grove of palms that seemed to reach the sky" (and there are many groves of tall royal palms there today), "there gushed forth two springs of water below it . . . and when the tide was on the flood, the water was so cold and of such goodness and so sweet, that no better could be found in the world, . . . and all rested there on the grass by those springs amid the scent of the flowers which was marvellous, and the sweetness of the singing of little birds, so many and so delightful, and under the shade of those palms so tall and fair that it was a wonder to see it all."

It reads like an idyl of Theocritus; only the nymphs and the shepherd's pipe are wanting. An imperfect idyl without these, yet as near as sun-baked mariners might attain to one of those scenes of absolute perfection in Sicily or in Cos that the Greek poet has preserved forever.

The most trying part of this voyage was ahead. Rounding (or perhaps cutting) Cayo Piedras, the fleet gaily crossed the Gulf of Cazones with a fair wind, and left the dark blue deeps for a shallow bank now called the Jardines. And suddenly they "entered a white sea, which was as white as milk, and as thick as the

water in which tanners treat their skins. And afterwards water
failed them, and they found themselves in two fathoms' depth, and
the wind drove them strongly on, and being in a channel very
dangerous to come about in, they could not anchor the ships,
because there was no room to shoot up into the wind and anchor;
nor was there holding ground, [for having dropped their anchors]
the ships went right on dragging them along the bottom. And so
they went on for ten leagues, through those channels behind these
islands until they reached an island where they found two and a
half fathoms of water and space for the caravels. There they anchored, in a state of extreme distress."

No wonder the men were dismayed. The Admiral had boldly
sailed into a tangled archipelago, the cays off the Zapata Peninsula, which are difficult enough to navigate today with chart and
beacons. Moreover, the people were baffled by the different colors
of the water. As they came upon the shoals from the deep blue of
the gulf, the water at first was clear as crystal, but suddenly turned
an opaque green; then after a few miles went milk-white, and
finally turned black as ink. And so it is today. Part of the gulf
has a bottom of fine white marl which becomes so roiled by the
waves that it mixes with the water right up to the surface, looking,
as Peter Martyr said, as if flour had been dredged into the sea.
I have myself seen the water a deep green, as in the Gulf of Maine,
although the depth was less than three fathoms, and the next time I
looked over the side it was black as ink under a bright sky, owing
I suppose to fine black sand on the bottom being stirred up by the
waves. All this was new to the Spaniards, and the more terrible
because it recalled old Arabic tales of the Green Sea of Gloom,
and interminable shoals that fringed the world's outermost edge.

Thirty miles of this — Columbus's leagues mean sea leagues this
time — and the fleet found good anchorage near an island. This was
probably one of the Cayos Providencias, near which the modern
chart promises 13 feet of water, near enough to the 2½ fathoms
that Bernáldez reports. Next day Columbus sent *San Juan* or
Cardera to the Cuban shore in search of fresh water, of which all

stood in need; the south coast of Cuba in summer, with a following breeze and the sun standing right overhead (so it seems) for
hours on end, is so hot that one is always thirsty. This caravel reported that the shore was all marsh, and on the edge of it bushes
"so thick that a cat couldn't get ashore" — a most vivid and accurate description of that mangrove- and mosquito-infested coastline. "The Admiral determined to go on" as usual, passed more
cays "so thickly wooded down to the seashore that they seemed to
be walls." That is one of the repellent features of mangrove: it completely covers the beaches with tangled roots, so that there is no
line of white or golden sand between vegetation and sea.

Later that day they arrived at a low headland, which the Admiral
named *Punta del Serafín,* because it was the Feast of All Angels,
May 27. From his description this must have been Punta Gorda,
the western point of the Zapata Peninsula. A more depressing and
repulsive place to name after the Heavenly Host he could hardly
have selected in all the Antilles.

"Within this point the land fell away to the eastward," Bernáldez correctly reports, "and to the north . . . were discovered
very high mountains, and the interval was clear of islands, all of
which lay to the southward and westward. Here they had fair
wind and found three fathoms of water, and the Admiral decided
to lay a course toward those mountains, where he arrived the following day, and they proceeded to anchor off a very fine and very
large palm grove, where there were springs of water, sweet and
very good, and signs that there were people about." This anchorage must have been at or very near the fishing port of Batabanó,
where the town called San Cristóbal de la Habana was founded
in 1514.

Here, according to all the raconteurs on the Second Voyage, occurred a strange and inexplicable incident. A crossbowman who
went hunting in the woods encountered a band of thirty Indians,
one of whom, dressed in a white tunic that came down to his
feet, the Spaniard at first glance took to be the friar of his own
ship's company. There then appeared two other light-complexioned

natives clothed in white tunics which ended at their knees. They shouted at the Spanish bowman, who took fright and ran toward the sea, hotly pursued by White Tunic No. 1, who disappeared when the Spaniard reached safety at the water's edge.

To the Admiral these apparitions meant Prester John, the legendary priest-king of Hither India or Ethiopia, whom he had hoped to meet if he missed the Grand Khan. On two successive days he sent men ashore to renew contact with the white-robed natives; they scouted the country for miles without meeting a human being, and returned with nothing but a basket of sea grapes and a tale of finding tracks of animals that some thought to be griffons and others lions. What then is the explanation? Michele de Cuneo says that the "holy men" of the Caribs (with whom he often confuses the Tainos) wore white cotton cloaks; but the function of these *sancti* was not to chase intruders, but to sit in "temples" and receive the amorous embraces of religiously inclined damsels. Probably the white-clad gentry and wild beasts' tracks were both imaginary; Castilian crossbowmen were not above pulling the longbow.

Columbus now headed his fleet into the Ensenada de la Broa, the northeast corner of the Gulf of Batabanó, but did not observe Hemingway's "Rio Encantado" that flows into it. Turning westward again, the fleet coasted the north shore of the Gulf. After they had gone 9 leagues they picked up a local cacique, who encouraged them to believe that deep water lay ahead; but that was false. The fleet now became involved in the worst shoals they had yet experienced, in the Canal de Cayamas. This channel, which in modern times has been dredged to 10 feet, then contained "scarcely a fathom of water." The caravels had to be kedged through by the laborious process of rowing a large anchor ahead in the ship's boat, letting it go, and then hauling in the cable on the windlass, while the keel plowed a channel in the soft bottom. Once past this shoal spot they found 3 fathoms' depth, and had no more trouble of that sort.

At this point, probably off the present village of Guanimar, "many canoes came out to the vessels, and the people in them said that the people of those mountains had a king of great estate . . . and that they called him holy, and that he wore a white tunic that trailed on the ground." Was that the white-clad Indian? Probably it was simply another case of "yessing" the Spaniards when they inquired in pantomime about the unexplained apparition of a few days before. But not all Cuban Indians were yessers. One that Diego talked with along this shore insisted that Cuba was an island, which was not at all what the Admiral wished to hear; yet even he followed up this geographical verity with a tale of a speechless cacique that Las Casas branded as false.

Columbus of course was stimulated by this cumulative "evidence" of the neighborhood of Prester John to make a minute and careful reconnaissance of the Gulf. Dropping the line of hills behind Batabanó, the fleet sailed westward four days before the faithful trade wind, anchoring every night. This southern shore of the Cuban province of Pinar del Rio is marshy and mangrove-covered, protected from ocean swells by a multitude of cays and by the Isle of Pines. No decent landing place could be found; but fortunately the water was deep enough for the caravels a short distance from shore.

The concluding days of the westward voyage are difficult if not impossible to plot from the information that we have. At the end of the four days' sail, off a marshy shore, the fleet "reached a bay where the land again trended eastward" — but there is no such bay; and "saw some very high mountains where the coast made a headland, 20 leagues distant"; but no mountains run down to a headland in that part of Cuba.

"They sailed along within many islands, and at the end of two days and nights came up to the mountains that they had seen, and found that it was a reddish range as great as that of the Aurea in the island of Corsica. They went all around it," but could not get ashore for the mud and mangroves, "stayed on that coast for several days seeking fresh water," and found it "on the eastern side in some very fine palm groves," and found big oysters, too. The mud and mangroves sound like the western part of the Gulf of Batabanó, but none of the bays there have an eastern side; and although the reddish range like Corsica is obviously the foothills of the Sierra de los Organos, these cannot be seen from along shore. It is all very puzzling. After refreshing themselves in the palm grove they steered south, then west, and then southwest, always following the coast of the "mainland" — that is, Cuba. These directions fit very neatly the shores of the Gulf of Batabanó from the Bahía Dayaniguas to the Bahía Cortés. "And to the south they saw the sea full of islands" — the Cayos San Felipe. Many birds were sighted, and turtles; and the air was filled with butterflies all one summer's day until the evening rainsquall blew them off.

It was somewhere about here, according to Peter Martyr, that the people found an old man ashore who was brought aboard, and whose language Diego could not understand. It was the first time that Columbus's Taino interpreter from the Bahamas had been baffled; and the ethnologists have found out why. The caravels had passed beyond the limit of Taino culture and entered the last stronghold of the Siboney, the primitive people who had been pushed westward by the Tainos not many years before. This incomprehensible old man must have been a Siboney.

It was now the second week in June. Although Columbus had begun this voyage with *Niña, San Juan* and *Cardera* as an exploring expedition, with the hope of proving Cuba to be part of the mainland, he had by this time, so he confessed to Bernáldez, developed a much more ambitious plan, anticipating Magellan. He would round the Golden Chersonese, stretch across the Indian Ocean, and either return in his little fleet to Spain around the Cape of Good Hope, or be set ashore by the Red Sea and make his way home overland, taking in Jerusalem en route. Such was the dream of Columbus the mystic and prophet, and the southward-trending coast on the Bahía Cortés looked as if he had actually reached the base of the Malay Peninsula. But the common sense of Columbus the practical seaman rejected any attempt to carry out so grandiose a plan with the equipment he had. The vessels were leaking owing to their frequent groundings in the shoals, running rigging wanted renewal, much of the hardtack and other supplies had been spoiled by sea water, and the seamen (who always hate running aground, it means so much extra work) were hungry, discontented and fearful lest they could never beat back to Hispaniola against the trades. The fleet had sailed westward, Columbus estimated, between 322 and 335 leagues from Cape Maisi, and although the actual distance was only about half that, each mile of shoal-water work was far more a strain on ships and men than a hundred miles off soundings.

If, as seems almost certain, Columbus had reached Bahía Cortés, he was less than 50 miles from Cape Corrientes, the southwestern promontory of Cuba. A little more perseverance in that direction and he could have ascertained that Cuba was an island; but of course that was not what he wanted. It was enough for him that the coast here trended southward. He had made up his mind from the length of his westerly voyage, from the stories of white-clad natives, and from the numerous islands that he had passed through, that (even without any sign of gold or spices) these islands were part of the Malay Archipelago, Cuba was the Chinese province of Mangi, and this southward-trending shore (which ended shortly at Cabo Francés) was the beginning of the Golden Chersonese, or Malay Peninsula. It is interesting to conjecture what would have happened if he had gone on. The Gulf Stream would almost certainly have swept the fleet within sight of the Florida cays; perhaps would have taken it so far north that the Hispanic peninsula would have been easier to make than Hispaniola. But the condition of the caravels and the sentiment of their officers and men made it imperative to turn back.

So Columbus, to save himself from blame for a premature return, caused the testimony of his gentlemen and seamen to be recorded, to the effect that Cuba was a peninsula, and it was no use going further. This procedure seems singular enough to us, and has aroused the ribald laughter of the Admiral's dry-land detractors; but he had good precedent. Six years earlier Bartholomew Dias had done exactly the same thing when his people forced him to turn back at the very gates of India; and as Columbus had been at Lisbon when Dias arrived there, he either saw the document or heard about the circumstances.

Pérez de Luna, chief scribe and notary public of Columbus's fleet, suitably equipped with pen, paper and inkhorn, visited all three vessels in turn, solemnly taking depositions. One and all (including Juan de la Cosa, who showed the contrary on his famous map) declared that they had never seen, heard or conceived of an island that extended 335 leagues from east to west; and Cuba is longer than any island in the Old World, even Britain. They were certain that Cuba was part of a continent, and that if they had sailed farther they would presently have encountered "civilized people of intelligence, who know the world." Having made this declaration, the men were warned that the Admiral would levy a fine of ten thousand maravedis on any one of them who ever said the contrary, and have his tongue cut out; or, if a boy, have a hundred lashes laid on his bare back.

Pérez de Luna declares in the preamble that the purpose of this declaration was to prevent anyone from maliciously belittling the voyage. Undoubtedly Columbus's main purpose was to save himself from blame for making insufficient efforts to find concrete evidence of Asia. I daresay he hoped to choke off waterfront tattle after the fleet returned to Castile, such as, "If the Old Man had sailed a few days further westward, as I advised him to do," etc., etc.

Naturally it settled nothing to record the opinion of seamen who were so eager to go home that they would gladly have subscribed to a statement that their Admiral had visited Cambaluk and been received in audience by the Grand Khan. And the learned were properly skeptical of this method of establishing geographical truth. Michele de Cuneo records that when the fleet reached Isabela in September, the question of Cuba's continental character was thrashed out by the Admiral with the Abbot of Lucerna, a learned astronomer and cosmographer who had lately arrived in

Hispaniola. The Abbot said that the Admiral was wrong, and Cuba "was only a very big island, in which judgment, considering the character of our navigation, most of us others concurred." Cuneo, to be sure, had never subscribed to the "Cuba no island" document; but Juan de la Cosa, who had, reneged, and depicted

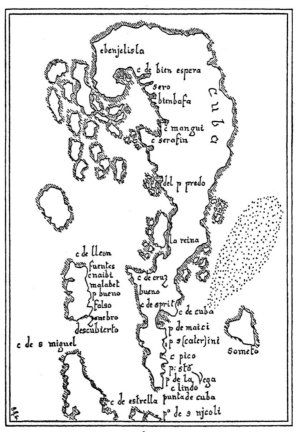

JUAN DE LA COSA'S MAP

Cuba as an island in his famous World Map. All that Columbus accomplished by this ill-judged effort was to befuddle the geography of the Caribbean for many years to come. On the Cantino map of 1502, and on a number of others as late as 1516, is found a continental region, on some labeled *Terra de Cuba Asiae Partis*, which seems to be an attempt to reconcile Columbus's erroneous belief with the facts.

Except for a few prophetic moments, it was Columbus's misfortune to ignore the significance of his discoveries that have given him immortal fame, and to advance geographical hypotheses that made him a laughingstock for fools. On this westward voyage, in seven weeks' time he had opened up the most valuable of Spain's insular colonies, and discovered another island that became the jewel of the old English Empire. From the navigator's point of view the most remarkable thing about this voyage was the Admiral's demonstration that his competence at coastal piloting, under the exceedingly difficult conditions of a labyrinth of uncharted cays and shoals, was fully equal to his ability as a deep-water navigator. Seldom in history, perhaps never again except in Captain James Cook, have the top grades of these two qualities been united in the same mariner. Columbus's exploration of the Queen's Garden and the Gulf of Batabanó, and his success in extricating *Niña, San Juan* and *Cardera* from them, is one of his outstanding feats of navigation.

CHAPTER XXXIV

Back to Isabela
June 13–September 29, 1494

*Illic naues pertransibunt. Draco iste, quem formasti ad
illudendum ei.*

There go the ships, there is that leviathan whom thou hast
made to play therein.

— PSALM ciii 26–27

NAMING the westernmost part of Cuba that his fleet reached,
in the Bahía Cortés, after Saint John the Evangelist, Columbus began his return voyage on June 13. He seems to have taken
a southerly course at first, seeking deep water and clear sailing
outside this submerged platform with its troublesome cays and
shoals over which he had come; but a strong sea turn of the wind
forced him again to become involved among the islands. On one
occasion the fleet, hopefully following a channel that seemed deep
enough, found itself completely surrounded by islands and lands
"as if in a corral," says Las Casas. That is a common delusion in
narrow waters; you are always looking ahead as you follow a
narrow, twisted channel, so that when it leads the ship into a closed
bay, and you look around for the entrance, it has vanished; seems as
if the land had moved in on you. Columbus's men were very much
frightened, says Las Casas; but "the Admiral cheered them all with
the best words he could muster, and they had trouble enough getting out by the way they came in." This gift for cheering the
fainthearted, and skill at pulling out of a hole, were among the
traits that made Columbus a great seaman.

They touched at an island to take on water, left there June 25 on
a NW course for some islands (the Mangles probably) that seemed

5 leagues distant, and were forced by the wind back to their turning point of June 13. *Vientos escasos*, head winds, compelled them "to return by an arm of the sea by which they had sailed up to the Punta del Serafín to the islands where they had first anchored in the white sea." Columbus would have liked nothing better than to seek sea room, but his caravels could do nothing against strong trade and set of current combined. So the discouraging business of tacking among the shoals and mangrove cays had to continue.

After two weeks of this, making very little progress, *Niña* ran aground on June 30, "and not being able to pull her off by the stern with the anchors and cables, they pulled her off by the bow, and, by reason of the shocks that the grounding gave her, she sustained considerable damage." Nor was this the end of their difficulties; for several days more they painfully beat to windward among the cays and shoals, "sailing all the time in that very white sea, and besides all these troubles and misadventures, every day at sunset they were visited by terrible rainsqualls that wore them out." Those evening rainsqualls off Cuba certainly do take the starch out of you, in more ways than one. The water seems to come down almost solid, and in an open boat you can hardly keep ahead of it by bailing.

This "milk-white gulf" was not devoid of interest and amusement. A mighty flock of *cuerbos marinos* (crows or cormorants) was sighted, and a multitude of turtles — so many, says Bernáldez, "that it seemed as if the ships would run aground on them, and their shells actually clattered" along the topsides. The Gulf of Batabanó is still a source of turtle meat for the Havana market, and I daresay of turtle stories as well. Conch shells "as large as a calf's head" could be seen on the bottom whenever the water cleared up; the men collected them by the boatload and boiled the meat, "as big as a man's arm," in sea water. And when they discovered oysters of the largest size, the men thought that their fortunes were made. Five or six boatloads of them were collected in the hope of their yielding mammoth pearls. Not a pearl was found, "but they were very good eating," says Cuneo. That genial gentleman adventurer never complained, but extracted interest or amusement from everything that happened. He was loyal to his *Signor Almirante*, but kept independent judgment. If I were to select a shipmate from all the companions of Columbus, he would be no haughty if heroic Castilian, but merry Michael of Savona.

Even though they were heading for home, this was the most weary and disheartening leg of the voyage. It required twenty-five days to make good about 200 miles to windward. Eventually the caravels worked clear of this nasty tangle of shoals and mangrove swamp, crossed the Gulf of Cochinos and reached what the natives called Ornofay, the bold, mountainous strip of coast between Cienfuegos and Casilda. On July 7 the fleet anchored in the Rio San Juan at the foot of the Sierra de Trinidad, where they had called on the voyage westward. Columbus now named it *El Rio de las Misas*, since the day was Sunday and the chaplain of the fleet celebrated Mass ashore.

As Columbus had used the Indians here well on his westward journey, they now came forward with gifts of fruit, cassava bread, hutías, parrots and savory wild pigeons. During the celebration of Mass Columbus noted the attention and interest evinced by an aged native "who seemed respectable although naked" (as Peter Martyr remarks), and who after the service thus addressed the Admiral. One must warn the reader that the ancient gaffer's speech has passed through Diego's interpretation as reported to Peter Martyr, the historian's Latin and Richard Eden's English: —

"I have bin advertised (most mighty prince) that you have of late with great power subdued many lands and regions, hitherto unknowne to you, and have brought no little feare uppon all the people and inhabitantes of the same: the which, your good fortune, you shall beare with lesse insolency if you remember that the soules of men have two journeyes after they are departed from this bodie. The one, foule and darke, prepared for such as are injurious and cruell to mankinde: the other, pleasant and delectable, ordeined for them which in their life time loved peace and quietnes. If therfore you acknowledge your selfe to be mortal, and consider that every man shal receive condigne rewarde or punishment for such thinges as he hath done in this life, you will wrongfully hurt no man." When he had saide these wordes and other like, which were declared to the Admirall by the interpretation, he marveiling at the judgment of the naked olde man, answered that he was glad to heare his opinion as touching the sundry journeies and rewards of soules departed from their bodyes, supposing that neither he, or any other of the inhabitantes of those regions, had had any knowledge thereof: declaring further, that the chiefe cause of his comming thither, was to instruct them in such godly knowledg and true religion: and that he was sent into those countreies by the Christian king of Spaine (his Lord and master) for the same purpose, and specially to subdue and punish the *Canibales*, and such other mischievous people, and to defend innocents against the violence of evill dooers, willing him, and all other such as imbrace vertue, in no case to be afraide, but rather to open his minde unto him, if eyther he, or any other such quiet men as he was, had susteined any wrong of their neighboures, and that he would see the same revenged. These comfortable words of the Admirall so pleased the olde man, that notwithstanding his extreme age, he would gladly have gone with the Admirall, as he had done indeede, if his wife and children had not hindered him of his purpose: but he marveiled not a little, that the Admirall was under the dominion of another: and much more when the interpretour tolde him of the glorie, magnificence, pompe, great power and furnimentes of warre of our kinges, and of the multitudes of cities and townes which were under their dominions. Intending therefore to have gone with the Admirall, his wife and children fell prostrate at his feete, with teares desiring him not to forsake them and leave them desolate; at whose pitifull requestes, the worthy olde man beeing moved, remained at home to the comfort of his people and familie, satisfying rather them then himselfe: for not yet ceasing to woonder, and of heavie countenance because he might not depart, he demaunded oftentimes if that lande was not Heaven, which brought foorth such a kinde of men? For it is certaine that among them the lande is as common as sunne and water, and that Mine and Thine (the seedes of all mischiefe) haue no place with them. They are content with so litle, that in so large a countrey they haue rather superfluitie then scarcenesse: so that (as we have sayde before) they seeme to live in the golden worlde without toyle, living in open gardens, not intrenched with ditches, divided with hedges, or defended with walles: they deale truely one with another without lawes, without booke, and without judges: they take him for an evill and mischievous man, which taketh pleasure in dooing hurt to other. And albeit that they delight not in superfluities, yet make they provision for the increase of such roots whereof they make their bread, as *Maizium, Iucca,* and *Ajes,* contended with such simple dyet, whereby health is preserued, and diseases auoyded. . . .

Peter Martyr never missed an opportunity to point out that the Indians were still in the Golden Age.

Beating to windward through the Queen's Garden was more than Columbus cared to contemplate, so he made one more try at fighting head wind and current outside. On taking his departure from the River of the Masses on July 8 he steered into blue water, leaving the Laberinto de Doze Leguas on the port hand. The fleet took a bad beating; it was almost worse than sand-scraping through the Garden. After rounding the reefs by Cayo Breton they took the trades on the nose, and ten days were required to make good 180 miles to windward. Foul weather all the way, men grumbling and fearing death by drowning or starvation, says Cuneo. It was a tough passage for the Admiral, too. "All the winds and waters," says Las Casas, "concerted to fatigue him and heap anxiety on anxiety, difficulty on difficulty, and surprise on surprise, for he had neither the time nor the opportunity to take breath; among many things that he suffered was a thundersquall so sudden, horrible and perilous that it threw the flagship on her beam ends, and with great difficulty, and it seems only with the help of God, did they strike the sails, and at the same time anchor with the heaviest anchors. Much water worked down below the floor timbers, which increased their danger, and the mariners could hardly pump it out, because at a time when all were exhausted by continual labor, provisions went so short that they had nothing to eat but a pound of putrid biscuit and a pint of wine or its dregs, except when they happened to catch some fish. . . . With these dangers and unceasing afflictions he arrived on July 18 at the cape which he had already named *Cabo de Cruz*, where the Indians received him well and brought him cassava bread, fish, fruits of the earth and everything they had, with great good will and pleasure. There they stayed and rested two or three days."

From this experience it was again proved that even small lateen-rigged caravels could do nothing dead to windward in Antillean conditions, when the trade wind, the sea and the current all set in the same direction.

With another hard beat in prospect along the ironbound coast east of Cape Cruz, Columbus wisely decided to ease off and complete his exploration of Jamaica. Departing from the Cape Cruz anchorage — where one can still see sailing vessels awaiting a change of wind — he steered S by W toward El Golfo de Bien Tiempo, whence the fleet had departed three months before; and as usual when returning to a spot by sea, he made it without difficulty.

From Montego Bay, as this "Fair Weather Gulf" is now called, the fleet sailed west, south and then east, anchoring every night; for Jamaica is well provided with harbors and roadsteads suitable for vessels of light draught. The Indians were friendly and generous with handouts of food — but every evening broke one of those dreaded thundersqualls. Other details are wanting until the second week of August, when the fleet anchored in Portland Bight, which Columbus named *Bahía de la Vaca* — Cow Bay; it contained seven islets, and near by there were many Indian villages.

Here the Indians were much more friendly than they had been on the north coast. The cacique of a large village on a mountain slope came down bearing food supplies and had a long conversation with the Admiral through Diego. But the cacique was not satisfied; and on the next day when the fleet was already under way in a light breeze, he overtook it with three canoes, one of them very long and brightly painted. Andrés Bernáldez' description of what followed is the best word picture that we have of any incident in this voyage: —

In the largest canoe he came in person with his wife and two daughters, one of whom was about eighteen years old, very beautiful, completely naked as they are accustomed to be, and very modest; the other was younger, and two stout sons and five brothers and other dependents; and all the rest must have been his vassals. In his canoe he carried a man as herald. This fellow stood alone at the canoe's prow wearing a cloak of red feathers shaped like a coat of arms, and on his head he wore a great coronet of feathers which looked very fine, and in his hand he carried a white banner without any design. Two or three men had their faces painted with colors in the same pattern, and each wore on his head a large feather helmet, and on his forehead a round disk as large as a plate, and each was painted like the other in the same design and colors, so that they were uniform as in their plumes. Each held in his hand a gadget which he tinkled. There were two other men painted in another manner, and these carried two wooden trumpets all covered with birds and other designs; the wood of which they were made was very black and fine. Each of them wore a very pretty helmet of green feathers very close and well put together. Six others wore helmets of white feathers, and all these were on guard over the cacique's effects. The cacique wore around his neck some ornaments of copper which they call *guaní*, from an island in the neighborhood, and which is very fine and looks like 8-carat gold.* It was in the shape of a fleur-de-lis, and as large as a plate. He wore it around his neck on a string of big beads of marble stone which they also consider of great value, and on his head he wore a coronet of small stones, green and red, arranged in order and interspersed with some bigger white ones, which looked fine; and he also wore a large jewel pendant over his forehead, and from his ears were hung two great disks of gold by some little strings of small green beads. Although he went naked he wore a girdle of the same workmanship as his coronet, but all the rest of his body was exposed. His wife was likewise adorned and naked, her body exposed except in the one spot of her pudendum, which was covered by a little cotton thing no bigger than an orange peel. She wore on her arms, going under the armpits, a roll of cotton like the shoulder-puffs of old-fashioned French doublets, and two similar but greater ones on each leg below the knee, like Moorish anklets. The elder and more beautiful daughter was completely nude. She only wore around her middle a single string of small

---

* See index, under *guanin*. All these gold objects must have been imported from Central America.

and very black stones, from which hung something like an ivy leaf, made of green and red stones fastened to woven cloth.

When this picturesque cavalcade drew alongside the Admiral was saying the office of tierce in his cabin, and did not know what was up until the cacique and suite were on deck and the canoes had been sent ashore. As soon as the chief saw the Admiral he approached with a joyful expression and declared that he and his family proposed to go home with him and visit the Catholic Sovereigns, whose majesty and power had been so eloquently described by Diego. For he had heard that nobody in the islands round about could withstand the Admiral and so, he said prophetically, "Before thou deprivest me of my land and sovereignty, I wish with my household to go in thy ships to behold the great King and Queen thy lords, and the most rich and opulent land in the world where they dwell, and to see the wonders of Castile, which are many, as thy man hath told me."

It is to Columbus's credit that humanity prevailed over glory. It must have been a temptation to parade this brilliant savage royalty with their gold and feather ornaments at court. But he thought of the cold weather in which they would suffer and die, of what the pretty daughters might expect from his seamen, of the disillusion that would await these innocent souls in Castile. So he took compassion on them, declined the cacique's request, and sent the Indians ashore in the ship's boat after receiving their homage and fealty.

Columbus apparently missed Port Royal Bay, the site of Kingston Harbor, through having a westerly wind. He steered directly from Portland Bight to the Blue Mountains, which rise 7300 feet directly from the sea at the east end of Jamaica. On August 19 the fleet passed Morant Point, which the Admiral named *Cabo del Farol*, Cape of the Lighthouse, or of the Signal Fire. Perhaps he was looking ahead to the day when a lighthouse would mark the point; or, more likely, some Indians lighted a watchfire there as the three caravels steered eastward into the darkness.

The Windward Passage, across which Diego Méndez and Fieschi made their famous canoe trip in 1503, was easily traversed in less than twenty-four hours by *Niña, San Juan* and *Cardera*. Michele de Cuneo of Savona was the first to sight land on August 20; so Columbus by way of *albricias* named this southwestern cape of Hispaniola after him, *Cabo de San Miguel de Saona*. The Admiral did not ascertain whether Cape San Miguel was part of a new island or of Hispaniola until three days later, when, coasting along the southern shore, a cacique came out in a canoe calling "Almirante! Almirante!" and put him right.

Although Columbus might have returned to Isabela more quickly by steering NE across the Gulf of Leogane and around Cape St. Nicolas, he wished to explore the southern coast of the island; and this part of the voyage, opening up some 400 miles of coast for the first time, was highly important for Spain. Unfortunately we have very few details. Apparently the fleet anchored in Jacmel Bay, since Columbus appears to have been familiar with it on his Fourth Voyage, under the name of Puerto Brazil. Afterwards the fleet became separated in a gale. At the end of August, when *Niña* reached Alta Vela, the isolated sail-like rock that marks the southernmost point of Hispaniola, Columbus sent men ashore to climb the hill and watch for his consorts. No sails could be seen, but the men killed immense birds and *lobos marinos* (seals) to splice out their scanty provisions. The larger inshore island, six miles cross-channel, Columbus named *Cathalina* after the lady cacique of Higuey. Natives came out in swarms, and gave Columbus good news of the Isabela colony. These subjects of the lady cacique were more deadly than other Tainos, for they used poisoned arrows, but fortunately they were peacefully inclined and gave the seamen food instead of fight. Six days later the little caravels caught up with *Niña*, and when the fleet reached the Rio Jaina in Santo Domingo Bay the Admiral sent nine men ashore with orders to cross the Vega Real, call at Santo Tomás and proceed by the Puerto de los Hidalgos to Isabela, in order to announce his coming. They appear to have made the journey successfully.

Our next definite news of the fleet is in the harbor behind Saona Island, at the southeastern tip of Hispaniola. A few days before, the fleet had encountered, says Las Casas, a repulsive sea monster, big as a medium-sized whale with a carapace like a turtle's, a horrible head like a barrel, and two wings. The Admiral observed that when such denizens of the deep came to the surface it was time to prepare for foul weather; a mariners' superstition not yet dead. Sure enough, a September gale struck in soon after, and the fleet was glad to take refuge behind Saona.

The name of this large island is explained by Michele de Cuneo. He had been the first to sight it as earlier he had sighted Cape San Miguel; so "out of love for me, the Lord Admiral called it *La Bella Saonese*. He made me a gift of it, and I took possession according to the appropriate modes and forms, as the Lord Admiral was doing of the other islands in the name of His Majesty, the King, that is, by virtue of a document signed by a notary public. On that island I uprooted grass and cut trees and planted the cross and also the gallows, and in the name of God baptized it with the name La Bella Saonese. And well may it be called beautiful, for in it there are 37 villages with at least 30,000 souls. And all this too the Lord Admiral noted down in his book."

A pretty picture, the two old friends and shipmates from the far-off Ligurian coast, recalling ancient Savona on this fair island of the New World, with Old World ceremonies of turf and twig. Michele did not live to take any profit of his isle and his highly overestimated vassals; but the island's name, Saona, still recalls his native city, and the pleasant ceremony on that September day so long ago.

Columbus observed a total eclipse of the moon on September 14, while the fleet lay anchored behind Saona, waiting for the weather to clear up. Having a Regiomontanus *Ephemerides* with him, which gave the time of the eclipse at Nuremberg, he was able to make a rough calculation of longitude, which gave him a difference in time of about five and a half hours between Saona and Cape St. Vincent. This would have placed Saona in about longitude 91°

30′ W, the meridian of the Pacific coast of Guatemala. Building on that, it was easy for him to persuade himself that he had come almost halfway around the world, and lay close to the heart of Asia when he turned back in Western Cuba.

After riding out the storm in this excellent harbor, the fleet set forth from Saona on September 24, and sailed to Cape Engaño, which the Admiral had named Cape San Rafael when westward bound in 1493. At this juncture Columbus made a sudden change of plan, very unusual for him, and suggesting that he was in poor physical condition. Instead of pursuing his course down-wind to Isabela, whence he had now been absent four months, he decided to embark on a punitive expedition against the Caribs with the avowed purpose of destroying their canoes so that they could no longer raid his gentle friends the Tainos. Probably his real object was to obtain Carib slaves for shipment home, in lieu of the gold that he had not found in Cuba or Jamaica.

The fleet turned SE toward Puerto Rico, approached and landed on Mona Island, which Las Casas describes as 6 leagues in circumference, rocky, but full of a yellow fertile soil where enormous manioc roots, from which cassava is made, grew in abundance. When already crossing the eastern side of Mona Passage and nearing Puerto Rico, the Admiral was laid low with a high fever accompanied by alternate coma and delirium. This attack, whose symptoms suggest the modern nervous breakdown, had probably been brought on by his extreme exertions, lack of sleep and bad nourishment. The officers of the fleet held a council, and unanimously decided to abandon the raid on the Caribbees, and make all haste to Isabela. On September 29 the caravels anchored in Isabela Roads, and the Admiral was carried ashore in the arms of his seamen, to be nursed back to health by his devoted brothers.

This is the first evidence we have of poor health in Columbus, except for a temporary indisposition on the day the fleet sailed from Cadiz. Las Casas tells us that he developed *la gota*, for which the modern name is arthritis. His next two voyages were carried out when he was suffering from that painful malady.

To have explored almost the entire south coast of Cuba, both shoals and deeps; to have discovered and circumnavigated Jamaica, and to have finished his periplus of Hispaniola, was sufficient adventure for one summer. Columbus, however, was mentally disturbed because he had found no certain evidence of being in the Orient. He might make everyone swear, under dreadful penalties, that Cuba was a peninsula of Asia and the Grand Khan just around the corner; that did not make it so. He had not brought home a pennyweight of gold or a single pearl, such as everyone expected from "The Indies." And things were at sixes and sevens at Isabela. For, as Peter Martyr concludes his account of another voyage, "As often times chaunceth in human things, among his so many prosperous, pleasant and luckie affayres fortune mingled some seedes of wormewood, and corrupted his pure corne with the malicious weedes of cocke."

CHAPTER XXXV

Hell in Hispaniola
1494–1496

Cierto no fué Dios servido de tan execrable injusticia.

Sure God was not served by such execrable injustice.
— LAS CASAS *Historia* ch. 104

THE FIRST MAN to board *Niña* when the fleet anchored off Isabela on September 29, 1494, was the Admiral's brother Bartholomew, whom he had not seen for five or six years. After being turned down by Henry VII of England, Bartholomew had gone to France, where the young king Charles VIII, having a nearer conquest than that of the Indies in mind, was not interested. Bartholomew then attached himself to the suite of Madame de Bourbon. The Admiral wrote to him after his return from the First Voyage begging him to come to Spain, but Bartholomew heard the great news first from the lips of the king, who graciously presented him with a purse of a hundred crowns for his traveling expenses. That must have been in the late summer of 1493 — another indication of how slowly news traveled beyond the Alps and the Pyrenees — for, in spite of making all convenient speed, Bartholomew arrived at Seville after the Admiral had sailed from Cadiz in September.

At Seville Bartholomew picked up a letter from his brother requesting him, among other things, to conduct his two sons Diego and Ferdinand to court, where the Queen had promised to make them pages to the Infante Don Juan. This he did early in 1494, the court then being resident at Valladolid. Bartholomew made an excellent impression on the Sovereigns. They created him *caballero* so that he could style himself Don Bartolomé; and when Antonio de Torres reported the instant need of Hispaniola for provisions and medicaments, Ferdinand and Isabella gave Bartholomew command over three caravels, which were promptly laden in order to relieve the colony. This fleet sailed from an Andalusian port in late April or early May, and arrived off Isabela on midsummer's day, 1494.

In spite of the Admiral's illness, the brothers' reunion must have been joyous. Christopher and Bartholomew had worked out the Great Enterprise together at Lisbon, had shared the same privations, been subjected to the same ridicule, and suffered a parallel series of rebuffs and disappointments. "El Adelantado" (the Leader), as Bartholomew is generally called from the office conferred on him by his brother and confirmed by the Sovereigns, would henceforth share the Admiral's triumphs and tribulations — mostly tribulations. The two brothers were complements to one another. Bartholomew had little originality and no mysticism, but he contributed the knowledge of a professional map maker and accomplished linguist, an innate sense of command both by land and by sea, strength of will, and absolute loyalty. Intelligent without being intellectual, he had the best qualities of a man of action, always dependable when others failed or turned traitor, always robust in health when others fell ill, always courageous when others faltered, always confident and hopeful when others lost heart. Never sparing of himself, he refused to spare others; severe toward his men and curt in his speech, he lacked what Las Casas called the "sweetness and benignity" of the Admiral, and perhaps erred on the side of rigor as his brother did on the side of gentleness. From now on, through good fortune and ill, he was the chief counselor and executive officer of his brother.

Bartholomew brought to the Admiral a flattering letter from the Sovereigns, the much needed supplies and reinforcements, and a promise of more. But this was the only good news that greeted the Admiral on his return from the voyage to Cuba and Jamaica. The mistakes he had made before departing in April had already borne bitter fruit. His brother Don Diego, a man more suited to the cloister than to a colony, had been unable to cope with the situation. Hojeda's savage punishment of the cacique who appropriated a few old clothes, in which Columbus must bear a good share of the blame, had alienated many of the natives. Even worse had been the result of turning Mosén Pedro Margarit loose.

Although Margarit's deplorable doings were contrary to the Admiral's wishes and commands, he had in a sense made them inevitable by sending this soldier to live off the country. Some 250 hidalgos and crossbowmen, 110 musketeers and 16 troopers, had only a pack of hawks' bells and other trinkets with which to purchase food. Columbus ordered Margarit to do the Indians no harm (unless they stole, when their noses and ears should be cropped), and told him to keep in mind that "Their Highnesses desire more the salvation of this people by making them Christians, than all the riches that can be obtained from them." But the Spaniards had to eat. And Columbus instructed Margarit to get Caonabó into his power by treachery through sending presents and a safe conduct. This he did not even attempt; nor did he obey a better instruction, to explore the island and report on its products.

While Hojeda held the fort of Santo Tomás, Margarit and his merry men roved the Vega Real, extorting gold from the natives, raping their women and quickly exhausting their food supplies. The Indians never kept much food on hand in a country of such natural bounty; and, as Las Casas said without much exaggeration, "one Spaniard ate more in a day than a whole family of natives would consume in a month." When the natives refused to furnish what they had not, Margarit's men resorted to threats and blows and whippings, "not only against the common people, but the noble and chief men who were called *nitaynos*"; they carried off many wives and daughters "with no respect to person or dignity, or marriage relation," and kidnaped young boys to serve them as slaves.

All this harsh and unwarranted treatment caused such unrest among the caciques and their subjects (always excepting the ever-faithful Guacanagarí) that the situation of the colony at Isabela became precarious. Don Diego as president of the council wrote to Margarit ordering him to mend his ways, and obey the Admiral's command to explore, and not to extort. Margarit regarded this as a reflection on his honor as a *caballero*, and a challenge to his authority. As to that, one must admit that he was right; for Columbus had expressly conferred on him "the same power that I hold from Their Highnesses of Viceroy and Captain General of these Indies for the present." He marched down to Isabela in a rage; and, when unable to bring the council to his way of thinking, joined forces with a faction of malcontents, seized the three caravels that Bartholomew had brought out from Spain and sailed for home. The most important person who joined him in this mutiny was his fellow Catalan Fray Buil, who had been given especial charge of converting the natives. Buil, initiator of a "hard-boiled" policy toward the Indians, was a bad egg indeed. He and the other friars under his orders had done absolutely nothing to convert and instruct the docile Tainos who lived near Isabela. It was not until September 21, 1496, that the first Indian was baptized in Hispaniola by Fray Ramón Pane, a modest and loyal Jeronymite who was doing his best to serve God instead of mammon.

This Catalan faction had sailed before the Admiral returned from Cuba, and their ships reached Spain some time in November, 1494. Fray Buil proceeded to court, where he circulated the most outrageous slanders against the Columbus brothers, and declared that there was neither gold nor anything else of profit in Hispaniola.

The Admiral, although suffering so acutely from arthritis that he kept his bed for weeks on end, took over the presidency of the council from Don Diego's weak hands, and endeavored to bring order out of anarchy. That was no easy task; things had gone too far. Gangs of soldiers abandoned by Margarit and discontented colonists were ranging the island, terrorizing the natives and committing every sort of licentiousness and brutality. Naturally some of them were ambushed and killed; but the Admiral, instead of outlawing these mutineers (which he probably feared to do in view of public opinion in Spain), adopted the principle that no

Christian could do wrong, held the Indians to strict accountability, sent a force into the interior, hunted down the natives with horses and hounds, rounded up over fifteen hundred of the poor creatures, and brought them to Isabela. Instead of punishing the authors of all this wickedness, he punished the innocent victims.

Worse was in store for the captives. Some time in the fall of 1494 the rest of the provision fleet, four caravels under command of Antonio de Torres, arrived at Isabela. Torres brought another letter from the Sovereigns (August 16, 1494) written after they had maturely considered and commented on the memorandum on colonial needs and policy that the Admiral had sent in February. Ferdinand and Isabella still approved everything the Admiral had done and recommended, except that they wished he might have been more explicit about the islands discovered on the outward voyage, "because you name some in your letters but not all" — a wish in which the historian heartily joins. They would also like to know more about the climate, which was probably a matter of pointed inquiry among intending colonists. The "affairs of Portugal" (the Treaty of Tordesillas) had gone so well that they suggested a monthly packet service between Spain and Hispaniola; they were a bit anxious about drawing the new line of demarcation, and suggested that the Admiral come home and help them. Yet, "if it be difficult for you to come, and if it would make some inconveniences for what you are about, see if you have not your brother or some other person there who knows, and instruct them well by writing, speech and diagrams, and in every other manner that they may be instructed, and send them hither promptly by the first caravels that come home."

Here was a chance of escape. Columbus might have taken this as a royal command and gone home immediately, leaving his brother in charge, and evading all the problems — the first colonial questions in modern history — that were rolling up on him. Would it not be wise to do so? Margarit and Fray Buil would soon be at court, telling lies to the Sovereigns. But Columbus refused to take the easy way out, nor could he spare Bartholomew. Drawing the line of demarcation could wait. It waited indefinitely, since the Portuguese and Spanish experts never could agree.

The immediate problem was what to send back by the Torres fleet. The much-publicized "mine of gold" in the Cibao had not been found; for none there was. As yet only insignificant quantities of gold had been collected for the crown, although every man jack in the colony had a small fortune concealed in the bush or on his person. None of the so-called spiceries or tropical hard-woods had found favor with the Spanish merchants. The Indian cotton cloth, of fine weave and texture, had found ready sale in Spain; but that did not amount to much. Something more profitable must be sent home, in order to repay part of the expenses and stop the mischievous propaganda of the Catalan faction for abandoning "The Indies" altogether. What was there to send but slaves?

In his Torres memorandum of February 1494, Columbus had outlined a plan for a regular trade in Carib slaves, in order to pay for supplies before the expected gold mine came into production. He believed that they could easily be captured with the *fustas de remos* or big rowing sailboats that he intended to build in the colony; and as the Caribs were mortal enemies of Their Highnesses' new subjects the Tainos, such traffic would be legitimate and even politic. Ferdinand and Isabella did not welcome this suggestion, for they noted against it, "This subject has been postponed for the present, until another voyage has come thence, and let the Admiral write what he thinks about it."

Far from being discouraged by this hint that the King and Queen did not look kindly on an American slave trade, even with the specious promise of making Christians and productive workers out of heathen cannibals, Columbus proceeded to establish a slave trade with the inhabitants of Hispaniola. And this, after he had declared time and again that the Tainos were the kindest, most peaceful and generous people in the world, who wanted nothing but a chance to become good subjects and good Christians. En-slaving these people in their own islands was no new idea to Co-lumbus; his first thought in 1492 was to clothe them and set them to work. But now he resorted to the monstrous expedient of sending hundreds of the wretched creatures overseas, to the slave mart of Seville.

Michele de Cuneo has preserved for us some of the distressing details. As a result of the recent punitive expedition, some fifteen hundred captives were driven down to Isabela. Of these about five hundred, "the best males and females," were loaded on the four caravels. Columbus then announced that any Christian might help himself to as many as he pleased of the remainder. After everyone had been supplied there were four hundred left, who were told to "scram." Among them were many women who had infants at the breast. "They, in order better to escape us, since they were afraid we would turn to catch them again, left their infants anywhere on the ground and started to flee like desperate people; and some fled so far that they were removed from our settlement of Isabela seven or eight days beyond mountains and across huge rivers." A cacique named Guatiguaná and two subordinate chiefs, who had been considered responsible for killing the Christian marauders, were tied up in preparation for being shot to death with arrows the following day; but they spoiled the fun by gnawing through each other's bonds with their teeth and escaping.

The four caravels, under the command of Antonio de Torres, set sail from Isabela on February 24, 1495. Michele de Cuneo was a passenger, and also Diego Columbus, whom the Admiral sent home as his advocate at court against the anticipated slanders of Buil and Margarit. Torres had not yet learned that the Admiral's homeward course in 1493, north to the latitude of Bermuda and east to Spain, should be a general rule. He attempted a more southerly route, and in consequence wasted a month beating among the Lesser Antilles. Finally, fearing lest the provisions be exhausted, Torres sailed northward for 150 leagues (says Cuneo), struck the westerlies which blow strong in March, and made Madeira in twenty-three days from Puerto Rico. The sufferings of Indians confined below hatches in stormy weather can better be imagined than described. On the last leg of the voyage from Madeira to Cadiz, writes Cuneo, "about two hundred of these Indians died, I believe because of the unaccustomed air, colder than theirs. We cast them into the sea. The first land we saw was Cape Spartel, and very soon after we reached Cadiz, in which place we disembarked all the slaves, half of whom were sick. For your information they are not working people and they very much fear cold, nor have they long life." Don Juan Fonseca put the survivors up for sale at Seville, where Bernáldez saw them "naked as they were born, with no more embarrassment than wild beasts. . . . They are not very profitable since almost all died, for the country did not agree with them." A nice beginning of overseas trade with the Indies!

The Tainos of Hispaniola were beginning to show more courage than they were credited with by Columbus, even though it was the courage of desperation. Guatiguaná, the cacique who had escaped by gnawing through his bonds, now attempted to drive the intruders into the sea. There is little doubt that if all the tribes of Hispaniola had united, they could have overwhelmed the Spaniards by sheer numbers despite their feeble weapons; but as in most wars between Indians and Europeans, they were unable to unite. Guacanagarí, whose people had suffered from Christian marauders like the others, remained steadfastly faithful to his unwritten pact with the Admiral, and the caciques at the other extremities of the island flattered themselves that they could remain safely in isolation if they did not trouble the white invaders. This was not their war.

Guatiguaná managed to assemble an army impressive for its size in the Vega Real. On March 27, 1495, the Admiral (who had recovered his strength), the Adelantado (who only wanted an opportunity to test his), and Alonso de Hojeda (who was always ready to fight) marched forth from Isabela to meet this host with two hundred foot, twenty horses and twenty hounds, and a force of Indian allies under Guacanagarí. By the Puerto de los Hidalgos the Spanish army descended into the great valley and took stations in ambush on the flanks of the close-huddled forces of Guatiguaná. The battle began with firing from ambush by the arquebusiers, which alarmed the natives more than it harmed them; then, at the word of command, Hojeda at the head of the cavalry troop dashed into the frightened, huddled mass, striking and cutting with lance and sword, while the hounds gave tongue. That was enough. The Indians, "who imagined that man and horse were one animal," were completely routed, and another big coffle of slaves was rounded up.

Caonabó still remained to be dealt with. By reputation he was the most daring and warlike of the caciques, and the Spaniards had a long score to settle with him for having murdered the garrison of Navidad.

Hojeda with only ten mounted men was sent to capture Caonabó by fair means or foul. He obtained access to the cacique at his headquarters on the southern slope of the Cibao mountains, invited him to visit Isabela and make a treaty with the Christians, and promised that on his arrival he should be presented with the bronze bell in the church. Caonabó had heard about that bell and fancied it; he accepted the bait, but prudently took an armed force of retainers to protect himself. When Spaniards and Indians were encamped together on a riverbank, Hojeda produced from his saddlebags a pair of burnished steel handcuffs and another of foot fetters, which he had brought in the hope of capturing Caonabó alive. The Indians greatly admired brass, which they called *turey*, and Hojeda told the cacique that these were made of *negro turey de Vizcaya* (black Biscay brass), and were such as the King of Spain wore on festival occasions when he rode horseback. Would the cacique like to wear them as the king did? Caonabó allowed that he would. So the cacique was mounted behind the conquistador, the "bracelets" and shackles were adjusted to hands and feet, and his body bound to Hojeda's so that he could not fall off. At a signal the troopers scattered Caonabó's astonished bodyguard, Hojeda dashed with his prisoner across the river, off and away. Halting only once to adjust the fetters, Hojeda brought the captive behind him into Isabela.

While Caonabó was left chained up in the Isabela calaboose,

"fretting and grating his teeth as if he had been a lion of Libya," Columbus sent Hojeda on a mopping-up expedition to the Cibao, where Caonabó's brother-in-law Behechio, cacique of Xaragua, was reported to be raising a hostile force. Hojeda garrisoned Santo Tomás once more, and marched over the mountains with his invincible troop of horse. Behechio put up the best fight of any, but the cavalry conquered as usual, and he too was brought in to Isabela as prisoner; but later he escaped. Columbus followed this up by a triumphal march through the country, which at last began to be pacified. Hispaniola was so thoroughly subdued by 1496, says Ferdinand, that a lone Spaniard could safely go wherever he pleased, and enjoy free food, women and pick-a-back rides.

Apparently some women and children, the first European women and children to reach the New World since the days of the Northmen, had been brought out by Torres in his fleet; for Ferdinand says that after the conquest of the island the white population numbered 630, "the major part sick, and many of them women and children." Now that Isabela began to take on the semblance of a settled colony, Columbus thought it was time for him to sail home and take care of his interests. But in June 1495 an early hurricane destroyed his shipping. Las Casas believed that this was a judgment of divine providence on the countless impieties and iniquities committed by the Spaniards. As Peter Martyr describes it: —

This same year in the month of June, they say there rose such a boisterous tempest of wind from the SE, as hath not lately been heard of. The violence hereof was such that it plucked up by the roots whatsoever great trees were within the force thereof. When this whirlwind came to the haven of the city, it beat down to the bottom of the sea three ships which lay at anchor, and broke the cables in sunder: and that (which is the greater marvel) without any storm or roughness of the sea, only turning them three or four times about. The inhabitants also affirm that the same year the sea extended itself further in to the land, and rose higher than ever it did before the memory of man, by the space of a cubit.

Stout little *Niña* weathered the hurricane, but the three others
— *San Juan, Cardera* and probably *Gallega* — were broken up.
Fortunately there were shipwrights at Isabela, and these the Admiral set to building a new vessel from salvaged portions of the
wrecks. In due course a handy little caravel of about 50 tons, as
nearly as possible a sister ship to *Niña*, was constructed, launched
and equipped with sails and gear from the others. Officially named
Santa Cruz, the seamen nicknamed her *India*, as the first vessel to be
constructed in the Indies.

For nine or ten months, from May 1495 to February or March
1496, the Columbus brothers were mainly occupied in subduing the
island. Las Casas had access to reports from the Admiral to the
Sovereigns which have since been lost, and which frankly reveal
his methods. Three more forts were built in the interior; and using
these as a base, the army marched about the island forcing the now
thoroughly terrified natives to submit to viceregal rule on condition of paying a tribute in gold.

Whoever thought up this ghastly system, Columbus was responsible for it, as the only means of producing gold for export.
Every native of fourteen years of age or upward who submitted
(as the only alternative to being killed) was required to furnish
every three months a Flanders hawk's bell full of gold dust; and
one of the caciques, Manicaotex, had to give a calabash full of gold
valued at 150 castellanos every two months. Natives who lived in
regions where no gold could be extracted from the river beds could
commute their tribute by one arroba (twenty-five pounds) of spun
or woven cotton in lieu of the trimonthly payment of gold dust.
Everyone who delivered his tribute to one of the armed posts was
given a stamped brass or copper token to hang about his neck in
order to protect him from fresh extortion. The system was irra-
tional, most burdensome, impossible, intolerable and abominable,
says Las Casas.

The truth of this can be appreciated when one realizes the difficulty of extracting gold from the soil and river beds of Hispaniola.
Those gold ornaments that seemed so abundant when the Spaniards

first came, represented the labor and accumulation of several generations, the Indians' family plate as it were. By this time all had been stripped from the Indians. Gold could now be obtained only by washing it out of the sand and gravel in the beds of rivers and streams, or by a still more laborious process, possible only with directed slave labor, of clearing the land of bushes and trees, trenching it, and through repeated experiment finding a place that showed "pay dirt." Individual Indians could only acquire the annual tribute of four hawks' bells full of gold in favored streams and by the most unremitting labor, to which they were not used. Occasionally they would make a lucky strike of a big nugget, but generally they were unable with the best will in the world to meet the tribute. The cacique Guarionex often told the Admiral that if he would assign him a tract of arable land from sea to sea, big enough (Las Casas estimates) to grow sufficient wheat to feed the whole kingdom of Castile ten times over, with all his subjects he could not collect enough gold there to satisfy the tribute. But the Admiral, "Christian and virtuous as he was, and full of good desires," was so anxious to repay the Sovereigns for their great expenses, and stop the mouths of his critics, that he refused to do more than cut down the tribute 50 per cent. Even that was exorbitant. "Some complied, and for others it was impossible; and so, falling into the most wretched way of living, some took refuge in the mountains whilst others, since the violence and provocation and injuries on the part of the Christians never ceased, killed some Christian for special damages and tortures that they suffered. Then straightway against them was taken the vengeance which the Christians called punishment; not only the murderers, but as many as might be in that village or region were punished with execution and torture, not respecting the human and divine justice and natural law under whose authority they did it."

Those who fled to the mountains were hunted with hounds, and of those who escaped, starvation and disease took toll, whilst thousands of the poor creatures in desperation took cassava poison to end their miseries. So the policy and acts of Columbus for which he alone was responsible began the depopulation of the terrestrial paradise that was Hispaniola in 1492. Of the original natives, estimated by a modern ethnologist at 300,000 in number, one third were killed off between 1494 and 1496. By 1508 an enumeration showed only 60,000 alive. Four years later that number was reduced by two thirds; and in 1548 Oviedo doubted whether 500 Indians remained. Today the blood of the Tainos only exists mingled with that of the more docile and laborious African Negroes who were imported to do the work that they could not and would not perform.

The fate of this gentle and almost defenseless people offers a terrible example to Americans who fancy they will be allowed to live in peace by people overseas who covet what they have.

In October 1495, a whole year since the last fleet had arrived from Spain, four caravels came scudding along the north coast of Hispaniola, and anchored in Isabela roads. They had sailed from Seville August 5, commanded by Juan Aguado, a former member of the Queen's household who had accompanied Columbus on the Second Voyage and later returned to Spain with Torres. He was charged to investigate and report on the Admiral's conduct as viceroy and governor. The Sovereigns could not ignore the complaints of Fray Buil and the other malcontents, several hundred in number, who had returned home; but they still had faith in the Admiral and chose this method of finding out the truth. Aguado brought much-needed supplies, and the expert metallurgist for whom Columbus had asked. To the Admiral he delivered a curt letter from the Sovereigns ordering him to reduce the colonists on the royal payroll to five hundred at most (which probably had already been done by natural causes), and commanding him to apportion the provisions equally, since it had been alleged that he had deprived some of their proper share as a punishment.

Aguado carried only the briefest letter of credence addressed to all noblemen, gentlemen and other persons in the Indies, introducing him as "our chamberlain who will speak to you on our part." Yet he made a pompous entry into Isabela with sound of trumpets, and at once began countermanding orders of the Adelantado (who had charge in the Admiral's absence inland), hearing complaints, arresting people, and in other ways assuming the functions of viceroy. Bartholomew sent word and warning to his brother, who returned to Isabela and adopted a patient and courteous attitude toward the usurper. Aguado and his scribes found plenty to do taking down testimony, since almost everyone in Isabela was sick or discontented and eager to go home. The healthy people, he tells us, were engaged in looting, hunting gold and catching slaves all over the island.

It seems extraordinary that after eighteen months' colonization of this rich and fertile island, after an abundance of seed, implements and laborers had been sent out from Spain, the Spaniards were still dependent on imported supplies; but the same condition lasted for years. Michele de Cuneo tells the essential reason. "Although the soil is very black and good they have not yet found the way nor the time to sow; *the reason is that nobody wants to live in these countries.*" This attitude was at the bottom of most of the trouble. Columbus planned a permanent settlement and the transfer of Hispanic culture and Catholic Christianity to the Indies; but nobody outside his family and a few faithful, humble souls like Fray Ramón Pane cared for that. Their object was to get gold quick and go home to spend it. By 1496, says Las Casas, the only oath heard in Isabela was *así Dios me lleva a Castilla,* "as God may take me to Castile!"

Columbus was not long coming to the conclusion that he too must return home in order to protect his interests, before Aguado could send in a report. He did not get off until March 1496, perhaps because *India* could not earlier be equipped for sea.

During these months of waiting a new and more suitable site was sought for the capital of Hispaniola. Isabela had proved unsatisfactory for many reasons. The anchorage afforded no protection from north winds; there was no gold-bearing soil within easy reach; and the near-by sections of the Vega Real had been devastated. Oviedo tells a romantic tale, which Las Casas brands as pure fable, of a

Spaniard named Miguel Díaz wandering across the island to the river Ozama, where he fell in love with the lady cacique Cathalina, who invited Columbus to build a new city in her territory. According to Las Casas the site of Santo Domingo was found by an exploring party sent out for that purpose under Díaz, and selected because of its good harbor, fertile land for agriculture, and gold-bearing rivers that had not yet been worked. However that may be, the last order of the Admiral to the Adelantado, after investigating one more site, was to found the new city in his absence; and the building of Santo Domingo was begun in 1496 or 1497.

Isabela, scene of so much suffering and disappointment, was abandoned. As early as Las Casas's day the ruins were said to be haunted. Terrible cries were heard by hunters who approached the place, and once in a deserted street a benighted traveler met two *caballeros* booted and spurred with swords by their sides and cloaked like courtiers of olden time, who on being saluted returned his courtesy with low and sweeping bows; but their heads came off with their hats, and their bodies disappeared. So men avoided the site of Isabela, and today it is a pasture by the sea with only a few stones above the ground to show that once it was the capital city of the Spanish Indies.

CHAPTER XXXVI

Crowded Crossing
March 10–June 11, 1496

Myrabiles elationes maris, myrabilis in altis Dominus.

Wonderful are the heavings of the sea; wonderful is the
Lord in the deeps.

— PSALM xcii 4

SANTA CLARA (alias *Niña*), in which Columbus returned
to Spain, and *Santa Cruz* (alias *India*) her consort, made a sad
little fleet in comparison with the splendid armada that the Admiral had commanded almost three years before. Pitiful it was to
think of the high spirits and great expectations of those days; for
the only joy aboard *Niña* and *India* lay in the prospect of leaving
the Indies forever, and returning to Spain. So many were eager to
go home that the caravels were dangerously overcrowded, with
two hundred and twenty-five Christians and thirty Indians aboard.
It staggers one's imagination to accommodate so many, for *Niña's*
company on the First Voyage numbered less than twenty-five, and
India was of the same burthen. Passengers must have slept on deck
in two shifts. How could the vessels have been worked, with their
decks covered with people? And how could so many have been
fed? Well, as we shall see, they almost weren't fed.

Niña, of which Columbus now owned a half share, still had
Alonso Medel as master and probably much the same crew as on
her Cuban voyage of 1494. *India* was commanded by Bartolomé
Colín, who had come out as captain in Aguado's fleet. The thirty
Indians aboard included captive Caonabó, who died at sea, his
brother and nephew, and a number of others selected to be trained
as interpreters. Except for those who were leaving their native land,

everyone was delighted to have a half interest in a two-by-six bit of deck space, and no tears were shed over leaving Isabela when the fleet set sail at daybreak March 10, 1496.

Considering the crowded condition of the caravels, it was incumbent on Columbus to make the quickest possible passage; perhaps that is why he waited until March, when the westerlies are strongest. If he had known as much of winds and currents as did Alonso de Santa Cruz in 1541, he would have scudded downwind through the Old Bahama Channel, and let the Gulf Stream carry him through the Straits of Florida to the latitude of Bermuda, where he would find plenty of westerly wind. This longest way round was the shortest way home to Spain, but it was many years before anyone discovered it. The second best route home was the one Columbus himself had taken in 1493; beating along Northern Hispaniola (which avoided the dangerous Silver Shoals where a great treasure fleet once foundered — the one fished for by Sir William Phips) to Samaná Bay, thence working northward closehauled on the trades into the zone of westerlies. Torres made a land-to-land passage of only twenty-five days on that route with his twelve vessels in 1494, and Oviedo declares that in 1525 four caravels made the entire voyage from Santo Domingo to Seville in just that space of time. Torres on his second homeward passage in March–April 1495 (the one that took Cuneo back to Spain) tried beating to the eastward and made very slow time, as Columbus must have learned from the captains and pilots of Aguado's fleet, who left Spain several months after Torres arrived. Why should the Admiral again attempt this bad course? Perhaps he feared losing touch with the land, in his overcrowded condition. Whatever the object, his route was very ill chosen, and Columbus was lucky not to get becalmed in the "horse latitudes" and lose half his passengers by starvation.

Bartholomew Columbus, whom the Admiral left in command as Adelantado, sailed aboard *Niña* to the first port of call, Puerto Plata. The brothers wished to look this place over as a possible site for the new capital. After a brief reconnaissance they decided in favor of the Ozama, and took affectionate leave of one another, the Adelantado returning to Isabela by land. Las Casas, who later became prior of the Dominican monastery on the mountain above Puerto Plata, is amusingly indignant about his home town being passed over. Bartholomew, he declares, was so prejudiced in favor of Santo Domingo that he maligned the streams which empty into Puerto Plata, telling the Admiral that their water was no good.

What with this call and the trade winds blowing parallel to the coast, it took *Niña* and *India* twelve days to beat along Hispaniola, and not until March 22 did they lose sight of Cape Engaño.

Trades continued to blow from the easterly quadrant, and the beating continued. It is not clear whether Columbus did his tacking inside or outside Puerto Rico and the Virgins; probably inside, as the water is smoother, and the wind sometimes draws off shore. On April 6, when already four weeks out from Isabela — enough to have reached Spain if they had taken the right route — provisions were running so alarmingly low that Columbus decided to call at Guadeloupe and lay in a supply of native food. On Saturday afternoon, April 9, 1496, *Niña* and *India* anchored off Mariegalante, the island where Columbus had taken formal possession of the Caribbees on his outward voyage. Next morning he gave orders to proceed to Guadeloupe. Seamen then as now objected to leaving port on a Sunday, and the Admiral's order occasioned the usual growling and grumbling. No doubt the sea lawyers and sky pilots were very smug and "I-told-you-so" over what happened next.

The vessels stood over to Guadeloupe, came to an anchor near the Admiral's old moorings in Grande Anse, and sent an armed boat ashore. Before it touched the beach, a multitude of women rushed out of the woods, and presented the visitors with a shower of arrows, but hit nobody. Columbus decided that this, not "Matinino," must be the isle of women he had heard of on the First Voyage.

Some of the women captives from Haiti were sent ashore to tell the Amazons that the Spaniards wished them no harm, and only wanted bread. They replied that they had none, but their husbands were at the north part of the island, and would doubtless furnish the Christians with what they needed. So *Niña* and *India* weighed anchors, and sailed round the southwestern cape of Guadeloupe, until they came to a cove (probably Anse à la Barque) where there was a village of palm-thatched huts with numerous natives. Again an armed boat was sent ashore, and the men walked right into an ambush. "Thousands of arrows" were shot at them and the natives stoutly resisted the landing party until a few well-placed lombard shots sent them scampering into the woods. The Spaniards looted and destroyed their huts, but found nothing of value, only some red parrots called *guacamayos* as big as chickens, and honey and wax, records Ferdinand; "but I don't believe it," says Las Casas, "as I never heard of honey or of wax in those islands, nor on the mainland." They also found a human arm roasting on a spit.

An armed party pursued the Indians into the mountains and managed to capture three boys and ten women, one of whom was either the ruler of the village or a wife of the cacique. Holding these as hostages, the Spaniards were able to do business. The women sold them a quantity of cassava roots and taught them how to make cassava bread by rasping the roots of the *yuca* or manioc on a wooden grater with flints imbedded in its surface, leaching out the hydrocyanic acid (which the Caribs used to make poison for their arrows), kneading the flour into dough, patting it into thin cakes, and baking it over the fire on a griddle made of earthenware. In Guadeloupe and Haiti the Negroes still make it much as the Indians did, except that they bray the roots in a mortar and cook the cakes on a bit of sheet iron over charcoal. Often have I bought a round of *pain de cassave* hot off the griddle from a roadside vendor, and saved a portion to toast for breakfast. It retains its flavor and freshness for a long time; for a year or more says Oviedo, who tells us that cassava was much used by the early navigators for ship's bread. In that respect it was far superior to corn bread, which was also available in the Antilles.

For nine days the two caravels remained at this anchorage in

Guadeloupe, baking their cassava bread, filling their water butts and cutting firewood. As the Admiral wished to keep the Indians friendly, knowing that other Spanish ships would pass that way, he returned all hostages except the lady cacique and her daughter, who (he said) stayed aboard of their own desire; "but this desire," says Las Casas, "God knows what it was, and how the natives deprived by their enemies of their Lady were consoled and satisfied."

On April 20 *Niña* and *India* left Guadeloupe for Spain, "with the wind ahead and much calm," says Ferdinand. This visit to Guadeloupe cost the fleet a month's time, for they took off for the ocean crossing in a zone and at a season when the trades blow fairly steadily from the easterly quadrant. Of the next month's sailing, April 20–May 20, we have not a single detail. The provisions must have been eked out by catching fish, for the caravels' progress could only have been slow on the wind; and in the horse latitudes, which they had to cross, the wind is always light. The next ship's news salvaged for us by Ferdinand is that on May 20 all hands were put on a short daily allowance of six ounces of cassava bread and a little cup of water, and nothing else. He adds: "And although there were eight or nine pilots aboard these two caravels, none of them knew where they were, but the Admiral was confident that their position lay somewhat to the westward of the Azores."

Niña and *India* rolled along a little to the southward of the Azores with fresh westerly breezes. Every day the crowded ships' companies were becoming hungrier and hungrier. By the end of the first week in June, six weeks out from Guadeloupe, some of the Spaniards proposed paying the Carib captives in their own coin and eating them, beginning with the plumpest (presumably the lady cacique and daughter). Others argued that Carib meat would make them sick, and proposed as a simpler expedient to heave all Indians overboard so that they would consume no more Christian food. Columbus stalled them along (says his son) with the plea that Caribs after all were human beings and should be used like the rest, a principle that might even better have been observed ashore.

An end was put to this debate by landfall on June 8. The pilots did not expect to sight land for several days, they were "going like lost men or blind" says Ferdinand, and their guesses of what land they would raise on that course ranged all the way from England to Galicia. But the Admiral the night before ordered sail taken in for fear of hitting Cape St. Vincent, "for which they all laughed at him." As usual in such matters, the Admiral had the last laugh. Next day they made land on the Portuguese coast near Odmira, about 35 miles north of Cape St. Vincent, for which Columbus had been aiming. Once more he had demonstrated the amazing accuracy of his dead-reckoning.

This seems to have been the neatest bit of navigation that Columbus ever did. If he was able to check his position at the Azores, a mistake of only 35 miles in the landfall on Portugal was excellent dead-reckoning. If, as is probable, he never saw the Azores, that slight error was phenomenal dead-reckoning. I doubt very much whether any navigator today could have come so close on so long a voyage, without taking sights on the heavenly bodies. It is no wonder, as Ferdinand said, that after this landfall the seamen regarded his father as "most expert and admirable in matters of navigation."

Turning their prows to the southward, and rounding Cape St. Vincent, the now weed-hung caravels crossed the "Sea of Spain" and on June 11 entered the Bay of Cadiz. A square meal in sight at last! The flag lockers were opened and every available banner and pendant was run up, to make as brave a showing as possible; but it was rather a pathetic homecoming in contrast to the gallant fleet that left Cadiz in 1493.

In Cadiz harbor and almost ready to sail were two caravels and a ship under command of Peralonso Niño, laden with provisions for the colony at Hispaniola. Peralonso would instantly have recognized *Niña*, which he had helped the Admiral to sail home in 1493; one may imagine his puzzled conjectures as to what and whence colonial-built *India* might be. The woebegone Indians and Spanish passengers with wasted bodies and "faces the color of lemon or saffron" must have been highly discouraging to Niño's people. One can imagine how the old salts would have growled to one another: — Guess the very magnificent Don Cristóbal is coming home, had enough. — Yes, and it looks like plenty of others had enough, too. — I'd give a hatful of gold castellanos to get out of this and safe ashore, if I had 'em. — Too late now, but if you take my advice, stay aboard in the Indies and eat ship's food, bad as it is; that junk you pick up ashore pizens a man. — Well, so I will if they let the wimmin come aboard. — Better let them alone too. I've heard . . . Well, I say it's a pity they ever started this Indies business. What do you get but lose your health, and the government takes all the gold you gain!

THE THIRD VOYAGE TO AMERICA

CHAPTER XXXVII

Preparations
June 11, 1496–May 25, 1498

Ad vesperum demorabitur fletus; et ad matutinum laetitia.

Heaviness may endure for a night, but joy cometh in the morning.

— PSALM xxix 6

A S SOON AS Columbus went ashore at Cadiz he adopted the coarse brown habit of a Minorite friar, which remained his usual costume when in Spain. Apparently he believed that his misfortunes were chastisements of divine providence for his pride, and so laid off the costly apparel proper to an Admiral of the Ocean Sea, and assumed the humble garb of his Franciscan friends as evidence of repentance and humility.

Columbus found his most loyal friends ashore among ecclesiastics, especially those in the monastic orders. He liked their piety, their conversation, and their simple way of living; and in his travels about Spain he preferred the hospitality of a monastery to that of caballero or grandee. While awaiting an invitation from the Sovereigns he lived in the house of Andrés Bernáldez, curate of Los Palacios and chaplain to the Archbishop. This simple and kindly man had a keen curiosity about far-off lands and strange people. In Bernáldez' house Columbus was able to rest, feed up and recruit his health after the crowded and debilitating voyage home; and at the same time to tell the story of his Cuban voyage and describe the marvels of the New World. With Bernáldez the Admiral deposited his journals of the Second Voyage, and other documents which the curate put to good use in the *Historia de los Reyes Católicos* that he was compiling.

Strange and pathetic is this picture of the Admiral of the Ocean Sea, discoverer of the Indies and (as he thought) of Cathay, founder of the first European colony in the New World, living quietly and unobtrusively, garbed like a humble friar, and seldom venturing forth except to perform his religious duties. Probably he could no longer walk the crowded *sierpes* of Seville without being insulted by disillusioned seekers after wealth and glory. Much harm had been done to his cause by Fermín Zedo, a Sevillian goldsmith who had gone out in 1493 but had been sent home as punishment for insubordination. Zedo told everyone that the golden nuggets and artifacts sent home by the Admiral were mere alloys, that there was no virgin gold in Hispaniola; Bernáldez was surprised to learn that neither statement was true, and pleased to see for himself the splendid articles of beaten gold that the Admiral brought home.

In due course there arrived a gracious note from the Sovereigns dated July 12, expressing pleasure at their Admiral's safe arrival, and desiring that he would come to them as soon as he could do so without inconvenience, "since in what has passed you have had much hardship." Unfortunately the court was at Almazán on the upper Douro, a good hundred miles northeast of Madrid. The Sovereigns always seemed to be at the other end of Spain when Columbus particularly needed to see them. But by this time the Admiral was well rested, and he set forth from Seville with a cavalcade well planned to convince the populace that Hispaniola gold was the genuine article.

Bernáldez, who saw him off, describes for us the "properties." A brother of Caonabó who had been christened "Don Diego" by the curate of Los Palacios, and a young nephew of the cacique who had been house-trained but not yet converted, accompanied the Admiral. Cages of brightly colored parrots acted as advance publicity by their screams, and whenever the Admiral was about to enter a town, jewelry was unpacked from the saddlebags and displayed on the Indians. "Don Diego" wore around his neck a collar of gold links weighing 600 castellanos, "and this I saw and held in my hands," says Bernáldez. The curate of Los Palacios describes "many things such as were used by the Indians, crowns, masks, girdles, collars, and many woven articles of cotton, and in all of them the devil was represented in the shape of a monkey or owl's head, or other worse shapes; some carved in wood, some made of cloth of the same cotton, or of a precious stone. He brought some winged crowns with golden eyes on their sides, and especially a crown that they said belonged to the cacique Caonabó, which was very big and tall, with wings on its sides like a shield and golden eyes as large as silver cups weighing half a mark, each one placed there as if enameled in a very strange and ingenious manner, and the devil too was represented on that crown; and I believe that so he appeared to them, and that they were idolaters and regarded the devil as lord." Would that someone had preserved these priceless examples of Taino art, instead of melting them all down!

Columbus probably took the north road through Merida and Salamanca, and made a detour to Guadalupe, for the records of the monastery there record the baptizing of some of his Indians in 1496. At Valladolid he must have learned that the court was on its way to Burgos, and thither he hastened to see his two sons, pages to the Infante D. Juan. The King and Queen, who arrived a few days after, received the Admiral graciously, and were presented with the Indians and the plunder, including a considerable quantity of gold dust and some nuggets as big as pigeons' eggs. Ferdinand and Isabella were keenly interested in all that he told them, and appeared to be satisfied with his conduct, although a report of Juan Aguado (which Columbus probably brought with him under seal) ventilated all manner of discontents. So far as the Admiral could discern, the calumnies of the Catalan clique had not impaired his credit with the Sovereigns. But these had had their effect on the court, where he found many adversaries.

Columbus lost no time in presenting proposals for a Third Voyage. Eight ships he asked for; two to return immediately to Hispaniola with provisions, and six to discover a mainland which the king of Portugal believed to exist in the ocean south or southeast of the islands, and of whose existence he himself had picked up sundry hints from the Indians. The Sovereigns replied that all should be as he wished, but it was many months before Columbus could bring them to give definite orders to that effect; and two years elapsed between landing at Cadiz and embarking on the Third Voyage to America.

This procrastination was in marked contrast to the promptness and energy that enabled the Second Voyage, with thrice the number of ships, to begin only six months after the First was concluded. At that time the Enterprise of the Indies had been a marvelous novelty, promising all manner of wealth and advantages for Sovereigns and subjects alike. Now, as far as the average Spaniard was concerned, it was a discredited racket, in which nobody cared to participate unless forced or very well paid. The Sovereigns, although full of good will toward their Admiral, were deeply concerned in liquidating the French invasion of Italy, and consolidating their dynasty by a series of marriage alliances. Charles was out of Italy well before Columbus arrived, but the surrender of his Neapolitan garrison to Gonsalvo de Cordova did not take place until July 20, 1496, when the Admiral was at Seville. A small border war between French and Spaniards was also under way, on both sides of the Pyrenees. On October 7 died the Neapolitan prince whom Gonsalvo's army had restored; and his successor, fifth king of Naples in three years, was so weak a creature that Ferdinand decided on a change of policy. He would now win the kingdom of Naples for himself; and as a means to that end arranged a series of royal marriages. Within a year the Infante D. Juan, heir to Ferdinand and Isabella, married the Archduchess Margarita of Austria, whose brother the Archduke Philip of Hapsburg married Doña Juana, one of the Catholic Sovereigns' younger daughters; and their eldest daughter, Doña Isabel, married D. Manuel, king of Portugal. All this, and the Naples question, occupied the Sovereigns' attention, cost immense sums of money, and (what affected Columbus most) required plenty of ships. A fleet of one hundred and thirty vessels, splendidly equipped, escorted Doña Juana to Flanders for her marriage to the Emperor's son, and brought back his sister Margarita to marry the heir apparent of the Spanish thrones. Ironically enough it was Columbus's slight service in connection with this pompous cortege, his successful prediction of the date when the Hapsburg princess would arrive at Laredo, that gave him the necessary credit with the crown to obtain maritime equipment for discovering the South American continent.

Columbus was present (not clad in the brown Franciscan robe, we hope) at the wedding of D. Juan and Margarita at Burgos on April 3, 1497. On the twenty-third the Sovereigns issued the first definite orders on preparations for the Third Voyage. First as to Hispaniola: Columbus is to send or take out three hundred persons at the royal expense, and up to fifty more if he can persuade them to come at their own charge. The number and pay of each class of colonist are rigorously prescribed: forty squires, thirty mariners and twenty artisans at thirty maravedis a day; thirty gromets, twenty gold diggers and one hundred foot soldiers' and day laborers at twenty maravedis a day; fifty farmers and ten gardeners at six thousand maravedis a year. Twelve maravedis a day keep is allowed for everyone except thirty women (one to every ten men), who were granted neither pay nor maintenance, but were expected to work their passages. These ladies, if they actually sailed, were probably the first Christian women in the Spanish colonies.

The Admiral's original rights, titles and privileges were confirmed, with the important concession that he was relieved of bearing one-eighth cost of the provision fleets of the last three years, and should have one-eighth gross proceeds and one-tenth net profits in future years. On June 15, 1497, the Sovereigns recapitulate what he is expected to do, recommend that he buy an old ship to take out some of the provisions immediately, and that he engage priests to administer the holy sacraments and "convert the Indians native of the said Indies to our Holy Catholic Faith." Apparently that alleged "first object" had been overlooked. Endless regulations about taking out and allotting cows and mares, about the local government of Hispaniola and control of the gold diggings were issued. All owners and masters of vessels wanted by the Admiral must charter them to him at the going price. Finally, Bartholomew Columbus is appointed and commissioned Adelantado of the Indies, with all powers appertaining to other Adelantados of the realms; and the Admiral is authorized to allot planting lands to individuals in Hispaniola, the crown reserving all logwood, gold and other precious metals.

The most interesting of these provisions was an offer of free pardon to all criminals and malefactors confined in jail (excepting those condemned for heresy, *lèse-majesté*, first-degree murder, treason, arson, counterfeiting and sodomy), who will "go with the said Admiral to Hispaniola, and the islands and mainland of the Indies," and spend a year or two; the greater the crime, the longer the stay that was necessary to procure a full pardon on returning. How many took advantage of this is not known. Unlike the other decrees preparatory to the Third Voyage, this became in principle a basic law of Spanish colonial policy. It appears in a somewhat altered form in a printed compilation of Spanish laws in 1503.

The obvious reason for this order was the reluctance of Spaniards to emigrate after the first stories of easy money had been punctured; but it was not an attempt to make a penal colony of Hispaniola as has sometimes been alleged. The released jailbirds were as free as anybody once they came aboard ship, and free to return if they chose after a year or two. Every colonizing power in America resorted to the same policy at one time or another in order to people its possessions. If Columbus took any of these criminals in his fleet of discovery, they made good; for he had less trouble with his men on this voyage than on any other.

A total sum of 2,824,326 maravedis was appropriated by the Sovereigns for the expenses of the Third Voyage, and of this Columbus acknowledged having received 350,094 maravedis on February 17, 1498. These sums were transferred in part through the

Seville branch of the Genoese house of Centurione that had employed Columbus in his youth.

Evidently it was the Sovereigns' will and pleasure to organize on a permanent basis their overseas possession, and to further the work of discovery. But Columbus might go down to Seville with his saddlebags stuffed with royal cedulas, duly signed "Yo el Rey, Yo la Reina," countersigned by secretary of state and chancellor, and sealed with the privy seal. That got him neither ships nor men. Don Juan de Fonseca, now Bishop of Badajoz, had charge of all such matters, and Don Juan was not only cool toward further voyaging, but resourceful in delay and obstruction. He could do nothing without money, and money was just what the Sovereigns were short of, with all these expensive wars, marriages and diplomatic negotiations under way. They even had to borrow from the dowry of their daughter the queen of Portugal to meet some necessary expenses of the fleet, and the proceeds of a cargo of Indian slaves that Peralonso Niño brought home from Hispaniola late in 1496 were turned over to the Admiral. Oftentimes Columbus must have longed for a few thousand maravedis in hand rather than two million in the treasury with his name on them. He often had no money to pay his men or the ship chandlers; he bought a cargo of wheat at Genoa on credit and when it arrived there was no money to pay for it; to the Adelantado he wrote that he had never experienced such anxieties, obstacles and fatigues.

Good old *Niña* and *India* were the first to clear. Since her return from the Second Voyage, *Niña* had had quite an adventure. During the Admiral's protracted absence at court Captains Alonso Medel and Bartolomé Colín thought they might as well make a little money, the demand for merchant shipping was so great. Accordingly they chartered *Niña* for a voyage to Rome, and *India* for a voyage to Flanders. *India* made out all right; but *Niña* was captured by a corsair when leaving the port of Cagliari, and brought to an anchor at Cape Pula, Sardinia, where she was stripped of her arms, and her people taken aboard the pirate. At night Alonso Medel and three men of Puerto Santa María stole a boat, rowed back to *Niña*, cut her cables, made sail and escaped. Thence arose several claims and counter claims. Columbus, who owned a half interest in each caravel, discharged Colín and Medel; and when *India* and *Niña* sailed from Sanlúcar as a victualing fleet on January 23, 1498, they were commanded respectively by Juan Bermúdez and Pedro Francés, with Pedro Fernández Coronel as Captain General. They arrived in due course, and *Niña* was still at Santo Domingo in 1500.

The six other ships were only procured by Columbus's exercising his prerogative of impressing what he wanted, at the usual rates of charter. It took the most of four months after *Niña* and *India* had sailed to get the discovery fleet ready for sea at Seville. Nobody who has not been through it can realize what it means to prepare a sailing fleet for sea, even in these days of quick communications. Stores don't come when they should, the stevedores dump them down anywhere, so that beachcombers help themselves; things you need before getting under way are buried under tons of cargo; rigging is rove wrong, sails are bent on the wrong yards; the cook gets discouraged and quits; a horrible stench arises from no. 1 hatch and you discover that some of the sea stores are spoiled and leaking; at the last moment the water tanks are mysteriously empty, and it is Saturday afternoon and everything is closed; seamen disappear and are brought aboard drunk and dirty; sailing day comes and it looks as if you might possibly get off next winter; whole weeks of fine sailing weather are wasted in delays, and finally when everything is aboard one hell of a gale blows up the coast. We are not surprised that before Columbus's third fleet got off he came to blows with a ship chandler who had provoked him by repeatedly failing to perform his promises.

Of this voyage we have more than enough documents on the preparations, but very little on the ships and personnel. Three caravels, whose names we do not know, were destined to proceed directly to Hispaniola with men and supplies. These were commanded respectively by Alonso Sánchez de Carvajal, the seagoing mayor of Baeza, who had been a captain on the Second Voyage;

by Pedro de Harana, brother to the Admiral's mistress; and by Giovanni Antonio Colombo of Genoa. This last was our old friend Giannetto ("Johnny") Colombo, son of Columbus's uncle Antonio, who had been sent to Spain at the expense of his Genoese brothers to see what he could pick up. Johnny evidently earned the Admiral's confidence, as he and Carvajal were later entrusted with collecting his percentage of Hispaniola gold and selling it in Spain.

The three vessels which Columbus reserved for discovery included two caravels, the smaller and swifter nicknamed *El Correo*, "The Mail," and one of 70 tons burthen called *La Vaqueños*, which suggests something bovine; but Columbus informs us that her half owner was a certain widow of Palos, whose name perhaps was Vasques. Pedro de Terreros, who had been the Admiral's steward on the First Voyage, was one of the captains, and Hernán Pérez the other. Columbus himself commanded the flagship, whose name he never once mentions; he merely refers to her as *la nao* (the ship) because she was not a caravel like the others. Like his first *Santa María*, which she resembled in burthen and in rig, she measured 100 tons or somewhat over.

One thing more remained for Columbus to do before his departure: to make provision for his family. In accordance with a special license from the Sovereigns, he created a *mayorazgo* (majorat or entail) of his property and privileges on February 22, 1498, in favor of his elder son Don Diego; and in case Diego died before him, the following should inherit and in this order: son Ferdinand, brother Bartholomew and his eldest son, brother Diego and his eldest son. The heir should inherit the office of Admiral and the one-eighth gross profits on the revenue of the Indies to which the Admiral believed that he was perpetually entitled by the recent confirmation of privileges. Diego is to give his brother and uncles a certain percentage of the revenue during their lifetime, to allow a fund to accumulate at the Bank of St. George in Genoa for the purpose of relieving the citizens from taxes, and to maintain a house in Genoa where some member of the Colombo family may live honorably. Yet no provision is made for the support of Beatriz Enríquez de Harana, the mother of Ferdinand Columbus.

This document proves not only the Admiral's loyalty to his native city, but his interest and faith in the future of the colony that he had founded. His heir is ordered to erect a church in Hispaniola, dedicate it to Santa María de la Concepción, and attach thereto a chapel where Masses might be said for his soul, and a hospital "as well planned as may be like those in Castile and Italy." He must further "maintain and support in Hispaniola four good Masters of Sacred Theology," whose main object shall be to work for the conversion of the natives. Columbus's wishes as to the church were carried out by D. Diego the second admiral, and theology was taught at Santo Domingo even before the University of St. Thomas Aquinas was founded there in 1538. Unfortunately by that time there were no Indians left to convert.

Finally, in the last week of May, 1498, everybody and everything was aboard at Seville. The six caravels then worked the tides down the Guadalquivir, and came to an anchor for the last time in Spain off the castle of Sanlúcar de Barrameda, at the river's mouth. There the Admiral joined the fleet, and another great voyage of discovery began.

CHAPTER XXXVIII

Trinidad

May 30–July 31, 1498

*Et dominabitur a mari usque ad mare, et a flumine usque
ad terminos orbis terrarum.*

He shall have dominion also from sea to sea, and from
the river unto the ends of the earth.

PSALM lxxi 8

ON May 30, 1498, the Third Voyage began at the bar of Sanlúcar de Barrameda at the mouth of the Guadalquivir. As
usual Columbus knew exactly what he wished to do; whether he
could do it was another question. He had been impressed by an
opinion of the king of Portugal that a great continent lay athwart
the equator, somewhere out in the Western Ocean; that was why
D. João II insisted on the line of demarcation being moved westward. The Admiral's primary purpose on this voyage was to test
the truth of this royal surmise; if the continent should appear by
dead-reckoning (there was no other way of computing longitude)
to lie east of the line of demarcation, Ferdinand and Isabella were
bound to hand it over to their son-in-law and heir presumptive,
D. Manuel of Portugal. If not, the new continent would be another jewel in the crown of Castile.

A secondary object of the voyage was to discover lands lying
more southerly than the Antilles. For, according to Aristotle's
doctrine of similar products in the same latitude, these if opposite
the Portuguese possessions in Guinea should prove far more profitable than overrated Hispaniola. Jaime Ferrer of Blanes, a lapidary
who dabbled in cosmography, wrote to Columbus that "within
the equinoctial regions there are great and precious things, such

as gems and gold and spicery and drugs," that in his business of gem collector he had heard from "many Indians and Arabs and Ethiopians that the majority of precious things come from a very hot region where the inhabitants are black or tan; and therefore, in my judgment, where your worship finds such people there shall he find a plenty of such things . . . I say this, Sir, because the Queen our Lady commanded me to write your worship what is in my mind." Accordingly Columbus planned to drop down to the latitude of Sierra Leone, where the Portuguese had first found gold, and follow that parallel up to the meridian of Hispaniola, in the hope of striking something — new islands, D. João's continent, or a part of Asia — where the "big money" would be found.

Columbus even had good reason to fear that, unless something new and valuable were discovered shortly, the whole Enterprise of the Indies would be abandoned by his Sovereigns, and his friends in Hispaniola left to their fate. When we recall that, a century later, the same thing happened to Raleigh's first colony in Virginia, we can appreciate that the Admiral's fears were well founded. "Truly this man had a good and Christian purpose," reflected Las Casas, "was thoroughly content with his station in life, and wished to live modestly therein and to rest from the great hardships which he had undergone so meritoriously. . . . But he saw that his signal services were held of slight value, and that suddenly the reputation that these Indies at first had enjoyed was sinking and declining, by reason of those who had the ear of the Sovereigns, so that day by day he feared greater disfavors, and that the Sovereigns might abandon the enterprise altogether, and that he might thus see his labor and travail go for naught, and he in the end die in poverty." Columbus sometimes compared himself to David, who was commanded to perform incredible tasks for Saul, and performed them; yet at each success fell deeper and deeper into disfavor. Columbus had discovered "The Indies," but that was not enough; he must colonize them and produce gold in quantities. He then successfully led a great fleet to Hispaniola, organized the colony there, discovered the Lesser Antilles, Puerto Rico and Jamaica, and explored the southern coast of Cuba; but these were not enough. He must now discover something more spectacular, and produce more gold; yet even when the continent and the Pearl Coast were discovered, these did not prevent his being sent home in disgrace. A fourth voyage in search of a passage to India was still necessary. Never could he do enough to satisfy his Sovereigns.

At the beginning of this voyage the Admiral was in a poor physical and mental condition, for the many vexations and vicissitudes of the last two years had prevented a complete cure of the arthritis contracted off the coast of Cuba. Yet, well or ill, it was good to be at sea again, in command of a stout little fleet, and free from courtiers, officials and land sharks. Sharks of another kind, however, lay in wait for him. Castile was then at war with France, and a French fleet was said to be lying off Cape St. Vincent, waiting to despoil the Columbian flotilla. Accordingly he made a wide sweep to the southward, passing near the African coast, instead of taking the straight course to Porto Santo, his first objective.

The fleet picked up Porto Santo on the eighth day out, June 7, after a sail of at least 650 miles. There Columbus proposed to take on wood and water, complete his supplies, and hear Mass. As this was the island of which the Perestrellos, his father-in-law and brother-in-law, had successively been captains, and where his son was born, Columbus expected a kind reception. Unfortunately the inhabitants mistook his fleet for French corsairs, and took to the hills with their flocks and herds. Unable to do business when no people were about, he set sail the same night for Madeira. That large island is usually visible from Porto Santo, and Funchal is no more than a 40-mile sail; but the fleet seems to have run into a soft spot, since it was not until June 10 that it anchored in Funchal roads.

Here had been the Admiral's home in his early married life. He had not called there since becoming famous, but the hospitable Madeirans had not forgotten him. "In the town he was given a very fine reception, and much entertainment," says the abstract Journal, "for he was very well known there, having been a resident thereof for some time. He stayed there six days, completing his lading of water, wood and other things necessary for his voyage." It was a delight for the Admiral to be among friends of his youth once more, recalling the days when he had been a simple merchant's factor and supercargo, before ambition and responsibility began to trouble him. Here in Funchal there were no enemies or detractors, nobody who wanted to do him down or get something out of him; simply old friends and their friends who wished to give him a good time.

Yet, as every garden has its weeds, so Madeira contributed unwittingly to the Admiral's sorrow as to his joy. It was there that he took on as pilot of one of his ships a Sevillian named Pedro de Ledesma, who behaved well enough on this voyage, but on the Fourth became a mutineer, and in after years, suborned by the Pinzons, told lies about the Admiral at the inquests, and denied that he had discovered the mainland.

Departing from Funchal the fleet found moderate and favorable winds for the 290-mile run southward to Gomera in the Canaries. They anchored in the familiar roadstead of San Sebastián on the third day out, June 19, the evening of new moon. But the romance with Doña Beatriz was dead. All that Columbus writes of Gomera this voyage is, "We took on cheeses, of which there are many and good ones there."

Gomera was the logical point for the Hispaniola squadron to part with the three vessels bent on discovery. Exact instructions were issued to the departing captains, Harana, Carvajal and Colombo. Each in turn was ordered to take command of the fleet for a week, and to show a light abaft for the others to follow by night. The Admiral set their course W by S before the trades, and predicted that after sailing 850 leagues they would make Dominica, as he had done on the same course (with Flemish compasses) in 1493. From Dominica they were ordered to steer WNW to Puerto Rico, then cross the Mona Passage, leaving Mona Island on the starboard hand, and follow the south coast of Hispaniola for 25 leagues, to the new city of Santo Domingo.

Although the correct course from the Canaries to Dominica was W by S ½S, this fleet, according to Las Casas, made it all right; probably they too had Flemish compasses. The next course set by the Admiral, WNW from Dominica to Puerto Rico, should have taken them to the middle of the south coast of that island, but the pilots managed to get lost somewhere between the Lesser Antilles and Hispaniola. They missed Santo Domingo altogether, and fetched up on Hispaniola so far to leeward, in the Province of Xaragua, that they got mixed up with Roldán's rebellion; and only after much beating to windward and many vicissitudes arrived at Santo Domingo after the Admiral.

Before the fleet split at Gomera they had a little excitement. Two French corsairs and two of their Spanish prizes were anchored at San Sebastián when the Admiral approached. The Frenchmen and one of their prizes slipped cables and made off, and when the captive Castilians saw one of Columbus's ships bearing down on them they were emboldened to overcome the French prize crew and recapture their own vessel.

Two days were enough for San Sebastián. After taking on a few more casks of water and filling all vacant spaces with firewood and Gomera cheeses, the flagship, *Vaqueños* and *Correo* departed for the Cape Verde Islands on June 21. The Hispaniola fleet accompanied them as far as Ferro, where the Admiral dismissed them "in the name of the Holy Trinity," whose special protection he invoked every day for this, his third great adventure.

From Ferro the Admiral set his course for the Cape Verdes, and on this leg of the voyage made excellent time; about 750 miles in six days, an average of better than 5 knots. Columbus seems never to have touched at the Cape Verdes in his earlier African voyages, for he expresses surprise at finding them dry and sterile, not verdant. Passing the island of Sal on June 27 without calling, the fleet proceeded another 22 miles to Boavista, and anchored in a bay nigh to an *ysleta chiquita*. This little island enables us to verify the bay as Porto Sal Rei or English Road, which is the best anchorage at Boavista. Before he had time to go ashore, the Admiral received a visit of courtesy from D. Rodrigo Afonso, the Portuguese captain of the island, who was given *refresco de Castilla* (probably liquid), which made him very merry, as well as generous. Unfortunately the island afforded nothing but wild goats, turtles and lepers. For some thirty years wealthy and distinguished lepers, of which there were no small number in fifteenth-century Europe, had been coming to Boavista and São Tiago to cure their foul disease, the cure being effected — so they imagined — by living on turtle meat and bathing in turtles' blood. The other inhabitants of Boavista were six or seven Portuguese, whose business was to kill goats and salt their pelts for export. The Admiral ordered his men to salt down for ship's stores some of the goat's flesh that the natives threw away. The result doubtless afforded Columbus's seamen a new and legitimate subject for grumbling, since salted goat mutton is one of the world's worst meats.

A very brief stay at Boavista satisfied the Admiral's curiosity. He set sail in the night of Saturday, June 30, as usual avoiding a Sunday departure, and anchored the next day off Ribeira Grande on the island of São Tiago, as the church bells were tolling for vespers. His object was to obtain a deckload of the wild black cattle of São Tiago, which would supposedly do well in Hispaniola; but the cattle appear to have been scarce or skittish since he could obtain none. That was a lucky break for the cattle, as they would undoubtedly have served only to feed the sharks in the doldrums. At São Tiago there was a considerable settlement of Portuguese and their African subjects. Some of the principal inhabitants told Columbus of a mysterious island that appeared southwesterly of Fogo, and which D. João II had planned to discover, and toward which canoes filled with merchandise from the west coast of Africa had been seen to navigate. This recalled the tales of the mythical St. Brendan's Isle that the Admiral had heard at Gomera on his First Voyage, and a similar crop of tales that circulated in the Azores.

Off São Tiago the fleet remained eight days, at the end of which, because the heat was so intense, the dust haze from the Sahara so suffocating and thick "that it seemed they could cut it with a knife," and the people falling sick, the Admiral decided to sail without any cattle. To this day the official *East Atlantic Pilot* warns mariners "sometimes the haze is so thick" about the Cape Verde Islands "that the surf is seen before any land can be recognized."

On July 4, 1498, the day after full moon, the fleet finally took off for the Indies. Columbus set a southwesterly course, in order, as he said, to prove the theory of D. João II "who said that there was a mainland to the south." The wind was so light that for three days Fogo, the high volcanic island 30 miles west of São Tiago, was clearly visible, emitting smoke and looking like a great church with its campanile. Departure was not taken until July 4 or 5. A moderate trade wind sprang up on July 7, and the fleet slowly made its way to the southward. These were not the first ships whose keels had plowed those waters. Almost a year before Vasco da Gama with his fleet of four vessels had taken his departure from "that isle which takes its name from the warrior saint, . . . to cross the lake immense of salty ocean," and by the time Columbus set forth, his great Portuguese rival had already completed the sea route to India.

Columbus's plan, as he explains at this point in his Journal, was to sail southwest until "he should be on a parallel with the lands of Sierra Leone and Cape St. Ann in Guinea, which is below the equator," since in south latitude "are found more gold and things of value." Having reached that parallel, he intended to sail due west to the meridian of Hispaniola, and then, if he had not yet struck land, to the south, to prove whether or not D. João II was right; and finally back north to Hispaniola. And that is just about what he did.

For eight days the fleet rolled along slowly before a soft summer trade wind, which grew more and more faint, and finally flattened out on an ominous date, Friday the thirteenth, when the Admiral's dead-reckoning showed a total distance run of 120 leagues, or 381 nautical miles. This course and distance from Fogo, diminished by the Admiral's normal overrun of 9 per cent, but

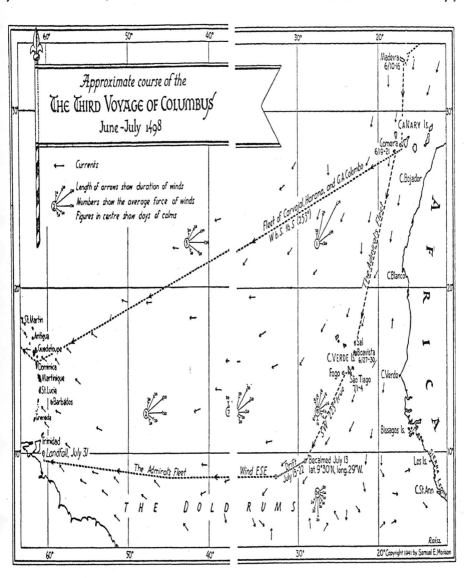

Approximate course of the

The Third Voyage of Columbus
June ~ July 1498

← Currents

Length of arrows show duration of winds
Numbers show the average force of winds
Figures in centre show days of calms

increased by 80 miles for the favoring equatorial current, would have brought the fleet to an approximate position of latitude 9° 30′ N, longitude 29° W on July 13.

This position, as the modern pilot chart of the North Atlantic for July shows, was well within the doldrums, the belt of calms and variables that extend from the southern limit of the northeast trades to the northern limit of the southwest monsoon and the southeast trades. It was, in fact, about the hottest and calmest spot on the entire ocean at that season. And the Admiral needed no pilot chart to tell him so. "The wind stopped so suddenly and unexpectedly and the supervening heat was so excessive and immoderate," he says, "that there was no one who dared go below to look

after the casks of wine and water, which burst, snapping the hoops of the pipes; the wheat burned like fire; the bacon and salted meat roasted and putrefied. This heat lasted eight days." Fortunately only the first day was sunny, the other seven were overcast with showers, "or many people must have perished."

There is no reason to suppose that the Admiral's account of his sufferings was overdrawn, but the impression he gives of heat in the doldrums is greatly exaggerated. Thousands of sailing vessels have passed through these waters, and been becalmed without experiencing any tremendous heat. I have noticed in many instances the sensitiveness of early European navigators to heat, and wonder whether it was not due to their wearing too much woolen clothing. Seamen never stripped down and acquired a tan in those days. Of course the doldrums were uncomfortable, and one of the greatest boons that mechanical propulsion has conferred on mariners is the power to get out of the soft spots on the ocean, instead of waiting around whistling and praying for a wind.

The Admiral profited by the first clear day in this depressing calm to break out the old wooden quadrant and make some celestial observations, the most detailed of his that have come down to us. At nightfall, he says, when the Guards of the Little Dipper stood at the "Head" position,* the altitude of the North Star was 6°. Six hours later, after midnight, the Guards passed "Left Arm" and Polaris stood 11° above the horizon. And at dawn, when the Guards had swung below the horizon, the North Star was elevated 16.°

From these observations the Admiral drew certain conclusions, one of which was correct, and the other fantastically wrong. What he should have done is to have thrown out the dawn observation. If the proper corrections (respectively +3° and −2°) had been applied to the altitudes of Polaris (6° and 11°) at the "Head" and "Left Arm" positions, the resulting latitude would have been 9° N. And that, as we have seen, is only 30′ south of where we have placed him by dead-reckoning; and it is quite possible that our

* See Chapter XII above, and diagram.

interpretation of his dead-reckoning is wrong, and his observation right. Columbus, however, did not know the proper corrections to apply, and deduced a latitude of 5° N, which he supposed to be that of Sierra Leone. Thirteen years before, he had been much impressed by a report that Mestre José Vizinho made to the king of Portugal in his or Bartholomew's presence, that the latitude of the Los Islands off Sierra Leone (really 9° 30′) was 5° and a few minutes north of the equator. Columbus's dead-reckoning told him that he was on the parallel of the Los Islands, and he cannot have been more than half a degree on either side of it. But his respect for Vizinho, the astronomer who sat on the Portuguese commission that turned down his project in 1485, was so great that he fudged his Polaris observations in order to make them agree with that of the learned Jew! Actually, at 9° to 10° N, he was at the lowest latitude in which Polaris can be observed with anything approaching accuracy; at 5° he could not have seen her with the naked eye. Mestre José's observation had been a solar one, which required declination tables to work out; and the use of tables was beyond the Admiral's mathematical competence.

On July 22, 1498, after eight days of calm and enervating heat, "at the lengthe an Eastsoutheaste wynde arose, and gave a prosperous blaste to his sayles." In a few minutes the whole scene and feeling and atmosphere changed. At one moment the three vessels were rolling in an oily swell, headed every which way, sails furled to prevent chafe, the people sick and bored, and no activity on deck save an occasional thrust with a sweep to prevent collision, with an accompaniment of oaths and ill-tempered insults. Some sharp-eyed lad espies a dark line on the eastern horizon. Can it be wind? The line widens into a belt — by San Fernando, it *is* wind! An "Irish pennant" high in the rigging is seen actually to flutter. Then, what a shaking-up of sleepers, what a joyous rush to cast off gaskets, heave-a-ho on halyards, brace yards and handle sheets to swing the ships on their new course set by the Admiral, *Oueste! Oueste!* which is gayly shouted to and fro between flagship and caravels. Now all miseries are forgotten as the ocean puts on her whitecaps again, the fresh cool trade wind bellies out the sails, and the vessels forge bravely ahead, each with a bone in her teeth. The Admiral, his orders executed, falls on his knees in the after cabin, ecstatically thanking the Holy, Blessed and Glorious Trinity for giving fresh impetus to this, his most important voyage. And well he might thank God, for the trades had struck in where they had no business to be at that season of the year.

During the week's calm the fleet had been idle, yet moving; the equatorial current carried it slowly southwesterly at a rate of 10 to 40 miles a day, so that Columbus was near latitude 8° 30′ when he took a fresh departure. A westerly course from that point — approximately latitude 8° 30′ N, longitude 32° to 33° W — would have carried the vessels quickly through the lines of 2° and 1° easterly variation to the zone of no variation; consequently the true course can have differed little from 270°. After reaching longitude 45° W, the equatorial current would have begun setting the fleet northwesterly, and consequently in a few days have brought it up to latitude 9° 30′, the parallel near which it was certainly sailing when the course was altered on July 31.

Columbus was in luck again, for the modern pilot chart shows that the SE trades in July do not commonly blow north of latitude 5° to 6° N in those longitudes, or the NE trades dip below 9° 30′ N, anywhere. The distance that his fleet made — roughly 1650 miles in nine days, an average speed of 6.8 knots — proves that the wind "gave a prosperous blaste to his sayles" the rest of the passage. Evidently the SE trades pushed considerably further north that year than he had a right to expect.

As he sailed along, the Admiral repeatedly made night observations of the pole star. He reported to the Sovereigns that at nightfall, the Guards being in the "Head" position, Polaris stood 5° above the horizon; at midnight, 10°, and at dawn, 15°. "In this matter of the North Star I felt great wonder," he says, "and accordingly for many nights with much care I repeated the observations of her with the quadrant; and I always found the thread and plummet fell to the same point." One read the altitude on these primitive quadrants from the point on the arc cut by a silk thread kept taut by a plumb-bob.* Allowing for an additional error because these observations were made from a live ship instead of as before in a flat calm, the evening and midnight altitudes were about as accurate as those of July 13-14, pointing to a latitude of 8° N. The correct latitude was probably between 8° 30′ and 9° N. But again, the dawn observation is curiously inaccurate.

This leg of the voyage must have been almost pure delight to the Admiral and his men; we know that as we followed the same route in our *Capitana*. The fleet sped along, making an average day's run of 183 miles. In the trades vessels always roll a good deal, but the steady and favorable wind singing in the rigging, the sapphire white-capped sea, the rush of great waters alongside, and the endless succession of fat, puffy trade-wind clouds, lift up the seaman's spirits and make him want to shout and sing. The old-time Spanish mariners called these broad waters *El Golfo de las Damas*, The Ladies' Sea, so easy is the navigation. As Von Humboldt wrote, "Nothing equals the beauty and mildness of the climate of the equinoctial region on the ocean." Occasionally a black rainsquall makes up from windward, but passes harmlessly with a brief lash of rain, and a slight change of wind. For days on end the sheets and braces need no attention. Flying fish and dorados play about the ship, and the pelagic birds, petrels and the like, pay brief visits. On moonless nights the sails stand out black against the star-studded firmament; and as the ship makes her southing, every night new stars and constellations appear — Canopus, Capricorn, Argo with her False Cross and the true Crux Australis. Columbus had already seen the Southern Cross in winter from Hispaniola; but most of his men were new to southern waters; and one can imagine them, as in Heredia's sonnet, leaning entranced over the bulwarks of the white caravels, and seeing in the phosphorescent sea an augury of the gold of the Indies.

Columbus seems to have had eyes for no star but the elusive Polaris; fortunately for himself and for us, he never allowed his

---

* See picture of a quadrant in Chapter XIII, above.

faulty observations of her position to interfere with sound practical navigation. As the days elapsed, and the good speed that the vessels made put them further and further from Spain, the spirit of the seamen changed, they became alarmed at the thought of the immense distance from home, and (as Pedro de Terreros remembered) urged the Admiral to return; never would he find land that way. "And when the Admiral asked the pilots for the position, some said they were in the sea of Spain and others in the sea of Scotland" — a grim sort of marine irony that still endures. "And all the seamen were in despair and said, 'what devil brought them with the Admiral?' and they were lost." But they were not lost. On Tuesday, July 31, nine days after the revived trade wind filled his sails, Columbus correctly estimated that the fleet lay almost due south of the Caribbee islands. As his supply of fresh water was growing scant, owing to the waste of it in the doldrums, he decided to steer for Dominica "or some of the *Canibales*," and fill the casks, before pursuing his search for the continent predicted by D. João II. So on the morning of the last day of July he ordered the course altered to *Norte quarta del nordeste*, North and by East.

At noon, " 'as His Divine Majesty ever useth mercy toward me, a seaman from Huelva my servant, named Alonso Pérez, climbed to the crow's nest and saw land to the westward, distant 15 leagues, and it appeared to be in the form of three rocks or mountains.' These are his words," says Las Casas. "He named this land *la ysla de la Trinidad* because he had determined that the first land he should discover should be so named." The fact that three hills were sighted after that vow seemed to him a miracle of the Triune God, for his especial benefit. "He gave infinite thanks to God, as is his custom, and all the people glorified the divine bounty, and with great joy and merriment they repeated, singing, the *Salve Regina*, with other devout canticles and prayers which glorify God and Our Lady, according to the custom of mariners, at least our mariners of Spain who are wont to say them in time of rejoicing as in time of tribulation."

The circumstances of this lucky or miraculous landfall are

such that one can fix the position whence the Three Hills were sighted within a mile or two. Columbus's belief in a miracle on this occasion was well justified, for if Alonso Pérez had not happened to go aloft at noon, Trinidad would have been missed, the fleet's course would have taken it further from Trinidad. It might have fallen afoul of the dangerous off-lying Darien Rock in the night, or, had it weathered that obstacle, sighted Tobago the following day, or even made its landfall on Barbados.

We in our *Capitana* approached the same corner of Trinidad on an overcast morning, with a light trade wind on our starboard quarter. As soon as we entered the triangle that I have plotted on the appended chart, Bob Armstrong in the cross-trees gave the "Land ho!" It was Trinity Hills bearing NW ¾ W, just as they had appeared to Alonso Pérez. A rainsquall promptly blotted them out; but by the time we had proceeded to a point near the northern apex of the triangle, the clouds lifted and we all sighted the triune hills looking like a distant mountain with three summits. No other land was then visible.

"Having seen the land, to the great cheer of all," reads Las Casas's abstract of the Journal, the Admiral altered his course again, "and headed toward the land which he had sighted, toward a cape which appeared to the westward, and which he called *Cabo de la Galera* from a great rock which it had, which from a distance looked like a galley under sail." About ten minutes after our second sight of the Three Hills we too picked up this Cape now called Galeota Point, and the resemblance of it to a many-masted galley under sail was striking. In addition to the bright-peaked cliffs which resemble lateen sails, there are diagonal marks on the rocks that look like a bank of oars. Columbus then noticed the eastern coast of Trinidad stretching out as far as the eye could reach. His fleet arrived off the Galley Cape "at the hour of compline," about 9 P.M. The moon was so bright that he ventured to look in at the mouth of Guayaguayare Bay, just inside the Galley Cape, and to heave the lead; but found it shoaling so rapidly that he decided to jog along westward all night. Sufficient for that day to have discovered a new island, and in so miraculous a manner.

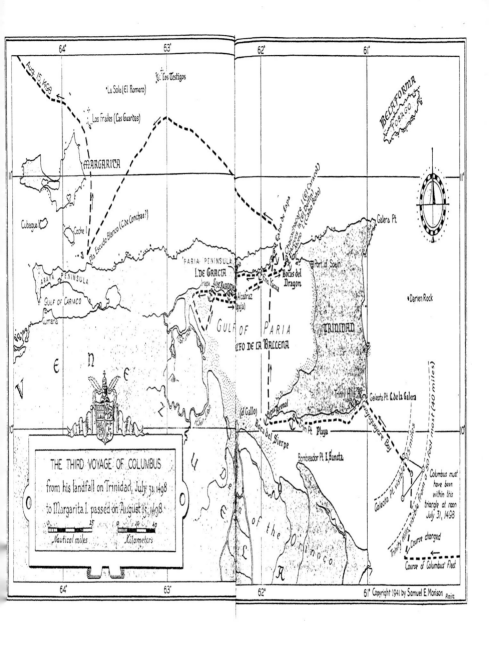

THE THIRD VOYAGE OF COLUMBUS
from his landfall on Trinidad, July 31, 1498
to Margarita I. passed on August 15, 1498

Nautical miles

Kilometers

Copyright 1941 by Samuel E. Morison

CHAPTER XXXIX

Paria

August 1–11, 1498

Viderunt insule et timuerunt; extrema terre obstupuerunt,
appropinquauerunt, et accesserunt.

The isles saw it, and feared; the ends of the earth were
afraid, drew near, and came.

— ISAIAH xli 5

COLUMBUS'S immediate object was to obtain water, only
one full cask being left aboard the flagship. So on Wednesday, August 1, he sailed some 15 miles along a coast "very pleasant
with trees down to the sea." "These lands are so fair," reported
Columbus, "and so verdant and full of trees and palms that they
are superior to the gardens of Valencia in May." Any land would
have looked good to him after a four weeks' ocean passage; yet
the south coast of Trinidad is indeed fair, though lacking the
picturesqueness of other Caribbean shores that are loftier. The
West Indian cedar, the red fustic or logwood, the acurel and the
moussara, common trees along that coast then as now, make a
splendid leafy coverage, and in places the palmiste or cabbage
palm thrusts its long trunks above the rest. Even today there are
so few signs of human habitation visible from the sea that one can
easily play discoverer when sailing along. But it makes a vast difference to know what is coming; and we wondered whether Columbus felt more apprehensive of the dangers ahead, knowing
nothing, than we did after consulting the rather alarming sailing
directions for the swift tideway that he named Boca de la Sierpe.

The Admiral was searching for a river, or a bay that looked as if
a river emptied into it. With his usual good judgment in these mat-

ters he chose the best watering place on the south coast of Trinidad. Behind Punta de la Playa, as he called the present Erin Point, lies Erin bay with several streams emptying into it, and good anchorage off a yellow sand beach. There the people went ashore "with great merriment," and filled their water-breakers at a pretty stream that crossed the beach. After their many days' short allowance of stale, lukewarm cask water, it was a wonderful refreshment for the men to drink their fill of fresh, sweet water, to wash the caked salt and sweat from their bodies, to wallow in a clear, cool river and scrape their backs on the pebbles, to wash their clouts and splash one another and shout and yell. Signs of people they saw none; footprints in the sand they thought to be of goats, but these must have been of the island deer. They examined the skeleton of an animal which, having no horns, they guessed to be that of a monkey; and very likely it was.

Just before rounding Erin Point, Columbus caught his first sight of the American mainland, probably the first sight of the continent vouchsafed to any European; but he failed to recognize it as mainland. The day was August 1, 1498, and the place sighted was Punta Bombeador of Venezuela, part of the alluvial land in the Orinoco delta. It looked like an island, and Columbus supposed it was one, and called it *Ysla Sancta*, Holy Isle. The distance from Erin Point is a scant 10 miles, and it looked no more than 15 at most to us; but Columbus made the extraordinary overestimate that it was 20 or 25 leagues away.

There seems to be something about Trinidad atmosphere which caused early navigators and geographers to make these gross overestimates of distance. Columbus, in his entry for August 2, declares that the length of the south coast of Trinidad is 35 leagues. If he meant his "land league" of about 1½ nautical miles, he was not far wrong, for the correct distance is 17½ sea leagues. Las Casas apologized for his hero's supposed underestimate and tacked on another 10 leagues; and Las Casas meant sea leagues. It was not until the late eighteenth century that Trinidad is depicted on any map with some approach to accuracy.

Venezuela and Trinidad approach each other like the claws of two fighting crabs, the space between them being the Gulf of Paria, into which the Rio Grande and the northern branches of the Orinoco empty themselves, commingling with the tides to make dangerous currents in the Bocas. The northern egress, with four channels, is still called Bocas del Dragón or the Dragon's Mouths; the southern and more dangerous one, with four separate channels separated by reefs, is called Boca de la Sierpe, or Serpent's Mouth. Columbus so named them.

As the Punta de la Playa afforded poor protection from the east wind, the Admiral weighed anchor the next day, August 2, sailed around Punta del Arenal (which he so named), around Icacos Point and into the Gulf of Paria, which for no apparent reason he called *Golfo de la Ballena* (of the Whale). Evidently he sailed through the Boca de la Sierpe at a time of slack water, since he then made no remark on the current; but he noted the high, barren Soldado Rock about five miles away in mid-Boca, and named it *El Gallo* (the Cock). It looks not unlike a rooster that has lost its head. On the north side of Icacos Point, the southwestern cape of Trinidad, the fleet anchored.

Columbus promptly ordered the people ashore to enjoy themselves, since, he says, they had become very wearied and fatigued by their long and trying voyage. Such entertainment as they had was furnished by the Indians. As the fleet lay at anchor a large canoe approached, containing about twenty-five young men. Columbus, having carefully followed the parallel of Sierra Leone, expected to encounter either Negroes or orientals, and was obviously disturbed to find that these were of the same race as the Caribs. Las Casas here allows himself a little fun at the expense of the Admiral: "I do not believe they wore much silk or brocade, with which I dare say the Spaniards and the Admiral would have been better pleased." One can well imagine the bitter disappointment of Columbus, all set for greeting sable potentates or servants of the Grand Khan. He took some consolation, however, from the fact that these handsome youths wore not only the usual loincloth, but a gay woven cotton bandanna on their heads. These, he said, resembled the *almaizar* worn by Moorish women in Spain — an oriental hint — and almost duplicated the native cotton kerchiefs that the Portuguese imported from Guinea and Sierra Leone. Aristotle's parallel-products idea was beginning to work out; if bandanna-wearing boys, why not gold and spices?

There was usually something comic as well as pathetic in Columbus's first contacts with natives. On this occasion, the Indian dugout ceased paddling at a safe distance from the ship, and the Indians began to halloo. Hoping to attract them, the Admiral caused "some brass *vacinetas* (chamber pots) and other shining things" to be temptingly displayed over the bulwarks, "with coaxing gestures and signs." The Indians approached a little nearer, but apparently had no use for chamber pots. The Admiral then put on a show for their benefit, causing a pipe-and-tabor player to perform, and the gromets to dance. Unfortunately the Indians took this demonstration to be a war dance, and let fly a shower of arrows. Quick curtain! Having made this gesture of defiance, the Indians were satisfied, since their canoe came right under the bows of *Vaqueños*, whose pilot, a bold fellow, jumped aboard bearing gifts; the Indians had nothing to offer in return but made signs that the Spaniards could have anything they liked ashore. Las Casas says that one of the ship's boys told him that the cacique made a visit to the flagship, wearing a golden diadem. He approached Columbus, who was wearing a scarlet cap, and made an exchange of headgear, which apparently pleased him and certainly profited the Admiral. It seems likely, however, that this incident took place later, on the other side of the gulf, where much friendlier relations were established with the Indians. Except for the one canoeful, which left them shortly and never returned, the Spaniards saw no natives along Trinidad; a great disappointment to seamen who were looking forward to sporting with the girls.

August 2 was the night of full moon. For two days the men played about Icacos Point fishing, gathering oysters, and catching "parrots as large as chickens." Only brackish water could be obtained from wells in the sand, but that did not matter as a good supply of sweet water had been secured at Punta de la Playa. In clear weather they could see thirty-five miles to the northward across the Gulf of Paria, the jagged Cerro Mejillones on the Venezuelan promontory, which runs out eastward from the mainland. Columbus believed this to be another island, and named it *Ysla de Gracia.* That, he decided, would be his next objective.

In the meantime, the Admiral was watching the currents in the Boca de la Sierpe with wonder, and no little apprehension. At slack water he sent out the ship's boat to take soundings, and found a least depth of 6 to 7 fathoms, which agrees with the modern chart. A current constantly set northward through the Boca, slacking at turn of tide, accelerating in full flood and ebb, roaring like the rote of surf, and "with as much fury as that of the Guadalquivir in flood." The rise and fall of tide were greater than he remembered anywhere in the West Indies; it reminded him of the range of tides at Sanlúcar de Barrameda, whose careening beach resembled the one off which he now lay. Clearly there could be no sailing back through this *angostura;* but within the Gulf, outside his anchorage, the water shoaled rapidly. So the only course was the bold one, to press on and pray God to afford another egress.

On August 4, just after the fleet had weighed anchors and begun to fill away on a northerly course, the Admiral and his men had one of the greatest scares of their lives. Here is his vivid description of it to the Sovereigns, written within three months of the occurrence: —

Standing on the ship's deck, I heard a terrible roaring which came from the southward toward the ship. And I stood by to watch, and I saw the sea lifting from west to east in the shape of a swell as high as the ship, and yet it came toward me little by little, and it was topped by a crest of white water which came roaring along with a very great noise, . . . and which sounded to me like the rote of surf on rocky ledges, so that even today I feel that fear in my body lest the ship be swamped when she came beneath it.

This great wave passed safely under the flagship, raising her as it seemed to an immense height and then dropping her down near the bottom. The only damage done was snapping *Vaqueños's* cable, she having been slow to weigh anchor. Naturally the Admiral made all haste to sail out into the gulf.

All writers who have noted this phenomenon have followed Las Casas in assuming that it was a tidal bore caused by the conflict of the Orinoco with the ocean tides, such as occurs at the mouths of several European rivers. But persons who have constantly navigated the Boca de la Sierpe, as well as a gentleman who lived for many years on Ícacos Point, have informed me that no tidal bores ever occur there. In October and November, when Orinoco floods coincide with spring tides, the currents are swift and treacherous, sometimes creating a wave that breaks with a great noise right over Wolf Rock; but Columbus visited the Boca in August. So it is certain that the wave which threatened him must have been caused by a volcanic disturbance. There are a number of little "mud volcanoes" boiling and steaming alongshore near the fleet's anchorage; and in Erin Bay, where they took on water, a mud islet has been thrown up at least twice in the present century; on such occasions there arises a wave that does considerable damage alongshore. Extraordinary waves like this occasionally occur in mid-ocean and on all the world's coasts. Columbus's description is not in the least exaggerated compared with hundreds of unaccountable waves of recent record.

Naturally the Admiral made haste to leave the Boca de la Sierpe, as he then named this treacherous channel; and the Serpent's Mouth it still is. Time has dealt more gently with his place names of the Third Voyage than with those of the other three.

After this terrifying experience the fleet had a peaceful sail across the Gulf of Paria toward the mountains sighted to the northward, and anchored in the evening of August 4 at a harbor which I believe to be the modern Bahía Celeste, near the extremity of the mainland. The tip of the Paria Peninsula Columbus called *Cabo de Lapa*, Barnacle Cape. The Bocas del Dragón, as he named them a

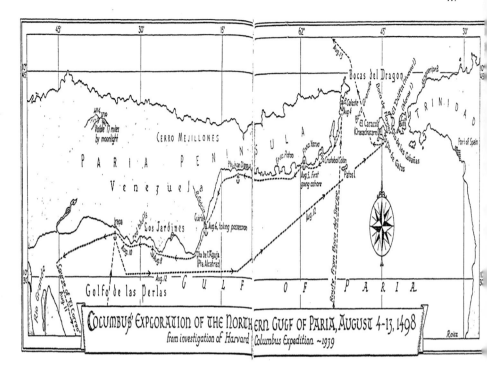

COLUMBUS' EXPLORATION OF THE NORTHERN GULF OF PARIA, AUGUST 4-13, 1498
from investigation of Harvard Columbus Expedition ~1939

few days later, are four in number, formed by three islands placed like giant steppingstones between Trinidad and the mainland. From the course that he sailed, Columbus could not see the easternmost and narrowest channel, the Boca de Monos; he believed Monos Island to be a part of Trinidad, and named it *Cabo Boto* (Cape Blunt) from the shape of its conspicuous headland. The next island (now Huevos) he named *El Delfín*, and when seen from the westward it is very like a dolphin fish or dorado, with a large head looking down the Gulf. The largest island, which now bears the formidable name Chacachacare, he called *El Caracol* (the Snail), probably because of its intricate outline.

Both at his last anchorage and at this one on the Bocas, the Admiral "took the North" with his quadrant, and obtained wrong latitudes as usual. "In that southern *boca*," he wrote to the Sovereigns, "which I called *de la Sierpe*, I found at nightfall that the North Star rose about 5°, and in that other northern one, which

I called *del Dragón*, she was about 7°." Hence, he concludes, the distance between them was 26 leagues, "And I cannot have made an error, because they were measured with a quadrant." This is an interesting example of Columbus's obstinate clinging to his erroneous belief that 56 2/3 Roman miles was the length of a degree, a 25 per cent underestimate which was necessary to prove that he had reached the Indies. According to these faulty observations he had sailed almost 2° due north, consequently he had covered a little less than 28 leagues. Actually the distance from anchorage to anchorage was about 37.5 nautical miles, a little less than 12 of Columbus's leagues! His eye estimate of 15 had been nearer the truth. Nor is this half the error. He still wrongly assumed that a twilight altitude of Polaris was equivalent to the latitude. Actually, he should have added about 3° to his nightfall observations, at that season, and should have reported the latitudes of the two Bocas as 8° and 10° respectively. Even then he would have been wrong, for the latitude of his anchorage near the Boca de la Sierpe was about 10° 05′, and the latitude of his northern anchorage was 10° 42′.5 (if we have correctly identified it as Bahía Celeste), and certainly not less than 10° 40′. Consequently there was a 2° error in the one observation, and a 0.7° error in the other. In sum, the Admiral made three separate and distinct sets of errors in this calculation which he so confidently reported to the Sovereigns as infallible!

As he entered Bahía Celeste near sundown on August 4, the Admiral had a gorgeous view. South of him lay the placid Gulf of Paria, with most of its shores out of sight, suggesting that he was in an archipelago, not a landlocked gulf. Westward stretched an endless succession of mountains and rugged headlands, which he resolved to coast along the following day in search of another channel out to sea. Eastward were the broken, picturesque islands of the Bocas del Dragón, Chacachacare, Huevos, and Monos, covered with the manchineel, the silk cotton, the butterwood, the Christmas Hope, and other tropical trees. Behind the islands, range after range, rose the mountains of Trinidad. Either that evening or the next morning, Columbus "saw an island of very high land to the NE, which might be 26 leagues from there, and named it *Belaforma.*" This island must have been Tobago, whose highest point, 1910 feet above sea level, is about 70 miles ENE of that point. I was told at Trinidad that nobody had ever sighted Tobago from the Bocas, and one writer has even demonstrated its impossibility by triangulation. Yet when we in *Capitana* were sailing out of the Boca de Navíos in the late afternoon of December 21, 1939, a sharp-eyed boy sighted Tobago from the topsail yard, bearing about NE by E, and subsequently two men saw it from the deck. We were then, to be sure, some 6 or 7 miles nearer Tobago than Columbus was at the Bahía Celeste, but we are satisfied that *Belaforma* was no mirage or other figment of the Admiral's imagination.

Sailing south and west from Bahía Celeste on Sunday, August 5, Columbus passed "a number of very good harbors, the one next the other," anchored in one "5 leagues" distant, and sent the boats ashore.

This harbor was the first place on the American continent where it can be positively stated that Europeans landed. I believe it to have been Ensenada Yacua, a little round cove where a sand beach stretches a white riband between two rocky headlands, covered with gray-green bushes and small trees. Behind the beach, a short valley through which runs a small stream slopes up to the Cerro Mejillones, a mountain screen between the Gulf of Paria and the Caribbean. The first going-ashore place may have been one of the *ensenadas* further west — Guinimita, Ucarito or Patao, all within 5 miles; my choice of Yacua is, I confess, based on intangibles; the beauty of this little harbor, the deep water almost up to the beach, lures one to come in and anchor.

In this, their first mainland harbor, the Spaniards "found fish and fire and signs of people and a great house"; fruits such as grapes, myrobalans, and "some like apples and others like oranges with the inside like figs." One recognizes from this decription the *uvero de playa* or sea grape, from which successive generations of Span-iards have unsuccessfully attempted to make good wine; the *hubo* or hog plum which Columbus was always mistaking for oriental myrobalans, and the guava, or perhaps the water lemon. The moun-tains were "covered with monkeys"; and monkeys obligingly chattered in the trees for us on December 19, 1939, as we lay at anchor off Yacua beach and tried to conjure up that momentous going-ashore on August 5, 1498. If the Indians had then stayed about instead of fleeing to the bush, they would have seen a formal taking-possession; but Columbus seldom put that show on without native witnesses; consequently it was postponed to the first port where the Indians would be trusting enough to furnish an audi-ence.

Since there was no reason to tarry, and wind came fair, the fleet weighed around noon and proceeded westward. "From here," says the abstract Journal, "he proceeded 8 leagues, where he found good harbors. This part of this Isle of Gracia is said to be very high land, and has many valleys, and 'all should be inhabited,' says he, because he saw it all cultivated." His description of this Paria Peninsula is exact. Between Yacua and the end of the mountains which he passed next day are at least six coves and harbors, each with its tiny valley and stream running down from the promontory's mountainous backbone. Other than a few ill-tended banana plantations and coconut groves at the heads of harbors, there is no cultivation today, and no roads. Undoubtedly the population is much less than in 1498; the contrast with the activity, enterprise and intense cultivation on the Trinidad side of the Gulf gives some point to Columbus's belief that right here the East begins.

That night his fleet probably anchored off shore (he could find good holding ground anywhere) somewhere near Punta San Diego; for the next day, writes Columbus, "I ran along this coast up to the end of the sierra." As one sails along that coast, the mountains appear to come to an abrupt end where the shore line makes an obtuse angle, on longitude 62° 15′; "and there," continues Columbus, "I anchored in a river; and many people came out, and told me that they called this land *Paria*." The first river beyond the mountains where the fleet could have anchored was the Rio Guiria, the mouth of which is about 8 miles alongshore from Punta San Diego. I have no doubt that their anchorage and place of taking-possession was the present Guiria roads, where a sizable river, now barred at the mouth, but probably navigable for a short distance in 1498, empties into the gulf. It is the only place of any activity today on this coast, a roadstead where oil tankers from the San Juan River complete loading from pipe lines.

Hardly had the fleet anchored inside the Rio Guiria on August 6 when a small canoe put out, containing three or four Indians. The bold pilot of *Correo* hailed them in order to be put ashore, but managed to capsize the little dugout in jumping aboard. He then captured some of the crew swimming — an amazing feat for a Spaniard — and brought them to the Admiral.

Details of the taking-possession are found in records of the inquest held by Don Diego Colón at Santo Domingo in 1512 and at Seville in 1513. The second admiral hoped thereby to kill the rumor that Hojeda or Vespucci or someone other than his father had discovered the mainland. Besides numerous persons who had "heard say" this or that, at least eight men who had been with the Admiral on the Third Voyage were examined, and of these only Pedro de Ledesma denied that Columbus had discovered the mainland. Hernán Pérez, captain of one of the caravels, and forty-one years old at the time, declared that he was the first to go ashore at the place of taking-possession, and that afterwards "the Admiral with about 50 men landed on the said country of Paria and took a sword in one hand and a banner in the other, saying that in the name of their Highnesses he took possession of the said province." All the others who testified denied that Columbus himself went ashore. Andrés del Corral, an eighteen-year-old page of the Admiral on this voyage, said that his master stayed aboard because of sore eyes; this checks with Columbus's complaint in his Letter to the Sovereigns, that his eyes were so inflamed from lack of sleep that he was almost blind. According to Andrés, it was Captain Pedro de Terreros who took possession for the Admiral; Hernando, another page-boy, added that they raised a great cross.

Columbus thus describes the natives of this place: "They are the color of all the others in the Indies; some of them wear their hair very long, others like us, but none have it cut as in Spain and the other lands. They are of very fair stature, and all well grown. They wear their genital member tied and covered, and the women all go naked as their mothers bore them." At this point Las Casas, who could not bear the thought of having missed something, interposes: "This is what the Admiral says; but I have been within 30 leagues of this land, and I never saw women who did not have at least their genitals covered; the Admiral must have meant to say that they went as their mothers bore them as to the rest of their bodies." But what is a breechclout among friends? The women were doubtless kind, and the mariners duly grateful.

Columbus says that he presented the first natives who came aboard with hawks' bells, beads and sugar, after which everybody wished to visit, and the vessels were soon surrounded by an "infinite number of canoes." The Indians, armed with bows and poisoned arrows, offered the Spaniards fruits of the country, and calabashes of *chicha,* a fermented drink made from maize, which is still a national beverage in Venezuela. They wore suspended around their necks polished disks of gold, which the Admiral thought were mirrors, and were ready to swop them for brass, "changey-changey" as seamen say, because the copper odor in the brass was agreeable to them. Here Columbus first saw in quantities the native alloy of copper and gold that the natives called *guanin,* and which modern archeologists call *tumbaga.* Guanin was an alloy of gold, silver and copper, the gold content varying in different objects from 9 to 89 per cent, and the copper from 11 to 74. The nose rings and disks, bird, frog and alligator pendants that the Spaniards called "eagles," and little tinkly bells and many other objects, were made of guanin by native artificers, and given either a gilt or a bronzelike finish. The objects containing a high proportion of gold were indistinguishable from pure gold, and naturally pleased the Spaniards most; but the natives had a different set of values. The advantage of guanin lay in the fact that when copper and gold are combined, if the proportion of copper is not less than 14 or more than 40 per cent, the melting point is lowered from an average of 1073° centigrade, that of pure gold, to 200°. Copper, which they obtained only by way of trade with Central America, was far more valuable to them than gold. Their custom, which Las Casas thought so odd, of sniffing every bit of metal offered to them, was simply an effort to detect the much-wanted copper in the Christians' hardware.

This discovery of guanin showed that Columbus had touched upon a new Indian culture area, of which he was to see more on his Fourth Voyage; the area stretching from the Guianas to Honduras, where the Indians were experts at cotton weaving and in metallurgy. Another sign of higher culture was the appearance of big freighting canoes with a cabin amidships.

Apart from their readiness to trade, and supply other elemental needs of the Spaniards, the natives of Paria could not make themselves understood. So the Admiral resorted to his usual method of kidnaping a few in order that they might learn Castilian and serve as interpreters. This is the occasion of one of Las Casas's most severe reflections on his hero. "It appears that the Admiral did this unscrupulously, as did he many other times on his First Voyage, it not appearing to him that it was an offense to God and his neighbor, to take free men against their will, separating fathers from sons and wives from husbands, . . . a mortal sin of which the Admiral was the efficient cause; and there was the further circumstance that they came out to the ships under tacit security and promised faith which should have been kept."

At Guiria the fleet spent two nights. On August 8 the Admiral "made sail toward a point that he called *del Aguja*" (of the Needle). This was the modern Punta Alcatraz or Guaraguara, which is about 4 miles from the Guiria anchorage. As one approaches it from the eastward, it has the appearance of a long sail needle, tapering down to a fine point. Thence he sighted "another island 15 leagues to the southward, very big, which ran SE–NW, and very high, and called it *Sabeta*, and in the evening he saw another to the westward, very high land." There is no high island or mainland to the southward of this part of Paria, and I cannot imagine what Sabeta was; but the high land to the westward was a part of the same coast, which as one sails along juts out as though it were a separate island.

When one passes Punta Alcatraz the whole character of the coast changes. It becomes a rich lowland, covered with big glossy-leaved tropical trees such as fustic and mahogany; Columbus was so impressed that he called this region *Los Jardines*, and it certainly is far more gardenlike than the Jardín de la Reina off Cuba. He anchored near a considerable Indian village, where the people were most friendly. Many of them wore neckpieces of gold as big as horseshoes which they offered for hawks' bells, but Columbus says that he refused to do business. This self-denial arouses the astonishment of Las Casas, who opines that the real obstacle to barter was the Admiral's suspiçion that this jewelry was composed of guanin;

but even a guanin horseshoe, one would suppose, was worth a few brass hawks' bells. There was real excitement among the Spaniards when women came aboard wearing necklaces of seeds interspersed with fine pearls, both round and baroque, which (they conveyed by signs) were gathered from the Caribbean side of Paria. These famous pearl fisheries between Margarita and the mainland were first exploited by Hojeda in 1499. Columbus ordered pearls to be collected against his return, when he expected to obtain whole bushels of them for a few trading goods.

At Los Jardines the natives were so gentle that a boat's crew readily accepted an invitation from two principal men of the village. The wondering seamen were conducted to a large house, built "not round like a tent as are those of the islands," and furnished with plenty of seats for guests and hosts; the men sat at one end and the women at the other. There they were tendered a savage banquet of bread and various fruits and *chicha* both white and red, and when this feast was consumed another like it was served at a second house, which apparently belonged to the son of host number one. Spaniards and Indians were unable to understand one another, but the language of gastronomy is universal, and the visitors returned to their ships replete and happy. Columbus reported that the natives here were lighter in color than at Trinidad, that the sea water was fresh, and the temperature so cool that morning and evening he felt the need of a lined gown. Las Casas, who spent several years on the Pearl Coast, remarked that even a fur collar was not unwelcome. Northern sojourners in the tropics quickly become sensible to slight changes of temperature which they would not have noticed at home.

As the Admiral still believed that he was coasting along an island, he ordered anchors aweigh on August 10, and sailed 5 leagues westward in search of a channel out to sea. More islands opened up to the west and south. In the Journal there are so many new names that Las Casas becomes impatient, saying it is apparent by the way the Admiral throws meaningless names about that he is a foreigner, unfamiliar with the niceties of the Castilian language. The shores here were lined by mangroves with tiny oysters on their roots; Columbus observed their shells to be open, supposedly to catch from the mangrove leaves the dewdrops that engendered pearls, as Pliny wrote in his *Natural History*. The waters of the gulf were shoaling rapidly, and had become fresh and muddy as the Guadalquivir; but the Admiral, who had made up his mind that the Paria Promontory was an island, still refused to believe that the fresh water came from a river; he expected any moment to find a channel out to sea. Anchoring the flagship and *Vaqueños* in a small horseshoe-shaped harbor because the ship could not navigate safely in less than 6 feet, he sent *El Correo* to reconnoiter on August 11. She returned that evening, reporting four river channels to the westward — the mouths of the Rio Grande.

Columbus was not yet ready to believe that Paria was a part of a continent, yet he did not dare to spend more time exploring the gulf. So, in order to get out to sea, the fleet had to return to the Bocas del Dragón. It irked the Admiral very much to change his course; he wished thoroughly to explore the entire Gulf of Paria and find out where the fresh water came from; but he suspected that the Adelantado would be needing his presence and wanting his supplies in Hispaniola.

At this point Columbus enters in his Journal one of those self-justifying *apologias* mingled with prophecy which became more common as he grew older; but this one happens to be remarkably farsighted. In spite of all his enemies, he has done more for the Sovereigns than any subject ever did for his prince, and at far less price in men and money than the Portuguese had paid for their sovereignty over Guinea. He has laid the foundation for a vast crown revenue. "And your Highnesses will win these lands, which are an Other World (*que son otro mundo*), and where Christianity will have so much enjoyment, and our faith in time so great an increase. All this I say with very honest intent, and because I desire that your Highnesses may be the greatest lords in the world, lords of it all I say; and that all be with much service to and satisfaction of the Holy Trinity."

Marvelous prophecy, superb faith! At a time when not fifty people of importance in Spain believed in Columbus or valued his discoveries, when the court doubtless hoped that shipwreck or other disaster would rid them forever of this importunate Genoese, when his name was a curse on the lips of the Spaniards in Hispaniola, he foresaw the vast revenue that his Sovereigns were about to secure. He foretold that Christianity, whose area had been shrinking since the rise of Islam, would here win new converts to the Cross, that the Catholic faith was destined to advance triumphantly into *Otro Mundo*, this Other and New World.

CHAPTER XL

Terrestrial Paradise

August 11–31, 1498

Plantaverat auten dominus Deus Paradisum voluptatis a principio.

And the Lord God planted a garden eastward in Eden.

GENESIS ii 8

HAVING made his decision, Columbus wasted no time in execution. A soft night breeze was blowing from the west, so at the rising of the moon on August 11, when it had just turned last quarter, he weighed anchor from the little horseshoe harbor near the northwest corner of the Gulf of Paria, made sail and steered eastward for the Bocas. Fortunately the land breeze held fair, and with a favoring current he made 50 miles by nightfall Sunday, August 12, anchoring "in a very good harbor which he called Puerto de Gatos (Monkey Harbor), which is next to the boca where are the two islands of Caracol and Delfín, between Cabo de Lapa and Cabo Boto. . . . He anchored near the said harbor, in order to go out by the boca in the morning. He found another harbor near there, and to view it he sent the ship's boat. It was very good. They found some fishermen's huts and much fresh water. He named it *El Puerto de las Cabañas* (Harbor of the Cabins)."

"Monkey harbor," in the outer part of which he anchored, was undoubtedly Chacachacare Bay on the island of that name, which Columbus called *El Caracol*. The port of the fishermen's cabins must have been one of the little bays on Huevos Island, "El Delfín."

In the small hours of the morning of Monday, August 13, at the rising of the moon, the fleet weighed and stood around Diamond

Rock into the Boca Grande, westernmost of the Bocas del Dragón, which Columbus correctly estimated to be a league and a half wide. By the hour of tierce, around 8 or 9 A.M., they were in mid-channel. The previous week they had sailed along the western edge of this Boca Grande in one of its rare calm moods. But on August 13 they found the usual turmoil between the fresh water flowing out and the salt tide seeking to get in, with such roaring tide-rips that "they thought to perish, no less than in the other Boca de la Sierpe." These Bocas are very dangerous bodies of water, even to steamers. There is usually an undercurrent running counter to the surface, and full of big logs that play havoc with small vessels. A ship can even remain stationary by dropping her anchor into the undercurrent, which is strong enough to tow her, as it were, through the surface current; and it was by some such means that Columbus's fleet was saved.

When the wind died on them, they tried to anchor, but could find no bottom (no wonder, as the depth is around 120 fathoms), and the surface current was setting toward the rocks. "It pleased the goodness of God to conduct them out of the same peril to safety and deliverance, for the fresh water prevailing over the salt, imperceptibly carried the ships out, and thus they were placed in safety; because when God wills that one or many be saved, water is the medicine." It was after this deliverance, Las Casas heard tell, that Columbus named the channel *Boca del Dragón* because they had escaped, as it were, from a dragon's mouth.

On going out to sea Columbus "saw to the north an island that might be 26 leagues from the Boca, and named it *Isla de la Asunción;* he saw another which he called *La Concepción.*" Next day was the vigil of the Assumption of the Virgin; the Admiral, whose adoration so far this voyage had been concentrated on the Trinity, evidently thought this was the proper occasion to honor Our Lady. Las Casas continues: ". . . And three small islands together he called *Los Testigos,* and these are so called today; another near them he called *El Romero;* other little islands he named *Las Guardias.*

Afterwards he arrived near the island *Margarita*, and so called it; and to another near it he gave the name *Martinet*."

We can only identify these islands by assuming that Asunción and Concepción were sighted as the fleet left the Boca del Dragón, and the others were seen in succession as they sailed westward along the coast. Asunción is obviously Grenada. Situated 70 miles (22 leagues) north of the Boca, and rising 2750 feet above sea level, Grenada cannot usually be sighted more than 60 miles away, but atmospheric conditions were probably exceptional on August 13, as on the fourth when Columbus saw Tobago from about the same place. Los Testigos (The Witnesses), as they are still called, are 70 miles NW of Boca Grande; their highest hill is only 600 feet above sea level, and Columbus cannot possibly have sighted them until the next day. La Concepción, I imagine, was only a cloud. El Romero (The Pilgrim) was probably the solitary islet now called *La Sola*. Las Guardias (The Sentinels or Watches) are obviously the group of islets now called *Los Frailes* near Margarita. Margarita we shall come to shortly; El Martinet (The Martlet) is identified by Las Casas as the island now called *Blanca* or *Blanquilla*, northwest of Margarita.

As soon as the fleet was well out of the Bocas del Dragón, Columbus set the course to the westward along the Paria Peninsula. He still considered it an island, and expected to discover from the north that channel to the gulf which *Correo* had been unable to locate on August 11. It was beginning to dawn on him that he had been sailing along the mainland right along; but he still could not believe that the great volume of fresh water he had observed came from rivers (as *Correo's* seamen insisted), "because neither the Ganges nor the Euphrates nor the Nile so far as he had heard carried so much fresh water." But the real reason for this incredulity, as Las Casas sagely remarked, was that Columbus had not seen lands sufficiently extensive, in his opinion, to give rise to such streams. Never in his life had the Admiral seen the mouth of one of the world's great rivers. He did not realize that they always flow to the sea between alluvial lowlands, which sink below the horizon as seen from the deck of a ship.

It had been his intention to keep close inshore, but he had lost so much sleep during the past month, and his eyes were so bloodshot, that he turned in that night, and the pilots cautiously edged off shore. Ferdinand says, "The Admiral then sailing to the westward along the coast of Paria continually tended off shore to the northwestward, because the calm and currents set him in that direction, so that on Wednesday, August 15, he left the cape which he called *de Conchas* to the south, and Margarita to the west. . . . He held on his course by six little islands which he called *Las Guardias*." Las Casas adds that he named four capes on the Paria Peninsula, the "Cape of Shells" being one of them. It was clear to us, as we followed Columbus's course through these scintillating waters of the Caribbean, where the trade wind holds its strength but the protection of islands to windward breaks the ocean swells, that Columbus was well off shore by the time he reached longitude 63° W. Otherwise he could never have seen Los Testigos. Moreover, it is only from at least 10 miles off this coast that it gives the appearance of having capes; for only from a distance do the mountains stand out and the lowlands between sink below the horizon. When day dawned on August 15, 1498, the mainland, Margarita and Los Frailes were all visible, and between the last two the fleet passed out to sea, bound for Hispaniola.

That decision was unfortunate, for Columbus was on the edge of the pearl fisheries behind Margarita, where Peralonso Niño secured a valuable cargo in 1500, and whence Spain drew vast wealth for a century or more. It is strange that he did not spare a day or two for exploration, since the natives of Los Jardines in the Gulf had indicated that this coast was the source of pearls. "I omitted to prove this," he admitted in his Letter to the Sovereigns, "because of the provisions and the soreness of my eyes, and because a great ship that I had was not suitable." All good seamanlike reasons for pressing on; but politics demanded pearls. A bushel or two of pearls sent home to the Sovereigns would have spoken louder than all the Admiral's description, far more authoritatively than his imaginary discovery of the terrestrial paradise. Pearls to the Queen would have stopped the mouths of his enemies at home and in Hispaniola. As it was, when the pearl fisheries were discovered by Hojeda, Columbus was falsely accused of having held back the information for his personal profit. It seems to have been his fate on each of his four voyages to have just missed something of vast importance, and to have been judged not by his great achievements, but by what he missed or did not do.

Just before leaving the coast for Hispaniola the Admiral became "conscious," says Las Casas, "that so great a land was not an island, but a continent." His dead-reckoning told him that he had passed along the outer coast more than twice the depth of the Gulf of Paria. No channel to it had appeared; the conclusion was inescapable. "And, as if speaking to the Sovereigns," says Las Casas, he makes this entry in his Journal for August 14 or 15: —

"I believe that this is a very great continent, which until today has been unknown. And reason aids me greatly because of that so great river and fresh-water sea, and next the saying of Esdras in his 4th book chapter 6, which says that the six parts of the world are of dry land, and one of water." Carib captives from Guadeloupe, St. Croix and Puerto Rico had told him that terra firma lay to the southward. "And if this be a continent," he concludes, "it is a marvellous thing, and will be so among all the wise, since so great a river flows that it makes a fresh-water sea of 48 leagues."

How typical is this passage of the workings of Columbus's mind! For two weeks he had been sailing along the very continent that he sought, and whose existence the king of Portugal suspected; but that part of South America, with its alluvial lowlands stretching away infinitely, failed to meet his mental specifications of how a continent should appear. And this, despite the evidence of fresh water from the mighty Orinoco and the Rios Grande and San Juan flowing daily under his keels. Suddenly he decides that the "Isla de Gracia" must be a continent; and at once verses from Esdras, vague gestures of Caribs and odd scraps of medieval learning fly together in his mind to prove it. In this mode of reasoning Columbus was a true child of his age. Roger Bacon had quoted Esdras to prove the "continental" theory of the distribution of land and water; but so, in 1505, did the great Portuguese navigator Duarte Pacheco Pereira, who had already made the Cape passage to India.

The conviction that he had found a new continent, an *Otro Mundo* or "Other World" unknown to the ancients or to Marco Polo, did not in the least alter the Admiral's conviction that he was in the East Indies. Nothing ever did. His brave new world lay south or southeast of the Chinese Province of Mangi (which he believed Cuba to be) and possibly was connected with it, as may be seen on the sketch map made by his brother in 1506, where *Serici Montes* (Chinese Mountains) rise up behind the coastline of Honduras. In 1498, however, Columbus believed that his Otro Mundo was insular; otherwise, how could Marco Polo have sailed from China to the Indian Ocean? And the special object of his Fourth Voyage was to find the strait through which Marco Polo sailed, which should lead directly to the Spice Islands.

Having made up his mind that this was indeed the long-sought continent, Columbus was all excitement to explore it further; and if he had done so, little would have been left for Hojeda and Vespucci to discover in 1499. But duty called the Admiral to Hispaniola. The supplies he was bringing to the colonists there were being spoiled and spent; his brother the Adelantado probably had need of his presence and authority — as indeed he had; the seamen were fagged out and grumbling; only one caravel of his fleet, *El Correo*, was small enough for coastwise discoveries; his eyes were inflamed from loss of sleep, and he sorely needed rest. And so, within sight of Margarita and the Pearl Coast on August 15, Columbus changed his course to the north of west, dropped the new-found continent astern, and passed between Margarita and Los Frailes in the direction of Hispaniola.

Margarita was so named by Columbus, says his son Ferdinand, as if inspired by God, because near it was the islet of Cubagua, center of the later pearl fisheries; and *margarita* is a Spanish word

for pearl. But Columbus as yet knew naught of the Cubagua pearl
fisheries. Undoubtedly he named the island after the Infanta Margarita of Austria, concerning whose voyage from Flanders to Spain
he had offered some navigational advice to Ferdinand and Isabella.
Princess Margaret was a gallant little lady and a wit. In her infancy
she had been betrothed to Charles VIII of France, who jilted her
in favor of Anne of Brittany; at the age of seventeen she was af-
fianced to D. Juan, Prince of the Asturias. In the course of her
voyage from Flanders to Spain in order to marry him, a violent
storm arose, in the midst of which Margaret composed an epitaph
for herself: —

> *Ci gist Margot la gentil demoiselle*
> *Qu'a deux maris et encore est pucelle.*
>
> Here lies Margot that proper young girl
> Who with husbands twain has preserved her pearl.

Margarita Island is worthy of its namesake — fertile and beautiful, with mountains at each end rising two and three thousand
feet from the sea, and lowlands between. Unfortunately the
Venezuelan government guards it with a jealousy worthy of its
royal namesake, and innocent yachtsmen who anchor there are
apt, on one pretext or another, to find themselves in the local calaboose. Columbus's course spared us that danger in 1939; as he did
not call, neither did we.

On August 15, the day that the fleet passed out to sea, it completed a good day's run. During the next twenty-four hours it
"sailed to the NW by N 26 leagues with the sea smooth, 'thanks
be to God,' as he always said." Some of our armchair navigators
are inclined to poke fun at this pious ejaculation with which Columbus always greeted a smooth sea, and to conclude that he was
"no sailor" in the modern use of that phrase; that he suffered from
seasickness. But I have never yet seen a deep-water sailor who does
not prefer smooth sea to rough. Not that motion makes them
squalmish, but that rough water is hard on gear, makes footing and
cooking difficult, and sends anything not properly lashed down

rolling into the scuppers. Smooth water is always something to be thankful for on a sailing vessel, provided it is not accompanied by light airs.

On August 16 Columbus records one of his rare observations of compass variation. The compass needles, which hitherto, he said, had not varied perceptibly from true North (as tested by Polaris or by the sun's shadow at the meridian), on the night of August 15–16 suddenly were seen to vary a point and a half to the westward, and some needles varied two points. "He also found," says Las Casas, "in the place where he now was, that the North Star rose 14° when the Guards had passed the 'head' two hours and a half." At that date the Guards were two and a half hours past the "Head" position at 6.30 P.M., a little early to observe them, especially for one suffering from ophthalmia; but let us assume that their reported position was correct. In order to translate that Polaris altitude into latitude Columbus should have added 1°, making 15° north. At nightfall August 16, according to my plotting of their course, the fleet was near latitude 13° north. Columbus's maximum error was certainly not more than 2°, and may have been less.

Since leaving the mainland Columbus had been cogitating about his Polaris observations on the ocean crossing, about the freshwater currents of the Gulf of Paria, the vegetation he had encountered there and the comparatively mild temperature for a place so near the equator. He had been wondering just how this Otro Mundo fitted in with world geography. He was not one to put two and two together to make four; rather, in the Admiral's way of reasoning, two and two made ten. Accordingly on August 17, when the fleet made 37 leagues in a smooth sea ("infinite thanks be to our Lord God!"), he confided to his Journal an astonishing deduction. "He says that not finding any islands now assures him that that land whence he came is a great continent where is located the Terrestrial Paradise, 'because all men say that it's at the end of the Orient, and that's where we are,' says he."

So Columbus had been skirting the Garden of Eden! The more

he thought over this hypothesis, the better he liked it, and in his Letter to the Sovereigns, written two months later at Santo Domingo, he elaborated on the reasons that convinced him. His favorite book, D'Ailly's *Imago Mundi*, placed the Terrestrial Paradise at the first point of the Far East, where the sun rose on the day of creation; and Columbus believed that Trinidad was on the meridian of Eastern Asia. According to the best authorities, the Garden of Eden lay just below the equator; and Columbus, as he thought, had touched 5° north latitude in the Serpent's Mouth. The Garden of Eden had a temperate climate; and the fleet had encountered no hot weather since escaping from the doldrums. In Eden grew every good plant and pleasant fruit; and had he not found strange but delicious fruits on the shores of Paria? "The gold of that land is good," and had he not found the natives wearing golden ornaments? "And a river went out of Eden to water the garden; and from thence it was parted, and became four" (Genesis ii 10); had not his men in *Correo* reported four rivers at the head of the gulf? The four rivers of Paradise, surely; the Nile, Euphrates, Tigris and Ganges.

On the ocean crossing, and when becalmed in the Doldrums, Columbus had been puzzled (as are we) by finding elevations of Polaris with his quadrant that varied ten degrees on the same latitude. Hence he concluded that the polar distance of the North Star — the radius of the circle that it describes around the celestial pole — was five degrees. But on his earlier voyages he had found it to be only half that. So Columbus jumped from a comparison of his two inaccurate sets of Polaris observations to the amazing conclusion that the earth was not round after all, but "in the shape of a pear," or, like a round ball "on one part of which is placed something like a woman's breast." This breast reached nearer Heaven than the rest of the world, and on the nipple the Terrestrial Paradise was located. The Admiral thought he had been sailing over the edge of this cosmic breast from the Doldrums to Trinidad, and the Pole Star's orbit seemed bigger because he was so much nearer Heaven.

It would be highly interesting to know what the Sovereigns thought of this hypothesis. There is no indication that even the pious Isabella was impressed with the notion that the Garden of Eden had been annexed to her empire; and Hojeda, when he set forth to explore Paria in 1499, was only interested in gold and pearls. Las Casas did not accept the Admiral's theory, but he pronounced it "neither absurd nor unreasonable." For, in addition to the Polaris observations — of whose accuracy Las Casas was unable to judge — the Admiral "experienced such freshness in the land, such green and pleasant trees, such mildness and amenity of soft airs, so great and so impetuous a confluence of sweet streams of water, and in addition, the goodness, generosity, simplicity and mansuetude of the people; so what else could he judge or conclude, save that there or thereabouts divine providence had placed the Terrestrial Paradise, and that this place so sweet was the source of the river and fountain of Paradise, whence the four rivers Euphrates, Ganges, Tigris and Nile had their origin?" Even the sophisticated Vespucci wrote of South America: "and surely in my opinion, if there be any earthly Paradyse in the worlde, it can not be farre from these regions of the south, where the heaven is so beneficiall and the elementes so temperate that they are neither bitten with coulde in winter, nor molested with heate in summer." Nor can I feel a modern scientific scorn at the Admiral's engrafting a beautiful literary myth onto his empirical observations. For Trinidad "the land of the humming-bird," and the Gulf of Paria in winter, are indeed a delight to the senses, and a satisfaction to the craving that all northern people have for lands of warmth, beauty, perfume and relaxation. If, as Vespucci said, there be a terrestrial paradise, it should lie somewhere on those shores bathed by the Carib Sea.

Even while indulging in these paradisiacal conceits the Admiral was not neglecting practical navigation. It is a striking testimony to the dualism in his nature that in the very same week of August 1498, when he was working up a fantastic cosmographical hypothesis, he should have been successfully concluding one of the finest bits of dead-reckoning in his maritime career — the navigation from Margarita to Hispaniola.

Taking his departure from Margarita on August 15, Columbus set the course NW by N for Hispaniola. That rhumb, if no currents or other factors had deflected the fleet, would have taken it to Saona Island, off the coast of Hispaniola, 25 leagues to windward (as Columbus had correctly informed Pedro de Harana) of Santo Domingo, the new island capital. Consider for a moment what infinite pains had been taken and what a careful reckoning had been kept to arrive at that NW by N course. Columbus was approaching Hispaniola by a new angle, from a newly discovered continent. He had left Isabela in March 1496, and had never visited the site of Santo Domingo. On the Third Voyage he had already sailed from Spain to Madeira and the Canaries and the Cape Verdes, southwest into the doldrums and west to the Boca de la Sierpe, and after circumnavigating the Gulf of Paria, along the Spanish Main to Margarita. Remember that since the Cape Verdes he had had no opportunity to check his position by any known land, all had been new, and his information placed the Cape Verdes 5° too far south. Yet all this time he had kept such accurate dead-reckoning that he knew the correct course for Hispaniola. Truly, as Jean Charcot said, this man *avait le sens marin*. He had that mysterious knowledge, partly intuitive, partly based on accumulated observation and experience, which has enabled so many unlettered mariners in days of sail to "smell their way" safely around the seven seas.

Making Santo Domingo was not to be so simple as setting a course NW by N. The trade wind, which seldom varies more than one point either side of east in August, served admirably. But there were currents to be reckoned with, and Columbus had no means of knowing their strength or direction. And as it was now in the dark of the moon, he wisely decided "to jog off-and-on every night, for fear of running afoul of islands or reefs." For aught he knew, islands might have been as thickly sown on this course as between Trinidad and the Virgins. This gave the fleet a sailing day of about fifteen hours. Nightfall August 15 found it at about latitude 12° N, longitude 65° W, 25 miles west of Blanquilla. It was that night, when jogging, that Columbus observed the compass variation of about a point and a half. This meant that he had been steering NW ½ W (310° true) instead of NW by N as the compass card said. Consequently, when he set sail at daybreak on the sixteenth, he must have altered his course a point and a half to the northward in order to make good NW by N true. Sailing on that course an average of 100 miles daily during three fifteen-hour days, with the equatorial current giving an average westerly set of 15 miles, and drifting an average of 25 miles westward every night, brought Columbus before nightfall on August 19 within sight of land. He recognized the landfall as an island he had passed on his Second Voyage in 1494, and then named after Saint Catherine; he now called it *Madama Beata*, after a more eminent virgin. Beata Island it still is.

On the morning of the twentieth the fleet closed with the land, and came to an anchor between Beata Island and "another smaller one next it with a steep little mountain which from afar looks like a sail, and he called it *Alto Velo*." Alta Vela, as we now call it, is one of the prominent landmarks of that coast.

One notes with amusement that Columbus's first reaction to this highly creditable landfall was extreme annoyance at fetching up 100 miles to leeward of Santo Domingo, instead of 75 miles to windward, as he had planned. *Pesóle de haber tanto decaýdo,* "it weighed on him to have fallen off so much," reports Las Casas; but the Admiral decided that his miscalculation was caused by "the currents, which are here very strong, setting toward terra firma and the West." He was absolutely right.

As soon as the fleet had anchored in the shelter of Beata Island, the flagship's boat was sent ashore to procure Indians as messengers to the Adelantado at Santo Domingo. An Indian came aboard carrying a crossbow, complete with cord, bolt and rack. A bad sign; for how did he obtain that lethal weapon? Had the tragedy of Navidad been repeated on a greater scale? But next day there was a joyful meeting. From Santo Domingo the three caravels from which Columbus had parted at Ferro had been sighted passing to leeward. Bartholomew, thinking his brother was aboard, set sail in pursuit; he missed them, but on August 21 encountered the Admiral at Beata. There was plenty of bad news to be told, but for the time being these two affectionate brothers felt only joy at finding each other alive, after a separation of two years and five months.

Las Casas informs us that he had known ships to take eight months to sail the hundred miles from Beata to Santo Domingo, beating against trade wind and currents, and lying in port awaiting a good chance. Columbus's fleet and the Adelantado's caravel were lucky. They left Beata August 22 and anchored in the Ozama River, the port of Santo Domingo, on the thirty-first.

One more voyage had been brilliantly carried through. A new continent, a new people and a pearl fishery had been discovered. No ship had been lost, no fights with the Indians had occurred. An Other World had been secured for Castile. Columbus had unlocked the door to a new home for the Spanish race and culture, a vast territory extending from California and New Mexico on the north to the Straits of Magellan. He had made it possible for the Catholic Faith to conquer a new world, for Christianity to enter on its first era of expansion in a thousand years. Yet this Discoverer returned to the country upon which he had conferred this immeasurable benefit as a prisoner, confined to his cabin and loaded with chains.

CHAPTER XLI

Terrestrial Inferno

1498–1500

Dominus Deus meus et refugium meum in die malorum.

O Lord, my strength and my fortress and my refuge in
the day of affliction.

— JEREMIAH xvi 19

COLUMBUS, on arriving at the new capital, Santo Domingo,
on the last day of August 1498 hoped rather than expected
to find peace and quiet in his viceroyalty, after the hardships of
the voyage; to recover from the arthritis that had been increasing
on him since the stormy passage home in the spring of 1493, and
especially to rest his eyes. Instead, he found the island in a far
worse condition than he had left it.

The Adelantado's first task after the Admiral's departure in
March 1496 had been to erect a fort in the Haina country, near
the site of Santo Domingo, which he named San Cristóbal. The
workmen nicknamed it La Torre Dorado, the Golden Tower, as
they found so much gold when digging and quarrying stone for
the foundations. But that hopeful sign proved to be no omen of
better things to come.

At the beginning of July 1496 the ship and two caravels under
Peralonso Niño, which Columbus had encountered in the port of
Cadiz on June 11, arrived at Isabela with a cargo of provisions.
As Las Casas says, nothing brought so much joy to the colonists
as a lucky find of gold, or the arrival of food from Spain. Niño
brought a dispatch from the Sovereigns giving definite orders for
the transference of the capital from Isabela to the Ozama River,
and a letter from the Admiral stating that the slave trade

could go on, provided the victims were genuine prisoners of war. Accordingly Bartholomew rounded up some 300 "prisoners" whom he sent to market aboard Niño's fleet. That summer began the building of Santo Domingo, or Isabela Nueva as it was often called in the earliest years. The site was uncommonly well chosen for a protected harbor, central location, fertility of the surrounding soil and easy access to the ocean. Santo Domingo was the first settlement of Europeans in the New World that proved permanent, and to this day it is one of the most important cities in the Caribbean.*

An idyllic interlude between these labors and the next calamity was a state visit of the Adelantado to the cacique Behechio of Xaragua, the southwestern section of Hispaniola. Bartholomew and men in armor marched through the splendid forests of that region, noting the scarlet-flowered *madre de cacao;* they crossed the Rio Yaque del Sur, met Behechio at the frontier of his "kingdom," and were conducted to his royal residence in the verdant basin around Lake Enriquillo. There the visitors were met by a cortege of Behechio's wives, clad only in cotton loincloths, and were entertained for three days by a succession of roast hutía and iguana feasts, mock battles, dances of naked maidens waving palm branches; and as a climax, Anacoana (Behechio's sister, Caonabó's widow), the fairest of the fair, was brought in on a litter, clad only in flower garlands. Xaragua seemed good enough terrestrial paradise for most of the Spaniards, and Bartholomew was so delighted with his entertainment that he let off Behechio with a tribute of hemp, cotton and cassava, since there was no gold in that region.

By the time Bartholomew returned to Isabela (for Santo Domingo was not yet ready for the transfer), rebellion had reared its ugly head. Francisco Roldán, a gentleman whom Columbus had appointed *alcalde mayor* or chief justice of the island, was the leader; the greed of the Spanish colonists for more gold, their discontent at a chronic insufficiency of food supplies from Spain,

---

* On recent maps Santo Domingo will be found under the new name Ciudad Trujillo, which it was given by a recent dictator of the Dominican Republic.

their dislike for the stern rule of that "foreigner" the Adelantado, were at the bottom of it. Roldán, like most leaders of revolt, promised all things to all men; the restive caciques were assured that no more tribute would be levied, and the Spaniards were promised a life of ease, with plenty of Indians to dig gold for them, free passage home and no taxes. He counted on the malcontents who had returned to Spain procuring the abolition of Columbus's privileges, and establishing a new regime on the island, perhaps with himself as governor.

Bartholomew was holding Roldán at bay in the Fortaleza de la Concepción de la Vega, on the mule track between Isabela and Santo Domingo, when the advance fleet of the Third Voyage under Pedro Fernández Coronel arrived at the new capital. News of the royal confirmation of the Admiral's privileges and of Bartholomew's appointment as Adelantado cut the ground from under Roldán's feet, and with his rebel army of seventy men he retired to Xaragua to enjoy the hospitality of Behechio and his women. Guarionex, the cacique of Magua who had joined Roldán, retreated to the mountains of the Samaná peninsula, where he was received by the arrow-shooting Ciguayos, whose men had threatened Columbus on the First Voyage. Thither with foot and horse marched the Adelantado. On this punitive expedition many native villages were burned; Guarionex and his host were delivered into Bartholomew's hands by treachery; and that part of the island was subdued.

This was the situation that confronted Columbus when he landed at Santo Domingo on the last day of August, 1498. The natives were superficially pacified, but suffering from cruel exploitation; Roldán was at large in Xaragua; the Spaniards were disaffected, and a hundred and sixty of them, which must have been 20 to 30 per cent of the total, were ill with syphilis. What made matters worse was the failure of the three caravels under Carvajal, Pedro de Harana and Giovanni Colombo, which Columbus had sent ahead from the Canaries in June, to turn up. They stupidly had overstood Santo Domingo and fetched up far to leeward on the

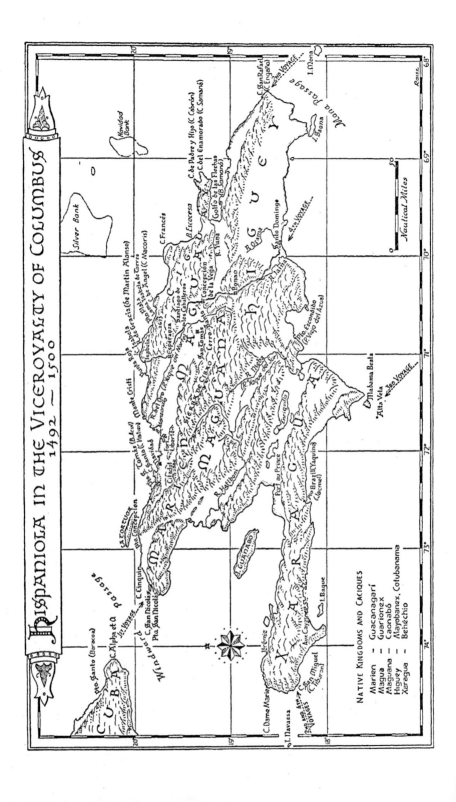

coast of Xaragua near Roldán's headquarters. Ignorant of his status, the captains allowed the rebel leader to come aboard and their men to go ashore; as a result Roldán managed to suborn a considerable number of the caravels' people and induce them to desert. As these included some very tough criminals from Spain, their defection was serious. Roldán, thus strengthened, marched forth from Xaragua into the Vega Real, where he proposed to attack the Concepción fortress, then in the hands of a loyal soldier named Miguel Ballester. Columbus could raise only seventy men-at-arms to go out against the rebels, and he was not sure of the loyalty of more than half·this force.

Retaining the caravel *Vaqueños* at Santo Domingo, Columbus dispatched his flagship and *Correo* to Spain on October 18, 1498. With them he sent the account of his voyage to the Terrestrial Paradise which we have frequently quoted, and letters to the Sovereigns on more practical matters. In order to defray the expenses of colonization, since the gold takings during his absence had as usual been disappointing, he proposed "to send in the name of the Holy Trinity, all the slaves that can be sold, and brazil-wood." Spain had enslaved the Canarians and Portugal the Africans; why make an exception of the Indians? He requests that devoted priests be sent out both to reform the Christians and to convert the natives, for Fray Ramón Pane was incapable of doing it all alone; so far he had a mere handful of catechumens, and had built but one chapel for them. An educated and experienced man is wanted to administer justice "since without royal justice the religious will profit little." The island can now provide its own cassava bread, pork, cattle and hutía meat, but wine and clothing are wanted. Let fifty or sixty good colonists be sent out every voyage, so that the weak and the rebellious may be packed off home. More men and ships are needed to reduce Roldán to order, and when that rebellion is liquidated, to enable the Adelantado to start a colony in Paria. He was already planning to colonize the Terrestrial Paradise.

In contrast to the straightforward and practical recommendations of his memoirs on the Second Voyage, these letters of Columbus in October 1498 are rambling and incoherent, impractical and evasive. They must have conveyed to the Sovereigns the feeling that the Admiral was "no longer the man he was." Nor was he. Whether his arthritis or some psychological disturbance was the cause, the firm and confident note of 1492–1494 was absent. At this juncture Columbus seemed incapable of vigorous and forthright action.

Perhaps Roldán's mutineers did outnumber the loyal forces. Nevertheless, Columbus had all the prestige of viceregal authority; and he should have dealt with the rebellion firmly. The only way to handle tough fellows is to be a little tougher than they are. Instead of taking the strong line, Columbus fancied that he could inveigle Roldán into being good. Two days after the ships sailed he addressed to him a placating letter, declaring that he wished to let his *caro amigo* go home but could detain the ships no longer as the Indian slaves were dying, and begging him to come to a peace conference. An interchange of notes followed, and in November an agreement was signed by which Roldán's followers could either submit or accept free passage home with their gold, concubines and slaves, for which Columbus promised to provide shipping within fifty days. He was unable to fulfill that condition, which unfortunately gave Roldán, now convinced that he had the Admiral on the run, an excuse to raise his terms. He demanded restoration to the office of chief justice, an official proclamation declaring that all the charges made against him were baseless, and free land grants in Xaragua for those who chose to remain. Columbus finally consented to these humiliating terms in September 1499. Moreover, he established in favor of the by no means repentant rebels a system of exploitation that became the basis of the social institutions of New Spain.

This was the system of *repartimientos*, later known as *encomiendas*. To each settler was allotted a large plot of cultivated land — ten thousand cassava plants was the first unit — with the Indians that were on it, to have and to hold and to exploit as the owner saw fit. The caciques consented to this in order to get rid of the intolerable burden of the gold tribute, and handed over their subjects to the conquerors.

Two caravels were sent back to Spain in October 1499, bearing letters from Columbus to the Sovereigns explaining these arrangements, excusing them as made under compulsion, and begging that a competent judge and discreet councilor be sent out to help him govern the island. Columbus might have returned himself, but for the sudden appearance of a new element of disturbance, Alonso de Hojeda. When the flagship and *Correo* returned to Spain in the fall of 1498 with news of the voyage to Paria, Hojeda managed to get possession of the Admiral's chart and to obtain a license from Don Juan de Fonseca for a voyage to that region. With Bartolomé Roldán (the amateur pilot of Columbus's First Voyage), Juan de la Cosa (the map maker of the Second) and a Florentine resident in Seville named Amerigo Vespucci (whose account of this voyage, predated two years and not mentioning his commander, led to the continent's being given his name), Hojeda reached the Gulf of Paria, continued his voyage along the mainland behind Margarita where Columbus had left off, discovered the valuable pearl fisheries, the islands of Aruba, Bonaire and Curaçao, the Gulf of Maracaibo (which he named *Venezuela*, Little Venice, from the native dwellings on piles), and the Cabo de la Vela to the west of that gulf. He then made for Hispaniola, landing at Puerto Brazil (Jacmel) on September 5, 1499, where he began without authority to cut logwood.

Francisco Roldán, who had no liking for a rival in his beloved Xaragua, consented under the Admiral's authority to round Hojeda up and bring him and his men captive to Santo Domingo. They met off the coast of Southwestern Hispaniola, but after an amusing play of capturing each other's people as hostages, and Hojeda's attempting to replace Roldán as leader of the discontented, the young conquistador sailed away to the Bahamas, where he loaded up with slaves, and returned safely to Spain.

In the same year 1499–1500 Peralonso Niño, former pilot of

Santa María and *Niña*, obtained a license for a voyage, and returned to Spain with a rich haul of pearls from around Margarita; and Vicente Yáñez Pinzón, former captain of *Niña*, in a very notable and courageous voyage, discovered the mouth of the Amazon, probably rounded Cape San Roque, the eastern extremity of Brazil, doubled back along the coast and through the Gulf of Paria to Santo Domingo. None of these voyages, by rights, should have been allowed without the Admiral's permission; that they took place showed that his influence at court was rapidly waning.

The Sovereigns were not unjustified in believing that the three Columbus brothers * had made a mess of things in Hispaniola. Seven years had elapsed since the Second Voyage set out with such great expectations of profit for the crown and all concerned, but the returns so far had come to but a small part of the expense. The King begrudged any enterprises that interfered with his balance-of-power politics in Europe; the Queen was disappointed with the small returns in the saving of souls, and offended by Columbus's repeated flouting of her wishes by shipping slaves home. Columbus's own policy may have been weak; but the malcontents and rebels, who had means of reaching the royal attention, represented it as tyrannical. As the old English translation of Peter Martyr puts it, they accused the Columbus brothers, more especially Bartholomew, of being "vniust men, cruel enemies and sheaders of the Spanyshe bludde"; who upon every or any occasion "wolde rackke them, hange them, and heade them: And that they tooke pleasure therin. And that they departed from them as from cruell tyrantes and wylde beastes reioysinge in bludde, also the kynges enemyes." Ferdinand Columbus remembered bitterly how in the summer of 1500 when he and his elder brother, both court pages, were at Granada, a crowd of repatriated rascals from Hispaniola, claiming that back wages were due them, sat down in the court of the Alhambra and shouted, "Pay! pay!" to the King whenever he passed; "and if my brother and I, who were pages to the Queen,

---

* Don Diego had returned to the colony as early as 1495 or 1496, and had been doing his feeble best to support the authority of the Admiral and the Adelantado.

should happen by, they followed us crying to Heaven, 'There go the sons of the Admiral of the Mosquitoes, of him who has found lands of vanity and delusion, the grave and ruin of Castilian gentlemen,' adding so many other insolencies that we took care not to pass before them."

In the spring of 1499, Ferdinand and Isabella selected Francisco de Bobadilla, a man of unblemished character and probity, an old servant of the crown and knight of one of the Spanish orders of chivalry, to go out to Hispaniola with powers of chief justice (as Columbus himself had asked), and also as royal commissioner to adjust grievances. He had powers to arrest rebels and sequester their effects, and to take over all forts and other royal property from the Admiral, who was commanded to obey his orders. These full and unlimited powers were conferred on Bobadilla by the Sovereigns before they knew that Roldán and the Admiral had come to terms, and when they naturally suspected him of weakness in dealing with rebellion against his and their authority. If Bobadilla had left for Hispaniola that year, he would have found matters fairly peaceable, and held a proper inquest into the causes of the trouble. Most unfortunately for Columbus his departure was delayed until July 1500, and he arrived at Santo Domingo on August 23, just after the Admiral had given a long-overdue exhibition of toughness in putting down (with Roldán's assistance) a new rebellion, led by one of Roldán's former lieutenants, Adrián de Moxica.

As Bobadilla entered the harbor his eyes were affronted by the spectacle of a gallows on which were hanging the corpses of seven rebel Spaniards; and when he landed, Don Diego, who was in charge of the city, informed him that five more were due for execution the next day. Bobadilla peremptorily ordered Don Diego to hand over the prisoners to him. Diego, with an unwonted display of firmness, refused to do anything until the Admiral's return to the city. Bobadilla insisted, read his commissions, summoned the rabble of Santo Domingo to obey his orders in the Sovereigns' name, took over the citadel, took possession of the Admiral's house, impounded all his papers and effects, established his own popularity by proclaiming liberty to gather gold and pay a reduced seigniorage to the crown, clapped Don Diego in irons; and, when Columbus appeared obediently in answer to his summons, had the Admiral of the Indies cast into jail and loaded with manacles and fetters. The Adelantado was still at large with an armed force, and capable of putting up a stout resistance, but on the advice of his brother, who trusted in the eventual justice of the Sovereigns, he too gave in his submission and was placed in irons aboard one of the ships. Bobadilla, who had by this time accumulated a stack of ex-parte testimony and perjured charges against the Columbus brothers, held some form of inquest and sentenced them to be returned to Spain for trial.

At the beginning of October 1500 the Admiral in chains was put aboard the caravel *La Gorda* and sent home to Spain. The captain offered as soon as they had cleared harbor to remove the irons, but Columbus refused. He had been chained in the Sovereigns' name, he said, and he would wear them until the Sovereigns ordered them removed. Don Diego was with him, also in chains; but Bartholomew seems to have been sent home on another ship. The Admiral's caravel fortunately made a quick passage, and entered the Bay of Cadiz before the end of October.

Although nothing can excuse the outrageous proceedings of Bobadilla, it must be admitted that Columbus as governor of a colony had been a failure. He had been weak when he should have been firm, and ruthless at the wrong time. Las Casas, who dismisses most of the charges against him as unfounded or frivolous, admits that the three brothers "did not show modesty and discretion in governing Spaniards which they should have done," being foreigners, and that they had been at fault in unjustly apportioning the provisions sent out from Spain as a means of rewarding the faithful and punishing the lazy and discontented. Possibly a Spaniard would have done better in dealing with Spaniards, who had a superabundance of "ego in the cosmos"; certainly Governor Ovando, Bobadilla's successor, acted with far greater severity than

Columbus had ever presumed, both toward Indians and toward colonists. Yet one may be permitted to think that nobody could have succeeded better than Columbus in ruling a band of adventurers who were only concerned in growing rich without work. Oviedo, who was a practical man and knew his Indies well, wrote that any early governor of Hispaniola, to have been a success, must have been "Angelic indeed and superhuman." We need seek no further than early Virginia to prove the extreme difficulty of governing undisciplined men who have undergone hardships with the sole hope of gain, and who want it quick.

The humiliation of these proceedings to Columbus, with his proud nature, and sensitiveness to slights on his honor, can hardly be grasped by any modern man. Yet not for a moment did he lose his dignity. The letter that he wrote on the homeward passage (or shortly after) to Doña Juana, sister of Antonio de Torres and *aya* or, governess to the Infante D. Juan, concludes with an admirable expression of his outraged sense of justice: —

"They judge me there as a governor who had gone to Sicily or to a city or town under a regular government, where the laws can be observed *in toto* without fear of losing all, and I am suffering grave injury. I should be judged as a captain who went from Spain to the Indies to conquer a people numerous and warlike, whose manners and religion are very different from ours, who live in sierras and mountains, without fixed settlements, and where by divine will I have placed under the sovereignty of the King and Queen our lords, an Other World, whereby Spain, which was reckoned poor, is become the richest of countries. . . .

"God our Lord is present with his strength and wisdom, as of old, and in the end especially punisheth ingratitude and injuries."

THE FOURTH VOYAGE TO AMERICA

CHAPTER XLII

Last Chance

October 1500–March 1502

O frati, dissi, che per cento milia
Perigli siete giunti all' occidente,
A questa tanto picciola vigilia
De' vostri sensi, ch' è del rimanente,
Non vogliate negar l'esperienza,
Diretro al Sol, del mondo senza gente

"Brothers," said I, "who with me face to face
through myriad dangers have attained this West,
and now remains but half a seaman's vigil
in all that's left of life's unceasing quest;
will ye refuse, for fear of further peril
westward the world unpeopled to explore?"
— INFERNO XXVI 112–117

FAIR WEATHER and favoring breezes attended the voyage home in *La Gorda*, as if the Ocean Sea had wished to shorten the miseries of her brave conqueror. Columbus was landed at Cadiz before the end of October, and at the invitation of his friend Fray Gaspar Gorricio went to stay at the Carthusian monastery of Las Cuevas in Seville, still in chains and accompanied by his jailer. His pathetic letter to Doña Juana de Torres, the Queen's confidante, was sent to her at court by messenger, together with one addressed to certain gentlemen of the court, beginning: —

It is now seventeen years since I came to serve these princes with the Enterprise of the Indies; they made me pass eight of them in discussion, and at the end rejected it as a thing of jest. None the less I persisted therein. . . .

Over there, I have placed under their sovereignty more land than there is in Africa and Europe, and more than seventeen hundred islands, without counting Hispaniola. . . . In seven years I, by the divine will, made that conquest. At a time when I was entitled to expect rewards and retirement, I was incontinently arrested and sent home loaded with chains, to my great dishonor and with slight service to their Highnesses.

The accusation was brought out of malice, on the basis of charges made by civilians who had revolted and wished to take possession of the land. And he who did it had the order to remain as governor if the testimony was grave. By whom and where would this be considered just? I have lost in this enterprise my youth, my proper share in these things, and my honor; but my deeds will not be judged outside Castille. . . .

I beg your graces, with the zeal of faithful Christians in whom their Highnesses have confidence, to read all my papers, and to consider how I who came from so far to serve these princes, . . . now at the end of my days have been despoiled of my honor and my property without cause, wherein is neither justice nor mercy.

The spectacle of the Admiral of the Ocean Sea in chains is said to have created a lamentable impression at Cadiz and Seville. Nevertheless almost six weeks elapsed before the Sovereigns, on December 12, ordered him to be released and summoned him to court. *Cosas de España.* They were preoccupied with heavy diplomacy. On November 11, 1500, in the secret Treaty of Granada, Ferdinand the Catholic and Louis XII of France agreed to divide between them the Kingdom of Naples, prelude to a new series of Italian wars.

This long delay at even recognizing the existence of injustice was somewhat softened by the Sovereigns' sending with their order the sum of two thousand ducats; for Columbus had not been permitted to take an ounce of gold home with him, and was dependent on charity for his food and lodging.

On December 17, 1500, the Admiral, the Adelantado and Don Diego presented themselves at court, in the Alhambra at Granada. "The Admiral," says Oviedo, "went to kiss the hands of the King and Queen, and with tears made his apologies as well as he could; and when they had heard him, with much clemency they consoled him and spoke such words that he was somewhat content. And since his services were so remarkable, although in some measure irregular, the royal majesty of such grateful princes could not suffer the Admiral to be maltreated; wherefore they commanded him straightway to be restored all the income and rights that he held here, which had been sequestered and detained when he was arrested. But never did they promise that he would be reinstated in the government." The Queen in particular consoled him, says Las Casas, "for in truth she more than the King ever favored and defended him, and so the Admiral trusted especially in her."

This was shortly before Christmas 1500; and no doubt the Columbus family had a happy reunion at Granada. Not only the three brothers, Christopher, Bartholomew and Diego, were there, but Christopher's son Diego, now in his twenty-first year, and Ferdinand, a boy of twelve, were resident at court. Both had become pages to the Queen after the death of the Infante D. Juan, to whose person they had formerly been attached.

What Columbus prayed for and expected as justice, was the recall and punishment of Bobadilla, the restoration of all his rights, privileges and offices; in a word, to have things put back exactly where they had been before 1500. But nothing happened. The new century dawned and weeks stretched out into months; long idle weeks passed in the sunny courts and fragrant gardens of Granada; excellent indeed for the Admiral's health, but irksome for a man of action. The Sovereigns were gracious but evasive. Columbus wrote to his friend Fray Gaspar Gorricio on February 26, 1501, that he had received the "writing" that he had kindly drawn up, but wanted it rewritten in a rounder hand, such as the King liked to read (for reading was not the King's strong point). This writing was probably the Book of Prophecies, Columbus's collection of every passage in the Bible, and many others, that might serve as a prediction of the discovery of America. He doubtless hoped that this would appeal to the mystical side of the Queen's nature as to his own, and convince her that he was the chosen man of destiny to conquer an Other World and bring home treasure wherewith to recover the Holy Sepulchre.

The Sovereigns' attention was held by more practical and pressing matters. Gonsalvo de Cordova, sent abroad to help Venice fight the Turks, was ordered back to Italy in order to see that King Ferdinand obtained his slice of the Neapolitan melon, and some of the French share too. "In the business of the Indies," wrote Columbus to Fray Gaspar, "nothing has been heard or is heard, not for our ill, but for our good." In other words, no news is good news. "But I think you should be glad and content since Our Lord is on our side, and so are their Highnesses. I wrote to you the other day concerning a book of voyages of the Indies which I sent to you by Ballester." The journals of his own last two voyages, no doubt; would that we had them! On May 24 he writes again to Fray Gaspar, "Here there is always something going on which puts all other matters in the background. The Lady Princess departed in the name of Our Lord, and it is believed that now something will be done about the Indies." This princess was the Sovereigns' youngest daughter, Catherine of Aragon, leaving for England with an immense dowry to marry Arthur, Prince of Wales; bride at fifteen, widow at sixteen, and subsequently first wife to Henry VIII. June 9: "Reverend and very dear father, I have received all your letters and the copy of the *mayorazgo* [the entail or majorat of his rights and privileges]. The Queen our Lady has told me she would like to read your writing at her leisure, which is very good and consoling. In the affairs of the Indies something is afoot, but no decision has yet been reached that I may be sure of, save that their Highnesses have told me that my property and offices shall not be touched. It is very certain that I have been expecting grace and I am expecting it. . . . Remember me to the reverend father prior and all those clergy whom I wish to please, and may they all remember me in their devoted prayers. . . ."

Other letters followed, undated. Always the same story; always something more urgent than the affairs of those boring and faraway

Indies for the Sovereigns' attention. In the meantime Rodrigo de Bastidas was sailing west from Venezuela to the Gulf of Darien, Gaspar Corte-Real had discovered Newfoundland for Portugal, Cabral had discovered Brazil, and three or four navigators, including Amerigo Vespucci, were ranging the southern continent as far as the River Plate; Juan de Escalante, who had been an officer on Columbus's Third Voyage, was allowed to make a voyage of his own; even that merry rascal Alonso de Hojeda, despite his piracies and kidnapings on his first voyage, was allowed to take four caravels to the Indies in search of gain. While everyone was chiseling in on the new world of Columbus's discovery, he was kept dancing attendance at court.

Really it was hopeless for Columbus to expect a complete restoration of his rights and privileges. Every voyage that returned from the New World to Spain or Portugal proved a greater extent of the southern continent. Duarte Pacheco Pereira rightly guessed that there was one continuous land mass from 70° North to 28° 30′ South. Juan de la Cosa's *Mappemonde* showed the same. It was preposterous to imagine that Columbus and his heirs could be viceroys and governors forever of the New World, with the right to tithe all its trade, nominate all officials and farm all revenues. True, he had been promised just that for whatever he should discover and hold, or whatever might be accomplished as a result of his discovery. This might have held good for an archipelago, or a few trading factories on the Asiatic mainland; but nobody, himself least of all, had expected to find a vast new undeveloped continent. Columbus, to be sure, had been promised permanent offices such as Admiral, Viceroy and Governor; but such promises were contingent on a reasonably good performance, which he had been unable to show in the single colony of Hispaniola. He could go on calling himself *El Almirante* or *El Virrey* if that was any use to him; but as for sending back an administrative failure to misgovern Hispaniola, no! Columbus would have been well advised at this juncture to settle for a good round pension and a castle in the conquered kingdom of Granada; to have renounced his rights for a reasonable dignity and security. But he was not that sort of man. If he had been, he would not have discovered America.

On September 3, 1501, the axe fell. Don Nicolás de Ovando, Commendador de Lares, was appointed by the Sovereigns governor and supreme justice of the islands and mainlands of the Indies, except over parts of the mainland which were placed under the jurisdiction of Vicente Yáñez Pinzón and Alonso de Hojeda. Ovando was not given the viceroyalty or the *almirantazgo*, that was some consolation. But this appointment meant that the exercise of Columbus's rights and privileges was definitely suspended. The only concession he could obtain was an order from the Sovereigns that Bobadilla make a proper accounting of the Admiral's property rights, and the privilege of sending an agent in Ovando's fleet to collect the proceeds of what was due to him from the trade and gold diggings. For factor, Columbus made an excellent choice in his veteran captain Alonso Sánchez de Carvajal, the seagoing mayor of Baeza, who served his interests to such good purpose that the Admiral died a comparatively wealthy man.

Ovando sailed from Cadiz on February 13, 1502, with a magnificent fleet of thirty sail — five ships of 90 to 150 tons burthen, twenty-four caravels and one *barco*, carrying twenty-five hundred mariners, colonists and men-at-arms. So that was that.

Columbus now decided to ask for ships, men and money to make a new voyage of discovery. Always uneasy and unhappy ashore, he longed to be at sea again; and although Ovando might hang himself with so long a length of rope, it would be two or three years at best before the Sovereigns could realize that Columbus alone was their only efficient (as he was the only rightful) governor of the Indies. On a new voyage, moreover, he stood a good chance of gathering further laurels, so that the Sovereigns would be forced to restore his rights and privileges and secure his family. A voyage whither, and for what ostensible purpose? With his knowledge of the New World, Columbus observed that the one region where something spectacular remained to be done was the Western Caribbean. Hojeda, Niño and Bastidas had not pushed discovery very far along the Spanish Main, owing either to their greed for pearls or to the difficulty of beating home. Nobody had been back to Cuba since 1494, and Columbus still believed that Cuba was the Chinese province of Mangi, and the western end of it the Golden Chersonese or the Malay Peninsula. Between the Isle of Pines and the eastern side of the Gulf of Darien, furthest west of the mainland explorers, lay a great undiscovered gulf. Here, Columbus believed, was the long-sought western passage to India. Marco Polo had sailed this way. If the Admiral could discover this strait or passage and sail home to Spain around the world, Vasco da Gama's voyage would be thrown in the shade.

For six months after Ovando's appointment, Columbus, now living under the hospitable roof of Las Cuevas at Seville, was pathetically calling attention to his existence. He wrote to the Pope asking for a supply of priests to carry the gospel to the Indians, hoping that His Holiness would request the Sovereigns to provide the ships, and appoint Columbus their captain general. But Alexander VI was more interested in mistresses than in missionaries. Columbus drew up a list of sea stores and other supplies for the Ovando fleet, with a little stinger at the end on the abominations of Bobadilla. But there is no evidence that Ovando paid any attention to this unasked-for advice. He wrote a little treatise on the Art of Navigation in the form of a letter to the Sovereigns, reminding them how his expert knowledge of wind and weather had predicted the arrival of the Spanish fleet bringing the Infante Margarita from Flanders, several years before. Finally, in a memorial of February 26, 1502, which unfortunately has not been preserved, he set forth his views of another voyage at length, and received so favorable and prompt action as to suggest that Ferdinand and Isabella were only too glad to be rid of so importunate a suppliant.

On March 14, 1502, the Sovereigns authorized the Fourth and last Voyage of Columbus. Their order came with a gracious covering letter. His imprisonment was very displeasing to them, and it was their will and pleasure that he should always and everywhere be treated with honor and courtesy. His privileges shall be pre-

served intact in order that he and his heirs may enjoy them without contravention, and they shall be confirmed anew if necessary;
but (this was not said though understood) he cannot for the present
exercise any of his functions. His sons and his brother Diego will
be looked after in his absence.

The Sovereigns' instructions are of the same date. D. Cristóbal
Colón, their Admiral of the Islands and Mainlands of the Ocean
Sea in the direction of the Indies, will sail on a voyage at their
command and cost. He shall have ten thousand pesos d'oro for the
expenses of fitting out, and all the artillery and munitions that he
wants. He is to make all convenient speed to the westward "since
the present season [March!] is very good for navigation." (One
reads between these lines the vulgar imperative "scram.") He is
to discover islands and continents "in the Indies in the part that belongs to us," that is, beyond the treaty line, take formal possession
thereof, and report on the nature of the land and the people. He
is to pay especial attention to their products of gold, silver, pearls,
precious stones and spiceries, and to allow no private trading for
such commodities, but to have everything of that nature brought
aboard entered by the official comptroller and placed in charge of
Francisco de Porras (of whom more anon) — as though he were
not to be trusted with anything of value. He must not carry off
natives as slaves; but if any wish to join him with promise of return, they may. No direct reference is made to the principal object
of this voyage, the search for a strait to the Indies. But an accom-
panying letter of introduction to Vasco da Gama, "Captain of the
most serene King of Portugal our son," * then outward bound to
India for a second time, declaring that their Admiral Don Cristóbal
Colón is sailing thither westward, "and it may be that you will meet
on your course," proves that the Sovereigns entertained a lively
hope that Columbus would find the strait, and sail home to Spain
around the world. In case he did not, he is authorized to call at
Hispaniola on the homeward voyage "if it appears to be neces-

* D. Manuel had recently married the Infanta Doña María, daughter of the
Spanish Sovereigns and his first wife's younger sister.

sary," but on no account to visit that island on the outward pas-sage. They well anticipated that his presence in Hispaniola at that juncture could only be distressing for him and disturbing to Ovando.

Columbus had hoped, if he made another voyage, to have some vessels especially built "in a new manner." Certain improvements in ship design he had in mind, in order to make headway when both wind and current ran against his course. But he had to take what the authorities were willing to charter for him. Perhaps this improved design that he wished to experiment with was incorporated in the type called *bergantina*, a light-draught vessel propelled by oars as well as sail, which within a few years was being built at Hispaniola and used by explorers such as Nicuesa and Balboa.

Happy in the knowledge that his privileges were not permanently withdrawn, and confident that eventually they would be confirmed to him and his heirs, Columbus spent much time and effort during his last months ashore completing and making copies of the Book of Privileges that he had begun to compile before his Third Voyage. Two of these copies he sent to the Bank of St. George in Genoa, one he left with his son; a fourth, with the original capitulations of 1492 and other important documents, he deposited in the hands of Fray Gaspar in the monastery of Las Cuevas. That copy, after being lost for over two centuries, has eventually found a safe resting place in the Library of Congress.

With a new will made, Beatriz Enríquez de Harana provided for, his elder son Diego in a safe position at court and his beloved younger son as a shipmate, happiness returned to the Admiral. He looked forward to another great and brilliant voyage, *el alto viaje* he called it, as the crowning glory of his maritime career.

CHAPTER XLIII

Hurricane

April 3–July 30, 1502

*Qui descendunt mare in nauibus, facientes operationem
in aquis multis. Ipsi viderunt opera Domini, et mirabilia eius
in profundo.*

They that go down to the sea in ships and occupy their
business in great waters, these men see the works of the
Lord, and his wonders in the deep.

— PSALM cvi 23–24

IN HIS fifty-first year, already an aged man according to the
notions of his day, Columbus embarked upon his most dangerous and least profitable voyage. El Alto Viaje ("the High Voyage"), as Columbus himself called it, offers a story of adventure
which imagination could hardly invent; a struggle between man
and the elements, in which the most splendid manifestations of
devotion, loyalty and courage are mingled with the vilest human
passions. Rightly related, as he and his son told it, this Fourth and
last Voyage is the one of highest interest to those who love the
sea and honor great seamen.

The fleet provided by the Sovereigns consisted of four caravels.
Ferdinand calls them "vessels with round-tops," indicating they
were rigged like the original *Santa María*, with main topsails. *La
caravela capitana* (the flag caravel) or simply *La Capitana* as she
was usually called — her real name we do not know — measured
70 tons and was chartered for 9000 maravedis a month. The Admiral and his son sailed aboard her; but the Admiral, perhaps because of his advancing age and precarious health, did not undertake to command her himself. Diego Tristán, a former shipmate and
loyal servant to Columbus, his major-domo in the interval between

voyages, was appointed captain with a salary of 4000 maravedis a month, which was double that of her master Ambrosio Sánchez, or of his brother Juan Sánchez, chief pilot of the fleet, who had been Hojeda's pilot in 1499. She carried fourteen able seamen (1000 maravedis a month), twenty gromets (666 maravedis), a cooper, a caulker, a carpenter, two gunners and two trumpeters, their wages running from 1000 to 1400 maravedis a month.

Santiago de Palos, nicknamed *Bermuda* after her owner-master Francisco Bermúdez, cost the crown 10,000 maravedis a month, more than *Capitana*; but she must have been smaller, as she carried less crew. And she proved so unsuitable that Columbus altered his course in the hope of getting rid of her. Bartholomew Columbus "The Adelantado" sailed aboard *Santiago*, and acted as her virtual captain, without pay. Francisco de Porras, her titular captain, touched 3666 maravedis a month, and was accompanied by his brother Diego as auditor, chief clerk and crown representative, with a yearly salary of 35,000 maravedis. The Porras brothers, who proved not only incompetent but disloyal, had been forced on Columbus by Alonso de Morales, treasurer of Castile, who was keeping their sister as mistress. Obviously one could not deny favors to a treasurer who had numerous means of hampering the voyage if his wishes were not met. *Santiago* carried eleven able seamen and a boatswain, six *escuderos* or gentlemen volunteers, including two Genoese and the intrepid Diego Méndez, twelve gromets, a cooper, a caulker, a carpenter and an Italian gunner.

El Gallego or *La Gallega* (The Galician), whose real name was *Santo* something or other, was chartered for 8333⅓ maravedis a month. By comparing her crew with those of the others, she probably measured about 60 tons, about that of the famous *Niña*; but she had four masts (fore, main, mizzen and bonaventure mizzen on the taffrail). Pedro de Terreros, her captain, was one of the highly paid officers, receiving 4000 maravedis a month; he had been on every one of Columbus's voyages. Juan Quintero, her master and probably her owner, received a monthly wage of 2000 maravedis. He was the same man who had been boatswain of *Pinta* on the

First Voyage. *Gallega* carried nine able seamen and a boatswain, one *escudero* and fourteen gromets; but no mention is made of any *oficiales* such as cooper and caulker, of which she stood greatly in need before the voyage was over.

Vizcaíno or *Vizcaína* (again a nickname, meaning "The Biscayan"), smallest of the fleet, measured 50 tons and cost 7000 a month charter money. She was commanded by Bartolomeo Fieschi, a young and adventurous member of a Genoese patrician family who had befriended the Colombos before Christopher was born. Her owner and master, Juan Pérez, sold her to the Admiral in the course of the voyage. She carried eight able seamen (including Pedro de Ledesma), a boatswain, two Genoese gentlemen, another of the Admiral's household, a chaplain (Fray Alexander), nine gromets and a page-boy.

All told there were one hundred and thirty-five men and boys on the payroll, according to a detailed list left by Diego de Porras. Of these about one quarter never returned. Four deserted at Hispaniola; thirty died by drowning or disease, or were killed by the Indians at Belén, or in the fight with the mutineers at Jamaica. Ferdinand gives the total personnel as one hundred and forty, which is probably correct, for besides himself and his father and uncle there may well have been a few others who were not "on the strength." Comparing the personnel with that of the First Voyage, the only other complete crew list that we have, one is struck by the recurrence of the old names from Palos and the Niebla; Gonzalo Díaz, for instance, was brother-in-law to Bartolomé García, boatswain of *Niña* on the First Voyage and able seaman on this. Certain detractors of Columbus have insisted that he did not inspire loyalty, and had to ship beachcombers and criminals; but in spite of his unpopularity among the settlers of Hispaniola, and his loss of favor at court, the local character of his crews on the Fourth Voyage proves that his reputation was still high among the seafaring population of Andalusia. One contrast between the crew lists of 1502 and those of ten years earlier, is the large proportion of gromets and page-boys to able seamen: 56 youngsters to 43 oldsters; the usual proportion was 3 to 4. Some of these boys, as afterwards appeared when they testified in court, were as young as twelve and thirteen; few if any of the gromets can have been over eighteen, and at least one of the *escuderos* was only seventeen. Strong, active and adventure-loving boys make better seamen on a voyage of adventure and discovery than conservative, grousing old "shellbacks," as hundreds of later navigators than Columbus have found out, provided there are enough oldsters along to teach them the mariner's art. Possibly Columbus had learned this from his earlier voyages; perhaps his choice of boys was dictated by a limited budget. In any event, the lads who survived this long and hard voyage, grew to manhood in the course of it.

This was the best-equipped fleet for exploration that the Admiral commanded on any of his voyages, as it appeared. He had often declared a preference for small, light caravels such as *Niña*, and three of the four were of her burthen or less. All were big enough to sail around the world, if the elusive strait were found. Yet one proved unseaworthy before the fleet reached Hispaniola, two were abandoned along the coast of terra firma, and the remaining two were only saved from sinking by being run ashore at Jamaica.

The fleet assembled at the port of Seville, hard by the Giralda. On April 3, 1502, under the Adelantado's command, they dropped down the Guadalquivir to Puebla Vieja, where there was a good beach for careening. After the bottoms had been scraped smooth and the caulking well paid, and the whole covered with black pitch, the four caravels were refloated. They then proceeded to Sanlúcar and to Cadiz. There the Admiral, his brother the Adelantado and his twelve-year-old son Ferdinand came aboard. Last Masses were heard, last confessions made, and "in the name of the Holy Trinity" the fleet set sail on May 9, 1502. But the *vendaval*, a strong southwesterly, forced them to put in at La Caleta, the anchorage under the fortress of Santa Catalina, which guards the approach to Cadiz. There they awaited a change of wind. On May 11 it came out of the north, and the caravels put to sea.

Just before leaving Cadiz the Admiral learned that the Moors were besieging the Portuguese fortress of Arzila on the coast of Morocco only 65 miles away, and he decided to call there and lend a hand. Either this was a bit of Quixotism, or, as is more likely, the Sovereigns so ordered him; for they were still on the best of terms with their son-in-law D. Manuel, king of Portugal. Whatever the motive, this slight detour cost the expedition nothing, for by the date of its arrival, May 13, the Moors had decamped. So, after exchanging civilities with the Governor of Arzila, and meeting some cousins of Dona Felipa de Moniz, his former wife, the Admiral set sail the same day and arrived at the Grand Canary on May 20, good time for a run of 675 miles. They anchored "at the Isleta," a peninsula which (with considerable help from a modern breakwater) makes the harbor of Santa Luz, the seaport of Las Palmas. On the twenty-fourth the fleet dropped down to Maspalomas road at the south end of the Grand Canary, to take on wood and water.

This move must have been dictated by the scarcity of these commodities at Las Palmas. There is a small lake of fresh water near the present lighthouse at Maspalomas, and a thicket behind it where Columbus's men cut their firewood.

The ocean crossing began from Maspalomas on the night of May 25, 1502, and on the following day a departure was taken from Ferro. *Oueste, quarta del sudoeste,* "West and by South," was the course set by the Admiral.

This was the same course that he had given to the Hispaniola squadron in 1498. It should have taken the caravels to Dominica with Flemish compasses, but actually they made the next island to the southward. After a quick and uneventful trade-wind passage of twenty-one days, the fastest ocean voyage that Columbus made, the fleet on June 15 reached Martinique. That was a good landfall. The trades were brisk and the sea was heavy, so the Admiral sought out a good lee, probably Fort-de-France Bay. Wherever it was, the first thing he did was to send the people ashore to fill the water casks, bathe in the streams, and wash their clothes. In the days of sail, no competent shipmaster neglected an opportunity for washing after an ocean voyage.

After three days' rest and refreshment, the fleet got under way June 18, called at Dominica, ran down the chain of Leeward Islands that Columbus had discovered on his Second Voyage, passed along the south coast of Puerto Rico on the twenty-fourth, and five days later found itself off the Ozama River, at the mouth of which was Santo Domingo, the new capital of Hispaniola.

Although Columbus's privileges had been restored before this voyage began, the Sovereigns forbade him to visit his viceroyalty until on the way home. But the Admiral had very good reasons for wishing to call at Santo Domingo, and there is no cause for suspecting, as some writers have, that these were mere excuses. He wished to send letters home by the fleet that was about to depart, and to induce some shipmaster of that fleet to make a trade for *Santiago*. She had proved to be crank and a dull sailer, unsuitable for exploration, although sound enough for a homeward passage in summer. Moreover, he sought refuge from a cyclonic storm that he saw was making up. Well he knew the signs, for he had ridden out a hurricane behind Saona Island in August 1494, and had witnessed a second when ashore on Hispaniola in October 1495. Oily swell rolling in from the southeastward, abnormal tide, an oppressive feeling in the air, low-pressure twinges in his rheumatic joints, veiled cirrus clouds tearing along in the upper air while light gusty winds blew on the surface of the water, gorgeous crimson sunset lighting up the whole sky; and, adds Las Casas, the large number of seals and dolphin fish on the surface of the ocean.

Don Nicolás de Ovando, Knight Commander of Lares and Governor of Hispaniola, had arrived at Santo Domingo in April with a magnificent armada of thirty sail. They were now anchored in the Ozama River ready to depart on the homeward passage. Columbus, coming to off the harbor mouth but not anchoring, sent Captain Terreros of *Gallega* ashore with a note to the governor, requesting permission to enter, and urging that the homeward-bound fleet be detained in port until the storm had blown over.

Ovando treated the request with insolent disdain, read the Admiral's letter aloud to his heelers, who mocked at the Admiral "as a prophet and soothsayer" in a manner that made honest Terreros long to knock them galley-west, refused Columbus access to the harbor, and, ignoring the storm warning, sent the homeward-bound fleet to sea forthwith.

Retribution was swift and terrible. This great and gallant fleet had just rounded into the Mona Passage, and had the wedge-shaped eastern end of Hispaniola under their lee, when a furious wind burst upon them from the northeastward, fairly tearing them apart; for the fleet was strung out along the track of the hurricane. Some ships foundered at sea, others that managed to heave-to in time were driven ashore and pounded to bits. Among those that went down with all hands was the flagship commanded by Columbus's friend and former second in command Antonio de Torres, bearing his enemy Bobadilla, Guarionex the conquered cacique, a cargo that included 200,000 castellanos' worth of gold, and the greatest nugget, weighing 3600 pesos, ever found in the West Indies. Nineteen other ships were lost with all hands, three or four weathered Saona Island and struggled into Santo Domingo in a sinking condition. Over five hundred lives were lost; and out of this once proud fleet only one, the *Aguja*, reached Spain. Because she had been reckoned the meanest, Ovando had assigned her to the Admiral's factor, who was bringing home some 4000 pesos of gold that Bobadilla had been forced to disgorge; and this considerable sum safely reached the hands of Don Diego Colón in Spain. No wonder that his enemies declared he had raised this hurricane by magic art!

The Admiral's squadron escaped unscathed. It is not to be supposed that Columbus, three centuries ahead of his time, knew the law of cyclonic storms; but he knew what to do. A West Indies hurricane is a mass of wind several hundred miles in diameter, whirling counter-clockwise and moving slowly along a broad curve from east to west. The indications are that the track of this one was similar to the hurricane of September 1928, which followed the central cordillera of Puerto Rico and passed through the Mona Passage to the northward of Hispaniola. Antonio de Torres's fleet, in the center and northern sector of the whirling wind, caught it at first from the NE and E, and was hurled upon a lee shore. Santo Domingo, being in the southern sector, had wind from the N, W and SW; and it was evidently not very far from the center, since we are told that the whole city — as yet built only of wood and thatch — was laid flat.

Columbus, when denied access to Santo Domingo harbor, finding the wind coming almost due N off the shore, took his fleet a few miles to the westward and anchored close under the land, possibly off the mouth of the Rio Jaina, where he had protection from the N and W; the men growling and grumbling, says Ferdinand, because they had been denied shore leave at the city. The fleet rode easily the next day, as the force of wind increased; but when night fell on June 30, and the storm devils began to shriek their loudest, only *Capitana's* ground tackle held. Each of the other ships was torn loose from her anchorage by the fearful gusts that came off the hills of Hispaniola, and driven out into a wild and foaming sea. Through black night and howling hurricane each caravel fought gamely for her life, believing that the others were lost; while the Admiral, after causing every bit of ironmongery aboard to be frapped to *Capitana's* cables, passed the night alternately cursing Ovando and praying to God. "What man ever born," he wrote, "not excepting Job, who would not have died of despair when in such weather, seeking safety for my son, brother, shipmates and myself, we were forbidden the land and the harbors that I, by God's will and sweating blood, had won for Spain?" Yet, by God's will and good seamanship, his fleet came through safely. Crank *Santiago*, the one he had tried to get rid of by exchange, was almost snatched from him, since Captain Porras, the political appointee, was useless in anything but fair weather. Fortunately the Adelantado, whom his nephew calls the best seaman in the fleet, took charge, boldly sought sea room, and managed to save her whole. *Gallega* lost her boat, which was in the water when she slipped out to sea; it swamped and the painter had to be cut, but Captain Terreros saw his vessel through. *Vizcaína* seems to have made out all right, under her Genoese Captain Fieschi.

It had been agreed before the storm struck home that in case they were separated, a rendezvous would be made in an excellent little landlocked harbor that Columbus knew, Puerto Escondido (now Puerto Viejo de Azua) at the head of Ocoa Bay. As the hurricane passed to the north and west the wind came SE, which was exactly right for getting there. And on Sunday, July 3, each member of this battered fleet of four in succession crawled into Azua and came safely to anchor. What a *Salve Regina* must have been sung on that Sabbath evening! The captains could not have done better if each had carried a meteorologist and a Bowditch.

Columbus was eager to get on, but wisely decided to take time out for repairs and recuperation. His lad Ferdinand remembered Azua best for the good fishing. One day they caught a manatee, which Ferdinand was clever enough to identify as a mammal, not a fish. On another occasion *Vizcaína's* boat came upon a giant ray, "as big as a medium-sized bed," lying asleep on the surface. The men struck home with a harping iron, the fish quickly drew the line taut, and towed the boat through the water at a great speed, so that the people aboard the caravels wondered by what witchcraft it moved so rapidly without sail or oars. Presently the great fish sounded, and died; he was then hauled alongside *Vizcaína* and hoisted aboard by tackles.

From Azua the fleet rounded Beata Island and the Alta Vela rock, Columbus's landfall in 1498, and put in at the roadstead of Jacmel to avoid another impending storm. That threat passed, they set sail July 14. None of these ships ever saw Hispaniola again.

Columbus's earlier and better plan for this voyage had been to pick up the continental coast near Margarita, where he had left it four years before, and coast down-wind until he found the strait. The decision to visit Santo Domingo and get rid of *Santiago* now made that course impracticable; he was too far north and west to beat back against trade wind and current. Consequently he decided to sail into the yet unknown western half of the Caribbean, hoping to strike land there and work back alongshore. He had no intention of stopping at Jamaica; but on the third day out from Jacmel the fleet ran into a flat calm, and was carried to the Morant Cays, a group of sand islets that lie about 33 miles SSE of the eastern point of Jamaica, within sight of the Blue Mountains in clear weather. They landed on one which Columbus named *Isla de las Pozas* (of the Pools), because the men found water by digging holes in the sand. Without further delay he resumed his course, but the SE wind and equatorial current carried him past Jamaica, and northwesterly between the Grand and Little Cayman, to the line of cays off Cuba and parallel to the Isle of Pines that he had discovered in 1494. From July 24 to 27 he was anchored off one of these cays, probably Cayo Largo, which they named *Anegada*. On the twenty-seventh the wind turned NE and the fleet made a run of some 360 miles W by W in the fast time of three days. When the wind moderated, one of the seamen climbed the mast to see if there was good bottom for swimming or any sharks about, and so sighted a fine high island ahead. This was Bonacca, one of the Bay Islands off the coast of Honduras.

CHAPTER XLIV

Search for a Strait
July 30–October 16, 1502

Misit ergo ei Hiram per manus servorum suorum naves,
et nautas gnaros maris, et abierunt cum servis Salomonis in
Ophyr, tuleruntque inde quadringenta quinquaginta talenta
auri, et attulerunt ad regem Salamonem.

And Hiram sent him by the hands of his servants ships
and servants that had knowledge of the sea; and they went
with the servants of Solomon to Ophir, and took thence four
hundred and fifty talents of gold, and brought them to
king Solomon.

— II CHRONICLES viii 18

B ONACCA is a handsome island about 8 miles long and rising
to 1200 feet, surrounded by a line of coral reefs through
which it is easy to pick out channels into protected waters. The
Spaniards found nothing profitable except tall pine trees, which
still stand up conspicuously on the upper ridges. Bartholomew
went ashore with two boats, met a crowd of Indians, and showed
them pearls and grains of gold; but the natives were so ignorant of
those precious things that they offered to buy instead of producing
more for sale. The Spaniards did indeed find what Ferdinand's trans-
lators call *terra calcide* or *lapis calaminaris*, which he says the Indians used to mix with copper. The seamen mistook it for true gold
and secured a quantity, "which they long kept concealed," since
private trading in gold was forbidden. Perhaps it was the same
iron pyrites or fool's gold which later in the century aroused
false hopes in Cartier, Gilbert and Frobisher.

At Bonacca Island the Admiral saw an interesting example of
Indian naval architecture. A large dugout canoe, long as a galley

and 8 feet broad, hove in sight. She had a crew of twenty-five men with numerous women and children passengers, who were sheltered by a waterproof palm-leaf awning amidships. The Spaniards captured her without difficulty, as the paddlers seemed stupefied by sight of the ships, and brought her alongside *Capitana*. Columbus allowed his people to help themselves to the cargo, which gave evidence of a far more civilized provenance than any New World regions heretofore visited. There were cotton coverings and sleeveless shirts curiously dyed and woven, colored shawls which resembled the Moorish women's garments at Granada; long wooden swords with flints let into their edges, which cut like steel; copper hatchets, bells and crucibles to melt copper; and for provisions, such roots and grains as the Arawaks used, together with a fermented liquor which tasted like English beer. What the Indians set most store by in their cargo were certain "nuts," undoubtedly *almendras de cacao* or cacao beans, which they used as currency. The Admiral was so struck by the modesty of the women, covering their faces like the pretty *Moras* of Granada, that he ordered his people to use them well, and gave them some of his truck in exchange for what the people had taken. But he forcibly retained their skipper, an old man named something like Iumbe, whom he wished to use as interpreter. Iumbe, renamed Juan Pérez, proved very intelligent and useful.

Whence came this canoe, and what people were in it? The encounter has been played up by Columbus's detractors to prove that he "missed the bus" for Yucatán, where he might have discovered the remarkable culture of the Mayas. Ferdinand says the canoe was "charged with merchandise of the western region around New Spain," by which he meant Mexico; but he wrote this thirty years after the event. Bartholomew, describing the incident in 1506, wrote that it came from "a certain province called *Maian*." Consequently almost everyone has assumed that Columbus encountered seagoing Mayas. But, as subsequently appears, that portion of the Honduran coast opposite Bonacca was called *Maia* by the Jicaque Indians (it having been a part of the Mayan empire of the Cocomes, who fell in A.D. 1485); and the type of canoe, the cotton clothes, flint-edged swords, copper hatchets and bells in the canoe's cargo are characteristic of the Honduran and not the Yucatán section of Mayapan. Nor does Bonacca Island lie on the alongshore canoe route from Honduras to Yucatán. These Indians were obviously trading between Bonacca and the Honduran mainland. It has taken North Americans almost a century to appreciate the splendors of Mayan civilization in Yucatán, so well depicted in 1843 by Stephens; but few yet realize that the natives of Central and of Northern South America smelted gold and silver and copper, made elaborate castings, and produced works of art in metal that may challenge comparison with the best of ancient Mexico.

To the Admiral these navigators conveyed by gestures such high notions of the "wealth, culture and industry" of people to the westward that he was tempted to change course and follow them thither. Had he done so, they would undoubtedly have conducted him to the Gulf of Honduras, and perhaps to El Mar Dulce, the famous inland sea of Guatemala. But, reflecting that it would be easy to visit that country later by running down-wind from Cuba, he decided to push on eastward in search of the strait. Although his opportunity to see the Gulf of Honduras never came, he encountered the same high culture later on this same voyage, along Costa Rica and Panama.

It was now early August, and Columbus made for the mainland, visible from Bonacca and about 30 miles distant. The fleet made terra firma at Cape Honduras, which Columbus named Punta Caxinas, from the Arawak name of a tree that they found there, bearing a fruit that Ferdinand describes as "rough like a spongy bone, and good eating, especially if cooked." This was probably the fruit of *Chrysobalanus Icaco*, which is common along the sea beaches of Honduras. The fleet anchored in the harbor to leeward of the cape, where the Spaniards a few years later founded the city of Trujillo, metropolis of colonial Honduras. There Columbus encountered Jicaque Indians dressed like those in the big trading canoe, some of them wearing thick quilted cotton jerkins that were sufficient protection against arrows. This was the Honduran kingdom of Maya; some of the Admiral's men later deposed that the Indians so called it.

The fleet now began a long beat to windward. On Sunday, August 14, they anchored off the mouth of a river which Columbus named Rio de la Posesión, because he there took formal possession of that mainland for his Sovereigns on the Wednesday following, and Fray Alexander celebrated Mass. The country was "verdant and beautiful, although low, and there were many pines, oaks, seven kinds of palms, and myrobalans like those in Hispaniola called *hobi*. They have an abundance of pumas, deer and gazelles."

Hundreds of Indians came down to view the taking-possession, and a lively trade followed with hawks' bells, beads and the usual truck. The Indians brought "fowls of the country, which are better than ours, roasted fish, red and white beans," and other commodities like those of Hispaniola. They were darker in color and more low-browed than the Arawaks, mostly naked, their bodies tattooed or painted with designs like lions, deer and turreted castles, "and their faces painted red and black to appear beautiful, but really they look like devils." Their ears were bored with holes large enough to insert a hen's egg; Columbus therefore named the region *La Costa de las Orejas*, "the Coast of the Ears." These were either the Paya or the Jicaque Indians, flesh-eating emigrants from a forested portion of South America.

Along the Miskito Coast of Honduras from the Rio Romano to Cape Gracias á Dios, the fleet bucked head winds and foul weather continuously for twenty-eight days, beating off shore by day and anchoring close to the land every night. "It was one continual rain, thunder, and lightning," wrote Columbus. "The ships lay exposed to the weather, with sails torn, and anchors, rigging, cables, boats and many of the stores lost; the people exhausted and so down in the mouth that they were all the time making vows to be good, to go on pilgrimages and all that; yea, even hearing one another's confessions! Other tempests I have seen, but none that lasted so long or so grim as this. Many old hands whom we looked

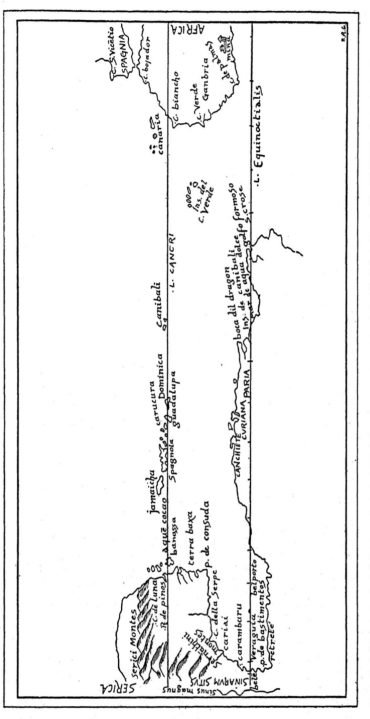

BARTHOLOMEW COLUMBUS'S SKETCH MAP OF THE COASTS OF
CENTRAL AMERICA, COLOMBIA AND VENEZUELA

Note "Serici Montes" (Chinese Mountains) and the Isthmus at Belén. Each space
on the equator equals one hour or fifteen degrees

on as stout fellows lost their courage. What griped me most were the sufferings of my son; to think that so young a lad, only thirteen, should go through so much. But Our Lord lent him such courage that he even heartened the rest, and he worked as though he had been to sea all of a long life. That comforted me. I was sick and many times lay at death's door, but gave orders from a dog-house that the people clapped together for me on the poop deck. My brother was in the worst of the ships, the cranky one, and I felt terribly having persuaded him to come against his will."

It was indeed a disheartening experience, much worse than being in deep water, where you can lay-to in such weather. Every morning at daylight the wind makes up from the eastward. Wolf a cold breakfast, heave up the anchor, hoist the yards on which the smallest sails in the locker are bent, claw off shore on the starboard tack in a smother of shoal-water waves that roll you down to leeward, under a rain so heavy that one ship cannot see the rest, and at times so torrential that each scupper is a waterfall and all distinction between sea and sky seems lost. Around noon the Admiral chooses an open spell and signals the fleet to wear. Around they come, dancing down-wind for a few brief moments, then hauled sharp up on the port tack and slogging along toward shore. No rest for anyone; watch below has to keep bailing, thirty fathom of sodden cable must be flaked in readiness for anchoring. More rain and thundersqualls, water shoaling, low coastline coming up at you, heave the lead, Admiral signals "Come to an anchor!" hard down helm (four hands on tiller), drop the anchor, and strike all sail but the mizzen. Anchor drags, pay out more scope, stand by to make sail if need be; finally the anchor bites, and the caravel rides to her cable. At this point some forecastle pessimist casts an eye ashore and growls out — There's that same goddam tree we left this morning!

Everything soaked, can't get the fire going on the hearth, just grab a wormy biscuit and a hunk of salt horse and roll up anywhere in your wet clothes while the caravel pitches and splashes and groans and creaks and rattles, and then the wind moderates and the mosquitoes fly out from the mangroves to gorge themselves on the blood of Spaniards too tired to brush them off.

During the twenty-eight days that this kept up the fleet made good only 165 to 170 miles. It is another example of Columbus's fortitude that he refused to declare himself beaten, change his plan, and slide down-wind to the land of gold and silver that he had heard about. What seaman, struggling in the teeth of wind and sea, tossed on a groaning and straining vessel, showered with spray, soaked by torrential rains, half drowned in breaking seas, exhausted by hauling on lines and working pumps, has not dreamed of that voluptuous pleasure of changing from a foul to a fair wind? A simple order — "Stand by braces! up with the helm! easy now!" — and Columbus's fleet would have passed from hell to heaven inside two minutes, the tempest have seemed a fair brisk gale, and the ships would have sailed fast and gaily before the wind without fuss or strain. But the Admiral of the Ocean Sea must seek the strait. That's what he came for. He could not afford to keep the sea at night, since that part of the Caribbean was still unexplored, might have been full of reefs and islands; and laying-to at night in the westerly current would have lost too much distance. Besides, the Admiral feared missing something; he was hoping and praying that God would soon spend His wrath; that some afternoon as the fleet approached this coast the sky would clear, the wind change; and as the Red Sea parted for Moses so here these sodden shores would seem to fly apart, the strait open up ahead, and the fleet go roaring through to the Indian Ocean, Taprobana, and everlasting glory.

Strait there was none to reward all this effort and anguish. But as seamen say, foul weather must end, luck must change; and so on September 14 the fleet found the coast trending southerly and rounded a cape beyond which the land actually fell away slightly to the westward; now the good Lord gave them favorable winds and currents. So the Admiral named this cape *Gracias á Dios*. Seamen who frequent that coast have asked me why so low and ill-favored a headland should bear so gracious a name. The Admiral's story is sufficient explanation; it was "Thanks be to God!" for a southward-trending coastline, and a chance to sail off the wind.

Having rounded Cape Gracias á Dios, the fleet coasted southward along the eastern shore of the present Republic of Nicaragua. It was a welcome relief to be able to sail on one tack, even to start the sheets a little, and to find protection from off-lying cays as the fleet shot through the Miskito Channel, and passed a bold red clay headland, now called Bragmans Bluff. Sixty miles further another line of cays (Man o' War and Pearl) gave a protected channel alongshore; and when the fleet reached the mouth of a wide and deep river on September 16, it anchored. The ships' boats were sent over the bar to procure wood and water. On coming out the wind, freshening from seaward, built up such a surf over the bar that one of the boats was swamped, and two of her crew drowned. For this reason the Admiral named it *Rio de los Desastres*. From Ferdinand's description of this place, it sounds like the Rio Grande; but from Diego de Porras's itinerary, it would appear to have been Bluefields. If Bluefields it was, they must have sailed continuously night and day since Cape Gracias á Dios.

During the next eight days they continued to skirt this coast to the southward for about 130 miles, passing the southern boundary of Nicaragua and coming upon the mountainous and picturesque Costa Rica. From the time they took it is evident that the fleet anchored every night, for fair anchorage was everywhere to be found in 5 to 7 fathoms at a safe distance from the shore. They passed a promontory that Porras called *Cabo de Rojas*, which must have been Monkey Point with its red cliffs; they passed the site of San Juan del Norte (Greytown), which was to have been the Caribbean terminus of the Nicaragua Canal. On September 25 they reached a region which the Indians called *Cariai*, and spent ten days anchored behind a pretty, wooded island which the Indians called *Quiriviri*, and the Admiral named *La Huerta*, the Garden. This island was probably Uva, and the place, the modern Puerto Limón, Costa Rica.

Here the Admiral decided to spend some time in order to give the men a good rest; and the indications are that they enjoyed themselves thoroughly. A great concourse of Talamanca Indians gathered on the shore, some armed with bows and arrows, others with palm-tree spears tipped with fish bones, and others with clubs. The men wore their hair braided and wound about their heads, and both they and the women had "eagles" of guanin pendent around their necks, "as we wear an *Agnus Dei* or other reliquary." The Admiral kept his people aboard, fearing trouble; but the Indians were so eager to trade that they swam out to the ships carrying a line of cotton jumpers and guanin ornaments. Columbus, however, soon sized up the local business situation, that the Indians had no pure gold. Consequently he refused to trade or to accept presents, but sent the visitors ashore laden with gifts. This appears to have offended them, as they left the truck tied together at the boat landing. The Indians then tried an ancient method of persuading visitors to trade. They sent aboard the flagship two virgins, one about eight and the other about fourteen years old, not knowing how tender the Spaniards liked their girls. "The damsels," says Ferdinand, "showed great courage; for although the Christians were complete strangers to them, they exhibited neither grief nor sorrow, but always looked pleasant and modest; hence they were well treated by the Admiral, who caused them to be clothed and fed, and sent them ashore, where the old man who had delivered them received them back with much satisfaction." Although the presence of the Admiral's thirteen-year-old son, rather than respect for maidenly modesty, explains this abnormal continence of the mariners, it astonished the natives, and caused them to endow their visitors with supernatural attributes.

On the following day the Adelantado went ashore attended by a secretary, in order to record what information he could obtain about Cariai. When he began to question two leading men who approached him as official greeters, and the scribe produced paper, pen and inkhorn to note the answers, this writing apparatus struck the natives as a form of sorcery; they fled in terror, tossing a powdered herb in the air to dispel the magic of these gods for whom fresh young virgins offered no temptation.

Columbus appears to have been very wary of these people, because not until October 2 did he send a landing expedition in force to reconnoiter the country. The men were impressed with the great abundance and variety of fauna, compared with that of the Antilles. They reported seeing deer, pumas and a sort of wild turkey, which Columbus describes as "a very great fowl with feathers like wool." But the most curious and interesting thing they saw was "a great palace of wood covered with canes, and within some tombs, in one of which was a corpse dried and embalmed, . . . with no bad odor, wrapped in cotton cloth; and over each tomb was a tablet carved with figures of beasts, and on some the effigy of the dead person, adorned with beads and *guanin,* and other things that they most value." The Castilians had, in fact, looked in on a native sepulchral ceremony; the corpse was awaiting the funeral dance by its relatives and friends before interment. Owing to the dampness of the soil, none of the wooden sepulchral tablets have been preserved; but many examples of the effigies that Ferdinand mentions have been excavated.

Wanting interpreters as usual (since "Juan Pérez" had been set free many days since, when they reached a point beyond his language zone), the Admiral caused two Indians to be captured and brought aboard. The others, thinking these were being held for ransom, dispatched messengers to make a deal, with a peace offering consisting of two peccaries, the wild boar of the country. Columbus sent the envoys ashore with gifts, but without their friends. The one peccary that he kept was so wild and fierce that it ran at everyone on deck; even forced an Irish wolfhound which belonged to the Admiral to go below and stay below. But before they sailed the peccary met his match in a large spider monkey which one of the crossbowmen wounded when hunting in the forest, and brought aboard with one fore leg cut off. The peccary, as soon as it saw the monkey, bristled and retreated; but Columbus ordered them to be thrown together. Monkey, although

bleeding to death, coiled his tail around piggy's snout, seized him
by the neck with his remaining fore claw, and bit the poor boar so
that he grunted with pain. All hands roared with laughter, for
tenderness toward animals was no part of human equipment
in the sixteenth century. Columbus even thought it worth relating
in his letter to the Sovereigns, as a novel incident and "such fine
sport."

From the abundant use of guanin ornaments by these Talamanca
Indians, Columbus concluded that they belonged to the nation of
the Massagetae, of whom he had read in the *Historia rerum ubique
gestarum* of Aeneas Sylvius. As usual, when he attempted to identify his discoveries in terms of ancient geography, he was several
thousand miles out.

On Wednesday, October 5, the fleet left Cariai and sailed alongshore in a southeasterly direction. Towards evening, when a little
over 50 miles from the last anchorage, they found a channel opening into a great bay. The strait at last! But it was only another
disappointment; the Boca del Dragón that leads into a great island-
studded bay, now named Almirante. On the eastern side of this
channel was an island now called Colón, but known to his two
Indian guides as Carambaru, Cerabaro, or Zorobaro, a name which
Columbus took to be that of the whole bay.

Quiriquetana, as the Indians called the mainland inside Almirante
Bay, gave our seagoing philologist a valuable clue, so he thought.
Just as on the First Voyage he deduced Cipangu from Cibao, so
here the Admiral tortured Quiriquetana into Ciamba, Marco Polo's
name for Cochin-China. Moreover he had passed beyond the belt
of guanin, the copper and gold alloy. In Almirante Bay "he
found the first sign of fine gold which an Indian wore like a large
medal on his breast, and traded it." Ferdinand tells us that this
gold disk, worth ten ducats (say $23), was exchanged for three
hawks' bells, worth about one cent, and some even heavier disks
were obtained for the same standard price.

Every explorer of the Atlantic coast of America from Davis
Straits to the River Plate, and over a period of at least two cen-

turies, was misled by the spacious gestures of Indians when pointing out the way. By spreading their arms and then touching their fingers, the Indians meant to convey the idea of a bay, lake or widening of the river; but the sanguine European understood them to mean the Indian Ocean, the Great South Sea or some ocean gateway thereto. On this occasion the Indians waved Columbus on to another great bay, Quiriquetana (Chiriqui Lagoon), which he understood to be the ocean. It was a strait all right; the caravels sailed "as it were in streets between one island and another, the foliage of the trees brushing the cordage of the vessels."

On January 14, 1940, we explored the passages in and between these two bays in a motor launch, seeking for one that would meet Ferdinand's description. Crawl Cay Channel, Sunwood Channel, and the passages in and out of Palos and Porras lagoons did not fill the specifications, as they were lined with low mangroves; but in Split Hill Channel we found the strait. Here there is a narrow and tortuous passage between high banks lined with lofty trees; and the channel passes so close to one shore that we could well imagine the rigging of the four caravels being brushed by branches. Today there are only 7 feet of water in Split Hill Channel; but an ancient pilot informed us that before the earthquake of 1912, which heaved up the bottom, he had taken vessels drawing 14 feet through there. *Capitana, Santiago, Gallega* and *Vizcaína* threaded this channel on October 6, 1502, believing it to be the Passage to India.

Again a disappointment. As the caravels issued from this narrow defile they entered a spacious landlocked bay some 30 miles long and 15 across. *Alburema*, as Columbus named it, Chiriqui Lagoon as we call it today, is a beautiful sheet of peacock-hued water, an inland salt lake cupped between a verdure-clad cordillera that rises 11,000 feet above sea level. Compensations there were for the Admiral. On October 7 a landing was made on the coast, a brisk barter began in gold disks, "eagles" and provisions, "and from here he began to go trading all along the coast." "The people were all painted on face and body in divers colors, white, black and red," remembered Ferdinand, "only covering their genitals with a narrow clout of cotton." These Indians were the Guaymies, who formerly occupied the coast in large numbers from Chiriqui to the Canal Zone. Their descendants, forced back by the Spaniards into forest clearings and high savannahs of the mountainous interior, still paint their faces black, red and white.

For ten days (October 6–16) the fleet idled about the beautiful Chiriqui Lagoon; fishing and visiting Indian villages to swap trading truck for gold and provisions. Much information was acquired through the interpreters from Cariai, who appear to have learned Castilian with surprising rapidity. They certainly performed the native interpreter's function of telling white men exactly what they wished to hear, which in this instance included a certain amount of truth. From them Columbus for the first time definitely learned that he was on an isthmus between two seas, and that an Indian province called *Ciguare* lay on the ocean nine days' march across the cordillera; he compared the situation of Ciguare in respect to Chiriqui with that of Venice in respect to Pisa. Apparently Ciguare, not Chiriqui, was the *Ciamba* (Cochin-China) of Marco Polo. The Ciguareans had an immense quantity of gold, he was told; obviously this was Ptolemy's Golden Chersonese. They wore coral ornaments as well; and Columbus had read somewhere that in Ciamba coral bits were used as money. Chili pepper, that persistent and never-failing clue to the Moluccas in the Admiral's eyes (or nostrils), they had of course. These Ciguareans or Ciambans were great traders, the interpreters relating by dumb show how they conducted business at local markets and fairs. The men of Ciguare were not naked savages, but went clothed in rich garments, armed with swords and cuirasses; and, as proof that they were civilized orientals, Columbus informs the Sovereigns that they used cavalry in battle, and had warships equipped with cannon. The River Ganges was but ten days' sail from their shores. At this point, in his *Lettera Rarissima* to the Sovereigns, Columbus reiterates the old arguments from Marinus of Tyre and from the total eclipse that he had observed off Cuba in 1494, to the effect that he had reached the longitude of Eastern China. He was then coasting along the Golden Chersonese, the Malay Peninsula, where Solomon sent Hiram for fine gold; he was near the center of the earth's greatest store of precious metal.

Strangely enough, this proof that he was on an isthmus seems to have ended Columbus's search for the strait. There is no more allusion to that quest in any account of the voyage, beyond Chiriqui. At Veragua the Admiral and his son remained over three months, in frequent communication with the natives, without once in their writings alluding to isthmus or strait. In a harbor where the Panama Canal begins he spent Christmas and New Year's without suspecting that the key to the Pacific lay in his hand. The only explanation I can offer for this incuriousness regarding the strait, in comparison with his earlier persistence through fair weather and foul, is that the reports of Ciguare convinced him that there was no watery strait; neither was there one! Of course he had no means to march across the cordillera; Balboa, on a less difficult crossing, required several hundred Spaniards and a thousand Indians.

Whatever the reasons may have been, Columbus from Chiriqui on concentrated on the secondary object of this voyage, the search for gold. The Search for the Strait was over.

CHAPTER XLV

Veragua

October 17–December 31, 1502

Ille autem dicit eis: Ego sum, nolite timere.

But he saith unto them, It is I; be not afraid.
— JOHN vi 20

TEN DAYS the fleet spent exploring this beautiful Chiriqui Lagoon, bartering for gold, and collecting tall tales of Ciguare. Probably the last harbor where they anchored was the present Bluefields Creek; it was the best they would find until they reached Porto Bello.

On October 17, choosing a day of westerly wind, the fleet passed out to sea by Tiger Channel (so called from the curious red cays at its entrance), rounded Punta Chiriqui and found a little island shaped like a Spanish escutcheon that Columbus named *El Escudo;* it is still called Escudo de Veragua. They were now in the harborless Golfo de los Mosquitos.

Turning southward toward the main they anchored off the mouth of a river called Guaiga, after a day's run of 38 miles. Here began the region that the natives called Veragua; an important source of gold, so they informed the Spaniards; and in this they told the truth. When in 1536 the Virreina Doña María de Colón y Toledo renounced in the name of her son D. Luis Colón (the Admiral's grandson) his hereditary titles and privileges over the whole of the Spanish Indies, he received as compensation a domain of 25 square leagues in this region from the Emperor Charles V, together with the title Duke of Veragua, which the Admiral's descendants bear to this day.

The fleet appears to have stayed several days at Guaiga in the hope of making contact with the natives; for the Indian villages of Veragua were situated on rivers some distance back of the coast. On October 20 the Spaniards had their wish, and found the Indians of Guaiga to be far more bellicose than any yet encountered on this voyage. Ferdinand (who was now a big boy of fourteen, and allowed to take part in everything) tells how the boats going ashore found over a hundred Indians on the beach, who assaulted them furiously, running into the water up to their middles, brandishing spears, blowing horns, beating a drum, splashing water toward the Christians, and squirting from their mouths some nasty herb that they were chewing. The Spaniards tried to appease them, and with some success, since they managed to draw near enough to exchange sixteen "mirrors" of pure gold worth 150 ducats for two or three hawks' bells apiece. Next day they tried again, but found the Indians on guard, occupying temporary shelters near the beach, and waiting, as it appeared, to ambush their visitors. As the Spaniards refused to land without some reassuring gesture, the Indians rushed out into the water in the same manner as the day before, and by signs threatened to hurl their spears if the boats did not quickly put back. One Spaniard wounded an Indian in the arm, and another fired a lombard, which so terrified the warriors that they ran ashore. After that three more gold disks were obtained, the Indians explaining that they had no more since they had come to the ocean's edge prepared to fight and not to trade. "But all the Admiral looked for on this leg of the voyage," said his son, "was to collect samples." He was certainly obtaining a good assortment from these Guaymi Indians.

Along the Veragua coast the fleet worked its way against the trade wind. This shore of the Golfo de los Mosquitos is superficially attractive, but fundamentally inhospitable. From Chiriqui Lagoon to Limón Bay (the Caribbean entrance to the Panama Canal), a distance of over 125 miles, there are no harbors, except where a river mouth happens to have a bar deep enough to admit vessels; and that is nowhere at present. The coastal plain is very narrow, not more than a few yards in some places; and behind it rises a high, rugged, broken country covered by an impenetrable jungle, and lofty, verdure-clad mountains. The trade wind beats in on the coast, which consists of long sand beaches separated by rocky bluffs; making it dangerous to anchor, and often impossible to land in small boats. Rainfall is so excessive as to make agriculture on any large scale unprofitable. The few people who live along that shore today have no means of communication with the outside world except dugout canoes; boats can be launched only when the sea is exceptionally calm. Canoes can penetrate far up into the interior by the rivers, but there are not even footpaths to connect them with the settled regions of the Republic. We on the Harvard Columbus Expedition found this the most difficult part of the Admiral's discoveries to get at, and only through the co-operation of the Panama government in providing us with a native sloop and native pilots did we manage to effect a landing (after sundry tumblings in the surf) at the Rio Belén.

Columbus's only interest in this coast was to locate the source of the golden ornaments worn by the Indians. Somewhere in that region, the interpreters informed him, were the mines whence came all this wealth. His progress eastward is impossible to follow with any exactness, because Ferdinand, who alone of the narrators affords any detail, gives no distances and few dates, and mentions only Indian place names which were not sufficiently persistent to get on the maps. The fleet's next call after Guaiga (probably the Chiriqui River) was a place called *Cateba* or *Cativa*, where they anchored "in the mouth of a great river." Here the natives raised another alarum with trumpets and drums, but promptly piped down, as mariners say, and traded gold disks. Their cacique, protected from the rain by a huge leaf, received the Christians ashore, and turned in one of his own disks for some of their truck.

Ferdinand reports a find at Cativa that reflects his later interests as a scholar and humanist. "This was the first place in the Indies where they saw signs of a building; it was a great mass of *stucco*, which appeared to have been built of stone and lime; the Admiral ordered a piece to be taken as a souvenir of that antiquity." This strange report is mentioned in no other narrative of the voyage. The Mayas never ranged that far east, and surely the Spaniards knew well enough the difference between a mass of natural rock and a ruined building. And, if Columbus had seen it, he would have mentioned it in his letter to the Sovereigns as evidence of some fallen oriental empire. I confess myself completely baffled for an explanation.

"From here," says Diego de Porras, "he pressed forward to another province called *Cobraba*, and there, because there was no harbor, he did not investigate but took an Indian as interpreter; he passed rapidly along this coast of Veragua without learning its secrets, save to go forward and discover more country, and as soon as he had passed beyond it, less gold appeared." After Cobrava, says Ferdinand, the fleet passed "five villages of great trade," one of which was *Veragua*, where the Indians said that the gold was collected and the "mirrors" were made; this was the village where the Adelantado kidnaped a cacique in February 1503. Next day they came to a village named *Cubiga*, where the Indians from Cariai said that the "trading country" which began at Almirante Bay, 50 leagues back along the coast, came to an end.

That being so, Columbus proposed to return to the center of auriferous activity near Veragua, and investigate further. Two months elapsed before he could do so. The rainy season had set in, and an unusually boisterous one it was, with gusty northers and strong westerlies. On the very night that he left Cubiga "there arose so violent a storm that we were forced to go wherever it drove us," wrote the Admiral. "I ran before the wind wherever it took me, without power to resist." On drove the fleet past the entrance to the future Panama Canal, and providentially into a fine harbor that opened up just where he wanted it. The Admiral named this harbor *Puerto Bello*, "because it is quite large, fair, inhabited and encompassed by a well tilled country." The fleet entered it on November 2, "passing between two islands; within the harbor vessels may lie close to shore, and beat out if they will. The country about this harbor is not very rough but cultivated and full of houses only a stone's throw or crossbow shot apart, pretty as a picture, the fairest thing you ever saw. During the seven days that we tarried there on account of the rain and foul weather, canoes came continually from the country round about to barter all sorts of eatables and skeins of fine spun cotton, which they gave for trifles of brass such as lace points and tags."

This description of Porto Bello still holds good, except that the jungle has grown up over the once well-tilled fields of the Cuna Cuna Indians. The harbor is so spacious, well-protected and easily entered that later in the century the Spaniards selected it as the Caribbean terminus of a mule track crossing the Isthmus of Panama. During the annual six weeks' fair, when the galleons from Spain exchanged their cargoes for the treasure from Peru and the products of Darien, Porto Bello became the most thriving town in the Americas; Sir Francis Drake died on shipboard when about to attack it, in 1596. Thomas Gage, who came there in 1637, reported seeing a train of two hundred mules come in laden with silver ingots, which were piled up in the market place like cordwood. In the eighteenth century, when the fairs ended, the town dwindled away almost to nothing; but the remains of several forts that once protected it, and the vast ruined *dogana* or customhouse, testify to the former grandeur of Porto Bello.

On November 9 the fleet left this pleasant place, sailed around Manzanillo Point, and made 15 or 20 more miles easting; but on the tenth the wind came easterly again and forced them back 13 miles, "and they put in among islets next the continent where Nombre de Dios now is: and because all these coasts and islets were full of maize, they called it *Puerto de Bastimentos*, Harbor of Provisions." There the fleet remained twelve days, repairing both the ships and the casks. Ferdinand reports an amusing incident of their stay. One of the ship's boats, seeing an Indian canoe full of paddlers, decided to hail it; but the Indians, when they approached, jumped overboard and dived like waterfowl. Whenever an Indian came to the surface the boat tried to row him down, but he always dived and came up a bowshot or two distant in another direction. For hours the boat continued this futile chase, while the men aboard the ships roared with laughter at the rage of the hounds and the skill of the hares.

On November 23 the fleet left Nombre de Dios (as Nicuesa renamed it in 1508, for the same reason as Columbus's "Gracias á Dios") and the same day put in at a place called *Guigua*, probably the mouth of the Rio Culebra. There the boats going ashore met a crowd of Indians and did a little trade. The Admiral does not mention this call, but states that after making 15 leagues "with great exertions" to the eastward of Nombre de Dios, the wind and current drove the fleet back. "But in again making for the port which I had quitted, I found on the way another port, which I named *Retrete*,* where I put in for shelter with great peril and regret, and very weary, both I and the ships and my people." It was now Saturday, November 26.

Porras also mentions *El Puerto del Retrete* as the next harbor, and calls it very small. Ferdinand gives the most detail. The fleet lay-to outside while the boats sounded the entrance and the harbor. This boat's crew brought back an over favorable report of the place, because they were tired of being tossed about, wished to trade with the Indians, and found steep-to banks inside against which the ships would have to lie, as the harbor was so small; "it could not contain five or six ships together." The entrance was only 75 to 100 feet wide with rocks "as sharp as diamonds" sticking up on either side; but the channel was so deep that if you favored either side when entering you could jump ashore on the rocks.

What was this tiny retired harbor? It has generally been identified as the modern Puerto Escribanos, about 20 miles east of Nombre de Dios. Visible from seaward, this was a natural place for Columbus to send in boats in the hope of finding shelter, which it well affords. One enters by a channel 10 to 12 feet deep between rocks, but nearer 100 yards than 100 feet wide. Ships can lie against either shore within. But this harbor is much larger than

* "Closet" or "small room." The word then had no scatological connotation.

Ferdinand describes, larger even than the modern charts indicate. At least thirty to forty sail of such vessels as Columbus had, could ride there in sufficient depth of water.

When searching for Retrete in January 1940, I read Ferdinand's description aloud to an intelligent local pilot, who at once said that it resembled a tiny harbor of refuge 2 miles west of Escribanos, between it and the Rio Culebra, named El Portete. This little hole in the reefs was of some local importance as a place for loading coconuts, early in this century. Schooners drawing 14 to 15 feet used to enter and lie alongside the bank. The country round about is flat, as Ferdinand describes the neighborhood of Retrete. El Portete has been much contracted in the last half century by the growth of coral reefs; the entrance is now barely 15 feet wide, and inside there would not now be room for the Columbian fleet, even if all four caravels were lashed together. They might barely have squeezed in there in 1502, and the place is a little "box" or "closet," which Escribanos is not. On the other hand, nobody sailing along-shore would suspect there to be a harbor at that place and send boats in to sound; and as Columbus approached from the eastward he would have seen Escribanos opening up first. And the earliest chart which shows Retrete as anything more than a spot, a French map of about 1570, has it cup-shaped, and in a position corresponding to Escribanos. Consequently the Harvard Columbus Expedition, after long debate, concluded that Puerto Escribanos, despite Ferdinand's understatement of its capacity, was the Admiral's Retrete; we think that an earthquake must have enlarged it greatly since his visit.

Owing to the small area of Retrete in 1502, the caravels had to lie alongside the banks as to a wharf; and this gave the men the opportunity for private trading that they wanted. At night, or whenever the officers were not vigilant, they slipped ashore by twos and threes. Following Indian trails to the native villages, they did considerable trading with a gun; and, says Ferdinand, "committed a thousand outrages, whence the Indians were provoked to alter their manners, and to break the peace, and some fights occurred between them." The Indians gathered in large numbers near the vessels, which lay alongside the shore. Columbus tried to win them over by patience and civility, but at last, "perceiving their arrogance, in order to strike terror into them caused some pieces of ordnance to be fired, to which they answered with shouts, beating the branches of the trees with staves, making sundry threats, and showing that they had no fear of his noise, because they thought it had been only a thundering to frighten them. Therefore, not to suffer so great pride, and lest they should contemn the Christians, the Admiral let fly a shot at a company of them as they were together on a little hill, and the ball falling in their midst, gave them to know that this thunder carried a thunderbolt. In the future they hardly dared peep out at us from behind the hills. The people of this country were the most proper built they had yet seen among the Indians, they were tall and spare, without any swelling of the belly, and of handsome countenances." They seem, then, to have been another race than the Cuna Cuna or San Blas Indians, who are square-built, broad in the chest, but with abnormally short legs attenuated by many generations of living in canoes. Yet the Cuna Cuna are supposed to have extended as far west as the Chagres.

Retrete is the first place on this voyage where Ferdinand mentions alligators. "In the harbor were vast great lizards or crocodiles, which go out to sleep ashore and scatter a certain odor as if all the musk in the world were collected; but they are so ravenous and cruel that if they find a man asleep ashore they will drag him into the water to devour him, though they are cowardly and flee when attacked. These lizards are found in many other parts of the mainland, and some do declare that they are crocodiles like those of the Nile."

Crocodiles — Nile — Terrestrial Paradise! So Columbus would have argued on his Third Voyage. But he was older now and disillusioned. This Otro Mundo was no paradise but a rough, wild shore where honest traders would find it hard to gain a living. If only a gap would appear in that eternal cordillera, and let him through to the Indian Ocean! He was so tired of beating along this rugged coast, felt sure there was no watery strait; you might dig one perhaps by enslaving the Indians, or build a road across the isthmus for pack mules — why not? Men travel daily from Genoa to Venice. But that would cost a mint of money and Columbus very well knew the frown he would get from the Queen and the cutting, ungracious words from the King if he came home with no gold to speak of, only a plan for spending it. So the best course was to seek more gold; gold and pearls were the only things that talked in Castile. So farewell Retrete, back to Veragua and exploit the mines.

"On Monday December 5 the Admiral, perceiving that the violence of the east and northeast winds abated not, and that no business could be done with these people, decided to turn back and verify what the Indians had said about the mines of Veragua, and therefore that day he went to sleep at Porto Bello 10 leagues to westward." The next day, December 6, the fleet had proceeded on its course but a few miles when the wind whipped around into the west again; and for a month the caravels were batted back and forth between Porto Bello and somewhere west of the Chagres River. The currents along this coast always run with the wind, as Ferdinand noted, and it was a winter wind; beating to windward got you nowhere.

Columbus writes of this dreadful month briefly but eloquently: "The tempest arose and wearied me so that I knew not where to turn; my old wound opened up, and for nine days I was as lost without hope of life; eyes never beheld the sea so high, angry and covered with foam. The wind not only prevented our progress, but offered no opportunity to run behind any headland for shelter; hence we were forced to keep out in this bloody ocean, seething like a pot on a hot fire. Never did the sky look more terrible; for one whole day and night it blazed like a furnace, and the lightning broke forth with such violence that each time I wondered if it had carried off my spars and sails; the flashes came with such fury and frightfulness that we all thought the ships would be blasted.

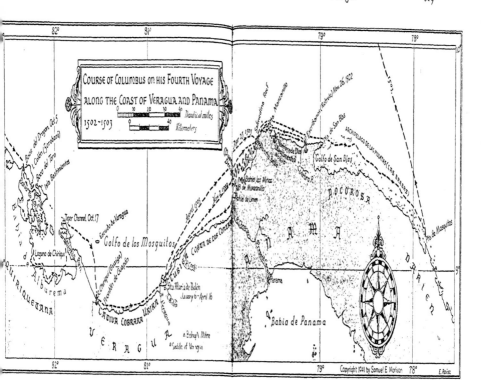

All this time the water never ceased to fall from the sky; I don't say it rained, because it was like another deluge. The people were so worn out that they longed for death to end their dreadful sufferings."

Ferdinand tells us of the frightful thunder and lightning, the torrential rain sluicing down, the men wet through for days on end, never getting half an hour's rest, "struggling with all the elements, and dreading them all; for in such terrible storms they dread the fire in lightning flashes, the air for its fury, the water for the waves, and the earth for the reefs and rocks of that unknown coast which sometimes come up at a man near the haven where he would be and not knowing the entrance, he chooses rather to contend with the other elements. . . . Besides these divers terrors there occurred one no less dangerous and wonderful, a waterspout which on Tuesday December 13 passed by the ships, the which had they

not dissolved by reciting the Gospel according to St. John, it would have swamped whatever it struck without a doubt; for, it draws the water up to the clouds in a column thicker than a water-butt, twisting it about like a whirlwind." It was the Admiral who exorcised the waterspout. From his Bible he read an account of that famous tempest off Capernaum, concluding, "Fear not, it is I!" Then, clasping the Bible in his left hand, with drawn sword he traced a cross in the sky and a circle around his whole fleet.

That same night *Vizcaína* lost sight of the other three, but had the good fortune to encounter them again after three very dark and dreadful days, during which she lost her boat and once anchored, but had to cut the cable. There followed two days of calm, which for the superstitious were almost as horrible as the tempest; for the caravels were surrounded by great schools of sharks. The men took and killed them by hook and chain, until they wearied of the bloody sport; and though some regarded shark meat as of evil omen, all were so ravenous and their stores so spent that fresh shark steak was a welcome feast. By this time, says Ferdinand, "what with the heat and dampness, our ship biscuit had become so wormy that, God help me, I saw many who waited for darkness to eat the porridge made of it, that they might not see the maggots; and others were so used to eating them that they didn't even trouble to pick them out, because they might lose their supper had they been so nice."

On Saturday, December 17, the fleet put in at a port called by the Indians *Huiva*, which lay 3 leagues east of a rock called *Peñón*. In this harbor like a great *canale* (channel) they rested three days. The Indians thereabouts were tree dwellers. On December 20 the fleet set sail with fair, but not settled weather; as soon as they were at sea the tempest began to rage again, and drove them into another port, "whence we departed on the third day, with weather that seemed to be on the mend, but which, like an enemy that lies in wait for a man, assaulted us again, and forced us to Peñón, where, when we were hoping to enter the harbor, the wind as if it were playing with us, started up so violently almost at the mouth of the harbor" that it blew the fleet into the harbor where it had been before! "And here we stayed from the second day of the feast of the Nativity (December 26) to the third day of January, 1503." Columbus says that they "returned to *Puerto Gordo* . . . on Christmas day at the hour of mass" because he dared not hold the sea owing to a predicted opposition of Saturn with Mars, which would make the weather even worse. This sinister opposition of the planets occurred on December 29. The Admiral did not neglect his almanac.

From a comparison of Columbus's account with that of his son, it seems that *Huiva* and *Puerto Gordo* were one and the same harbor, probably Limón Bay, now the harbor of the Canal Zone port of Cristóbal; or the adjacent Manzanilla Bay, which makes a harbor for the Panamanian city of Colón. Puerto Gordo is described in one of the *pleitos* as being between the Rio de los Lagartos (Columbus's name for the Chagres, now used for its southern branch) and Porto Bello. There is only one other harbor between these two points, and that, Las Minas Bay eastward of Manzanilla, we think would have seemed rather a small than a large "channel" to the Spaniards. *Peñón,* meaning a rocky cliff or cape, must be the headland at the Chagres mouth, where the ancient Fort Lorenzo is located. Another circumstance pointing to Limón or Manzanilla Bay as Puerto Gordo is that *Gallega* was there put on the beach to be graved; and in both bays there are suitable careening beaches.

So we may regard it as certain that Columbus's fleet kept Christmas and New Year riding at anchor off the site of our Coco Solo naval base, or within sight of the Panama Canal entrance at Cristóbal, while *Gallega* was hove-down on a near-by beach, her bottom being graved and her seams payed with pitch. Ferdinand was a prophet unawares in calling this place a *canale.* But it is sad to consider what Columbus missed. Had he now been as keen about the strait as he was for gold, had he questioned the Indians closely here as he had in Chiriqui, he might have sent his boats 5 miles around Toro Point and up the Chagres, and proceeded by dugout canoe to a point only 10 or 12 miles distant from the Pacific tides. One can well understand why he did not. There are times when, after a terrible buffeting at sea, a seaman can only lie in port like a dog licking his wounds after a bear fight. Columbus was so exhausted and humbled that he had no energy for exploration, and his officers and men were only too glad to relax. So it was left for Vasco Núñez de Balboa to "gaze with wild surmise" on the Pacific, from a height in Darien.

CHAPTER XLVI

Belén

January 1–April 16, 1503

Quare fremuerunt Gentes, et populi meditati sunt inania?

Why do the heathen so furiously rage together, and why
do the people imagine a vain thing?

— PSALM ii 1

SATURN'S opposition to Mars passed off with no untoward
events; a happy omen for the New Year 1503. *Capitana,
Santiago, Vizcaína* and patched-up *Gallega* took on maize and
wood and water, and put to sea from Puerto Gordo near the future
Panama Canal entrance on January 3, 1503. Ferdinand declares that
the wind promptly turned contrary, and gave the fleet another
tossing, so that the Admiral named this shore *La Costa de los Con-
trastes,* "The Coast of Contrarieties." But the Admiral himself reports fair weather, "although the ships were unseaworthy and the
men lifeless." In any case, it took the fleet three days to recover
60 miles. On January 6 they dropped anchors off a river that Columbus named *Belén* (Bethlehem) after that day, the Epiphany or
Feast of the Three Kings.

Owing to the position of this river and that of the Rio Veragua
becoming a bone of contention between Panama and Costa Rica
in their long boundary controversy, much doubt has been expressed as to whether the present Rio Belén is the same as the one
so named by Columbus. For that reason, the Harvard Columbus
Expedition made a point of examining the rivers along that part of
the Golfo de los Mosquitos, in order to identify Columbus's
"Bethlehem River." After enduring several very rough anchorages,
being spilled when landing in the surf, and walking many miles

along beaches heaped knee-high with driftwood, we are able to report confidently that the river now called Belén perfectly fits Ferdinand's description of the one that he and his father discovered.

While the fleet lay anchored in the open roadstead off the mouth of Rio Belén, Columbus had its bar and that of the Rio Veragua (a league further west) sounded from the boats. Finding ten *palmos* (about 7 feet) of water on the Belén bar and much less at Veragua, the Admiral decided to make the Belén his headquarters while he explored the region in search of gold mines. "I got inside with great difficulty," he says, "and the following day the tempest returned. If I had been outside I could never have got over the bar." *Capitana* and *Vizcaína* passed over on January 9, and their boats at once rowed up-river to trade; *Gallego* and *Santiago* missed flood tide that day, but crossed the bar on the tenth.

Just inside the bar the Rio Belén forms a basin, where there is over 3 fathoms' depth of water today, and plenty of room for twenty or thirty sail of such ships as the Admiral's. Above there is a straight, deep reach of the river some 2 miles long. Boats can row up-river 10 or 11 miles, we were told, and canoes may penetrate much farther into the highlands. These were ideal headquarters for exploring Veragua. Columbus decided to stay at least until the rainy season was over; and it rained without stopping for more than a month.

The Guaymi Indians, whose villages were on the upper reaches of the Belén and the Veragua, were unfriendly and seemed little inclined to trade. Fortunately an interpreter, probably one who had talked with the Spaniards at Chiriqui, offered his services and told the local Indians that the Spaniards were good people. On January 12 the Adelantado took all the ships' boats a few miles down the coast and ascended the Rio Veragua to the headquarters of a cacique known as *El Quibián*, who came downstream with his canoes and warriors to meet the distinguished visitors. "When the conference had hardly begun, the servants of the cacique, mindful of his royal majesty," and fearing lest he demean himself "in standing up to do business, fetched a rock from the neighboring stream-side, washed and dried it with care, and respectfully placed it under the royal bottom. Once seated, the cacique by nodding assent gave us to understand that he would allow us to explore his rivers." Next day the Quibián returned the visit aboard *Capitana*, discoursed with the Admiral for about an hour through the interpreter, and received suitable gifts.

"We being thus very easy and secure," says Ferdinand, "on Tuesday January 24 the Rio de Belén suddenly flooded, so that before we could prepare for it or run a hawser ashore, the fury of that water struck *Capitana* with such force that she broke one of her two cables, and drove with such impetus against *Gallega* which lay astern, as to carry away her bonaventure mizzen; then, fouling one another, they drifted so as to be in great peril of perishing with all hands." These floods are characteristic of that region. The mountains pick up so much moisture from the trade winds that the ground is usually saturated, and heavy rain has to run off in a freshet. That is the reason why the gold resources of Veragua, the wealth of which Columbus did not exaggerate, have never been successfully exploited. For, as an old prospector told us, no sooner does one build sluice boxes or other gear than a freshet occurs, and carries them "to hell-and-gone."

Driving rain, floods, and seas breaking on the bar prevented further exploration for two weeks. The men had nothing to occupy them but re-rigging and caulking the caravels. By February 6, when the sea had flattened down sufficiently so that the boats could cross the bar, Bartholomew with all three boats and sixty-eight men rowed along the coast a league, and then up the Rio Veragua. They passed a night at the Quibián's village, and marched upcountry with Indian guides, crossing the river forty-four times in one day. On the second day they reached a heavily wooded region of auriferous earth where the Guaymis obtained their gold; and in one day the Spaniards without any tools other than their knives collected two or three castellanos' worth (say $6 to $9) of gold. The party returned in safety, much pleased with themselves; and this discovery of the "mines of gold" so impressed the Admiral that he decided to build a town and leave his brother in charge, while he returned to Spain for reinforcements. He had missed the strait, but no matter; for he had found a much richer gold deposit than any in Hispaniola.

Exploration proceeded apace. On February 14 the Adelantado with fifty-four men rowed some 22 miles westward along the coast to a region and river that the Indians called *Urirá;* probably the modern Rio Culovebora. They met a friendly reception from the local cacique, whose men continually chewed a dry herb (possibly the coca plant); spent the night in a great house, met a second cacique, and bartered for gold disks, which were sent back to the ships. The indefatigable Adelantado with thirty men pressed on by foot to villages called Cobrava and Cativa where he found extensive cornfields, and procured a great quantity of gold disks "like the paten of a chalice; they wear them hanging by a string about their necks, as we do an *Agnus Dei.*"

As soon as Bartholomew returned, work began on the new settlement, which Columbus named *Santa María de Belén.* Ferdinand describes it as situated on the west bank of the river, a lombard shot from the mouth, "beyond a gully that comes down to the river, at the foot of which there is a *monticello.*" Standing on the opposite bank of the Belén on January 12, 1940, I found it easy to locate the spot, but was not much impressed with its defensive possibilities; for the *monticello* or hillock on the river is commanded by higher wooded hills. Houses and a magazine or storehouse were constructed of timber and thatched with palm leaf; but all provisions that came from Spain, such as wine, biscuit, oil, vinegar, cheese and grain, were stored aboard *Gallega,* which the Admiral intended to leave for his brother's use.

Ferdinand here interpolates a most interesting account of the Guaymis and their ways. They turn their backs when they speak, and are always chewing an herb which rots their teeth. Their main food is fish, which they take in nets and on hooks cut out of tortoise shell with a stout thread. Small fishes called *titi* and others like sardines they catch near the surface in small nets, wrap them in leaves as apothecaries roll electuaries in paper, and dry them in ovens. Sardines are taken by beating the water with paddles, which causes them to leap toward the canoes, where palm-leaf screens are erected to make them fall aboard. A fermented drink (*chicha*) is made from maize, and a sharp, brisk wine, resembling the wine of Gascony, from the juice of a kind of palm. Wine is also made from pineapples which they cultivate for that purpose, and from the mamey or mammee apple.

When ten or twelve houses had been put up at Santa María de Belén, and everything was set for the Admiral to depart, it stopped raining and the water level in the river dropped sharply, leaving only two feet over the bar. Now the caravels could not get out. "We had nothing left," says Ferdinand, "but to pray God for rain, as formerly we prayed for fair weather." And at this juncture, when the fleet was trapped inside, there came that inevitable change of attitude characteristic of all American Indians when they realized that "men from Heaven" meant to settle down. "They were very simple (*rústicos*) and our people very importunate," said Columbus. No doubt, as at Retrete, Spaniards in twos and threes had been stealing off to the bush, and by arms extorting gold from the natives. Veragua had no communication with Retrete, but feral instinct was enough; the Spaniards must go.

Pretty soon the fleet began to be visited by parties of Indians in warlike array, pretending that they were joining the Quibián to make war on Cobrava and other places to the westward. Diego Méndez, one of the gentleman volunteers on *Santiago*, told the Admiral that he did not like the look of it, something was in the wind; the Admiral thought so too. Diego volunteered to row along the coast toward Veragua in search of the encampment whence these armed parties appeared to come. A mile or two around the headland he found a thousand warriors encamped on the shore, chattering and howling and very much pleased with what they were planning. Diego, with that amazing coolness of the Spaniard which came from his overweening sense of superiority to all heathen, stepped ashore alone to speak with them. Then, returning to the boat, he had the oarsmen keep her just off shore, so that the Indians were under observation all night. They dared not move on Belén, knowing he could get there first by water and give the alarm. In the morning the oarsmen gave way, and within an hour Diego reported to the Admiral.

This should have given Columbus a hint that his proposed colony was impracticable without overwhelming force; but he refused to abandon the plan without more definite information. Diego Méndez volunteered to procure it. This time he walked along the beach with only one companion. Near the mouth of the Veragua he found two canoes of strange Indians who frankly told him that the assembled warriors, who had shifted camp, intended to attack the caravels in two days' time. Diego, who seems to have applied himself to learning the Guaymi language during the past six weeks, induced these people, much against their will, to paddle him up-river to the Quibián's village, where the war party was encamped. By pretending that he had come to cure an arrow wound of the cacique, he obtained access to the compound around "the palace," as he calls the cacique's elaborate hut. Upon his approach a dreadful uproar broke out among the women and children, and a son of the cacique rushed out, saying very nasty things in his own language and giving Diego a push that almost knocked him down. Diego, perfectly disciplined and completely poised, concealed his resentment at this rude handling, and coolly staged a little act that he had rehearsed. Knowing the Indians' curiosity over anything new, Méndez had brought a simple barber's kit — a pocket mirror, comb and a pair of shears; he sat on the ground while his companion, Rodrigo de Escobar, solemnly combed and cut his hair. As had been expected, this process so interested the Quibián that he gladly had his hair trimmed (surely Rodrigo was an expert, the comb stout, and the shears of Toledo steel!), and was then presented with the barber's outfit. Diego asked for something to eat, food and drink were produced, and he and Escobar had a friendly dinner with the cacique. They returned to the ships with certain news that the Indians were planning to exterminate their visitors.

Columbus again took counsel with Diego Méndez, who advised that the only safe course was to seize the Quibián and his lieutenants and hold them as hostages; and this he proposed to effect by stratagem. The Adelantado, Diego Méndez, and about eighty men rowed up to the Quibián's village. Dispersing the bulk of their force in ambush about the hill where the cacique's hut was pitched, the two leaders with three attendants marched boldly up and demanded audience. The Quibián came out to meet the Adelantado, who pretended to be solicitous about his wound, and grasped him by the arm. One of Diego's advance party fired a gun as a signal, when the other Spaniards rushed from their ambush, beset the hut, and captured and carried off the cacique together with almost thirty members of his household, including wives and children.

Quibián and some of the more important prisoners were bound and entrusted to the chief pilot of the fleet, Juan Sánchez, to carry to Belén, while most of the Spaniards remained to mop up. But the cacique was too wily for his captor. Complaining that his bonds were hurting him, he induced Sánchez to set him free from all ropes but one, which the Spaniard held. At nightfall, when they were still descending the river, he jumped overboard, forcing Sánchez to let go the rope rather than be drawn in after him. The Quibián made good his escape, but the Adelantado and Diego Méndez returned unscathed to Belén, bearing three hundred ducats' worth of booty in the shape of gold disks, "eagles" and "gold cords that they put about their heads in guise of coronets." All this plunder was divided among the party, except for 20 per cent saved as the crown's share.

A bold stratagem, well executed; but the cacique's escape spoiled it, for he promptly raised the country against the Spaniards. They in the meantime, profiting by a rain that raised the water on the bar, were towing out the three caravels intended for the homeward passage. Bartholomew was to be left as commander of the settlement with Diego Méndez as his lieutenant and some seventy men. On April 6, when the bulk of their force were saying farewell aboard the caravels outside, and only twenty men and the Irish wolfhound were left to guard Santa María de Belén, there suddenly appeared on the hills overlooking the village four hundred warriors armed with bows and arrows, slingshots and spears, which they hurled through the wattles of the huts. They killed one and wounded several, including the Adelantado; but, "punished by the edge of the sword, and by the dog who pursued them furiously," fled. "This fight lasted three full hours, and Our Lord gave us the victory miraculously, we being so few and they so numerous," records Diego Méndez.

The sequel was tragic. Just before the attack Captain Diego Tristán of *Capitana* had been sent ashore with a ship's boat to take on a final supply of water. During the fight he and his men remained stolidly in the boat looking on, because, he said, his orders were to obtain water and nothing else. When the fight was over the captain calmly rowed up the Belén to obtain good sweet water. He was warned that the Indians might get him; but no matter, said Diego, he had his orders from the Admiral and could take care of himself. When the boats were about a league upstream, where heavy foliage lined both banks, the Indians sprang out at them. They killed Tristán by a spear stroke through the eye and slaughtered his entire company, save one man who swam under water beyond spear shot, and so escaped to tell the bad news. And the Indians also broke up the boat.

Here was a pretty fix. The three caravels lying in an open roadstead with but one boat between them; Indians raising horrible whoops and yells around the settlement; and the depressing spectacle of the corpses of Diego Tristán and his men floating downstream, covered with hideous wounds and attended by carrion crows. The whole garrison would gladly have made its escape, but they could not get *Gallega* over the bar, and had no boat; nor could the Admiral send his one boat in for them.

While the fight was going on Columbus was left alone aboard *Capitana*, anchored more than a mile off shore. Already shaken by a malarial fever, he was rendered delirious by the sounds of battle, the grim silence that followed, and the failure of his captain to return. "I climbed," he says, "to the highest part of the ship; and in a fearful voice cried out for help to Your Highnesses' war captains in every direction; but none replied. At length, groaning with exhaustion, I fell asleep, and heard a compassionate voice saying: 'O fool and slow to believe and serve thy God, the God of every man! What more did he do for Moses, or for David his servant, than for thee? From thy birth he hath ever held thee in special charge. When he saw thee arrive at man's estate, marvellously did he cause thy name to resound over the earth. The Indies, so rich a portion of the world, he gave thee for thine own, and thou hast divided them as it pleased thee. Of those barriers of the Ocean Sea, which were closed with such mighty chains, he gave thee the keys. What more did he do for the people of Israel, or for David who from a shepherd he raised to be king over Judea? Turn to him and acknowledge thy fault; thine old age shall not hinder thee from mighty deeds, for many and vast heritages he holdeth. . . . Fear not, but have trust; all these tribulations are written on tablets of marble, and not without cause.' I heard all this, as in a swoon, but I had no answer to give in definite words, only to weep for my transgressions."

A skeleton crew had to be provided for *Capitana* from the other two ships that were riding off shore. For eight days matters remained at an impasse, the weather improving so that there was no need to shift anchorage, but not enough to get a boat across the bar. Fortunately the Quibián had acquired a healthy respect for the Spaniards' dogs and firearms, so after three days of alarums and excursions the Indians retired.

In the meantime, the other natives captured in the Veragua raid were becoming very restive in their prison aboard *Santiago*. At night they were confined below deck, and the hatch cover fastened down by a chain. But one night the anchor watch grew careless, and failed to secure the chain, because the hatch provided a nice flat surface on which to sleep. Some of the more enterprising captives heaped up ballast below, and standing on the stones forced the hatch off with their shoulders, tumbling the sleepy sailors on deck; and before the alarm was given, they had leaped overboard and were swimming ashore. The watch then secured the hatch. When it was removed at daylight to give the other captives air, a ghastly sight met the seamen's eyes. During the night these poor wretches, some of them women, had collected ropes in the hold and hanged themselves to the deck beams, courageously bending their knees while they strangled, as there was insufficient headroom for a proper straight-legged hanging.

Columbus now reflected that, having no hostages with which to secure the Quibián's good conduct, his brother's situation ashore must be pretty desperate; yet the river bar was still breaking all across, and no boat could get inside. Pedro de Ledesma volunteered, if the one remaining boat would take him where the water broke, to swim across and obtain news of the settlement. This he courageously did, bringing back word that the garrison were not only quarreling among themselves, but in a bad way for defense, and begging the Admiral to take them aboard. This meant giving up Santa María de Belén. But there was nothing else for Columbus to do, as he valued the lives of his brother and shipmates. Well he remembered the fate of Navidad. Diego Méndez, by fashioning a raft out of two dugouts and timber, managed in two days to lighter over the bar the whole garrison, stores and gear, abandoning the worm-eaten hulk of *Gallega*. For this and his other labors, Diego was embraced by the Admiral on both cheeks, and promoted captain of *Capitana* in place of Diego Tristán.

Finally, on Easter night, April 16, 1503, the reduced fleet of three ships set sail from this ill-fated spot for Hispaniola — as they hoped. This village, which had cost the lives of ten good men, was abandoned forever. From time to time, during the next three and a half centuries, the Spaniards attempted settlements up the valleys of the Belén and Veragua; but the difficulties of extracting gold proved insuperable, the climate was murderous to white men, and one by one these mining camps were abandoned. The surviving Guaymi Indians, whose ancestors were long since driven from their vil-

lages and cornfields, now live far up in the mountains; and except
for a few clearings of palm-thatched huts where a handful of half-
breeds live miserably, the lower reaches of the Belén and the Veragua are more wild and wooded now than when Columbus first
saw them on the Day of the Three Kings, 1503.

CHAPTER XLVII

At Sea in a Sieve
April 16–June 25, 1503

Et cum coepisset mergi, clamauit dicens, Domine, saluum me fac.

And beginning to sink, he cried, saying, Lord, save me.
— MATTHEW xiv 30

COLUMBUS'S plan, when he set sail from the Rio de Belén on Easter night, 1503, was to call at Santo Domingo for refreshment and repairs, and thence proceed home to Spain. All the pilots of the fleet believed that Hispaniola or Puerto Rico lay due north of them; whilst actually they were on the meridian of Cienfuegos, Cuba, and the nearest point of Hispaniola lay northeast, in the teeth of the prevailing wind. Columbus, observing that the equatorial current made it impossible to execute a long beat to windward, especially with ships in the condition that his were, decided to work eastward along the coast until he reached a point whence there was some chance of reaching Hispaniola on one tack. This sensible and seamanlike decision caused the people to grumble, because they believed the pilots. They charged the Admiral with intending to sail a direct route to Spain with unfit and ill-provisioned vessels.

While the fleet had been lying idle inside the Belén bar, the teredos or shipworms had been getting in their deadly work. Why Columbus had not careened and pitched the whole fleet at Puerto Gordo instead of only *Gallega*, is not explained. Possibly he had pitch enough for only one ship, and applied it to the one that was in the worst way. By that time it was probably too late to save them; for pitch to a teredo is like a boy's first cigar; if he gets past

it, he will go on. And once into a ship's bottom, nothing can stop
a teredo until he works through, and the planking is completely
riddled. Why did not the Admiral heave down and cleanse the
entire fleet when he touched at Cuba, as he had done on the First
Voyage; or at Bonacca Island or Cape Honduras? Even with modern copper paint, it is unsafe to leave a wooden ship in tropical
waters longer than six months without a hauling-out; and the Admiral's fleet, when it left Belén, had been afloat for over a year.
However, it may have been an unusually bad year for teredos, and
Columbus answered our post-mortem criticisms in his *Lettera
Rarissima* to the Sovereigns: —

"Let those who are fond of blaming and finding fault, while
they sit safely at home, ask, 'Why did you not do thus and so?' I
wish they were on this voyage; I well believe that another voyage
of a different kind awaits them, or our faith is naught."

In other words, to hell with them!

Vizcaína had to be abandoned at Porto Bello on April 23, and the
other two, *Capitana* and *Santiago*, were not much better off. Diego
Méndez recalled that "all the people with pumps, kettles and other
vessels were insufficient to bail out the water that entered by the
worm-holes." With two rotten ships, only one boat left for shore
service, and short of provisions, the situation was far from cheerful.

Rounding the rocky headlands beyond Porto Bello, the crippled
vessels proceeded eastward past Retrete, into the Gulf of San
Blas. According to our tastes, this is the most beautiful country
that Columbus discovered on his Fourth Voyage, and the finest
winter cruising ground that any of us ever expect to see. At San
Blas Point the eastward-trending coastline steps southward about
7 miles, and the peninsula itself breaks off into a ragged line of
wooded sand cays which Columbus appropriately named *Las
Barbas* (The Whiskers). They lay a league or so from the mainland, and were then uninhabited; the fleet spent a night anchored
off one of Las Barbas, and someone made a bad shot at Polaris,
reporting the latitude as 13° 30', four degrees too much. The

modern name of these islands, *Archipelago de las Mulatas* (of the Mulatto Wenches), is singularly inappropriate, for the Cuna Cuna or San Blas Indians who inhabit them today (having learned by experience that the islands are free from malaria) have kept their language, their customs, their blood and their dignity. During the building of the Panama Canal, a high official attempted to purchase the sand of one of the cays in this region, to use in construction. The reigning cacique replied: "He who made this sand made it for the Cuna Cuna who live no longer, for those who are here today and also for those to come. So it is not ours only, and we could not sell it."

Pocorosa, we learn, was the name of the Cuna Cuna cacique in 1503, but Columbus was too anxious about his ships to take time out for barter. Nor does he mention the jagged cordillera whose sky line comes within 10 miles of the coast, or the magnificent forest covering of valuable woods, where good mast pines are mingled with mahogany, cedar, silk cotton, ebony, satinwood, rosewood, and the *brazil* or logwood which in colonial days was the chief export of this region. Every so often one tree thrusts itself above the rolling sea of green foliage and bursts into a mass of pink or orange blossoms, bright as though a torch were being held up from the dark jungle below.

On May 1, eight days and about 125 miles from Porto Bello, the fleet reached a continental headland that Columbus for no apparent reason named *Marmóreo* (Marble). In all probability this was Punta de Mosquito in latitude 9° 07′ N, longitude 77° 52′ W. Since the coast here began definitely to trend southeasterly into the Gulf of Darien, the pilots and captains, who thought they were already *east* of the Caribbee Islands, prevailed upon Columbus to leave the mainland and strike out for Hispaniola. Their actual position was due south of Jamaica, and about 900 miles *west* of the Caribbee Islands! Columbus would have done better to have crossed the Gulf of Darien and worked along the coast as far as Cabo de la Vela before taking his departure; thus he would have had a fair chance of making Hispaniola on one board, taking abeam the light easterly trades which prevail in summer. Hojeda made Jacmel, Haiti, from Cabo de la Vela in 1499, and weathered Beata Island on the same course in 1502.

Columbus himself remarks at this point that it was no use trying to sail on the wind in the Western Caribbean, not because the ships were ill-designed or clumsy — even Portuguese caravels would not serve, he said — but because the wind, current and sea running together render it impossible to make progress sailing "on the bowline," close-hauled. Hence it was highly advisable for the fleet to make further easting alongshore, where they could catch counter currents, have occasional protection from islands, and use the land breeze at night. From a point a few hundred miles to the eastward they could have a good slant to Hispaniola. But the coastline from Las Mulatas to Cabo de la Vela was yet unknown, and even an Admiral must sometimes respect public opinion. It is very difficult to run a ship when the crew believes that the commanding officer is doing something absolutely wrong, and heading them to certain death. Apparently the pilots had persuaded the people that if they did not turn north soon, they would miss the Windward Islands; and with planking becoming spongier every day, that meant drowning. So, against his better judgment, Columbus said his last farewell to the American continent, and with sheets close-hauled, headed as near north as the wind would permit.

Of the next leg of this voyage we have only the barest details. "On Monday the first of May 1503, we stood to the northward, with winds and currents easterly," says Ferdinand, "always endeavoring to sail as close to the wind as we could. And although all the pilots insisted that we had passed eastward of the Caribbee Islands, the Admiral feared we should not manage to fetch Hispaniola. It so turned out, because on Wednesday May 10 we raised two very small and low islands full of turtles (as was all the sea about, so that they looked like little rocks); whence these islands were called *Las Tortugas*." These were Little Cayman and Cayman Brac, about 115 miles northwestward from Jamaica, and still a great center of the turtle industry. The direct course thither from Mosquito Point is 650 miles 349° true or N by W; but the actual course following the wind must have been very much longer, since the wind would have varied several points, and the equatorial current ran from east to west at a rate varying from 10 to 50 miles a day. Under these circumstances, and with planking like honeycomb tripe, *Capitana* and *Santiago* did very well to make good an average of 72 miles a day. And they had the good fortune to pass safely between the Pedro, Serranilla and other breaking reefs.

No stop was made at the Caymans. "On the evening of the following Friday (May 12), 30 leagues beyond, we arrived at the Jardín de la Reina, which is a very great collection of islands on the south side of Cuba." So says the realistic Ferdinand, but his father characteristically reported to the Sovereigns, "I arrived on May 13 in the province of Mangi, which is a part of Cathay." Never would he relinquish the notion that Cuba belonged to the Asiatic mainland.

This place where they made Cuba was the northwestern part of the Laberinto de Doze Leguas, southwestern edge of the group that Columbus named El Jardín de la Reina on his Second Voyage. There the Bretón and Cinco Balas Cays form a narrow, rocky harbor which we investigated in 1940, and decided to be the most likely spot for the fleet to have found shelter. Diego Méndez, despite his loyalty to the Admiral, believed that the pilots were right, and at this point in his narrative remarks, "Thus we were over 300 leagues further from Castile than when we left Veragua to go thither." Actually Columbus had lost about 90 miles easting, but gained over 700 miles northing; no man could have done better with the ships he had.

"Being here at anchor ten leagues from Cuba," says Ferdinand, "full of hunger and trouble, because they had nothing to eat but hard-tack and a little oil and vinegar, and exhausted by working three pumps day and night because the vessels were ready to sink from the multitude of worms that had bored into them; there came on in the night a great blow, in which the ship *Bermuda* [*Santiago*], being unable to ride it out, fouled us and broke our stem, nor did she get off whole, but smashed her stern almost to the helm. With great labor owing to the heavy rain and high wind it pleased God that they got clear of one another; and although we let go all the anchors and cables that we had, none held but the flagship's sheet anchor. When day dawned, we found intact but one strand of her cable, which must have parted had the night lasted an hour longer; and that being a hard place, full of rocks, we could not have missed fetching up on some of those astern of us. But it pleased God to deliver us there, as already He had from many other dangers." Columbus adds that they lost three anchors on that treacherous coral bottom.

After six days, which would bring us to about May 20, the weather moderated and Columbus continued his voyage to the eastward, "having already lost all the spare ground tackle, the ships pierced by borers worse than a honeycomb, the people spiritless and desperate." They put in at two harbors; the first impossible to identify, the second, which Porras says was near Cape Cruz, and Ferdinand calls *Macaca*, was probably Puerto Pilón. Apparently only one anchor was left for the two ships; *Santiago* had to lay astern of *Capitana* on a painter, or in a calm harbor lash herself to the flagship with bow and stern lines and breastfasts.

Diego Porras, in a very ungenerous conclusion to his narrative, declares that Columbus could "very easily have gone" from this harbor to Hispaniola, which he alleged was but 50 leagues (159 miles) distant. Actually from Puerto Pilón to the nearest Haitian anchorage at Jérémie was 200 miles ESE *against wind and current*. The ships could never have made it by straight beating, for every day they leaked worse, as more teredos worked through their skins. Columbus planned the most sensible course to save his voyage: to stand over toward Jamaica on the port tack, making that island as far to windward as possible; and then, if the ships could still float, await a chance for the last jump to Hispaniola. If they could go no further, Jamaica would be a gain to windward, and at least no worse a place to be marooned in than Cuba. The men believed that they could keep the caravels afloat a few weeks more, and preferred to continue their monotonous labors at the pumps on the chance of reaching a Christian country.

Almost a month had elapsed from the day they reached the Cuban cays when the two half-sinking caravels set forth from Puerto Pilón on their last voyage. "Day and night," says Ferdinand, "we never ceased working three pumps in each of them; and if any broke down, we had to supply its place by bailing with kettles while it was being patched up." Of all melancholy work on shipboard, pumping a hopelessly leaky vessel is the worst; the labor is back-breaking, there is no respite, and you know it can never improve. Columbus admitted in his Letter to the Sovereigns that he made a mistake in not running over to Jamaica as quickly as possible. In the hope of making Hispaniola he steered by the wind on the port tack until he had reached a point which according to his dead-reckoning was 28 leagues from Haiti. Water then began to gain on *Santiago* at so alarming a rate that both ships squared their yards and ran desperately down-wind for Jamaica. On the night of June 22–23, the water was almost up to the deck of *Capitana;* but in the morning they made Puerto Bueno, as they supposed.

As Dry Harbor, the modern name of this port, indicates, there was no fresh water available, and no Indian village near by as a source of supplies. Consequently the caravels were kept afloat over St. John's Day, and on the twenty-fifth with a land breeze sailed 12½ miles eastward into the harbor "enclosed with reefs" that Columbus had named Puerto Santa Gloria in 1494.

Ferdinand continues: "Having got in, and no longer able to keep the ships afloat, we ran them ashore as far as we could, grounding them close together board and board, and shoring them up on both sides so they could not budge; and in this position the tide rose almost to the decks. Upon these and the fore and stern castles cabins were built where the people might lodge, intending to make them strong that the Indians might do no damage; because at that time the island was not yet inhabited or subdued by Christians."

And there they stayed.

CHAPTER XLVIII

Marooned

June 25, 1503–March 7, 1504

Et dixit Sion: Dereliquit me Dominus, et Dominus oblitus est mei.

But Zion said, The Lord hath forsaken me, and my Lord hath forgotten me.

— ISAIAH xlix 14

THE LOCATION of this spot where *Capitana* and *Santiago* were run ashore to end their lives ingloriously as houseboats was one of the last tasks of the Harvard Columbus Expedition in January 1940. Under the guidance of Mr. Charles S. Cotter of Lime Hall, a former seaman and civil engineer who has studied the problem, we followed Columbus's reduced and waterlogged squadron to its last resting place. On the west side of St. Ann's Bay (as Santa Gloria was renamed a few years later) a channel of sufficient depth leads into a lagoon, so well protected by a line of coral reefs that on the day of our inspection, when a norther was making up, it was perfectly secure. On the south shore of this lagoon is a sand beach, shelving into deep water, and with an ocean outlook over an arc of some 150°. Behind the beach there is a slight eminence where a watch could be kept; and on the rising ground above, the Spaniards pitched Sevilla Nueva, their first Jamaican settlement, in 1508. The straight beach and low shores offered the Indians no opportunity to attack the grounded vessels from ambush, and the wide sea view made it likely that any passing sail would be sighted and hailed.

One can easily imagine the process of beaching the caravels. First *Capitana* and then *Santiago* was anchored off the beach, their heavy stores taken ashore, and the stone ballast hove overboard. A line was passed from a tree to the windlass of the first ship, both crews formed a bucket brigade to bail her out dry so as to lessen her draught, and at high water all hands worked windlass and sweeps in order to bring her onto the beach with as much way on as possible. Before the tide dropped she was shored up with newly cut timbers, and at low water sand ballast was shoveled into the hold. At the next daylight high tide, the same process

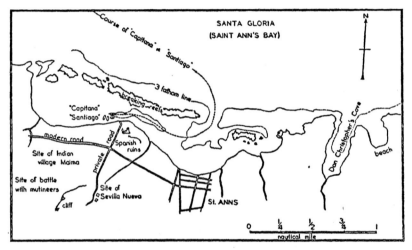

would be repeated with the other caravel. While the worm-eaten hulks settled into the sand, palm-thatched cabins were built on deck for shelter, and the artillery and small arms so disposed that the men could beat off attack either from the shore or from a flotilla of canoes.

The two caravels thus planted "board and board," as Ferdinand says, made a dry home, and no mean fortress. There were two good streams of fresh water near by, and a large Indian village, Maima, lay about half a mile away, convenient as a source of supply. No more suitable place for the purpose could have been found on the north shore of Jamaica.

The crew were now pretty well fixed for safety; Diego Méndez remarked that the only danger lay in the possibility that the Indians might steal upon them at night and set fire to their cabins. The immediate problem was food, for the ship's stores were all spoiled or spent. Of the original complement of 140 men and boys, 6 had died or deserted before reaching Veragua, 12 had been killed in the fight at Belén, and 6 had since died, leaving 116 mouths to be fed; and Spaniards of those days were no mean feeders. Columbus knew that Jamaica was thickly populated, and although the natives were of the same Taino culture as those of Cuba and the Bahamas, and although they were protected by having absolutely no gold, they had shown fight on his Second Voyage; and the Admiral knew by experience that even a Taino could be driven to desperation by the deeds of Spaniards. If he let his people, who were "naturally disobedient," go "running about the country and into the Indians' houses to take from them what they found and stir up the women and children," he would have the native population about his ears — as had happened at Retrete. Consequently the men were ordered to stay aboard, "and there was no going ashore without permission." Captain Diego Méndez with three companions was sent off to try what he could do by diplomacy to procure food.

Méndez tells how he gave out the last rations of biscuit and wine, and "with sword in hand and three companions" struck off into the interior. "And it pleased God that I found people so gentle that they did me no harm, but were friendly and gave me to eat with good will." In a village called Aguacadiba he agreed with the Indians that they should take cassava bread and hunt and fish and deliver to the ships what they made or took in return for trading truck. Ferdinand informs us that the agreed price was two of the big rodents called hutía for a lace-point, a cake of cassava bread for two or three glass beads, a hawk's bell for a great quantity of anything, with an occasional gift to caciques or other important persons of a red cap, mirror or pair of scissors. Méndez sent back one of his men to inform the Admiral. He then proceeded to another village, made a similar agreement, and sent the second man back. Thence to a great cacique called Huareo at a village on the site of Mellila. This chief was eager to trade, and the third Christian was sent back to inform the Admiral. Huareo then furnished

Méndez with two Indians to accompany him as porters, "one to carry the hammock in which I slept, and the other the food." At the eastern end of the island Méndez met a cacique named Ameyro with whom he entered into close friendship, even exchanging names. For a brass helmet, a cloak and a shirt, Méndez purchased from Ameyro an excellent dugout canoe in which, propelled by six Indian paddlers and carrying a supply of provisions, he returned by sea to Santa Gloria in triumph. Columbus embraced him, as well he might; for there was not a crust left to eat aboard the grounded caravels, and the Spaniards were starving. I cannot understand why they were unable to catch fish, or to buy maize and cassava from the Indians of the near-by village of Maima. However, Indians from near and far now came daily with food supplies, and for several months the question "when do we eat?" did not arise.

The next problem was how to get home. Later navigators, warned by what happened to their predecessors, always brought axes, adzes, and other tools for converting trees into ship timber; but Columbus had none of these, and both his caulkers had been killed at Belén. His men were incapable of replanking *Capitana* and *Santiago*, much less of building a new vessel. There was no expectation of any ship being sent out from Hispaniola to look for them, and the chance of any explorer coming that way was nil. No Spaniard, so far as we have record, had even visited Cuba or Jamaica since 1494, excepting two caravels of Hojeda's second fleet which sailed to the south coast of Jamaica from the Cabo de la Vela in 1502 in search of provisions; and the reason is obvious. Columbus had reported no gold there. Consequently the only possible means of rescue was to send a messenger by Indian canoe to Hispaniola, and there charter a caravel. A canoe it must be, because the only ship's boat rescued from the fight at Belén had been lost in the big wind at Cayo Bretón.

Columbus spoke his mind on the subject to Diego Méndez in July, urging haste. At any time the fickle natives might tire of the provision trade and attack the ships, or the Spaniards, bored and disgusted in their forced confinement on shipboard, might get out of hand. Méndez demurred, and no wonder; for the passage from the eastern end of Jamaica to the western cape of Hispaniola was 105 miles against wind and current, with another 350 miles to paddle alongshore before reaching Santo Domingo. He declared, moreover, that the trust the Admiral had placed in him on sundry occasions had aroused jealousy. Accordingly he suggested that the Admiral call together all his officers and propose the canoe journey; and if none volunteered, he, Diego Méndez, would again expose his life for the Admiral's service. It happened just as he predicted. All refused to go, and Méndez volunteered.

Very hastily, for Diego wished to be off at once, Columbus in his deck cabin composed the letter to his Sovereigns which is called *Lettera Rarissima*. It is the work of a man suffering both in mind and in body; incoherent, exaggerated, interspersed with discussions of cosmography and the visions of Belén; then there suddenly intrudes an earthy anecdote like the peccary and monkey fight at Cariai. He urges the Sovereigns to pay his men who "have passed through incredible toil and danger," but gives credit to no individual except his brother; he insists that the gold mines of Veragua were "the best news that ever was carried to Spain," and adverts to the humiliation of being imprisoned and sent home in irons. Yet this incoherent screed concludes with a noble and eloquent peroration: —

I came to serve [Your Highnesses] at the age of twenty-eight, and now I have no hair upon me that is not white, and my body is infirm and exhausted. All that was left to me and to my brothers has been taken away and sold, even to the cloak that I wore, to my great dishonor. It is believed that this was not done by your royal command. The restitution of my honor and losses, and the punishment of those who have inflicted them, of those who plundered me of my pearls, and who have disparaged my admiral's privileges, will redound to the honor of your royal dignity. The highest virtue, unexampled fame as grateful and just princes will redound to Your Highnesses if you do this; and the glorious memory will survive for Spain. The honest purpose which I have always shown in Your Highnesses' service, [coupled with] such unmerited outrage, will not permit my soul to keep silence, even though I might so wish. I implore Your Highnesses' pardon. I am as ruined as I have said. Hitherto I have wept for others; now have pity upon me, Heaven, and weep for me, earth! Of things material I have not even a *blanca* * to offer; in things spiritual, I have even ceased observing the forms here in the Indies. Isolated in this pain, infirm, daily expecting death, surrounded by a million savages full of cruelty and our enemies, and thus separated from the holy sacraments of holy Church, how neglected will be this soul if here it part from the body! Weep for me, whoever has charity, truth and justice! I did not come on this voyage to navigate for gain, honor or wealth, that is certain; for then the hope of all such things was dead. I came to Your Highnesses with honest purpose and sincere zeal, and I do not lie. I humbly beg Your Highnesses that, if it please God to remove me hence, you will aid me to go to Rome and on other pilgrimages. May the Holy Trinity guard and increase Your lives and high estate.

Done in the Indies, in the island of Jamaica, on the seventh of July, in the year one thousand five hundred and three.

Our feeling that this was not the sort of letter to elicit royal favor is confirmed by its reception. It had so little effect that Columbus was not invited to court for several months after his return, despite the presence of his son there. His despoilers and persecutors were never punished, his viceroyalty was not restored in his lifetime, and the stories of the gold mines at Veragua left the Sovereigns cold. He had not found the strait, not reached the Spice Islands; from the Sovereigns' point of view this voyage was a waste of money, and the Admiral an importunate bore.

More to modern taste is the brief note that Columbus just had time to scratch off to his friend Fray Gaspar Gorricio of the Monastery of Las Cuevas, Seville.

Reverend and very dear Father,

If my voyage were to be as conducive to the health of my person and the welfare of my house as it gives promise of being for the advantage of the royal crown and the King and Queen my Lords, I should hope to live more than a hundred jubilees. I have no time to write more at

* A small copper coin; see table at beginning of this work.

length. I hope that the bearer may be a person who may tell you more
by word of mouth than may be said in a thousand letters. Don Diego
will also give information.

I beseech the reverend Prior and all the brethren that they may
graciously remember me in all their prayers.

Done in the island of Jamaica on the 7th of July 1503.

At your reverence's orders,

· S ·

S · A · S ·

X   M   ϒ

Xρo   FERENS.

Diego Méndez hauled out the big dugout he had bought from
Ameyro, fixed a false keel to her, pitched and greased the bottom,
raised washboards on bow and stern to keep out breaking seas, and
fitted a mast and sail. Taking one Christian and six Indians he set
bravely forth. He passed some of the finest scenery in the Caribbean: white coral beaches lined by palms, waterfalls tumbling over
rocks into the sea, deeply cleft valleys leading up to the Blue Mountains, whose summits collected great blankets of cloud; tiny harbors offering safe refuge for the night, and Port San Antonio,
where a wooded island gives perfect protection. Somewhere near
Northeast Point, which he believed to be the nearest to Hispaniola,
Diego Méndez with customary boldness left the canoe and walked
into the forest. Suddenly he was surrounded by Indians who, he
gathered, intended to kill him and seize the canoe and cargo. While
they were playing a game of chance, of which the winner was
evidently to have the privilege of killing him, Diego escaped to
the canoe and paddled back to Santa Gloria.

Columbus, if he was disappointed at the failure of this attempt,
tactfully concealed it, and expressed great joy at seeing Méndez
alive; but begged him to try again. This he agreed to do, if the
Admiral would send an armed guard to protect him from those
hostile Indians at his intended take-off. Accordingly the Adelantado with a considerable force accompanied Méndez to the eastern
end of Jamaica in a fleet of dugouts.

On this second attempt, Méndez was accompanied by another big canoe commanded by Bartolomeo Fieschi. "Flisco," as Columbus called him, belonged to a Genoese patrician family which more than once had befriended the Colombos in their days of poverty and obscurity. Bartolomeo happened to be in Seville when Columbus was recruiting men for this voyage, and as the Admiral always liked to give responsible positions to his compatriots, Fieschi was appointed captain of *Vizcaína*.

It was agreed that Méndez and Fieschi should each take six Christians and ten Indians, in the hope that at least one dugout could make the passage to Hispaniola; and that if both made it, Méndez should press on to Santo Domingo to charter a ship, and Fieschi return to Jamaica with the news that help was forthcoming. At or near Northeast Point, Diego Méndez commended himself to God and Our Lady of Antigua; Fieschi doubtless prayed to his city's patron, Saint George, and farewells were exchanged with the Adelantado *con hartas lágrimas*, "with abundant tears," on both sides. Strong men in those days were not ashamed to weep when they felt like it. The Adelantado watched the two canoes out of sight on the glassy sea, and returned to Santa Gloria for a long, long wait.

Diego Méndez is as laconic about the actual crossing as he is voluble on the preparations; fortunately we have Fieschi's story, by way of Ferdinand. From Northeast Point, Jamaica, to the nearest land on Hispaniola, between Cape Dame Marie and Cape Tiburon, is about 108 nautical miles; but the journey can be broken 78 miles from Jamaica on the island of Navassa, a flat, level rock about 300 feet high and 2 miles long, where the United States now maintains a lighthouse. Although the canoers started in a flat calm, they had no reason to expect it to last; for July is a month of brisk trade winds in that region.

Each canoe carried six Christians besides the captain, and about ten Indians to do the work. Presumably each took a compass from the abandoned ships. On the first day the heat troubled the men most; even the Indians could not bear it, and had to take turns at swimming to refresh themselves. By sunset, when the Blue Mountains had disappeared, the watch was changed, and the canoes paddled on eastward. After breakfast next morning it was discovered that all the water brought by the Indians for their own use was gone, and by noon they were so thirsty as to be unable to work. Fortunately each captain had reserved a water-breaker for his private use, and from it served out just enough to keep the men going, encouraging them with the hope of raising Navassa before dark. Sunset came and no Navassa. Everyone was deeply discouraged; for according to their reckoning they had paddled 64 miles, and should have sighted the island if the course had been correct. "It was exhaustion and faintness that deceived them," says Ferdinand, "because a canoe cannot make good more than 10 leagues in 24 hours on account of the currents running counter to the course from Jamaica to Hispaniola." On the second night out an Indian died of thirst, and others were too weak and dejected to do anything but lie on the bottom. From time to time they washed out their mouths with salt water. This, says Ferdinand, "was the comfort afforded Our Lord when he said 'I thirst' "; and with such saline comfort they managed to push along during the third day. Night fell again with no sign of Navassa. But when the moon rose Diego Méndez observed that "a little island covered its lower limb like an eclipse." That encouraged them, and by the morning of the fourth day, seventy-two hours from Jamaica, the canoes were up to the island. "Landing there as best they could," says Ferdinand, — and landing on those rocky cliffs is difficult at best, — they first thanked God and then went in search of fresh water, which was found in the hollows of rocks. Some of the Indians drank so much that they died, and others "got desperate distempers." Diego Méndez kindled a fire with flint and steel, shellfish were gathered and cooked; but what cheered the men most was the sight of high Cape Tiburon to the eastward. So in the cool of the evening the canoes were launched again, and the remaining 30 miles to Hispaniola were covered before morning.

After resting two days on the shores of Cape Tiburon, Bartolomeo

Fieschi, "who was a gentleman that stood on his honor," proposed to begin the return voyage; but not a man could be persuaded to come with him. The Indians preferred risking death in Hispaniola rather than make the passage, and the Christians, regarding themselves as "having been delivered from out of the whale's belly, their three days and nights corresponding to those of the prophet Jonah," declared it would affront God to try their luck again. In comparison with the canoe voyages regularly made by Polynesians, and with many small-boat voyages made by English and Americans, especially in the present war, this hundred-mile crossing of the Windward Passage was "nothing to write home about." But the American Indians were not used to such journeys, and it was the first occasion that we know of when South Europeans had done anything of the sort. Diego Méndez had performed many brave deeds in a long and honorable life; but in his will, where these exploits are recounted, he left the following directions for his tombstone and epitaph: —

Here lies the Honorable Gentleman Diego Méndez, who greatly served the Royal Crown of Spain in the Discovery and Conquest of the Indies with the Admiral Don Cristóbal Colón of Glorious Memory, who discovered them, and afterwards with his own Ships and at his own Cost. He died   . He begs for Charity's sake a Pater Noster and an Ave Maria.

In the middle of the said stone let there be carved a canoe, which is a dug-out tree in which the Indians navigate, for in such a one I navigated three hundred leagues; and above it let them set the letters that say CANOA.

"I beached my canoe on a very fine beach," says Méndez in his narrative, "where many natives came down and brought many things to eat." He secured six fresh Indian paddlers and though suffering from a quartan ague proceeded along the coast toward Santo Domingo. After reaching Azua, on or near the harbor where the fleet had put in after the hurricane over a year before, he learned that Governor Ovando had gone to the province of

Xaragua to pacify it. Abandoning the canoe, Méndez struck inland, and met the Governor at his field headquarters.

The news that Columbus was marooned at Jamaica was by no
means displeasing to Ovando, who feared that the Admiral's arrival, with the fresh glory of new discoveries, would cause the
Sovereigns to restore his viceregal powers; and that would mean
Ovando's retirement from a highly lucrative position. He detained
Méndez at his headquarters for seven months, while he put down
the Indians' revolt in a most bloody and thoroughgoing manner
that even a modern conqueror could not surpass, hanging or burning alive some eighty caciques and other leaders, including the
beautiful lady cacique Anacoana. It must have been August 1503
when Méndez reached Ovando, and March 1504 when he was
finally allowed to proceed afoot to Santo Domingo. There he had
to wait two months or more for ships to arrive from Spain. The
government had a small caravel at Santo Domingo, but Ovando
would not let him use it. Of Fieschi we hear nothing further until
he returned with Columbus to Spain. Apparently he found it impossible to engage paddlers for a return journey. He witnessed the
Admiral's last will and testament in 1506, and later returned to
Genoa, where several years later we find him commanding a fleet
of fifteen galleys in a war against France.

At Santa Gloria Columbus and his men were waiting and hoping;
and the longer they waited the lower fell their hopes that the messengers had reached Hispaniola. Summer turned to fall, and fall to
winter; this made little difference in the vegetation, but a good deal
in terms of comfort. For with winter came the northers, and the
caravels' beach in Santa Gloria Bay, though protected from heavy
seas by the coral reefs, was exposed to north wind and rain. The
Spaniards, always by their Admiral's strict command confined to
the beached ships, became fearful, uneasy and discontented, ripe
for mutiny; and around the persons of the Porras brothers a conspiracy formed.

Captain Francisco de Porras of *Santiago*, and Diego the crown representative and comptroller, were political appointees; and like many men of that kidney had never done a fair share of the work. Bartholomew Columbus had been the effective though unsalaried captain of *Santiago*, and Diego Porras, except for keeping account of gold coming aboard, had been an idler the entire voyage. Ignorant of seamanship, they were incapable of understanding the good reasons for running the ships ashore; and the men, in their depressed and discontented condition, were only too ready to hear suggestions of foul play. Why, they asked one another, was the Admiral keeping them in Jamaica? He could perfectly well have sailed the caravels to Hispaniola, if he chose; of course they were no good now, but Captain Porras would have taken them there if that Genoese had only let him. There was nothing much wrong with good old *Santiago*, until the Admiral ran her ashore! The root of the matter was this: Colón was serving out a term of banishment — didn't you notice how they wouldn't let him land at Santo Domingo? He can't return there, has no intention of doing so, and the canoes were sent purely to fix up his business, gold or what not; much he cared for our interests! Quite likely, if a ship does come, he will leave us here to be massacred by Indians, as happened to those poor devils at Navidad. Indeed, that's what would have happened to us at Belén if the Adelantado hadn't wanted to save his skin. The only sensible course for us is to seize canoes, kidnap a few Indians to work them, and escape to Hispaniola. What, in Heaven's name, is the sense of lying here rotting, to please these beggarly Genoese adventurers? — All right, suppose we reach Hispaniola, what about being tried for mutiny? — Not a chance. Governor Ovando is the Admiral's enemy, he would be delighted to see us without him. — Well, perhaps; but how about *Los Reyes*, Ferdinand and Isabella; the Admiral seems to stand in pretty well with them, and after all these are their ships and they pay our wages. — Who pays our wages? The very magnificent Don Alonso de Morales, High Treasurer of Castile, whose lady love is sister to me, Francisco de Porras, gentleman!

Of course that clinches the argument. That means that the Porras brothers can get away with mutiny and murder, and that's just what they do.

Out of the hundred or so men and boys left at Santa Gloria, forty-eight joined the conspiracy; and as the Admiral was laid low with arthritis, there was a good chance of their success. After a dismal Christmas and an unhappy New Year's Day, with no wine to celebrate, not a morsel of proper Christian food, the Porras brothers set January 2, 1504, for the big blow-up. In the morning Francisco came aboard *Capitana*, entered the Admiral's cabin un-invited, and said, "Señor, what do you mean by not trying to get to Castile, do you wish to keep us here perishing?" Columbus, catching from his insolent tone what was up, replied calmly that he wanted to go home as much as anyone, but did not see how they could until a ship was sent; if he had any other plan to propose, let it be submitted to a council of officers. To which Porras replied, "It's no time to talk; embark quickly, or stay here with God," and then turning to the men who were gathering about within earshot cried, "I'm for Castile, with those who will follow me!" That was the signal to the conspirators, who all began to shout, "We're with you!" and quickly took possession of the fore and stern castles and the round-tops on the mainmasts, crying *á Castilla! á Castilla!* Although the Admiral was in bed he came tottering out at this uproar, and would probably have been murdered if three or four of his devoted servants had not laid hold of him and forced him back. Bartholomew now came running out with a lance in hand; the Admiral's servants wrested it from him and pushed him into his brother's cabin, while they begged Porras to get going if he would, but to commit no murder for which he would certainly be punished if he ever reached home.

The mutineers now piled into ten dugout canoes which were tied up to the ships, and many not in the conspiracy went with them, to the great distress of the few loyal and faithful seamen, and of the sick. Without doubt, says Ferdinand, if all the company had been in good health, not twenty men would have remained with the Admiral. As it was, the men who stayed about equaled the mutineers.

The Porras brothers and their merry men started eastward along the coast "as gaily as if they had been in some harbor of Castile," robbing the Indians wherever they called, and telling them to collect their pay from the Admiral, or kill him if they would. After waiting some days at Northeast Point, they chose the first calm day and shoved off for Hispaniola, as they thought. But it never stays calm very long in those waters, in January. Four leagues out the breeze freshened from the eastward, and they decided to put back. It was so rough that everything except their arms was thrown overboard, and after the goods they threw the Indian paddlers, who clung piteously to the gunwales, only to have their hands hacked off. A few only were spared to steer the canoes. The mutineers remained a month at the easternmost Indian village of Jamaica, living off the natives and making two more attempts to cross, both failures. So at last, very down-in-the-mouth, they abandoned their boats and started back to Santa Gloria on foot, living off the country and abusing the Indians as they went along.

At Santa Gloria all went well for a time with the Admiral and his fifty loyal men. Indians continued to bring in provisions to barter, and the sick recovered their full health. But after a few weeks the Indian trade began to decline, "they being a people who take small pains in cultivation," as Ferdinand said, "and we consuming more in a day than they ate in twenty, and besides, their demand for our truck fell off." Every Taino had all the hawks' bells, glass beads, brass rings and lace-points that he wanted; so why trade? Less and less food was brought in daily; and the Spaniards, who for some unknown reason were never able to supply themselves with fish or kill game, rapidly approached starvation. And to allow forays on the Indians' stores of food would invite massacre.

At this juncture Columbus bethought himself of a stratagem. Among the few books aboard ship was a Regiomontanus *Ephe-*

merides, printed at Nuremberg before the end of the century, but containing predictions of eclipses for thirty years ahead. In three days' time, on the night of February 29, 1504, Regiomontanus predicted a total eclipse of the moon. So, sending an Indian as messenger, Columbus summoned the caciques and chief men of that region to a conference. On the twenty-ninth they assembled aboard *Capitana.* The Admiral through the interpreter made a little speech. Christians worshiped God in Heaven, who rewarded the good and punished the wicked. God, disapproving the Porras rebellion, had not permitted the mutineers to cross over to Hispaniola, but had sent them through all those trials and dangers of which the island was well aware. As for the Indians, God observed with deep disapproval how negligent they were in bringing provisions to the faithful, and had determined to chastise them with famine and pestilence. He would presently send them a clear token from Heaven of the punishment they were about to receive. Wherefore the Admiral bade them attend well that night the rising of the moon. She will rise bloody and enflamed, denoting the mischief that the Indians will incur for their neglect to feed the Christians properly.

Columbus having spoken, the Indians departed, some in fear and others scoffing. "But, the eclipse beginning at the rising of the moon, and augmenting as she ascended, the Indians took heed, and were so frightened that with great howling and lamentation they came running from every direction to the ships laden with provisions, praying the Admiral to intercede by all means with God on their behalf; that he might not visit his wrath upon them, promising for the future diligently to furnish all that they stood in need of. To this the Admiral replied that he wished to converse somewhat with God; and retired while the eclipse lasted, they all the while crying out to him to aid them. And when the Admiral observed that the totality of the eclipse was finished, and that the moon would soon shine forth, he issued from his cabin, saying that he had supplicated his God and made prayers for them, and had promised Him in their names that henceforth they would be good and use the

Christians well, fetching them provisions and necessary things, and that therefore God had forgiven them, in token of which pardon they would see the wrath and inflammation of the moon pass away. This taking effect with his words, they rendered many thanks to the Admiral and praised his God, so continuing until the eclipse was ended. From that time forward they always took care to provide what they had need of."

When he retired to his cabin the Admiral was not putting in his time praying, but measuring with his *ampolleta* or half-hour glass the duration of the eclipse, in order that he might compute the longitude of Jamaica. The result is thus recorded in his Book of Prophecies: —

"Thursday 29 February 1504, I being in the Indies on the Island of Jamaica in the harbor called Santa Gloria which is almost in the middle of the island on the north side, there was an eclipse of the moon, and as the beginning thereof was before the sun set, I could only note the end of it, when the moon had just returned to its light, and this was certainly two hours and a half after the night [fell], five *ampolletas* most certainly. The difference between the middle of the island of Jamaica in the Indies and the island of Cadiz in Spain is seven hours and fifteen minutes, so that in Cadiz the sun sets seven hours and fifteen minutes earlier than in Jamaica (see almanac)."

Following the eclipse entry in the Book of Prophecies there is a calculation of latitude for Santa Gloria that is very nearly correct. "In the harbor of Santa Gloria in Jamaica, the altitude of the Pole was 18 degrees when the Guards were on the Arm." The actual latitude of that beach in St. Ann's Bay is 18° 26′ 45″. Columbus therefore made an error of less than half a degree. Considering that he now had a perfectly stable platform to "shoot" from, and a whole year to make repeated observations and average them, this was nothing to boast about; but it does show that the Admiral's technique with the quadrant had improved since his previous voyage. After all, it was one of the best latitude observations on record for the early years of the sixteenth century.

CHAPTER XLIX

Rescue and End

1504–1506

Et clamauerunt ad Dominum cum tribularentur: et de necessitatibus eorum eripuit eos.

Then they cried unto the Lord in their trouble — and he delivered them out of their distresses.

— PSALM cvi 6

ALTHOUGH the food problem was now solved for the time being, the question of how to get home was not, and the mutineers were still roving about the island making trouble. At the end of March 1504 over eight months had passed since Méndez and Fieschi left for Hispaniola, but nothing had been heard of them; and a report by some Indians of a big empty canoe drifting ashore started mutinous talk among the men at Santa Gloria. One Bernal, an apothecary from Valencia, was fomenting another conspiracy when a small caravel suddenly came in from the sea and anchored near the grounded ships. She proved a cruel disappointment, for Ovando had not sent her to take Columbus off, but merely to spy on him and report; and she sailed the same evening. Her captain, Diego de Escobar, came aboard the grounded *Capitana* and gave the Admiral two casks of wine and a slab of salt pork with the governor's compliments, and delivered a message from Diego Méndez to the effect that he had safely reached Hispaniola and would send a rescue party as soon as he could obtain a ship. Columbus just had time to write a dignified letter of thanks to the governor, hoping "for the succor of God and yourselves."

Even the choice of Escobar as an emissary was an affront to Columbus, for he had been one of the leading rebels under Roldán.

Ovando doubtless hoped he would report that Columbus was dead, which would leave the viceroyalty of the Indies vacant; that, at least, was a firm opinion of Las Casas, who was then in Hispaniola. Columbus put a good face on the caravel's departure, telling the men that since she was too small to take them all, he preferred to stay with them until Diego Méndez sent a proper ship for everyone. So this brief and mysterious visit quenched the Bernal conspiracy. Now, with commendable magnanimity, the Admiral made advances to the Porras mutineers. Two men were sent to their camp, bearing a generous slice of Ovando's salt pork as proof of the caravel's visit, and offering a general pardon. Porras dickered for terms — so much food and clothing, so much space on the ship, and the like — which so disgusted the messengers that they broke off the parley. The mutineers then marched on Santa Gloria hoping to conquer the loyalists and seize the houseboats. On May 19, when they reached Maima, the Indian village hard by the ships, Columbus sent his brother to offer war or peace, with fifty armed men to back him up. Porras, who regarded all those who did not join his mutiny as invalids or weaklings, chose to fight. A small-scale pitched battle then took place, fought largely (for want of powder) with swords, while the Indians stood by and enjoyed the spectacle of Christians carving each other up.

The loyalists won. Porras was captured, Juan Sánchez the former chief pilot was killed, others were wounded and several taken prisoners. Pedro de Ledesma, champion swimmer of the fleet, fell over a cliff, and moreover was so badly sliced that one could see his brains; one arm hung limp, part of one calf hung down like a loose stocking, and the sole of one foot was sliced from heel to toe so that it resembled a slipper, says Ferdinand. Yet he recovered, and lived to do the Admiral another bad turn. The following day the rest submitted, received full pardon, and were allowed to stay ashore under a leader appointed by the Admiral, while Francisco de Porras was placed in irons on board.

At that time Diego Méndez was fitting out a rescue ship. Ovando had refused to let him have the caravel on station at Santo

Domingo, so he had to await the arrival of ships from Spain. At length a fleet of three came in. One of them, which Columbus refers to as a *caravelón*, a little caravel, Méndez chartered, provisioned and sent to Jamaica under command of Diego de Salcedo, a loyal servant of the Admiral. Méndez returned to Spain in one of the other ships, as Columbus had commanded, in order to deliver his letters to the Sovereigns, Padre Gorricio and Don Diego.

The *caravelón* arrived at Santa Gloria toward the end of June 1504 and on the twenty-ninth departed for Hispaniola with all the survivors, about one hundred strong. They had been in Jamaica a year and five days. The voyage against wind and current to Santa Domingo was long and tedious, and the *caravelón* was not in good condition. Her mainmast was sprung, the sails rotten, the bottom foul; and she leaked so rapidly, owing to bad or old caulking, that they had some difficulty keeping her afloat. For a long time she was detained by foul weather at Puerto Brazil (Jacmel) and Beata Island, whence Columbus sent by messenger a grateful letter to Ovando on August 3. Ten days later the ship reached Santo Domingo — a passage of six and a half weeks. Ovando, making great pretense of joy at seeing the Admiral, took him into his own house, but showed his real sentiments by setting the Porrases at liberty; this precious pair of brothers was never punished for the mutiny, and when Jamaica was settled Francisco received a government job there.

At Santo Domingo another ship was chartered, and aboard her the Admiral, his son and brother and twenty-two others embarked for Spain September 12. Most of the survivors of the Fourth Voyage chose to stay in Hispaniola rather than indulge in more seafaring at present; some of them later became the first settlers of Puerto Rico. A few took passage home in the *caravelón* that brought them from Jamaica; she sailed at the same time, broke her mast outside the Ozama and put back, and finally arrived in Spain about the end of November. Apparently the Porrases sailed in her.

The Admiral's homeward passage on his chartered ship was long and troublesome, but we have no hint of what course she followed.

On October 19 the mainmast broke in four pieces; but the ingenuity of the Columbus brothers contrived a jury mast out of yard, well fished with ropes and bits of plank. The foremast was sprung in another storm. On November 7, 1504, after a passage of fifty-six days from Santo Domingo, the Admiral's last voyage ended safely in the roadstead of Sanlúcar de Barrameda.

Ferdinand, who was not yet fourteen years old when the voyage began, had now passed his sixteenth birthday. The Adelantado was still hale, vigorous and ready for more adventure; but the Admiral, at fifty-three, was broken in health, if not in spirit. He knew very well that he had not done what was expected; no strait had been found. But he had discovered the isthmus, and a much richer gold-bearing region than Hispaniola. And his conscience was satisfied that he had done his best. As he wrote to his son shortly after arrival: —

Certain it is that I have served Their Highnesses with as great diligence and love as I might have employed to win paradise and more; and if in somewhat I have been wanting, that was impossible, or much beyond my knowledge and strength. Our Lord God in such cases asketh no more of men than good will. . . .

Thy father who loveth thee more than himself

· S ·
· S · A · S ·
X   M   ϒ
Xῥo FERENS

It were well had the rest been silence.

Instead of being summoned to court to tell his story, a favor accorded to less distinguished leaders of comparatively insignificant voyages, Columbus had absolutely no notice taken of him by the Sovereigns. The ostensible reason was the Queen's illness. Actually she was on her deathbed, which made her refusal to send him word the more distressing; for she could well have spared Columbus a moment to kiss her hands, when every court official and hanger-on had access to her bedside. Doubtless the real reason why Columbus received no invitation to court was the suspicion that he would use the occasion to unfold a tale of woe, rather than beguile the sinking Queen with an amusing story of discovery and adventure.

He might have afforded the Queen a little pleasure with the "eagles" and "mirrors" and other golden gadgets that he brought home from Veragua; but it is quite true that his main desire was to complain of his shabby treatment by Ovando, of mutiny led by the treasurer's cronies, and to beg for a restoration of his rights. The Sovereigns had heard plenty of that sort of thing from Columbus before, and they proposed to do nothing about it. So why let themselves be confronted by a bad conscience in the shape of that heroic but tiresome old seaman?

The death of Isabella on November 26, 1504, meant that Columbus's last chance was gone, and that his Fourth and last Voyage had been sailed in vain, so far as any profit to himself was concerned. She had always believed in him, had consoled him in affliction and relieved his necessities; the King's conception of royal policy left no place for sentiment. Ovando was doing very well for the crown in Hispaniola; the increasing supplies of gold that he sent home proved it, and there was no sense in replacing him by a broken-down discoverer who had found Hispaniola too hot before. Nor would this act of abstract justice have helped matters in the colony. "Neither the Admiral nor his brother should come here to these islands" is the emphatic statement of a colonist whose first interest was the conversion of the natives. The Columbus family were far too unpopular.

Columbus was too sick to travel by the time the news of Isabella's death reached him. But he had a devoted and interested advocate at court, his elder son, who well knew by long experience the ropes of that particular ship. During the period of the Fourth Voyage Don Diego outgrew his office of page, and became a soldier of the Queen's bodyguard. That corps was dissolved by her death, but the young man (now about twenty-four) stood in well with the King, and received an appointment to his own guard. Nobody could be better situated than Don Diego to do business for his father, but there was little that could be done. This we learn from a remarkable sequence of letters from Columbus to his son, written between November 21, 1504, and February 25, 1505.

During that period of three months, Columbus was living in a hired house in the parish of Santa María, Seville, and well supplied with money, servants and attendants. For, it must be remembered, Columbus had not only brought home a rich haul of gold objects from Veragua, but he was deriving a substantial revenue from his "tenths" of the gold diggings in Hispaniola. Carvajal had safely transferred a substantial sum of gold for him on the ship that escaped the hurricane of 1502, and we have a record of what Carvajal and Giovanni Antonio ("Johnny") Colombo sold for the Admiral's account in 1503–1504, 22 marcos (worth about $3300) in gold. In addition, Ovando handed over to Columbus a chest of specie to take home on his last voyage, and Columbus claimed to have left 60,000 pesos d'oro (roughly $180,000) in Hispaniola, against which the Genoese bankers at Seville allowed him to draw. All this fell far short of what the Admiral believed to be his just due; nevertheless, during the last two years of his life he was a comparatively rich man. Yet with monotonous persistence, every letter of this period to his son urged him to obtain orders from the King for prompt and honest payment of his "tenth, eighth and third."

Columbus, it must be admitted, would have passed a far happier old age if he had entertained a less exalted estimate of his pecuniary "rights"; and the King might have been disposed to confirm his titles and honors, if such action had not involved a perpetual lien on the crown's colonial revenues. In one letter to his son, Columbus said that the titles and offices should first be restored, when pecuniary privileges would follow, and to the King he sent a strong petition to that effect. Columbus doubtless would have been happy to be confirmed in his charges, even if not permitted to exercise them, like a bishop *in partibus*. But the King very well knew that any such favor would strengthen Columbus's pecuniary claims, and paid no attention to the request.

It is so long since we have spoken of Columbus's property rights that the reader has probably forgotten what the Admiral meant by his tenth, eighth and third. The *tenth* was his right guaranteed by the "capitulations" of 1493 to 10 per cent of the net production of the world that he discovered. That right had never formally been abrogated, but Columbus complained that the Sovereigns allowed him only a tenth of their fifth of the gold (the only product that counted) — that is, 2 instead of 10 per cent. The *eighth* meant the profits of Columbus's own ventures on outward voyages, which the capitulations of 1492 gave him the option of making; no particulars as to these have come down to us, but it is probable that Columbus had sent out provisions and Spanish goods as a speculation, and Bobadilla or Ovando had impounded the receipts. The *third* was one of his presumed prerogatives as Admiral. When compiling his Book of Privileges, Columbus discovered that the Grand Admiral of Castile was entitled to levy a 33⅓ per cent tax on the trade of places within his jurisdiction; so Columbus claimed the same privilege for himself from the trade of the Indies. This extravagant claim had never been admitted by the Sovereigns, and never was exercised.

Columbus was also worried lest the Porras brothers reach the King's ears first with their story of the Fourth Voyage; but his greatest concern was for pecuniary matters. He pressed for repayment of the sums he had advanced out of his own pocket to charter and provision the rescue ship, and to take his crew home. Nor was he exclusively concerned with his own losses. Thrice he urges D. Diego to persuade treasurer Morales to pay the wages of his "poor people," the mariners who had "passed through infinite perils and hardships." Everyone in the fleet had received six months' advance wages in March 1502; but the voyage lasted thirty-two months, and most of the survivors who came home with the Admiral arrived penniless. Some picked up odd jobs in Seville, while waiting for their pay; others were living on the Admiral's charity. On his advice a delegation of them made the long journey to court, bearing from the Admiral a strong letter to Don Juan de Fonseca, now Bishop of Palencia. Columbus asks D. Diego to do all he can to see that the men are paid promptly, "although there are some among them" (the mutineers) "who deserve punishment more than favors."

Many human and even humorous touches are found in these letters. In December Columbus sends his brother the Adelantado and his son Ferdinand on ahead of him to court. He is evidently worried lest they seem uncouth sailors to Don Diego, the smooth courtier. So the Admiral requests Diego to treat his uncle with respect, and his younger brother with affection, and to remember that he is no longer a "kid," that the voyage has made a man of little Ferdinand. The Adelantado, who had been a courtier himself at Fontainebleau, was certainly nobody to be ashamed of at the court of Spain; but one imagines that sixteen-year-old Ferdinand had to be told more than once by his elder brother to cut out his tales of waterspouts and hurricanes, caballeros were not interested in such matters; it's high time the brat bought a suit of armor and learned the practice and language of chivalry.

Columbus wrote an account of his voyage for the new pope, Julius II, and sent it unsealed to Don Diego with instructions that it be shown to Diego de Deza, now Archbishop of Seville; ostensibly to see that it was couched in proper terms for the eyes of the Holy Father, but really to remind the now magnificent Archbishop of his old friend's services and sufferings. A rumor had reached Seville that bishops were to be appointed for the Indies, and Columbus hoped to have a hand in their selection. He would dearly like to reward Fray Gaspar, Fray Juan Pérez, or other ecclesiastics who had been kind to him. But the only friend of Columbus ever appointed to an episcopal see in the New World was Alessandro Geraldini, and that was fifteen years after the Admiral's death.

Among the ex-mutineers, Gonzalo Camacho, gentleman volunteer aboard *Gallego*, made the most trouble ashore, next to the Porras brothers. A particular crony of Captain Pedro de Terreros, who died in Jamaica, he produced a forged will making himself the captain's sole heir, although Terreros had left a family and a genuine will at home. Camacho, moreover, spread "a thousand falsehoods" about Columbus around Seville. The Admiral had warrants sworn out against him on both counts, which so alarmed Camacho that he sought asylum in a church of Seville. Columbus gave his son an amusing picture of this rascal having to spend the Christmas holidays inside this church, not daring to leave the sacred precincts lest he be clapped into jail.

During this winter of 1504–1505 in Seville, Columbus was suffering tortures from *la gota*, the arthritis which had grown on him with age and the hard life of the sea. Otherwise he would have proceeded to Segovia in mid-November, shown himself at the Queen's funeral, and sought an audience with the King. As the weeks slipped by, and no reassurance of the progress of his cause came from D. Diego, Columbus began to think of ways and means by which he could cross Spain in spite of his infirmities. In Seville Cathedral there was a splendid wheeled catafalque which had been used in the sumptuous funeral of the very magnificent Don Diego Hurtado de Mendoza, Duke of Infantado and Prince of the Church. Just the thing, thought Columbus, for his cross-country journey. The Cathedral chapter, applied to for the loan of the catafalque, consented under condition that its return be guaranteed. Fortunately "the weather appeared so violent that it appeared impossible to start," so the populace were spared the ludicrous and pathetic spectacle of a gouty old admiral proceeding to court in a hearse.

Columbus then abandoned his somewhat exalted notions of transportation, and requested royal permission to ride a mule. The Andalusian horse-raising interests, it appears, had become so alarmed at the increasing employment of mules as saddle animals that a law had been passed forbidding their use for such a purpose. Columbus believed that he could endure the gentle gaits of a mule, but not the somewhat jittery paces of an Andalusian horse; so he applied to the King for a mule permit, and it was granted. But it was not until May 1505 that he felt well enough to use this gracious privilege – the only favor that King Ferdinand ever granted to the Discoverer of America.

By New Year's Day 1505, Columbus decided that it was no use

making any further effort to be restored as active administrator of Hispaniola. His age and infirmities would no longer permit him to sail on another transatlantic voyage. Consequently he and his son simultaneously petitioned the Sovereign to confer the governorship and viceroyalty on Don Diego, Columbus making a characteristically tactless allusion to the "miracle" of the 1502 hurricane, proving divine disapproval of his supercession by Bobadilla. The King made no reply. He had his eye on Don Diego, a fine tall strapping fellow of twenty-five, with a long face like his father. But it was out of the question to make so young a man who had never seen action, a courtier by training and temperament, governor of a turbulent colony like Hispaniola.

Eventually the King met Columbus's wishes. He made no objection to Don Diego assuming the title of Admiral after his father's death, and three years later, in 1509, appointed him governor of Hispaniola. But this belated favor was due rather to Diego's marriage to a lady of the court, Doña María de Toledo, who was a cousin of the King. Don Diego, generally known as the second Admiral of the Indies, remained in Hispaniola long enough to prove that he was a capable enough head of an administration which Ovando had brought into order and regularity, and to build the massive stone castle whose ruins still dominate the harborside at Santo Domingo. But he spent most of his life in Spain, endeavoring to secure his hereditary rights as Viceroy of all "The Indies"; and in Spain he died in 1526. The Virreina Doña María de Colón y Toledo then became regent for their infant son Don Luis, who turned out to be completely worthless. It was she who on his behalf wisely renounced his ephemeral titles, offices and pecuniary privileges as heir of Christopher Columbus, in exchange for the Duchy of Veragua.

Columbus had several people working for him at court — his two sons, his brother the Adelantado, the ever-faithful and loyal Diego Méndez, Juan de Coloma who had concluded the agreement of 1492, and (at least so he expected and believed) Amerigo Vespucci. Columbus's letter of February 25, 1505, to his son was forwarded to Segovia in the hands of Vespucci, who had returned from another voyage to South America and been summoned to court "on matters of navigation." "He is a very honorable man and always desirous of pleasing me," says the Admiral, "and is determined to do everything possible for me. See what he can do to profit me there and try to have him do it." Columbus little suspected that Vespucci's predated account of his voyage with Hojeda, just published as *Mundus Novus,* would cause the Florentine to be hailed as the discoverer of a New World, or that in consequence of this faked-up narrative the world of Columbus's discovery would be named America.

What, if anything, Vespucci did for Columbus is not known. All that the King did for Columbus's family in 1505 was to order that Ferdinand receive his back pay as the Queen's page during the Fourth Voyage, since he had not been on the fleet's payroll. On the other hand, he sent word to Ovando to sell the movables of the Admiral in Hispaniola, and a secret order was issued to the effect that any proceeds of this sale, or other property of the Admiral sent over to Spain, should be impounded by the royal treasury to pay Columbus's debts. These last documents fairly stink of the Porras brothers and their dishonorable connection with treasurer Morales of Castile. Happily, Columbus never seems to have learned of them. He noted the arrival of ships from the Indies laden with chests of gold, "but none for me"; and blamed Ovando, not the King.

In May 1505, Columbus at last felt equal to mule travel, and a long spell of fair weather was predicted, so he set out on the long journey to the court at Segovia in Old Castile, across the Sierra de Guadarrama from Madrid. In due course he was graciously permitted to see the King, but this personal appearance availed him nothing. His Majesty was ever bland and courteous, but always noncommittal. He did indeed propose that an arbiter be appointed to settle the Admiral's claims, and fell in with Columbus's suggestion that his former protector, Diego de Deza, Archbishop of Seville, be the man. Deza was spared this embarrassing charge because Columbus understood that only his pecuniary claims should be arbitrated, whilst the King insisted that the admiralty and viceroyalty be cast into the pot; and Columbus refused to admit that those rights were arbitrable. The King might as justly ask a man whom he had created duke to arbitrate his dukedom. Columbus had been created admiral, viceroy and governor by the King and Queen, he had a clear legal right to these offices for himself and his heirs, and he would admit no other side to the question. The King also dropped the hint that if Columbus would renounce these titles and the revenues appertaining thereto, he would be granted a handsome estate in Castile with a fat rent roll. Often the Admiral's descendants must have wished that he had accepted this exchange. But Columbus's wounded sense of honor, and that same inflexibility and stubbornness in his make-up which enabled him to surmount every human and material obstacle and make four of the greatest voyages in the world's history, prevented him from sacrificing the promised fruits of his conquests. He would have all or nothing. And it was nothing that he got.

During the year 1505 the court moved to Salamanca and then to Valladolid, and Columbus painfully followed. The arthritis was growing worse, and most of the time he was confined to bed. Were these racking pains the only return he was to have for all his discoveries and the hardships he had endured? Often and often he must have sought some explanation from the inscrutable divine will that decreed his many sufferings. Was God still angry over the Admiral's pride in those brave days when he had a whole new world at his feet? Would not the divine compassion put an end to these tortures, and vouchsafe him some mark of royal clemency before he passed to yet another world? Evidently this was what the Admiral expected, since almost to the last day of his life we find him planning the expenditure of his future revenues: legacies to repay ancient debts of his improvident father; a chapel in Hispaniola perpetually endowed where Masses might be said for the repose of his soul; a sinking fund to be used for the recovery of the Holy Sepulchre. So certain was Columbus of the justice of his claims that he seemed to have no doubt that God would see them confirmed to his son and heir, if not to himself. If God wished to punish him, His will be done; but surely God would approve these pious dispositions of the Admiral's last will and testament, and so see that his descendants were put in a way to fulfill them.

Almost at the last moment came a new glimmer of hope. Since the death of Queen Isabella, the King had been ruling her kingdom of Castile as regent for their daughter the Infanta Juana ("la Loca") and her husband the Archduke Philip of Austria. Ferdinand, the old fox, proposed to cheat them out of their inheritance by marrying a young niece of Louis XII of France, in the hope of producing a son and heir to the throne of Castile; and this marriage gave Philip and Juana the hint that they had better secure their rights without further delay. Late in April 1506, they landed at Corunna. Columbus now hoped to obtain the justice from Juana that he was denied by her father. After all, she was the daughter of Isabella; the Infanta Doña Juana had sat open-mouthed by her mother's side when Columbus brought home the first Indians, and told the first marvelous tales of the golden Indies. Had he been well enough, he would have sought out the new Queen and thrown himself at her feet, but he could not be moved. So the Adelantado was sent ahead in the Admiral's name to kiss the hands of the young sovereigns of Castile, and to beseech their favor for his wronged though distinguished brother.

By this time the Admiral's malady was increasing rapidly, and his attendants knew that the end was near; the seamen among them were wagging their beards and saying that the Admiral would go out with the next ebb tide, as a seaman should. On May 19, 1506, Columbus ratified his last will and testament, creating Don Diego heir to all his property and privileges, commending all other surviving members of his immediate family, and Beatriz Enríquez de Harana, to his benevolence; and leaving small legacies to pay debts of conscience at Genoa and Lisbon. Nor was the long-hoped-for crusade to Jerusalem forgotten on this, the penultimate day of the pious Admiral's life.

On May 20, the vigil of the Feast of the Ascension, Columbus suddenly grew worse. No news yet from the Adelantado at the new sovereigns' camp, alas. Please God to prosper his suit! Diego the beloved younger brother, Don Diego the son and heir, Ferdinand the son and shipmate, Diego Méndez and Fieschi, valiant captains of *Capitana* and *Vizcaína* and leaders of the canoe journey, and a few faithful domestics, rallied around the bedside of the dying man. It was a poor enough deathbed for the Admiral of the Ocean Sea and Viceroy and Governor of the Islands and Mainlands therein; but no pomp or circumstance could help him now. A priest was summoned, a Mass said, and everyone in this little circle of friends and relatives received the sacrament. The viaticum was administered to the dying Admiral; and after the concluding prayer of this last office, remembering the last words of his Lord and Saviour, to whose sufferings he sometimes ventured to compare his own, Columbus was heard to say *in manus tuas, Domine, commendo spiritum meum*.

"And having said this, he gave up the ghost."

.   .   .   .

So died the man who had done more to direct the course of history than any individual since Augustus Caesar. Yet the life of the Admiral closed on a note of frustration. He had not found the Strait, or met the Grand Khan, or converted any great number of heathen, or regained Jerusalem. He had not even secured the future of his family. And the significance of what he had accomplished was only slightly less obscure to him than to the chroniclers who neglected to record his death, or to the courtiers who failed to attend his modest funeral at Valladolid. The vast extent and immense resources of the Americas were but dimly seen; the mighty ocean that laved their western shores had not yet yielded her secret.

America would eventually have been discovered if the Great Enterprise of Columbus had been rejected; yet who can predict what would have been the outcome? The voyage that took him to "The Indies" and home was no blind chance, but the creation of his own brain and soul, long studied, carefully planned, repeatedly urged on indifferent princes, and carried through by virtue of his courage, sea-knowledge and indomitable will. No later voyage could ever have such spectacular results, and Columbus's fame would have been secure had he retired from the sea in 1493. Yet a lofty ambition to explore further, to organize the territories won for Castile, and to complete the circuit of the globe, sent him thrice more to America. These voyages, even more than the first, proved him to be the greatest navigator of his age, and enabled him to train the captains and pilots who were to display the banners of Spain off every American cape and island between Fifty North and Fifty South. The ease with which he dissipated the unknown terrors of the Ocean, the skill with which he found his way out and home, again and again, led thousands of men from every Western European nation into maritime adventure and exploration. And if Columbus was a failure as a colonial administrator, it was partly because his conception of a colony transcended the desire of his followers to impart, and the capacity of natives to receive, the institutions and culture of Renaissance Europe.

Columbus had a proud, passionate and sensitive nature that suffered deeply from the contempt to which he was early subjected, and the envy, disloyalty, ingratitude and injustice which he met as a discoverer. He wrote so freely out of the abundance of his complaint, as to give the impression that his life was more full of woe than of weal. That impression is false. As with other mariners, a month at sea healed the wounds of a year ashore, and a fair wind blew away the memory of foul weather. Command of a tall and gallant ship speeding over blue water before a fresh trade wind, shaping her course for some new and marvelous land where gold is abundant and the women are kind, is a mariner's dream of the good life. Columbus had a Hellenic sense of wonder at the new and strange, combined with an artist's appreciation of natural beauty; and his voyages to this strange new world brought him to some of the most gorgeous coastlines on the earth's surface. Moreover, Columbus had a deep conviction of the immanence, the sovereignty and the infinite wisdom of God, which transcended all his suffering, and enhanced all his triumphs. Waste no pity on the Admiral of the Ocean Sea! He enjoyed long stretches of pure delight such as only a seaman may know, and moments of high, proud exultation that only a discoverer can experience.

One only wishes that the Admiral might have been afforded the sense of fulfillment that would have come from foreseeing all that flowed from his discoveries; that would have turned all the sorrows of his last years to joy. The whole history of the Americas stems from the Four Voyages of Columbus; and as the Greek city-states looked back to the deathless gods as their founders, so today a score of independent nations and dominions unite in homage to Christopher the stout-hearted son of Genoa, who carried Christian civilization across the Ocean Sea.

FINIS

Index

The Maps and Illustrations are not indexed. See list at p. xi.

ABBREVIATIONS

B. Bahía, Bay
C. Cabo, Cape
C. C. Christopher Columbus
D. Don, Dom, Doña, Dona
Fr. Fray, Brother

V. Voyage

G. Golfo, Gulf
Is. Isleo, Island, Islands
Pta. Punta, Point
Pto. Puerto, Harbor
R. Rio, River

CPSIA information can be obtained at www.ICGtesting.com
Printed in the USA
LVOW08*1419020514

384215LV00006B/21/A